Mediation in International Commercial and Investment Disputes

Mediation in International Commercial and Investment Disputes

Edited by

CATHARINE TITI
KATIA FACH GÓMEZ

OXFORD
UNIVERSITY PRESS

OXFORD
UNIVERSITY PRESS

Great Clarendon Street, Oxford, OX2 6DP,
United Kingdom

Oxford University Press is a department of the University of Oxford.
It furthers the University's objective of excellence in research, scholarship,
and education by publishing worldwide. Oxford is a registered trade mark of
Oxford University Press in the UK and in certain other countries

First Edition published in 2019

Published in the United States of America by Oxford University Press
198 Madison Avenue, New York, NY 10016, United States of America

British Library Cataloguing in Publication Data
Data available

Library of Congress Control Number: 2019937071

ISBN 978-0-19-882795-5

Foreword

Edna Sussman

This book will serve an important need. While mediation has been a subject of discussion in international circles for many years, it is now poised to grow dramatically. Relatively little has been published that comprehensively covers the subject. This book fills that gap.

A review of the many efforts made over the course of the past ten years to encourage mediation for cross-border disputes and the repeated statements by users of a preference for collaborative resolution of disputes confirms the importance of the contribution the book's authors offer practitioners and users.

In recognition of the fact that mediation can provide a cost-effective and quick extrajudicial resolution of disputes in civil and commercial matters through processes tailored to the needs of the parties, and is more likely to be complied with voluntarily and to preserve an amicable and sustainable relationship between the parties, the European Union issued its Mediation Directive in 2008. In recognition of those same factors and the contribution of mediation to producing savings in the administration of justice, court-annexed mediation is increasingly being implemented in jurisdictions around the world. The introduction of mediation laws is also on the rise, as exemplified by Brazil's successful enactment of its mediation law in 2015. The World Bank issued its Mediation Series in 2016, offering learning resources to assist states in developing mediation policy and law, understanding mediation essentials, and assisting in conflict management design.

Responses from users across jurisdictions highlight the current interest in mediation. The 2015 Queen Mary University of London and White & Case survey found that users felt that counsel could do more to encourage settlement, including the use of mediation during an arbitration. The Global Pound Conference, which convened 4,000 dispute resolution stakeholders in twenty-eight conferences across twenty-four countries throughout 2016 and 2017 identified as a key insight that users sought greater use of non-adjudicative protocols to resolve disputes.

The most significant development in the field of international mediation is the completion in 2018 by the United Nations Commission on International Trade Law (UNCITRAL) of the Convention on International Settlement Agreements Resulting from Mediation, to be commonly known as the Singapore Convention. The new convention, which many view similarly to the New York Convention for mediation, will assure both enforcement and recognition of mediated settlement agreements and is intended not only to enable users of mediation to reap the benefits of their solutions, but also to drive the increased use of mediation, just as the New York Convention drove the increased use of arbitration. In a parallel instrument, UNCITRAL completed the development of an amendment to the 2002 Model Law on International Commercial Conciliation to add provisions related to enforcement of mediated settlement agreements.

Historically, while mediation was largely limited to commercial disputes and those dealt with by diplomacy between states with respect to disputes of geopolitical consequences, the burgeoning caseload of investor–state disputes over the past ten years has brought mediation to this arena as well. The early discussions of mediation for investor–state disputes at the Fordham International Arbitration and Mediation Conference in 2008 was followed by the development in 2012 of the International Bar Association (IBA) Rules for Investor–State Mediation. In 2013, the United Nations Conference on Trade and Development (UNCTAD) published a roadmap of five paths for reform of investor–state disputes settlement, listing first the need to promote alternative dispute resolution as the preferred process. In recognition of the importance of mediation, in 2018 the ICSID proposed amendments to its conciliation rules in order to improve the process it offers.

These are just a few of the developments driving the growth of mediation to which this book responds. The authors address the necessary subjects. Chapters discuss both commercial and investor–state disputes, as well as innovative ways in which the process can be designed to maximize the chances of a successful resolution. Procedures for the conduct of mediation at the major institutions, as well as information about mediation in various geographic areas, are thoughtfully presented. The need for a uniform cross-border ethical framework for the conduct of mediation is a cogently presented call to action. The authors not only discuss mediation in industry sectors in which mediation is now frequently used, but also include areas where mediation has to date not been extensively utilized but that would benefit from the use of processes for amicable resolutions, e.g. financial disputes. Finally, the authors offer practical guidance, e.g. on the selection of mediators and confidentiality versus transparency in commercial and investment mediation.

This book is an excellent and wide-ranging contribution that will serve to inform practitioners and users, as mediation is increasingly utilized to maximize user satisfaction with a process that is less costly, more efficient, and can enable tailored solutions that are not available in an adjudicative process.

Summary

In recent decades, the resolution of international commercial and investment disputes has been dominated by international arbitration. Mediation and conciliation have remained quietly in the background. While a complementary mechanism, international mediation and conciliation have become wide currency compared to the past. Mediation rules that have been in disuse have gained momentum; dispute settlement centres now introduce and promote new mediation rules; the European Union is encouraging international mediation both in the commercial and investment sphere, and mediation provisions are included in secondary EU legislation and in the new EU international investment agreements (IIAs); a new initiative in the United Nations Commission on International Trade Law (UNCITRAL) aims to ensure enforcement of international commercial settlement agreements resulting from conciliation; the first investor–state disputes are mediated under the IBA rules; the International Centre for Settlement of Investment Disputes (ICSID)'s conciliation mechanism is used more often than in the past; the International Chamber of Commerce (ICC) has recently administered its first mediation case based on a bilateral investment treaty; and a new training market on mediation is flourishing. As a consequence, academics, investment treaty negotiators, lawyers, and disputing parties are becoming increasingly aware of this alternative method of dispute settlement.

Mediation in Commercial and Investment Disputes addresses this highly topical theme. It brings together a group of outstanding, highly qualified experts from academia, mediation, arbitration institutions, and international legal practice who address the subject in all its complexity from a variety of angles.

Catharine Titi is Research Associate Professor at the French National Centre for Scientific Research (CNRS)-CERSA, University Paris II Panthéon-Assas, France.

Katia Fach Gómez is Tenured Professor (*Profesora Titular*) at the Law School, University of Zaragoza, Spain.

Contents

List of Contributors

Hal Abramson, *Professor of Law, Touro Law Center (New York)*

Charles H. Brower II, *Professor, Wayne State University Law School*

Chester Brown, *Professor, University of Sydney*

Peter D. Cameron, *Professor and Director, Centre for Energy, Petroleum, Mineral Law and Policy, University of Dundee*

Jack J. Coe, Jr, *Professor, Pepperdine Law School*

Ignacio de Castro, *Deputy Director, World Intellectual Property Organization (WIPO) Arbitration and Mediation Center*

Andrija Erac, *Deputy Manager, International Chamber of Commerce (ICC) International Centre for ADR*

Katia Fach Gómez, *Tenured Professor (Profesora Titular), University of Zaragoza*

Ilaria Forestieri, *Post-Doctoral Researcher, University of Florence*

Alberto Fortún, *Partner, Cuatrecasas*

Tracey B. Frisch, *Senior Counsel, American Arbitration Association (AAA)*

Kaj Hobér, *Chair, Stockholm Chamber of Commerce (SCC) Board*

Alfonso Iglesia, *Head of the Litigation & Arbitration Practice, Cuatrecasas*

Abba Kolo, *Associate Professor, British University in Dubai*

Alina Leoveanu, *Manager, International Chamber of Commerce (ICC) International Centre for ADR*

Danny McFadden, *Ambassador, Centre for Effective Dispute Resolution (CEDR) Asia Pacific*

Giovanna Micheli, *Director, International Centre for Dispute Resolution (ICDR)*

Frauke Nitschke, *Senior Counsel, International Centre for Settlement of Investment Disputes (ICSID)*

Philipp Paech, *Associate Professor, London School of Economics*

Yanett Quiroz, *Director, International Centre for Dispute Resolution (ICDR)*

S. I. Strong, *Manley O. Hudson Professor of Law, University of Missouri*

Calliope M. Sudborough, *Academic Director and Lecturer, IÉSEG School of Management*

Edna Sussman, *Distinguished ADR Practitioner in Residence, Fordham University School of Law*

Joe Tirado, *Partner and Global Co-Head of International Arbitration and ADR, Garrigues*

Catharine Titi, *Research Associate Professor, French National Centre for Scientific Research (CNRS)-CERSA, University Paris II Panthéon-Assas*

Eric P. Tuchmann, *General Counsel and Corporate Secretary, American Arbitration Association (AAA) and Senior Vice President, International Centre for Dispute Resolution (ICDR)*

Karen Vandekerckhove, *Head of Unit, DG-Justice and Consumers, European Commission*

Elisa Vicente Maravall, *Senior Associate, Garrigues*

Phoebe Winch, *Legal Officer, Office of International Law, Attorney-General's Department, Canberra*

Heike Wollgast, *Head, IP Disputes Section, World Intellectual Property Organization (WIPO) Arbitration and Mediation Center*

PART I

COMMERCIAL AND INVESTMENT MEDIATION

BOUNDARIES, TRENDS, AND OUTLOOK

1

The Role of Mediation in International Commercial Disputes

Reflections on some Technological, Ethical, and Educational Challenges

*Katia Fach Gómez**

I. Introduction

This chapter reflects on the role currently played by mediation in the resolution of international commercial disputes. This objective is both broad and ambitious and the chapter benefits from the fact that this book contains over a dozen contributions from prestigious authors in the mediation sector who all adroitly address a broad range of aspects of international commercial mediation. The chapter's main focus is consequently the outlining and discussing of a specific series of issues that aim to complement the analysis developed by the other contributors in this edited volume.

Section II therefore explores the new meaning that some scholars have attached to the widely used acronym ADR (alternative dispute resolution). Considering mediation an important part of the 'appropriate dispute resolution' mechanisms available to commercial disputants suggests that a new light is shining through this important sector and the principles that it embraces, such as access to justice. This central idea is developed in Section III, which addresses various highly topical issues in the framework of commercial mediation: the dilemma of compulsory mediation in non-family contexts; the impact of developments in information and communication technology on the mediation milieu; the role of ethics in the contemporary mediation world; and the structure and main objectives of training schemes in international commercial mediation. Section IV concludes the discussion and leads on to the thematic studies of international commercial mediation.

* Member of the Spanish research project DER2017-85585-P and the regional research project LegMIBIO S12_17R DGA.

II. Mediation as a Cornerstone of a Holistic International Dispute Resolution Scheme

The legal term *mediation*, which has raised so many uncertainties with regard to definition and scope, is linked to the broader notion of ADR. This term's use has frequently implied a clear boundary dividing litigation before public judicial bodies on the one hand, and options that have typically been classed as 'alternatives' on the other. One of the outcomes of this dualist approach may be that part of the traditional academic debate has revolved around justifying the benefits of ADR mechanisms such as mediation and reflecting on the dangers that ADR may pose for national public justice systems.

A series of phenomena have recently converged in defence of a far more holistic approach to dispute resolution, especially at the international level. What were formerly known as ADR mechanisms have increasingly shed their 'alternative' label[1] and gained recognition and become part of a truly multi-faceted dispute resolution system. As argued elsewhere in this book,[2] the development has brought about the creation of new resolution mechanisms which are becoming interdependent to some extent,[3] all of which is driven by the desire of the newly flexible dispute resolution system to provide its users with tailor-made solutions.

Fully aware of this reality, enclaves like Singapore have implemented a range of measures with the aim of becoming all-embracing international dispute resolution hubs. Not only does Singapore possess a well-developed national judicial system, which includes the Singapore International Commercial Court (SICC),[4] but it also has powerful arbitration and mediation institutions, e.g. the Singapore International Arbitration Centre (SIAC) and the Singapore International Mediation Centre (SIMC).[5] In the view of the creators of this composite system,

[1] Lord Briggs, Justice of the Supreme Court of the UK, suggested that 'the use of technology is vital 'in taking the A out of ADR' in order to make ADR more normative'. Lord Briggs, 'DAS Convention 2017: Technology and ADR—The Risks and Opportunities', 20 November 2017, https://www.cedr.com/blog/opportunities-and-risks-of-technology-for-use-in-mediation-2/. Carrie Menkel-Meadow proposes to keep the 'A' but to give it another meaning: 'appropriate dispute resolution'. Carrie Menkel-Meadow, 'Is ODR ADR? Reflections of an ADR Founder from the 15th ODR Conference, The Hague, the Netherlands, 22–23 May 2016' (2016) 3 International Journal of Online Dispute Resolution 4.

[2] See Chapter 3, this volume.

[3] Jacqueline Nolan-Haley, 'Mediation: The 'New Arbitration' (2012) 17 Harvard Negotiation Law Review 61.

[4] This is a hybrid national court, clearly showing influence from commercial arbitration. Andrew Godwin, Ian Ramsay, and Miranda Webster, 'International Commercial Courts: The Singapore Experience' (2017) 18 Melbourne Journal of International Law 1; Man Yip, 'The Resolution of Disputes Before the Singapore International Commercial Court' (2016) 65 International and Comparative Law Quarterly 439; Johannes Landbrecht, 'The Singapore International Commercial Court (SICC)-An Alternative to International Arbitration?' (2016) 34 ASA Bulletin 112.

[5] Singapore International Commercial Court Committee, Report, November 2013, https://www.mlaw.gov.sg/content/dam/minlaw/corp/News/Annex%20A%20-%20SICC%20Committee%20Report.pdf. It is highly symptomatic that 'in Singapore the Supreme Court and the Singapore Mediation Centre are housed in the same modern building, providing a true 'multi-door courthouse', as Professor Frank Sander originally imagined it'. Carrie Menkel-Meadow, 'The Case for Mediation: The Things that

instead of competing with each other, the separate parts work together to attract the largest possible volume of legal business at the global level.[6] One author has even coined the meaningful term 'international dispute resolution tourist destination'[7] for such places.[8]

The systemic evolution of public and private dispute resolution mechanisms towards a non-hierarchical coexistence is also expected to produce effects in terms of the principle of access to justice. This key principle, which is alluded to various times throughout this chapter, is likely to become broader in scope in the future. If it is concluded that access to justice no longer refers solely to access to state court justice but to non-adjudicative protection mechanisms as well, many relevant changes are going to occur (e.g. the drafting and judicial interpretation of various international and regional provisions addressing this major issue will need to be modified).[9] Scholars state that a new paradigm of 'integral justice' has been created in the twenty-first century, based on a system of 'shared justice'. In its detractors' view, this system may actually mean the public authorities' abandonment of one of their core functions: the administration of justice and the control of the way in which it is imparted.[10]

III. Contemporary Key Challenges in the Field of International Commercial Mediation

This section reflects on a number of contemporary challenges in international commercial mediation. As will be explained, one factor that is common to them all is their contribution via various mechanisms to locating mediation as a cornerstone of a holistic international dispute resolution scheme.

Mediators should be Learning and Doing' (2016) 82 Arbitration: International Journal of Arbitration, Mediation and Dispute Management 22, 30. On Singapore, see Chapter 9, this volume.

[6] Sundaresh Menon, 'International Commercial Courts: Towards a Transnational System of Dispute Resolution'. Opening Lecture for the DIFC Courts Lecture Series 2015, https://www.supremecourt.gov.sg/docs/default-source/default-document-library/media-room/opening-lecture---difc-lecture-series-2015.pdf.

[7] Eunice Chua, 'Feel the Earth Move: Shifts in the International Dispute Resolution Landscape', 14 August 2018, http://mediationblog.kluwerarbitration.com/2018/08/14/feel-earth-move-shifts-international-dispute-resolution-landscape/.

[8] Shannon Salter, 'Online Dispute Resolution and Justice System Integration: British Columbia's Civil Resolution Tribunal' (2017) 34 (1) Windsor Yearbook of Access to Justice 112.

[9] Reflecting on these arguments: Carlos Esplugues, 'Civil and Commercial Mediation and National Courts: Towards a New Concept of Justice for the XXI Century?', in M. Schauer and B. Verschraegen (eds), *General Reports of the XIXth Congress of the International Academy of Comparative Law, Ius Comparatum—Global Studies in Comparative Law* (Springer, 2017), 213, 215, 218.

[10] Silvia Barona Vilar (ed.), *Mediación, arbitraje y jurisdicción en el actual paradigma de justicia* (Civitas Thomson-Reuters, 2016).

A. The Compulsory Mediation Dilemma

The question frequently arises as to why mediation is not more successful in quantitative terms.[11] It is sometimes pointed out in answer that mediation is not an especially well-known practice throughout the business sector;[12] that not all lawyers recommend it to their clients in commercial disputes,[13] and that the level of stakeholder confidence in mediation providers and mediators leaves room for improvement.[14]

All this begs the question as to whether the public authorities should give mediation in commercial disputes the final push by using mandatory mechanisms such as imposing a legal obligation to mediate as a pre-condition of access to the courts in some cases (via out-of-court mediation); establishing mediation as a requirement during legal proceedings (via court-referred or court-annexed mediation); or by using *quasi*-compulsory means in the sense of resorting to persuasive instruments such as cost orders.[15]

Policies of this type may be justified because mediation has extremely convincing intrinsic benefits, or because it is actually seen as an effective option for reducing the burden on national judicial systems. While such approaches are defended in the mediation community,[16] they also have stalwart detractors who highlight mediation's firm basis in party autonomy. These critics also feel that the notion of compulsory mediation is an oxymoron that could clash with the right

[11] European Commission, 'Rebooting the Mediation Directive: Assessing the Limited Impact of its Implementation and Proposing Measures to Increase the Number of Mediations in the EU' 2014, http://www.europarl.europa.eu/thinktank/en/document.html?reference=IPOL-JURI_ET(2014)493042. This does not prevent statistics offered by some mediation providers such as the Singapore Mediation Centre from showing a constant increase in the number of cases that have been raised, as well as in the disputed sums. Tan Tam Mei, 'Record Year for Mediation Centre in 2017', https://www.straitstimes.com/singapore/record-year-for-mediation-centre-in-2017.

[12] However, the 2018 International Arbitration Survey, 'The Evolution of International Arbitration', reveals that there might be a change where this issue is concerned, since 'The in-house counsel subgroup reflects a clear preference for international arbitration together with ADR (60%) over international arbitration as a stand-alone (32%) [...] as the preferred method of resolving cross-border disputes'. https://www.whitecase.com/publications/insight/2018-international-arbitration-survey-evolution-international-arbitration.

[13] Nevertheless, a 2016 survey indicates that '[u]sers are dramatically more familiar with mediation (50%) than their advisors perceive them to be (6%) [...]. Advisors are more familiar with mediation (40%) than Users perceive them to be (30%), and recommend mediation more often (70%) than Users perceive they do (47%)'. International Mediation Institute, '2016 International Mediation & ADR Survey. Census of Conflict Management Stakeholders and Trends', http://www.odreurope.com/assets/site/content/IMI_survey_2016.pdf.

[14] Thomas Stipanowich and J. Ryan Lamare, 'Living with "ADR": Evolving Perceptions and Use of Mediation, Arbitration and Conflict Management in Fortune 1,000 Corporations' (2013) 19 Harvard Negotiation Law Review 1.

[15] As indicated, the notion of mandatory mediation, an issue that falls outside the hard core of this chapter, can be defined according to varying degrees of potential imperativeness.

[16] Julian Sidoli del Ceno, 'Compulsory Mediation: Civil Justice, Human Rights and Proportionality' (2014) 6 (3) International Journal of Law in the Built Environment 286.

of access to the judicial system, for instance, or simply be less effective due to lack of party will.[17]

The debate is far from closed. Public sector advisory bodies like the UK's Civil Justice Council[18] are contributing to the creation of an intense legal, professional, and social discussion around compulsory mediation.[19] Meanwhile, the legislatures of EU-member states like Italy[20] and Greece[21] have recently made effective use of the room for manoeuvre provided by Article 5.2 of the Mediation Directive,[22] enacting mandatory mediation in a range of different types of civil and commercial disputes.[23] Countries like Australia, which is outside this EU Directive's scope,

[17] See Chapter 10, this volume. Reflecting on these arguments, Esplugues (n 9) 220; Jacqueline Nolan-Haley, 'Is Europe Headed Down the Primrose Path with Mandatory Mediation?' (2012) 37 North Carolina Journal of International Law and Commercial Regulation.

[18] The CJC is an Advisory Public Body which was established under the Civil Procedure Act 1997 with responsibility for overseeing and co-ordinating the modernisation of the civil justice system, https://www.judiciary.uk/related-offices-and-bodies/advisory-bodies/cjc/.

[19] Civil Justice Council, ADR and Civil Justice, Interim Report, October 2017, https://www.judiciary.uk/wp-content/uploads/2017/10/interim-report-future-role-of-adr-in-civil-justice-20171017.pdf. Announcing a possible study on the subject, the Joint Project Group established by The European Law Institute (ELI) and the European Network of Councils for the Judiciary (ENCJ), 'The Relationship between Formal and Informal Justice: the Courts and Alternative Dispute Resolution', https://www.europeanlawinstitute.eu/fileadmin/user_upload/p_eli/Publications/ADR_Statement.pdf, 8.

[20] Giuseppe Conte, 'The Italian Way of Mediation' (2014) 6 Yearbook on Arbitration & Mediation 180.

[21] Nevertheless, the provisions of the Greek Mediation Act proclaiming compulsory mediation have been placed on hold until 16 September 2019. Haris Meidanis, 'Greece: Mediation Going Compulsory. For Good or for Bad?', Kluwer Mediation Blog, 31 May 2018, http://mediationblog.kluwerarbitration.com/2018/05/31/greece-mediation-going-compulsory-good-bad/; Haris Meidanis, 'Greece: Mediation Going Compulsory. The Sequel', 12 October 2018, http://mediationblog.kluwerarbitration.com/2018/10/12/greece-mediation-going-compulsory-sequel/. A 'mandatory mediation attempt' included in Romanian Mediation Law also raised constitutional problems there. Constantin-Adi Gavrila, 'Mandatory 'Mediation Attempt', http://mediationblog.kluwerarbitration.com/2018/09/14/mandatory-mediation-attempt/.

[22] Article 5.2 (Recourse to Mediation): 'This Directive is without prejudice to national legislation making the use of mediation compulsory or subject to incentives or sanctions, whether before or after judicial proceedings have started, provided that such legislation does not prevent the parties from exercising their right of access to the judicial system'. Directive 2008/52/EC of the European Parliament and of the Council of 21 May 2008 on certain aspects of mediation in civil and commercial matters.

[23] The European Court of Justice's interpretation of this topic is as follows: 'Nor do the principles of equivalence and effectiveness or the principle of effective judicial protection preclude national legislation which imposes, in respect of such disputes, prior implementation of an out-of-court settlement procedure, provided that that procedure does not result in a decision which is binding on the parties, that it does not cause a substantial delay for the purposes of bringing legal proceedings, that it suspends the period for the time-barring of claims and that it does not give rise to costs—or gives rise to very low costs—for the parties, and only if electronic means is not the only means by which the settlement procedure may be accessed and interim measures are possible in exceptional cases where the urgency of the situation so requires.' Judgment of the Court (Fourth Chamber) of 18 March 2010 (references for a preliminary ruling from the Giudice di Pace di Ischia, Italy)—*Rosalba Alassini v Telecom Italia SpA* (C-317/08), *Filomena Califano v Wind SpA* (C-318/08), *Lucia Anna Giorgia Iacono v Telecom Italia SpA* (C-319/08), and *Multiservice Srl v Telecom Italia SpA* (C-320/08) ('*Alassini*'). Dealing with these issues, Antonio Maria Marzocco and Michele Nino, 'The EU Directive on Mediation in Civil and Commercial Matters and the Principle of Effective Judicial Protection' (2012) Lex et Scientia. Juridical Series 105; Pablo Cortés, 'Can I Afford Not to Mediate? Mandatory Online Mediation for European Consumers: Legal Constraints and Policy Issues' (2008) 35 Rutgers Computer & Technology Law Journal 1.

have also implemented various mandatory mediation schemes.[24] Time will tell whether such initiatives, temporary or not, are capable of producing the desired results in terms of consolidating mediation as an ADR mechanism in the resolution of commercial disputes.

B. Mediation in the Information and Communication Technology Era

Our daily lives have changed considerably in just a few decades, mainly as a result of a range of new technologies, from Facebook, Siri, Alexa, 3-D printers, wearable tech, and exoskeletons to self-driving cars, to name but a few. It is also indisputable that the global economy and its commercial transactions now operate transnationally and are increasingly reliant on technologies that enable commercial transactions to be carried out in nanoseconds. Taking all these factors into account, it seems clear that commercial mediation cannot, and should not, remain on the periphery of the many advances driven by Information and Communication Technologies (ICTs). This section therefore contains a few observations on this highly complex and fast-moving topic.

The starting point is that new technologies have been incorporated into commercial mediation processes at many different levels. ICT facilitates user access to dispute resolution services and enables both disputants and the neutral party to use technological tools at many points of the mediation process: electronic filing; email and video-conferencing; document management and information sharing software; private online conversations instead of in-person caucuses; electronic signatures; and more.[25] These options no longer come as a surprise to anyone.

As this book shows,[26] online dispute resolution (ODR) of consumer disputes can be viewed as the tip of the iceberg in the process of interconnecting new technologies and non-family ADR schemes.[27] Much has already been written about these

[24] Alan Limbury, 'Compulsory Mediation—The Australian Experience, 22 October 2018', http://mediationblog.kluwerarbitration.com/2018/10/22/compulsory-mediation-australian-experience/; Melissa Hanks, 'Perspectives on Mandatory Mediation' (2012) 35 (2) University of New South Wales Law Journal 929.

[25] Most mediation providers already provide online dockets for their users; see, for example, the WIPO Electronic Case Facility. See also Chapter 14, this volume. Likewise, the Australian Resolution Institute has created MODRON, https://www.resolution.institute/membership-information/odr-online-dispute-resolution. This type of initiative is called a document-oriented approach, as opposed to the case-oriented approach that in turn develops into predictive systems.

[26] See Chapter 10, this volume.

[27] Likewise, family mediation has spearheaded the increasing use of technology in ADR, with projects such as the Dutch divorce platform Rechtwijzer (https://rechtwijzer.nl/). From this perspective, commercial mediation is harvesting the fruits of pioneering advances in the field of family mediation. The following reflection is relevant in this context: 'In England & Wales, we have a major court reform project that is introducing Online Dispute Resolution for small claims up to £25,000, for divorce, for guilty pleas in criminal cases, and for many tribunal claims in relation to social entitlements and other issues. We should not kid ourselves that commercial disputes will not ultimately follow. We need to get our online dispute resolution processes right, so that they can take their place in the court structure

ODR-type resources, usually focused on business-to-consumer e-commerce[28] and with an emphasis on improving the global community's access to justice—including disadvantaged groups who can rely on ODR as a social inclusion tool.[29] It is unquestionable that traditional justice mechanisms used to be out of reach for a large part of the global population, and that nowadays these types of digital justice fill this this gap.[30] What is not so clear, as will be discussed later, is whether or not these ODRs are eroding the quality of deeply rooted ADR mechanisms and other guarantees that should accompany them.

On a separate issue, implementing of commercial contracts executed via blockchain undoubtedly generates legal controversies, some of them derived directly from the technological peculiarities of these contracts. For this reason, resolving them in an offline mediation environment does not seem to be the optimal solution. Dispute resolution platforms such as the Decentralized Arbitration and Mediation Network (DAMN)[31] and new protocols created by traditional ADR providers, such as JAMS,[32] are therefore promoting the application of 'smart ADR mechanisms' such as mediation for solving problems arising from 'smart contacts'.

In addition, the international commercial mediation field's current reality and potential are both much broader than these non-jurisdictional e-initiatives and innovative software options. Artificial intelligence (AI) brings us to the mainly uncharted waters of a technological utopia (or otherwise), in which not only have geographical frontiers disappeared but technology also develops without limits. Big data, for instance, allows disputants to make informed decisions, which can lead to the escalation or abandonment of the controversy.[33] Furthermore,

to speed up the delivery of justice and bring our justice systems into the 21st century.' Sir Geoffrey Vos, 'Presentation to a Legal Business Seminar in Frankfurt: The Future for the UK's Jurisdiction and English Law after Brexit', 28 November 2017, https://www.judiciary.uk/wp-content/uploads/2017/11/chc-frankfurt-presentation-nov2017.pdf.

[28] The figures supplied by the eBay Resolution Center, which resolves more than 60 million disputes per year, are paradigmatic in this sense. A detailed study of the multi-tier system (problem diagnosis followed by automated negotiation that may end with mediation and arbitration) can be found in: Colin Rule, 'Designing a Global Online Dispute Resolution System: Lessons Learned from eBay' (2017) 13 University of St. Thomas Law Journal 354.

[29] From a global institutional perspective, interested readers are referred to the work on Online Dispute Resolution implemented by the UNCITRAL Working Group III 2010–2016: http://www.uncitral.org/uncitral/en/commission/working_groups/3Online_Dispute_Resolution.html.

[30] Nadja Alexander, 'Mobile Mediation: How Technology is Driving the Globalization of ADR' (2006) 27 Hamline Journal of Law and Public Policy 243; Michael Legg, 'The Future of Dispute Resolution: Online ADR and Online Courts' (2016) 27 Australasian Dispute Resolution Journal 277; http://classic.austlii.edu.au/au/journals/UNSWLRS/2016/71.pdf.

[31] DAMN, https://github.com/thirdkey-solutions/damn/blob/master/proposal.asciidoc.

[32] JAMS has created protocols supporting the use of ADR (among them mediation) in disputes arising from blockchain activities, including smart contracts. JAMS, 'ADR and Blockchain Technology', https://www.jamsadr.com/smartcontracts.

[33] The authors referred to here analyse AI systems that 'keep the parties informed about the possible consequences of their litigation if their problems are to be settled in court. Moreover, it makes use of a case-based reasoning algorithm that searches for solutions for the litigation considering past known similar cases, as a way to enhance the negotiation process. When parties have access to all this information and are aware of the consequences of their choices, they can take better decisions that encompass all

AI resources may enable the implementation of algorithm-driven mediation based on predictive analytics[34] or may lead to human mediators being replaced by a multi-agent system in the shape of an empathetic hologram, avatar, or android.[35]

With regard to these highly advanced situations in terms of AI, a not insignificant group of contemporary authors seems to consider that complex AI innovations are not yet mature enough to be applied in the commercial mediation field.[36] The digital divide and the importance of both the human element and cultural and gender-focused nuances in mediation mechanisms in fact converge in the defence of a mediation system in which AI developments should not play essential roles. At best, some authors consider commercial mediation combining 'great computer design and human interfaces' to be an optimum solution.[37] This approach, therefore, focuses on complementarity rather than replacement[38]—or, to use typical jargon from the sector, it conceives technology as the 'fourth party'.

the important aspects of a litigation process.' Davide Carneiro, Paulo Novais, Francisco Andrade, John Zeleznikow, and José Neves, 'Using Case-Based Reasoning to Support Alternative Dispute Resolution', in Andre Carvalho, Sara Rod-González, Juan Paz, and Juan M. Corchado (eds), *Distributed Computing and Artificial Intelligence. 7th International Symposium on Distributed Computing and Artificial Intelligence* (Springer, 2010) 123.

[34] It is remarkable that the Case Cruncher Alpha programme has obtained better results than highly-qualified lawyers predicting the results of 775 non-payment disputes in the insurance context, which were to be resolved by a financial ombudsman, see https://www.case-crunch.com/index.html#progress-bars3-o. Tests of this type have also been carried out in the construction mediation context. Chun-Yi Hwang and Nie-Jia Yau, 'An Experimental Case-Based Reasoning Mechanism for Construction Mediation', http://www.iaarc.org/publications/fulltext/S06-3.pdf.

[35] A multi-agent system is defined as 'a group of entities (may be software or hardware) which will "feel" the circumstances they are in and make intelligent decisions in order to achieve some common goal (like proposing a solution for the parties in dispute) based on knowledge from every agent in the system. For an agent to be considered so, it must show some basic abilities: autonomy, reactivity, pro-activity and sociability which means agents must operate on their own, read their environment and react accordingly, they must show initiative and take their own actions and be able to relate to other agents in order to achieve their goals. Additionally, an agent may show characteristics such as mobility, learning, veracity, emotions, among others'. Francisco Andrade, Paulo Novais, Davide Carneiro, and José Neves, 'Conflict Resolution In Virtual Locations', in Irene Portela and Maria Manuela Cunha (eds), *Information Communication Technology Law, Protection and Access Rights: Global Approaches and Issues* (IGI Global, 2010) 33. Sophia, developed by Hanson Robotics, might be an example of this; see http://www.hansonrobotics.com/sophia/.

[36] It has recently been declared that, '[d]espite the existence of some automated systems that operate on well delimited legal domains, the development of fully autonomous ODR systems is still far from what was initially envisioned. In fact, nowadays we cannot talk about intelligent or intuitive ODR tools'. Davide Carneiro, Paulo Novais, Francisco Andrade, John Zeleznikow, and José Neves, 'Online Dispute Resolution: An Artificial Intelligence Perspective' (2014) 41 Artificial Intelligence Review 211, 237–8. Ethan Katsh, considered to be one of the founders of the field of IDR, has made the following distinction between simple and complex disputes: 'there are actually only a limited number of categories of dispute [on eBay]. The thing broke, it wasn't what it was advertised to be, whatever. Five or six or seven or eight of those. If you can figure out what categories these disputes are likely to fall into, you can set up systems to them, but it is harder to do that with more complex disputes. I think that's one of the big challenges'. Aled Davies, 'The Evolution of ODR Mediator—Ethan Katsh', https://www.judiciary.uk/wp-content/uploads/2015/02/ethan_katsh_int2_evo_of_odr.pdf.

[37] Menkel-Meadow (n 1) 4, 5.

[38] In the words of Samantha Hardy: 'It seems more probable that we may see the increased use of automated systems to supplement the traditional mediation process whereby second-generation systems are used to facilitate some aspects of the mediation process'. Samantha Hardy, 'Avatars as

While awaiting future developments, it cannot be ignored that in a few years the digital native generation will occupy important positions in the global mediation market as disputants or mediation providers. This is likely to bring about radical changes in perception and the corresponding shifts in the mediation policy of private and public stakeholders. In contrast to older generations' less-than-favourable attitude towards ICT-driven mediation, new generations will probably not feel that human mediators' cognitive processes are more reliable than those of AI-driven devices. In short, provided that the appropriate technological means are available, feelings such as trust, a sense of security, and confidence will no longer be exclusively created by human mediators.

One consequence of all of this is that the shape of commercial mediation has become more complex due to the impact of these myriad new technologies. New agents come into play in the classical relationship between the disputants and the third-party neutral: the technological elements themselves, referred to as the 'fourth party', and the technological service provider, also known as the 'fifth party'.[39]

Many legal challenges arise inside and around this multi-faceted and technologically assisted mediation ecosystem, among which are confidentiality linked to information security, and mediation quality. Whereas confidentiality has always been considered one of offline mediation's great assets, with a limited number of well-justified exceptions,[40] the current technologically driven mediation scenario generates a series of risks regarding this fundamental aspect. For instance, a software security virus or an external contractor error can make information about a mediation process public; a subject involved in a mediation case may leak confidential information via the Internet; data may be hacked by someone from outside the dispute; or the massive amount of data collected by an ODR platform could be misused. Examples like these show that a range of effective legal responses are required in the face of controversial situations regarding data retention, transfer, and destruction in a technology-driven mediation environment.[41] These responses also need to take the transnational character of these situations into account, as this chapter has consistently highlighted.

So far, initiatives that address this type of technological issue in the mediation sphere are still a minority; nonetheless, it is worth mentioning some pioneering examples. In the private sphere, the detailed Competency Criteria for e-Mediators

Third-Party Neutral? Opportunities and Challenges for Technology in Mediation', 22 November 2017, https://adrresearch.net/2017/11/22/avatars-as-third-party-neutral-opportunities-and-challenges-for-technology-in-mediation/.

[39] This term was coined by Ethan Katsh and Janet Rifkin, *Online Dispute Resolution: Resolving Conflicts in Cyberspace* (Wiley, 2011).

[40] See Chapter 17, this volume.

[41] David Allen Larson, Artificial Intelligence: Robots, Avatars and the Demise of the Human Mediator (2010) 25 Ohio State Journal on Dispute Resolution 105, 162.

drawn up by the International Mediation Institute (IMI),[42] and the Advice for mediators working with technology produced by the Centre for Effective Dispute Resolution (CEDR)[43] are both significant. In the public sphere, this statement from the Practice Standards of the 2015 Australian National Mediator Accreditation System (NMAS) is worth noting: 'a mediator must take care to preserve confidentiality in the storage and disposal of written and electronic notes and records of the mediation and must take reasonable steps to ensure that administrative staff preserve such confidentiality'.[44]

Where the quality of technology-assisted mediation is concerned, some authors fear that the promotion of ODR as a broad equal access portal to conflict resolution[45] may have a negative side: a decline in the quality of mediation mechanisms. There is a danger that procedural justice, clearly identified through principles such as due process in more classical contexts, like litigation or international arbitration, may be diluted in the framework of ODR mechanisms.[46] Various soft law documents have been produced to promote and protect ODR quality, such as the International Council for ODR (ICODR) Standards dealing with ODR programme quality[47] and the previous work developed by the National Center for Technology and Dispute Resolution on principles for ODR practice.[48] It is clear that technology-assisted mediation raises a series of uncertainties with ethical roots, which currently seem under-regulated.

C. Ethics in a Changing Mediation World

Another chapter of this book discusses the fact that multiple private and public initiatives have been implemented in the mediation field to create codes of conduct for mediators.[49] These ethical codes are justified in terms of increasing the consistency, credibility, and confidence levels within the mediation world. In addition, these codes of conduct have a further merit: they have served and continue to serve

[42] IMI Certification in e-Mediation Competency Criteria for e-Mediators, Annex I and Annex II, https://www.imimediation.org/about-imi/who-are-imi/online-dispute-resolution-task-force/.

[43] Advice for mediators working with technology: https://www.cedr.com/about_us/modeldocs/?id=70.

[44] Provision 9.5, see https://www.ipaustralia.gov.au/sites/g/files/net856/f/certification_rules/1842587_170804_initial_rules.pdf.

[45] According to statistics, the dispute resolution website Mediate.com has over six million annual site visitors. 'Comparative Data on Mediator Directory Websites', 26 June 2018, https://www.mediate.com/articles/comparative.cfm.

[46] Suzanne Van Arsdale, 'User Protections in Online Dispute Resolution' (2015) 21 Harvard Negotiation Law Review 107, 127–8; Arno R. Lodder and John Zeleznikow, 'Artificial Intelligence and Online Dispute Resolution', in Mohamed Abdel Wahab, Ethan Katsh, and Daniel Rainey (eds), *Online Dispute Resolution Theory and Practice* (Eleven International Publishing, 2013) 91.

[47] ICODR Standards, http://icodr.org/index.php/standards/.

[48] Ethical Principles for ODR, http://odr.info/ethics-and-odr/.

[49] See Chapter 18, this volume.

as useful inspiration in the ethical context of international commercial and investment arbitration.[50]

However, the existence of these mediator codes does not in any way mean that ethical controversies have disappeared from the mediation ecosystem. On the contrary, a consequence of a combination of circumstances, they are clearly on the increase. Firstly, we are far from having a global and harmonized code for mediators. In fact, the multiple existing codes neither have identical content nor specify their scope of application in all cases, which creates abundant problems at a practical level. Secondly, the codes are widely said to be characterized by vagueness, to lack key definitions,[51] and to be less than exhaustive in their inclusion of the relevant ethical issues.[52] This would explain, for example, the doubts that still exist as to which ethical rules should be applied to professionals such as lawyer-mediators, who are, in theory, subject to two different sets of ethical rules.[53] Thirdly, the codes' effectiveness is also questioned, especially if they belong to the soft law field and are not always accompanied by effective grievance processes for complaints about a mediator breaching rules of conduct.[54] A fourth and final factor that would explain the abundance of ethical controversies in contemporary mediation is its incorporation of ICT.

To look more closely at some of the issues already addressed in section B of this chapter on ICT, with the aim of reflecting on the ethical consequences of this new mediation configuration, it is worth returning to the idea that contemporary mediation is a complex multi-faceted phenomenon that involves an ever-increasing number of parties. Rather than supporting the hypothesis that the ethical parameters traditionally applicable to offline mediation have lost their validity in the modern context of technology-assisted mediation, it seems more reasonable to argue that the ethical parameters applicable to mediators remain essentially valid, but that they are in need of continued and flexible reinterpretation.[55] Expressed

[50] Katia Fach Gómez, *Key Duties of International Investment Arbitrators* (Springer, 2018).

[51] These vaguely expressed codes have promoted initiatives such as the non-binding opinions issued by the Committee on Mediator Ethical Guidance of the ABA Dispute Resolution Section. An interesting online resource on this subject is the National Clearinghouse for Mediator Ethics Opinions, https://www.americanbar.org/groups/dispute_resolution/resources/Ethics/.

[52] Scholars have affirmed: 'because general codes like the *Model Standards* reduce the mediator's ethical landscape to generic and commonly undisputed principles, they poorly inform the more common and difficult mediator choices. Provisions are substantively vague, and the framework is arguably problematic.' Andrea C. Yang, 'Ethics Codes for Mediator Conduct: Necessary but Still Insufficient' (2009) 22 The Georgetown Journal of Legal Ethics 1229. In the same sense: Susan Nauss Exon, 'How Can a Mediator Be Both Impartial and Fair: Why Ethical Standards of Conduct Create Chaos for Mediators' (2006) 2 Journal of Dispute Resolution 1.

[53] Maureen E. Laflin, 'Preserving the Integrity of Mediation through the Adoption of Ethical Rules for Lawyer-Mediators' (2014) 14 Notre Dame Journal of Law, Ethics & Public Policy 479; Melvin A. Rubin and Brian F. Spector, 'Ethical Conundrums for the 21st-Century Lawyer/Mediator' (2008) 2 American Journal of Mediation 73.

[54] Focused on the US context, Sharon Press, 'Mediator Ethical Breaches: Implication for Public Policy' (2014) 6 Yearbook on Arbitration & Mediation 107.

[55] In the words of Rainey, '[t]he adjustment in ethical standards will be evolutionary, not revolutionary, and will be accomplished over time through dialogue with practitioners who are facing the new demands, restrictions and freedoms brought to third-party by technology'. Daniel Rainey, 'Third-Party

very simply, ICT's entry into the mediation context requires mediators to be aware of the content newly re-acquired by traditional ethical principles, since this brings with it new obligations for the neutral third party. As an example, the principle of mediator impartiality and independence may currently be affected by various circumstances originating in technology (for example, if a professional does not fully inform the parties regarding which ICT is used in the course of the mediation, or a mediator has a conflict of interest regarding the automated provider). Likewise, the principle of party autonomy in contemporary mediation needs to include the disputants' acceptance of the mediator's choices of technology.[56]

Another key idea in the understanding of contemporary commercial mediation and its ethical challenges is that non-legal professionals play an extremely important role in the design, use, and monitoring of ICT-driven mediation.[57] Multidisciplinarity has permanently permeated the essence of this ADR mechanism.[58] From an ethical perspective, if the general claim is that mediator ethics is still an under-regulated area,[59] the same can be argued even more fervently with regard to the ethical standards applicable to other mediation-connected professions, such as ODR developers. Although there are professional bodies, for example, the Australian Computer Society, that have developed ethical codes for their members,[60] practice shows that many non-legal professionals who dedicate themselves to the mediation field are neither certified nor members of these bodies; thus, their ethical standards are currently little short of nebulous.

This scenario justifies initiatives like that presented in 2018 by the Institute of Electrical and Electronics Engineers (IEEE): the drafting of a 266-page document entitled 'Ethically Aligned Design: A Vision for Prioritizing Human Well-Being with Autonomous and Intelligent Systems'.[61] Many of the issues addressed in this text will undoubtedly require in-depth discussion by mediation's legal and non-legal professionals.

Ethics in the Age of the Fourth Party' (2014) 1 International Journal of Online Dispute Resolution 37–56, 38.

---

[56] Ibid., 46–9.

[57] Philip Hanke, 'Computers with Law Degrees? The Role of Artificial Intelligence in Transnational Dispute Resolution, and its Implications for the Legal Profession' (2017) 2 Transnational Dispute Management; see also Katia Fach Gómez and Weiwei Zhang, 'Non-Legal Adjudicators in National and International Disputes' (2017) 2 Transnational Dispute Management; Leah Wing, 'Ethical Principles for Online Dispute Resolution: A GPS Device for the Field' (2017) 3 (1) International Journal of Online Dispute Resolution 12.

[58] Darin Thompson, 'Creating New Pathways to Justice Using Simple Artificial Intelligence and Online Dispute Resolution' (2015) 1 International Journal of Online Dispute Resolution.

[59] Omer Shapira, *A Theory of Mediator's Ethics: Foundations, Rationale, and Application* (Cambridge University Press, 2016).

[60] ACS Code of Ethics, https://www.acs.org.au/content/dam/acs/acs-documents/Code-of-Ethics.pdf.

[61] IEEE, 'Ethically Aligned Design: A Vision for Prioritizing Human Well-Being with Autonomous and Intelligent Systems', https://ethicsinaction.ieee.org/.

D. Training for International Commercial Mediation

This book aims to be an educational tool for use on the mediation and ADR courses that are increasingly being run by universities, dispute resolution providers, bar associations, and other institutions worldwide. Its practical nature is the result of clear drafting, the reference to many leading cases and relevant examples, and the inclusion of a commercial mediation fact pattern.[62]

What follows is a series of observations on university-taught commercial mediation, which is believed to be a pivotal element for creating a pro-mediation culture. Leaving aside the multiple financial, sociological, cultural, and university policy-related factors that may shape these studies' specific characteristics in particular countries or regions, any course focusing on commercial mediation should be a priori characterized by the following features:

1) Offering varied and interactive teaching tools aimed at developing the students' practical skills and that have to be mastered by the experts teaching the courses.

Apart from lectures, workshops, and a wide range of drafting exercises, commercial mediation courses usually offer live role-plays, mock mediations, and participation in mediation clinics.

2) Experts teaching mediation must have well-developed ICT skills.

Directly connected with the first criterion, and as mentioned previously in this chapter, all mediation courses today are supported to a great extent by new technologies. Students are encouraged to make use of online environments and distance learning platforms in the same way that lecturers use mediation cartoons, online conflict style inventories, and filmed mediations.[63]

3) While the primary aim of university mediation courses is obviously to train future mediators, this should not be their only goal.

The mediation market is still limited[64] and mediation courses therefore also need to meet other broader and equally praiseworthy objectives, such as training

[62] See Chapter 4, this volume.

[63] Sabine Walsh, 'Educating the Dispute Resolvers of the Future; 'The Highs and Lows of Mediation Training. Part 1: The Mediation Trainer's Toolbox', http://mediationblog.kluwerarbitration.com.

[64] Nevertheless, it has been argued that the use and understanding of social media shown by young professionals may help them to gain a professional access to the mediation world. Gregg Relyea, 'Social Media-tion: A Bridge for Young Mediators to Enter and Re-Define the Profession?', April 2018, https://www.mediate.com/articles/relyeag8.cfm.

different types of professionals who will incorporate the mediation culture into their work habits.

4) Mediation courses must also benefit from multidisciplinary groups.

It is crucial for non-law students with economics, business, management, or engineering expertise[65] to also master commercial mediation. It follows from this that mediation courses need not necessarily be taught in law faculties.

5) The syllabi should also reflect the highly diverse nature of this non-adversarial discipline.

In line with no. 4, and without neglecting the important legal bedrock of commercial mediation, mediation courses should also offer socio-psychological training, i.e. include content on communication skills,[66] as well as the technological aspects of contemporary mediation and the ethical challenges connected to it;

6) All mediation courses must give international perspective the importance it deserves.

The fact that commercial mediation with international aspects is becoming increasingly common has already been highlighted.[67]

As mentioned earlier, these university courses are sometimes directly linked to commercial mediation competitions.[68] There is no better way to implement the learning-by-doing approach that is so inherent to the mediation context than by student participation in these international competitions. The International Chamber of Commerce (ICC) undoubtedly plays a pioneering role worldwide in this field, as shown by the magnificent data from the fourteen

[65] In contexts such as construction, the contractual regulation of this kind of business is usually carried out through model contracts developed by private sector professional institutions such as the International Federation of Consulting Engineers (FIDIC). The contracts usually address dispute resolution via multi-tier clauses, which have traditionally attached great importance to the figure of the engineer in their initial phase. This example clearly justifies the need for these professionals to have specialist training in ADR. Maria R. Lamari, 'The Role of Alternative Dispute Resolution in Government Construction Contract Disputes' (1994) 23 Hofstra Law Review 205. See also Chapter 15, this volume.

[66] Luigi Cominelli, 'Training Young Lawyers in the European Mediation Framework: It's Time to Devise a New Pedagogy for Conflict Management and Dispute Resolution' (2016) 2 The Italian Law Journal 163–73.

[67] The relevant private international law issues that international commercial mediation may raise are addressed, for example, in: Horst Eidenmüller and Helge Großerichter, 'Alternative Dispute Resolution', in Jürgen Basedow, Giesela Rühl, Franco Ferrari, and Pedro de Miguel Asensio, *Encyclopedia of Private International Law* (Edward Elgar, 2017).

[68] By way of example, https://www.handbook.unsw.edu.au/undergraduate/courses/2019/LAWS3510/.

editions of its mediation moot in Paris,[69] as well as the proliferation of regional pre-moots.[70]

In relation to these observations, it is useful at this point to look briefly at the study of commercial mediation as a means of becoming a certified mediator. The two key principles that need to be referred to in this context are on the one hand party autonomy in mediator selection[71] and on the other state intervention in mediator selection and training. Although these principles may be viewed a priori as contradictory, an analysis of comparative law shows that they have, in fact, managed to coexist in different ways in multiple national legislations. For instance, some national provisions limit the parties' freedom of choice in the context of court-annexed mediation or when mediating on specific issues relating to business areas in which the state has a specific interest. Likewise, the parties' freedom to select their preferred mediator may be affected by a range of different requirements regarding his/her professional or academic qualifications or training (which are sometimes pre-requisites for allowing mediators to be included in a register or qualify as certified mediators).[72] Underlying all these impositions is the state's interest in establishing and guaranteeing a certain level of quality in mediation services.[73]

The United States is a pioneer in the mediation certification field, as in many other commercial mediation-related issues.[74] A long-running debate began there several decades ago regarding the need to provide the mediation process with legitimacy through mediator credentialing.[75] The major benefits such professionalization is expected to bring about—which can also be extrapolated to many other countries—include increased harmonization of mediation quality; enhanced mediator credibility as a result of an external statement of quality; and the creation of

[69] See Chapter 5, this volume.

[70] The interest that the ICC is showing in Asia via pre-moots deserves to be highlighted (https://iccwbo.org/event/icc-international-commercial-mediation-competition-hong-kong/), as it is another example of a reality that is revealed throughout this book: the region's dynamism and growing weight in the international commercial mediation field. See also Chapter 9, this volume.

[71] The choice of mediator (or co-mediators) is a key issue, as it is in the international arbitration context. See also Chapter 16, this volume.

[72] Esplugues (n 9) 236–9 provides a thorough analysis of comparative law in the subject matter.

[73] Developing this statement, Moffit indicates four possible quality assurance mechanisms in the mediation context: public front-end mechanisms, private front-end mechanisms, public back-end mechanisms, and private back-end mechanisms. Michael L. Moffitt, 'The Four Ways to Assure Mediator Quality (And Why None of Them Work)' (2009) 24 (2) Ohio State Journal on Dispute Resolution 191.

[74] Mary Ellen O'Connell, 'Introduction to the Symposium Issue on the Americanization of International Dispute Resolution' (2003–2004) 9 Ohio State Journal on Dispute Resolution 1.

[75] Among these pioneering articles are: Ellen A. Waldman, 'The Challenge of Certification: How to Ensure Mediator Competence While Preserving Diversity' (1995–1996) 30 University of San Francisco Law Review 723; Donald T. Weckstein, 'Mediator Certification: Why and How' (1995–1996) 30 University of San Francisco Law Review 757; Dana Shaw, 'Mediation Certification: An Analysis of the Aspects of Mediator Certification and an Outlook on the Trend of Formulation Qualifications for Mediators' (1998) 29 University of Toledo Law Review 328.

greater awareness within the professional group of certified mediators, positioning them as a more skilful lobby to foster mediation practices.[76]

With respect to the substantive content of and methodological approach to such specialist professional training, the logical starting point is that the applicable regulation must be complied with. However, it is not uncommon for national or sub-national legislations to provide nothing more than brief general indications,[77] leaving those offering this type of training in the mediation market enough room for manoeuvre. Thus, international harmonization in the certified training field is currently far from being a real possibility; in fact, in some paradigmatic cases a nation-wide mediator certification has not yet been achieved.[78] In practice, the regulatory gaps left by public bodies are being addressed through soft law means by important private institutions, e.g. the American Bar Association (ABA)[79] or the International Mediation Institute (IMI), both of which have made significant efforts in this field.[80]

One of the outcomes of the scant standardization in mediation certification requirements is the large number of professional mediation training courses currently available. In principle, it seems that the essence of the courses in this burgeoning market should not differ substantially content-wise from the university courses referred to above in this chapter.[81] Nevertheless, vis-à-vis academic freedom, in the professional context many stakeholders wish their own approaches to training to prevail in terms of course content and methodology, with the aim of guaranteeing their perspective on quality of mediation training. For all these reasons, any individual wishing to work in the mediation field needs to weigh a great many factors before choosing a commercial mediation training course, including the geographical context in which the neutral third party would act.

[76] In greater detail, see Michelle Robinson, 'Mediator Certification: Realizing its Potentials and Coping with its Limitations' (2007) American Journal of Mediation 51.

[77] In the case of Spain, see Alberto José Lafuente Torralba, 'La formación del mediador y el coste de la mediación: dos aspectos cruciales aunque menospreciados por la Ley 5/2012 de 6 de julio', in Juan Pablo Murga Fernández and Salvador Tomás Tomás (eds), *Il diritto patrimoniale di fronte alla crisi economica in Italia e in Spagna* (CEDAM, 2014) 385.

[78] Mandy Zhang, 'To Certify or Not to Certify: A Comparison of Australia and the U.S. in Achieving National Mediator Certification' (2008) 8 (2) Pepperdine Dispute Resolution Law Journal 307. In the Spanish context, in which the autonomous communities have dictated their own rules on the matter, see Manuel Álvarez Torres, Beatriz Gil Vallejo, and Juan Jesús Morcillo Jiménez, *Mediación civil y mercantil* (Dykinson, 2013).

[79] Recommendations of the ABA Section of Dispute Resolution Task Force on Mediator Credentialing, https://www.americanbar.org/content/dam/aba/migrated/dispute/taksforce_report_2003.authcheckdam.pdf.

[80] For instance, the ODR Task Force of the IMI has released a document detailing a measurable set of criteria for competency in e-mediation aimed at professionals participating in qualifying assessment programs. IMI Certification in E-Mediation Competency Criteria for e-Mediators, https://www.imimediation.org/about-imi/who-are-imi/online-dispute-resolution-task-force/.

[81] Joseph B. Stulberg, Donald C. Peters, Tracy L. Allen, and Judith P. Meyer, 'Creating and Certifying the Professional Mediator-Education and Credentialing' (2004) 28 (1) American Journal of Trial Advocacy 75; Fern Smith, 'Critical Components for Mediation Training' in Arthur W. Rovine (ed.), *Contemporary Issues in International Arbitration and Mediation: The Fordham Papers* (Brill, 2007) 265.

Another important aspect is that, regardless of the formal educational requirements imposed by public or private institutions on those wishing to enter the profession, it seems reasonable to envisage training as a life-long commitment for mediators,[82] whose requirements may harden over time. Principle 1.1 of the European Code of Conduct for Mediators addressed this issue in 2004: 'Mediators must be competent and knowledgeable in the process of mediation. Relevant factors include proper training and continuous updating of their education and practice in mediation skills, having regard to any relevant standards or accreditation schemes'.[83] This question was also deal with a year later in the Model Standards of Conduct for Mediators adopted by the American Arbitration Association (AAA), the American Bar Association (ABA), and the Association for Conflict Resolution (ACR): 'A mediator should attend educational programs and related activities to maintain and enhance the mediator's knowledge and skills related to mediation'.[84] The notion of continuous training is also reflected in the 2018 Edinburgh Declaration of International Mediators' statement: 'We are committed to maintaining and raising professional standards through training, continuing development and sharing of best practice'.[85] On a practical level, some mediation training providers have already instituted re-certification processes.[86]

Finally, it should be noted that mediation training is also required of other groups such as judges.[87] In 2018, the European Law Institute (ELI) and the European Network of Councils for the Judiciary (ENCJ) approved a Statement of European Best Practice in relation to the approach that courts and judges should adopt in interacting with all types of ADR processes. It states that, '[i]n encouraging ADR, Courts and Judges should […] be provided with training and continuing professional education in ADR, so that they understand those domestic and EU ADR processes currently available in their Member State'.[88]

[82] Dwight Golann, 'What Can Training Do for an Experienced Mediator?' (2005–2006) 12 Dispute Resolution Magazine 9.

[83] European Code of Conduct for Mediators, http://ec.europa.eu/civiljustice/adr/adr_ec_code_conduct_en.pdf.

[84] Standard IV, Competence, A. 2, https://www.mediate.com/articles/model_standards_of_conflict.cfm. Analysing the origins of this extensive proposal, see John D. Feerick, 'Toward Uniform Standards of Conduct for Mediators' (1997) 38 South Texas Law Review 455.

[85] See http://mediationblog.kluwerarbitration.com/2018/05/28/edinburgh-declaration-international-mediators-may-2018/.

[86] For instance, the National Association of Certified Mediators (NACM), http://www.mediatorcertification.org.

[87] Other professional groups, e.g. lawyers, should not distance themselves from the study of these subjects, including their technological component. David Syme, 'Keeping Pace: On-Line Technology and ADR Services' (2006) 23 Conflict Resolution Quarterly 343. In this sense, in 2012 the ABA amended Section 1.1 of its Model Rules of Professional Conduct, which now reads as follows: 'to maintain the requisite knowledge and skill, a lawyer should keep abreast of changes in the law and its practice including the benefits and risks associated with relevant technology, engage in continuing study and education to comply with all continuing legal education requirements to which the lawyer is subject'. See https://www.americanbar.org/groups/professional_responsibility/publications/model_rules_of_professional_conduct/model_rules_of_professional_conduct_table_of_contents/.

[88] https://www.europeanlawinstitute.eu/fileadmin/user_upload/p_eli/Publications/ADR_Statement.pdf.

IV. Concluding Remarks

It would be fallacious to state that all commercial controversies with a foreign connection are nowadays resolved thanks to the classical legal tools provided by private international law. Traditional international litigation remains in good health, but reality shows that ADR mechanisms are still growing at a remarkable rate in the international business field and that they have consequently attracted increasing interest from legal and non-legal scholars.

On the basis that the monopoly on the resolution of international commercial disputes disappeared a long time ago, this chapter has focused its attention on international commercial mediation. This specific ADR mechanism has proved to be a useful instrument for various types of disputants and conflicts, as well as being sufficiently flexible to adapt with a certain speed to the radical changes taking place at technological and social levels. Mapping the profiles and main characteristics of contemporary commercial mediation, as this chapter and the book itself aims to do, also makes it possible to predict how this institution will position itself in the face of future challenges.

2

Mediation and the Settlement of International Investment Disputes

Between Utopia and Realism

Catharine Titi

I. Introduction

Investment arbitration is the default mode of settling international investment disputes. So while in other contexts arbitration is discussed as an alternative dispute resolution (ADR) mechanism, in international investment law, *alternative* is typically that which is not arbitration—or national court proceedings.[1] More particularly, ADR in this context tends to refer to 'soft', non-binding procedures, such as negotiations, consultations, and mediation.[2] ADR is also sometimes used to refer to dispute prevention policies (DPPs).[3] This chapter focuses on investment mediation, and discusses some DPPs to the extent that they resemble mediation.

The advantages of mediation are well known. Mediation is voluntary. The parties are the masters of the game, drive the process, and have control over the outcome.[4] Mediation is less formal and more flexible than arbitration. Jeswald Salacuse has presented this in the following terms. Disputants can theoretically resort to four 'ideal' types of dispute settlement: negotiation, mediation, arbitration, and

[1] United Nations Conference on Trade and Development (UNCTAD), 'Investor-State Disputes: Prevention and Alternatives to Arbitration', *UNCTAD Series on International Investment Policies for Development* (United Nations, 2010) xii.

[2] No distinction is made in this chapter between the terms 'mediation' and 'conciliation'. In line with the overall approach taken in this book, the term 'mediation' is used to also refer to 'conciliation'. Although 'mediation' and 'conciliation' are not coterminous, the difference between them is one of degree rather than of substance. Conciliation is often described as a more formal process than mediation ('very formal, structured and result oriented'), with the conciliator assuming a more directive or interventionist role, to the extent that it has been described as 'non-binding arbitration'. Mediation is more flexible and less formal, and it is sometimes likened to a process of 'assisted negotiation' (UNCTAD (n 1) xiii–xiv, xix). The line between the two can be unclear.

[3] E.g. UNCTAD (n 1) xii, where DPPs are termed 'preventative ADR'. Similarly, in Susan D. Franck, 'Challenges Facing Investment Disputes: Reconsidering Dispute Resolution in International Investment Agreements', in Karl P. Sauvant (ed.), *Appeals Mechanism in International Investment Disputes* (Oxford University Press, 2008) 143, 160.

[4] Jack J. Coe, Jr, 'Towards a Complementary Use of Conciliation in Investor-State Disputes—A Preliminary Sketch', (2005) 12 UC Davis Journal of International Law 7, 15; Note, 'Mediation of Investor-State Conflicts' (2014) 127 Harvard Law Review 2543, 2549.

adjudication.[5] These ideal types exist on a continuum from negotiation to adjudication and as parties move along the continuum, they increasingly lose flexibility and control over their dispute.[6] Salacuse's construct is useful to place mediation in context. In contrast with negotiations, in mediation the parties do not have *absolute* control over their dispute; the presence of a third-party neutral alters the dynamics between the parties.[7] But contrary to arbitration, the mediator does not have the power to impose a solution on the parties.[8] Adjudication offers the least degree of flexibility to the parties, since both the court's jurisdiction and the process is determined by the applicable law and not, as in arbitration, by the agreement of the parties.[9]

Other oft-cited advantages of mediation include that it is cheaper and faster than arbitration.[10] Over time investment arbitration has become expensive and time-consuming. In 2012, average arbitration costs were calculated at 8 million US dollars per case[11] and in 2014, at 10 million US dollars.[12] In reality, the average amount appears to be lower: a 2017 study found that average party costs were 6,019,000 US dollars for the claimant and 4,855,000 US dollars for the respondent, while average tribunal costs were 933,000 US dollars.[13] Mediation tends to be cheaper than arbitration. It involves both lower party costs, partly because mediation is less pleadings-intensive than arbitration,[14] and lower institutional/third-party neutral costs. For example, the average institutional costs of concluded conciliation proceedings at the International Centre for Settlement of Investment

[5] Jeswald W. Salacuse, 'Is There a Better Way? Alternative Methods of Treaty-Based, Investor-State Dispute Resolution' (2007) 31 Fordham International Law Journal 138, 154.

[6] Ibid., 154–5.

[7] Ibid., 154.

[8] Cf. (n 3) on the role of conciliators.

[9] Salacuse (n 5) 154–5.

[10] E.g. ibid., 155; Thomas W. Walde, Proactive Mediation of International Business and Investment Disputes Involving Long-Term Contracts: From Zero-Sum Litigation to Efficient Dispute Management (2004) 5 Business Law International 99, 100–1.

[11] David Gaukrodger and Kathryn Gordon, 'Investor-State Dispute Settlement: A Scoping Paper for the Investment Policy Community' (2012) OECD Working Papers on International Investment 2012/03, 19; Anna Joubin-Bret and Barton Legum, 'A Set of Rules Dedicated to Investor-State Mediation: The IBA Investor-State Mediation Rules', (2014) 29 (1) ICSID Review–Foreign Investment Law Journal 17, 19.

[12] Joachim Pohl, 'Societal Benefits and Costs of International Investment Agreements: A Critical Review of Aspects and Available Empirical Evidence' (2018) OECD Working Papers on International Investment 2018/01, 46.

[13] Party costs typically refer to fees and expenses of counsel, experts, and witnesses, while tribunal costs refer to the fees and expenses of arbitrators and the arbitral institution, if relevant. For the cited amounts, see Matthew Hodgson and Alistair Campbell, 'Damages and Costs in Investment Treaty Arbitration Revisited' Allen & Overy, 14 December 2017, http://www.allenovery.com/SiteCollectionDocuments/14-12-17_Damages_and_costs_in_investment_treaty_arbitration_revisited_.pdf. See also Luke Nottage and Ana Ubilava, 'Costs, Outcomes and Transparency in ISDS Arbitrations: Evidence for an Investment Treaty Parliamentary Inquiry' (2018) 21 International Arbitration Law Review 4 ff; Jeffery P. Commission, 'How Much Does an ICSID Arbitration Cost? A Snapshot of the Last Five Years' (2016) Kluwer Arbitration Blog, http://arbitrationblog.kluwerarbitration.com/2016/02/29/how-much-does-an-icsid-arbitration-cost-a-snapshot-of-the-last-five-years/.

[14] Coe (n 4) 16.

Disputes (ICSID) are 182,000 US dollars, i.e. less than 20 percent of estimated tribunal costs in arbitration.[15] In addition, cost allocation in investment arbitration was found to be unpredictable.[16] By comparison, costs incurred in mediation, such as in conciliation proceedings at ICSID, are 'borne equally by the parties'.[17] The length of investment arbitrations is another disadvantage. In 2012, this was calculated at over three years at 'first instance', and about two years for ICSID annulment.[18] By contrast, investment mediation proceedings are shorter. According to ICSID data, all but one of concluded investment mediations were completed in under two years.[19] One case was settled in a little under three years,[20] while in one case the conciliation commission rendered its report less than six months after the case was registered.[21]

Another advantage of mediation is that the parties can preserve their business relationship going forward.[22] Building an investment relationship typically requires a significant commitment of capital and other resources, and mediation can help the disputing parties preserve their economic relationship.[23] It has further been argued that mediation has the potential to improve business relationships, if the disputing parties use it as an opportunity not only to solve their dispute but also to share information about their needs and interests and build trust in each other.[24]

Mediation may be appropriate for disputes that involve very sensitive issues and where the parties wish to retain control of the outcome, including notably when the claimant seeks more than compensation. Indeed, it may be more useful for the investment to reverse, for example, a decision to recall a licence rather than to obtain compensation. But retaining control can also be particularly important from the viewpoint of the host state. Consider the following example: while restitution is not a remedy regularly sought in investment arbitration (and much less is it granted),[25] sometimes investors do seek specific performance. In *Philip Morris*

[15] See Chapter 7, this volume. Notice that the amount for tribunal costs given above (933,000 US dollars) is the average for investment arbitration irrespective of the applicable arbitration rules or administering arbitral institution; arbitration tribunal costs at ICSID are slightly lower (at 920,000 US dollars). But the discrepancy with ICSID conciliation is still significant. For the amounts, see Hodgson and Campbell (n 13).

[16] Suzan Franck, 'Rationalizing Costs in Investment Treaty Arbitration' (2011) 88 Washington University Law Review 769.

[17] Article 61(1) of the ICSID Convention. See also Chapter 7, this volume.

[18] Times vary for review proceedings before national courts for non-ICSID arbitrations. Gaukrodger and Gordon (n 11) 71.

[19] See https://icsid.worldbank.org/en/.

[20] *Republic of Equatorial Guinea v CMS Energy Corporation and others*, ICSID Case No. CONC(AF)/12/2, registered 29 June 2012, sole conciliator report rendered on 12 May 2015.

[21] *Société d'Energie et d'Eau du Gabon v Gabonese Republic*, ICSID Case No. CONC/18/1, registered 30 March 2018, conciliation commission report rendered on 19 September 2018.

[22] Coe (n 4) 15. Nancy A. Welsh and Andrea K. Schneider, 'The Thoughtful Integration of Mediation into Bilateral Investment Treaty Arbitration' (2013) 18 Harvard Negotiation Law Review 71, 77.

[23] Salacuse (n 5) 155.

[24] Welsh and Schneider (n 22) 77.

[25] There is at least one case where the tribunal granted specific performance in lieu of damages. This is *ATA Construction v Jordan*, ICSID Case No. ARB/08/2, Award (18 May 2010), see Susan D. Franck and Lindsey E. Wylie, 'Predicting Outcomes in Investment Treaty Arbitration' (2015) 65 Duke Law

v Uruguay and *Philip Morris v Australia*, the claimant asked that the respondent withdraw the legislative measures it had adopted or refrain from applying them to the claimant's investment, and only in the alternative did it request compensation.[26] Where specific performance is sought, mediation may be desirable, particularly if the state party wants to ensure that a tribunal does not enjoin it to act in a certain way (as opposed to ordering compensation). In the two *Philip Morris* cases, claims were eventually rejected.[27] Given the facts at issue, it seems unlikely that a tribunal would have ordered specific performance, i.e. that the state withdraw its public health legislation, or that it render it inapplicable to the claimant.

But mediation also has several disadvantages. Precisely because it is a voluntary process, it is not possible to make a party comply with its outcome[28] and the mediation agreement is not enforceable in the way an arbitral award is—although the Convention on International Settlement Agreements Resulting from Mediation (Singapore Mediation Convention) is set to change the landscape in this respect.[29] There is further no certainty that mediation will yield a settlement, and the process may turn out to be a waste of time and resources.[30] In addition, mediation as a non-adjudicative means of dispute settlement is said to retard 'jurisprudential growth'; in other words, it does not contribute to the development of the law. [31] Mediation produces neither 'soft' precedents, nor guidance, nor legal certainty going forward for the issues resolved.

Moreover, mediation leaves the contested state measures, which may affect other investors too, under a shadow of doubt as to their conformity with international law. Contrast this with the example of the above-mentioned arbitration in *Philip Morris v Uruguay*, where it was made clear that the state had no responsibility under international law for the health measures it adopted. Finally, mediation assumes that the investment relationship is not in such dire straits or that the crux of the dispute is not so important to the disputing parties that they are not prepared to make any concessions or even sit around the same table to discuss. In some cases, mediation may be simply unworkable. For these reasons, investment mediation cannot replace arbitration in general,[32]

Journal 459, 485, n 116. In reality, specific performance is probably not granted in investment arbitration, both because an award granting it is difficult to enforce and because it raises questions about the respect of the sovereignty of the state.

[26] *Philip Morris Brands Sàrl, Philip Morris Products S.A. and Abal Hermanos S.A. v Uruguay*, ICSID Case No. ARB/10/7, Award (8 July 2016), para. 12; *Philip Morris Asia Ltd v Australia*, UNCITRAL, PCA Case No 2012-12, Award on Jurisdiction and Admissibility (17 December 2015), para. 89.

[27] In *Philip Morris v Uruguay* on the merits, and in *Philip Morris v Australia* at jurisdiction.

[28] Coe (n 4) 17.

[29] See Chapter 19, this volume.

[30] Coe (n 4) 17.

[31] Ibid., 25; Salacuse (n 5) 179.

[32] Ibid., 32, where the author stated that the idea 'that conciliation might fully replace arbitration is both unrealistic and undesirable'.

but it is certainly useful as a complementary option that the parties can consider in specific cases.[33]

The remainder of this chapter canvasses the existing options for mediation under investment agreements, and some options outside these treaties, and the institutional developments that reveal that mediation is on the rise. Subsequently, it considers the co-existence of mediation and arbitration and presents the former as an alternative that, while it cannot—and should not—displace arbitration, can be a very useful complement for a number of disputes. Indeed some disputes may never be resolved without mediation, e.g. because of arbitration's prohibitive costs. Next, it considers some of the challenges presented by investment mediation, and the final section concludes.

II. The Status Quo of Mediation under Investment Treaties (and Some Options outside Treaties)

A. Mediation under Investment Treaties

Although mediation has not gained much currency as a method of settling investor–state disputes when compared to arbitration, means of amicable settlement are generally a preliminary step before the investor can seise an arbitral tribunal. Some treaties make this step an apparently *quasi*-compulsory precondition to arbitration through the use of so-called 'waiting' or 'cooling-off' periods.[34] Waiting or cooling-off periods generally last from three to six months and are intended to encourage the amicable settlement of the dispute.[35] It has been argued that the term is somewhat of a misnomer and that in fact the parties do not just have to wait but must take positive action to avert the need to arbitrate their dispute.[36] However, international investment agreements (IIAs) do not impose on disputing parties an actual obligation to engage in amicable procedures. For example, the 2012 US model bilateral investment treaty (BIT) provides in an article entitled 'Consultation and Negotiation' that:

[33] Cf. Salacuse (n 5) 176.

[34] In reality, the extent to which a step is treated as 'compulsory' or not depends on the tribunal. Two contradictory strains currently exist in arbitral case law. According to one of them, waiting periods can be bypassed by the application of the most-favoured-nation treatment. See Lars Markert and Catharine Titi, 'States Strike Back—Old and New Ways for Host States to Defend Against Investment Arbitrations', in Andrea Bjorklund (ed.), *Yearbook on International Investment Law & Policy 2013–2014* (Oxford University Press, 2015) 409.

[35] E.g. see Articles 23 and 24(3) of the US Model BIT (2012); Article 22 of the Canadian Model BIT (2012 version); Article 8 of the UK–Egypt BIT (1975) and Article 8 of the UK–Ethiopia BIT (2009).

[36] Christoph Schreuer, 'Travelling the BIT Route—Of Waiting Periods, Umbrella Clauses and Forks in the Road' (2004) 5 Journal of World Investment & Trade 231, 238–9.

> In the event of an investment dispute, the claimant and the respondent should initially seek to resolve the dispute through consultation and negotiation, which may include the use of non-binding, third-party procedures.[37]

The use of mediation is clearly, if not expressly, included in the provision for 'non-binding, third-party procedures'. Even absent this specification, provision for 'amicable settlement' would include mediation. However, an initial doubt is raised about the existence of an *obligation* to pursue such procedures by the use of the hortatory 'should' (e.g. instead of a more directive 'must', 'shall', etc.). This is confirmed by the ensuing article in the US model BIT, which allows a disputing party to initiate arbitration '[i]n the event that [it] considers that an investment dispute cannot be settled by consultation and negotiation'.[38] Provided that six months have elapsed since the dispute arose, the claim can be submitted to arbitration.[39]

Investment treaties expressly mention arbitration, but only exceptionally do they refer to mediation or conciliation. For example, the BIT concluded between the United Kingdom and Kenya in 1999 provides the contracting parties' consent to submit any investor–state dispute to ICSID 'for settlement by conciliation or arbitration'.[40] In fact, a number of BITs concluded by the United Kingdom and the United States give the parties' consent to conciliation.[41] Some French BITs make reference to the jurisdiction of ICSID, thereby also including their consent to ICSID conciliation.[42] A somewhat different provision exists in the 1992 Germany–Jamaica BIT, which states that nothing in the agreement shall be construed as preventing the disputing parties from agreeing to submit their dispute to conciliation or arbitration.[43] This treaty does not provide the states' offer to submit disputes to conciliation or arbitration, but rather requires that the disputing parties subsequently agree to conciliation or arbitration. Some Indian BITs also make reference to conciliation, especially under the Conciliation Rules of the United Nations Commission on International Trade Law (UNCITRAL), and a few give advance consent to conciliation.[44] Analogous provisions have existed for a long time in numerous BITs involving various parties around the world.[45]

This trend is confirmed and to a small degree expanded in new investment agreements that expressly mention mediation (or conciliation) as a dispute settlement

[37] Article 23 of the US Model BIT (2012).
[38] Article 24 of the US Model BIT (2012).
[39] Article 24(3) of the US Model BIT (2012).
[40] Article 8(1) of the Kenya–United Kingdom BIT.
[41] For examples, see Gabriel Bottini and Veronica Lavista, 'Conciliation and BITs', in Arthur W. Rovine (ed.), *Contemporary Issues in International Arbitration and Mediation: The Fordham Papers 2009* (Brill, 2010) 370–2. E.g. see Article 8 of the UK–Egypt BIT (1975) and Article 8 of the UK Model BIT (2008).
[42] Bottini and Lavista (n 41) 365–6.
[43] Article 11(3) of the Germany–Jamaica BIT.
[44] Bottini and Lavista (n 41) 367.
[45] For examples until 2010, see, in general, ibid.

option. For example, the 2018 Comprehensive and Progressive Agreement for Trans-Pacific Partnership (CPTPP) provides that:

> [i]n the event of an investment dispute, the claimant and the respondent should initially seek to resolve the dispute through consultation and negotiation, which may include the use of non-binding, third-party procedures, such as good offices, conciliation, or mediation.[46]

The 2017 Pacific Agreement on Closer Economic Relations (PACER) Plus goes one step further. Its provision on 'Good Offices, Conciliation and Mediation' is worth citing in full. It states:

> 1. The Parties to the dispute may at any time agree to good offices, conciliation or mediation. Procedures for good offices, conciliation or mediation may begin at any time and be terminated at any time.
> 2. If the Parties to the dispute agree, procedures for good offices, conciliation or mediation may continue while the matter is being examined by a Panel established or reconvened under this Chapter.
> 3. Proceedings involving good offices, conciliation or mediation and positions taken by the Parties to the dispute during these proceedings shall be confidential and without prejudice to the rights of any Parties to the dispute in any further or other proceedings.
> 4. The Secretary-General of the Pacific Islands Forum Secretariat or their nominee may, acting in an ex officio capacity, offer good offices, conciliation or mediation with a view to assisting Parties to reach a mutually satisfactory solution.[47]

The 2016 Comprehensive Economic and Trade Agreement (CETA) between the EU and Canada contains a similar provision. Article 8.20 on 'Mediation' provides that:

> 1. The disputing parties may at any time agree to have recourse to mediation.
> 2. Recourse to mediation is without prejudice to the legal position or rights of either disputing party under this Chapter and is governed by the rules agreed to by the disputing parties including, if available, the rules for mediation adopted by the Committee on Services and Investment pursuant to Article 8.44.3(c).[48]

[46] Article 9.18 of the CPTPP. A similar provision exists in Article 10.15(1) of the Pacific Alliance Additional Protocol.

[47] Article 6 of Chapter 14 of PACER Plus.

[48] According to this provision, the Committee on Services and Investment may, if the contracting parties agree, 'adopt rules for mediation for use by disputing parties'.

3. The mediator is appointed by agreement of the disputing parties. The disputing parties may also request that the Secretary General of ICSID appoint the mediator.
4. The disputing parties shall endeavour to reach a resolution of the dispute within 60 days from the appointment of the mediator.
5. If the disputing parties agree to have recourse to mediation, Articles 8.19.6 and 8.19.8 shall not apply[49] from the date on which the disputing parties agreed to have recourse to mediation to the date on which either disputing party decides to terminate the mediation. A decision by a disputing party to terminate the mediation shall be transmitted by way of a letter to the mediator and the other disputing party.

The EU–Singapore Investment Protection Agreement (IPA)[50] includes an annex (Annex 6) on the 'Mediation Mechanism for Disputes between Investors and Parties'. The objective of the mechanism is to 'facilitate the finding of a mutually agreed solution through a comprehensive and expeditious procedure with the assistance of a mediator'.[51] Detailed provisions follow on practical and procedural issues, notably on the selection of the mediator, the initiation and conduct of the procedure, the implementation of the settlement agreement, the relationship with dispute settlement, and time limits and costs.[52] Like CETA, the EU–Singapore IPA specifies that the mediation mechanism is without prejudice to the parties' legal positions under investor–state dispute settlement (ISDS) or state–state dispute settlement (SSDS).[53] The IIA expressly protects the confidentiality of the mediation procedure (although any disputing party may disclose that a mediation is taking place).[54] Last, but not least, the treaty specifies that in the event of another dispute settlement procedure under the agreement, disputing parties

> shall not rely on or introduce as evidence in such dispute settlement procedures, nor shall any adjudicatory body, tribunal or panel take into consideration:
>
> (a) positions taken by the other disputing party in the course of the mediation procedure;
> (b) the fact that the other disputing party has indicated its willingness to accept a solution to the measure subject to mediation; or
> (c) advice given or proposals made by the mediator.[55]

[49] These provisions concern time limits and withdrawal of a request for consultations.
[50] The EU–Singapore IIA has been separated from the EU–Singapore FTA, following Opinion 2/15 of the Court of Justice of the European Union (CJEU) on the division of competences between the EU and its member states in relation to the EU–Singapore FTA, as envisaged at the time.
[51] Article 1 of Annex 6 of the EU–Singapore IPA.
[52] Articles 2–8 of Annex 6 of the EU–Singapore IPA.
[53] Article 6(2) of Annex 6 of the EU–Singapore IPA.
[54] Article 6(3) of Annex 6 of the EU–Singapore IPA.
[55] Article 6(1) of Annex 6 of the EU–Singapore IPA.

Both CETA and the EU–Singapore IPA further incorporate a code of conduct for arbitrators and mediators.[56] The codes describe various responsibilities, disclosure obligations, duties, independence and impartiality, obligations of persons formerly acting as mediators, confidentiality, and expenses.[57] The provisions refer to arbitrators, but apply *mutatis mutandis* to mediators.[58]

B. Dispute Prevention Policies under Investment Treaties

Some investment treaties provide for dispute prevention mechanisms that resemble mediation. This is notably the case of Brazilian cooperation and facilitation investment agreements (CFIAs). Between 2015 and the spring of 2018, Brazil signed nine such agreements, including the plurilateral Intra-MERCOSUR Investment Facilitation Protocol (2017). The CFIA concluded between Brazil and Angola in 2015 became the first Brazilian investment treaty to enter into force in October 2017. CFIAs focus on DPPs that aim to minimize the number of conflicts that escalate into formal disputes.[59] If DPPs in the Brazilian model fail, the contracting parties, but not the investor, can submit the dispute to interstate dispute settlement. A particular DPP that has been inserted in the CFIAs is recourse to ombudsmen or national focal points.[60] Focal points are *not* mediators; indeed, their role in this respect is one of dispute *prevention*, rather than settlement, but their functions undeniably overlap with some form of mediation.

National focal points are designated by each party.[61] In this respect they are not third-party neutrals and they are established at the national, rather than the international, level. For instance, in Brazil focal points are established within the Chamber of Foreign Trade (CAMEX),[62] the Council of Ministers of the Brazilian Chamber of Commerce, an inter-ministerial body for foreign trade presided over by the Minister of Development, Industry and Foreign Trade.[63] Their principal task is to assist investors from the other party in their territory.[64] They are tasked with investment promotion and facilitation and with dispute prevention. It is only with respect to that latter part (dispute prevention) that their function is redolent of mediation. Their responsibilities comprise: assessing, in consultation with relevant

[56] Annex 29-B of CETA and 7 and 11 of the EU–Singapore IPA.
[57] Ibid.
[58] Ibid.
[59] UNCTAD (n 1) xiv. On Brazil's investment policy, see, in general, Catharine Titi, 'International Investment Law and the Protection of Foreign Investment in Brazil' (2016) 2 (1) Transnational Dispute Management: Special Issue on Latin America, Ignacio Torterola and Quinn Smith (eds).
[60] The terms are used interchangeably in the chapter.
[61] Article 17(1) of the Brazilian Model CFIA of 3 March 2016 (version 2.3.1) (hereinafter Brazilian Model CFIA).
[62] Article 17(2) of the Brazilian Model CFIA.
[63] CAMEX's functions are established by Decree n. 4.732/2003.
[64] Article 17(1) of the Brazilian Model CFIA.

public authorities, suggestions and complaints of the other party or investors of the other party and recommending actions to improve the investment environment; seeking to prevent disputes in investment matters, in collaboration with public authorities and relevant private entities.[65]

The Brazilian model CFIA's national focal points or ombudsmen are inspired by the Korean Office of the Foreign Investment Ombudsman, introduced in 1999 to resolve grievances of foreign investors operating in Korea.[66] Besides Korea, other countries have established analogous mechanisms, including Georgia,[67] Greece,[68] Japan,[69] the Philippines,[70] and the United States.[71] Some countries have developed particular systems to assist them in responding to disputes. For example, Peru developed a coordination and response system, which includes a Special Commission tasked with, among others, hearing separately both disputing parties when a dispute arises (prior to arbitration).[72] Colombia, a state that until 2016 had not faced any investment claims,[73] established a national agency, tasked with, among others, facilitating discussions between the parties and assuming a *quasi*-mediating role.[74] These systems are generally to be distinguished from the focal points in the Brazilian model insomuch as they are established unilaterally by a country without reciprocity. They are national mechanisms not provided for in the investment treaty. For this reason, they are at a further remove from mediation.

While there is some overlap between mediation and dispute prevention policies, the two are certainly not coterminous. Dispute prevention policies are generally one-sided, and even Brazilian CFIAs' focal points are established within each partner country. Trust in the mediators is key,[75] and this is where dispute prevention mechanisms, such as focal points, may be at a disadvantage when compared to mediation. If investors perceive these national dispute prevention agencies as

[65] Article 17(4) of the Brazilian Model CFIA. On the focal points, see, in general, Titi (n 59); Catharine Titi, 'Non-Adjudicatory State-State Mechanisms in Investment Dispute Prevention and Dispute Settlement: Joint Interpretations, Filters and Focal Points' (2017) 14 (2) International Investment Law, Brazilian Journal of International Law/Revista de Direito Internacional: Special Issue 37, Hervé Ascensio, Nitish Monebhurrun, and Catharine Titi (eds), 45–7.

[66] See http://ombudsman.kotra.or.kr/eng/au/poelb.do.

[67] See http://businessombudsman.ge/en.

[68] See http://www.enterprisegreece.gov.gr/en/about-us-/profile.

[69] See http://www.invest-japan.go.jp/link/contact/en_index.html.

[70] See http://www.ombudsman.gov.ph/docs/investmentOmbudsman/investmentomb.pdf.

[71] See https://www.selectusa.gov/welcome.

[72] Rodrigo Polanco Lazo, 'Systems of Legal Defence Used by Latin American Countries in Investment Disputes' (2016) 17 (4) The Latin American Challenge to the Current System of Investor-State Dispute Settlement, Journal of World Investment & Trade: Special Issue 562, Katia Fach Gómez and Catharine Titi (eds), 583–4. Carlos José Valderrama, Peru—Best Practices for Confronting International Lawsuits Brought by Private Investors, (2018) 33 (1) ICSID Review–Foreign Investment Law Journal. More information about Peru's coordination and response system (*Sistema de Coordinación y Respuesta del Estado en Controversias Internacionales de Inversión - SICRECI*) can be found on the website of Peru's Ministry of the Economy and Finance https://www.mef.gob.pe/es/acerca-de-las-asociaciones-publico-privadas-apps/sicreci.

[73] See UNCTAD's ISDS Navigator http://investmentpolicyhub.unctad.org/ISDS.

[74] Welsh and Schneider (n 22) 118.

[75] Ibid.

biased, their effectiveness will be reduced.[76] At the same time, in contrast with Brazilian CFIAs' focal points, the other mechanisms (e.g. the Korean Office of the Foreign Investment Ombudsman or Peru's coordination and response system) do not replace investor–state dispute settlement, but are complementary to it.

C. Mediation outside Investment Treaties

Mediation can also take place outside IIAs, notably in the context of contractual relationships or under political risk insurance.[77] Mediation in the latter case, such as in the Multilateral Investment Guarantee Agency (MIGA), forms part of an 'umbrella of deterrence' against governmental measures that can interfere with insured assets provided by investment guarantee schemes; it is a selling-point of political risk insurance.[78] In *ABCI v Tunisia*, the investor, before filing the dispute with ICSID, had asked MIGA to mediate the dispute.[79] *In casu*, Tunisia had refused to participate,[80] while a second attempt for MIGA mediation following the tribunal's jurisdictional decision also failed.[81] Amicable settlement can also take place during an investment arbitration and exceptionally even *after* an award on the merits has been rendered.[82] Mediation itself can take place in parallel with the conduct of an arbitration.[83]

III. The New Status Quo under Institutional Rules

If states have been making incremental changes to their investment treaties for a larger acknowledgment of mediation, other developments and, notably, institutional rules show that investment mediation and conciliation are gaining momentum—or at least that the conditions are in place to allow them to do so.

[76] Ibid., 119.

[77] On mediation and political risk insurance, see Chapter 8, this volume.

[78] See https://www.miga.org/dispute-resolution.

[79] *ABCI Investments NV v Tunisia*, ICSID Case No. ARB/02/12, Decision on Jurisdiction, 18 February 2011, para. 40 and *passim*.

[80] Ibid.

[81] This is recorded in Sébastien Manciaux, 'Le recours à la médiation pour le règlement des différends relatifs aux investissements', in Walid Benhamida and Sami Bostanji (eds), *La médiation dans tous ses états* (Pédone, 2018), 215.

[82] Catharine Titi, 'Investment Arbitration in Latin America: The Uncertain Veracity of Preconceived Ideas' (2014) 30 (2) Arbitration International 357, 377.

[83] Prima facie, Article 26 of the ICSID Convention prevents parallel arbitration and mediation proceedings. It provides that '[c]onsent of the parties to arbitration under this Convention shall, unless otherwise stated, be deemed consent to such arbitration to the exclusion of any other remedy'. However, the 'unless otherwise stated' proviso may allow the parties to specifically provide for alternative relations to other remedies. See also Frauke Nitschke, 'The IBA's Investor-State Mediation Rules and the ICSID Dispute Settlement Framework' (2014) 29 (1) ICSID Review–Foreign Investment Law Journal 112, n 151.

A number of institutions provide mediation rules; some of them have existed for years. In the ICSID framework, conciliation is provided for in the ICSID Convention and in the Additional Facility (Conciliation) Rules.[84] Eleven conciliation cases have been registered to date, nine of which under the ICSID Convention and two under the Additional Facility (Conciliation) Rules.[85] Almost half of these (five out of eleven cases) were registered in the last seven years.[86] UNCITRAL's Conciliation Rules date from 1980.[87] It has been suggested that, while mediation probably takes place more often under institutional conciliation rules rather than UNCITRAL's Conciliation Rules, some of the latter's key provisions have been emulated in other institutional mediation rules.[88] Claimant investors' preference for the UNCITRAL Arbitration Rules over the Conciliation Rules is seen as simply reflective of a general preference for arbitration over conciliation, rather than as passing judgment on the Conciliation Rules.[89] The Hong Kong International Arbitration Centre's (HKIAC) Mediation Rules[90] and the Optional Conciliation Rules of the Permanent Court of Arbitration (PCA)[91] have also been in effect for some time.

Alongside these rules that have existed for a few decades, more recently, arbitral and other institutions show a renewed or intensified interest in mediation. In 2012, the International Bar Association (IBA) adopted the IBA Investor–State Mediation Rules.[92] Earlier in that same year, the 2012 Mediation Rules of the London Court of International Arbitration (LCIA) came into effect.[93] In 2014, the Mediation Rules of the International Chamber of Commerce (ICC) came into force, integrating the best practices of the ICC in relation to alternative dispute resolution (ADR).[94] The Mediation Rules replaced the 2001 Amicable Dispute Resolution Rules and are administered by the ICC International Centre for ADR.[95]

[84] See Chapter 7, this volume.
[85] Ibid.
[86] See https://icsid.worldbank.org.
[87] See http://www.uncitral.org/uncitral/en/uncitral_texts/arbitration/1980Conciliation_rules.html.
[88] Howard Holtzmann, 'Recent Work on Dispute Resolution by the United Nations Commission on International Trade Law' (1999) 5 ILSA Journal of International and Comparative Law 425, 426. The Optional Conciliation Rules of the Permanent Court of Arbitration (PCA) are an example of mediation rules based on the UNCITRAL Conciliation Rules, see https://pca-cpa.org/en/services/mediation-conciliation/.
[89] Gavan Griffith and Andrew D Mitchell, 'Contractual Dispute Resolution in International Trade: The UNCITRAL Arbitration Rules (1976) and the UNCITRAL Conciliation Rules (1980)' (2002) 3 Melbourne Journal of International Law 184, 199.
[90] See http://www.hkiac.org/mediation/rules/hkiac-mediation-rules. For mediation in Asia, see Chapter 9, this volume.
[91] Effective as of 1 July 1996.
[92] For a discussion, see e.g. Joubin-Bret and Legum (n 11); Welsh and Schneider (n 22) 83–4; see Nitschke (n 83).
[93] See http://www.lcia.org/Dispute_Resolution_Services/LCIA_Mediation_Rules.aspx.
[94] See Chapter 5, this volume.
[95] Article 1 of the ICC Mediation Rules. See also https://iccwbo.org/dispute-resolution-services/mediation/mediation-rules/.

The Centre has administered one of the few known mediations on the basis of a BIT.[96] The Arbitration Institute of the Stockholm Chamber of Commerce (SCC) also amended its 1999 Mediation Rules in 2014.[97]

In July 2016, the Energy Charter Conference adopted a Guide on Investment Mediation, a document prepared to help investors and governments decide whether to use mediation.[98] The Guide was prepared with the support of a number of arbitral institutions, including ICSID, the Arbitration Institute of the SCC, the PCA, and UNCITRAL.[99] The aim was to provide 'an explanatory document that could be voluntarily used by governments and companies to take the decision on whether to go for mediation and how to prepare for it'.[100] Mediation also received a formal backing from the European Commission, which stated in 2015 that the EU aims to provide incentives for investors to pursue among others 'amicable solutions—such as mediation'.[101]

IV. Investment Mediation as a Complementary Mechanism for Dispute Settlement

Despite these developments, thus far mediation has not moved centre stage in the way investment arbitration did. But it certainly has a lot of (underused) potential. In 2009, Gabriel Bottini and Veronica Lavista discussed their experience with Argentina's settlements following negotiations with discontented investors.[102] They argued that, while it was not possible to know how many of the investment claims could have been resolved through mediation, the important number of claims where the parties eventually did settle seemed to indicate that mediation could have been 'a valuable alternative' in at least some of the cases.[103] Drawing on experience from the United States, two other authors have argued that, because

[96] See Chapter 5, this volume; Luke Peterson, 'In An Apparent First, Investor and Host-State Agree to Mediation Under IBA Rules to Resolve in Investment Treaty Dispute' Investment Arbitration Reporter, 14 April 2016.

[97] Samuel Carey, 'SCC Practice Note: Mediation Proceedings 2003–2017' (2017) https://sccinstitute.com/media/231969/scc-practice-note-mediation-final.pdf, 2.

[98] See https://energycharter.org/media/news/article/conference-endorses-guide-on-investment-mediation/.

[99] Energy Charter Secretariat, 'Decision of the Energy Charter Conference: Adoption by correspondence of the Guide on Investment Mediation', 19 July 2016, https://energycharter.org/fileadmin/DocumentsMedia/CCDECS/2016/CCDEC201612.pdf (unnumbered).

[100] Ibid.

[101] European Commission, 'Online Public Consultation on Investment Protection and Investor-To-State Dispute Settlement (ISDS) in the Transatlantic Trade and Investment Partnership Agreement (TTIP)', 13 January 2015, http://trade.ec.europa.eu/doclib/docs/2015/january/tradoc_153044.pdf, 89.

[102] Bottini and Lavista (n 41) 365. Argentina, possibly because of the sheer volume of investment claims that were registered against it in the aftermath of its 2001 economic and political crisis, sought to settle investment disputes through negotiations. See Titi (n 82) 377.

[103] Bottini and Lavista (n 41) 365.

mandating compulsory mediation increases the number of disputes that are being mediated, mandatory mediation would raise the number of settlements.[104]

The investment treaties considered previously provide for mediation of investor–state disputes in a non-binding manner and as a complementary method of settling disputes. This soft mechanism remains voluntary and does not, beyond the requirement to respect a waiting period, constitute a precondition to arbitration. Because mediation is by definition a voluntary process, it cannot be imposed upon the parties. In other words, it would be a logical contradiction to consider introducing compulsory mediation for investment disputes.[105] Even if the procedure could be imposed on the parties, there would be no way to ensure their good faith, nor could the parties be under an obligation to arrive at a mediation agreement. While it is possible to encourage mediation, its use should remain complementary.[106] In cases where the relationship between the parties is irreparably damaged, imposing mediation would not add a realistic remedy and could contribute to raising the costs of dispute resolution. But mediation should be encouraged and new IIAs seem to move in this direction.

V. The Role of Consent in Investment Mediation

Mediation, like arbitration, requires the parties' consent. To take the example of the ICSID Convention, pursuant to Article 25, the jurisdiction of the Centre extends to investment disputes that the parties 'consent in writing' to submit to it. This provision applies to both arbitration and conciliation proceedings under the ICSID Convention. Investment treaties typically provide the parties' consent to arbitration, but, as discussed in section IV, only some of them grant consent to mediate future disputes. Nonetheless, the significance of consent given in advance in an investment treaty for mediation is not the same as consent given for arbitration.

The significance of consent to investment arbitration given in advance lies in the fact that arbitration proceedings are adversarial. If the state has not given its advance consent, once the dispute arises, it may prove unwilling to do so. There is a substantive difference with mediation. While for investment arbitration consent is necessary as a formal agreement of the parties to submit their dispute to an investment tribunal, in mediation, because it is a consensual proceeding, substantive consent to the process is required not only as to the initiation of the proceedings

[104] Welsh and Schneider (n 22) 129–30.

[105] Contrast Chapter 1, this volume, in which the author discusses commercial mediation.

[106] The author joins others who have previously expressed scepticism about investment mediation as a mandatory process, e.g. Coe (n 4); Lucy Reed, 'Synopsis of Closing Remarks', in Susan D. Franck and Anna Joubin-Bret (eds), *Investor–State Disputes: Prevention and Alternatives to Arbitration II. Proceedings of the Washington and Lee University and UNCTAD Joint Symposium on International Investment and Alternative Dispute Resolution. 29 March 2010, Lexington, VA.* (United Nations, 2010) 30.

and at every moment of the dispute settlement process, but also as to the outcome of the mediation. In the absence of pre-existing consent in an investment treaty, nothing prevents the parties from agreeing to institute mediation proceedings. At the same time, the value of granting advance consent to mediation is limited. Advance consent would allow the mediation procedure to commence but by itself would do little to ensure its successful conclusion. For these reasons, the argument that 'the entire legal regime would have to be restructured' for mediation to be added as a viable dispute settlement option does not appear to be confirmed.[107]

Because of the particularity of the role of consent, mediation does not require consent in an investment treaty and can be initiated even in the absence of one. For the same reason, it is possible to envisage mediation initiated by the host state, instead of by the investor. Finally, in traditional investor–state proceedings, the notification of a claim could encourage a host state to seek to mediate the dispute in order to avoid arbitration.

VI. Some Challenges

Despite the desirability of facilitating access to mediation, some challenges remain, including transparency and the appropriateness of mediation when one of the disputing parties is a state.

In recent years, the calls for transparency of ISDS have led to related reforms. The UNCITRAL Rules on Transparency in Treaty-Based Investor-State Arbitration[108], the United Nations Convention on Transparency in Treaty-Based Investor–State Arbitration (Mauritius Convention on Transparency),[109] and transparency concerns as evidenced in the proposed amendments to the ICSID Rules are all examples of how the system has tried to deal with the criticism of 'secrecy'.[110] In contrast, the confidentiality of the mediation process (sometimes discussed as an advantage of mediation,[111] at least in part because arbitration can have a negative reputational impact on both investor and host state)[112] jars with the new tendency for transparency in ISDS. We must ask to what extent the increased transparency in ISDS impacts the generally confidential mediation process. Specifically, how can we coherently live with these two systems where we have (more) transparency in one, and in the other we value confidentiality? Mediation requires trust and

[107] Welsh and Schneider (n 22) 86 ('Some commentators argue that the entire legal regime would have to be restructured if mediation were added. Hundreds of BITs would require renegotiation and the rules and procedures of ICSID and other bodies would need to be revised').

[108] Entered into force on 1 April 2014.

[109] Entered into force on 18 October 2017.

[110] ICSID, 'Proposals for Amendment of the ICSID Rules – Working Paper' 3, 2 August 2018, 205–19.

[111] Susan D. Franck, 'Using Investor-State Mediation Rules to Promote Conflict Management: An Introductory Guide' (2014) 29 (1) ICSID Review–Foreign Investment Law Journal 66, 78; Coe (n 4) 23, but cf. 26–7; Salacuse (n 5) 177.

[112] Ibid.

therefore confidentiality *is* essential. However, just as in investment arbitration, the dispute involves a sovereign state and concessions made through mediation can have an impact on the state's population. And yet, it is difficult to envisage mediation that would work without the guarantee of confidentiality.[113] Transparency (or the lack of) in mediation therefore remains a challenge that may need to be addressed.

Another challenge relates to whether mediation is a realistic option for states. Michael Reisman argues that mediation does not work where the respondent is a state entity.[114] According to Reisman, 'large and complex organizations in which authority is allocated among many different departments will experience difficulty in making major decisions'.[115] This is especially so in the context of investor–state disputes, where 'active political oppositions' may be 'waiting for an opportunity to pounce on the incumbents for having "betrayed" the national patrimony by settling with an investor'.[116] The more sensitive the state measure and the purpose for which it was adopted, the more difficult settlement will be. The decision to voluntarily compensate harmed investors for measures the state has taken for the public good can be difficult to 'sell to constituents'.[117]

Claims brought against Argentina in the immediate aftermath of its economic and financial crisis have been used as examples of where mediation could be impracticable.[118] The claims were triggered when Argentina defaulted on its debt and devalued its currency, previously on a par with the dollar, leading to the *pesification* of the economy, although prominent economists argued that Argentina 'had no choice but to default' and that the currency devaluation was 'inevitable'.[119] It has been argued that in such situations the decision to voluntarily settle and agree to disburse funds to foreign investors would have made for difficult political decisions.[120] Although there does not appear to have been mediation, Argentina did pursue settlements of the claims brought against it, and did so very successfully. This may disprove the point made at the beginning of this paragraph about the difficulty of resorting to mediation,[121] especially if the state fears that arbitration

[113] On the transparency versus confidentiality debate in this context, see Chapter 17, this volume.

[114] W. Michael Reisman, 'International Investment Arbitration and ADR: Married but Best Living Apart', in Susan D. Franck and Anna Joubin-Bret (eds), *Investor-State Disputes: Prevention and Alternatives to Arbitration II*. Proceedings of the Washington and Lee University and UNCTAD Joint Symposium on International Investment and Alternative Dispute Resolution. 29 March 2010, Lexington, VA (United Nations, 2010) 26.

[115] Ibid.

[116] Ibid.

[117] Welsh and Schneider (n 22) 86–7.

[118] Ibid., 87.

[119] Joseph E. Stiglitz, 'Argentina, Shortchanged', The Washington Post, 12 May 2002, https://www.washingtonpost.com/archive/opinions/2002/05/12/argentina-shortchanged/82965939-1ef1-44b3-9485-c1208517b022/?utm_term=.2eaba928cbe1.

[120] Welsh and Schneider (n 22) 87 ('How could the government negotiate the payment of millions of dollars to a foreign company to compensate it (and its domestic partners) for its economic loss when Argentina's citizens and wholly owned domestic companies clearly had lost so much more?').

[121] This is also backed by the argument made by Bottini and Lavista (n 41) 365.

will be unfavourable to it. However, arbitration could be more useful to the state than mediation if the tribunal were to confirm that the state did not have responsibility under international law. In the author's view, this might have proved to be the case in *Abaclat v Argentina*,[122] where there was no known mediation but the parties settled while an arbitration was ongoing. However, it is impossible to know for certain.

Apart from difficulties due to the political nature of a decision to settle, mediation involving state entities may prove difficult for other reasons. Public officials are often unaware of the facts that led to the dispute and preparation for the state typically starts when it receives the actual request for arbitration.[123] In addition, the agency responsible for the measures that gave rise to the claim is generally not the same as the agency responsible for defending the state against potential claims.[124] It has been argued that it may be weeks or even months before officials in the agency responsible for defending the state can identify their counterparts in the agency at the origin of the claim; it can take even longer before the former makes a first assessment of the merits of the claim.[125] Consequently, at the early stages of the dispute, the agency charged with defending the state will have little information about the strength of the state's case.[126] In other words, there may be slowness in the reaction of ministry officials for endogenous reasons, such as the uncertainty about which ministry is responsible, and response may eventually come when a request for arbitration makes it clear that the problem will not go away if the state just turns a blind eye.

This is further complicated for the following reasons. Government officials may not be at liberty to settle with foreign investors; even where they are habilitated to do so, they may bear potential liability (legal and financial) for settlements they reach with investors.[127] While typically there is authorization to pay for adverse decisions against the state (and it is clear which agency budget will bear the brunt), this is not necessarily true for payments in relation to settlement agreements in international proceedings and a special authorization may be required before the agency can agree to a settlement.[128] The upshot of it all is that a decision imposed by a third party may appear preferable.

[122] *Abaclat and others v Argentine Republic*, ICSID Case No. ARB/07/5 Decision on Jurisdiction and Admissibility (4 August 2011).

[123] Barton Legum and Anna Crevon, 'An Outline of Procedure in an Investment Treaty Arbitration: Strategy and Choices', in Chiara Giorgetti (ed.), *Litigating International Investment Disputes: A Practitioner's Guide* (Brill Nijhoff, 2014) 3; Jeremy K. Sharpe, 'Representing a Respondent State in Investment Arbitration', in Giorgetti (n 123) 43–5.

[124] Barton Legum, 'The Difficulties of Conciliation in Investment Treaty Cases: A Comment on Professor Jack C. Coe's 'Toward a Complementary Use of Conciliation in Investor-State Disputes—A Preliminary Sketch' (2006) 21 (4) MEALEY's International Arbitration Report 1.

[125] Ibid.

[126] Ibid. See also Coe (n 4) 41.

[127] Silvia Constain, 'Mediation in Investor-State Dispute Settlement: Government Policy and the Changing Landscape' (2014) 29 (1) ICSID Review–Foreign Investment Law Journal 25, 34.

[128] Legum (n 124) 2.

An example cited in this context is *SPP v Egypt* (the Pyramids case),[129] where at some point a tentative settlement agreement of 10 million US dollars was rejected in favour of arbitration by the Egyptian Prime Minister, who considered that to settle for 10 million US dollars 'would open him to attack by opponents and the media'.[130] The parties later settled, after going through arbitration, for 17.5 million US dollars.[131] In reality, decision-makers in the management of multinationals can face similar difficulties. Multinationals, like states, often engage the services of consultants in order to blame difficult decisions on third parties. These challenges need to be addressed if mediation is to become more mainstream, but they also show that, in many cases, arbitration will appear preferable to mediation.

VII. Conclusion

Investment cases settled through mediation represent only an inconsequential fragment of international investment disputes and mediation in this field remains relatively unexplored. At the same time, recent developments show that alternative dispute resolution is gaining traction at a time when the traditional ISDS system brims with critiques and efforts are made to reform it. Investment treaties often make provision for amicable dispute settlement, including mediation, as a precondition to arbitration. In reality, the relevant clauses impose a waiting period rather than an actual obligation to pursue dispute resolution in ADR. Investment mediation could be a helpful tool to resolve some disputes that might otherwise end in arbitration. But its limitations must also be borne in mind. Mediation is not appropriate for all disputes. Where the relationship between the disputing parties has entirely disintegrated, mediation is unlikely to be of much use, and can add to the costs and time necessary to settle the dispute. But there is certainly room to encourage mediation as a complimentary, non-binding option in investment treaties, and it is likely that an increasing number of investment cases will be resolved in mediation going forward.

[129] *Southern Pacific Properties (SPP) v Egypt*, ICSID Case No. ARB/84/3.

[130] Salacuse (n 5) 150.

[131] Ibid. But Salacuse uses this case as an argument in favour of mediation, noting that '[t]his result might have been avoided if, at an earlier stage, Egypt and the investor had agreed to the intervention of a distinguished conciliator who would have provided an expert opinion on a fair settlement of the conflict, thereby giving the Prime Minister the political cover that he felt he needed' (idem).

3

Applying the Lessons of International Commercial Arbitration to International Commercial Mediation

A Dispute System Design Analysis

S. I. Strong

I. Introduction

Over the last sixty years, arbitration has become the preferred means of resolving cross-border business disputes, replacing both litigation and mediation (conciliation) as the international dispute resolution mechanism of choice. However, the international community has become somewhat disenchanted with the costs, delays, and procedural formality associated with contemporary arbitration, and some individuals and institutions have begun to search for a better way of resolving cross-border commercial disputes. Of the various options, mediation has established itself as the leading alternative to both transnational litigation and international commercial arbitration.[1]

In some ways, this phenomenon appears to be a case of history repeating itself, since mediation was the preferred means of resolving international business disputes in the years prior to the Second World War.[2] However, contemporary calls for international commercial mediation appear to arise out of the alternative dispute resolution (ADR) movement that began in the United States in 1976 with the Pound Conference on the Causes of Popular Dissatisfaction with the Administration of Justice[3] and moved to other jurisdictions in the following years.[4] Indeed, one of the leading organizations involved in promoting the appropriate use

[1] Jacqueline Nolan-Haley, 'Mediation: The "New Arbitration"' (2012) 17 Harvard Negotiation Law Review 61, 66–7.

[2] Eric A. Schwartz, 'International Conciliation and the ICC' (1995) 10 ICSID Review–Foreign Investment Law Journal 98, 99, 107.

[3] William H. Erickson, 'The Pound Conference Recommendations: A Blueprint for the Justice System in the Twenty-First Century' (1977–1978) 76 Federal Rules Decisions 277, 279–81.

[4] For example, England and Wales incorporated ADR into their court procedures pursuant to the Woolf Reforms, which implemented in 1999 in the Civil Procedure Rules. See S. I. Strong, 'Defining the Litigation Default' (2018) 37 Civil Justice Quarterly 463.

of international commercial mediation is known as the Global Pound Conference in conscious recognition of the 1976 conclave.[5]

As interest in international commercial mediation has grown, so, too, has the number of scholarly inquiries and practical proposals. For example, the last few years have seen several empirical studies dedicated to international commercial mediation[6] as well as increasing support for mediation from the international business community. Thousands of multinational corporations,[7] most notably General Electric[8] and Siemens,[9] have endorsed the use of early dispute resolution strategies like mediation, and a range of intergovernmental actors, including the World Bank[10] and the United Nations Commission on International Trade Law (UNCITRAL),[11] have sought to promote international mediation through various formal and informal initiatives. The most recent effort in this regard is the United Nations Convention on International Settlement Agreements Resulting from Mediation (Singapore Convention on Mediation), which was opened for signature on August 7, 2019.[12]

As positive as these developments may appear, certain lacunae exist. Perhaps the most important omission involves the significant shortage of any comprehensive scholarly analyses of the international mediation regime, such as those that are recommended by experts in dispute systems design (DSD).[13] DSD is a somewhat unique area of study within the dispute resolution field, since it does not seek to promote or analyse a particular methodology or process, but instead focuses on

[5] Global Pound Conference, http://globalpound.org/.

[6] S. I. Strong, 'Realizing Rationality: An Empirical Assessment of International Commercial Mediation' (2016) 73 Washington and Lee Law Review 1973; Grant Morris, 'From Anecdote to Evidence: The New Zealand Commercial Mediation Market' (2016) 22 New Zealand Business Law Quarterly 10.

[7] CPR, Corporate Pledge, https://www.cpradr.org/resource-center/adr-pledges.

[8] Michael A. Wheeler and Gillian Morris, 'GE's Early Dispute Resolution Initiative (A)' (2001) 801-395 Harvard Business School Case Collection 9 (discussing General Electric's domestic dispute resolution strategy, based on the Six Sigma approach); Michael A. Wheeler and Gillian Morris, 'GE's Early Dispute Resolution Initiative (B)' (2001) 801-453 Harvard Business School Case Collection 9 (discussing the internationalization of General Electric's dispute resolution strategy).

[9] Walter G. Gans and David Stryker, 'ADR: The Siemens' Experience' (1996) 51 Dispute Resolution Journal 40, 41.

[10] See e.g. Understanding IFC's Alternative Dispute Resolution Program in South Europe (1 January 2011), http://documents.worldbank.org/curated/en/954361468113938354/Understanding-IFCs-Alternative-Dispute-Resolution-Program-in-Southern-Europe.

[11] UNCITRAL, Working Group II (Dispute Settlement), Sixty-eighth Session, Annotated Provisional Agenda, 2-4, UN Document A/CN.9/WG.II/WP.204 (22 November 2017) (UNCITRAL Provisional Agenda) (outlining historical consideration of international mediation [conciliation] by UNCITRAL).

[12] U.N. Comm. on Int'l Trade Law, Report of the U.N. Comm. on Int'l Trade Law, Fifty-first session, U.N. Doc. A/73/17 (2018) at Annex I (Singapore Convention). See also S. I. Strong, 'The Role of Empirical Research and Dispute System Design in Developing International Treaties: A Case Study of the Singapore Convention on Mediation' (forthcoming 2019) 20 Cardozo Journal of Conflict Resolution; Chapter 19, this volume.

[13] Nancy H. Rogers, Robert C. Bordone, Frank A. E. Sander, and Craig A. McEwan, *Designing Systems and Processes for Managing Disputes* (Wolters Kluwer, 2013) 4–5 (describing DSD).

larger structural issues so as to improve dispute resolution at a systemic level.[14] That goal is achieved by:

> (1) analysing parties' patterns of disputing to diagnose the current system, (2) designing methods to manage conflict more effectively with practical principles, (3) approving and implementing the design architecture, and (4) testing and evaluating the new design to make appropriate revisions prior to disseminating the process to the rest of the system.[15]

A full DSD analysis requires consideration of numerous variables and is beyond the scope of the current discussion.[16] However, a number of key issues usefully can be considered even within the space available, since the inquiry here can build on a recent large-scale empirical study conducted by the author in the area of international commercial mediation.[17] This material not only provides useful insights into how the structure of the international dispute resolution system currently operates, but also suggests how the existing system might be redesigned to create a more effective means of managing cross-border business conflicts.

The chapter proceeds as follows. First, section II provides a structural analysis of how the international commercial dispute resolution regime currently operates by outlining the differences and similarities in the legal environments surrounding international commercial litigation, arbitration, and mediation. Next, section III describes how various features of the existing legal regime nudge parties toward certain procedures, even if that behaviour is not necessarily rational. Section IV then discusses how the world of international dispute resolution can be redesigned to make the system more effective and optimize certain values considered important by states and other international actors. Finally, section V draws together the various strands of analysis and provides some forward-looking observations.

Although this analysis hopes to break new ground, space restrictions require the imposition of certain limitations. Most importantly, this discussion focuses on mediation in international commercial cases, not on mediation in international investment or domestic settings, since the procedures reflect a number of key differences as a matter of law and fact. However, some of the observations contained herein may also be applicable in those contexts.

[14] Susan D. Franck, 'Integrating Investment Treaty Conflict and Dispute Systems Design' (2007) 92 Minnesota Law Review 161, 177–8 (noting DSD 'is not a dispute resolution methodology itself' but instead reflects 'the intentional and systematic creation of an effective, efficient, and fair dispute resolution process based upon the unique needs of a particular system').

[15] Ibid., 178.

[16] Rogers et al. (n 13) 6, 8.

[17] Strong (n 6) 1994–2006.

II. Structural Analysis of International Commercial Dispute Resolution

Traditional dispute resolution analyses focus on individual procedures, meaning the step-by-step process associated with resolution of particular disputes or the relative merits of one particular mechanism over other alternatives. However, the current inquiry adopts a very different perspective by analysing international commercial dispute resolution not at the individual or institutional level, but at the systemic level. Only through this type of comprehensive evaluation can certain structural pressures be assessed in rational terms. When considering these issues, it is important to identify not only those elements that push parties toward a particular mechanism, but also those that push them away from the same procedure. Furthermore, it is critical to study the ways in which the various legal environments are both similar and dissimilar, since differences often drive the decision-making process.[18]

Conventional analyses of international dispute resolution typically compare the public nature of litigation to the private nature of both arbitration and mediation, or contrast the cooperative and consensual elements of mediation with the win-lose, zero-sum aspects of litigation and arbitration. However, a DSD analysis goes beyond a comparison of the hallmarks of the individual procedures and instead focuses on larger systemic concerns involving the legal environments in which the three processes (litigation, arbitration, and mediation) operate.

The analysis begins at the level of individual disputes. Here, the three procedures appear somewhat similar. While arbitration and mediation may at one time have been relatively lax in their procedural requirements (and may still be somewhat loose in their domestic incarnations), international commercial disputes are subject to highly sophisticated procedural rules promulgated by public, *quasi*-public, or private institutions and adopted by the parties. For example, international arbitration is often referred to as 'Rolls Royce justice' (in contract to the purported 'second-class justice' delivered in domestic arbitration),[19] while international mediation is often highly legalistic and conducted like a 'mini-arbitration'.[20]

However, the three procedures reflect a number of differences, even at the individual level. For example, the rules for transnational litigation are set by a public body such as a legislature or court[21] while the rules in international commercial mediation and arbitration are primarily set by private institutions (e.g. the International Chamber of Commerce (ICC), the London Court of International

[18] Peter B. Rutledge, 'Convergence and Divergence in International Dispute Resolution' (2012) Journal of Dispute Resolution 49, 50–2.

[19] Russell J. Weintraub, *International Litigation and Arbitration* (Carolina Academic Press, 1994) 455.

[20] Schwartz (n 2) 112.

[21] Although these rules are primarily established for domestic disputes, they are equally applicable to international disputes, e.g. Civil Procedure Rules (England); Federal Rules of Civil Procedure (US).

Arbitration (LCIA), or the International Centre for Dispute Resolution (ICDR), which is the international arm of the American Arbitration Association (AAA))[22] or *quasi*-public bodies such as UNCITRAL[23] and selected by the parties.

Although litigation is admittedly distinct from arbitration and mediation in some key regards, conventional analyses of international procedural rules often fail to recognize that all three mechanisms involve a mix of public and private elements. For example, states provide guidance on individual procedural issues in international commercial mediation and arbitration through laws identifying the procedural boundaries of the two processes[24] and through various default rules that apply in the absence of party agreement.[25] Furthermore, individual parties in litigation exercise autonomy when they adopt a forum selection provision that identifies which jurisdiction—and thus, which procedural rules—will govern the dispute in question.[26] Some jurisdictions even allow parties in litigation to alter certain aspects of the applicable rules of civil procedure through party agreement.[27]

Another important structural element to consider involves the interaction or relationship between different national laws affecting international commercial dispute resolution. In particular, it is useful to consider whether and to what extent the international community has sought to harmonize or coordinate national laws on dispute resolution to facilitate multinational proceedings and avoid conflict of laws concerns.

[22] See International Centre for Dispute Resolution, International Dispute Resolution Procedures (Including mediation and Arbitration Rules), in effect 1 June 2014, https://www.adr.org; International Chamber of Commerce, ICC Arbitration Rules, in effect 1 March 2017, http://www.iccwbo.org; International Chamber of Commerce, ICC Mediation Rules, in effect 1 January 2014, http://www.iccwbo.org; London Court of International Arbitration, LCIA Arbitration Rules, in effect 1 October 2014, http://www.lcia.org/dispute_resolution_services/lcia-arbitration-rules-2014.aspx; London Court of International Arbitration, LCIA Mediation Rules, in effect 1 July 2012, http://www.lcia.org/dispute_resolution_services/lcia_mediation_rules.aspx.

[23] UNCITRAL initially promulgated its arbitration rules in 1976, but revised them in 2010. UNCITRAL Arbitration Rules, GA Resolution 31/98, UNCITRAL, 31st Session, Supplement No 17 at 34, UN Document A/31/17 (28 April 1976), http://www.uncitral.org/pdf/english/texts/arbitration/arb-rules/arb-rules.pdf; UNCITRAL Arbitration Rules, GA Resolution 65/22, UN Document A/RES/65/22 (10 January 2011), http://www.uncitral.org/pdf/english/texts/arbitration/arb-rules-revised/arb-rules-revised-2010-e.pdf. UNCITRAL's rules on mediation were promulgated in 1980. Conciliation Rules of the United Nations Commission on International Trade, UN GAOR, 35th Session, 81st plenary meeting at 260, UN Document A/35/52 (1980), http://www.uncitral.org/pdf/english/texts/arbitration/conc-rules/conc-rules-e.pdf.

[24] E.g. Arbitration Act 1996 (England); 9 USC ss 1-307 (US Federal Arbitration Act); Uniform Law Commission (US), Uniform Mediation Act; S. I. Strong, 'General Principles of Procedural Law and Procedural *Jus Cogens*' (2018) 122 Penn State Law Review 347, 395.

[25] The most well-known of these default rules is found in the Panama Convention. See Art 3 of the Inter-American Convention on International Commercial Arbitration (Panama Convention), 30 January 1975, OASTS No 42, 14 ILM 336 (1975) (Panama Convention); see also Inter-American Commercial Arbitration Commission Rules, in effect 1 April 2002, https://www.adr.org/sites/default/files/Inter-American%20Commercial%20Arbitration%20Commission%20Rules-%20English.pdf.

[26] S. I. Strong, 'Limits of Procedural Choice of Law' (2014) 39 Brooklyn Journal of International Law 1027, 1028–36.

[27] Ibid.

As it turns out, the international legal community has taken significant steps to promote arbitration and mediation in cross-border disputes through the promulgation of the UNCITRAL Model Law on International Commercial Conciliation (Model Conciliation Law (revised in 2018 and renamed as the Model Mediation Law)) and the UNCITRAL Model Law on International Commercial Arbitration (Model Arbitration Law).[28] These initiatives not only facilitate the adoption of national legislation involving international arbitration and mediation, they also help ensure global consistency in the treatment of parties involved in multinational disputes.[29]

Efforts to adopt similar provisions involving litigation have been far less successful, although it is unclear why that is so. For example, some states may not see a need for international reform because they believe their national rules of civil procedure are capable of handling any cross-border cases that arise, while other states may not wish to engage in harmonization efforts due to the parochialism and exceptionalism that is the hallmark of national civil procedure.[30] At this point, the only initiatives to have garnered even a modicum of success have been the Principles of Transnational Civil Procedure (ALI/UNIDROIT Principles) and Rules of Transnational Civil Procedure (ALI/UNIDROIT Rules), which were promulgated by the American Law Institute (ALI) and the International Institute for the Unification of Private Law (UNIDROIT) as part of an effort to harmonize civil procedural norms applicable to cross-border commercial cases.[31] Unfortunately, the project has met with only limited practical success, as illustrated by the fact that ten years after their promulgation, neither the ALI/UNIDROIT Principles nor the ALI/UNIDROIT Rules have been formally adopted by any jurisdiction.[32] This is not to say that the project was a complete failure, since the European Law Institute is relying heavily on the ALI/UNIDROIT Principles in a project seeking

[28] U.N. Comm. on Int'l Trade Law, Report of the U.N. Comm. on Int'l Trade Law, Fifty-first session, U.N. Doc. A/73/17 (2018) at Annex II (Model Mediation Law); Model Law on International Commercial Conciliation of the United Nations Commission on International Trade Law, GA Res 57/18, UN Document A/Res/57/18, UN GAOR, 57th Session (24 January 2003), https://undocs.org/en/A/RES/57/18; UNCITRAL Model Law on International Commercial Arbitration, UN Commission on International Trade Law, 18th Session, Annex I, UN Document A/40/17 (21 June 1985), revised by Report of the UN Commission on International Trade Law, 39th Session, 17 June–7 July 2006, Annex I (Article 34), UN Document A/61/17, United Nations GAOR, 61st Session, Supplement No 17 (2006). The Model Conciliation Law was revised to make it consistent with the Singapore Convention on Mediation, although most of the amendments merely reflected a change in nomenclature (e.g., replacing 'conciliation' or 'conciliator' with 'mediation' and 'mediator').

[29] Gary B. Born, *International Commercial Arbitration* (2nd edn, Kluwer Law International, 2014) 134–41.

[30] Kevin M. Clermont, 'Integrating Transnational Perspectives into Civil Procedure: What Not to Teach' (2006) 56 Journal of Legal Education 524, 530 (discussing 'the parochialism that so affects US procedure'); Richard L. Marcus, 'Putting American Procedural Exceptionalism into A Globalized Context' (2005) 53 American Journal of Comparative Law 709, 740 ('The problem in the US is that comparative procedure is barely on the map.').

[31] ALI and UNIDROIT, *Principles of Transnational Civil Procedure* (Cambridge University Press, 2006).

[32] Ibid., xxix, xxxviii–xxxix.

to establish will be known as the European Rules of Civil Procedure, but the lack of widespread global support for the ALI/UNIDROIT initiative is telling.[33]

Furthermore, the failure to harmonize or at least coordinate national rules on transnational litigation has long been considered to have a negative effect on party behaviour. Differences in national procedure often give one party a significant 'home court' advantage, which can create an impasse when negotiating a forum selection provision in a commercial contract.[34] However, the failure to agree to a forum selection provision *ex ante* can be even more problematic, since parties will then file suit in competing jurisdictions, leading to an expensive and time-consuming battle about where a particular dispute will be heard. Predictability in terms of forum has been at least as important as procedural autonomy in driving the field of international dispute resolution toward arbitration, which suggests that states' failure to consider the structural aspects of international dispute resolution, particularly vis-à-vis litigation, has created an incentive to the parties to contract out of national courts.

This argument becomes even more compelling when the analysis moves to the level of public international law. Structurally, arbitration is the most developed of the three procedures as a result of various international treaties that facilitate the international recognition and enforcement of both arbitration agreements and arbitral awards. The most notable of these instruments is the United Nations Convention on the Recognition and Enforcement of Foreign Arbitral Awards (New York Convention), which has been ratified or adhered to by 157 states parties,[35] but the international arbitral regime is also supported by several equally beneficial regional agreements.[36] As discussed further in section III, these treaties have been extremely effective in overcoming the legal and psychological pull toward litigation and in making arbitration the dispute resolution mechanism of choice in the international commercial context.[37]

Cognizant of the benefits commonly associated with international arbitration, some law- and policymakers are taking steps to eliminate the structural advantages of international commercial arbitration by promulgating various international instruments that seek to endow transnational litigation with certain attributes more

[33] UNIDROIT, Transnational Civil Procedure—Formulation of Regional Rules, https://www.unidroit.org/work-in-progress/transnational-civil-procedure.

[34] Gary B. Born, *International Arbitration and Forum Selection Agreements: Drafting and Enforcing* (5th edn, Wolters Kluwer, 2016), Ch. 1.D.1.

[35] United Nations Convention on the Recognition and Enforcement of Foreign Arbitral Awards, 10 June 1958, 330 UNTS 3; UNCITRAL, Status: 1958 Convention on the Recognition and Enforcement of Foreign Arbitral Awards, http://www.uncitral.org/uncitral/en/uncitral_texts/arbitration/NYConvention_status.html.

[36] European Convention on International Commercial Arbitration, 21 April 1964, 484 UNTS 364; Panama Convention (n 25); Organization of American States, Inter-American Convention on Extraterritorial Validity of Foreign Judgments and Arbitral Awards, 14 May 1979, 1439 UNTS 87.

[37] S. I. Strong, 'Truth in a Post-Truth Society: How Sticky Defaults, Status Quo Bias and the Sovereign Prerogative Influence the Perceived Legitimacy of International Arbitration' (2018) University of Illinois Law Review 533, 554–6.

commonly associated with international commercial arbitration. Thus, for example, the Hague Conference on Private International Law (Hague Conference) promulgated the Convention on Choice of Court Agreements (COCA) in 2005 as a means of offsetting the New York Convention's ability to facilitate party autonomy regarding choice of venue.[38] However, COCA still has only a very small number of states parties and has thus far failed to shift party preference away from arbitration in matters involving international commercial law.[39]

In 2015, the Hague Conference again sought to bolster litigation's status in the world of transnational dispute resolution, this time by promulgating the Principles on Choice of Law in International Commercial Contracts, which increases party autonomy in a variety of ways and seeks to provide litigants in national court with a number of freedoms that are routinely reflected in international arbitration.[40] Because this document is non-binding in nature, it does not need to wait until a certain number of states adhere to it before going into effect. However, it is as yet unclear whether and to what extent this initiative will have any effect in practice, given different national approaches to the interpretation and application of choice of law provisions.[41]

At this point, there is no international instrument involving litigation that challenges the New York Convention's predominance in the area of recognition and enforcement of the outcome of the dispute. However, the Hague Conference has been working for the last several years on the 'Judgments Project', which seeks to identify a means of facilitating cross-border enforcement of foreign judgments.[42] At the time of writing, a draft convention had been circulated for discussion, with a diplomatic meeting anticipated for 2019. However, the historic difficulties associated with this initiative suggest that the process of adherence and ratification may take a while, which suggests that arbitration will remain far easier to enforce internationally than court judgments, at least for the foreseeable future, and will therefore continue to enjoy significant structural superiority over litigation.[43]

The status of international commercial mediation differs from that of both litigation and arbitration. At this point, there are no international instruments concerning the enforcement of mediation or settlement agreements, a phenomenon that commentators believe has significantly affected international commercial

[38] Convention on Choice of Court Agreements, 30 June 2005, 44 ILM 1294 (entered into force 1 October 2015).

[39] See COCA, Status, https://www.hcch.net/en/instruments/conventions/status-table/?cid=98.

[40] Hague Conference on Private International Law, Principles on Choice of Law in International Commercial Contracts, 19 March 2015, https://www.hcch.net/en/instruments/conventions/full-text/?cid=135; Born (n 29) 73, 76.

[41] Sarah Leval, 'A Comparative Study of Party Autonomy and its Limitations in Commercial Contracts: American and European Law, with Reference to the Hague Principles, 2015' (2016) 25 Cardozo Journal of International and Comparative Law 29, 39.

[42] The Judgments Project, Hague Conference, https://www.hcch.net/en/projects/legislative-projects/judgments.

[43] Born (n 29) 77–80.

actors' decision-making processes.[44] In 2015, after considering recent research in the field,[45] the United States Department of State submitted a proposal to UNCITRAL for a new convention concerning the enforcement of settlement agreements arising out of international commercial arbitration.[46] Although the final product (the Singapore Convention on Mediation) only addresses issues at the back end of the mediation process (i.e. the settlement agreement) and does not affect the front end of the process (i.e. the mediation agreement), this project marks significant progress toward redressing certain structural inequities in the area of international commercial dispute resolution and begins to provide parties in mediation with some of the type of benefits commonly associated with the New York Convention.[47]

Nevertheless, some obstacles still remain. For example, although the Singapore Convention on Mediation is binding, states parties are allowed to enter a reservation indicating that the instrument will apply 'only to the extent that the parties to the settlement agreement have agreed to the application of the Convention'.[48] Although this type of 'opt-in' approach was part of a necessary compromise that grew out of the negotiations at UNCITRAL, it could diminish the global impact of the Convention.[49] Hopefully the reservation will not be used frequently, since recent empirical research suggests that most practitioners, neutrals, academics and users working in the field support the creation of a binding instrument of this area of law.[50]

III. Incentives, Defaults, and Other 'Nudges' in International Dispute Resolution

Although the legal literature overflows with discussions of why and when litigation, arbitration, or mediation are superior to other alternatives in international commercial cases, most of those analyses focus on the benefits that accrue to individual parties. For example, commentators frequently emphasize how certain

[44] S. I. Strong, 'Beyond International Commercial Arbitration? The Promise of International Commercial Mediation' (2014) 45 Washington University Journal of Law and Policy 11, 29–38 (citing sources).

[45] Public Meeting on International Arbitration and Conciliation, US Department of State, http://www.state.gov/s/l/229037.htm (noting the genesis of the US proposal).

[46] Proposal by the Government of the United States of America: Future Work for Working Group II, UN Document A/CN.9/822 (2 June 2014) (US Proposal).

[47] Singapore Convention (n 12).

[48] Article 8(1)(b) of the Singapore Convention.

[49] Timothy Schnabel, 'The Singapore Convention on Mediation: A Framework for the Cross-Border Recognition and Enforcement of Mediated Settlements', (2019) 19 Pepperdine Dispute Resolution Law Journal, 1, 57.

[50] Timothy Schnabel, 'Implementation of the Singapore Convention: Federalism, Self-Execution, and Private Law Treaties' (forthcoming 2019) American Review of International Arbitration; Strong (n 6) 2056–61 (citing survey data).

procedures can save time or money, increase the predictability and validity of the outcome, and/or provide various social benefits ranging from creative and collaborative solutions to publicly accountable procedures.[51] Although many of these arguments are now so familiar as to constitute conventional wisdom, a number of principles—most notably the claim that mediation is faster and cheaper than other alternatives—have never been adequately tested through empirical research that takes the special nature of international commercial law and practice properly into account.[52]

This lacuna is extremely problematic, since cross-border commercial actors have indicated that the most important issue in the realm of international dispute resolution is the reduction of the time and cost associated with resolving individual matters.[53] Indeed, a recent study of the cross-border business and legal communities suggests that international commercial actors would be willing to consider the use of international commercial mediation if they could be assured that it would result in the savings of time or money, as proponents of the procedure often claim.[54] However, empirical research in the domestic realm suggests that mediation actually decreases client costs in only about half of the disputes in which it is used (a percentage that may not be as persuasive to practitioners as it is to scholars),[55] and savings of time and money may be even less likely to occur in international commercial matters, where there is a tendency for counsel to conduct mediations like 'mini arbitrations'.[56] This information suggests that international commercial actors' hesitation about mediation is highly rational, particularly if—as the data suggests—time and money are the most important drivers of decisions about dispute resolution procedures in cross-border commercial cases.[57]

Although some people may interpret this material as suggesting that parties are simply unwilling to try a new procedure (mediation) unless and until they can be assured of its efficacy, other inferences are possible, particularly if the issue is considered from a DSD perspective. For example, acknowledged concerns about the cost of international commercial arbitration have not generated a widespread return to litigation, even though the cost and time differential between the two procedures may no longer be as pronounced as it once was or was believed to be. This phenomenon suggests that commercial parties are likely motivated by factors other than savings of time and money, despite their claim that those attributes are of primary importance, and raises the question of whether those other motivating features also exist (or can be made to exist) in international commercial mediation.

[51] Nolan-Haley (n 1) 66–7; Strong (n 44) 24–8 (citing sources); Strong (n 6) 2007–16 (citing sources).
[52] Strong (n 6) 2007–16 (outlining problems in literature).
[53] Ibid., 2036.
[54] Ibid., 2031, 2036.
[55] Roselle L. Wissler, 'Court-Connected Mediation in General Civil Cases: What We Know from Empirical Research' (2002) 17 Ohio State Journal on Dispute Resolution 641, 672.
[56] Schwartz (n 2) 112.
[57] Strong (n 6) 2031, 2036.

One common explanation for the continuing preference for international commercial arbitration over mediation involves a purported party preference for adjudicative, rather than consensual, forms of dispute resolution. Although this hypothesis may appear logical at first glance, the alleged bias in favour of adjudication does not explain the preference for arbitration over litigation.[58] Instead, the success of international commercial arbitration appears to be attributable to the superiority of arbitration's legal infrastructure, particularly with respect to the New York Convention and related instruments supporting the easy enforceability of arbitration agreements and awards.[59] This conclusion is not only consistent with allegations about the importance of saving time and money (since a system of easy international enforcement of arbitration agreements and awards results in time and cost savings), but also takes cognizance of the one area (international enforcement) where international commercial arbitration is markedly different from international commercial litigation and mediation as a structural matter.

Although the inability to control for different variables makes it difficult to study structural issues at an empirical level, interdisciplinary research can provide important insights into the questions discussed here. One particularly useful paradigm involves default theory, which was initially developed by law and economics scholars as a means of evaluating decision-making in the area of contract law.[60] Default theory grew out of empirical research in behavioural economics and psychology and has been used in a variety of areas of law, including those involving procedure.[61]

Although default theory has never previously been applied to international commercial mediation, this paradigm is actually very useful, since the overwhelming majority of cross-border mediations arise as a matter of contract.[62] Furthermore, international commercial litigation and arbitration also reflect contractual considerations. For example, parties in litigation can and often do enter into contractual agreements regarding both choice of law and choice of forum, while parties in arbitration must have an 'arbitral clause in a contract or an arbitration agreement, signed by the parties or contained in an exchange of letters or telegrams', if the proceedings are to be enforced under the New York Convention.[63] Thus, default theory is an appropriate framework for analysing why international commercial actors behave as they do.

[58] Strong (n 37) 554–6.

[59] Born (n 29) 134–41.

[60] Ian Ayres and Robert Gertner, 'Filling Gaps in Incomplete Contracts: An Economic Theory of Default Rules' (1989) 99 Yale Law Journal 87, 87–8.

[61] Maurits Barendrecht and Berend R. de Vries, 'Fitting the Forum to the Fuss with Sticky Defaults: Failure in the Market for Dispute Resolution Services?' (2005) 7 Cardozo Journal of Conflict Resolution 83, 83–4; Strong (n 37) 533

[62] Strong (n 6) 2026.

[63] Article II (2) of the New York Convention.

One of the most fundamental aspects of default theory involves the notion that default provisions enjoy certain legal and psychological benefits. For example, Russell Korobkin has noted that:

> when lawmakers anoint a contract term the default, the substantive preferences of contracting parties shift—that term becomes more desirable, and other competing terms becoming less desirable. Put another way, contracting parties view default terms as part of the status quo, and they prefer the status quo to alternative states, all other things equal.[64]

When considering the world of international dispute resolution, it is clear that litigation operates as the legal default.[65] Not only is litigation the legal fall-back position should parties fail to agree to arbitration or mediation, but parties seeking to avoid litigation also must incur various types of transaction costs to avoid judicial procedures. Litigation's status as the legal default is also evident in the fact that litigation provides the jurisprudential standard by which procedural justice is measured.[66]

In some ways, litigation's position as the legal default appears to be at odds with descriptions of arbitration as the international commercial dispute resolution mechanism of choice. Indeed, some scholars have suggested that up to 90 percent of all international commercial contracts include an arbitration provision,[67] which would appear to deny any psychological pull toward the default.[68] However, it is also possible, if not probable, that the force of the litigation default in cross-border business disputes is offset in practice by various legal and policy initiatives favouring arbitration.[69] Indeed, international commercial arbitration enjoys a number of structural benefits (most notably the New York Convention and Model Arbitration Law) that do not exist in mediation or litigation and that have undoubtedly increased the incentives associated with arbitration.[70] However, other, less visible, influences also exist. For example, arbitration has undoubtedly benefitted from the highly deferential, pro-arbitration policy adopted by courts around the world.[71] This deference is illustrated in a variety of ways, including the doctrine of separability, support for *competence-competence* and negative *competence-competence*, and the increasingly expansive approach to non-signatories.

[64] Russell Korobkin, 'The Status Quo Bias and Contract Default Rules' (1998) 83 Cornell Law Review 608, 611–12 (1998).
[65] Strong (n 37) 533.
[66] Ibid.
[67] Otto Sandrock, 'The Choice Between Forum Selection, Mediation and Arbitration Clauses: European Perspectives' (2009) 20 American Review of International Arbitration 7, 37. But see Born (n 29) 93–7 (disputing figures).
[68] Strong (n 37) 564.
[69] Born (n 29) 98.
[70] Strong (n 37) 564.
[71] Born (n 29) 98.

The tension between the legal default (litigation) and the psychological preference for arbitration has inspired some commentators to suggest making arbitration the legal default in cross-border business disputes. The boldest proposal has come from Gary Born, who has recommended the adoption of an international treaty establishing arbitration as the default for international commercial conflicts,[72] but other people have proposed similar outcomes through changes to national laws[73] or as a matter of judicial interpretation.[74]

Although early analysts in this field focused exclusively on default rules themselves, scholars have now expanded their research to include the concept of 'nudges', defined by Richard Thaler and Cass Sunstein 'as interventions that maintain freedom of choice, that do not impose mandates or bans, but that nonetheless incline people's choices in a particular direction'.[75] According to Thaler and Sunstein, 'default rules, even or perhaps especially if they appear to be invisible, count as prime "nudges"', although other devices—such as positive incentives—can also help shift individual and institutional behaviour.[76] The concept of nudges is particularly helpful in the current context because it helps describe how the structural advantages associated with international commercial arbitration can and do offset the effect of the litigation default and because it highlights the role of the 'choice architect' in designing the system in question.[77]

When considering nudges in international commercial dispute resolution, it is important to recognize that every country responds to government interventions in a slightly different manner.[78] For example, '[t]here appears to be a large category of nations where majorities are likely to approve of nudges so long as they have legitimate ends and are consistent with the interests and values of most people'; these countries are referred to as 'principled pro-nudge nations'.[79] Research has also identified a relatively small group of nations (referred to as 'overwhelmingly

[72] Draft Model Bilateral Arbitration Treaty, https://www.wilmerhale.com/en/insights/news/2015-03-13-model-bilateral-arbitration-treaty-released-for-public-comment; Gary Born, 'BITS, BATS, and Buts: Reflections on International Dispute Resolution' (speech at the University of Pennsylvania) https://www.wilmerhale.com/uploadedFiles/Shared_Content/Editorial/News/Documents/BITs-BATs-and-Buts.pdf.

[73] Gilles Cuniberti, 'Beyond Contract: The Case for Default Arbitration in International Commercial Disputes' (2009) 32 Fordham International Law Journal 417, 487; Jack M. Graves, 'Arbitration as Contract: The Need for a Fully Developed and Comprehensive Set of Statutory Default Legal Rules' (2011) 2 William and Mary Business Law Review 227, 233–4.

[74] Jack Graves, 'Court Litigation Over Arbitration Agreements: Is it Time for a New Default Rule?' (2012) 23 American Review of International Arbitration 113, 114 (advocating the adoption of a 'strong' version of negative *competence-competence*).

[75] Richard H. Thaler and Cass R Sunstein, *Nudge: Improving Decisions About Health, Wealth, and Happiness* (Yale University Press, 2008) 6.

[76] Cass R. Sunstein, 'Deciding by Default' (2013) 162 University of Pennsylvania Law Review 1, 5.

[77] Richard H. Thaler, 'Do You Need a Nudge?' Yale Insights (4 November 2009).

[78] Lucia A. Reisch and Cass R. Sunstein, 'Do Europeans Like Nudges?' (2016) 11 Judgment and Decision-Making 310, 321; Cass R. Sunstein, Lucia A. Reisch, and Julius Rauber, 'Behavioral Insights All Over the World? Public Attitudes Toward Nudging in a Multi-Country Study', https://papers.ssrn.com/sol3/Papers.cfm?abstract_id=2921217.

[79] Sunstein, Reisch, and Rauber (n 78) 17, 19.

pro-nudge nations') that reflect 'overwhelming majorities [that] approve of nearly all nudges'[80] as well as another small group of nations (referred to as 'cautiously pro-nudge' countries) that 'generally support nudges, but where the level of support is markedly lower than in nations that fall in category (1)'.[81] Thus, governments seeking to change party behaviour through nudges must be aware of the type of nudge (or default), the purpose of the nudge (or default), and the psychological make-up of their particular jurisdiction before adopting any particular strategy.

One issue that is not relevant to this analysis is how the nudge (or default) was adopted. Researchers have noted that defaults can be established consciously or unconsciously by choice architects, but the method of determining the default has no effect on the strength of the rule in question.[82] Thus, the fact that the systemic default in favour of litigation appears to have been historically set without considering other alternatives[83] does not change the extent or the nature of the benefits conferred by litigation's status as the legal default.[84]

Traditionally, defaults have been defined in a rather monochromatic manner as 'settings or rules about the way products, policies, or legal relationships function that apply unless users, affected citizens, or parties take action to change them'.[85] However, the contemporary understanding of defaults includes a more detailed appreciation of the different types of defaults and how they operate within a particular legal system. At one time, scholars considered defaults to be nothing more than simple gap fillers that provided a normative rule in situations where parties had not affirmatively chosen a particular option.[86] However, refinements in default theory have allowed analysts to distinguish between several different types of defaults, thereby helping law and policymakers make more appropriate choices when designing dispute systems.

For example, researchers have found that some defaults, often referred to as 'policy defaults,' are adopted 'with an explicit purpose to alter the ultimate position of the parties'.[87] These mechanisms also establish a position that is assumed to be 'good for most individuals, under the assumption that only the minority who have clear preferences to the contrary will opt out'.[88] On the other end of the spectrum lie 'penalty defaults', which reflect rules that one or more parties dislike and which are expected to result in increased efforts by parties to contract around the default.[89] Penalty defaults typically arise when policymakers are unsure of the rule that would be chosen by an informed individual.[90]

[80] Ibid., 18–19.
[81] Ibid., 17, 19.
[82] Thaler (n 77).
[83] Strong (n 4); Thaler (n 77).
[84] Cass R. Sunstein, 'Switching the Default Rule' (2002) 77 New York University Law Review 106, 109.
[85] Lauren E. Willis, 'When Nudges Fail: Slippery Defaults' (2013) 80 University of Chicago Law Review 1155, 1157.
[86] Ibid.
[87] Ibid.
[88] Ibid.
[89] Sunstein (n 76) 35.
[90] Ibid., 5.

States use policy and penalty defaults to nudge parties toward certain types of behaviour.[91] However, some jurisdictions may respond more favourably to one type of default over the other, depending on whether they are a principled pro-nudge nation, an overwhelmingly pro-nudge nation, or a cautiously pro-nudge nation.[92] For example, policy defaults may be more effective in principled or overwhelmingly pro-nudge nations, since people in those jurisdictions are generally predisposed to adopt government initiatives, whereas penalty defaults may be more effective in countries that are only cautiously pro-nudge, since people in those countries are relatively sceptical about government interventions and thus may be more inclined to act autonomously or in opposition to government policies.

Defaults do not have to be visible or particularly heavy-handed to influence individual or institutional choice. To the contrary, the cumulative effect of numerous small, seemingly insignificant nudges can have a measurable effect on the process in question and can even overcome what might otherwise be characterized as a rational choice.[93] Choice architects involved in designing or redesigning a dispute system must also consider the fact that different defaults generate different levels of intensity.[94]

For example, policy defaults are usually described as 'sticky', meaning that more people adopt the behaviour in question than would be expected if the rule were not in place.[95] 'Stickiness' is achieved through various measures, including the imposition of relatively high transaction costs on those seeking to avoid the default and the relatively strict attitude adopted by adjudicators involved in interpreting and applying the norm in question. This approach can be justified on the grounds that policy defaults reflect a position that the state considers optimal for most individuals.[96] Penalty defaults, on the other hand, tend to be relatively 'slippery' and can be easily avoided by parties.[97] Penalty defaults also generate fewer transaction costs, due, in part, to the fact that adjudicators are less inclined to protect the default through rigorous rules of interpretation.

At this point, it is not clear what type of default litigation is meant to reflect in the international commercial context.[98] On the one hand, courts and legislatures from around the world have made it very easy for parties to avoid litigation through arbitration, which suggests that litigation operates as a penalty default. However, other factors (such as the role litigation plays in the constitutional order) suggest that litigation operates as a policy default. Many commentators also consider litigation

91 Thaler and Sunstein (n 75) 6; Willis (n 85) 1157.
92 Sunstein, Reisch, and Rauber (n 78) 17–19.
93 Korobkin (n 64) 611–12; Thaler (n 77).
94 Stephanie Smith and Janet Martinez, 'An Analytic Framework for Dispute Systems Design' (2009) 14 Harvard Negotiation Law Review 123, 125.
95 Willis (n 85) 1157.
96 Ibid.
97 Ibid 1157, n 3.
98 Strong (n 37) 564; Strong (n 4).

to be superior to other dispute resolution mechanisms, although that debate (occasionally framed as involving the 'privatization' of civil justice) often focuses on normative, rather than descriptive, concerns.[99]

It would be very useful to determine how the litigation default currently operates in international commercial cases so as to avoid structural elements that generate perverse incentives for sub-optimal behaviour.[100] Although comprehensive consideration of such matters is beyond the scope of the current analysis, section IV demonstrates how default theory can be integrated into discussions about the structure of the international commercial dispute resolution regime so as to maximize those values that are considered important from a policy perspective and avoid creation of unanticipated or undesired results.

IV. Applying Default and Structural Analyses to the International Commercial Dispute Resolution Regime

When undertaking a DSD analysis, choice architects must identify the values most important to the system's sponsors and participants, as those principles will need to be prioritized in the new system design. At this point, one of the clearest policy goals enunciated in the world of international dispute resolution involves party autonomy.[101] While this rationale is most often associated with the desire to allow parties in arbitration to choose how to structure their individual proceedings, the concept of autonomy also refers to the freedom to choose which dispute resolution procedure to adopt, a notion that includes the freedom to choose mediation. However, as sections II and III demonstrate, there are numerous structural features that effectively nudge parties away from using mediation to resolve their cross-border business disputes. If autonomy is indeed an important value in international dispute resolution, then the system must set all three procedures—litigation, arbitration, and mediation—on a level playing field.

One of the ways that states have consciously or unconsciously nudged parties toward international commercial arbitration is by making the process predictable, as well as time- and cost-effective through the adoption of various mechanisms that facilitate enforcement of arbitration agreements and awards. Numerous empirical studies, including those focusing on party motivation regarding mediation, have shown the importance of these features to international commercial actors,[102] which suggests that the best way to encourage mediation in cross-border

[99] Tracey E. George and Chris Guthrie, 'Induced Litigation' (2004) 98 Northwestern University Law Review 545, 547–8; Judith Resnik, 'Diffusing Disputes: The Public in the Private of Arbitration, the Private in Courts, and the Erasure of Rights' (2015) 124 Yale Law Journal 2804, 2706–7.

[100] Strong (n 4).

[101] Born (n 29) 76–7.

[102] Strong (n 6) 2031, 2036.

business disputes is to ensure that the process is predictable as well as time- and cost-efficient.

Although there are a variety of ways to achieve that particular end, the most logical technique involves the elimination of certain structural obstacles to the international enforcement of both mediation agreements and settlement agreements through the adoption of binding international instruments providing for easy enforcement of both types of agreements.[103] Indeed, empirical research suggests not only that international actors perceive the enforcement of mediation and settlement agreements associated with international commercial disputes to be extremely difficult, but also that adoption of one or more international instruments involving enforcement of those agreements would be extremely beneficial.[104] One major international study conducted by the author indicates that 75 percent of respondents believe that an international convention to facilitate recognition and enforcement of both mediation agreements (i.e. agreements on the front end of the mediation process) and settlement agreements (i.e. agreements at the back end of the mediation process) would be desirable.[105] An additional 19 percent of respondents thought that a convention only addressing settlement agreements would be desirable, while an additional 6 percent thought that a convention only addressing mediation agreements would be desirable.[106] This data was presented to UNCITRAL Working Group II (Dispute Settlement) as part of the early deliberations on the Singapore Convention on Mediation and doubtless played a role in the delegates' decision to move forward with the initiative.[107]

Although the Singapore Convention on Mediation has been formally opened for signature,[108] it is still too early to know how effective it will be in overcoming the structural bias in favour of international arbitration. Much will depend on whether states parties use the opt-in reservation included in Article 8(1)(b) and whether courts asked to apply the instrument adopt the same type of robust interpretive approach used in the arbitral context. While the outcome to these questions will not transpire for a number of years, the future appears promising.

As encouraging as the work at UNCITRAL is, it only addresses half the problem. Empirical research shows that the vast majority of commercial mediations are currently triggered by standalone or multi-tier mediation clauses,[109] and many of these provisions have proven difficult to interpret and enforce in practice. As a result, adoption of a binding international instrument facilitating the enforcement

[103] Strong (n 44) 29–38.
[104] Strong (n 6) 2047–56, 2056–61.
[105] Ibid., 2057.
[106] Ibid.
[107] Settlement Agreements Resulting from International Commercial Conciliation/Mediation, Note by the Secretariat, 6 ft16, UN Document A/CN.9/WG.II/WP.187 (27 November 2014). See also Singapore Convention (n 12); Strong (n 12).
[108] Singapore Convention (n 12). See also Chapter 19, this volume.
[109] Strong (n 6) 2026.

of agreements to engage in cross-border commercial mediation would not only decrease the time and cost of engaging in mediation and increase the predictability of the process, but also it would also create a more level playing field between international commercial arbitration and international commercial mediation by reflecting the second major benefit of the New York Convention (i.e. the easy enforceability of arbitration agreements).

In many ways, drafting this type of convention will be easier than drafting the Singapore Convention on Mediation. As a rule, UNCITRAL considers it a 'best practice' to reinforce legal principles by adopting consistent language in related documents, as has been done with the New York Convention and the Model Arbitration Law in the arbitral realm.[110] However, the significant shortage of UNCITRAL enactments concerning international enforcement of settlement agreements meant that delegates had to create the new instrument almost entirely from whole cloth.[111]

The situation is very different with respect to a possible instrument on the international enforcement of agreements to mediate, since UNCITRAL can look to a number of provisions in the Model Mediation Law for inspiration. Indeed, the Model Mediation Law—like the Model Conciliation Law before it—is very useful in this regard because it reflects a significant 'effort to put together a comprehensive [mediation] act that covers virtually all relevant issues (a) to set minimum standards for the internal aspects of conciliation and (b) to regulate the aspects of conciliation that relate to contemporaneous or subsequent court, arbitral, or similar proceedings'.[112]

First, those interested in drafting an international convention on enforcement and recognition of international commercial mediation agreements can look to the Model Mediation Law for the definition of mediation. According to Article 1(3), mediation

> means a process, whether referred to by the expression mediation, conciliation, or an expression of similar import, whereby parties request a third person or persons ('the mediator') to assist them in their attempt to reach an amicable settlement of their dispute arising out of or relating to a contractual or other legal

[110] Guide to Enactment and Use of the UNCITRAL Model Law 2002, 13, http://www.uncitral.org/pdf/english/texts/arbitration/ml-conc/03-90953_Ebook.pdf.

[111] The original Model Conciliation Law, enacted in 2002, mentions enforcement of settlement agreements only in passing, since there was not a great deal of consensus on settlement procedures or the nature of settlement agreements at the time the Model Conciliation Law was adopted; see Art 14 of the Model Conciliation Law, paras 88–91. The Model Conciliation Law was revised and renamed as the Model Mediation Law in 2018 to take into account various elements reflected in the Singapore Convention on Mediation.

[112] Eric van Ginkel, 'The UNCITRAL Model Law on International Commercial Conciliation: A Critical Appraisal' (2004) 21 Journal of International Arbitration 1, 58 (referring to the Model Conciliation Act).

> relationship. The mediator does not have the authority to impose upon the parties a solution to the dispute.

Article 3(2) goes on to state that:

> [a] mediation is 'international' if:
>
> (a) The parties to an agreement to mediate have, at the time of the conclusion of that agreement, their places of business in different States; or
> (b) The State in which the parties have their places of business is different from either:
>   (i) The State in which a substantial part of the obligations of the commercial relationship is to be performed; or
>   (ii) The State with which the subject matter of the dispute is most closely connected.

The usefulness of the Model Mediation Law is not limited to definitional issues. Instead, drafters of a new instrument on international enforcement of mediation agreements can also look to the Model Mediation Law for assistance on certain operative provisions. For example, a considerable amount of debate exists in the international realm about what constitutes rejection or termination of mediation.[113] Article 5(2) of the Model Mediation Law offers some helpful insight into that particular issue, and states that:

> [i]f a party that invited another party to mediate does not receive an acceptance of the invitation within 30 days from the day on which the invitation was sent, or within such other period of time as specified in the invitation, the party may elect to treat this as a rejection of the invitation to mediate.

The identification of a firm deadline creates a clear default rule and ensures that a recalcitrant party does not hold the other party hostage to a particular process.

International commercial actors have also found it difficult to determine when a mediation proceeding can be considered complete. Again, the Model Mediation Law offers some helpful language, e.g. in Article 12, that mediation proceedings can be terminated:

> (a) By the conclusion of a settlement agreement by the parties, on the date of the agreement;
> (b) By a declaration of the mediator, after consultation with the parties, to the effect that further efforts at mediation are no longer justified, on the date of the declaration;

[113] Born (n 29) 928–35.

(c) By a declaration of the parties addressed to the mediator to the effect that the mediation proceedings are terminated, on the date of the declaration; or
(d) By a declaration of a party to the other party or parties and the mediator, if appointed, to the effect that the mediation proceedings are terminated, on the date of the declaration.

Although it is important to know when the obligation to engage in mediation has been fulfilled, termination of the mediation does not always equate to resolution of the dispute. In fact, empirical evidence suggests that significant numbers of mediation agreements in international commercial disputes arise as part of a multi-tier (step) process that contemplate a binding dispute resolution procedure (either arbitration or litigation) should mediation fail to achieve results.[114] Multi-tier provisions have proven extremely challenging in the cross-border business setting, since it is not clear whether mediation is to be considered a condition precedent (precondition) to arbitration or litigation, and what effect that determination might have.[115] Fortunately, the Model Mediation Law contemplated that issue in Article 14, which indicates that:

> [w]here the parties have agreed to mediate and have expressly undertaken not to initiate during a specified period of time or until a specified event has occurred arbitral or judicial proceedings with respect to an existing or future dispute, such an undertaking shall be given effect by the arbitral tribunal or the court until the terms of the undertaking have been complied with, except to the extent necessary for a party, in its opinion, to preserve its rights. Initiation of such proceedings is not of itself to be regarded as a waiver of the agreement to mediate or as a termination of the mediation proceedings.

These provisions obviously do not address all of the issues that would have to be considered in a new international instrument on the enforcement of international commercial mediation agreements. However, the Model Mediation Law, like the Model Conciliation Law before it, nevertheless offers a helpful starting point should UNCITRAL decide to take up that particular task.

V. Conclusion

Scholarly and practical interest in international commercial mediation is on the rise around the world, leading to numerous studies and initiatives. Many of these projects have focused on the procedure itself, as is both right and proper. However,

[114] Strong (n 6) 2026.
[115] Born (n 29) 928–35.

it is important that law and policymakers do not lose sight of the need also to consider high-level structural issues, since experience and empirical research both suggest that the failure to appreciate how mediation fits into the overall international dispute resolution regime has been one of the primary reasons why mediation has failed to flourish in the post-Second World War era.

Specialists in DSD have shown that research into civil justice cannot be limited to the nuances of individual procedures, but also must include comprehensive study of the legal, social, economic, and cultural environments in which a particular mechanism operates. Only by considering a variety of factors, including both visible and invisible nudges, can choice architects truly appreciate the forces that drive individual and institutional decisions involving international dispute resolution.

Although space restrictions precluded a full DSD analysis, this chapter has nevertheless provided important insights for dispute system designers in the area of international civil justice by using an innovative default theoretic analysis to demonstrate how various structural elements consciously or unconsciously push parties toward certain dispute resolution procedures. While it is not unusual for states to engage in 'nudging' behaviour, the international dispute resolution regime appears to have been constructed without much conscious thought regarding the way in which different procedural alternatives interact.

This study has identified a number of important questions that must be answered before a truly coherent means of resolving cross-border commercial disputes can be constructed. For example, states need to decide whether the default in favour of litigation is intended to operate in international commercial cases as a policy or penalty default. States also need to determine whether they wish to place international commercial mediation on the same level as international commercial arbitration and why that decision is appropriate. This information is critical to the construction of an effective and enduring system of civil justice.

Although this chapter has shown that systemic reform is both logical and desirable, not everyone is or will be in favour of such efforts. Indeed, proponents of international commercial mediation have already experienced resistance to various initiatives, including the Singapore Convention on Mediation.[116] Opposition has come from various quarters, including some that were completely unanticipated, and involves perceived threats to a variety of individual and institutional interests, including those of a personal, professional, financial, or reputational nature.[117] Fortunately, the DSD process is adept at identifying and responding to these types of concerns.[118]

116 Schnabel (n 49) 5; S. I. Strong, 'Clash of Cultures: Epistemic Communities, Negotiation Theory, and International Lawmaking' (2017) 50 Akron Law Review 495, 511–12.

117 Ibid.

118 Rogers et al. (n 16) 6, 8; Strong (n 12).

When considering the form and nature of civil justice, it is important to consider the role played by unconscious cognitive distortions (such as the status quo bias) and historic influences, even if the latter are no longer based in reality.[119] For example, the long-standing hostility of English judges to arbitration was once described by Lord Campbell as having

> its origin in the interests of the judges. There was no disguising the fact that, as formerly, the emoluments of the Judges depended mainly, or almost entirely, on fees, and as they had no fixed salaries there was great competition to get as much as possible of litigation into Westminster Hall and there was a great scramble in Westminster Hall for the division of the spoil. [. . .] And they had great jealousy of arbitration whereby Westminster Hall was robbed of those cases.[120]

Although judges no longer retain a direct financial interest in the cases they hear, DSD analyses suggest that they do enjoy a variety of intangible benefits, e.g. those of a reputational nature, that arise from litigation's preferential status in the panoply of dispute resolution alternatives. This phenomenon may explain the animosity exhibited by some judges to non-judicial dispute resolution processes, including both arbitration and mediation.

While it can be difficult to overcome these types of unconscious or hidden biases, DSD analyses can be very helpful in this regard, since the DSD framework promotes increased rationality of debate and discussion about systemic reform in the area of civil justice.[121] While this chapter has only been able to provide a limited glimpse into certain aspects of the DSD process, it is hoped that the discussion reflected herein will help law- and policymakers appreciate how comprehensive structural considerations affect the development and use of international commercial mediation.

[119] Strong (n 37) 552.
[120] *Scott v Avery* [1856] 5 HL Cas 811, 853 (Lord Campbell).
[121] Smith and Martinez (n 94) 129–33.

4

Concurrent Co-Mediation

Toward a More Collaborative Centre of Gravity in Investor–State Dispute Resolution

Jack J. Coe, Jr

I. Introduction

As has been much discussed,[1] over the past two decades investment treaty arbitration has been transformed from a largely untested dispute resolution regime to one regularly invoked by investors. The claims that have been involved, now numbering in the hundreds, have been often quite large—sometimes staggeringly so. As might have been expected, when pressed by an avalanche of proceedings, the investor–state arbitration system has proven to be imperfect, although the extent to which its flaws are fundamental is subject to debate. Those expressing misgivings about the current system have included the disputants themselves (not least states), scholars (to varying degrees) and—it seems increasingly—various casual observers (often with great conviction).[2]

Among the more often-cited shortcomings of investor–state arbitration is that, as a mechanism for confirming rights and duties, the system underperforms, producing jurisprudence that is too indeterminate. Under a popular line of reasoning, it follows from such legal insecurity that states will exercise uncalled-for self-restraint when regulating in the public interest because they are uncertain what an arbitral tribunal later will deem to be the content of their investment treaty undertakings. Concurrently, so goes the argument, elasticity in treaty terms such as 'fair and equitable treatment' encourage claimants to advance exorbitant putative theories of recovery.

[1] See International Centre for the Settlement of Investment Disputes (ICSID), 'Bibliography on Investment Law and Procedure' https://icsid.worldbank.org/en/Pages/resources/Bibliography-on-Investment-Law-and-Procedure.aspx#.

[2] See Elizabeth Warren, 'The Trans-Pacific Partnership Clause Everyone Should Oppose' *The Washington Post* (25 February 2015) ('[B]uried in the fine print of the closely guarded draft [is] an increasingly common feature of trade agreements, […] called "Investor–State Dispute Settlement," or ISDS. The name may sound mild, but don't be fooled.') https://www.washingtonpost.com/opinions/kill-the-dispute-settlement-language-in-the-trans-pacific-partnership/2015/02/25/ec7705a2-bd1e-11e4-b274-e5209a3bc9a9_story.html?utmterm=3e12cf2c3ee8.

Aside from issues of legal certainty, there have also been complaints about the adjudicative process used to decide investor claims. These are not deficiencies exclusive to investment arbitration, but rather are associated with international commercial arbitration in general (i.e. it is slow, expensive, highly combative, involves limited review of arbitral work-product, and is designed to produce a winner and a corresponding loser).[3]

Heightened interest in reforming the prevailing investor–state disputes regime has led to earnest consideration by policymakers of numerous reforms,[4] including the use of third-party assisted non-arbitral problem-solving, particularly mediation (conciliation).[5] Most often what is envisioned is the use of mediation as a process that supplements arbitration in some fashion.

As part of a continuing examination of the many questions raised by investor–state mediation, this chapter returns to the topic of concurrent (or 'shadow') mediation.[6] The terms 'concurrent' or 'shadow' here mean that the activities of the third-party neutrals would coincide with those of the arbitrators (or arbitrator). The emphasis is on a model that employs two mediators, rather than one—an approach variously referred to as 'team mediation' or 'co-mediation'.

II. The General Proposal

Elsewhere,[7] this author has suggested that mediation ought to be routinely and purposefully made available in investor–state disputes, not as a substitute for

[3] Other process-related critiques have targeted the standard arbitration model's failure to account for the public nature of investment disputes and the corresponding need for greater transparency. See Jack J. Coe, Jr, 'Transparency in the Resolution of Investor-State Disputes—Adoption, Adaptation, and NAFTA Leadership' (2006) 54 University of Kansas Law Review 1339; UNCITRAL, *United Nations Convention on Transparency in Treaty-Based Investor-State Arbitration*, U.N. Doc. A/69/496 (2015) https://www.uncitral.org/pdf/english/texts/arbitration/transparency-convention/Transparency-Convention-e.pdf.

[4] For an overview of the present investor–state system and current thinking about concrete reform options viewed from the state's perspective, see United Nations Commission on Trade and Development (UNCTAD), 'UNCTAD's Reform Package for the International Investment Regime' (United Nations, 2017), http://investmentpolicyhub.unctad.org/News/Hub/Home/1576 [hereinafter Reform Package.

[5] This chapter uses 'mediation' and 'conciliation' interchangeably to refer to the process in which one or more neutrals use various techniques to achieve settlement of a dispute.

[6] For an earlier assessment, see Jack J. Coe, Jr, 'Concurrent Med-Arb (CMA): Some Further Reflections on a Work in Progress', in Susan D. Franck and Anna Joubin-Bret (eds), *Investor-State Disputes: Prevention and Alternatives to Arbitration II.* Proceedings of the Washington and Lee University and UNCTAD Joint Symposium on International Investment and Alternative Dispute Resolution. 29 March 2010, Lexington, VA. (United Nations, 2010) 43.

[7] See Jack J. Coe, Jr, 'Toward a Complementary Role for Conciliation in Investor-State Disputes: A Preliminary Sketch' (2005) 12 University of California Davis Journal of International Law and Policy 7; Jack J. Coe, Jr, 'Settlement of Investor-State Disputes through Mediation: Preliminary Remarks on Processes, Problems and Prospects', in R. Doak Bishop (ed.), *Enforcement Of Arbitral Awards Against Sovereigns* (JurisNet, 2009) Ch. 4; Jack J. Coe, Jr, 'Should Mediation of Investment Disputes Be Encouraged, and if So, by Whom and How?', in Arthur W. Rovine (ed.), *Contemporary Issues In International Arbitration And Mediation* (Brill, 2010) 339.

arbitration, and not merely as a precursor to be exhausted before arbitration begins, but as a parallel process. Thus, the mediation would coincide with the arbitration in question, and indeed might extend into the post-award sphere (remaining at the disposal of the disputants even after the arbitral tribunal is *functus officio*).[8] Under the model envisioned, the two processes would be coordinated, at least to a degree; the two types of neutrals—arbitrators and mediators—would be aware of and accommodate the others' activities.[9] The process would be triggered by prompts in the bilateral investment treaty (BIT) involved and supported by the rules available to the parties through an administering institution or otherwise.

It is a fact that a percentage of investor–state arbitrations settle, and do so without the help of one or more third-party neutrals. This author's thesis remains that one or more skilful and well-prepared[10] mediators would likely add to the number of investor–state disputes that settle,[11] and would often produce outcomes that are more authoritative, inventive, and attentive to individual party interests than those accomplished through unassisted negotiation.

Additionally, mediation will likely prove more able than arbitration to accommodate the interests of non-parties to the legal dispute; that is, the mediation process and a mediated settlement may include various types of third parties, either directly or indirectly.[12]

Importantly, even when not achieving a full settlement, mediation would enhance the arbitration process that it shadows. In particular, mediation might assist the parties in navigating the many instances during an arbitration in which successful bilateral give-and-take is to be preferred to defaulting to the arbitral tribunal, such as when particular issues of documentary disclosure arise, or when there is deadlock in agreeing on the structure and content of a confidentiality agreement, or when a disputant intends to press motions or substantive arguments

[8] The rendition of the award often marks a new round of negotiations between the parties. See e.g. Reuters Staff, 'ConocoPhillips to receive $337 million in accord with Ecuador', *Reuters* (4 December 2017) https://www.reuters.com/article/us-conocophillips-ecuador/conocophillips-to-receive-337-million-in-accord-with-ecuador-idUSKBN1DY1KP.

[9] This coordination might be reflected in allowing the mediators to receive briefs and to attend hearings, and in scheduling accommodations.

[10] I have in mind mediators with notable standing in the investor–state arbitration or related communities; that is, persons who enjoy excellent stature and authoritativeness on par with the arbitrator or arbitrators forming the tribunal; they should have a very good grasp of investment law and arbitral practice. Relatedly, and putting aside arguments about labels, my view of mediation is that the process is most promising when mediators are equipped to give, when appropriate, a specialist's evaluation of each side's case, both in general and as to selected issues and arguments.

[11] The settlement rate has been variously calculated depending on how one defines settlement. A reliable premise is that about one third of the filed cases settle. See e.g. Rachel Wellhausen, 'Recent Trends in Investor State Dispute Settlement' (2016) 7 (1) Journal of International Dispute Settlement 117 (153 of 461 studied cases settled).

[12] Such third parties might include subsidiary divisions of the host state or third-party funders. At least as to the mediation *process* (as opposed to the result), in appropriate circumstances the investor's home state and relevant non-governmental organizations (NGOs) might profitably be included. By contrast, an arbitral tribunal is highly limited in its ability to bind, or directly consider the interests of, various third-party stakeholders, despite the advent of amicus briefs and more transparent hearings.

with little chance of succeeding. Equally, the mediation process will often also help the parties to better understand their respective cases, thus promoting higher-quality arguments before the arbitral tribunal.

To the extent that mediation becomes embedded in disputant expectations and routine, greater sophistication and best practices should emerge, allowing its users to more fully to realize mediation's 'value-adding' potential.[13]

III. How It Might Work: Water Delivery in Ruritania

A. The Dispute

Having had its concession to retrieve, purify, and deliver water revoked by a local municipality, the American company Watertime, Inc. delivered to Ruritania its Notice of Intent to file a claim under the Ruritania–US BIT. As authorized under that BIT, in that Notice Watertime signified its intent to elect the optional process set forth in fictional Appendix D (Nonbinding, Concurrent, Third-Party Procedures).[14]

By virtue of the Notice, Ruritania's central government became aware of the dispute for the first time. After less than systematic correspondence with the Municipality and officials of the province in which it operates, Ruritania's Ministries of Justice and Foreign Affairs developed a general sense of the local government's reasons for revocation. Based thereon, it informed Watertime that it would resist the claim vigorously.

B. The Mediation Underway

Within one month of the Notice, two mediators had been provisionally appointed pursuant to Appendix D. Both were appointed by an institution, both had government experience, and both had at some point served as counsel and arbitrators in investor–state matters. Neither was Ruritanian nor American. With the parties'

[13] Regarding the use of mediation's ability to promote agreements that do more than settle the legal dispute before the arbitrators, see Kimberlee Kovach, *Mediation Principles and Practice* (3rd edn, Thompson-West, 2004) 196–8.

[14] 'That election establishes that, subject to a different appointment procedure agreed by the disputants, the claimant (with or without the help of an institution) shall nominate within one month of issuing the Notice of Intent, a mediator to be attached to the case. Upon notification of the claimant's election to invoke Appendix D, the state may nominate a mediator, who will be the co-mediator, or instead may affirm its intention to let the one-mediator default govern. If upon giving its Notice of Intent the claimant does not elect Appendix D, the state may nevertheless do so. Either disputant may, but need not, enlist the Permanent Court of Arbitration (PCA), ICSID or other institution to assist in identifying its nominee for mediator. Nominees for mediator are subject to disclosure and challenge procedures analogous to those applicable to any arbitrator that serves.'

agreement, the two affirmed that they would be guided, but not strictly bound, by the International Bar Association (IBA) Rules for Investor–State Mediation.[15]

After both sides had summarized their respective cases in ten-page memos (simultaneously submitted) the disputants and mediators met, first in short private caucuses during which the mediators assessed the feasibility of moving to joint sessions, then in two joint sessions lasting four hours each. The joint meetings did not end in settlement, but the mediators and the two disputants learned a great deal. Among other things, Ruritania came to better understand the basis upon which Watertime would press not only expropriation and fair and equitable treatment claims, but also national treatment and most-favoured nation (MFN) theories of recovery. Those theories were rooted in Watertime's belief that both local companies and third-country concessionaires who provided trash collection services to the municipality were allowed to operate significantly older trucks than those used by Watertime and that, like Watertime, the third-country service providers had employed local agents to help them formulate their initial bids without being accused of improper influence.

For its part, Watertime learned that Ruritania would rely on myriad jurisdiction-related defences and, in particular, specific BIT provisions excluding from BIT protections certain measures maintained by municipalities. The mediators, in turn, came to better understand each side's case, if still at a preliminary level, and, as importantly, to know more about the personalities involved.

When the notice and cooling-off periods had elapsed,[16] Watertime initiated arbitration under the ICSID Convention, one of the options offered under the BIT.[17] As contemplated in Appendix D, both disputants affirmed that the mediators who had served during the cooling-off period could continue to serve. Additionally, Ruritania failed to insist on a three-arbitrator tribunal, so that under the Appendix D default rule, the tribunal would consist of one arbitrator, appointed by the parties or ICSID, as needed.

As foreshadowed during the earlier mediation sessions, however, Ruritania urged that ICSID not register the request for arbitration. It advanced several admissibility and jurisdiction-related arguments.[18] After receiving from Watertime

[15] The IBA Mediation Rules are available at https://icsid.worldbank.org/en/Documents/process/IBA%20Rules%20for%20Investor-State%20Mediation%20(Approved%20by%20IBA%20Council%204%20Oct%202012).pdf.

[16] Under the fictional BIT, the cooling off period is 'six months [...] since the events giving rise to the claim'.

[17] According to Section B of the fictional BIT, the investor may choose whichever form of ICSID arbitration is available (Additional Facility or ICSID Convention) or United Nations Commission on International Trade Law (UNCITRAL) Rules arbitration. If either disputant has set in motion Appendix D mediation, the default assumption is that one arbitrator will serve and will be jointly appointed by the parties (or, if needed, by ICSID or the PCA, depending upon which arbitration format the claimant chose). Either disputant may supplant the default rule by requesting that three arbitrators serve, in which case, the mode of appointment established in the governing arbitration rules will be followed.

[18] Ruritania insisted, in correspondence with the Secretariat, that under both the BIT and ICSID Convention jurisprudence, Watertime was neither an investor, nor had an investment in Ruritania; that the acts it complained of were, at most, merely garden-variety breaches of contract (not BIT breaches);

certain clarifications, the ICSID Secretariat registered the Request, citing its limited role in the process, and emphasizing the word 'manifestly' in Article 36 of the ICSID Convention.[19] Soon thereafter, the two mediators resumed joint sessions. With the help of a list procedure suggested by the two mediators, a sole arbitrator was institutionally appointed.[20]

Soon after her appointment, the arbitrator immediately scheduled an 'organizational' meeting. The agenda contemplated consideration of the usual matters that lead to an initial procedural order and also indicated that the parties would be invited to give a brief overview of their respective cases. During the intervening two weeks, the mediators jointly caucused with both parties. Each was persuaded to streamline its case. Watertime agreed not to introduce a performance requirements theory (which, in caucus, both mediators insisted was very weak) and Ruritania agreed, inter alia, that it would not rely on the BIT's denial of benefits provision, nor its reservation for certain existing municipal measures, both of which arguments the mediators had in caucus described as so fanciful as to alienate the tribunal.[21]

The procedural order that followed the arbitrator's subsequent meeting with the parties anticipated a bifurcated proceeding addressing admissibility and jurisdictional defences only. Shortly after the one round of pleadings had been completed, but before the prehearing conference, the mediators re-engaged. In a joint session, each disputant evinced complete confidence that it would prevail. Then followed additional private caucuses.

During those separate caucuses, after probing questions by the mediators, each party conceded some weaknesses in their jurisdictional cases. Watertime agreed with the mediators that, while no bribery had been alleged, under the domestic jurisprudence upon which both sides relied, the investment might be deemed to have been procured in violation of local law because Watertime had employed as a consultant a former government official. Much would depend on how the tribunal interpreted the facts and Ruritania's recently enacted 'influence' statute.

that Watertime could be denied protection under the denial of benefits clause found in the BIT; and that the Municipality's insistence on modern equipment for delivering water was a health and safety measure that fell under the BIT's essential security provision. It also relied on clauses in the concession designating domestic courts and Ruritanian law in the event of disputes under the concession, which according to Ruritania, meant that Watertime had in any event 'contracted away' any BIT protections it might have had.

[19] Article 36(3) of the ICSID Convention provides in the relevant part: 'The Secretary-General shall register the request unless he finds, on the basis of the information contained in the request, that the dispute is manifestly outside the jurisdiction of the Centre'.

[20] The initial list comprised five names proposed by the mediators; Ruritania declined two; Watertime declined one of those two, and also rejected one other name. From the remaining two names, the appointment was made by the ICSID (acting as appointing authority under Appendix D).

[21] The legal team for Ruritania in fact welcomed the assessment offered by the two mediators, as those theories had been insisted upon over the legal team's objection by an influential cabinet person serving in Ruritania.

Ruritania agreed in private that despite its pleadings, Watertime's concession and related activities most probably met the definition of 'investment' both under the BIT and under ICSID Convention jurisprudence. On its illegal-procurement-of-investment argument, Ruritania disclosed in caucus that it needed more time to gather further critical facts and that the witness on whose written statement it relied had become unavailable. Armed with these confidential disclosures, the mediators proposed to the parties that they indicate to the tribunal their shared preference that the question of illegal acquisition be deferred to the merits; persuaded, they did so jointly. At the prehearing conference, Ruritania also advised the tribunal that, while it was not abandoning its argument based on the BIT's definition of 'investment', it would 'use its limited hearing time to focus on the meaning of investment under the ICSID Convention'.

The hearing was held. Immediately after the hearing, as prefigured in the agreed mediation 'pre-sets',[22] the parties were invited by the mediators to join in a joint session. Watertime agreed, but Ruritania declined. The mediators decided not to caucus with the investor, but to re-propose a joint meeting after the tribunal had ruled on jurisdiction. One month later, the tribunal did so rule.

The arbitrator determined that Watertown had an investment under both the BIT and ICSID jurisprudence. It joined to the merits, however, all remaining admissibility and jurisdiction-related questions. Its contemporaneous procedural order set a schedule for submissions on the merits. In accordance with a mediation pre-set, the mediators again invited the parties to participate in a joint session; again the investor was willing, but the state declined.

After the parties had completed a round of written arbitration submissions on the merits, and another invitation to mediate was declined by Ruritania, the mediator with the more pronounced government service background visited the capital to urge Ruritania to re-engage. That meeting ultimately functioned as a private caucus in which the other mediator was not present. At that session, the situation faced by the government lawyers became clear. About the time of the jurisdictional hearing, management of the case had been transferred from the Ministry of Foreign Affairs to the Ministry of Justice; the latter was unconvinced that mediation was a productive use of state resources. Lawyers at the Ministry of Justice also believed that continued participation in mediation would be characterized as weakness both by Watertime and, of equal concern, by Ruritanian voters. There was, after all, an election scheduled to occur in a few months. Moreover, both politically and legally, many of the potential solutions already broached by the mediators could not be effectuated without the direct involvement of the Municipality.

The dispute had indeed become politically significant. The political party not in power used it as an example of why BITs were harmful to Ruritanian sovereignty.

[22] Here, 'pre-set' means a designated juncture at which the mediators will invite the parties to re-engage. Pres-sets are soft commitments to convene at future benchmarks; they make the process more predictable, and trigger mediation without either disputant having to instigate it.

In particular, much had been made publicly of the 100 million US dollars in damages sought in Watertown's Request for Arbitration. The mediator nevertheless expressed her confidence that settlement could be had through mediation on terms favourable to the state, such that it could claim victory, while also ending the arbitration (which had been an evergreen inspiration for news stories and opposition talking-points). The mediator affirmed her understanding that because the Ruritanian press and public had fixated on the 100 million US dollar figure, any settlement amount approaching that figure was out of the question. In part on the strength of the mediator's urgings, and her undertaking to allow the Municipality to be directly involved in mediation sessions, the state agreed to attend further sessions.[23]

The two mediators next met in caucus with Watertime. That meeting confirmed that, as the mediators had suspected, a sophisticated analysis of damages had not been undertaken yet by the investor, who had arrived at the 100 US dollar million number based on several questionable assumptions, including that the concession (initially granted for a five-year term), would be renewed for at least two successive five-year terms.[24] It also had applied a rather relaxed discount rate in arriving at present value, assumed the cost of fuel would remain constant over the fifteen-year period, and adopted a highly optimistic useful life for its fleet of trucks.

When asked about these assumptions in caucus, Watertime intimated that it had endeavoured to reach the highest possible number to signal its seriousness and to maximize settlement value. The mediators then proposed that Watertime undertake, on a confidential basis, the same exercise that the tribunal might perform, i.e. to consider to what damages it would be entitled if the concession (already entering year three) ended at the completion of year five and to discount the expected cash flow using a more realistic discount rate. Additionally, the mediators suggested that Watertime consider the possibility that it might have to bear its own legal fees, both as to the current proceeding, and for any annulment proceeding that might follow. The next day, Watertime returned to a caucus session with numbers ranging between 16 and 20 million US dollars (not adjusted downward to account for legal fees).

After the investor accused the mediators of favouring the state, the mediators spent some time disabusing the claimant of that belief. The caucus ended with the mediators confirming that they would not share with Ruritania any disclosures

[23] In keeping with best practices, the attending mediator fully briefed the absent mediator after the caucus. See Article 8(5) of the IBA Mediation Rules ('co-mediator shall share with the other co-mediator all written or oral communications received from a party or parties').

[24] In its briefs, it had argued that Ruritania was obliged to renew because the trash concessions held by third-country investors had been repeatedly renewed. The investor's assumption, of course, was that trash collection and water delivery were sufficiently analogous to constitute 'like circumstances'.

made during the caucus.[25] The two mediators were, however, authorized to continue exploring settlement options with the state.

The presence in the mediation of the Municipality added another dimension to the dispute. From that direct municipality involvement, for a first time, an alternative justification for cancellation of the concession emerged: municipal officials had suspected that Watertime had, in violation of Ruritanian law, become engaged in local politics, and in particular was thought to have supported the opposition party's bid to retake power in the next election. According to those officials, those suspicions provided a legitimate reason for cancelling the concession. It was not lost on either the claimant or the government lawyers attending the session that such a basis for cancellation might not be consistent with Ruritania's treaty undertakings.

C. In the Fullness of Times: Settlement

As might have been expected, the above fictional case settled for an amount far less than 100 million US dollars. Indeed, the settlement did not involve the state issuing a check to Watertime. Instead, the mediators orchestrated an outcome in which the concession was renegotiated for a term of three years, with a second five-year term to be granted automatically absent a showing of 'cause' (carefully defined in the new concession).

Although no money was paid directly to Watertime, at a cost of 5 million US dollars the federal government purchased a fleet of new water trucks, which it leased to the Municipality; the Municipality in turn subleased the fleet to Watertime on favourable terms. The service fee structure contemplated in the original concession was maintained in the new arrangement, as adjusted by the lease payments to be made by Watertime.

As part of the settlement, Watertime supplied the federal government with several dozen three-year-old computers, which it had just decommissioned in favour of newer technology. In turn, those computers were placed in libraries, schools, and government offices (mostly in the Municipality). Watertime also expressly affirmed that it had not, and would not in the future, involve itself in political activities of any kind.[26]

Additionally, at the request of both parties, the mediators issued a joint written opinion concluding, inter alia, that: 1) the outcome of the case in the hands of the

[25] See Article 8(4) of the IBA Mediation Rules ('No information provided orally by a party to the mediator during a separate meeting may be disclosed to any other party by the mediator, unless the party explicitly so authorizes the mediator.').

[26] The federal government's investigation of the alleged illegal campaign activity uncovered only that some of Watertime's employees (Ruritanian nationals) had been active, quite lawfully, in supporting candidates, but that the company itself had no involvement in political activities.

arbitrator was very difficult to predict; 2) the arbitration might last another four years (including, possibly, a period needed to conclude annulment proceedings under the Convention); 3) the manner in which the tribunal and ad hoc committee would allocate costs could not be forecast; 4) Watertime had not involved itself in local politics; and 5) as a result of the settlement agreement, Ruritanian public safety would likely be enhanced.

IV. Reflections on the Scenario

A. Generally

It is an essential feature of mediation that the parties may control the outcome of the process, just as they do when negotiating.[27] When an advancing arbitration forms the backdrop of such paralleling collaborative processes, those processes are the means by which the parties not only to end the dispute but also avoid an uncontrollable approaching result the substance of which they cannot fully predict. In modern corporate practice, settlements have long been viewed as a business decision.[28] While states face considerations in contemplating settlement different from those driving businesses, ultimately, as with companies, the exercise involves an assessment of the risks of settlement in comparison with the risks of non-settlement.[29]

Mediation is a more powerful settlement tool than bilateral settlement negotiations alone because mediators, as problem-solving neutrals, can perform functions that partisans generally do not pursue. While the factual and legal issues in the Watertime case supplied an important backdrop for the mediators' work, ultimately, their goal was to deemphasize those issues in favour of identifying as to each disputant the obstacles to a mutually beneficial end to the dispute.

B. Selected Features

Despite its simplicity, the Watertime scenario demonstrates several features of a successful shadow co-mediation. These features would also be involved in managing much larger, more complex, disputes.

[27] Alan W. Kowalchyk, 'Resolving Intellectual Property Disputes Outside of Court: Using ADR to Take Control of Your Case' (2006) 61 (2) Dispute Resolution Journal 28, 36 ('mediation provides parties with the greatest amount of control over [. . .] resolution of their dispute').

[28] On the evolving attitudes of corporations toward alternative dispute resolution (ADR) and the tendency for such disputes increasingly to be seen in business terms, see Jean Claude Najar, 'Corporate Counsel in the Era of Dispute Management 2.0.' (2014) 15 (2) Business Law International 37.

[29] See generally Jessica Notini, 'Effective Alternatives Analysis in Mediation: "BATNA/WATNA" Analysis Demystified', https://www.mediate.com/articles/notini1.cfm.

1. Triggering

First, the expectation that mediation might occur was expressly prefigured in the BIT's text: in the negotiation and consultation provision,[30] and in the fictional Appendix D. Commercial entities often associate mediation with contract triggers;[31] the treaty provisions perform the same function, while not purporting to require mediation as an obligatory first step.[32] Rule formulae in turn may redouble the invitation to mediate.[33] The agreed-upon pre-sets also serve as triggers throughout the process.

2. Counsel and mediators

The scenario did not focus on the often-critical role played, for good or for ill, by counsel.[34] Writing in 1982, and presumably referring to the US Bar, Professor Leonard Riskin opined that, '[m]ost lawyers neither understand nor perform mediation nor have a strong interest in doing either'.[35] Nearly four decades later, Riskin's assessment is no doubt less accurate than when he wrote it. One finds today many lawyers who have a very sophisticated understanding of mediation and who have developed skills to harness mediation's potential on behalf of their clients.[36]

Nevertheless, party representatives who view arbitration to be the principal enterprise for which they have been engaged may be reluctant to involve mediators in that already-challenging process. The available anecdotes suggest several potential explanations. Chief among them is that lawyers understandably wish to maintain as much control of the process and of client expectations as possible. They also may assume, often with justification, that their negotiation skills will suffice to bring

[30] See, e.g. Article 23 of the US Model BIT 2012 ('[C]onsultation and negotiation ... *may include the use of nonbinding, third-party procedures*' [emphasis added]). The fictional scenario's counterpart might add: 'in accordance with Appendix D, or as otherwise agreed'.

[31] For data consistent with one's anecdotal sense that mediation provisions formalized before dispute arises improve the likelihood that mediation will occur, see Tom Stipanowich and J. Ryan Lamare, 'Living with ADR: Evolving Perceptions and Use of Mediation, Arbitration, and Conflict Management in Fortune 1000 Corporations' (2013) 19 Harvard Negotiation Law Review 1, 34–6 (for commercial disputes, 54 percent of responders identified contract provisions as ADR triggers (arbitration and mediation not distinguished)).

[32] The extent to which parties should be urged to pursue what is supposed to be a consensual process is an important, and nuanced, question. See Coe, 2005 (n 7) 100–2.

[33] Such rule provisions might invite the parties to state that pursuit of mediation is not inconsistent with arbitration; invite the parties to notify the arbitrators of any mediation, planned or underway; and direct the tribunal to remind the parties of the possible appropriateness of mediation at the initial procedural meeting.

[34] The role of counsel in mediation is now the subject of considerable literature, ranging from highly academic to very tradecraft oriented. For an example of the latter, see Eileen Carrol and Karl Mackie, *The Art of Business Diplomacy: International Mediation* (Kluwer Law International, 2000) 61–3.

[35] Leonard L. Riskin, 'Mediation and Lawyers' (1982) 43 Ohio State Law Journal 29, 43.

[36] See Thomas J. Stipanowich, 'Living the Dream of ADR: Reflection on Four Decades of Quiet Revolution in Dispute Resolution' (2017) 18 Cardozo Journal of Conflict Resolution 513, 524 (citing a 2014 survey of mediators by International Academy of Mediations (IMA) confirming mediator perception that the majority of lawyers encountered in mediation seemed to have substantial mediation experience).

about settlement, if settlement is warranted. Counsel may also simply regard mediation to be an unwelcome distraction and diversion of resources from the arbitration that is their specialty and chief assignment.

Counsel will nevertheless sometimes overlook or undervalue certain opportunities to end a dispute on beneficial terms. They may do so because of their emotional investment in a particular theory of the case, or because they enjoy only such access to information about their counterpart's case as the arbitral mechanism allows them, in contrast to mediators who are informed by a wider range of data than counsel. Despite the increasing presence of alternative dispute resolution (ADR) courses available to lawyers-in-training, counsel may still be expected to give primacy to the legal case, whereas in the hands of mediators the legal merits of the case are merely one element in the mix of considerations driving the process.

Consider, for example, Watertime's 'donation' to the Municipality of its used, but still useful, computers. It would have been unlikely to suggest itself to either legal team. And, why would it?[37] Certainly, it is hard to imagine that the prospect of free computers, and the pre-election good will they might generate, fundamentally altered the state's negotiating position. But, at the margin, that gesture may have helped mollify an essential stakeholder—the Municipality. In addition to helping generate good will, they added value to an integrative bargain[38] that was reached with no new money being paid directly to the investor, and that made it unnecessary for the Municipality to find replacement water delivery concessionaires. Adding computers to the bargaining conversation is also a good example of how the methods and thought processes of mediators may supplement, and not merely duplicate, those of counsel.[39] It is also a classic example of mediators adding to the mix an item of little value to one party, but of tangible value to the other.

3. Number of mediators

Consistent with the focus of this essay, the Watertime scenario involved two neutral[40] mediators, operating as a team and paralleling the arbitration. Although

[37] Riskin observed that, by their training, lawyers have a 'rule orientation' that causes them to evaluate factual elements in terms of legal meaning (their bearing on rights and duties) and that they assume that these analytics govern most situations, thus encouraging them to overlook, or regard as detrimental, other modes of problem solving. See Riskin (n 35) 43–8.

[38] See Kovach (n 13) 196–8; Dwight Golann and Jay Folberg, *Mediation: The Role of Advocate and Neutral* (Aspen Publishers, 2006) 58–62, 184–7.

[39] The mediators' suggestion to contribute computers to Ruritania started with a joint session; both lawyers and mediators were present when a Watertime executive, struggling to navigate his new computer, lamented the loss of his more familiar but decommissioned laptop. For the lawyers, it was of no interest, but for the mediators, it was a fact that corresponded to another fact, also irrelevant to the legal case but noticed by the mediators: Ruritanian public libraries, classrooms, and government offices seemed to have only a few, outdated, computers.

[40] One can imagine a co-mediation model in which each mediator is expected to be a partisan on behalf of the party that appointed him or her. That is not the norm. See Article 3(1) of the IBA Mediation Rules ('The mediator shall be impartial and independent.'); ibid., at Article 7(1) ('The mediator shall be guided by principles of fairness, objectivity, independence and impartiality'). Partisanship would undercut the trust that allows both disputants to consider mediator proposals without suspicion and the ability of the two mediators to rely on each other; partisanship would also impede mediator synergy.

having multiple mediators is by no means indispensable to mediation success, there are good reasons to employ a team approach—reasons that parallel those often offered to explain the common preference for three arbitrators: the additional mediator might bring to the process linguistic, subject-matter, and cultural traits that complement those of her co-mediator;[41] there can occur a division of labour[42] between the two that produces a more complete understanding of the dispute and harnesses the respective skill sets of both mediators. There is also the non-negligible possibility that each disputant will be more likely to deem the process legitimate, and to engage fully in it, if at least one of the mediators seems already familiar with the concerns, values, and strictures that are important to that party.[43] Co-mediation,[44] of course, is not untested. It has been used successfully in complex disputes, e.g. those that arise from large construction projects, which generally involve multiple parties and short time frames.[45] It has also served well when cross-cultural dynamics are at work.[46]

The arguments against using two mediators include that the introduction of an additional person increases the likelihood that personality conflicts will impede the process, i.e. conflicts between a party and a mediator and those between the mediators themselves. The prospect of conflicts in style, method,[47] and personality raises important questions, not least those that bear on the mediator appointment process.[48] Ultimately, however, the system must depend on the neutrals themselves

A co-mediator may, of course, have a particular affinity for a party by virtue of shared cultural or linguistic traits, or familiarity with vicissitudes affecting that disputant, such as might result from having been (as the case may be) a government, or corporate in-house, lawyer.

[41] Ibid. See also Kowalchyk (n 27) 33 (using co-mediators might eliminate the need to employ experts).

[42] Often involving protracted sessions, mediation can be exhausting for all the participants. See Carrol and Mackie (n 34) 37 (co-mediators 'can share the energy demands').

[43] Thus, in the hypothetical, one of the two mediators was singular in attempts to re-establish momentum in the mediation process when the state had disengaged for internal reasons.

[44] Roy E. Wagner and Terry F. Peppard, 'Mediating Complex Construction Claims' (2008) State Bar of Wisconsin https://www.wisbar.org/NewsPublications/WisconsinLawyer/pages/article.aspx?Volume=81&Issue=6& ArticleID=1558.exercise. See also Article 6 of the IBA Mediation Rules.

[45] See Wagner and Peppard (n 44).

[46] See generally Bianka Keys, 'Co-Mediation: Positives, Pitfalls and Lessons Learned' (2009) 11 (4) ADR Bulletin, Article 3 ff; Cf. Bruce E. Barnes, 'Co-Facilitation and Team Facilitation: Core Skills for Leading Restorative Justice and Circle Processes to Expand Our Range of Peacemaking Skills in Indigenous and Multicultural Settings' http://www.uaf.edu/files/justice/adr-symposium/symposium-papers/Co-Facilitation-and-Team-Facilitation-Barnes.pdf 4 February 2012 (co-mediation has been used 'regularly and successfully for over 30 years' in the Hawaii mediation centres, especially in cross-gender disputes).

[47] Individual mediator views vary concerning, for instance, the timing and number of caucuses, when and how to evaluate the merits of the controversy, and the role of counsel.

[48] There are good arguments for letting an institution designate the mediators who will serve. Increasingly, institutions, e.g. ICSID, know capable and authoritative persons with backgrounds in investor–state disputes who also have mediation skills. Significant substantive background and high standing in the field, taken together, greatly improve the chances of mediation success. Under a co-mediation model, moreover, an institution's thoughtful pairing of mediators can improve complementarity. If each mediator is appointed by a party, by contrast, it is unlikely that the parties will coordinate their appointments to optimize intermediator teamwork and associated possibilities. Additionally, in

to assess if and how they can function well enough together to carry out their mandate. As to budgeting, two mediators, of course, imply two fees. Cost as an argument for not using the second mediator, however, seems unpersuasive in all but the smallest value cases. Especially in a larger case, the additional cost of the second neutral will ordinarily seem modest, and indeed well spent, if settlement results.

4. Number of arbitrators

Instead of the established three-arbitrator pattern evident in investor–state arbitration, the Watertime arbitration involved a sole arbitrator. While single arbitrator tribunals are not the norm in investment arbitration, the advantages of using a sole arbitrator, when shadowed by two co-mediators, are worth considering. A sole-arbitrator tribunal can usually be formed more quickly than a standard three-arbitrator panel, and with fewer calendars to reconcile and persons to consult the tribunal can more nimbly advance the arbitration. In addition, there are the obvious cost-savings that result in terms of arbitrators' fees when only one arbitrator serves.[49]

5. Mediator authoritativeness and vouching

As broached in the Watertime scenario, the difficulty of getting and keeping the state engaged in the mediation process is a recurrent theme among those who study the prospect of investor–state mediation. With respect to both bilateral negotiations and mediation, it is sometimes suggested that government officials lack incentives to settle sufficient to outweigh the perceived risks of doing so. Nevertheless, in comparison to simple settlement negotiations, mediation conducted by two authoritative neutrals who are attuned to the below-the-surface obstacles facing government representatives can help ameliorate the risks. In particular, mediated outcomes can be packaged to forestall unfounded charges that incompetency or corruption has tainted the settlement; in this connection, the vouching function performed by the mediators would be an important part of a strategy for satisfying the various government (and, for that matter, corporate) oversight mechanisms through which such an agreement must pass.

comparison to a party-appointment model, tasking an institution with making mediator appointments should greatly reduce the potential for a party to expect partisanship, or for one mediator to feel obliged to align herself with one disputant rather than another. On the other hand, party appointment, for all its faults, is the common method employed to form investor–state arbitral tribunals. In investor–state arbitration, just as in international commercial arbitration, the practice persists because disputants—ever risk averse—tend to favour it.

---

[49] One might be tempted to add that, to the extent the party-appointed arbitrators would have disagreed as to the outcome, the chair is the deciding vote in any event. It is not necessarily true, however, that a chair faced with opposing wing arbitrators will always, or even most often, produce the same award as a sole arbitrator would. The dynamics of three-arbitrator decision-making processes can differ significantly from those involving a sole arbitrator taking her own counsel. It is in part this dynamic that disputants may hope for when opting for three arbitrators instead of one.

6. Concurrency

Because the mediation was concurrent with the arbitration, the former had an opportunity to fully function while not delaying the latter; the process leading toward an award moved forward apace while mediation was pursued. By contrast, mediation limited to a single segment early in or before the arbitration may be handicapped by a lack of the information: states cannot be expected to settle without sufficient information to justify doing so, and if not fully informed claimants may suffer from unwarranted optimism. By contrast, a parallel process can account for (and capitalize upon) changes in the circumstances occurring throughout the arbitration process that impact the disputants' respective views on settlement.[50]

7. Roles and methods

In some ways, the Watertime-Ruritania dispute entrusted to the mediators was different from that placed before the arbitrator. The tribunal's mandate was to determine what the Municipality had done, and perhaps the reasons for its actions; that conduct (generally equated to state acts under international law) would then have been assessed in light of the standards set by the BIT and related jurisprudence. Ruritania the State, and not the Municipality, was before the tribunal, and the burden of any award rendered against Ruritania would be allocated to the Municipality, if at all, in accordance with Ruritania's internal law and politics.

The assignment given to the mediators overlapped with, but ultimately looked very different from, that before the arbitrators. The mediators, too, had to consider the extent to which the Municipality's conduct seemed to violate the BIT, viewed not in light of the information before them, but by reference to the information before the arbitral tribunal. That evaluation (whether shared with the disputants or not) was merely one element, however, in an overall cataloguing of the interests (and vulnerabilities) of the parties; it influenced, but did not dictate, the mediation's outcome. Moreover, the mediation succeeded in part because the Municipality, as a key stakeholder, was directly involved in the process (in a manner it would not have been in the arbitration).

8. Evaluative, or purely facilitative?

In the Watertime scenario, the mediators, when invited, selectively offered the parties educated assessments of the merits, without purporting to predict conclusively the outcome concerning any of the substantive and procedural issues that arose. Across legal cultures there are differing views as to when, if ever, mediators should attempt to evaluate the merits.[51]

[50] Rulings on jurisdiction or liability, for example, are major events that can change momentum. External factors, such as a change of government or a fundamental corporate change, may also induce pro-settlement attitudes among disputants. Mounting legal costs, of course, also exert settlement pressure simply by virtue of the process advancing.

[51] If one adopts a broad definition of evaluation, it might be said to be occurring in any event when a mediator uses well-informed questions to point to weaknesses in each side's case. Under a model in

The arguments for allowing evaluation in appropriate circumstances are that it may give the disputants a means of confirming the assessment given by their respective legal teams and may provide needed support for the company or government representatives responsible for sponsoring the mediated agreement, both internally and before other constituencies.[52]

The arguments against evaluation, which seem less persuasive, include that mediators may not be able to predict reliably what the arbitral tribunal will later decide, creating a risk of misdirecting the parties. The risk is heightened moreover to the extent that the request for an evaluation comes early in the process and thus may be based on evolving circumstances[53] or to the extent the evaluation is based on information known to the mediators, but not to the arbitral tribunal. To offset these risks, experienced mediators generally will not speak in absolutes; rather, they will opine in terms of probabilities.

9. Caucusing

The mediator team serving in the Watertime dispute made liberal use of caucusing (having *ex parte* meetings with each side). There is a debate among mediators as to whether heavy emphasis on caucusing is desirable. Some mediation styles, particularly among American mediators, rely extensively on caucuses to lay the groundwork for joint sessions. The mediators serve as buffers, filters, and interpreters as they shuttle between camps. Caucuses are more easily managed than joint sessions as a rule; the advance work done is intended to make joint sessions more productive.

The argument against caucusing is that it may allow skilful lawyers to manipulate the process (and the mediators) by shaping the narrative without the other party present to object or offer needed context. However, experienced mediators can be relied upon to resist effectively attempts by counsel to commandeer the process at any given point. Whereas, to limit the use of caucusing would be to encumber the mediators in critical respects; there are simply important facts revealed in caucus that do not emerge in joint session.

which the mediators do not have deep exposure to investment law, the opportunities for evaluation are highly limited.

[52] Those responsible for approving the settlements may perceive certain risks. See National University of Singapore Center for International Law, 'Report: Survey on Obstacles to Settlement of Investor-State Disputes' (CIL, 2017) https://cil.nus.edu.sg/wp-content/uploads/2017/08/Final-Report-of-CIL-Obstacle-Survey-26-May-2017.pdf. The most frequently mentioned obstacles to settlement were: 'the desire to avoid or defer responsibility', 'the fear of allegations of or future prosecution for corruption', and 'the fear of public and/or political criticism'.

[53] After all, witnesses may ultimately prove to be weak, authenticity of a key document may become doubtful, or lawyers from one side may simply be more persuasive than those on the other.

V. Conclusion

Proposals that mediation should play a greater supporting role in investment disputes are not new.[54] At least as early as 2005, for example, the United Nations Conference on Trade and Development (UNCTAD) alerted its constituencies to the notion that, principally as a pre-arbitration exercise, use of mediation should be considered.[55] In 2018, mediation continues to be discussed in connection with investor–state disputes,[56] reflecting continuing pressure to reform the current system, the long-standing success enjoyed by mediation in other commercial sectors,[57] and the sense among those familiar with mediation that it remains underexplored in connection with investment disputes. The continuing work of UNCTAD, the growing interest in mediation evident at ICSID,[58] the existence of supporting texts specific to investor–state mediation,[59] and the systematic inquiries beginning to be undertaken by academic institutions[60] are significant markers. UNCITRAL's efforts toward instituting a global enforcement regime for mediated agreements is also a promising development.[61] Indeed, at this point, it

[54] Among the earlier discussions by commentators are Clyde C. Pearce and Jack J. Coe, Jr, 'Arbitration under NAFTA Chapter Eleven: Some Pragmatic Reflections upon the First Case Filed Against Mexico' (2000) 23 Hastings International and Comparative Law Review 311, 343 (proposing that pre-arbitration mediation be required); Barton Legum, 'The Difficulties of Conciliation in Investment Treaty Cases: A Comment on Professor Jack [J.] Coe's "Toward a Complementary Use of Conciliation in Investor–State Disputes: A Preliminary Sketch"' (2006) International Arbitration Quarterly Law Review 81, 82–3; Ucheora Onwuamaegbu, 'The Role of ADR in Investor–State Dispute Settlement: The ICSID Experience' (2005) 22 (2) News From ICSID, 12.

[55] UNCTAD, *Investor–State Disputes Arising from Investment Treaties: A Review* (United Nations, 2005) 53–4.

[56] Quite appreciably, the literature on the subject has grown steadily. Examples include: Monde Marshall, 'Investor–State Dispute Settlement Reconceptionalized: Regulation of Disputes, Standards and Mediation' (2017) 17 Pepperdine Dispute Resolution Law Journal 233; Jan K. Schäfer, 'Alternatives to Investment Arbitration', in Marc Bungenberg, Jorn Griebel, Stephan Hobe, and August Reinisch (eds), *International Investment Law* (Nomos/Hart, 2015) 186; Anna Joubin-Bret, 'International Dispatch: Investor–State Disputes' (2013) 20 Dispute Resolution Magazine 37; Margrete Stevens and Ben Love, 'Investor–State Mediation: Observations on the Role of Institutions', in Arthur W. Rovine (ed.), *Contemporary Issues in International Arbitration and Mediation: The Fordham Papers 2010* (Martinus Nijhoff, 2011) 389; Nancy A. Welsh and Andrea Kupfer Schneider, 'The Thoughtful Integration Of Mediation Into Bilateral Investment Treaty Arbitration' (2013) 18 Harvard Negotiation Law Review 71.

[57] CEDR Reports a high success rate. See 'Mediation Market Grows by 5%: The 2016 Mediation Audit' *CEDR News* (11 May 2016) https://www.cedr.com/news/?item=Mediation-Market-grows-by-5-percent-The-CEDR-2016-Mediation-Audit (2016 CEDR Audit demonstrated an 'aggregate settlement rate from mediations of around 86%.').

[58] Mediation is now a searchable topic on the ICSID website.

[59] Regarding the IBA-sponsored Investor–State Mediation Rules, see Anna Joubin-Bret (n 56) 40 (summarizing the Rules); and see *Competency Criteria for Investor–State Mediators* (sponsored by an Investor–State Mediation Task Force of International Mediation Institute (IMI)), see 'IMI Competency Criteria for Investor–State Mediators' http://www.imimediation.org/about-imi/who-are-imi/investor-state-mediation-task-force/ (19 September 2016).

[60] See National University of Singapore Center for International Law (n 52).

[61] See UNCITRAL Working Group II (Dispute Settlement), 6–10 February 2017, *International Commercial Conciliation: Preparation of an Instrument on Enforcement of International Commercial Settlement Agreements Resulting from Conciliation*, UN Doc. A/CN.9/WG.II/WP.200, GAOR, 66th Session, Note by the Secretariat (2017).

may not be unrealistic to expect UNCITRAL to consider the topic as part of its newly commissioned study of investor–state disputes.[62]

Mediation is not a stand-alone solution to all that ails the current system. Rather, it should be part of an overall coordinated set of strategies that include not only various refinements to prevailing arbitration regimes and improved precision in the way substantive treaty protections are delimited, but also more pervasive use of host-state systems for detecting and managing inchoate disputes.[63]

Relatedly, the difficulties states face given the public nature of investor–state disputes,[64] and the intra-governmental intricacies involved in agreeing to settlements, should not be underestimated. Yet, somehow, roughly one out of three investor–state cases already settle.[65] As there is nothing inherent in investor–state disputes that renders them inappropriate for settlement per se, the question is whether introducing concurrent co-mediation into the process will lead to a higher percentage of settlements, or a cheaper process overall, or greater satisfaction with the process, or some other benefit that would make the effort worthwhile.

Quite arguably, the principal challenge is not how to make attempts at mediation worthy exercises, but rather, how to convene the parties in the first instance. Treaty and rule text triggers are a partial answer. Institutional encouragement must also play a role. Ultimately, however, the more important ingredient in mediation's wider use will be attitudinal changes, reflected in new standard operating procedures, among states in particular; these new habits will generate and reinforce new best practices and new expectations that will in turn encourage the mastery of new, quite powerful, techniques.

[62] See 'UNCITRAL to Consider Possible Reform of Investor–State Dispute Settlement', *UN Press Release* (14 July 2017) http://www.unis.unvienna.org/unis/en/pressrels/2017/unisl250.html.

[63] See, e.g. Françoise Nicolas, Stephen Thomsen, and Mi-Hyun Bang, *Lessons from Investment Policy Reform in Korea* (OECD, 2013) 24–5. (Post-investment, Office of Foreign Investment Ombudsman focuses on services for foreign investors and, inter alia, 'resolves grievances reported by foreign investors not only directly by sending experts who are licensed and experienced to business sites but also by taking pre-emptive measures to prevent future grievances by encouraging systemic improvements and legal amendments'). Korea has had few investor claims brought against it. The post-investment regime in place there may explain that fact. Broad adoption of this kind of early-warning system might be facilitated by model regimes sponsored, perhaps by UNCITRAL, analogous to its Model Arbitration and Conciliation Laws. It remains to be seen whether this kind of project will be considered in UNCITRAL's work under its investor–state disputes initiative. See (n 62).

[64] See Mark Clodfelter, 'Why Aren't More Investor–State Treaty Disputes Settled Amicably?', in Franck and Joubin-Bret (n 6) 38, 40 ('The public nature of the parties and the measures at issue in most investor–state disputes makes them very different from commercial disputes').

[65] See Wellhausen (n 11) (153 of 461 investment arbitrations settled).

PART II

MEDIATION RULES AND MEDIATION IN PRACTICE

5

ICC Mediation

Paving the Way Forward

*Alina Leoveanu and Andrija Erac**

I. 100 Years of ICC Amicable Settlement of Disputes

In the field of alternative dispute resolution (ADR), the International Chamber of Commerce (ICC) is recognized worldwide for its International Court of Arbitration (Court). However, the amicable settlement of disputes is also ingrained in the ICC's DNA and its history, be it through conciliation or mediation.[1] The first ever ICC Congress, held in London in June 1921, discussed a set of regulations which established early ICC arbitration and conciliation rules.[2] During the first Congress, the ICC International Committee on Arbitration drew up a document under the chairmanship of Mr Lyon-Caen[3] with the participation of lawyers and business representatives from Belgium, Great Britain, Italy, the Netherlands, and the United States. Its title, 'Proposed Plan for Conciliation and Arbitration between Traders of Different Countries', as well as the following provisions, both demonstrate how the ICC envisaged conciliation and arbitration as being complementary and destined for the same purpose:

> In view of the advantages which would accrue to the business world from the creation of an international organization whereby commercial disputes between men of different countries may be settled by Conciliation or by Arbitration, the International Chamber of Commerce is of the belief that it should encourage the use of Conciliation and Arbitration.
>
> It puts itself therefore freely at the disposal of financiers, manufacturers and business men of all countries, to facilitate, in so far as possible through the

* The views and opinions expressed herein are those of the authors and do not necessarily reflect those of the ICC International Centre for ADR. The authors express their gratitude to Cameron McColl, Graciela Iñigo Perez, Akhil Chowdary Unnam, and Martin Méric for their valuable support in the preparation of this chapter.

[1] This chapter uses the two terms 'mediation' and 'conciliation' interchangeably. Both are considered as extra-judicial dispute resolution techniques.

[2] Stuart Hamilton, 'ICC Conciliation: A Glimpse into History' (2001) ICC Court Bulletin, ADR: International Applications: Special Supplement 2001 23.

[3] At the time Permanent Secretary of L'Académie des sciences morales et politiques and former Dean of the Paris Faculty of Law.

> exercise of its good offices, the settlement of disputes by conciliation; and to facilitate, in every way, requests for arbitration ...
>
> [...]
>
> The moral force which the International Chamber of Commerce is in a position to exert by its many points of contact in all the countries of the world justifies the hope that the instances in which it is called upon to conciliate will become more and more frequent and that, in these cases, the effect of this moral influence will be great.

This plan was followed by a scheme of rules for conciliation and arbitration.[4] These were subsequently and continuously developed and they evolved over the course of the following century into the respective ICC Arbitration Rules and ICC Mediation Rules as we know them today.

In the early days, conciliation was considered to be of equal importance to arbitration and was in fact the more prominent of the two services. Out of the first forty disputes referred to the Court that settled, around 80 percent did so by informal means, including ICC conciliation.[5] Back then, conciliation was an informal process managed by the ICC Commission of Conciliation. A dispute would be referred to the Commission, which would then select a Chairman and two commissioners to assess the case. Commissioners were representatives chosen by the ICC National Committees and were selected to assess a case based on their nationality—a dispute between a French and a Dutch party would mean the selection of French and Dutch commissioners. Interestingly, the parties and/or their representatives came to the ICC in person to submit their disputes, which allowed for 'a settlement to be reached directly and rapidly'.[6] It was not until 1923 that a dispute 'was decided on the basis of documents only'.[7]

The earliest decision in the ICC's archives, dated 28 December 1922, was amicably resolved by conciliation. It concerned a dispute between Dutch and British parties. The parties decided to cancel the contract and agreed that the British party would be paid compensation. A subsequent decision from 22 June 1923 involved a dispute between French and Belgian parties regarding the payment for the delivery of wood. With the help of the ICC Commission of Conciliation, an agreement was reached on the amount which the French seller was entitled to receive.[8]

Remarkably, suggestions provided by the ICC Commission of Conciliation in early cases almost always resulted in settlements the parties observed, as mentioned in a decision from April 1925:

[4] Drafted by Mr S. G. Archibald (USA), Mr T. Carlander (Sweden), Mr R. Pozzi (Italy), and Mr R. Streat (Great Britain), approved by the ICC Congress on 10 July 1922.

[5] Hamilton (n 2).

[6] Ibid.

[7] Ibid.

[8] Ibid.

> The Administrative Commission has frequently solicited the aid of local chambers of commerce, requesting them to make friendly suggestions to the parties concerned, and this moral action has always had the most happy results, as the proposals submitted to the two parties by the Commission of Conciliation have nearly always been accepted. This friendly and inexpensive procedure can therefore be of great use to commerce in general.[9]

Even the earliest arbitration awards rendered under the auspices of the ICC reveal how arbitration proceedings adopted conciliation techniques similar to those in ICC Mediation today. Decisions in early arbitral awards resembled amicable settlement agreements. For example, in a 1922 arbitration case between a British company and a French merchant concerning a delivery of faulty carding machines, the award stated that the parties jointly agreed upon the amount of compensation, as well as on the costs of repairing the machines, as suggested by the arbitrator. The parties considered that this agreement completely settled their dispute. Although this decision would probably be more akin today to an award by consent, this agreement demonstrates how interchangeably arbitration and mediation techniques were used to arrive at flexible solutions.

The gradual evolution of conciliation and other methods of amicable dispute resolution were somewhat overshadowed by the advent of arbitration, prompted by the New York Convention on the Enforcement of Arbitral Awards of 1958. Yet, over the course of the last century at the ICC, amicable dispute resolution has garnered importance at its own pace, evolving and reshaping itself and taking on different forms, from the ICC Rules of Optional Conciliation[10] to the ICC Rules on Alternative Dispute Resolution,[11] finally arriving at the current ICC Mediation Rules.[12]

Current rules embody the spirit of the plans set out in the ICC's first Congress. In 1921, the ICC Congress envisaged the moral influence that was to be exerted by the ICC as a neutral body, capable of efficiently and flexibly resolving disputes between parties from different countries and commercial areas around the world.[13] The sentiment is just as pertinent now as it was then; it is this mission statement that remains central to the Centre's commitment to engage parties worldwide and facilitate the resolution of their disputes. The ICC Mediation Rules are paving stones which help direct parties towards an amicable and timely resolution to disputes.

[9] Arbitration Report No. 3, (1924) 1 Journal of the International Chamber of Commerce 2.
[10] ICC Rules of Conciliation, entry into force 1 January 1988.
[11] ICC ADR Rules, entry into force 1 July 2001.
[12] ICC Mediation Rules, entry into force 1 January 2014.
[13] International Chamber of Commerce First Congress London (June 27 to July 1, 1921), Brochure No. 13, Commercial Arbitration at 23.

This chapter attempts to contribute to the reflection around international commercial and investor-state mediation from the ICC perspective. After presenting the main features of the ICC Mediation Rules and the flexibility of the ICC Mediation services, it looks at some of the trends relating to cases referred to the ICC International Centre for ADR. Although the numbers that result from the authors' research are applicable only to ICC cases, the hope is that, together with the findings of other institutions, they will contribute to the scholarly study of cross-border commercial and investment mediation. The chapter also looks at the source of most of the ICC's mediation caseload—the mediation clauses. It also attempts to share with the reader the ICC's experience regarding their proper drafting and their use. It provides two interesting examples of mediations involving states that may also be a valuable tool in spreading the use of investment mediation. The chapter concludes by showing that better and greater use of international commercial and investment mediation will only come with the investment in educating future generations of dispute resolvers, such as the ICC's International Commercial Mediation Competition.

II. 2014 ICC Mediation Rules: The Right Paving Stones

The ICC Mediation Rules (Rules) entered into force in January 2014, and are the outcome of a revision carried out by the ICC Commission on Arbitration and ADR[14] of the previous ICC ADR Rules. The revision had three main objectives: 1) to better reflect the Centre's current practices in administering proceedings under the ICC ADR Rules, while maintaining flexibility; 2) to update the Rules in order to reflect developments in ADR and mediation practice; and 3) to make the new Rules and clauses consistent with the ICC Arbitration Rules.

The Rules integrate best practice developed by the ICC through the evolution of ADR. They are a modern and flexible set of rules that fix clear parameters for the conduct of the proceedings.[15] Since their entry into force, the Rules have been primarily used for conducting mediations (hence, the modification of their name from ADR Rules to Mediation Rules), as well as other procedures aimed at amicably settling disputes, e.g. neutral evaluation, co-mediation, or any combination of such procedures.

[14] The ICC Commission on Arbitration and ADR is the body responsible for continuously improving the services that the ICC offers in the field of dispute resolution. The Commission is a think-tank and rule-making body composed of one thousand members from more than ninety countries, comprising lawyers, in-house counsel, arbitrators, mediators, law professors, and experts in various dispute resolution fields.

[15] ICC, (2003) 24 (2) International Court of Arbitration Bulletin.

III. A Walk through the Main Provisions

A. Articles 2 and 3: Commencement of Proceedings

Parties may commence an ICC mediation irrespective of whether their contract contains an ICC mediation clause (Article 2) or not. Article 3 of the Rules deals with the commencement of proceedings where the parties have no prior agreement to refer their dispute to mediation under the Rules. Whereas under Article 2, the request for mediation is usually notified directly by the requesting party to the responding party, under Article 3, the Centre will act as an intermediary between the parties and will notify the request for mediation to the responding party. In doing so, the Centre conveys the proposals of the requesting party to the responding party, invites its answer and, where appropriate, explains the principles governing the administered mediation proceedings, the role of the mediator, the role of the Centre, and how mediation differs from other proceedings. In both cases, 'the Centre can play an especially important role in helping to bridge cultural gaps between the parties and make them equally informed'.[16]

B. Flexibility throughout the Rules

The Rules are designed to be as flexible as mediation itself. They 'do not prescribe how mediations should be conducted but are deliberately flexible in this respect'.[17] Preserving the parties' will in the context of an ICC is are made possible through the following features of the Rules.

1. Article 7: conduct of the mediation

Parties are free to choose the settlement technique that is most useful to help them resolve their disputes, as well as the most appropriate type of neutral, or multiple neutrals. 'The Rules do not prescribe how the mediation or other settlement techniques should be conducted, which makes ICC mediation a very flexible process.'[18] The parties and the mediator are free to decide the technique and the approach to their mediation through the course of the proceedings (Article 7(1)), as long as they are compatible with the spirit of the Rules.

The first discussion with the mediator focuses on the way the mediation will be conducted. After such discussion, the mediator promptly provides the parties with a written note informing them of this decision. Each party, by agreeing to refer a dispute to the Rules, agrees to participate in the Proceedings at least until receipt of such note from the mediator (Article 7(2)).

[16] Ibid.
[17] Ibid.
[18] Ibid.

The only limitation set forth in the Rules is that the mediator shall be guided by the wishes of the parties and shall treat them with fairness and impartiality when establishing and conducting the mediation (Article 7(3)).

The Rules are accompanied by the ICC Mediation Guidance Notes, which are designed to help the parties, mediators, and counsel. They offer suggestions on how to take advantage of the flexibility of mediation and to organize the proceedings in such a way that takes account of the parties' needs, their cultural and legal backgrounds and the particularities of the dispute.

Under the Rules, the parties may agree to suspend the mediation proceedings. This may prove useful in situations where the parties wish to negotiate certain issues directly between themselves, or where they need some time to prepare and exchange information (e.g. carry out a joint expertise in order to determine the causality of an event).

Confidentiality marks another shift from the ADR Rules. Under Article 9 of the Rules, proceedings conducted are confidential. Nonetheless, the fact that settlement proceedings are taking place is no longer confidential in itself, unless all the parties have agreed otherwise, or the applicable law provides otherwise.

2. Article 5: selection of the mediator

Parties may either jointly nominate the mediator, or she/he may be appointed by the ICC. The Centre may also propose a list of mediators to the parties. This allows the parties to keep their autonomy in the selection of the neutral while making it easy for them to choose from the right candidates. The list provided by the Centre includes candidates who fulfil the specific requirements agreed upon by the parties. All the potential candidates contacted by the Centre are invited to complete a statement, whereby the Centre verifies their qualifications, as well as their availability, impartiality, and independence, before proposing them to the parties.

The Centre does not have a pre-established list of mediators. For each mediation case, the Centre conducts a new search in order to identify individuals who fit the particular criteria in that specific case. Pursuant to Article 5(5) of the Rules 'when the Centre appoints a Mediator, it shall do so either on the basis of a proposal by an ICC National Committee or Group, or otherwise'.

When selecting candidates for appointment as mediator, the Centre always invites the parties to make proposals with regard to the attributes of the mediator. From the experience of the Centre, these attributes are often focused on the knowledge of a particular industry (e.g. construction, intellectual property), field of law (e.g. distribution, design, and construction agreements), and language.

The Centre seeks to identify candidates having experience acting as mediators, ideally in international cross-border commercial disputes. The reason for such a requirement is that the disputes referred to ICC under the Mediation Rules are usually complex. Energy, telecoms, and construction disputes often arise out of a multiplicity of contracts entered into by multiple parties and amended several times. Such business relationships may involve various contractors, subcontractors, legal successors, investors, numerous related entities and individuals. In such contexts, the selection of an appropriate mediator who has substantial experience in dealing with complex cases, is vital.

Complex disputes can make for longer durations of mediation proceedings. Some mediation cases administered by the Centre related to failures in equipment and machinery can endure for several months and even up to a year. On a few occasions, the Centre was requested to stay the proceedings and allow the parties to carry out an expertise or retrieve pieces of missing information.

More often than not, parties ask the Centre to keep the proceedings open and the mediator to remain in place until the settlement agreement is fully implemented. The relationship between the mediator and the parties grows stronger as the prospects for a settlement become more likely. Once a settlement is signed, the mediator is seen as a moral guarantor. By keeping him/her in place, the parties commit to maintaining the same level of mutual respect that they built together during the mediation.

As the Centre does not have a pre-established list of mediators, any mediator interested in being considered for future cases may either reach out to the ICC National Committee or Group of their home country, or approach the Centre directly. The Centre does maintain an open database of dispute resolution professionals having acted as mediators in previous ICC cases or having expressed their interest to be included in the open database.

3. Article 4: place and language of the mediation

Parties are free to choose both the place and the language of the mediation. Whenever there is a disagreement over any of the two, pursuant to the Rules, the Centre will either determine the place/language of the proceedings or will invite the mediator to do so after receipt of the case file. Unlike the ADR Rules, the Mediation Rules allow for these issues to be decided by the Centre and not just by the mediator. This can avoid 'the need for the mediator to make a decision that might damage the mediator´s relations with one or more of the parties early in the proceedings.'[19] In practice, the Centre will always first make all reasonable efforts to encourage the parties to reach an agreement on these issues before making a decision itself or inviting the mediator to do it.

4. Article 10(2): parallel proceedings

The initiation of mediation proceedings does not impede the initiation of other proceedings, e.g. litigation or arbitration. Article 10(2) states that the parties may commence or continue any judicial, arbitral, or similar proceedings in respect of the dispute, notwithstanding the proceedings under the Rules.

[19] Ibid.

C. Costs

The costs of the ICC mediation proceedings are composed of 1) administrative expenses and 2) mediator's fees and expenses. The filing fee is 3,000 US dollars (as of 1 January 2018). Article 2 of the Appendix to the Rules sets the guidelines for the Centre to fix the amount of the administrative expenses, depending on the work carried out by the Centre and the amount in dispute. Article 3(1) of the Appendix to the Rules provides that the fees of the mediator shall be calculated on the basis of the time reasonably spent by the mediator in the proceedings. These fees are based on an hourly rate or single fee fixed by the Centre when appointing or confirming the mediator and after having consulted with the mediator and the parties.

The average cost of an ICC mediation is around 20,000 US dollars (covering both the ICC administrative expenses and the mediator's fees and expenses). Thus, when compared to arbitration, mediation remains far less expensive. Although the cost of the proceedings is usually borne by the parties in equal shares, the Rules allow for one party to finance the entirety of the proceedings.

In order to encourage the use of mediation before or throughout the arbitration proceedings, two references have been added in the Mediation and Arbitration Rules:

1) When unsuccessful, an ICC mediation may continue to an ICC arbitration. In such case, the parties will benefit from cross-crediting and one half of the administrative expenses paid in the mediation case will be transferred to the arbitration case (Article 2 (12) of the Appendix III to the Arbitration Rules).
2) If the parties refer their dispute to mediation after having filed a request for arbitration with the ICC, the amount of 5,000 US dollars paid as the filing fee in arbitration will be credited towards the administrative expenses of the mediation, if the total administrative expenses paid with respect to the arbitration exceed 7,500 US dollars (Article 4 of the Appendix to the Mediation Rules). Such a provision in the Rules makes a mediation window less costly and perhaps more appealing to the parties already engaged in an arbitration.

IV. A Look at the Trends

The core business of the ICC Dispute Resolution Services is arbitration, with over 800 new cases filed with the Secretariat of the ICC International Court of Arbitration every year. However, over the last decade, ICC users are showing increased interest in mediation. The ICC International Centre for ADR has

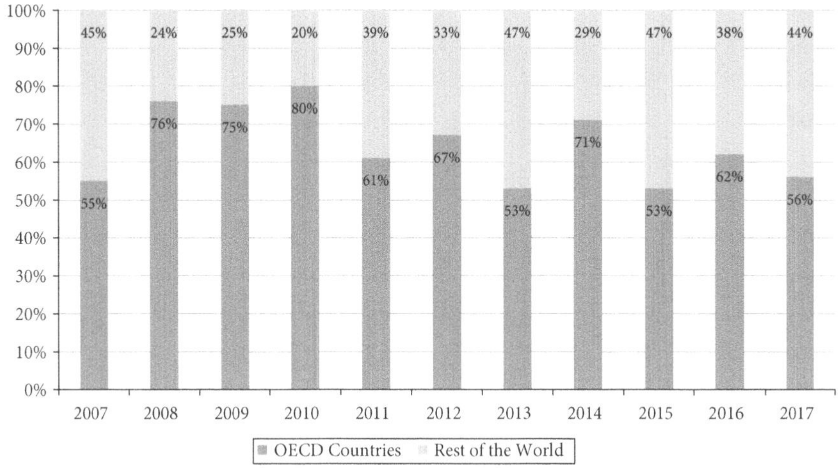

Figure 5.1 Parties from OECD Countries in ICC Mediations from 2007 to 2017.

been administering a steadily growing number of cases, with 2018 being a record year.

A. Parties

In 2018, disputes involving 100 parties from thirty-six different nationalities around the world were referred to the Centre for mediation proceedings.

Drawing from the Centre's experience with cross-border commercial disputes, mediation is mostly used by more advanced economies, but not exclusively. Figure 5.1 shows that a number of disputes emanating from non-OECD[20] countries have been referred to the ICC for mediation proceedings.

Figure 5.2 shows that traditionally Europe has been the most represented continent in ICC mediations. However, in 2017, the percentage of parties from Europe was historically low, whereas the percentage of parties from the Americas peaked.

B. Sectors

Energy, telecommunications, and construction are the three most mediated sectors at the Centre, amounting to nearly half of all disputes referred to the ICC

[20] For the purpose of this chapter, the authors chose to look at the OECD member countries as those being considered as developed. A similar partition could also be made by referring to the classification of countries of the United Nations or the World Bank.

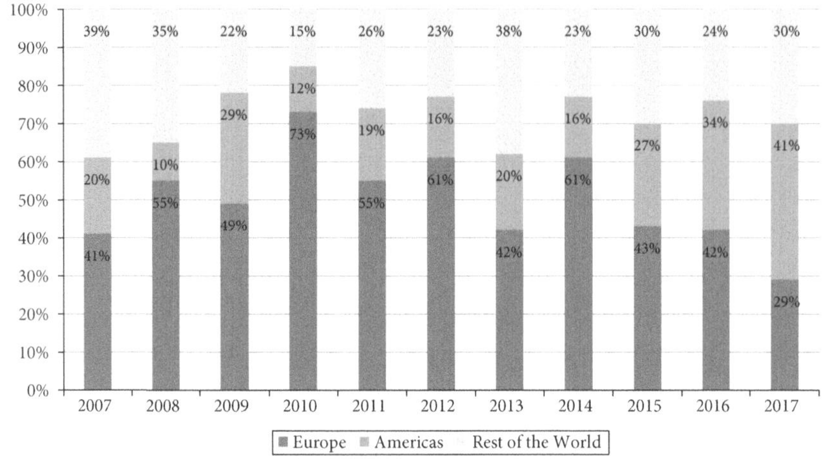

Figure 5.2 Parties from Europe and the Americas in ICC Mediations from 2007 to 2017.

for mediation proceedings between 2015 and 2017. They are followed by finance and insurance (8 percent), industrial equipment (7 percent) and transportation (6 percent). In these sectors, disputes are often high in value and very complex. These sectors are also the most prevalent in arbitrations administered by the ICC International Court of Arbitration.[21]

C. Mediators' Hourly Rate

As mentioned previously, the Centre fixes mediator fees upon consultation with the parties. Mediators either suggest an hourly rate or a single fee that covers their entire work during the proceedings. The average hourly rate of the mediators is around 550 US dollars (Figure 5.3). However, there can be significant disparities in the rates of mediators operating in different countries around the world. For instance, higher legal fees in countries like the United States, United Kingdom, Switzerland, the United Arab Emirates, and Singapore result in higher rates requested by mediators—upwards of 800 or 900 US dollars per hour in some cases. In comparison, mediators operating in countries like Italy, Mexico, or Brazil tend to charge rates between 300 and 400 US dollars per hour.

[21] ICC (2018) 2 ICC Dispute Resolution Bulletin.

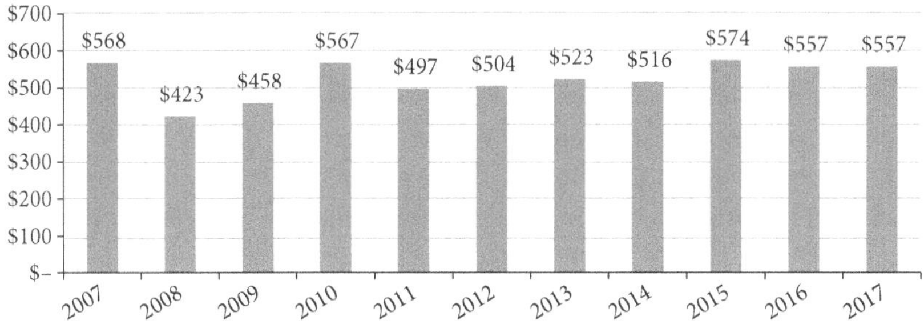

Figure 5.3 Average Hourly Rate of Mediators Acting in ICC Mediations from 2007 to 2017.

D. Diversity of Mediators

From 2007 to 2017, the top three nationalities of mediators acting in ICC cases were British, Swiss, and French, and accounted for almost half of the mediators acting in ICC mediations. This is mostly due to the nationalities of the parties, the place of the proceedings, and knowledge of the applicable law of the contract concerned.

The ICC has made considerable efforts to promote and encourage gender diversity; it is an important consideration in the process of selecting mediators. The Centre makes a conscious effort to identify suitable female candidates and expressly reminds the ICC National Committees to respect gender diversity when proposing candidates to the Centre. Needless to say, there are always improvements to be made. Female mediators were chosen in only 23 percent of cases administered by the Centre in 2017. Nevertheless, the Centre is strongly engaged with this issue, and is confident that it can continue to improve gender diversity in mediation and set an example to be followed.

Another major focus of the Centre's commitment to diversity concerns the age of mediators. The average age of mediators appointed in 2017 was 61. Unfortunately, younger mediators often lack substantial experience in dealing with complex, high-value commercial disputes, and this level of experience is often demanded by the parties in their list of relevant attributes required of potential candidates. As the number and variety of cases increases, the Centre is committed to promoting diversity in its selection of mediators in terms of age as well as of sex and nationality, among other factors.

E. Amounts in Dispute

Between 2007 and 2017, a total of nearly 5.4 billion US dollars' worth of disputes were referred to mediation under the ICC Rules. This impressive number is based on those cases in which the amount in dispute was actually quantified and communicated to the ICC by the parties or by the mediator. The actual number is therefore undoubtedly higher. Over the observed period, the average amount in dispute was over 27 million US dollars. However, the median is significantly lower—around 2.3 million US dollars. While there is a disparity among the amounts in disputes referred to mediation under the ICC Rules, these figures show that mediation is undoubtedly well suited to high-value commercial disputes.

V. Mediation Clauses: Getting them Right

Ninety percent of the requests for mediation filed with the Centre are based on a pre-existing agreement to refer a dispute to the ICC Mediation Rules.[22] Such pre-existing agreements are most often made in the form of a dispute resolution clause contained in the parties' contract. In 2017, out of the mediation agreements pursuant to which disputes were referred to ICC, 96 percent were multi-tier clauses that provided for arbitration as the next step. In August 2018, the figure stood at 83 percent.

However, it may be that not enough importance is attached to the drafting of mediation clauses in contracts. When arbitration is taught in law schools, one of the key subjects covered is the drafting of arbitration clauses. As almost any arbitration is bound to start with a clause, considerable attention is paid to the clause's clarity and practicability. A special expression was coined to describe poorly drafted, ambiguous, and impracticable contractual provisions—the so-called 'pathological clauses'.

Mediation clauses can also be pathological. If enough attention is not paid to the drafting of a mediation clause, the will of the parties may not translate suitably into the mediation proceedings once they begin. Questions may come up as to the mandatory nature of the clause, the dispute resolution technique that is envisioned, the rules applicable to the dispute, and the length of the proceedings. Frequently, the Centre has the complicated task of interpreting and translating a mediation clause into a practicable and efficient process compatible with the Rules, while at the same time respecting the parties' wishes as incorporated in their contract.

In order to avoid such difficulties, the ICC has prepared model mediation clauses, which can be found in the ICC Mediation Rules (translated into several languages) and can be applied by users around the world.

[22] Statistics based on the cases filed in 2017.

A. Model Multi-Tiered Clauses: ICC's Best Seller

The two most used model mediation clauses are the multi-tier clauses that provide for a combination of mediation and arbitration.[23] The first multi-tiered clause provides for *an obligation* to refer any dispute to the ICC Mediation Rules, while permitting parallel arbitration proceedings:

> (x) In the event of any dispute arising out of or in connection with the present contract, the parties shall first refer the dispute to proceedings under the ICC Mediation Rules. The commencement of proceedings under the ICC Mediation Rules shall not prevent any party from commencing arbitration in accordance with sub-clause (y) below.
>
> (y) All disputes arising out of or in connection with the present contract shall be finally settled under the Rules of Arbitration of the International Chamber of Commerce by one or more arbitrators appointed in accordance with the said Rules.

This model clause is designed to ensure that when a dispute arises, the parties will first attempt to settle the dispute under the ICC Mediation Rules. Although the ICC often encounters this type of clause and its variations in its cases, it is rare that the parties choose to engage in mediation and arbitration proceedings at the same time.

The model clause also makes it clear that the parties do not need to conclude the proceedings under the ICC Mediation Rules, or wait for an agreed period of time, before commencing arbitration proceedings. This is the default position under Article 10(2) of the Rules, which provides the following:

> Unless all of the parties have agreed otherwise in writing or unless prohibited by applicable law, the parties may commence or continue any judicial, arbitral or similar proceedings in respect of the dispute, notwithstanding the Proceedings under the Rules.

The second multi-tiered clause, most widely used, *also provides for an obligation* of the parties to first refer any dispute to the ICC Mediation Rules, followed by arbitration, if required:

> In the event of any dispute arising out of or in connection with the present contract, the parties shall first refer the dispute to proceedings under the ICC Mediation Rules. If the dispute has not been settled pursuant to the said Rules

[23] In total, the ICC Mediation Rules provide for four model clauses. While clauses A and B provide for optional mediation, clauses C and D foresee an obligation to refer a dispute to the Mediation Rules.

> within [45] days following the filing of a Request for Mediation or within such other period as the parties may agree in writing, such dispute shall thereafter be finally settled under the Rules of Arbitration of the International Chamber of Commerce by one or more arbitrators appointed in accordance with the said Rules of Arbitration.

Unlike the first multi-tiered clause, this second clause provides that arbitration proceedings may not be commenced until an agreed period has elapsed following the filing of a request for mediation and changes the default position under Article 10(2) of the ICC Mediation Rules. In all cases, companies are free to modify the model clauses and adapt them to the particularities of their business relationships.

B. A Few Examples of 'Pathological' Clauses

1. Mediation led by experts

The clause cited below (Clause 1) provided for mediation as the dispute resolution technique to be conducted under the 'ICC Rules'. Unusually, Clause 1 also provided for the mediation proceedings to be conducted by a panel of three experts, as follows:

> Both parties agree to give a *mediation mission to three experts* knowing that those experts will have to work out an agreement acceptable by both parties. *Each party will have to nominate their own expert and both experts will nominate a third independent expert.* These nominations have to be done within 8 days following the identification of the source of disagreement by both parties. If a third expert is not found by the first two experts he will be nominated by the president of the commercial court of Paris in France under the request of one of the parties. *Each party will support the cost of his own expert and half the cost of the third expert.* The mediation shall be conducted under the ICC rules. The mediation shall have come to a conclusion within two months. In the case the mediation proved to be unsuccessful an arbitration procedure will be initiated (emphasis added).

The requesting party submitted the dispute to the ICC International Centre for ADR in accordance with Article 2 of the ICC Mediation Rules. In accordance with the aforementioned Clause 1, both parties designated the first two experts and the two jointly designated a third one. Following the agreement of the parties, the Centre confirmed the three experts as mediators in the dispute.

Although the wording of the clause was not incompatible with the provisions of the Rules, the proceedings were difficult to run and administer for the following reasons. The three experts who were designated as mediators had a strong technical background, but they had never acted as mediators before. Therefore, in order to help them conduct a mediation in accordance with the Rules, the Centre held several teleconferences with them, explained the process to them, as well as the objective of the mediation. That the two parties each designated one expert, and that each party was to bear the costs of their own expert's fees, made it difficult to ensure the independence and impartiality of the mediators and to make them work together toward the common goal of helping the parties reach a settlement. It is very likely that, in the drafting of this clause, the parties were inspired by a specific procedure known in France as *expertise contradictoire,* particular to insurance disputes.

2. Co-mediation with party-appointed mediators

Following a disagreement between two undertakings engaged in a supplier agreement, a dispute was referred to the Centre. The agreement between the parties (Clause 2) included a dispute resolution procedure that firstly required the parties to settle any dispute through two internal 'Steering Committee' meetings. If the dispute could not be solved during these meetings, the parties would then each appoint a mediator with a view to help them resolve their dispute:

> This Agreement shall be governed by the rules of France and the Parties shall strive to settle amicably any dispute arising therefrom and in connection herewith or therewith via no fewer than two (2) meetings of the Steering Committee.
>
> To this effect the Parties shall *each appoint a mediator* with a view to helping them solve any dispute which would not have been settled after the two meetings of the Steering Committee; in the absence of appointment of the second mediator by any arty within fifteen (15) days following the appointment of the first by the first Party, said first Party shall be entitled to seek the appointment of said second mediator by the International Chamber of Commerce (ICC) in accordance with the ICC ADR Rules in force as at that date. Within fifteen (15) days following the appointment of the second mediator, each Party shall set forth in writing to the mediators its position with respect to the disputed matter with a copy to the other Party. The mediators shall then have thirty (30) days within which to render an opinion as to the disputed matter. The Parties shall make all commercially reasonable efforts to try to solve their dispute with the assistance of the mediators as above (emphasis added).

Co-mediation is by no means incompatible with the Rules. However, as Clause 2 demonstrates, having each party appoint a mediator may turn problematic when one of the parties chooses to appoint a trusted professional with whom it had previously worked in the past, but who does not have any mediation experience. In this case, the proposed mediator was, of course, obliged to disclose in his Statement of Acceptance, Availability, Independence and Impartiality his past and current relationship with the party that had nominated him. Following the opposing party's objections against him, the Centre did not confirm him and invited the requesting party to nominate another mediator.

3. Adjudicator deciding the settlement agreement

Another interesting example involves Clause 3 providing for *adjudication* under the ADR Rules, but which was filed as a request for mediation. On the face of it, Clause 3 (set out here) is incompatible with the ICC Mediation Rules:

> Adjudication
>
> [. . .] the Parties shall attempt to settle the Dispute in accordance with the ADR rules[24] published by the International Chamber of Commerce (the ICC). Unless otherwise agreed between the Parties, *the adjudicator will be appointed by ICC. The adjudication will take place in Zürich, Switzerland and the language of the adjudication will be English.*
>
> [. . .] *The adjudicator's decision shall be binding on the Parties, unless any of the Parties commences arbitration pursuant to sub-article 14.3 below within 45 days following receipt of the adjudicator's decision.* For the avoidance of doubt, for the purposes of [X] law, this sub-article shall represent an agreement on a future settlement agreement, where *the content of the settlement agreement is to be determined by the adjudicator in its decision* (emphasis added).

Here, an immediate problem lies in the ambiguity of the clause. On the one hand, it provides that the parties should attempt to *settle* the dispute in accordance with the ADR Rules, and on the other, it is entitled 'Adjudication' and provides that the ICC shall appoint an *adjudicator*, who would render a *decision binding* on the parties.

The sub-article mentioned in the clause 'represents an agreement on a future settlement agreement, where *the content of the settlement is to be determined by the adjudicator in its decision*' (emphasis added).

The requesting party filed a request for mediation to the Centre, in which it stated that the parties' intention had always been to submit their dispute to mediation and, accordingly, requested the appointment of a mediator. Consequently, the Centre invited the responding party's comments on the applicable rules and the settlement procedure. The parties subsequently agreed to submit their dispute to mediation and discussed the possibility of the mediator issuing a non-binding recommendation.[25]

[24] Pursuant to Article 10(1) of the ICC Mediation Rules, where a clause dated prior to the date of entry into force of the ICC Mediation Rules makes reference to 'ADR Rules', the parties will be deemed to have referred their dispute to the ICC Mediation Rules.

[25] As provided for in paragraph 40 of the ICC Mediation Guidance Notes: 'Without imposing terms of settlement on the parties, the mediator may, if requested by all parties, recommend terms of settlement for their consideration.'

Mediation and adjudication are different dispute resolution procedures. Whereas mediation is a flexible settlement technique in which a mediator acts as a neutral facilitator to help the parties try to arrive at a negotiated settlement of their dispute, adjudication focuses more on the parties' legal rights, and is consequently more akin to arbitration or litigation. However, the mediator may, if agreed by all parties, recommend terms of settlement for their consideration, the decision to settle, and the terms of any settlement agreement remain with the parties. Unlike an adjudicator, the mediator has no power to impose a settlement on the parties through a binding decision.

Therefore, adjudication proceedings, in which an adjudicator issues a binding decision on the parties, cannot be administered under the ICC Rules for Mediation. Had the parties decided to opt for adjudication, the Centre could have appointed an adjudicator and administered the proceedings, but under a different set of rules, i.e. the ICC Rules for the Administration of Expert Proceedings.

VI. Mediating with States

There has been a rising interest in the mediation of investment treaty disputes.[26] Companies having entered into contracts with states look for solutions other than arbitration; this allows them to settle their disputes while, at the same time, continuing their commercial dealings with states. The Centre has administered one of the only known mediations initiated under a bilateral investment treaty (BIT).[27] Bringing an investor and a state closer in a dispute can be very complicated. The next two cases illustrate the challenges and the benefits of mediating with states.

A. The First ICC Mediation under a BIT

In this case, the bilateral agreement on the promotion and protection of investments was entered into by a Western European state and a South-East Asian state. The BIT provided for arbitration as the dispute resolution procedure. Nonetheless, the investor proposed an opt-in mediation to the South-East Asian state. The request for mediation was filed pursuant to Article 3 of the ICC Mediation Rules of 2014 and the IBA Rules for Investor–State Mediation of 2012. Given the flexibility

[26] Esme Shirlow, 'The Rising Interest in the Mediation of Investment Treaty Disputes, and Scope for Increasing Interaction between Mediation and Arbitration', Kluwer Arbitration Blog, 29 September 2016, http://arbitrationblog.kluwerarbitration.com/2016/09/29/the-rising-interest-in-the-mediation-of-investment-treaty-disputes-and-scope-for-increasing-interaction-between-mediation-and-arbitration/.

[27] Luke Peterson, 'In an Apparent First, Investor and Host-State Agree to Mediation Under IBA Rules to Resolve in Investment Treaty Dispute', Investment Arbitration Reporter, 14 April 2016.

of the ICC Rules, the Centre was in a position to accept such a request and apply the IBA Rules insofar as they were not inconsistent with the ICC Rules. As both sets of rules contain rather general provisions on the conduct of the mediation, the Centre did not encounter any difficulties in applying the two at the same time.[28]

The mediation lasted for nearly two and a half years, making it one of the longest mediations in the history of the ICC International Centre for ADR. During this time, the mediator, who was jointly nominated by the parties, was in place for a total of 764 days. The biggest challenge throughout the mediation was ensuring the government's participation. Two months elapsed between the notification of the request for mediation by the Centre to the state and the latter's agreement to participate. During this time, the Centre had to identify the appropriate contact person within the state, to engage them in communication, and ensure that they would provide an answer to the request for mediation. At this stage, the Centre played an instrumental role. The Manager and Deputy Manager of the Centre guided state representatives through the mediation process by explaining to them the principles governing mediation, provisions contained in the Rules, and their interplay with the IBA Rules, as well as the ICC Mediation procedure and its differences with other settlement techniques. The sheer quantity of exchanges between all of the players involved (the parties, the mediator, and the Centre) demonstrates how difficult it was to reach out and get a response from the state. Overall, nearly 200 pieces of correspondence were exchanged and at least four teleconferences were held.

A further obstacle came in the form of a general election, which took place in the state during the mediation proceedings. This resulted in a change of administration and of the representatives of the relevant departments participating in the proceedings and significantly delayed the progress of the mediation. Ultimately, the parties fell short of settling their dispute. Yet, the parties achieved significant progress in their negotiations and the mediation proceedings helped them to re-establish communication, potentially leaving the door open for future business opportunities. Furthermore, despite its significant duration, the mediation was still cost efficient for the parties. For an amount in dispute of around 2.5 million US dollars, the total cost of the proceedings fixed by the Centre was 40,000 US dollars (13,000 US dollars in administrative costs and the remaining amount for the Mediator's fees and expenses).

B. Getting to YES with a State

This case involved a dispute between a state and a satellite communications company (Company). The Company was awarded a contract by the state following a

[28] For example, prior to agreeing on a joint nomination of a mediator, the parties suggested that the qualifications of the mediators listed in Annex B of the IBA Rules should be taken into consideration.

tender process, according to which it would provide the state with an end-to-end satellite communications system. The contract was still ongoing at the time of the dispute. Having incurred additional costs due to delays attributed to the state, the Company submitted a request for equitable adjustment, pursuant to the terms of the contract, followed by a formal request for reimbursement. The parties were not able to agree on the amount the Company was entitled to recover.

The contract provided for ICC Arbitration as the dispute resolution procedure. However, the Company had an interest in continuing to perform its contractual obligations and in being considered in future public tenders with the state. Both parties sought to maintain a positive working relationship and reach an amicable agreement. Accordingly, they agreed upon and signed a mediation agreement under the ICC Mediation Rules and referred their dispute to mediation. They agreed to nominate jointly a mediator who was then confirmed by the Centre. The Company also agreed to cap its request for equitable readjustment at a certain amount.

Less than three months after the request for mediation was submitted to the Centre, the parties reached a full and complete settlement of all disputed issues in this matter, both before the time limit for the proceedings had expired and after just two days of mediation totalling roughly twenty hours of the mediator's time. The mediator, a retired judge with experience chairing arbitrations, suggested an amount for the equitable re-adjustment based on what he would have decided had he presided over the case as a judge or arbitrator. The parties subsequently agreed upon a settlement by which the equitable readjustment was to be incorporated into the payment schedule of the contract. Following the settlement, they continued their business relationship. The total cost of the mediation proceedings was 37,000 US dollars.

Both of the above-mentioned cases demonstrate the willingness of the parties, both investors and states, to explore a new means of dispute settlement that allows them to continue their commercial relationships. Opt-in mediation was successful in the second example and the parties' decision to incorporate the settlement as an amendment to the contract was a creative solution that avoided potential issues with enforceability. Once again, mediation has proved to be successful where parties have ongoing, long-term relationships.

VII. Paving the Way for the Future

Promoting the use and practice of mediation in cross-border disputes is very much a question of education. Mediation will not become a regular option for the resolution of international commercial disputes until it becomes a familiar process for all dispute resolution professionals. Lawyers, contract and project managers, in-house counsel, arbitrators, adjudicators—all need awareness of the advantages, potential, challenges, and limits of mediation. At present, dispute resolution professionals far too often have a distorted or incomplete understanding of mediation. To this end, the ICC has taken on an educational role in the field over the years, teaching critical mediation advocacy skills to new generations through the annual ICC International Commercial Mediation Competition.

The ICC Mediation Competition is the ICC's biggest educational event. Over its thirteen series it has gathered more than 3,200 students from 196 different universities in fifty-four countries. They competed in approximately ninety-five different mock disputes. The latest competitions have involved over 140 professionals from various backgrounds and countries. Organizing this event requires substantial efforts and logistical coordination from our project manager and team, with the help of multiple sponsors.

The foremost success of the ICC Mediation Competition is that many participating students have since gone on to pursue careers in the dispute resolution field, with a focus on mediation. Furthermore, the ICC Mediation Competition has also inspired the creation of several regional pre-moots that are now being organized worldwide. Promotion of mediation on an international scale has significantly contributed to the ICC's wider mission of facilitating international trade and investment.

In the midst of growing trends of protectionism and nativism, a neutral, international body capable of bringing parties together from different countries and commercial areas seems more relevant and important than ever. In 1921, the first ICC Congress, in the face of similar international challenges, committed itself to exerting a moral influence on the world stage through its ability to help parties resolve their disputes in an ever-growing neutral forum. Such is the commitment of the Centre today: to resolve disputes through its effective, flexible, and efficient methods of amicable dispute resolution.

6

The International Centre for Dispute Resolution's Mediation Practice and Experience

Eric P. Tuchmann, Tracey B. Frisch, Giovanna Micheli, and Yanett Quiroz

I. Introduction: ICDR Background Information

The International Centre for Dispute Resolution (ICDR) is the international division of the American Arbitration Association (AAA), which administers international arbitrations, mediations, and other dispute resolution services under its various rules and procedures.[1] The ICDR was launched in 1996 as a distinct and separately staffed centre specializing in international disputes and as a response to rapid growth in world trade and the increasingly global business environment. However, the ICDR operates under the AAA umbrella, which itself was involved in international dispute resolution since it was founded in 1926 and issued specific Rules and Standards of the Voluntary International Arbitration Tribunals in 1951.

The ICDR is headquartered in New York City and maintains additional offices in Singapore, Miami, and Houston, where ICDR staff are also located to administer cases. Mediations can take place in these offices, or in any other location the parties agree to and where hearing rooms are available. The ICDR administers cases under the ICDR's International Rules, UNCITRAL Rules, and a variety of other rules, e.g. the Inter-American Commercial Arbitration Commission (IACAC) Rules, Internet Corporation for Assigned Names and Numbers (ICANN) Rules, and the various AAA rules where the dispute involves one or more foreign parties.

The ICDR is staffed with multi-lingual attorneys with backgrounds or expertise in international alternative dispute resolution, and the ICDR provides a full range of conflict management services to businesses, government agencies, and other organizations around the world. These services are enhanced by a network of eighty-five cooperative agreements with other arbitration institutions in fifty-two countries and key alliances located around the globe, all of which support the

[1] The AAA was founded in 1926 as a New York not-for-profit corporation and has retained that corporate structure throughout its history.

ICDR's international administration and educational initiatives. The ICDR maintains a roster of experienced and expert mediators from around the world and is also able to access the roster of mediators that are maintained on the AAA's domestic roster.

In the five-year period between 2012 and 2017, the ICDR administered over 4,300 cases, and while the vast majority of those cases were arbitrations, mediation is specifically addressed in the ICDR's International Rules and most other rules that apply to ICDR-administered matters. The ICDR International Arbitration Rules, effective 1 June 2014, placed an increased emphasis on mediation by including language specifically suggesting that the ICDR 'may invite the parties to mediate […] At any stage of the proceedings, the parties may agree to mediate. […] Unless the parties agree otherwise, the mediation shall proceed concurrently with arbitration and the mediator shall not be an arbitrator appointed to the case'.[2]

With regard to mediation, it is important to note that the ICDR's International Mediation Rules (hereinafter the ICDR Mediation Rules, or Rules) were developed to provide a roadmap to parties, mediators, and other participants in ICDR mediations. The Rules outline a small number of procedures that, consistent with the flexible character of the mediation process, are subject to modification by the parties. Nonetheless, the Rules provide a handful of basic default procedures the ICDR views as important to the mediation process. Specifically, the Rules indicate, among other things, how the parties can agree to mediation, provide guidance on how to initiate the mediation process, outline the mediator appointment process, specify how mediators are appointed and what their responsibilities are, and the importance of confidentiality in mediations.

II. The International Mediation Caseload

From 2012 through 2018, 739 international mediations were administered, representing an average of approximately 100 mediations per year. Although the number of mediations administered from year to year has not been consistent (Table 6.1), it does not appear that the caseload modulations were the result of any particular set of factors.

Approximately half the mediations administered each year resulted from cases that were filed by a party specifically seeking mediation alone. The other half of the mediations resulted from cases proceeding as arbitrations where the parties subsequently agreed to mediate their dispute in an attempt to settle their respective claims without a full arbitration proceeding. Mediations involved subject-matter

[2] Article 5 (Mediation) of the ICDR International Arbitration Rules.

Table 6.1 Number of mediations administered per year.

Year	# of Mediations
2018	101
2017	128
2016	97
2015	127
2014	107
2013	74
2012	105

areas that included construction, energy, technology, financial services, entertainment, pharma/biotech, and a variety of other commercial disputes. Other mediations involved advertising/marketing, commercial real estate, transportation, insurance, and hospitality.

With regard to the nationality of parties to international mediations for the years 2012 to 2016, the ICDR assisted parties with mediation from all different parts of the world. Most mediations involved one party from the United States, and parties from other countries included South America (19), Central America (7), Non-US Caribbean (25), Europe (198), Asia (110), Africa (7), Middle East (19), Canada (55), and Mexico (11).

III. The Agreement to Mediate

The great majority of the mediations administered by the ICDR arise out of contracts containing clauses requiring future disputes to be mediated under the auspices of the ICDR. Those mediation clauses are frequently a part of a multi-stepped dispute resolution process in which the parties agree to mediate as a condition precedent to arbitrating. Additional, but less-common, features of these stepped clauses are to require that the parties negotiate prior to mediation, or to provide that litigation, and not arbitration, is the final step in the process. In addition, in a handful of cases each year, the parties will agree to ICDR-administered mediation through a post-dispute submission agreement where the parties are either heading toward or are actively involved in litigation. In smaller number of cases, the ICDR is made aware that mediation previously occurred in the course of administering an arbitration, but the ICDR was not otherwise involved in that mediation in any way.

The following shows the standard mediation clause provisions suggested by the ICDR for incorporation into the dispute resolution clause in the parties' contract, or in their post-dispute submission agreement to mediate:

1) Pre-Dispute provision:

In the event of any controversy or claim arising out of or relating to this contract, or a breach thereof, the parties hereto agree first to try and settle the dispute by mediation, administered by the International Centre for Dispute Resolution under its Mediation Rules, before resorting to arbitration, litigation, or some other dispute resolution procedure.

The parties should consider adding:

a. The place of mediation shall be [city, (province or state), country]; and
b. The language(s) of the mediation shall be ___________.

2) For an existing dispute:

The parties hereby submit the following dispute to mediation administered by the International Centre for Dispute Resolution in accordance with its International Mediation Rules. (The clause may also provide for the qualifications of the mediator(s), the place of mediation, and any other item of concern to the parties.)

3) For concurrent mediation:

Any controversy or claim arising out of or relating to this contract, or the breach thereof, shall be determined by arbitration administered by the International Centre for Dispute Resolution in accordance with its International Arbitration Rules. Once the demand for arbitration is initiated, the parties agree to attempt to settle any controversy or claim arising out of or relating to this contract, or a breach thereof, by mediation administered by the International Centre for Dispute Resolution under its International Mediation Rules at the request of either party. Mediation may proceed concurrently with arbitration and shall not be a condition precedent to any stage of the arbitration process.

The parties may wish to consider adding:

a. The place of mediation shall be (city and/or country); and
b. The language(s) of the mediation shall be [3]_________.

Because mediation is a voluntary alternative dispute resolution proceeding, the formalities associated with arbitration are not essential with mediation. Mediation can be attempted at any stage while a litigation or arbitration is pending, and parties generally can unilaterally withdraw from a mediation proceeding at any point in the process. In terms of timing, ICDR-administered mediations generally take

[3] International Dispute Resolution Procedures (Including Mediation and Arbitration Rules), Amended and Effective 1 June 2014.

place shortly after an arbitration has started, although they can occur at any time during the arbitration process. Further mediations can proceed concurrently with arbitration to avoid any potential delay, or if the parties desire, an arbitration proceeding can be suspended while the mediation take place.

A. The Enforceability of Mediation Clauses

Court decisions from various jurisdictions around the world reflect that mediation clauses that are definitive regarding the parties' obligation to mediate are likely to be enforced. This is particularly so where the mediation is to be administered pursuant to the rules of an institution.

For example, the First Circuit found that a clause incorporating the AAA's Construction Industry Mediation Rules and stating that the parties 'shall endeavor to resolve their disputes by mediation' was enforceable as a condition precedent to arbitration.[4] US State courts have likewise upheld pre-dispute agreements to mediate. The Nevada State Supreme Court held that a mediation provision contained in the parties' contract was enforceable. It stated that 'parties agree that any disputes or questions arising hereunder [. . .] shall be submitted to mediation [. . .] with the rules of the American Arbitration Association'.[5] As the court explained, since 'the provision at issue unambiguously addresses mediation as a condition precedent to litigation, the terms are given their "usual and ordinary" signification'.[6]

In *Cable & Wireless Plc v IBM United Kingdom Ltd.*,[7] the court enforced a pre-dispute ADR clause as an agreement to mediate that called for good faith negotiations followed by a good faith attempt to resolve the matter through an 'alternative dispute resolution' as recommended by the institution Centre for Effective Dispute Resolution (CEDR). The court held that the hearing of the claim should be 'adjourned until after the parties have referred all their outstanding disputes to ADR'. Likewise, in *Hooper Bailie Assoc. Ltd v Natcon Group Party Ltd*,[8] the Supreme Court of New South Wales enforced a pre-dispute agreement to mediate after examining English, Australian, and United States authorities. Lastly, Hong Kong courts have also held that definitive pre-dispute agreements to mediate should be enforced. *Hyundai Engineering and Construction Co Lts v Vigour Ltd*[9] provides useful guidance. The Hong Kong Court of Appeal held that an agreement that parties would 'agree and submit to Third Party Mediation procedure' was not enforceable because it lacked specific measures such as reference to an institutional rule set and

[4] *HIM Portland, LLC v Devito Builders, Inc.*, 317 F.3d 41, 44 (1st Cir. 2003).
[5] *MBAm., Inc. v Alaska Pac. Leasing Co.*, 367 P.3d 1286, 1289 (Nev. 2016).
[6] Ibid., 1288, citing *Traffic Control Servs., Inc. v United Rentals Nw., Inc.*, 87 P.3d 1054 (Nev. 2004) (internal quotations omitted).
[7] England and Wales High Court, (2002) EWHC 2059 (Comm) (11 October 2002).
[8] New South Wales Law Reports, (1992) 28 NSWLR 194-13 (13 April 1992).
[9] (2005) 1 HKC 579.

timetable. However, the court stated that had the clause made more specific reference to mediation procedures it would be an enforceable pre-dispute mediation provision.

B. The ICDR Encourages Mediation

The ICDR's policy is to discuss the possibility of mediation at least in every administrative conference call that takes place at the outset of an arbitration. While the primary purpose of the ICDR's administrative conference is to discuss matters such as the nature of the case, arbitrator selection, the parties' claims, and preliminary scheduling, the ICDR takes the opportunity very early in the case to both discuss the parties' willingness to consider mediating their dispute, and (as appropriate) to describe the ICDR's capabilities and mediation roster. ICDR staff are proactive in discussing the benefits of mediation, and to emphasize that it is a process that can be successfully initiated at any stage of the arbitration proceeding. The ICDR's experience is that very commonly the parties do not feel ready to mediate at a very early stage of the arbitration proceeding. However, it is the ICDR's experience that time and cost savings are maximized the earlier mediation is engaged to resolve the parties dispute.

Nonetheless, many parties proceed with the arbitration first, and indicate that before they can properly evaluate if they would agree to mediate, they need better understand their own case and that of the other party or parties. Having the benefit of information exchange and more detailed examination of the law and facts of the case may often lead to more informed parties and representatives who would be willing to discuss settlement. Consequently, the ICDR will approach parties a second time at the conclusion of the exchange of information stage to gauge their interest in attempting mediation at that time. Since the time between the conclusion of information exchange and the actual hearings may be several weeks or more, there is sufficient time to select a mediator and conduct a session without ever having to disrupt the arbitration schedule.

C. Initiating Mediation with the ICDR

Most ICDR mediations are initiated because of a pre-dispute contractual agreement that requires the parties to mediate their dispute with the ICDR before, or concurrent with, proceeding to arbitration or litigation. However, some ICDR mediations are initiated as a result of the parties' post-dispute agreement to mediation, which can result from the parties' independent agreement, or from the ICDR prompting the parties to consider mediation.

1. Pre-existing agreements to mediate

Where there is a pre-existing agreement to mediate, any or all of the parties can commence the mediation process by making a request for mediation to any ICDR or AAA office via telephone, email, regular mail, fax, or through the AAA's online filing platform, AAA WebFile[10] at http://www.icdr.org. The request for mediation must contain: 1) the mediation provision of the parties' contract or stipulation to mediate; 2) the contact information of all parties and representatives, if any; 3) a brief statement of the nature of the dispute and requested relief; and, 4) any qualifications required in the mediator.[11]

2. No pre-existing agreement to mediate

Where there is no pre-existing agreement to mediate with the ICDR, any party may nonetheless request that the ICDR invite another party to voluntarily submit their dispute to mediation. Since mediation is a voluntary process, all parties must agree to participate in order for the ICDR to proceed with the administration of the mediation. For this reason, the ICDR will seek information about any prior discussions about mediating the dispute, and if so, the outcomes of the discussions and an articulation of the responding parties' objections, if any.

When the ICDR contacts the opposing parties, an effort is made to explain the mediation process from the view of a neutral administrative body, to discuss the benefits of the process, and the qualifications and types of mediators that could be considered for appointment.

IV. The Mediation Proceeding

Once all parties have agreed to mediate, the ICDR contacts them immediately to schedule a joint conference call to discuss the following issues, in addition to others that may be specific to the particular dispute: 1) mediator selection; 2) date and place of the mediation conference; 3) allocation of costs; 4) preferred method of communication; and 5) nature of the dispute and amount or type of relief sought. The ICDR prefers that the organizing conference call take place within a few days of filing. During this call, and the whole proceeding, any party may be represented by a person of their choice, unless the applicable law provides for certain limitations.

[10] AAA WebFile is an online case filing platform where parties can file their case with the AAA–ICDR and view case documents online.

[11] Rule 2(2) of International Mediation Rules, Amended and Effective 1 June 2014.

A. Appointment of the Mediator

After the administrative conference call with the parties and based on their description of the dispute and their referred mediator qualifications, including geographical limits, and if the parties have not previously mutually agreed upon a mediator or a specific method of appointment, the ICDR will prepare a list of mediators for their consideration and discussion.[12]

1. Mediator appointment using the list process

The ICDR's practice is to provide a list of approximately five suitable mediator candidates who are members of the mediation roster. The list, along with their resumes, are sent to the parties, who then have three business days to agree upon a mediator, or in the absence of agreement, for each party to strike the unacceptable names from the list, number the remaining names in order of preference, and return the list to the ICDR.[13] From among the mediators mutually accepted by the parties and in accordance with order of mutual preference, a mediator will be invited to serve. If the parties have provided a specific date when the mediation conference must be held, the mediators appearing on the list can be screened in advance by the ICDR to ensure their availability on that date. The parties can also access https://www.aaamediation.org, a publicly accessible mediator search tool that was created by the AAA used to search for additional suitable candidates.

ICDR mediators are recognized for their experience and expertise through training and experience interacting with parties with adverse positions, or unreasonable expectations. The ICDR also offers specific mediation training. The mediators on the ICDR's roster are not only well trained in the mediation process, they are respected professional experts in business, industry, and law, and are skilled and selected as appropriate for each individual dispute.

The Rules also provide a mechanism for the appointment of a mediator in the event that the parties fail to agree to a mediator on their own or fail to agree on any of the mediators suggested by the ICDR. While the ICDR makes significant efforts to provide a list of potential mediators that will be acceptable to the parties, including providing supplemental names or list of potential mediators, the ICDR does nonetheless have the authority to appoint a mediator without doing so.[14]

Once a mediator has been identified, the ICDR invites that individual to serve and advises the mediator of the names of the parties, their principals, and representatives if known. The mediator is also asked to confirm possession of any special qualifications specified by the parties, and availability if the parties have requested a specific date for the mediation. If the parties have not provided a date for the

[12] Rule 4(a) of The International Mediation Rules, Amended and Effective 1 June 2014.
[13] Rule 4(b) The International Mediation Rules, Amended and Effective 1 June 2014.
[14] Rule 4(c) The International Mediation Rules, Amended and Effective 1 June 2014.

mediation conference, the ICDR will still inquire about the mediator's availability in the near future. The ICDR will also advise of the location for the mediation.

2. Ethical obligations of mediators

The ICDR imposes important ethical obligations on mediators appointed in the mediations that it administers. Specifically, mediators are required to abide by the Model Standards of Conduct for Mediators (Model Standards).[15] The Model Standards contain a number of important guiding principles regarding the mediation process, e.g. the requirement that a mediator conduct a mediation based on the principle of self-determination, which is the act of coming to a voluntary, uncoerced decision. Additional provisions of the Model Standards address mediator impartiality, conflicts of interest, competence, confidentiality, and other elements of mediator conduct.[16]

The ICDR is particularly proactive with regard to the issue of mediator impartiality. Because a mediator's effectiveness relies in the parties' trust that the individual serving in that role is neutral and not aligned with the interest of any party to the dispute, the ICDR's rules require that mediators 'disclose as soon as practicable, all actual and potential conflicts of interest that are reasonably known to the mediator and could reasonably be seen as raising a question about the mediator's impartiality.'[17]

Consequently, even though mediators do not have any authority to render any type of decision with regard to the merits of the parties' dispute that is binding in the manner that an arbitrator does, disclosures take a high priority in ICDR cases. Mediators are 'required to make a reasonable inquiry to determine whether there are any facts that a reasonable individual would consider likely to create a potential or actual conflict of interest for the mediator. ICDR mediators are required to disclose any circumstance likely to create a presumption of bias or prevent a resolution of the parties' dispute within the time frame desired by the parties.'[18] To assist mediators with their disclosure obligations, the ICDR provides them with forms that prompt the necessary inquiries, including those which relate to business, personal, social, or familial relationships.

Whatever disclosures are received from the mediator are communicated to the parties for their comments. Parties may waive any disclosures made by the mediator and proceed with the mediation; however, if any party objects to the mediators' continued service, the mediator shall be replaced.[19] Upon completion of the mediator's appointment, the ICDR also provides the mediator with online access

[15] Rule 5(1) The International Mediation Rules, Amended and Effective 1 June 2014.
[16] See https://www.americanbar.org/content/dam/aba/migrated/2011_build/dispute_resolution/model_standards_conduct_april2007.authcheckdam.pdf.
[17] Rule 5(1) of The International Mediation Rules, Amended and Effective 1 June 2014.
[18] Rule 5(2) of The International Mediation Rules, Amended and Effective 1 June 2014.
[19] Rule 5(3) of The International Mediation Rules, Amended and Effective 1 June 2014.

to the mediation file via the AAA–ICDR's eCenter, which contains documents related to the mediation, including any filing documents, the request for mediation, notice of mediator appointment, or mediation briefs to the extent that they exist. If a mediator is removed because of a conflict of interest or is otherwise unwilling or unable to serve, the ICDR will appoint another mediator using the list method, unless the parties agree otherwise.[20]

B. The Mediation Process

The ICDR expects mediation to be completed in an expedited time frame with limited exchange of information, and the time spent by a mediator on preparation for a mediation session will be considerably less than the time spent by an arbitrator reviewing submissions. Similarly, the time spent in the actual mediation session is usually significantly less than the time spent in an arbitration hearing.

It is essential that the mediator conduct the mediation based on the voluntary participation of the parties, leaving them to make free and informed choices as to process and outcome.[21] For that reason, the parties need to actively participate in the design of the proceeding and its resolution. The mediator does not have the authority to impose a settlement on the parties, and instead will attempt to help them reach a satisfactory resolution of their dispute. Under the ICDR mediation proceeding, the mediator may, upon the parties' agreement, make oral or written recommendations for settlement to a party privately or to all parties jointly.[22]

Immediately after the mediator's appointment is finalized, the ICDR will ask the mediator about scheduling a pre-mediation conference call with the parties. During that conference, the mediator discusses with the parties if pre-mediation memoranda will be filed, and, if so, whether the parties are to exchange the memoranda. The memoranda frequently include a brief description of the relief requested, the main issues in the dispute, any underlying interests, and the history of the parties' negotiations. Separate meetings and communications with the mediator, including *ex parte* communications, are permissible. The place and date for the mediation session is also decided during this conference. The ICDR coordinates these meetings whether in person, by phone, or otherwise, and sends related notices.

The parties also have responsibilities under the ICDR Mediation Rules, and they are to ensure that the representatives attending the mediation have the authority to consummate a settlement and attend the mediation conference.[23] Because

[20] Rule 6 of The International Mediation Rules, Amended and Effective 1 June 2014.
[21] Rule 7(1) of The International Mediation Rules, Amended and Effective 1 June 2014.
[22] Rule 7(4) of The International Mediation Rules, Amended and Effective 1 June 2014.
[23] Rule 8(1) of The International Mediation Rules, Amended and Effective 1 June 2014.

mediation is party-controlled, its success depends on the parties' desire to participate in good faith with a genuine intent to reach a resolution. Furthermore, as they have a stake by participating in the development of the settlement, they usually have more of a personal interest in compliance.

One of the most critical aspects of mediation is that it is a confidential process, and the ability of parties to fully exchange their views and settlement offers is the understanding that such views, offers, and other confidential information divulged during the mediation will remain confidential. It is also the case that a mediator in most jurisdictions is protected from testifying before any subsequent tribunal regarding the matter. The purpose of this protection is to invite the parties to participate in a truly meaningful interaction with a comfort level that enables them to be forthright in terms of their position regarding the dispute. The ICDR's Mediation Rules also incorporate these perspectives regarding confidentiality.[24] The language of the mediation shall be the one of the documents containing the mediation agreement, unless the parties agree otherwise.

C. Costs of Mediation

There is a 250 US dollar non-refundable deposit to initiate mediation and appoint a mediator. The cost of mediation is based on the hourly or daily mediation rate published on the mediator's resume. In addition, the parties will be charged an administrative fee for the AAA–ICDR's services of 75 US dollars for each hour charged by the mediator.

Based on the parties' estimates of how long the mediation will take, the ICDR will ask the mediator what funds the parties are required to place in deposit and the ICDR will invoice parties in advance of the mediation conference. An invoice for the parties will be generated and sent via email with instructions to process payment prior to the mediation conference. If the mediation conference is scheduled with very short notice, the ICDR can approach the mediators for their approval to allow the parties permission to make payment after the conclusion of the mediation conference. A final accounting will be rendered to the parties at the end of the case, and any unexpended balance will be refunded.

There is a four-hour minimum charge for a mediation conference, and if a matter submitted to mediation is withdrawn or cancelled, or results in a settlement after the request to initiate mediation is filed but prior to the mediation conference, a 250 US dollar charge will be incurred in addition to any mediator charges. These costs shall be borne by the initiating party unless the parties agree otherwise.

[24] Rule 10 of The International Mediation Rules, Amended and Effective 1 June 2014.

D. Termination of the Mediation

The ICDR will contact the mediator within 24 to 48 hours after the mediation conference to obtain the disposition of the case, i.e. settled, impasse, or impasse but continuing. If the parties settle, the ICDR will close the finances of the case and request any additional payments required to complete the mediator's compensation; the mediator will be paid after receiving the funds, and the ICDR will notify the termination of the mediation. If the mediator notifies that no agreement can be reached and further efforts will not contribute to a resolution of the dispute, or all the parties declare that the mediation has been terminated, the ICDR will close its file.

It may also happen that the mediation conference does not result in a settlement but that the mediator indicates he or she will continue with efforts to follow up with the parties for a certain period of time. In that case, the ICDR will schedule a case follow-up until the final disposition of the matter. The ICDR may also request additional deposits from the parties during that period of time. However, if there is no communication between the mediator and any party or party's representative for 21 days following the conclusion of the mediation session, the mediation shall be terminated.[25] This termination procedure was put in place to avoid delay tactics from a party that intends to avoid other dispute resolution proceedings, e.g. arbitration or litigation.

V. The ICDR'S Experiences Identifying Cases Suitable for Mediation

Understanding the dynamics behind a given dispute is fundamental to determining if mediation may assist the parties in resolving their dispute. In the end, settlements are viewed by parties as a win–win solution, particularly where those parties are able to maintain a continuing business relationship. In contrast, a win–lose scenario reached a few months later in arbitration, or years in a litigation, comes at a higher price, coupled with the risk of potential additional litigation to enforce the outcome. Being a structured, confidential, and voluntary procedure, the ICDR's view is that mediation should be embraced by parties. Surprisingly, it is not always an easy task for the ICDR to motivate parties to attempt mediation in the alternative or on a parallel track to a pending arbitration.

International commercial mediation cases usually involve multiple parties from different countries with different cultural backgrounds and languages. Virtually all international commercial cases can be mediated, but many parties are not willing to do so. Some of the most frequently raised objections not to proceed

[25] Rule 12 of The International Mediation Rules, Amended and Effective 1 June 2014.

with mediation include that the relationship between the parties has deteriorated to the extent that mediation could not be fruitful; suspicion about mediation and lack of knowledge among one or more parties about the process; legal uncertainty regarding the settlement agreement if reached; fear of showing weakness in proposing mediation; the parties have engaged in negotiations already and mediation will not offer a different outcome; and that the process is being offered too early in the dispute and the parties need to learn more about their respective positions before they can consider mediation.

Conversely, the ICDR has taken numerous steps to promote mediation. It has devoted time and resources to further develop staff knowledge through internally organized mediator skills trainings, as well as private and public seminars and working groups on mediation. This has significantly enhanced the ICDR staff's skill set to profile a case suitable for mediation. The addition of mediation provisions in some of the AAA's arbitration rules and the simplicity of introducing mediation in a pending ICDR arbitration have further displaced some of the negative perceptions towards mediation held by certain parties.

At the outset of any arbitration matter, the ICDR organizes an administrative conference call with the parties during which the ICDR offers mediation as an alternative or on a parallel track to arbitration. In preparation for the call, the ICDR case administrator reviews the main pleadings, the contract, and any pertinent correspondence exchanged between the parties. It is at this early stage that a knowledgeable ICDR case administrator can engage the parties in a conversation as to whether or not they will agree to mediate their dispute.

A. Factors Favouring Mediation in Cases Filed as Arbitrations

1. Cost

One of the primary reasons parties attempt to settle disputes with a neutral mediator is the cost savings that results from avoiding full arbitration or litigation. Particularly when the dispute is limited to a few, relatively uncontroversial issues, or the various issues and facts are easy to ascertain and typically relate to the mere calculation of damages or the valuation of assets, a third party with no connection to any of the participants can be most helpful to resolve the dispute. Similarly, when the claimed amount is sufficiently small so that the costs of arbitration or litigation cannot be justified, parties are inclined to explore mediation. Conversely, when a dispute is particularly complex or the stakes are very high, some parties may seek mediation as to better control the outcome, even though they may have high confidence in their case. Some parties simply feel that, with large amount of money at stake, it may be too risky to submit a dispute to arbitration or litigation. Accordingly, when a demand for arbitration illustrates a case with these characteristics, there is a high likelihood that parties may consider mediation at the beginning of the case. The parties will only have to pay for the services rendered by the mediator at their hourly rate, which includes a portion for ICDR services. Since a dispute can be resolved in many cases in just one mediation conference day, the savings can be considerable. Thus, parties are generally positively inclined to entertain this option, mostly placing the pending arbitration in abeyance until the outcome of the mediation is known.

2. Collaboration, preparation, and flexibility of counsel

An important factor in the success of mediation is counsel's participation and collaboration in the administrative conference call with sufficient knowledge of the background of the matter and history between the parties. Less-experienced parties and representatives tend to be averse to the idea of mediating the dispute merely because they are not as familiar with previous negotiations or working relationships among the parties. Also, entrenched litigators often lack the willingness to be receptive to alternative avenues of dispute resolution. Thus, counsel's experience, preparedness, reasonability, and willingness to reach an agreement play a key role in these cases.

It is also crucial that counsel be flexible enough to adapt and evolve as the path of a given case may change. In fact, when choosing mediation, the arbitration is usually not placed into abeyance automatically to avoid the perception that it would derail or otherwise slow down the pending arbitration. Rather, it will move along on a parallel track with the mediation procedure. Yet, an ongoing arbitration may change the dynamics of the mediation proceeding. To address both concerns, the ICDR offers, and usually the parties agree, to proceed with the arbitration on a parallel track—at least until the arbitral tribunal is fully constituted so that no additional costs will be incurred should the mediation prove successful. If the mediation fails, the arbitral tribunal is prepared to resume the arbitration and organize the preliminary hearing conference with the parties in short order.

3. *Pro se* cases

To the extent that *pro se* parties agree to mediate, the vast majority do so at the very outset of a case, particularly if the claims sought are relatively small and the pending arbitration is placed into abeyance pending outcome of the mediation. *Pro se* arbitrations are by no means less contentious. In fact, the opposite is often the case. That said, the promotion of mediation is fairly successful, which may be rooted in the fact that unrepresented parties are often not too familiar with the difficulties they will face in an international arbitration context. The costs of the process are again one of the main concerns, along with the lack of experience with the arbitration process and the issues related to the enforceability of a foreign award at an international level. That said, the lack of experience of *pro se* parties with the intricacies and culture of the mediation process may still create significant problems. This usually manifests itself in the finding of a suitable mediator for their dispute and the expectations of what a mediator can and cannot do for both sides. At times, the ICDR may then need to intervene and remind the parties that the mediator's role is to facilitate a settlement between them, rather than to take sides.

4. Previous settlement attempts

At times, the parties' initial submissions or the administrative conference call reveal that they entertained, albeit unsuccessfully, settlement negotiations before the arbitration was filed. In those instances, the parties are generally receptive to mediation. The resistance is then often a different one in that one party, usually the claimant, perceives that further attempts to settle the dispute are futile while the other party, usually the respondent, still hopes the dispute can be resolved amicably. As long as at least one party entertains the idea of an amicable solution, the door to mediation remains open and the ICDR will attempt to obtain the parties' agreement to appoint a mediator. The ICDR will also remind the parties that mediation can be attempted at any time during the life of an arbitration and that, given the success rate, there will be obvious economic advantages to the parties. Given the previous disposition, the ICDR may follow up whenever a new attempt to persuade the parties to mediate may be appropriate. This may likely occur after the exchange of information and/or the exchange of witness lists/statements, as the parties then usually know their case's strength better than they did at the outset.

5. The possibility of narrowing the issues submitted to arbitration

Experienced counsel in multi-party, multi-contract, and multi-claim disputes often use mediation to create a framework for these types of complex international arbitration disputes and to limit the costs while maximizing the benefits for their clients. Counsel will, however, use this approach when there is a likelihood of reaching a settlement via mediation for some of the issues. A side benefit is that it also helps the parties to better understand the complete case, as well as its strengths and weaknesses. In many instances where this approach is used, the parties have not only already selected their mediator, but they have already decided when and where the mediation will take place. The two proceedings run on parallel tracks as they address separate claims of the same dispute. Mediation being a faster process, it will conclude in short order and shape the pending arbitration accordingly. Furthermore, mediation being a confidential process, the information used during mediation will not be admitted in arbitration, which is certainly a key factor for the parties.

6. The need to maintain business relationships

Another typical scenario of arbitration-to-mediation conversion is when the parties involved want/need to keep their business relationship intact. It is, therefore, in their best interest to limit the damages and find an amicable solution via mediation. In case of an impasse, the parties will retain control of the option to arbitrate, but they will have the greater advantage of rearranging their business relationship via a new individualized solution, a new contract, a new partnership agreement, etc. While these cases are easy to spot in initial submissions, the major task for the ICDR is to find a suitable mediator who understands what needs to happen in order to salvage the business relationship.

7. 'Required' mediation

One of the most important incentives for the parties to agree to mediation is that mediation is required under certain AAA rules such as the Commercial Arbitration Rules (Section R-9) and the Construction Industry Arbitration Rules (Section R-10). These provisions allow any party to an arbitration to unilaterally opt out of mediation, but they do reflect the presumption that the parties will mediate at some point during the arbitration process. For example:

> Section R-9. Mediation
>
> In all cases where a claim or counterclaim exceeds $75,000, upon the AAA's administration of the arbitration or at any time while the arbitration is pending, *the parties shall mediate* their dispute pursuant to the applicable provisions of the AAA's Commercial Mediation Procedures, or as otherwise agreed by the parties. Absent an agreement of the parties to the contrary, the mediation shall take place concurrently with the arbitration and shall not serve to delay the arbitration proceedings. However, *any party to an arbitration may unilaterally opt out of this rule* upon notification to the AAA and the other parties to the arbitration' (emphasis added).

When the parties have a rule that imposes on them the obligation to consider and then take a position on mediating their dispute, they must take some action. Frequently, that action is to ask for more time to make this decision as neither party wants to eliminate the option or appear to be too eager in the eye of the opposing party. It is equally true that perhaps the parties who do not want to appear lenient towards settlement may find in this provision an elegant way to promote mediation without implying that the case in the pending arbitration lacks substance. Since R-9 was first introduced in late 2013, mediations have consistently increased overall at the AAA, although that increase remains relatively gradual.

8. Concerns about enforcing mediated settlements

Particularly in countries where the use of mediation is not highly developed, parties may share concerns that disputes settled in mediation will be unenforceable, or that they will be unable to seek remedies for any breach of a settlement agreement. To overcome this issue, parties may consider adding an arbitration provision within the settlement agreement. Thus, if the settlement agreement is breached a party can seek recourse in arbitration and subsequently confirm an award. Another less frequently used approach is to have the settlement agreement converted to the terms of a consent award by a separately appointed arbitrator. In turn, the consent award can be confirmed in the same manner as if the dispute had been arbitrated.

9. Delay

Additional concerns raised by parties are the possible delay of the pending arbitration coupled with the additional investment of resources or any previous negative experiences with the opposing party. In some cases, it is also the inexperience and the lack of knowledge of the case. Sometimes it is simply too early to engage in mediating a case not knowing whether a counterclaim may be filed. The best approach is then to wait for the exchange of information stage to be completed. Further concerns are the lack of negotiability, or the fact that the conflict escalated too far during the arbitration and too much has already been invested.

Other cases are simply not fit for mediation because of the type of claim, the declaratory relief requested, or the specific legal issue involved. Also, an impending statute of limitation or cancellation period provided for in the underlying contract or the applicable law can make mediation less suitable. However, the possibility to mediate after an application for emergency measures has been filed remains an option. Even those cases may become suitable for mediation as, most of the time, the main procedure will close as the underlying issues become moot and the parties may sometimes be interested in reaching an agreement. This is another opportunity for the parties to pursue mediation.

VI. The ICDR's Roster of Mediators

It is paramount to identify and select a mediator best suited for a particular dispute and subject matter expertise does not always define suitability. In international mediations, an experienced mediator will work closely with the parties to identify the appropriate method of bargaining to use in the particular dispute at hand. A reality check of a case's strength or weakness is often much needed to find common ground. Also, an accurate and comprehensive risk assessment is often useful, as parties are influenced by their own assessment of their alternatives to a negotiated agreement. A well-trained mediator, in a distributive or in a directive mediation, will be able to assist the parties in this regard by helping them to analyse any alternative paths with an eye on the best and worst outcomes. A good mediator will also ground the parties in reality by focusing them on objective criteria and actual possibilities, rather than chasing uninformed or one-sided ideas.

The ICDR recognizes that mediators undertake serious responsibilities and have ethical obligations to the parties and the process itself. To address the need for suitable mediators, over many decades the ICDR has formed a panel composed of geographically diverse international dispute resolution specialists, all of whom are highly regarded professionals from business and legal communities. The ICDR has also created tools and internal search capabilities that allow for customized mediator searches by fields of expertise, geographic area, cultural background, and language.

Common areas of expertise of the ICDR mediators are those involving 1) significant business relationships, e.g. contractual disputes relating to performance (typically in constructions cases), services, employment, commercial leases, etc.; 2) fiduciary relationships, e.g. partnerships, joint ventures, professional malpractice relating to doctors, lawyers, accountants, etc.; 3) areas of law practice, including banking and generally financial services, pharmaceuticals/patent licensing/supply agreement, maritime/shipping, product liability, information technology, corporate, business, insurance/reinsurance, aviation and construction; and 4) personal/family business, e.g. closed corporations, family partnerships, as well as trust-related issues, etc.

The ICDR roster of mediators provides professionals with substantial experience in cases of an international and cross-cultural nature. An overview of the biographical information provided by the ICDR's international mediators shows how comprehensive their resumes are; they describe not only the mediators' expertise, but also their philosophy that a mediator 'is a facilitator in the composition of interests between the parties' and takes an 'objective view for the interests at stake, together with suggestions of possible solutions', and that the technique they use 'keep[s] the initiative and control in the parties' hands' etc. Some mediator resumes even explain at the start any concerns before, during, and after the mediation that the parties should review together with the mediator (e.g. prepare your case, obtain as much information as possible, keep always neutral in words and attitudes, etc.).

Some mediator resumes also describe their mediation experience and include details like the number of parties, party nationalities, any specific issues in dispute, and the place of mediation. Examples include:

- Mediation took place over several months with meetings in Frankfurt, Milan, Dubai, and finally London with on-line mediation in the intervening periods. Settled with a new forward trading agreement;
- High value Oil & Gas dispute (£25 million) between worldwide oil major and oil refinery
- Challenge to accounting firm partner appointed to arbitrate post-closing adjustments in sale of international building materials corporation;
- Mediated over a number of months at high level and trading level to bring about a forward trading solution;
- A settlement agreement was reached following 1.5 days of mediation and using a consecutive interpreter.

To be added to the ICDR Panel, a candidate must undergo a rigorous selection process that includes both an internal and external review committee. The internal committee consists of ICDR executives and case management staff who can identify the type of mediators most frequently sought by the party. External reviews may consist of AAA council members, or other leaders in the field of alternative dispute resolution. Both screen candidates for their case management skills, substantive expertise, commitment, ethics, training, and suitability to the caseload. ICDR mediators must have the highest regard by peers for integrity, fairness, and good judgment. ICDR mediators have achieved academic and professional honours that mark them as leaders in their respective fields. Once on the ICDR panel, stringent standards of ethics and experience must be met and maintained.[26]

VII. Mediator Characteristics Most Frequently Sought by Parties

Through experience, the ICDR has learned that mediator skills and qualifications most often requested by parties are quite different from those found in arbitrators. Arbitrators are generally expected to be experts in the subject matter of the dispute. While mediators are also required to have knowledge, but also they are expected to have interpersonal skills and the ability to aid the parties in the decision-making process. The most frequently selected ICDR mediators have evaluative mediation approaches, credibility, and a personality that reflects the ability to build rapport.

For international disputes, it is also important that the mediator has an intercultural background that allows them to understand the cultural and jurisdictional differences at issue. This background also helps to conduct mediations under different models that the parties select and adapt the proceeding to their specific and unique needs.

VIII. Vision for the Future

It is the ICDR's hope that the international community will embrace mediation as a valuable dispute resolution process and that parties will include mediation in their contract clauses and seek out mediation to address international disputes. Mediation, as a party driven process, allows disputants to actively participate in

[26] See Model Standard of Conduct for Mediators, September 2005.

the outcome of their dispute. Owning the process and the outcome is a powerful and universal benefit of mediation. International disputants would be wise to consider mediation as a viable alternative to adjudicated resolutions. The ICDR is well situated to assist parties make that decision and guide them through the mediation process.

7

The ICSID Conciliation Rules in Practice

*Frauke Nitschke**

I. Introduction

In 1966, the Convention on the Settlement of Investment Disputes Between States and Nationals of Other States (the ICSID Convention) established an international forum for the settlement of investment disputes through conciliation and arbitration.[1] Article 25 of the ICSID Convention defines the jurisdiction of ICSID as extending 'to any legal dispute arising directly out of an investment, between a Contracting State (or any constituent subdivision or agency of a Contracting State designated to the Centre by that State) and a national of another Contracting Sate, which the parties to the dispute consent in writing to submit to the Centre.' As of 1 April 2019, 154 states have ratified the ICSID Convention to become contracting states.[2] In 1978, the Administrative Council of ICSID adopted the Additional Facility Rules, authorizing the Secretariat to administer certain categories of proceedings between states and nationals of other states that fell outside the scope of the Convention.[3] By 28 February 2019, ICSID had registered 711 cases; 645 cases were registered under the ICSID Convention and 66 under the Additional Facility Rules. Seven hundred cases were arbitrations, and eleven cases were conciliations.

This chapter reviews the historical background and drafting history related to the conciliation provisions in the ICSID Convention (section II), before summarizing the similarities (section III) and differences (section IV) between the Convention's conciliation and arbitration framework. ICSID conciliation practice will subsequently be examined (section V), before providing an outlook on amicable settlement of investment disputes (section VI).

* The views expressed in this article are those of the author and should not be attributed to International Centre for Settlement of Investment Disputes (ICSID). The author thanks Ms Phoebe Ngan, whose tireless support was instrumental during the preparation of this article.

[1] Article 1(2) of the Convention on the Settlement of Investment Disputes between States and Nationals of Other States (opened for signature 18 March 1965, entered into force 14 October 1966) (ICSID Convention).

[2] ICSID, List of Contracting States and Other Signatories of the Convention, https://icsid.worldbank.org/en/Documents/icsiddocs/List%20of%20Contracting%20States%20and%20Other%20Signatories%20of%20the%20Convention%20-%20Latest.pdf.

[3] Rules Governing the Additional Facility for the Administration of Proceedings by the Secretariat of the International Centre for Settlement of Investment Disputes (Additional Facility Rules). These types of proceedings include inter alia arbitration, conciliation, and fact-finding proceedings involving parties, one of which is not a contracting state or a national of a contracting state.

II. Historical Context and Drafting History

Following the end of the Second World War, the international community established what came to be known the World Bank.[4]

Between 1949 and 1962, investors and governments requested the World Bank—or its President Eugene R. Black in his personal capacity—to assist in the settlement of their disputes,[5] either through full-scale conciliation, the appointment of arbitrators or referees, or by assisting parties in finding a mutually agreeable dispute settlement methodology.[6] Among these disputes were 1) a dispute relating to the expropriation of the Suez Canal; 2) a dispute relating to the expropriation of companies in Tunisia; and 3) a 1958 dispute between the City of Tokyo and French nationals who held bonds issued by the city.[7] In the latter dispute, the parties requested President Black to serve as conciliator and 'to draft a concrete and workable plan for settling ... the controversy'.[8] A number of these disputes were successfully settled.[9]

Peaceful settlement of investment disputes was recognized as encouraging foreign investment flows[10] and considered to be part of the World Bank's mandate. However, in 1961, President Black noted that 'the Bank is not really equipped to handle this sort of business in the course of its regular routine' and that 'a very useful contribution could be made by some sort of special forum for the conciliation or arbitration of these disputes'.[11] Preceding this speech was a note that Aron Broches, the World Bank's General Counsel, had sent to the Executive Directors in August 1961,[12] which envisioned the creation of an 'international machinery' for the conduct of arbitration and conciliation proceedings. Following exchanges with the World Bank's Executive Directors, Broches prepared in June of 1962 a Draft Convention.[13] In these early communications, it was noted that

> many governments do include provisions for international conciliation and/or arbitration in certain types of agreements with foreign investors and that many governments are willing in principle to consider international adjustment of disputes arising with foreign investors [...] This is the justification for exploring

[4] The term World Bank refers to the International Bank for Reconstruction and Development and the International Development Association.

[5] Paul Szasz, 'Arbitration under the Auspices of the World Bank' (1969) 3 (2) The International Lawyer 312.

[6] ICSID, *History of the ICSID Convention: Documents Concerning the Origin and the Formulation of the Convention on the Settlement of Investment Disputes between States and Nationals of Other States*, Vol. 2, Part 1 (ICSID first published in 1968, reprinted 2009) 7 para. 5; ibid., 3.

[7] Szasz (n 5) 312.

[8] World Bank Press Release: City of Tokyo Bonds of 1912, UN 60/167, 4 April 1960.

[9] ICSID (n 6) 508–9:

[10] Ibid., 4, para. 3; see Antonio R. Parra, *The History of ICSID* (OUP, 2012) 21, n 78.

[11] ICSID (n 6) Vol. II, Part I, 3.

[12] Ibid., 1–3.

[13] Ibid., 19.

> the possibilities of an international agreement which would facilitate recourse to these methods of dispute settlement.[14]

At the outset, conciliation was considered the preferred method for investment dispute settlement

> because (a) the Bank has had successful experience with conciliation; and (b) conciliation did not in any way infringe or appear to infringe upon a country's sovereignty. [. . .] Conciliation being more acceptable than arbitration, it was likely to be more effective.[15]

The drafters considered that the terms 'conciliation' and 'mediation' could be used interchangeably, stating that 'mediation recommends, arbitration decides'. Ultimately, the term 'conciliation' was chosen, and defined as:

> any proceeding or method for the adjustment of a dispute, aimed at bringing the parties to an agreed solution with the assistance of one or more persons ('conciliators') empowered to make recommendations.[16]

Conciliation and arbitration were envisioned to be available on equal footing.[17] However, the relationship between the two led to some discussion.[18] It was ultimately decided to give maximum flexibility to the disputing parties, allowing for a choice between arbitration or conciliation, or a combination of both.[19] The Convention's arbitration and conciliation chapters were modelled closely after one another to create almost identical systems,[20] with the main difference being the functions and powers of the commission or tribunal, and the legal nature of the final instrument to be issued: a binding award by the arbitral tribunal and a non-binding report by the conciliation commission.[21]

[14] Ibid., 9, para. 20.

[15] Ibid., 14, para. 8.

[16] Ibid., 6, para. 2. There does not appear to have been much discussion regarding other, non-evaluative approaches to conciliation, e.g. a facilitative conciliation model. See generally, Leonard L. Riskin, 'Mediator Orientations, Strategies and Techniques' (1994) 12 Alternatives to the High Cost of Litigation, 111–14.

[17] ICSID (n 6) Vol. II, Part I, 413. During the final drafting stages of the Convention, Aron Broches indeed explained that 'conciliation [under the ICSID Convention] could in certain cases be a disguised form of arbitration'. ICSID (n 6) Vol. II, Part II, 782.

[18] Ibid., 14, para. 7. Some thought ICSID should be limited to conciliation only, while others thought conciliation should be no more than a first step. See ibid., 570. See also ICSID (n 6) Vol. II, Part I, 251–2, 263.

[19] Ibid., 419.

[20] Contribution of Mr Sapateiro, ICSID (n 6) Vol. II, Part II, 783.

[21] See ICSID (n 6) Vol. II, Part I, 38, Section 4 (Working Paper in the form of a Draft Convention, 5 June 1962); ibid., 156, Article 6 of the Annotated First Preliminary Draft Convention, 9 August 1963; ibid., 209, Section 5 (Preliminary Draft Convention: Working Paper for the Consultative Meetings of Legal Experts,15 October 1963; ibid., 627, Article 38 of the Draft Convention: Working Paper for the

The drafters' choice that a conciliation commission's function was to 'clarify the points in dispute between the parties and to endeavor to bring about an agreement between them upon mutually acceptable terms' as well as the commission's ability to make recommendations to the parties at any stage of the proceedings[22] was largely influenced by two treaties: the General Act for the Pacific Settlement of International Disputes of 1928[23] and the American Treaty on Pacific Settlement of 1948.[24] The decision may also have been influenced by the World Bank's successful assistance with the settlement of the Tokyo dispute in 1958.[25]

During the regional consultative meetings on the Draft Convention[26] it became clear that conciliation would be more acceptable than arbitration, especially for Latin American countries, which considered that affording foreign investors the 'right to sue a sovereign state outside its national territory'[27] would put domestic investors in a position of inferiority and afford foreign investors greater rights.

The final text of the ICSID Convention was opened for signature on 18 March 1965 and the Convention entered into force on 14 October 1966.

III. Similarities between ICSID Arbitration and Conciliation

ICSID conciliation and arbitration have a number of similarities. First, consent to ICSID conciliation or arbitration is binding upon the parties, and may not be withdrawn unilaterally.[28] Conciliation and arbitration proceedings are instituted by a written request addressed to the Secretary-General, who shall register such request unless it is found to be manifestly outside the Centre's jurisdiction.[29] The content requirements of such a request are the same for conciliation and arbitration.[30]

Legal Committee, 11 September 1964; ICSID (n 6) Vol. II, Part II, 921, Article 35(1) of the Revised Draft of the Convention, 11 December 1964.

[22] Ibid., 154.

[23] Article 15(1): '[t]he task of the Conciliation Commission shall be to elucidate the questions in dispute, to collect with that object all necessary information by means of enquiry or otherwise, and to endeavor to bring the parties to an agreement. It may, after the case has been examined, inform the parties of the terms of settlement which seem suitable to it, and lay down the period within which they are to make their decision.'

[24] Article XXII: 'it shall be the duty of the Commission of Investigation and Conciliation to clarify the points in dispute between the parties and to endeavor to bring about an agreement between them upon mutually acceptable terms. The Commission shall institute such investigations of the facts involved in the controversy as it may deem necessary for the purpose of proposing acceptable bases of settlement.'

[25] World Bank Press Release (n 8).

[26] ICSID (n 6) Vol. II, Part I, 236 ff, 298 ff, 367 ff, 367 ff, 458 ff.

[27] Ibid., 606, 370.

[28] Article 25(1) of the ICSID Convention. Once parties have consented to ICSID conciliation, they are obligated to participate; Article 34(1) of the ICSID Convention.

[29] Articles 28 and 36 of the ICSID Convention.

[30] Ibid. ICSID Rules of Procedure for the Institution of Conciliation and Arbitration Proceedings (ICSID Institution Rules) adopted by the Administrative Council of ICSID pursuant to Article 6(1)(b) of ICSID Convention are the same for both types of proceedings.

Conciliation commissions and arbitral tribunals are to be constituted 'as soon as possible' following registration of a request.[31] The provisions on the constitution of the commission and tribunal are almost identical,[32] except for the so-called nationality rule in Article 39, which does not apply to conciliators.[33]

Parties to conciliations and arbitrations have ample flexibility regarding the method of constitution and composition of commissions and tribunals. If the parties do not agree on the number of conciliators or arbitrators and the method of their appointment, the Convention provides for a default procedure that is identical in arbitration and conciliation.[34] The qualities required of conciliators and arbitrators are largely the same.[35] The Convention envisions that both conciliation commissions and arbitral tribunals shall be the judge of their own competence,[36] and that parties may file objections to such competence.[37] ICSID conciliation and arbitration proceedings shall be conducted in accordance with the Convention and, except as the parties otherwise agree, in accordance with the conciliation and arbitration rules in effect on the date of the parties' consent. Commissions and tribunals may decide 'any question of procedure' not covered under the Convention.[38]

The Convention further provides the same procedure for the filling of vacancies on the commission/tribunal if a conciliator or arbitrator resigns, dies, or becomes incapacitated.[39] Similarly, the Convention envisions the same procedures in the event that a party files a proposal for the disqualification of an arbitrator or conciliator.[40] The provisions on the amounts to be paid by the parties to cover the cost of the proceeding are the same.[41] The Convention's provisions on the place of proceedings do not differentiate between arbitration or conciliation procedures.[42]

[31] Articles 29(1) and 37(1) of the ICSID Convention.

[32] Articles 29(2) and 37(2) of the ICSID Convention.

[33] See Article 39 of the ICSID Convention for arbitration proceedings. See also Rule 1(3) of the ICSID Rules of Procedure for Arbitration Proceedings (ICSID Arbitration Rules) (April 2006). Rule 1(4) makes clear that no person who previously served as conciliator may serve as a member of the tribunal absent a party agreement.

[34] Articles 29(2)(b) and 30; and 37(2)(b) and 383 of the ICSID Convention.

[35] They 'shall be persons of high moral character and recognized competence in the fields of law, commerce, industry or finance, who may be relied upon to exercise independent judgment' with the only difference being that for ICSID arbitrators, the '[c]ompetence in the field of law shall be of particular importance'. Articles 31 and 40 of the ICSID Convention. Articles 31(2) and 40(2) refer to Article 14(1).

[36] Articles 32(1) and 41(1) of the ICSID Convention. During the drafting of the Convention, there was no separate discussion regarding the competence of commissions and those of tribunals. See ICSID (n 6) Vol. II, Part I, 399, 408, 508.

[37] Articles 32(2) and 40(2) of the ICSID Convention.

[38] Articles 33 and 44 of the ICSID Convention.

[39] Article 56(1) of the ICSID Convention. No conciliator has resigned to date.

[40] Articles 57 and 58 of the ICSID Convention. No disqualification proposal has been filed thus far.

[41] Articles 59 and 60 of the ICSID Convention.

[42] Articles 62 and 63 of the ICSID Convention.

IV. Differences between ICSID Arbitration and Conciliation

While the drafters decided to create largely identical systems, there are, given the nature of the proceedings, considerable differences between the conciliation and arbitration frameworks. The most notable difference is reflected in the functions and powers of conciliation commissions and arbitral tribunals. In contrast to an arbitral tribunal, which is empowered to decide a dispute in accordance with the applicable law, the role of a conciliation commission is to clarify the disputed issues and assist the parties in reaching a settlement.[43] Procedurally, the Convention's conciliation framework allows for more flexibility compared to its arbitration counterpart.[44]

In terms of outcomes, the Convention envisions that arbitral tribunals will render a final and binding award dealing with every question submitted.[45] Each party shall abide by and comply with such award.[46] By contrast, a conciliation commission is to issue a non-binding report, which may contain recommendations for settlement. The parties are obligated to 'give their most serious consideration' to such report.[47] The commission's reports do not benefit from the Convention's simplified enforcement regime established by Articles 53 and 54, which only apply to awards rendered by a tribunal.

Another difference relates to the use of information revealed during a proceeding. Pursuant to Article 35 of the Convention and unless agreed otherwise by the parties, neither party may invoke or rely on any views, statements, admissions, or settlement offers made by the other party during the conciliation, or invoke or rely on any recommendation or the Report issued by the commission. In contrast, the Convention does not contain a similar 'without prejudice' provision in its arbitration framework.[48]

[43] Article 34(1) of the ICSID Convention.

[44] The differences are less apparent in the ICSID Convention but are spelled out in the ICSID Rules of Procedure for Conciliation Proceedings (ICSID Conciliation Rules) (April 2006) and Arbitration Rules, namely the provisions on oral and written procedures, evidence, and the award. See chapters IV, V, and VI of the ICSID Arbitration Rules.

[45] Article 48(3) of the ICSID Convention.

[46] Article 53(1) of the ICSID Convention.

[47] Article 43 of the ICSID Convention.

[48] Non-disclosure of information in arbitrations is typically addressed by party agreement, confidentiality undertakings, and/or tribunal rulings. ICSID's obligations regarding publication of case-related information are, however, the same in arbitrations and conciliations; Regulations 23(1) and 22(1) of the ICSID Administrative and Financial Regulations.

V. ICSID Conciliation in Practice

Much has been written in the past decades about ICSID arbitration practice; however, ICSID conciliation practice has not received the same attention. Section A reviews the ICSID conciliation procedure under the Convention and the ICSID Conciliation Rules and provides examples of their practical application.

A. Institution of Conciliation Proceedings

ICSID conciliation is initiated by the filing of a request for conciliation with the Secretary-General.[49] The request provides information concerning the issues in dispute, the parties, and their written consent to ICSID conciliation.[50] A request must be registered by the Secretary-General unless the dispute is manifestly outside the jurisdiction of ICSID.[51] Eleven conciliation cases have been registered to date; eight were initiated under the ICSID Convention and two on the basis of the Additional Facility (Conciliation) Rules.[52] These cases make up 2 percent of the overall ICSID caseload, with 700 arbitrations registered by ICSID as of 28 February 2019. Two of these conciliation cases are currently pending (as of 28 February 2019).[53]

All but one of the registered conciliations sought to establish ICSID jurisdiction on the basis of investment contracts with the host state. In one case, the requesting party relied on ICSID dispute settlement provisions in a bilateral investment treaty and in an investment law. Five conciliations involved the oil, gas, and mining sector; while two cases concerned the textile industry,[54] one case involved the forestry sector, one the construction sector, and two cases related to electric power and other energy.

Nine cases involved state parties from Sub-Saharan Africa, one case involved a state party from the Central America and Caribbean region, and one case named a state in the European Union. Investors involved in conciliations asserted nationality of the Bahamas, Gabon, Germany, Greece, Togo, the United Kingdom, and the United States. Two conciliation cases were initiated by a locally incorporated

[49] Article 28(1) of the ICSID Convention.

[50] The requirements for requests for arbitration and conciliation are the same. See Articles 28(1) and 28(2) and Articles 36(1) and 36(2) and the Institution Rules.

[51] Article 28(3) of the ICSID Convention. No request for conciliation has been refused registration.

[52] The subsequent text will refer to ICSID Convention conciliation. The framework for conciliation proceedings under the Conciliation (Additional Facility) Rules is largely similar.

[53] *Hess Equatorial Guinea, Inc. and Tullow Equatorial Guinea Limited v Equatorial Guinea*, ICSID Case No. CONC(AF)/12/1, and *Xenofon Karagiannis v Albania*, ICSID Case No. CONC/16/1 (*Karagiannis*).

[54] These two cases were brought by the same investor, i.e. *SEDITEX Engineering Beratungsgesellschaft für die Textilindustrie mbH v Madagascar*, ICSID Case No. CONC/82/1 (*SEDITEX I*) and *SEDITEX Engineering Beratungsgesellschaft für die Textilindustrie mbH v Madagascar*, ICSID Case No. CONC/94/1 (*SEDITEX II*).

company relying for ICSID Convention purposes on its foreign control and the provision in Article 25(2)(b) of the ICSID Convention.[55] Ten conciliation proceedings were brought by juridical persons and one by an individual. Ten of the conciliations were commenced by a foreign investor against the state party to the dispute, and one case was initiated jointly by the investor and the state.[56]

B. Constitution of the Conciliation Commission

As contemplated by Article 29(1) of the ICSID Convention, the conciliation commission shall be constituted as soon as possible following the registration of the conciliation request.

1. Conciliator qualifications

Parties may agree on any candidate to serve as conciliator so long as this person is 'of high moral character and recognized competence in the field of law, commerce, industry or finance, who may be relied upon to exercise independent judgment'.[57] The selection of the conciliator is of great importance given the role and function of the conciliation commission: if both parties have confidence in the conciliator(s), it is likely that the process will run more smoothly, and resolution might be more likely. Of the seventeen individuals who have served on conciliation commissions, eleven have been nationals of Western Europe (Belgium, France, Germany, Portugal, Switzerland, and the UK), three were nationals of North America (Canada, Mexico, and the US), two were from the Sub-Saharan Africa region (Madagascar and Central African Republic), and one from North Africa (Egypt). Two women have been appointed as a member of a conciliation commission to date, both of them in 2018.[58] In terms of appointing authority, four conciliators have been appointed by the Chairman of the Administrative Council pursuant to the agreement of the parties, four have been appointed by investors, four by state parties, and five jointly by the parties.

The ICSID conciliation framework does not exclude candidates with the same nationality as the disputing parties, nor does it require a party agreement for such appointments.[59] It was felt that conciliators of the same nationality as the disputing parties might indeed be well placed, given their likely familiarity with the parties

[55] Article 25(2) of the ICSID Convention reads: '"National of another Contracting State" means: (b) any juridical person which had the nationality of [...] the Contracting State party to the dispute on [the date of consent] which, because of foreign control, the parties have agreed should be treated as a national of another Contracting State for the purposes of this Convention'.

[56] *Equatorial Guinea v CMS Energy Corporation and others*, ICSID Case No. CONC(AF)/12/2 (*CMS*).

[57] Articles 14(1) and 31(2) of the ICSID Convention.

[58] *Société d'Energie et d'Eau du Gabon v Gabonese Republic* (ICSID Case No. CONC/18/1, 30 March 2018) (*Société d'Energie*).

[59] But see Rule 1(3) of the ICSID Arbitration Rules for arbitrator appointments.

and issues in dispute.[60] ICSID conciliation practice indicates that co-nationals have been appointed in only three cases. All other appointments involved nationals from states other than the state of the investor or the state party to the dispute.[61]

2. Method of constitution

Unless the request for conciliation sets forth a party agreement regarding the number of conciliators and the method of their appointment, the parties shall communicate any such agreement in this regard to the Secretary-General.[62] Conciliation Rule 2 sets out the method of constituting the conciliation commission in the absence of such prior agreement.[63] If no agreement on another procedure for constituting the conciliation commission is reached within 60 days following the registration of the request, either party may inform the Secretary-General that it chooses the formula provided for in Article 29(2)(b) of the ICSID Convention,[64] i.e. that the commission shall consist of three conciliators, one appointed by each party and the third presiding conciliator to be appointed by agreement of the parties.[65]

Of the eleven conciliation proceedings registered, conciliation commissions were constituted in seven cases.[66] On average, the constitution of the commission took 13 weeks following the registration of the request, which is much faster than the time typically required for the constitution of tribunals in investment arbitration. The conciliation commissions consisted of three members in five cases.[67] Two of these three-member commissions were constituted on the basis of a party agreement.[68] In three of these cases, a party invoked the default provision set out in Article 29(2)(b) of the ICSID Convention.[69] In two further cases, parties agreed to appoint a sole conciliator.[70]

[60] ICSID (n 6) Vol. II, Part I, 266 (Preliminary Draft Convention: Working Paper for the Consultative Meetings of Legal Experts, 15 October 1963).

[61] In *SEDITEX I* (n 54), the state party appointed one of its nationals; in *Shareholders of SESAM v Central African Republic*, ICSID Case No. CONC/07/1 (*SESAM*), the investor appointed a national of the investor's home state, the state appointed one of its nationals, and the parties agreed on a presiding conciliator possessing the nationality of the investor. In *RSM Production Company v Cameroon*, ICSID Case No. CONC/11/1 (*RSM*), the investor appointed a co-national.

[62] Rule 2 of the ICSID Conciliation Rules.

[63] Conciliation Rule 2 sets out the procedure to be followed.

[64] Rule 2(3) of the ICSID Conciliation Rules.

[65] Conciliation Rule 3 sets out the applicable procedure.

[66] *CMS* (n 56); *RSM* (n 61); *SESAM* (n 61); *Togo Electricité v Togo*, ICSID Case No. CONC/05/1 (*Togo Electricité*); *SEDITEX II* (n 54); *Tesoro Petroleum Corporation v Trinidad and Tobago*, ICSID Case No. CONC/83/1 (*Tesoro*); *Société d'Energie* (n 58). In the two pending cases, no commission had been constituted at the time of drafting (1 April 2019).

[67] *RSM* (n 61); *SESAM* (n 61); *Togo Electricité* (n 66); *SEDITEX II* (n 54); *Société d'Energie* (n 58).

[68] *RSM* (n 61); *Société d'Energie* (n 58).

[69] *Togo Electricité* (n 66); *SEDITEX II* (n 54); and *SESAM* (n 61).

[70] *CMS* (n 56); *Tesoro* (n 66). Lester Nurick and Stephen J. Schnably, 'The First ICSID Conciliation: *Tesoro Petroleum Corporation v Trinidad and Tobago*' (1986) 1 (2) ICSID Review–Foreign Investment Law Journal 340 cite cost and increased efficiency for the appointment of a sole conciliator.

3. Default procedure

If the conciliation commission is not constituted within 90 days following the registration of the request, or such other period as the parties may agree,[71] either party may request that the Chairman of the Administrative Council appoint the conciliator(s) not yet appointed.[72] To date, only one such request was filed; however, as the parties subsequently agreed to terminate the proceeding no appointment was made.[73]

C. Function and Role of the Conciliation Commission

The function and role of the conciliation commission are described in Article 34(2) of the ICSID Convention and Rule 22 of the ICSID Conciliation Rules.

1. General function and role of the conciliation commission

Article 34(2) of the Convention provides that the function of the commission is 'to clarify the issues in dispute between the parties and to endeavor to bring about agreement between them upon mutually acceptable terms'. Conciliation Rule 22(1) specifies that the commission shall hear the parties and shall endeavour to obtain any information that might be helpful in exercising its function. In the often-cited *Tesoro* case, the sole conciliator considered that

> his task [...] is to examine the contentions raised by the parties, to clarify the issues, and to endeavor to evaluate their respective merits and the likelihood of their being accepted, or rejected, in Arbitration or Court proceedings, in the hope that such evaluation may assist the parties in reaching an agreed settlement.[74]

The conciliator appeared to have considered his role to be limited to a legal assessment, evaluating the merits of the parties' legal arguments based on the law as it might be applied by an arbitral tribunal or domestic court. The plain wording of Article 34 of the ICSID Convention and Rule 22 of the ICSID Conciliation Rules does not appear to limit the commission's function and evaluative powers to a mere legal assessment. Indeed, given the plain wording, it seems that the commission's task was intended to be broader. Such reading also finds support in the fact that the ICSID Convention does not contain any guiding provision on the law to be applied in conciliation proceedings.[75] Indeed, in the 1960s, the period of the Convention's drafting, international conciliation was generally defined as

[71] Parties reached an agreement to extend this period in *Tesoro* (n 66).

[72] Article 30 of the ICSID Convention. The procedure is set out in Rule 4 of the ICSID Conciliation Rules.

[73] *SEDITEX II* (n 54).

[74] Nurick and Schnably (n 70) 348.

[75] See Article 42 of the ICSID Convention for arbitrations.

> [i]ntervention in the settlement of an international dispute by a body having no political authority of its own, but enjoying the confidence of the parties to the dispute and entrusted with the task of investigating every aspect of the dispute and of proposing a solution which is not binding on the parties.[76]

The function of an international conciliation commission was further understood to encompass the examination of 'the entire dispute, including clarification of the facts and a survey of both the applicable law and the non-juridical elements'. Any recommendations by a commission 'need not be based purely on the application of law', and 'relevant legal principles may be supplementary grounds or may be absent altogether'.[77] The conciliation experiences of the World Bank in the 1950s[78] further suggests that the commission's function was indeed intended to go beyond a legal analysis when attempting to 'bring about amicable settlement on mutually acceptable terms'.

2. Settlement recommendations by the commission

Article 34(1) of the ICSID Convention specifies that the conciliation commission may 'at any stage of the proceedings and from time to time' recommend specific settlement terms to the parties. Such recommendations may be made orally or in writing and shall set out the underlying reasons.[79] In six of the seven cases in which a conciliation commission was constituted, the commissions made recommendations during the proceedings and/or in their final reports. In one case, it is publicly reported that the parties negotiated based on the commission's recommendations and reached a settlement.[80] In a number of other cases, the commission's settlement recommendations were discussed by the parties in written statements and/or oral presentations at the hearing.

3. Recommendations to preserve the status quo

Rule 22(2) of the ICSID Conciliation Rules further confers on the conciliation commission the ability to recommend measures to preserve the status quo, i.e. the conciliation commission may provide a reasoned recommendation to the parties that they refrain 'from specific acts that might aggravate the dispute'.[81] Contrary to

[76] Jean-Pierre Cot, *La conciliation internationale* (Pedone, 1968) 9, cited in Linda C. Reif, 'Conciliation as a Mechanism for the Resolution of International Economic and Business Disputes' (1990) 14 (3) Fordham International Law Journal 578, 582.

[77] Reif (n 76) 583. More recent dispute resolution theory considers that the law is not so much to serve as support for each party's 'claim' but to provide objective criteria against which each party may assess the 'fairness' of the agreed settlement. Roger Fisher and William Ury, *Getting to Yes: How to Negotiate Agreement Without Giving In* (2nd edn, Penguin, 1991) 81 ff.

[78] See section II above.

[79] Rule 22 of the ICSID Conciliation Rules. The power of the Commission to make such recommendations was not much discussed during the various drafting stages of the Convention. See (n 22) and accompanying text.

[80] Nurick and Schnably (n 70) 348.

[81] Rule 22(1) of the ICSID Conciliation Rules.

the considerable number of requests for provisional measures aimed at preserving the status quo filed in arbitrations,[82] only one conciliation commission has been requested to issue such recommendation to date.

4. Decisions of the commission

The Convention empowers the commission to decide any question of procedure not covered by the provisions in the ICSID Convention, the Conciliation Rules, or any rules agreed by the parties.[83] The Conciliation Rules specify that decisions of the commission shall be taken by a majority of votes[84] and may take the form of procedural orders.[85]

D. Parties' Obligation to Cooperate

The very nature of conciliation requires the parties' active participation. Therefore, Article 34(1) of the Convention sets out a legal obligation for the parties to 'co-operate in good faith with the commission and, in particular, at its request furnish all relevant documents, information and explanations'.[86] The parties are further required to 'use the means at their disposal' to tender witnesses and experts the conciliation commission wishes to hear[87] and to comply with any time limits.[88] Conciliation proceedings are futile if a party fails to appear or participate.[89] Such situation is recognized in Article 34(2) of the ICSID Convention and Rule 30(3) of the ICSID Conciliation Rules: 'absent the cooperation of both parties, the commission shall, following a notice to the parties, terminate the proceedings by issuing a report recording the failure of the party to appear or participate'.[90]

E. The Conciliation Procedure

Several provisions prominent in the arbitration framework are absent in the conciliation regime, such as detailed rules on evidence, default, ancillary claims, and, for obvious reasons, the award. Furthermore, the conciliation framework does not

[82] Article 47 of the ICSID Convention and Rule 39 of the ICSID Arbitration Rules. See Anthony C. Sinclair and Odysseas G. Repousis, 'An Overview of Provisional Measures in ICSID Proceedings' (2017) 32 (2) ICSID Review–Foreign Investment Law Journal 431.

[83] Article 33 of the ICSID Convention. Article 33 is similar in substance to Article 44.

[84] Rule 16(1) of the ICSID Conciliation Rules.

[85] Rule 19 of the ICSID Conciliation Rules.

[86] Rule 23(1) of the ICSID Conciliation Rules.

[87] Note A to Rule 23 of the ICSID Rules of Procedure for Conciliation Proceedings (in effect on 1 January 1968) (1968 Conciliation Rules).

[88] Rule 23(2) of the ICSID Conciliation Rules.

[89] Note D to Rule 31 of the 1968 Conciliation Rules.

[90] This is different from ICSID arbitration where a failure of a party to appear does not prevent a tribunal from rendering an award pursuant to Article 45 of the ICSID Convention.

envision any proceedings for the rectification, supplementation, interpretation, revision, or annulment of a conciliation report. The rules on written statements, supporting documentation, and evidence are overall less elaborative, allowing for a flexible conduct of the conciliation procedure.

1. Commencement of proceedings and first session

Upon the constitution of the conciliation commission, proceedings are deemed to have begun. Rule 13(1) of the ICSID Conciliation Rules contemplates that the commission's first session be held within 60 days following its constitution, unless another period is agreed to by the parties. Such sessions may be held in person or by use of remote technologies, including audio or video conferencing. In the conciliation cases registered to date, first sessions have all been conducted as in-person meetings held in London,[91] New York,[92] and Paris.[93] Five first sessions were held within the 60-day timeframe, while the 60-day timeline was extended pursuant to a party agreement in the remaining cases in which a first session was conducted.

During the first session, the basic procedural framework is determined. The matters typically addressed are listed in Rule 20 of the ICSID Conciliation Rules, including, inter alia, the language and place of proceedings, routing of communications, number of written statements, and record keeping.[94] First sessions also include discussions on the format of the written and oral procedure and a determination of the procedural calendar. A record of such first sessions is typically kept by the ICSID Secretariat in the form of a procedural order.[95]

2. The written procedure

The Conciliation Rules envision that the procedure commences with a written statement by each party to be filed within 30 days of the commission's constitution or such other timeline as the president of the commission deems appropriate. The parties' written statements may contain explanations, summaries of facts, new information, or observations on the other party's views or on the conciliation commission's recommendations.[96] Such statements were expressly envisioned to take a different form than a 'pleading' in a technical sense.[97] Additional written statements may be filed by the parties or requested by the commission at any stage to assist the commission in clarifying the issues in dispute or to seek the parties' views on proposed recommendations.[98]

[91] *Tesoro* (n 66).
[92] *CMS* (n 56).
[93] *RSM* (n 61); *SESAM* (n 61); *Togo Electricité* (n 66); *SEDITEX II* (n 54); *Société d'Energie* (n 58).
[94] The points addressed are largely similar to those of arbitration proceedings, see Rule 20 of the ICSID Arbitration Rules.
[95] Rule 19 of the ICSID Conciliation Rules.
[96] Note B to Rule 25 of the 1968 Conciliation Rules.
[97] Ibid.
[98] Rule 25(1) of the ICSID Conciliation Rules.

In all but two conciliations, the procedure commenced with a written statement by the party who had initiated the proceeding.[99] These first statements were filed within one to two months following the first session. In these cases, the initial statement was followed by a response from the respondent, filed in most cases between one to two months after the initial submission. There was a further statement by one party in one, and a full round of written submissions by both parties in another case.[100] Simultaneous submissions were filed by the parties at the outset in two cases.[101] The parties' submissions typically contained the information envisaged by the rules for such statement, at times responding to specific questions posed by the commission. In some instances, the commission requested the parties' views on settlement recommendations, which, once received, were not shared with the other party, but were meant to assist the commission in formulating further recommendation for settlement.[102]

3. Supporting documentation and evidence

The ICSID Conciliation Rules offer ample flexibility to the parties regarding the information they wish to provide to support their respective statements. Such supporting documentation may include factual exhibits, legal authorities, or written witness statements.[103] The commission is free to decide if it wishes to receive further written statements or witness or expert testimony—which may be supplied throughout the proceeding either by a party or upon the commission's request.[104] In some, but not all cases, the parties provided documentary evidence in support of their respective written submissions. Evidence in the form of witness statements or expert reports have rarely been filed in the conciliation proceedings registered to date.

4. Hearings

Hearings are expressly envisioned and 'shall take place in private and, except as the parties otherwise agree, shall remain secret'.[105] With the consent of the parties, the

[99] In *RSM* (n 61), the parties filed prior to the first written submission a request to join a third party. The conciliation commission decided the matter in a procedural order. Following this order, the claimant filed its first written submission. In *Société d'Energie* (n 58), the parties filed simultaneous submissions.

[100] *SESAM* (n 61); *CMS* (n 56); and *Tesoro* (n 66).

[101] *CMS* (n 56); *Société d'Energie* (n 58).

[102] In effect, the relevant commissions were applying the caucus principle for written submissions. For further information on caucus, see (n 112) and (n 113) and accompanying text.

[103] Rule 26(1) of the ICSID Conciliation Rules.

[104] Note D to Rule 22 of the 1968 Conciliation Rules; the parties may at any stage of the proceeding ask the commission to hear expert evidence which 'the party considers relevant'. See Conciliation Rule 28(2) and (3). Note D to Rule 28 of the 1968 Conciliation Rules. Rule 23(1) of the ICSID Conciliation Rules makes clear that the parties shall 'use the means at their disposal to enable the Commission to hear witnesses and experts whom it desires to call'; See Rule 23(1) of the ICSID Conciliation Rules, which makes clear that the parties shall 'use the means at their disposal to enable the Commission to hear witnesses and experts whom it desires to call'.

[105] Rule 27(1) of the ICSID Conciliation Rules.

commission may decide which other persons besides the parties, their representatives, and witnesses and experts may attend hearings.[106] Hearings were intended to

> permit the oral development of the arguments of the parties, the presentation of oral evidence […] and, what is more important, an opportunity for the Commission to explore informally with the parties the possibilities of settling the dispute. To preserve flexibility and adequate discretion for the Commission, these Rules contain no specific guidance as to their conduct.[107]

In five cases in which a conciliation commission was constituted, the written exchange of statements was followed by an in-person hearing spanning between one to three days.[108] In two cases, the hearing was followed by a second hearing of an additional two days.[109] In one further conciliation, the parties conducted one in-person meeting in the form of a 'Status Conference' with 'fairly extensive oral presentations of their positions and arguments'.[110] In another case, no in-person meeting occurred following the first session.[111]

5. Separate meetings/caucuses

Many alternative dispute resolution methods envision confidential meetings between the third-party neutral and one of the disputing parties. Such meetings are typically referred to as a 'caucus' and are considered an effective tool to break an impasse or to obtain further information that one party is reluctant to share openly.[112] While not expressly mentioned in the ICSID conciliation framework, such an approach was contemplated by the drafters of the Conciliation Rules.[113] To date, more than half of the conciliation commissions have conducted such caucuses in the course of the conciliation proceeding.

6. Site visits

A conciliation commission may, at any stage of the proceeding, visit the place connected with the dispute, provided that the parties may participate.[114] Parties are, in fact, obliged to facilitate such site visits.[115] In the conciliation cases registered to date, only one such site visit was conducted.[116]

106 Rule 27(2) of the ICSID Conciliation Rules.
107 Note B to Rule 27 of the 1968 Conciliation Rules.
108 *SEDITEX II* (n 54): 1 day; *Togo Electricité* (n 66): 2 days; *RSM* (n 61): 2 days followed by another 2 days approximately 6 weeks later; *CMS* (n 56): 3 days; *Société d'Energie* (n 58): 2 days.
109 *SEDITEX II* (n 54) and *CMS* (n 56).
110 Nurick and Schnably (n 70) 347–8.
111 *SESAM* (n 61).
112 Typically, any information obtained in such meetings may only be disclosed to the other party with the express consent of the disclosing party.
113 Note A to Rule 22 of the 1968 Conciliation Rules.
114 Rule 22(3)(c) of the ICSID Conciliation Rules.
115 Rule 23(1) of the ICSID Conciliation Rules.
116 *CMS* (n 56).

F. Objections to Jurisdiction

The function of ICSID is defined in Chapter II of the Convention, entitled 'Jurisdiction of the Centre'. As noted, the drafters decided that Article 25 was to apply to both arbitration and conciliation proceedings. In the early drafting stages, it was debated to submit the question of a conciliation commission's 'jurisdiction' to an arbitral tribunal; however, that proposal was later dropped.[117] The concept of 'jurisdiction of a conciliation commission' may give pause. The idea behind a commission's jurisdiction might perhaps best be explained as relating to the commission's 'competence' and rooted in the states' desire to define the scope of the international forum for the resolution of investment disputes between private parties and states which they wished to create in the 1960s.

1. Procedure

Pursuant to Article 32(1) of the ICSID Convention, the commission shall be the judge of its own competence.[118] Any objection by a party to the commission's competence is to be 'made as early as possible', and no later than the earlier of that party's first written statement or the first hearing.[119] Upon the raising of an objection, 'the proceeding on the merits shall be suspended'.[120] However, the commission may decide to join the jurisdictional objection(s) to the merits of the dispute. Parties have raised objections to jurisdiction in only two conciliations; in both cases these objections were joined to the examination of the disputed issues.[121]

2. Decision

It is clear from Rule 29(5) of the ICSID Conciliation Rules that a finding by the commission that the dispute is *not* within the commission's competence is to be rendered in the form of a reasoned report.[122] However, the conciliation framework is silent as to the form and nature of a commission's finding that it *has* jurisdiction. The drafting history of the ICSID Convention is inconclusive in this regard.[123] In practice, conciliation commissions' decisions on competence have been included in their final reports, which are non-binding absent a party agreement to the contrary.[124]

[117] ICSID (n 6) Vol. II, Part I, 156.

[118] Rule 29(2) of the ICSID Conciliation Rules establishes that the commission may consider its competence at any stage of the proceeding, and also on its own initiative.

[119] Unless the facts on which the objection is based are unknown to the party at that time. Rule 29(1) of the ICSID Conciliation Rules.

[120] Rule 29(3) of the ICSID Conciliation Rules.

[121] *SESAM* (n 61) and *Tesoro* (n 66).

[122] Rule 29(5) of the ICSID Conciliation Rules.

[123] Christoph H. Schreuer, Loretta Malintoppi, August Reinisch, and Anthony Sinclair (eds), *The ICSID Convention: A Commentary* (2nd edn, CUP, 2009) 439, Article 32, para. 3.

[124] For publicly available information, see Nurick and Schnably (n 70) 348.

G. Outcomes

The ICSID Convention envisions a conciliation proceeding to conclude with a report by the commission.

1. Commission reports

Rule 32 of the ICSID Conciliation Rules specifies the formal content of a conciliation report, which must include a precise designation of each party and its representatives; the names of the conciliator(s); a statement regarding the commission's constitution; the method of constitution applied; the dates and place of sittings; and a summary of the proceeding.[125] The report shall also record any agreement of the parties concerning the disclosure of information in subsequent proceedings pursuant to Article 35 of the Convention.[126]

If the parties reached a settlement on some or all issues in dispute, the commission shall note the disputed matters and record the fact that the parties have reached a settlement agreement. The terms of the parties' settlement shall only be included in the report upon the parties' request.[127] If the commission determines that 'there is no likelihood of agreement between the parties', the commission shall merely note the submission of the dispute to conciliation and record the parties' failure to reach agreement.[128] If a party fails to appear or participate in the proceeding, the commission shall, after notice to the parties, issue a report noting the failure of the party to appear or participate.[129]

If a conciliation commission determines that the dispute does not fall within its competence, it shall issue a report to that effect which states the commission's reasons for such finding.[130] Reports by conciliation commissions have been issued in seven cases. One report noted the parties' settlement agreement and five reports recorded the parties' failure to reach agreement. In one further case, the commission noted the parties' agreement on some, but not all, issues.

2. Discontinuance

Conciliations may be discontinued pursuant to Regulation 14(3)(d) of the ICSID Administrative and Financial Regulations for failure of the parties to pay the advances required to defray the costs of the proceeding. No conciliation case has been discontinued on this basis to date. The ICSID Conciliation Rules do not contain

[125] Rule 32(1) of the ICSID Conciliation Rules. Since the commission's report does not have binding effect on the disputing parties (unless the parties agree otherwise), the formal requirements are less strict than those applying to an award by an ICSID tribunal. See Rule 47 of the ICSID Arbitration Rules.

[126] Article 35 of the ICSID Convention and Rule 32(2) of the ICSID Conciliation Rules.

[127] Rule 30(1) of the ICSID Conciliation Rules.

[128] Rule 30(2) of the ICSID Conciliation Rules.

[129] Rule 30(3) of the ICSID Conciliation Rules. For a default award in ICSID arbitration, see (n 90).

[130] Rule 29(5) of the ICSID Conciliation Rules.

other discontinuance provisions, in particular, none similar to ICSID Arbitration Rules 43–45, which envision the discontinuance of an arbitration proceeding either pursuant to a party request or due to the parties' failure to act. Parties in two conciliations requested the discontinuance of the proceeding prior to the constitution of the conciliation commission and such discontinuance was recorded by the Secretary-General.[131]

H. Confidentiality and without Prejudice Principle

As noted, Article 35 of the ICSID Convention provides that neither disputing party may 'invoke or rely on any views expressed or statements or admissions or offers of settlement made' in the course of the conciliation, unless this is agreed to by the disputing parties.[132] This prohibition also includes the report or any recommendations made by the conciliation commission.[133] The limitation on the use of information obtained in a conciliation was intended to afford parties the opportunity to move beyond their legal positioning and allow the parties to freely negotiate.[134] Any agreements reached by the parties regarding the disclosure of information are to be reflected in the commission's report.[135]

To date, there is little public information on conciliations available besides the information provided by ICSID on its website[136] or in selected publications.[137] In one case, the parties agreed to provide information about the proceeding in a press release. Counsel for the government subsequently published an article providing considerable insights into the procedure and its outcome.[138]

[131] *SEDITEX I* (n 54) and *TG World Petroleum Limited v Niger*, ICSID Case No. CONC/03/1 (*TG World*). In *TG World*, the parties had reached a settlement of their dispute, see *TG World* in ICSID Annual Report 2005 (ICSID 2005) 29.

[132] Article 35 of the ICSID Convention. Article 35 contains an express reference to arbitration or court proceedings, but also contains a general 'or otherwise' provision which clarifies the broad scope of the concept.

[133] Ibid. The principle is also expressly provided for in the context of hearings. Hearings are to be held in private and, except as the parties otherwise agree, shall remain secret; Rule 27(1) of the ICSID Conciliation Rules. This extends the concept of confidentiality to also apply to persons other than the disputing parties present during the hearing.

[134] Schreuer (n 123) 453, Article 35, para. 3.

[135] Rule 32(2) of the ICSID Conciliation Rules.

[136] Regulation 23 of the ICSID Administrative and Financial Regulations provides that the ICSID Secretariat shall maintain registers containing significant data on ICSID conciliation proceedings. Such registers are accessible to the general public and are available in the 'Cases' section of the ICSID website.

[137] E.g. Nurick and Schnably (n 70); Nassib G. Ziadé, 'ICSID Conciliation' (1996) 13 (2) News from ICSID 3.

[138] Nurick and Schnably (n 70).

I. Representation, Procedural Languages, Duration, and Costs

Parties to ICSID conciliations may be represented or assisted by agents, counsel, or advocates.[139] Investors sought representation by external counsel in all conciliations registered to date; whereas state parties relied on external counsel in all but two conciliation proceedings.[140]

Conciliations may be conducted in one or two of the official languages of ICSID, which are English, French, and Spanish.[141] Parties may also agree to use another language with the approval of the conciliation commission.[142] Of the conciliation cases registered to date, six have been conducted in French, four in English, and one in English and French.

ICSID conciliation proceedings took on average 18 months from the date of registration to the date of conclusion of the proceeding, which is significantly shorter than the average duration of an arbitration. The commission reports were issued between 4 weeks and 14 months following the last procedural step.

Provisions on costs of conciliations are set out in Chapter VI of the Convention, and the ICSID Schedule of Fees.[143] Article 61(1) of the Convention provides that the cost of a conciliation proceeding 'shall be borne equally by the parties and that each party shall bear any other expenses it incurs in connection with the proceedings'.[144] The current fee for lodging requests for conciliation is 25,000 US dollars, which is non-refundable.[145] Conciliators are entitled to receive a fee of 3,000 US dollars per day of meetings or other work performed, as well as subsistence allowances.[146] ICSID's administrative fee is 42,000 US dollars per year. The average cost of concluded conciliation proceedings is 182,000 US dollars, i.e. 91,000 US dollars per party.[147] This includes the fees and expenses of the commission, the cost of the proceeding, and ICSID's administrative fee. Legal fees and expenses by the parties are not included.

[139] Rule 18 of the ICSID Conciliation Rules.

[140] *Karagiannis* (n 53) and *TG World* (n 131).

[141] Regulation 34(1) of the ICSID Administrative and Financial Regulations. Rule 21(2) of the ICSID Conciliation Rules.

[142] Rule 21(1) of the ICSID Conciliation Rules.

[143] The ICSID Schedule of Fees is available at https://icsid.worldbank.org/en/Pages/icsiddocs/Schedule-of-Fees.aspx.

[144] Article 61(1) of the ICSID Convention. Whereas in arbitration proceedings, unless otherwise agreed by the parties, the Arbitral Tribunal shall assess the expenses incurred and decide how and by whom the parties' expenses and the costs of the arbitration shall be paid, Article 61(2) of the ICSID Convention.

[145] ICSID (n 143) para. 1.

[146] Ibid., para. 3.

[147] In contrast, recent studies identify that the average cost per party for an investment arbitration, including counsel fees, ranges between 4 to 6 million US dollars. See Matthew Hodgson, 'Counting the Costs of Investment Treaty Arbitration' (24 March 2014) *Global Arbitration Review*; Matthew Hodgson, 'Costs in Investment Treaty Arbitration: The Case for Reform' (2014) 11 (1) Transnational Dispute Management, https://www.transnational-dispute-management.com/article.asp?key=2088.

J. Relationship between ICSID Conciliation and ICSID Arbitration

As mentioned, ICSID conciliation and arbitration are provided on equal footing, and it is left to the disputing parties to decide in their consent to ICSID dispute settlement which of these procedures they wish to pursue, or whether they wish to combine both.[148] Most ICSID cases have either been conciliations or arbitrations; however, in three cases, parties first conducted a conciliation followed by an arbitration.[149] One of these subsequent arbitrations resulted in an award by the tribunal,[150] one further arbitration was discontinued at the joint request of the parties,[151] and one arbitration resulted in an award embodying the parties' settlement agreement.[152] Under the ICSID framework, parties could, if desired, initiate an ICSID conciliation while an ICSID arbitration is ongoing, and, should such conciliation be unsuccessful, continue with the arbitration process. This option is specifically provided for in Article 26 of the ICSID Convention.[153]

In 1984, ICSID introduced the possibility for the parties to request a 'pre-hearing conference' with the tribunal to consider the issues in dispute with the view to reaching an amicable settlement. Arbitration Rule 21(2) has not been widely used in practice. However, in one case, parties requested the tribunal's assistance during their settlement discussions. The parties agreed for the president to serve as mediator for a specific period, following which the parties agreed to report to the entire tribunal on the progress achieved. The parties eventually agreed on some issues and requested the tribunal to decide the remaining matters.[154]

VI. Amicable Dispute Settlement: An Outlook

Some commentators have suggested that the ICSID conciliation framework is not sufficiently flexible and too closely resembles the arbitration framework.[155] While

[148] See (n 19) and accompanying text.

[149] *Togo Electricité* (n 66) and *Togo Electricité and GDF-Suez Energie Services v Togo*, ICSID Case No ARB/06/7 (*Togo Electricité and GDF-Suez Energie Services*); *RSM* (n 61); and *RSM Production Company v Cameroon*, ICSID Case No. ARB/13/14 (*RSM Production Company*).

[150] *Togo Electricité and GDF-Suez Energie Services* (n 149).

[151] *RSM Production Company* (n 149).

[152] *Société d'Energie* (n 58); *Société d'Energie et d'Eau du Gabon and Veolia Africa v Gabonese Republic* (ICSID Case No. ARB/18/36, 16 October 2018).

[153] Article 26 reads: 'Consent of the parties to *arbitration under this Convention* shall, *unless otherwise stated*, be *deemed* consent to such arbitration to the exclusion of any other remedy' (emphasis added). Article 26 creates a presumption; however, parties may explicitly address the relationship to other remedies.

[154] See Eloïse Obadia, 'How Proactive Arbitrators Really Are in Conducting Arbitral Proceedings: An ICSID Perspective' (1999) 16 (2) News from ICSID 8, 10.

[155] E.g. Michael E. Schneider, 'Investor-State Disputes: Moving Beyond Arbitration', in Laurence Boisson de Chazournes, Marcelo G. Kohen, and Georges E. Viñuales (eds), *Diplomatic and Judicial Means of Dispute Settlement* (Brill, 2013) 120, 148; 'Mediation of Investor–State Conflicts' (2014) 127 (8) Harvard Law Review 2543.

it is true that the institution of conciliation proceedings as well as the default procedure for the constitution of the commission and the ability to challenge the commission' competence is almost identical to the Convention's arbitration provisions, the procedure before the conciliation commission is not, and it builds in ample flexibility. For example, there is substantial room to tailor the scheduling and scope of written statements, combination of oral hearings and written exchanges, joint meetings and caucuses, or shared or confidential written exchanges on settlement recommendations. The ICSID Conciliation Rules allow for many ways to conduct the proceeding, and can accommodate the needs of the parties and the circumstances of their dispute.[156] As set out above, the commission's role was not intended to be reduced to a legal evaluation, but to provide comprehensive assistance for the parties to find an amicable resolution to the disputed issues.

In 2016, ICSID commenced a Rules amendment project and sought public and state input on potential changes. On 3 August 2018, the ICSID Secretariat proposed comprehensive changes to modernize its rules for resolving disputes between foreign investors and states, including a comprehensive working paper outlining proposed changes to the ICSID conciliation framework under the Convention and the Additional Facility.[157] On 15 March 2019, the ICSID Secretariat published its second working paper on proposals for rule amendments (Working Paper #2).[158] The paper builds on the proposals that were originally published in August 2018 (Working Paper #1) and follows extensive consultations with ICSID member States and the public.

The proposed amendments to the ICSID conciliation process aim to make the rules more user-friendly and the conciliation process even more flexible. It is further proposed to integrate the Conciliation Rules into the multilateral framework that is being created by the Convention on the Recognition and Enforcement for Mediated Settlements (Singapore Convention).[159] Working Paper #1 proposed to restructure the Conciliation Rules and introduce a chapter on general provisions at the outset, addressing matters related to parties and party representation, routing of communications, procedural languages, payment of advances, and cost of the conciliation, as well as confidentiality and disclosure of information in subsequent proceedings.

The proposed provisions relating to the appointment of conciliators and constitution of the commission have been updated; it has been clarified that the method of constitution of the commission needs to be determined before any action may

[156] For example, in one conciliation, the parties reportedly agreed to apply the 2012 International Bar Association's Investor–State Mediation Rules to the proceeding.

[157] World Bank, 'Proposals for Amendment of the ICSID Rules' (2018) Working Paper 1, Vol. 3, https://icsid.worldbank.org/en/amendments/Pages/Proposals/Working-Paper.aspx. The text addresses only the proposed changes to the ICSID Convention conciliation framework.

[158] World Bank, 'Proposals for Amendment of the ICSID Rules' (2019) Working Paper 2, https://icsid.worldbank.org/en/Documents/Vol_1.pdf, 335 ff, 625 ff.

[159] See Chapter 19, this volume.

be taken on the appointment of conciliators. Further, parties may request the assistance of the Secretary-General with any of the appointments to be made. Each conciliator is asked to provide a comprehensive declaration of independence and impartiality and the parties are asked to provide third-party funding disclosure. A provision has been added identifying that a conciliator may step down prior to constitution of the commission, a situation not explicitly addressed in the current rules. The rules regarding the disqualification of conciliators have further been streamlined and provide timelines for the parties' observations on the proposal. Conciliators may resign at any time, but must provide reasons.

Most changes have been made to the chapter dealing with the conduct of the conciliation. The role of the commission remains unchanged as set out in Article 34 of the ICSID Convention. It is clarified that recommendations by the commission require prior consultations with the parties and that the recommendations may be made orally or in writing. Parties also may request reasons to be provided. This change is intended to make the process less formal and more time-efficient.

The commission may request that the parties provide information, explanations, or documents, and site visits may be conducted with the parties' consent. It has been codified that the commission may further communicate with the parties jointly or separately. The duties of the commission have been specified, i.e. that the commission shall treat the parties equally, act expeditiously, and provide the parties a reasonable opportunity to the parties to participate. The parties are to cooperate with the commission, and provide the requested information or explanations and give utmost consideration to the commission's recommendation—a duty also set out in Article 34 of the Convention.

The process commences with written statements by each party, filed simultaneously within 30 days of the commission's constitution. Such initial statements shall contain a description of the issues in dispute and the parties' views on them and on procedure. The initial written statements are intended to assist with the conduct of the first session and to provide a basis for the commission, immediately following the first session, to commence its work on the issues in dispute between the parties.

The items to be discussed at the first session have been expanded, and include, inter alia, any agreement between the parties (i) concerning the treatment of information disclosed by one party in caucus to the other party; (ii) not to initiate or pursue during the conciliation any other proceeding in respect of the dispute; (iii) concerning the application of prescription or limitation periods that toll during the conciliation; and (iv) pursuant to Article 35 of the Convention. In addition, each party is to identify at the first session or shortly thereafter a representative authorized to settle the dispute and to describe the process required to implement a settlement. This provision aims at assisting to facilitate the conclusion of a settlement agreement, as often those who are representatives in the conciliation differ from those who are involved in the implementation of an eventual settlement agreement.

'Hearings' are now called 'meetings' between the commission and the parties and are more flexible in scope and conduct.

The process regarding preliminary objections has been updated to remove the automatic suspension of the conciliation upon the raising of an objection. It is further clarified that the non-raising of an objection to jurisdiction in a conciliation is covered by the without-prejudice principle set out in Article 35 of the Convention. In terms of the termination, provisions have been added that cover the discontinuance of the conciliation prior to the commission's constitution upon party request or failure of the parties to act. In addition, it has been clarified that the conciliation may be terminated by party agreement following the commission's constitution. In terms of the commission's report, a provision has been included to the effect that the complete and signed settlement agreement may be embodied in the commission's report. This provision is intended to allow the parties to benefit from the enforcement mechanism of the draft Singapore Convention.

The proposed changes to the Conciliation Rules have been positively received by ICSID member states and the public. The ICSID Administrative Council may adopt these rules at its annual meeting in October 2019.

Amicable settlement of investor–state disputes at ICSID goes beyond the conciliation framework: about 40 percent of ICSID arbitrations are either settled amicably or otherwise discontinued.[160] While investors most often pursue the arbitration route, this does not necessarily mean that an amicable settlement is per se impossible; rather, it may be settlement 'in the shadow of arbitration'. States' desire for amicable settlement of investment disputes is reflected in the provisions on conciliation and mediation included in a number of bilateral or multilateral treaties. A new generation of treaties refer specifically to mediation and as an alternative or additional means of solving investment disputes.[161] ICSID, with its considerable practical expertise in the administration of investor–state dispute settlement procedures under its own and other procedural frameworks, appears to be best suited to provide assistance to states and investors to amicably settle their disputes—either through the well-established arbitration or conciliation route, or through investment mediation under ICSID's newly proposed ICSID Mediation Rules.[162]

[160] ICSID, 'The ICSID Caseload-Statistics' (Issue 2017-2), https://icsid.worldbank.org/en/Pages/resources/ICSID-Caseload-Statistics.aspx.

[161] For example, the EU–Canada Comprehensive Economic and Trade Agreement (CETA) provides a standalone mediation provision. Article 10.15 of the Central American Free Trade Agreement (CAFTA) provides that the disputing parties shall 'initially seek to resolve the [investment] dispute through consultation and negotiation, which may include the use of non-binding, third-party procedures such as conciliation and mediation'. Article 26 of the Investment Agreement for the Common Investment Area of the Common Market for Eastern and Southern Africa (COMESA) requires a six-month cooling-off period, during which the parties 'shall seek the assistance of a mediator', unless an alternative method of dispute settlement is agreed upon.

[162] World Bank, 'Proposals for Amendment of the ICSID Rules — Working Paper' (2018) Working Paper Vol. 3, https://icsid.worldbank.org/en/Documents/X.Amendments_Vol_3_AFMR.pdf 765 ff.

8

Political Risk Insurance and Mediation

Kaj Hobér

I. Introduction

The general world trend toward market liberalization also embraces foreign investment, direct and indirect. Foreign direct investment will continue to grow in developing nations. Although developing nations may be the most interesting for investors, they also, typically, present the greatest amount of risk due to unstable legal, social, economic, and political environments. An investor can often calculate with some precision the *commercial* risk of both domestic and foreign investments. However, the *political* risk of international investment, particularly in developing countries, is usually more difficult to foresee.

Foreign investments are different in nature from domestic investments and from international trade transactions. The international nature of an investment means that the investor will, to varying degrees, be dependent on the relationship with the host state and the economic, political, and legal frameworks provided by it. Foreign investments usually result in a long-term relationship with the host state. At any rate, the relationship is more long-term than a typical trade transaction, which usually is limited to a one-off exchange of goods and money.

The longer the foreign investment lasts, the more dependent the investor will be on the relationship with the host state. Once the investor has completed its investment, and the project is up and running, the critical risk for the investor is that the host state might change the rules of the game, e.g. by introducing new legislation or taking other measures, which may affect the benefits of the project. It is in such a situation that the question of political risk comes to the forefront.

This chapter explores the role mediation might play in the context of political risk insurance. Its focus is not on mediation per se: its rules, principles, and techniques. This is amply covered by other contributors to this volume. The focus is rather on identifying situations in the political risk insurance context where mediation could be used to resolve disputes. Section V discusses such situations. In order to be able to identify these situations, it is necessary first to go through a few preliminary steps. First, Section II addresses the definition of political risk. Section III then discusses methods of protecting against political risk. Finally, Section IV briefly describes some of the leading providers of political risk insurance.

II. What Is Political Risk?

There does not seem to be any generally accepted definition of political risk. At the conceptual level, however, it is submitted that political risk is typically the likelihood of the host state taking extraordinary measures negatively affecting foreign investments.

In broad terms, there are three basic categories of political risk. First, expropriation in different forms, which includes indirect and creeping expropriation, as well as the situation where the state can be said to have expropriated contractual rights by terminating a contract to which the state itself is a party. Second, currency risk, i.e. the risk that the host state will prohibit the investor from converting local currency into hard currency, or that it will increase controls of the exchange of money. Issues concerning currency are typically under the control of the host state. It should be pointed out that government-caused inflation and devaluation of currency are usually viewed as commercial rather than political risk. Third, political violence, which includes war, terrorism, revolution, insurrection, civil strike, and sabotage. These events are characterized as political risks, even though the host state usually has relatively little control over them.

The Multilateral Investment Guarantee Agency (MIGA), the leading international foreign direct investment agency, broadly defines political risk as the probability of disruption of the operations of multinational enterprises by political forces or events, whether they occur in host countries or result from changes in the international environment.[1] Political risk is defined as the possibility that political decisions, or political or social events, in a country will affect the business climate in such a way that investors lose a portion of their investment or expected return.[2]

Accordingly:

> Political risk is distinct from commercial risk, which refers to those risks arising in the normal course of business. Commercial risks include, but are not limited to: the prices of inputs and outputs; new technologies; legal risk; financial risks such as interest rate and foreign exchange risk, liquidity management and capital structure decisions; production risk; market demand and general changes in the overall competitive situation.[3]

Closely connected with the definition of political risk is how to evaluate or measure it. Over the years several models have been developed with a view to trying to

[1] MIGA, World Investment and Political Risk Report, 2010, 19 citing from MIGA, World Investment and Political Risk Report, 2009; for a brief account of MIGA, see 7 ff.

[2] S.E.A. Global Enterprises Corporation, 'What is Political Risk', available at http://www.sea-enterprises.com/consulting/sea-consulting/political-risk (Adapted from Llewellyn Howell, *The Handbook of Country and Political Risk Analysis* (3rd edn, PRS Group, 2001).

[3] Ibid.

evaluate the nature, likelihood, and degree of political risks. Generally speaking, these models try to identify and attach values to factors that may affect an investment. Such factors would typically include: the political stability of the host state, including local political structures as well as familiarity with local political leaders and their respective policies; the legal structure and infrastructure of the host state, including familiarity with local legislation in areas such as investment laws, taxation, labour regulations, intellectual property, and anti-trust legislation, as well as an evaluation of the local court system and the judiciary; a review of investment protection treaties—bilateral as well as multilateral—signed by the host state; and long-term and short-term economic stability of the country, including an analysis of inflation rates, price stability, balance of payment problems, sovereign debt, and foreign exchange problems.

While these models are undoubtedly both helpful and useful, as well as necessary, it is probably impossible to avoid a relatively high degree of subjectivity with respect to the individual investment. At the end of the day, the evaluation of the political risks very much depends on the ambitions and objectives of the given investor with respect to the specific investment. At a minimum, however, once political risks have been identified, most investors seek to obtain some form of protection against them.

III. Protection against Political Risk

There are several ways for an investor to protect itself against political risks. Already when planning a foreign direct investment (FDI) the investor should seek to structure its transaction—both from a commercial and legal perspective—so as to minimize any exposure to political risks. Depending on the investment in question this can be done in different ways, e.g. by investing together with a local partner in a jointly owned company, or in other forms of joint ventures, thereby—at least theoretically—reducing the risk of the host state interfering with the investment. Another approach would be to minimize the number and value of assets physically located in the host state.

With respect to certain investments, it may be possible to enter into an investor-state agreement, a so-called 'investment agreement', with the host state. Such an agreement would involve the host state directly in the investment and may be used to minimize the political risks involved. Needless to say, the level of protection obtained through such agreements will depend on the specific clauses included therein.

At the international law level, investors enjoy protection under customary international law and under investment protection treaties, bilateral as well as multilateral. The heart and soul of most investment protection treaties—be they bilateral or multilateral—is protection against political risk. There are several areas where there is substantial and important interaction between political risk insurance and investment protection treaties. First, it is the practice of many insurers to ascertain whether there is an investment protection treaty in place with the host state. Some insurers rely on such a treaty as a condition for granting political risk insurance.[4] Secondly, many investment protection treaties have subrogation clauses allowing the insurer having paid insurance compensation to take up the investor's claim against the host state.[5] Subrogation rights can also be regulated in separate agreements. Thirdly, determination by insurers concerning claims from insured investors often address public international law issues, which may be of relevance to, and are sometimes taken into account by, arbitral tribunals sitting under investment protection treaties.

A simple, direct, and effective method of obtaining protection against political risks is for the investor to purchase political risk insurance. In many respects, political risk insurance is similar to ordinary business risk insurance. It is available from a number of sources, including private insurers, state-sponsored insurance agencies, and international agencies.

National state-sponsored insurance programmes are usually tied to the promotion of the national economy of the investor. This means that protection is typically granted only to national companies and usually only to their investments in countries that are friendly with the host state.[6]

As a rule, private insurers have more flexibility than government-sponsored agencies. Private insurers can thus adapt their products to the specific needs of the individual investor. This means that both coverage and price can vary considerably from one private insurer to another. The private sector, on the other hand, seems to be less willing to provide coverage for longer periods of time. It is not unusual for governmental sponsored agencies to offer protection for up to twenty years, and beyond, whereas this seems to be unusual in the private sector.[7]

While political risk insurance does provide certain coverage for investors, it does not always cover investments existing at the time of the entry into force of the insurance contract, or all risks that are commonly protected by investment protection treaties. However, unlike in some investment arbitrations, political risk insurance does not present the jurisdictional hurdles sometimes faced by investors, or factors such as challenges to party-appointed arbitrators and annulment procedures that may significantly prolong the arbitral process. Similar to bilateral and multilateral investment treaties, political risk insurance not only benefits the investor by securing protection for its investment, but also benefits the host state by encouraging foreign direct investment from potential investors.

[4] Cf. e.g. § 2197(a) USC, with respect to OPIC.

[5] See, e.g. Article 15 of the Energy Charter Treaty.

[6] Cf. e.g. http:/www.agaportal.de/en/dia/grundlagen/garantievoraussetzungen.html.

[7] Cf. e.g. Zurich Insurance, where the time period is usually not longer than 15 years; https://www.zurichna.com/en/prodsols/trade/politicalrisk.

IV. Political Risk Insurance Providers

There are several actors providing political risk insurance. At the international level, MIGA is the most important actor. At the national level, the Overseas Private Investment Corporation (OPIC) in the United States plays an important role, as does the German equivalent, Investment Guarantees, which is managed by PricewaterhouseCoopers–Euler Hermes. Both OPIC and Hermes are backed by their respective governments. In addition, there is currently a multitude of private-sector providers of political insurance.[8] In order to properly understand the environment and scenarios under which mediation may be relevant, it is necessary to have a basic understanding of how the providers of political risk insurance function.

A. MIGA

MIGA was created to promote foreign investment by establishing a method to provide political risk insurance to companies whose governments did not have national programmes affording such coverage and to complement those that did provide coverage.[9] The draft convention establishing the Agency was submitted to the Board of Governors of the International Bank for Reconstruction and Development on 11 October 1985, and went into effect on 12 April 1988 (the 'MIGA Convention' or the 'Convention'). It entered into force upon ratification by five industrialized countries (referred to in the MIGA Convention as Category 1 countries) and fifteen developing countries (Category 2 countries), which were required to subscribe to one-third of MIGA's capital (approximately USD360 million).[10] Pursuant to Article 4(a), membership is open to all members of the World Bank and to Switzerland.

The MIGA Convention was amended by the Council of Governors of MIGA; the amendment was effective as of 14 November 2010. Under its amended provisions, Article 12(v) now enables the Agency to cover existing investments 'where there is an improvement or enhancement of the underlying project or the investor otherwise demonstrates medium- or long-term commitment to the project and

[8] One estimate indicates that in 2016 there were approximately seventy private political risk insurers; see Clint Peinhardt and Todd Allee, 'Political Risk Insurance as Dispute Resolution' (2016) 7 Journal of International Dispute Resolution 208.

[9] Doak R. Bishop, James Crawford, and W. Michael Reisman (eds), *Foreign Investment Disputes: Cases, Materials and Commentary* (Kluwer Law International, 2005) 491–2; more information is available at http://www.miga.org.

[10] See Article 61 of the MIGA Convention; S. Linn Williams, 'Political and Other Risk Insurance: OPIC, MIGA, EXIMBANK and Other Providers' (1993) 5 Pace International Law Review 59, 82.

the Agency is satisfied that the project continues to have a high developmental impact in the host country.'

The object and purpose of MIGA is to support the flow of investments for productive purposes among its member countries, and in particular to *developing member countries*.[11] To reach this objective, the founders provided MIGA with the authority to issue guarantees against political risks in respect of investments between member countries.[12]

Article 11 of the Convention sets forth the specific political risks against which the Agency may guarantee eligible investments, including currency inconvertibility and transfer restriction,[13] expropriation and similar measures,[14] breach of contract,[15] war, terrorism, and civil disturbance.[16] In addition, the Board of Directors may, by special majority, extend the coverage beyond these specific political risks.[17] It is important to note that investors cannot be insured against the risks of devaluation or depreciation of currency.[18] Furthermore, a loss is not covered if the host government action or omission has been agreed to by the investor, or if the host government action or omission occurred before the conclusion of the guarantee agreement.[19]

Pursuant to Article 11(a)(i) of the Convention, coverage may be provided for losses arising from any introduction, attributable to the host government, of restrictions on the conversion of local currency into a freely usable currency, or on the foreign currency into which the local currency was converted.[20] This includes a failure of the host government to act within a reasonable period of time on an application by a holder for such a transfer.[21]

[11] The Convention Establishing the Multilateral Investment Guarantee Agency, 11 October 1985, 1508 UNTS 99, Article 2 (MIGA Convention) (emphasis added).

[12] Preamble, Article 2(a) of the MIGA Convention.

[13] Article 11(a)(i) of the MIGA Convention ('any introduction attributable to the host government of restrictions on the transfer outside the host country of its currency into a freely usable currency or another currency acceptable to the holder of the guarantee, including a failure of the host government to act within a reasonable period of time on an application by such holder for such transfer.').

[14] Article 11(a)(ii) of the MIGA Convention ('any legislative action or administrative action or omission attributable to the host government which has the effect of depriving the holder of a guarantee of his ownership or control of, or a substantial benefit from, his investment, with the exception of non-discriminatory measures of general application which governments normally take for the purpose of regulating economic activity in their territories.').

[15] Article 11(a)(iii) of the MIGA Convention ('any repudiation or breach by the host government of a contract with the holder of a guarantee, when (a) the holder of a guarantee does not have recourse to a judicial or arbitral forum to determine the claim of repudiation or breach, or (b) a decision by such forum is not rendered within such reasonable period of time as shall be prescribed in the contracts of guarantee pursuant to the Agency's regulations, or (c) such a decision cannot be enforced.').

[16] Article 11(a)(iv) of the MIGA Convention ('any military action or civil disturbance in any territory of the host country to which this Convention shall be applicable as provided in Article 66'); see also MIGA's Non-Honoring of Sovereign Financial Obligations Product (July 2011) available at https://www.miga.org/sites/default/files/2018-06/NHFObrief%20%281%29.pdf.

[17] Article 11(b) of the MIGA Convention.

[18] Ibid.

[19] Article 11(c)(i) and (ii) of the MIGA Convention.

[20] Section 1.23 of the MIGA Operational Regulations (22 June 1988 as amended by the Board of Directors through 4 February 2011) (MIGA Operational Regulations).

[21] See Sections 1.24–1.25 of the MIGA Operational Regulations.

As set forth in Article 11(a)(ii) of the Convention, coverage may be provided for losses arising from measures attributable to the host government which have the effect of depriving the guarantee owner of his ownership or control of, or a substantial benefit from, his investment. This includes, but is not limited to, measures of expropriation, nationalization, confiscation, sequestration, seizure, attachment, and freezing of assets.[22] With respect to creeping expropriation, coverage may also be provided against a series of measures by the host government, which in their combined effect are expropriatory.[23]

In order to qualify for political risk insurance under the Convention, certain requirements must be met with respect to the type of investor, the resources invested, and the type of the investment.[24] Investors eligible to receive a guarantee may be either natural or juridical persons.[25] Pursuant to Article 13, eligible investors include a national of a member other than the host country, an entity incorporated with the principal place of business in a member country, or the majority of its capital owned by a member or members or nationals thereof, and nationals of the host country if the assets to be invested are obtained from abroad.[26] Investments by state-owned corporations are also eligible if they operate on a commercial basis; investments by non-profit organizations may be eligible if it is established that the specific investment will be carried out on a commercial basis.[27]

Article 12 of the Convention sets out the requirements for eligible investments. Coverage is provided for both equity interests and non-equity direct investment.[28] Investments that can be covered include equity, shareholder and non-shareholder loans, and loan guarantees, provided the loans have a minimum maturity of more than one year.[29] Other forms of investments—such as technical assistance and

[22] Section 1.29 of the MIGA Operational Regulations.

[23] Section 1.37 of the MIGA Operational Regulations.

[24] Section 1.01 of the MIGA Operational Regulations; see also Section 2.04(a)(b)(c) of the MIGA Operational Regulations ('The period of guarantee for equity investments and non-equity direct investments shall not be less than 3 years or more than 15 years, while the period of guarantee for loans should have a minimum tenor of more than 1 year and a maximum tenor of 15 years and other medium to long term forms of investment shall be more than 1 year and not more than 15 years').

[25] Section 1.14 of the MIGA Operational Regulations ('Partnerships, which are not treated in essential respects as juridical persons under the law governing them, unincorporated associations and branches are not eligible as such. In such cases, eligibility is confined to the individual partners, members of the association and owners of the branch. Where in these cases some investors are eligible while others are not, a guarantee may be issued for such portion of the investment as corresponds to the eligible investors' share in the Investment Project').

[26] Article 13(a) of the MIGA Convention.

[27] MIGA Investment Guarantee Guide (November 2010) 4.

[28] Article 12(a) of the MIGA Convention; see also Section 1.02 of the MIGA Operational Regulations.

[29] Section 1.04 of the MIGA Operational Regulations ('With respect to equity interests, coverage extends to, *inter alia*, shares or ownership interests in a corporation established in the host country, rights arising out of the profits and liquidation of any joint venture in the host country, rights in the assets of an unincorporated branch in the host country, portfolio and direct equity investments resulting from the conversion of debt instruments, and specified loans meeting certain requirements').

management contracts, turnkey contracts, profit-sharing contracts, or franchising and licensing agreements—may also be eligible subject to them having terms of at least three years and depending on how substantial are the revenues of the project.[30]

Pursuant to Article 12(e), in assessing the risks of the project the agency shall satisfy itself that the investment will contribute to the economic development of the host country, comply with the host country's laws and regulations, be consistent with the declared development objects and priorities of the host country, and that the conditions in the host country provide for legal protection and fair and equitable treatment.[31] The Agency will determine if there is adequate legal protection in the host state and if the investment is duly protected under a relevant investment treaty.

Article 15 requires the host state to approve the investment before the Agency concludes any guarantee agreement against the risks designated for cover. Pursuant to Article 18(a) of the Convention, upon paying or agreeing to pay compensation to a holder of a guarantee, MIGA becomes subrogated to such rights or claims related to the guaranteed investment as the insured investor may have had against the host state. The details of this form of subrogation are left to be determined in the insurance contract and are dealt with in the Operational Regulations, Chapter 4, Sections III and IV.

Under the Convention, if there is a dispute between the Agency and a member, the Agency acting as subrogee of an investor steps into the shoes of the investor and can rely on the investor's rights against the host country.[32] Pursuant to Article 18 of the Convention, the Agency shall succeed to any rights or claims related to the guaranteed investment that the investor may have against the host country and other obligors.

As a means of dispute resolution subsequent to subrogation, the Convention refers to arbitration, but also provides for an alternative method for the settlement of disputes. Pursuant to Articles 3 and 4 of Annex II, for most disputes between a member and the Agency, the MIGA Convention establishes a framework of negotiations and conciliation, and if this fails, subsequent arbitration under ICSID-like rules.

[30] MIGA Investment Guarantee Guide (November 2010) 5. See also Sections 1.05 and 1.06 of the MIGA Operational Regulations ('In this respect, special attention shall be given to investment arrangements of long duration and high developmental potential. In no case shall the Agency provide coverage of this type, which, in its judgment and in the light of appropriate consultation, can be obtained from a government or an official export credit insurance agency of a member').

[31] See also Sections 3.15 and 3. 16 of the MIGA Operational Regulations (amended 4 February 2011) ('Such assessment shall be conducted in strict confidentiality and its outcome shall be shared only with the government concerned with a view to enabling it to improve the investment conditions in its territory').

[32] Article 57(b) of the MIGA Convention.

B. OPIC

OPIC was chartered by the US Congress in order to provide support for US businesses investing in developing countries. It is fully owned by the US government.[33] It was established in 1971 after raising 40 million US dollars in capital through an issuance of shares to the US Treasury.[34] OPIC provides political risk insurance against losses mainly resulting from currency inconvertibility, expropriation, political violence, war, revolution and civil strife. Political risk insurance provided by OPIC is backed by the full faith and credit of the US Government.[35]

OPIC's aim is to assist US businesses investing overseas, to foster economic development in new and emerging markets, complement the private sector in managing risks associated with foreign direct investment, and to support US foreign policy.[36] An important aspect of OPIC is that it seeks to utilize, and cooperate with, private sector political risk insurers. Its goals are to encourage economic development abroad and assist American investors abroad.[37]

In order to obtain political risk insurance from OPIC, investors must meet certain criteria.[38] Eligible investors must be US citizens, entities, or other associations incorporated in the United States, foreign corporations that are more than 95 percent owned by investors who are US citizens or eligible corporations, and other foreign entities that are 100 percent US owned.[39] OPIC can insure different forms of investment, including conventional equity investments and loans, construction and service contracts, production-sharing agreements, leases, various contractual arrangements such as consigned inventory, licensing, franchising and technical assistance agreements, and other special agreements that investors may devise.[40]

OPIC's political risk insurance generally covers currency inconvertibility, expropriation/improper government interference, and political violence.[41] In order to issue political risk insurance, specific risks must meet certain requirements set forth by OPIC. OPIC's currency inconvertibility compensates investors if new

[33] For a historical background of OPIC, see John S. Diaconis, 'Political Risk Insurance; OPIC's Use of a "Fiduciary Agent" to Facilitate Resolution of Subrogation of Claims' (1989) 23 International Lawyer 271; for more information, see http://www.opic.gov/Sites.

[34] Maura B. Perry, 'A Model for Efficient Foreign Aid: The Case for the Political Risk Insurance Activities of the Overseas Private Investment Corporation' (1996) 36 Virginia Journal of International Law 511, 518.

[35] 22 USC § 2197(c).

[36] See https://www.opic.gov/who-we-are/overview.

[37] Elizabeth A. Kessler, 'Political Risk Insurance and the Overseas Private Investment Corporation: What Happened to the Private Sector' (1992) 13 New York Law School Journal of International and Comparative Law 203–27, 204; 22 USC § 2191. (Its mandate is to mobilize and facilitate the participation of United States private capital and skills in the economic and social development of less-developed countries and areas, and countries in transition from nonmarket to market economies, thereby complementing the development assistance objectives of the United States.)

[38] 22 USC § 2198(c) 1988.

[39] Ibid.

[40] See generally OPIC's website https://www.opic.gov .

[41] Ibid., 18–20.

currency restrictions, or other government action or inaction, prevent the conversion or transfer of investment returns from insured investments.[42] Currency inconvertibility protects an investor against the inability to convert into US dollars other currencies, or credits in such currencies, received as earnings or profits from the approved project, as repayment or return of the investment therein, in whole or in part, or as compensation for the sale or disposition of all or any part thereof.[43]

OPIC's provisions regarding currency inconvertibility, do not provide coverage when a host state decides to devalue its currency, because devaluation is generally viewed as a commercial risk.[44] OPIC's expropriation coverage includes nationalization, confiscation, or expropriation of an investment, including 'creeping' expropriation, due to unlawful government acts, or a series of acts, that deprive the investor of its fundamental rights in a project.[45] It excludes losses due to lawful regulation or taxation by host governments and actions provoked by the investor or the foreign enterprise.[46]

Pursuant to § 2197(a) of the US Code, OPIC may only cover investments made in connection with projects in a less-developed, friendly country, or area with which the government of which the President of the United States has agreed to institute a programme for insurance, guaranties, or reinsurance. Therefore, if the US does not have an investment agreement with a particular country, OPIC is prohibited from covering investments made in the said state. OPIC requires its investors to invest in host countries that have subrogation treaties with the United States, allowing OPIC to attempt to reclaim its expenditure from the host country, usually through a fiduciary agent located in the host country.

OPIC is required to enter into 'satisfactory arrangements' with a host government before it can offer insurance programmes. Typically, these arrangements take the form of *bilateral investment guarantee agreements*. These agreements establish the basic relationship between OPIC and the host government. Among other things, the agreements provide that OPIC will be subrogated to the rights of its insureds and that disputes between OPIC and the host government will be resolved by international arbitration in accordance with international law.

[42] See https://www.opic.gov/what-we-offer/political-risk-insurance/types-of-coverage/currency-inconvertability.

[43] 22 USC § 2194(a)(1)(A).

[44] Alex Khachaturian, 'Note: "Are We in Good Hands?" The Adequacy of American and Multilateral Political Risk Insurance Programs in Fostering International Development' (2006) 38 Connecticut Law Review 1041–62, 1057.

[45] See OPIC's website (n 40). See also 22 USC § 2198(b) ('the term "expropriation" includes, but is not limited to, any abrogation, repudiation, or impairment by a foreign government, a political subdivision of a foreign government, or a corporation owned or controlled by a foreign government, of its own contract with an investor with respect to a project, where such abrogation, repudiation, or impairment is not caused by the investor's own fault or misconduct, and materially adversely affects the continued operation of the project.').

[46] See OPIC's website (n 40). See also 22 USC § 2194.

C. Investment Guarantees of the Federal Republic of Germany

Similar to OPIC provided for by the US Government,[47] the Federal German government provides political risk coverage for investments made in developing nations through a consortium formed by PricewaterhouseCoopers Aktiengesellschaft Wirtschaftsprüfungs-gesellschaft, as lead partner, and Euler Hermes Kreditversicherungs-AG.[48] Its investment guarantee programme covers losses resulting from expropriation, breach of contract, war, moratorium, and inconvertibility.[49] To qualify for coverage:

> the investor must be domiciled in Germany, there must be an explicit German interest in the realization of the project abroad, the project must be a new direct investment (no portfolio investment), the investment must be an economically feasible and sound project, the project must contribute to host country development, appropriate environmental standards are to be observed, there must be positive reverse effects on Germany, the investment must enjoy sufficient legal protection in the host country, the application for a guarantee must be handed in before the first contribution is made.[50]

D. Private Risk Insurance

Private risk insurance (PRI) has been said to be derived from marine insurance provided by Lloyd's. Although it gradually evolved over time, it became popular in the 1970s.[51] The private market covers both export, or trade credit, and investment insurance. While the large private risk insurer American International Group had liquidity problems in 2008 due to the financial crisis, the private risk insurance market still includes about twenty Lloyd's syndicates and about eight private insurance companies, which are predominantly located in London, Bermuda, and the United States.[52]

[47] For an overview of institutions providing public risk insurance for governments, see Kathryn Gordon, 'Investment Guarantees and Political Risk Insurance: Institutions, Incentives and Development', *OECD Investment Policy Perspectives* (OECD Publishing, 2008).

[48] See http://www.agaportal.de/en/dia/index.html.

[49] See http://www.agaportal.de/en/dia/grundlagen/gedeckte_risiken.html. ('The question whether one of these risks has occurred is evaluated in the event of loss by verifying the actual circumstances on the basis of the German principles of law and in consideration of international law').

[50] See http://www.agaportal.de/en/dia/grundlagen/garantievoraussetzungen.html.

[51] See Perry (n 34) 532; see also Rudolf Dolzer and Christoph Schreuer, *Principles of Investment Law* (OUP, 2008) 207.

[52] MIGA, World Investment and Political Risk Report, 2010, 55 ('As well as traditional equity PRI, the private market offers protection for a wide variety of developing-country payment risks, either for political perils alone or comprehensive non-payment cover. Brokers play an important role in promoting and sourcing PRI for the private market. This market segment is dynamic: over the past year, some players have exited the PRI market, while new entrants have appeared').

Private risk insurance presents certain differences compared to the coverage provided by national or multilateral insurers. Private risk insurance coverage is available on a commercial basis without the environmental, labour, and human rights restrictions often involved with MIGA or OPIC. The coverage is also available on short notice without the lengthy negotiation period that often characterizes national programmes.[53] On the other hand, there are similarities between public and private risk insurances. For example, similarly to the period of guarantee provided by the MIGA Convention,[54] the private risk insurance provider Zurich Insurance may extend its coverage for up to 15 years.[55]

The public and private risk insurance contracts are similar in their definitions of triggering events, exclusions, limitations, and qualification requirements for payment of a claim. In many cases, the drafters of private insurance contracts appear to have read through the OPIC jurisprudence before writing particular clauses.[56] For example, Zurich's specimen policy contains similar language to that found in the MIGA Convention and OPIC's mandate. In Article 3.1(b), Zurich covers creeping expropriation for investors, financial institutions, project developers, and contractors by stating that expropriation means an act or a series of acts taken by the host government that 'effectively prevents or restricts, through financial, regulatory or other measures, the operation of the Foreign Enterprise relating to the Project, causing the total cessation of the Foreign Enterprise's operations relating to the Project'. Furthermore, Zurich includes language similar to that of OPIC in relation to its coverage for political violence.

Also, it should be noted again that OPIC encourages cooperation with private risk insurers. For example, while OPIC may not be able to ensure an existing investment, the investor may be able to obtain the political risk protection it needs by insuring new investments with OPIC and securing coverage through the private market for its existing exposures. In addition, when OPIC policies reach their twenty year expiration date, they may be continued if a US insurer is willing to assume at least one-half of the risk.[57] Some investors utilize both public and private risk insurance.

[53] Bishop, Crawford, and Reisman (n 9) 491 (citations omitted).

[54] Section 2.04 of the MIGA Operational Regulations.

[55] See https://www.zurichna.com/en/prodsols/trade/politicalrisk.

[56] Jennifer M. DeLeonardo, 'Are Public and Private Risk Insurance TWD of a Kind? Suggestions for a New Direction for Government Coverage' (2005) 45 Virginia Journal of International Law 746 ('The coverage with regard to currency inconvertibility is substantially the same under both public and private source form contracts').

[57] See http://www.opic.gov/publications/reports-handbooks/guides/sources.

V. The Role of Mediation

As mentioned in the introduction, the purpose of this chapter is not to discuss the mediation process per se, but rather to identify various situations in the context of political risk insurance where mediation can be used as a dispute settlement mechanism. There is no lack of articles and books on mediation in international disputes, including investment disputes. The basic principles and rules of mediation remain the same. An absolutely essential condition is the will of all the involved parties to try to reach a settlement. A *bona fide* approach to the mediation is thus necessary. It is reasonable to assume that also the techniques of mediation remain more or less the same when disputes relate to political risk insurance. A great deal will depend on the facts and circumstances of the individual case. Exactly how a mediation relating to political risk insurance unfolds will also depend on the involved parties and on their commercial and financial objectives, as well as on the mediators.

It must also be kept in mind that mediation is confidential in nature. In fact, this is a hallmark of most successful mediations. Any mediation involves a giving and taking from the parties involved. For a number of reasons, most parties are willing to do so only if the process of mediation is confidential. While there is a high degree of transparency today with respect to investment disputes in general, this does not seem to be the case in the field of political risk insurance. It is thus very difficult, if not impossible, to ascertain with any degree of certainty exactly *how* mediations are done in this field. Very little information reaches the public domain.

It is, however, possible to identify several situations or scenarios where mediation could be used to settle disputes among the involved parties. The following four situations describe where mediation could be relevant.

A. Determinations by the Insurer

One such situation occurs when the investor—the insured—requests payment from the insurer under the insurance contract in question. Differences of opinion may arise as to the eligibility requirements under the insurance contract. Such disputes may concern the type of investor, the resources invested, the type of investment, as well as the amount of payment requested. Rather than proceeding to a formal determination by the insurer, it may be in the interest of both parties to have the differences of opinion resolved through mediation. Many insurance contracts have dispute settlement clauses covering these kinds of situations. Such clauses often provide for arbitration, and sometimes for mediation. Also, when there is no direct reference to arbitration, the parties are free to agree on mediation in some form. Depending on the circumstances of the individual case this may be more appropriate and efficient than other forms of dispute settlement.

B. Subrogation

Another situation when mediation may come into play is when the insurer exercises its rights following from subrogation. Most insurance contracts and many investment protection treaties provide for subrogation. A fairly typical subrogation clause is found in Article 15 of the Energy Charter Treaty. It reads:

> (1) If a Contracting Party or its designated agency (hereinafter referred to as the 'Indemnifying Party') makes a payment under an indemnity or guarantee given in respect of an Investment of an Investor (hereinafter referred to as the 'Party Indemnified') in the Area of another Contracting Party (hereinafter referred to as the 'Host Party'), the Host Party shall recognise:
> (a) the assignment to the Indemnifying Party of all the rights and claims in respect of such Investment; and
> (b) the right of the Indemnifying Party to exercise all such rights and enforce such claims by virtue of subrogation.
> (2) The Indemnifying Party shall be entitled in all circumstances to:
> (a) the same treatment in respect of the rights and claims acquired by it by virtue of the assignment referred to in paragraph (1); and
> (b) the same payments due pursuant to those rights and claims,
> as the Party Indemnified was entitled to receive by virtue of this Treaty in respect of the Investment concerned.
> (3) In any proceeding under Article 26, a Contracting Party shall not assert as a defence, counterclaim, right of set-off or for any other reason, that indemnification or other compensation for all or part of the alleged damages has been received or will be received pursuant to an insurance or guarantee contract.

Subrogation means that the claims of the investor/insured are transferred to the insurer. The insurer thus steps into the shoes of the insured with respect to the claims against the host state. In most cases subrogation takes place automatically. In other words, as soon as the insurer has compensated the insured, the former takes over the rights of the latter.

In the context of an investment protection treaty, this means that the insurer can avail itself of the arbitration clause found in most such treaties. Prior to commencing arbitration most such treaties prescribe a so-called 'cooling-off period'—usually between three to six months—during which the parties are expected to try to reach a settlement. During this time period, mediation, in one form or the other, may well be used by the parties. Mediation can of course be resorted to also prior to the commencement of the cooling-off period, as well as during any arbitration proceeding.

In the situation described, any mediation will take place between the insurer—also referred to as the subrogee—and the host state. From a legal perspective, no difference is made between public sector and private insurers in this respect. From a practical point of view, however, this difference usually matters, particularly if the insurer is a government-owned, or -sponsored, entity domiciled in a powerful state. The economic and political pressure that such an entity can exercise during negotiations, and any mediation, should not be underestimated. The situation is probably the same if the insurer is a multilateral agency, such as MIGA. Private sector insurers usually have fewer possibilities to exert political and economic pressure. This fact is likely to influence the conduct, and maybe the length, of negotiations and mediations.

C. Pre-Dispute Activities

A third situation where mediation may become relevant is the following. Under many insurance contracts, the insured investor has an obligation to keep the insurer informed of events that may affect the insurance, e.g. political events and developments, proposed legislation, regulatory reforms, etc. If such events transpire, they might cause the political risk insurer to intervene with the host state—with or without the assistance of the investor—with a view to trying to prevent the situation from escalating to a level requiring payment under the insurance contract. In such a scenario, it is typically in the interest both of the insured investor and the insurer to avoid escalation. This would seem to be a situation where mediation could be an efficient way of solving a problem at an early stage, before it develops into a dispute. It is likely that all parties involved would be interested in an informal and confidential way of coming to an agreement.

In the situation described, mediation would primarily take place between the insurer and the host state. It is also possible that mediation would be suitable for solving issues that might arise between the insurer and the insured investor under this scenario. There may, for example, be different opinions between the insured and the insurer as to the coverage of the insurance contract, concerning the nature of the acts performed by the host state, the extent to which the insured investor should, or must, participate in the discussions/negotiations with the host state, and as regards the party responsible for bearing the cost for such negotiations.

D. Recovery by the Insured Investor

Most political risk insurance arrangements are combined with some form of subrogation rights for the insurer. Many investment protection treaties have subrogation clauses. Subrogation rights may also be provided for in separate agreements, as is usually the case with respect to OPIC. As mentioned, for insurers from powerful states, and for multilateral agencies, subrogation rights usually allow them to exert economic and political pressure on the host state in question. Usually they can therefore conduct negotiations and mediations from a position of strength.

The situation may be different for political risk insurers from the private sector. They usually do not have the same possibilities to exert political and economic pressure. At the same time, they must recover from the host state what they have paid the insured investor under the insurance contract. It is also not unusual for private insurers not to have cooperation partners or agents in the host state. For these reasons, private insurers sometimes require the insured investor to negotiate, litigate, or arbitrate with the host state with a view to recovering the insurance payment made by it to the insured investor. This is often done with the backing and support of the insurer. In such a situation, it is possible that the investor and the host state would rather commence mediation to try to reach agreement.

Also, the relationship between the insured investor and the insurer may give rise to differences of opinion in this situation, e.g. how to conduct negotiations with the host state, which might be best settled through mediation.

VI. Concluding Remarks

The political risk insurance business is confidential and secretive by nature. It is therefore very difficult to ascertain what role mediation plays in this economic sector. Given the flexible and informal character of the mediation process, there are several situations where mediation could be—and is in fact—used to resolve problems arising out of political risk insurance arrangements.

9

The Growing Importance of Regional Mediation Centres in Asia

Danny McFadden

I. Introduction

The modern model of commercial mediation popularized first in the United States and later taken up primarily by other common law jurisdictions, e.g. Australia, the United Kingdom, and New Zealand, has been studied with interest in Asia for some time but only in the past decade has it really taken off as a forum of choice for parties in dispute in the region. In turn, this success has led to the creation of regional mediation centres and a concentrated effort by arbitration bodies, governments, law and bar societies, and others to promote their local services in the Asian region.[1]

II. Support for Western Stand-Alone Commercial Mediation in Asia

In the last twenty years in Hong Kong and Singapore, there has been a re-examination of the value of Western mediation processes, in particular, the stand-alone facilitative mediation model.[2] These Asian jurisdictions have closely followed the development of mediation in commercial disputes in other countries. China has also been aware of mediation's global development and it has payed particular attention to Hong Kong and Singapore's embracing of the Western mediation model. Singapore was an early adopter of modern mediation with what one might say is a 'Singapore twist'. In 1997, the then-Chief Justice of Singapore Yong Poon How stated that it was time to 'relearn mediation from the West' but then develop a model that 'suits our culture and diverse ethnic backgrounds'.[3] In Hong

[1] Although Northern Asia India, Bangladesh, and Pakistan, for example, are in the process of developing mediation centres, this chapter is focused on South-East Asian jurisdictions, primarily China, Hong Kong SAR, and Singapore; and to a lesser degree Indonesia, Japan, Korea, and Thailand.

[2] Cao Lijun, 'Combining Conciliation and Arbitration in China: Overview and Latest Developments' (2006) 3 Asian Legal Review 85.

[3] Michael Moser, *Businesss Disputes in China* (3rd edition, Juris Publishing, 2011), Chief Justice Yong Pung How, Opening speech Singapore Mediation Centre (1997) 14.

Kong, which has made sweeping changes to its civil procedure rules to accommodate mediation, the Secretary of Justice Wong Yan Lung said in 2005:

> It has been suggested that there is something distinctly Asian about mediation, as there is a strong element of compromise and harmony. So in promoting mediation, we may well be embarking on a process of cultural awakening.

Other centres and jurisdictions in Asia are also currently either adapting new mediation models from the West or re-invigorating their efforts to promote mediation in the commercial area. Recent developments would suggest that Asian dispute resolution bodies in countries like Indonesia, Japan, Korea, and Thailand do not want to be left behind in establishing their own modern mediation services. Adding extra impetus of late is the introduction by China of its Belt and Road initiatives, which have not only caused excitement among many countries and commercial entities, but also spurred dispute resolution bodies in Asia to examine if they are ready and able to offer a full raft of dispute resolution services, including modern mediation.

A. Mediation in China

1. Background to China's development of mediation

A close look at mediation in China reveals that much about the underpinnings of mediation practice throughout Asia is due to the huge influence China has had on the region for centuries. Throughout its history China has cultivated a national system of institutional mediation that has its roots in Chinese custom and philosophy. As far back as the Qing dynasty, if a dispute arose the local judge would often return the complaint and request the parties to mediate in order to discourage unnecessary litigation. This ethos continues to this day, and Chinese judges are empowered to employ mediation as part of their practice in dealing with cases.[4]

The philosophy of Confucius has had an immense influence throughout South East Asia.[5] It is particularly important in countries like Korea and Japan. It is a philosophy that sets out to give direction and instruction to society, from the ruler to the ruled, on how to live and also to provide guidance on dealing with conflict. In Confucianism, concepts such as harmony (*he*) and yielding to others (*rang*) are highly valued, whereas aggression and argument are seen as character defects.[6]

[4] 'Judicial Mediation in China Explained', Herbert Smith 30 July 2012 med-arb s://hsfnotes.com/adr/2012/07/30/judicial-mediation-in-mainland-china-explained/.

[5] Danny McFadden, *Mediation in Greater China: The New Frontier for Commercial Mediation* (Wolters Kluwer/CCH Hong Kong, 2013) 195.

[6] Wang Wenying, 'The Role of Conciliation in Resolving Disputes: A PRC Perspective' (2005) 20 (2) Ohio State Journal of Dispute Resolution 427.

This emphasis on harmony (*he*) is reflected in Chinese social interaction and conflict resolution. Confucius believed in a society governed by the principles of *li* (right behaviour), not *fa* (law). Recourse to law or argument amounted to a complete failure by the parties involved to observe ethical principles and amounted to a severe loss of face. This deeply embedded distaste for confrontation in relationships still reverberates strongly in China and other Asian countries today

After 1979, when China began to open itself to world trade again, it needed to quickly establish a means to settle international trade disputes, which resulted in the introduction of the Arbitration Law of the People's Republic of China (PRC) (Arbitration Law) in 1995. Arbitration in China received a great deal of support. China's first arbitration body, the China International Economic and Trade Arbitration Commission (CIETAC), was established in Beijing and CIETAC year on year conducts more arbitration cases than any other arbitration body in the world. [7]

The previous legal system was abolished not long after the People's Republic of China (PRC) was founded in 1949, as the new government did not see the need to have civil, criminal, and procedural law.[8] However, both the PRC and the Chinese Communist Party (CCP) encouraged the use of mediation, which they saw as being informal and non-legalistic in nature. In fact, according to Eric Glassman, further emphasizing mediation's role the PRC became 'the first modern nation to sanction mediation as the preferred method of dispute settlement'.[9]

In 1982, China's Constitution reinstituted the People's Mediation Committees (PMC), which conduct mediations at the local level in neighbourhoods and villages; it is a system that continues to this day. In 2013, the Ministry of Justice stated that China has more than 4.9 million mediators working in more than 800,000 mediation committees, handling more than 7.67 million disputes per year.[10] However, it should not be deduced that litigation is not accepted or used as a means of resolving disputes in China. As the Chinese economy has grown, the number of cases filed each year has continued to rise.[11] In 2015, the Supreme Court of China advised that through the end of September 2015, civil cases were up almost

[7] Markus Altenkirch and Jan Frohloff 'Global Arbitration Cases Still Rise – Arbitral Institutions' Caseload Statistics for 2015, Global Arbitration News, 25 August 2016, https://globalarbitrationnews.com/global-arbitration-cases-still-rise-arbitral-institutions-caseload-statistics-2015/#page=1.

[8] Hungdah Chiu, 'Chinese Law and Justice: Trends over Three Decades' (1982) 7 Maryland Series in Contemporary Asian Studies 1, 4–5.

[9] Eric J Glassman, 'The Function of Mediation in China: Examining the Impact of Regulations Governing the People's Mediation Committees' (1992) 10 (2) UCLA Pacific Basin Law Journal P 463

[10] 'Chinese Legislature Passes People's Mediation Law', Chinese People's Daily (23 June 2010) 1, http://www.chinadaily.com.cn/china. For information, *The China's People's Daily* is the voice of the Chinese government, so anything quoted as information has been vetted by the Chinese government.

[11] Pitman Potter 'Legal Reform in China: Institutions, Culture, and Selective Adaptation' (2004) 29 (2) Law and Social Enquiry: Journal of the American Bar Foundation 484.

23 percent, administrative cases up 76 percent, and private prosecutions of criminal cases up 60 percent. [12]

The modern mediation model as practised in the United States and other common law countries has only recently begun to be used in China, primarily in international cases. In China, a mediation process forms part of both arbitration and court hearings. In arbitration, for example, a hybrid model of dispute resolution (which includes both arbitration and mediation) has been practised widely for many years. This mediation–arbitration model (med–arb) has been much debated in common law legal circles,[13] where it is not popular; there are believed to be some inherent problems with the neutral in the roles of both mediator and arbitrator. Likewise, Chinese courts use a similar model, where judges can choose to switch roles and act as both judge and mediator. However, of late, international dispute resolution in China has changed tack and many cities and provinces are now experiencing a wave of engagement with the Western stand-alone mediation model, driven by interest from institutional and private dispute resolution bodies. [14]

According to Yuwen Li, mediation in China saw 'a rise in the 1980s, a fall in the 1990s and then its partial revival in the 2000s'.[15] What is called 'mediation' in China today includes a wide variety of actions, ranging from the purely facilitative to the substantially adjudicative, which includes a mediation component.[16] All of these activities will be labelled 'mediation' and if the case settles it will be deemed to have settled at mediation. China currently has four types of mediation sanctioned by the government and the courts.

It should be noted that in China (and elsewhere in Asia), the pre-eminent model and style of mediation is evaluative, not the Western more facilitative mode. A Chinese mediator/judge–mediator/arbitrator–mediator is usually quite comfortable giving his or her opinion on the merits of the case. Culture also plays a factor. In China, the mediator is expected to be a 'wise counsellor' who will guide the parties to a solution (often with what would be considered in a Western facilitative model as a lecturing or authoritarian directive style). Therefore, changing to a more facilitative Western model is contrary to local mediation practice and partly explains why the uptake of a facilitative model has been slow.

[12] Susan Finder, 'Update on Case Filing Reform and Other Challenges for Chinese Courts and Judges', Supreme People's Court Monitor [blog] 3 December 2015, https://supremepeoplescourtmonitor.com/2015/12/03/update-on-case-filing-reform-and-other-challenges-for-chinese-courts-and-judges.

[13] See Chapter 4, this volume.

[14] Meg Utterback, 'Mediating Disputes in China', in Michael Moser (ed.), *Dispute Resolution in China* (Jurisnet LLC, 2012) 373.

[15] Yuwen Li, *The Judicial System and Reform in Post-Mao China: Stumbling Towards Justice* (Routledge Press, 2014) 136.

[16] Philip C. C. Huang, 'Court Mediation in China, Past and Present' (2006) 32 (3) Modern China 275.

2. The main types of mediation in China

There are currently four types of mediation practiced in China.[17] The first is civil mediation, which is mediation by PMCs outside of the court system.[18] Secondly, there is judicial or court mediation, which is conducted by a court of law in civil and economic disputes and minor criminal cases, and which takes place during the court proceedings. For marital cases, inside-court mediation is a necessary procedure. Whether or not to seek judicial mediation is for the litigants to decide. Mediation is not a mandatory procedure. However, if the case settles during the court mediation process, the settlement agreement can be enforced as an order of the court. The court mediation process allows the judge–mediator to use the evaluative power inherent in their office to a degree unheard of in Western mediation practice. Nonetheless, it does allow for greater flexibility in arriving at a decision. Thirdly, China has introduced administrative mediation which is usually outside-the-court mediation by grassroots governments, such as a township government in ordinary civil disputes, or outside-the-court mediation by government departments in compliance with legal provisions in specific civil disputes, economic disputes, or labour disputes. Fourthly, China has arbitration mediation, which is mediation by arbitration bodies in arbitration cases. In China, both domestic and international arbitration permits mediation before commencing arbitration. Arbitration is used only when the parties are unable to resolve their dispute using mediation. This arb–med or arb–med–arb process is an outside-the-court mediation process. Even where the parties' commercial contract dispute resolution clause states that in the event of a dispute the matter must be arbitrated, Chinese arbitrators may suggest and encourage the use of mediation prior to arbitration. The acceptance of arb–med is partly attributable to China's own tradition of evaluative mediation practice, where the mediator is often asked to give an opinion on the merits of the case if the dispute does not settle.[19]

3. Chinese governmental support for mediation

In 2010, the Chinese government moved to streamline mediation procedures and, on 28 August 2010, the National People's Congress Standing Committee passed the first People's Mediation Law (PML), effective on 1 January 2011.[20] In a speech presenting the draft law for approval, Minister of Justice Wu Aiying told the Standing

[17] Ibid.

[18] Information Office of the State Council of the People's Republic of China, 'The Judicial System and Reform Process', (8 October 2012) 1, http://www.china.org.cn/government/whitepaper/2012-10/09/content_26733733.htm.

[19] Yuning Wu, 'People's Mediation in China', in Cao Lijun, Ivany Sun, and Bill Henenton (eds), *The Routledge Handbook of Chinese Criminology* (Routledge, 2014) 118.

[20] People's Mediation Law of the People's Republic of China (promulgated by Standing Committee of the National People's Congress, 28 August 2010, effective on 1 January 2011).

Committee that 'mediation should be the first line of defense to maintain social stability and promote harmony'.[21]

Then in August 2012, the Standing Committee of the National People's Congress of the PRC approved significant Amendments to the PRC's Civil Procedure Law (CPL), which came into effect on 1 January 2013.[22] The rules made changes with regards to the legal status of a mediation settlement agreement. Under previous civil procedure rules, a private settlement outside the court room was considered a contract. This meant that, as in other jurisdictions like Hong Kong and the United Kingdom, the breach of such a mediation settlement meant the parties had to bring the case back to litigation proceedings all over again. Pursuant to the Amendments (Articles 194 and 195), the parties may, in accordance with the PML, apply to the basic People's court where the mediation institution is located, to obtain judicial recognition of the mediation settlement within 30 days after such mediation settlement becomes effective.[23]

4. Interest in the Western standalone mediation model in China by Chinese mediation organisations

A sign of the awakening interest in Western mediation models in China is evidenced by important dispute resolution bodies, such as the China Council for the Promotion of International Trade (CCPIT/CCOIC) Mediation Centre in Beijing, conducting training in modern commercial mediation processes and offering mediation services to foreign companies.[24]

The CCPIT Mediation Centre was established in 1987 and has over fifty sub-council mediation centres in provinces, municipalities, and autonomous regions throughout the country, constituting a nationwide conciliation network. The Centre's network has handled cases involving over thirty countries and regions; the Mediation Centre says that over 80 percent of the cases have been successfully settled through mediation. Also, in Northern China, the Beijing Arbitration Commission (BAC) opened the BAC Mediation Centre in 2011 in order to administer cases and conduct research into mediation best practice.[25]

[21] Margaret Woo, 'Court Reform with Chinese Characteristics' (2017) 27 Washington International Law Journal 241, 254, quoting Zhu Zhe and Lan Tian, 'Mediation Draft Law Could Ease Tension', China Daily (23 June 2010), www.chinadaily.com.cn/china/2010-06/23/content_10005555.htm.

[22] Amendments Civil Procedure Law of the People's Republic of China (Amendments) (Revised), Order No.59 of the President of the People's Republic of China (31 August 2012).

[23] 'People's Mediation Law of the People's Republic of China' (Adopted at the 16th meeting of the Standing Committee of the 11th National People's Congress of the People's Republic of China on 28 August 2010).

[24] CCPIT/CCOIC, 'CCPIT/CCOIC Mediation Center and Xicheng District People's Court of Beijing Launched Commercial Disputes Mediation Linking Mechanism' (3 August 2017), http://adr.ccpit.org/EN/News/ec0bcbc6-dd74-4c58-b197-2677793feaf2.html.

[25] Jun Wu, 'Annual Review on Commercial Mediation' in *Commercial Dispute Resolution in China: An Annual Review and Preview*. Beijing Arbitration Commission, Queen Mary, University of London Institute of Advanced Legal Studies (May 2014) 45–75; See http://www.bjac.org.cn/attached/file/20160217/2014.pdf.

In 2015 two major mediation alliances were established separately in the South and North of China. The Beijing Mediation Alliance (BMA) was established in Beijing on 27 April 2015, co-initiated by sixteen organizations. The aim of the BMA is to enhance communication and cooperation between the current dispute settlement organizations, and promote the quality of mediation. In Southern China, the Commercial Mediation Alliance between the Guangdong, Hong Kong, and Macao regions was established at Qianhai in Shenzhen on 7 December 2014 as part of the Shenzhen, Qianhai, and Hong Kong Industry Cooperation Zone established in the region. The Regulations on the Qianhai Shenzhen–Hong Kong Modern Service Industry Cooperation Zone in Shenzhen Special Economic Zone state that it will 'encourage cooperation of non-governmental mediation organisations between Hong Kong and Shenzhen, in order to offer commercial mediation services in the Qianhai Cooperation Zone'.[26] Finally, Shanghai (one of China's great commercial cities) is not far behind in its efforts to become a dominant player in dispute resolution. The Shanghai Commercial Mediation Centre (SCMC) was created in 2011 and is strongly supported by the Shanghai government and promotes mediation and supports training in the region.[27]

B. Hong Kong

Beginning in 2006, the Hong Kong government, judiciary, and legal bodies started a process of re-examining the ADR environment in Hong Kong. Thus began the creation of what today is an increasingly sophisticated mediation infrastructure in Hong Kong.

1. Background

In 2009 the promotion of mediation was included as part of a raft of new changes to the Civil Justice Reforms (CJR) of the High Court 'with a view to ensuring and improving access to justice at a reasonable cost and speed'.[28] These reforms resulted in lawyers and their clients in Hong Kong being forced to re-examine the way they conduct litigation, particularly how mediation may form part of their legal strategy.

The CJR introduced a number of new rules to the existing High Court Rules; the new rules were aimed at making litigation fairer, more efficient, and cost effective. Unlike the UK, where following the Woolf Reforms an entirely new set of rules were adopted, the existing High Court Rules were kept with selective amendments

[26] Yifan Tan, 'Mediation Center Set Up for International Disputes', Shenzhen Qianhai, People's Cooperation Zone Court, http://enmobile.szqhcourt.gov.cn/NEWS/Detail/192.html.

[27] 'About SCMC', Shanghai Commercial Mediation Centre. See http://www.scmc.org.cn/.

[28] 'Interim Report and Consultation Paper', Terms of Reference, Civil Justice Reform, Feb 2000, https://www.civiljustice.hk/ir/paperHTML/WorkingParty.html.

grafted on to them.[29] The Courts in Hong Kong are currently advising parties that, before taking legal action, they should consider other ways to resolve their disputes: 'Court action should be your last resort.'[30]

2. Mediation: 'Practice Direction 31'

Practice Direction 31 (PD 31) came into effect on 1 January 2010. PD 31 states that the underlying objective of the Rules of the High Court and the District Court (as amended under the CJR) is to facilitate the settlement of disputes.[31] The Court has a duty as part of active case management to further that objective by encouraging disputing parties to use ADR if the Court considers it is appropriate and that the Court should facilitate its use.[32] The Court also has a duty to help the parties settle their case.[33] The parties and their legal representatives must assist the Court to discharge the duty in question.[34]

One key element is that, pursuant to PD 31, the courts in Hong Kong are able to impose any adverse costs order on any party that unreasonably fails to engage in the mediation process.[35] Closely followed by the Hong Kong courts, English legal precedent provides clear evidence that litigants who refuse to mediate can suffer greatly if their refusal is seen as unreasonable when costs are being decided.[36]

3. Hong Kong Mediation Bill

The Mediation Bill (the Bill) was introduced to the Legislative Council on 30 November 2011. Then in June 2012, the Mediation Ordinance was enacted which gave effect to the Mediation Bill.[37] The introduction of this bill was intended to be an indication of the government's desire to encourage parties to adopt mediation as a favoured alternative dispute resolution (ADR) avenue. Under the Bill, the meaning of mediation is defined as

> a structured process comprising one or more sessions in which one or more impartial individuals, without adjudicating the dispute, assists the parties to do any or all of the following: identify the issues in dispute; explore and generate options;

[29] 'The Final Report of the Working Party on Civil Justice Reform Hong Kong' (3 March 2004) http://www.info.gov.hk/gia/general/200403/03/0303195.htm.

[30] 'Frequently Asked Questions: Civil Justice Reforms – Hong Kong Government Information' (2 April 2009), https://www.civiljustice.hk/eng/home.html.

[31] 'General Guide to Practice Direction 31–Mediation', effective 1 January 2010, https://mediation.judiciary.hk/en/doc/GeneralGuide_PD31-Eng.pdf.

[32] Ibid.

[33] Ibid.

[34] Practice Direction 31 (Part A, 1), https://legalref.judiciary.hk/lrs/common/pd/pdcontent.jsp?pdn=PD31.htm.

[35] General Guide to Practice Direction 31 (n 31) 5.

[36] Justice Yeung JA, Hong Kong Court of Appeal, *iRiver Hong Kong Limited v Thakral Corporation (HK) Limited*, CACV 252 of 2007, Judgment (8 August 2008) referred to English cases such as *Dunnet v Railtrack* [2002], *Burchell v Bullard* [2005], and *Halsey v Milton Keynes General NHS Trust* [2004].

[37] See https://www.elegislation.gov.hk/hk/cap620.

communicate with one another; and reach agreement regarding the resolution of the whole or part of the dispute.[38]

This definition is consistent with the facilitative model of mediation provided for in PD 31, namely, the mediator is there to assist the parties to reach their own resolution of the dispute, rather than to impose his or her own views or decisions on them. However, the Department of Justice's Steering Committee on Mediation is currently considering whether or not the Ordinance needs to be changed, because some are suggesting that an evaluative (rather than facilitative) model of mediation may be appropriate in certain cases, e.g. intellectual property disputes.[39]

4. Hong Kong Mediation Accreditation Association Limited

In 2013, the establishment of Hong Kong Mediation Accreditation Association Limited (HKMAAL), an umbrella regulatory body for mediation in Hong Kong, was a first for Asia in that, up until that point, no other jurisdiction previously had tried to bring all mediators under one roof.[40] Although currently not a statutory body, most mediators in Hong Kong seek to become HKMAAL accredited mediators. The main function of the HKMAAL is to establish an accreditation system for mediators in Hong Kong with a view to maintaining and unifying the standards of mediators and ensuring the professionalism of mediators in Hong Kong.[41]

The aims of the HKMAAL are to set standards for accredited mediators, supervisors, assessors, trainers, coaches, and other professionals involved in mediation in Hong Kong, and to accredit them on satisfying the requisite standard; to set standards for relevant mediation training courses in Hong Kong, and to approve them on satisfying the requisite standards; and to promote a culture of best practice and professionalism in mediation in Hong Kong.[42] The institution is now collating a set of accreditation standards and guidelines in consultation with the mediation profession in Hong Kong.

A KPMG General Counsel Survey found that 48 percent of General Counsels surveyed believe that mediation will grow significantly ahead of litigation and arbitration in the region. They suggest that cultural factors, such as a tradition of family owned and run organisations, and an associated need for privacy, make mediation an especially attractive way of settling disputes.[43]

[38] Ibid.

[39] Hong Kong Mediation Accreditation Association Limited (HKMAAL), http://www.hkmaal.org.hk/en/index.php.

[40] Nicholas Seymour, '1st Session: A Review of the Latest Global Developments', in Mediate First, Advance with the Times, Hong Kong, China, 13 May 2016.

[41] Ibid.

[42] The author is Vice Chair and a Council Member of HKMAAL.

[43] KPMG, 'Beyond the Law', KPMG Global General Counsel Survey 2012, 36. https://assets.kpmg/content/dam/kpmg/pdf/2013/01/general-counsel-survey-v5.pdf.

According to the Hong Kong government there are three main reasons why the use of mediation has grown so enthusiastically in Hong Kong.[44] It is part of a growing regional, and indeed global, trend for settling disputes without resorting to litigation; it fits neatly with Hong Kong's cultural tradition and legal history, influenced by both British and mainland Chinese ideas; and it is part of a demand circle—international law firms have imported the practice from other jurisdictions, which has creating increased local demand.

5. Apology legislation and mediation in Hong Kong

Hong Kong is the first jurisdiction in Asia to enact apology legislation and its Apology Ordinance[45] is the broadest enacted to date worldwide.[46] A Steering Committee on Mediation, chaired by the Secretary for Justice Mr Rimsky Yuen, was set up by the Department of Justice in late 2012 to further foster the development of mediation in the Hong Kong Special Administrative Region. The Steering Committee is comprised of members from different sectors including legal professionals, mediation experts, medical practitioners, academics, administrators, social workers, and insurers.[47]

The Steering Committee's Working Group on Mediation recommended, among other things, that there should be apology legislation for the purpose of enhancing mediation settlement. The main objective of this type of legislation in Hong Kong is to promote and encourage apologies in order to facilitate the amicable settlement of disputes.[48] Although an apology made during mediation would be already protected by the confidentiality provisions in the Mediation Ordinance, the Apology Ordinance is far broader in scope and covers all apologies made at any time between parties in dispute. In June 2015, the Steering Committee on Mediation launched a six-week public consultation to seek views on whether to enact apology legislation in Hong Kong. The Consultation Paper noted that

> [i]t appears that there is a general reluctance in both the public and the private sectors of our community to apologize, particularly when the issue of liability is yet to be decided. Such an attitude is not conducive to the prevention of escalation of disputes or the amicable settlement thereof.[49]

[44] Danny McFadden, 'No Hidden Dragon' (2012) New Law Journal 7542.

[45] The Apology Legislation, 1 December 2017, L.N. 148 of 2017, https://www.elegislation.gov.hk/hk/cap631.

[46] Herbert Smith Freehills, 'Apology Legislation Passed in Hong Kong: What Does it Mean for You?', Legal Briefing, 19 July 2017.

[47] Steering Committee on Mediation, Department of Justice, Hong Kong SAR, Revised 14 September 2018, https://www.doj.gov.hk/eng/public/mediation.html.

[48] Ibid.

[49] Hong Kong Department of Justice, 'Consultation Paper: Enactment of Apology Legislation in Hong Kong', Revised January 2018, https://www.doj.gov.hk/eng/public/apology.html.

The Apology Ordinance (Cap. 631) (Ordinance) was passed on 13 July 2017 and became effective on 1 December 2017. Section 7 states that an apology does not constitute an admission of fault or liability. Section 8 states that an apology must not be taken into account in determining fault, liability, or any other issue in connection with the matter to the prejudice of the person. Furthermore, Section 9 states that an apology does not constitute an 'acknowledgment' for purposes Section 23 of the Limitation Ordinance (Cap. 347), and Section 10 affirms that apologies do not void a contract of insurance or indemnity. The Ordinance seeks to change the current dispute resolution culture from one which is primarily adversarial to one that is more conciliatory in nature. It is hoped that it will encourage open and direct dialogue between disputing parties and offer an avenue to reduce tension, antagonism, and anger. It is noteworthy that an initiative born in the Mediation Steering Committee will potentially impact the manner in which Hong Kong parties, whether they mediate or not, choose to handle their disputes.

The promotion of commercial mediation in Hong Kong has certainly not let up and in May 2018, during Hong Kong's annual Mediation Week, the Department of Justice and the Hong Kong Trade Development Council (HKTDC) held the 'Mediate First—Exploring New Horizons Conference', which attracted a record 580 participants.[50] In October 2018, the first Hong Kong ICC Mediation Competition was held, which was the first time the ICC Mediation Competition (the Competition) was held in Asia.[51] Law school university teams from eight countries took part in the Competition.

C. Singapore

As noted, Singapore was an early adaptor and champion of modern commercial mediation practice. After introducing modern mediation practice and developing institutions to handle cases in the 1990s, Singapore has 'kicked on' again. In the last three or four years, it has refreshed and revived its mediation institutions, including by introducing a new mediation act. There are two types of commercial mediation practice in Singapore: court-based mediation and private mediation. Court-based mediation is mediation that takes place in the courts after parties have commenced litigation proceedings.

1. Court-based dispute resolution

Court dispute resolution (CDR) at the Primary Dispute Resolution Centre (PDRC) was introduced in a pilot project in 1994. The Court Mediation Centre was established in 1995. It was renamed the Primary Dispute Resolution Centre in

[50] See https://www.doj.gov.hk/mediatefirst/eng/programme2018.html.
[51] See https://iccwbo.org/event/icc-international-commercial-mediation-competition-hong-kong/.

May 1998, as CDR expanded to include processes other than mediation, e.g. early neutral evaluation and binding and non-binding evaluation, and special forms of mediation like CDR-international, co-mediation with experts, mini-trial, and mediation-arbitration. CDR has had an enormous positive impact on Singapore's judicial system.[52]

A multi-door courthouse was established within the Primary Dispute Resolution Centre in 1999. Its purpose is to assist and direct disputants in finding the appropriate dispute resolution mechanism within or outside the court system. Court-connected mediation refers to mediation held in court or conducted by a judicial officer or court official once legal proceedings have commenced. Apart from mediation under CDR, mediation may be employed within pre-trial conferences. However, the majority of all court-based mediation is handled under CDR. The vast majority of cases in the subordinate courts undergo CDR.

2. Private mediation

a) *The Singapore Mediation Centre*

It was recognized in Singapore that in spite of the success of the CDR system there was a need for mediation to be made available outside the court system. Some cases could be mediated before trial and other cases need more time than the CDR process allows. Therefore, in 1997, the Singapore Academy of Law (SAL) established the Singapore Mediation Centre (SMC), which was launched by the then-Chief Justice Yong Pung How.

As of 2017, more than 3,600 matters have been mediated at the SMC. The rate of settlement is about 70 percent, with 90 percent of them being resolved within one working day. Since its inception, about 3.3 billion US dollars' worth of disputes have been mediated at the SMC, the highest quantum being 209 million US dollars.[53] Of the more than 1,700 disputants who have taken part in the mediations held at the SMC, more than 84 percent reported saving costs, while more than 88 percent said they saved time. Also, more than 94 percent claimed that they would recommend the process to other persons in similar conflict situations.[54] In 2017, there were 538 matters filed for mediation at the SMC, an 8 percent increase from 2016. Of these, 465 were eventually mediated, a 15 percent rise from the previous year.

b) *Recent mediation initiatives*

After successfully developing the Singapore International Arbitration Center (SIAC) into one of the most popular arbitration centres in the world, thus enhancing Singapore's claim as a hub for global dispute resolution, the Singapore

[52] Dorcas Quek and Loong Seng Onn, Singapore Law Watch, Chapter 3, Section 1: Mediation, 2015 https://www.singaporelawwatch.sg/About-Singapore-Law/Overview/ch-03-mediation.

[53] Tan Lee Ming (ed.), 'Singapore Law Watch', 2017, https://www.singaporelawwatch.sg/About-Singapore-Law/Arbitration-ADR.

[54] Ibid.

Ministry of Justice turned its attention to mediation. The following are some highlights of Singapore's more recent mediation initiatives.[55]

The Singapore International Mediation Centre (SIMC) was established in 2104 to focus primarily on international cases.[56] Therefore, after 2014, SMC began to focus solely on local domestic commercial mediation cases. In 2017, SIMC had a panel of 73 expert mediators from fourteen countries and administered cases from diverse jurisdictions.[57]

In conjunction with SIAC, the SIMC also offers a hybrid arb-med-arb process, which allows settlement agreements that have been finalized in mediation to be rendered into an arbitration award and to become enforceable under the New York Convention.

The Singapore International Mediation Institute (SIMI) was established to 'act as a standards body for mediation in Singapore'.[58] SIMI is not a statutory body but is *quasi*-official in nature since it is supported by the Singaporean government. SIMI has developed a credentialing system for mediators and, in an educational role, provides information to prospective users of mediation. SIMI is similar to the International Mediation Institute (IMI). It promulgates qualification and credentialing standards to contribute to the professionalization of the mediation practice in the region.[59]

In 2016, the Singapore International Dispute Resolution Academy (SIDRA) was established to provide a platform for developing ideas on theory, practice, and research into mediation. The Singapore Mediation Act (Act), passed in 2017, is intended to bring clarity into the law with regard to mediation. Significantly, the Act allows for the recording of a mediated settlement agreement as an order of the court, which should make enforcement easier absent an arbitral award. Under the Act, where a mediated settlement agreement has been achieved in relation to a dispute for which no proceedings have been commenced in a court, any party to the agreement may, with the consent of all the other parties to that agreement, apply to a court to record the agreement as an order of court.[60] Under Section 12(5), a mediated settlement agreement that is recorded as an order of court may be enforced in the same manner as a judgment given or an order made by a court.

[55] SIAC, 'Singapore International Mediation Centre (SIAC) Announces New Records 2017', http://www.siac.org.sg/69-siac-news/560-siac-announces-new-records-for-2017.

[56] Peter Phillips, 'Singapore: The Hub of International Commercial Dispute Resolution', Business Conflict Management [blog] 30 October 2017, http://www.businessconflictmanagement.com/blog/2017/10/singapore-the-hub-of-international-commercial-dispute-resolution/.

[57] Joel Lee, 'Singapore Developments – The Singapore International Mediation Institute and the Singapore International Mediation Centre' Kluwer Mediation Blog [blog] 14 November 2014, http://mediationblog.kluwerarbitration.com/2014/11/14/singapore-developments-the-singapore-international-mediation-institute-and-the-singapore-international-mediation-centre/.

[58] See https://www.simi.or.sg.

[59] Ibid.

[60] See Singapore Mediation Act 2017, https://sso.agc.gov.sg/Act/MA2017.

D. Indonesia

Currently, the leading centre for commercial mediation in Indonesia is the Pusat Mediasi Indonesia (the Indonesian Mediation Centre, or PMN), which was established in 2003.[61] The PMN is a non-profit foundation providing mediation training and services. It is staffed with experienced mediators drawn from diverse areas of law, banking, engineering, and business. The PMN promotes the use of mediation and since its inception has provided many training programmes for Indonesian lawyers and judges. The organization is deeply involved with the Asian mediation community and in October 2018 hosted the 5th Asian Mediation Conference, which was attended by 220 delegates from the Asian region.[62]

The Asian Mediation Association (AMA) is a regional membership body comprising thirteen mediation centres, all based in Asia. The founding members of AMA are the PMN, the HKMC, the Malaysian Mediation Centre (MMC), the Philippine Mediation Centre (PMC), and the SMC. The PMN currently serves as the AMA Secretariat. The AMA aims to promote and facilitate the use of mediation to amicably settle disputes in Asia, and hopes to provide a regional dispute resolution infrastructure for conflict management and dispute resolution that will support the increasing cross-border investment and trade activities of the fast-growing Asian economies.[63]

The prospects for the PMN are bright as Indonesia is undergoing a massive modernization programme and the economy has been strong for some years. It is hoped that this will encourage the use of modern mediation in non-domestic cases and that foreign businesses will be comfortable with Jakarta as a centre for dispute resolution.

E. Thailand

In 2000, Thailand's Office of the Judiciary established the Thai Mediation Centre (TMC) to promote dispute resolution as a means of settling conflicts and to help develop the professional skills of Thai mediators for court-annexed cases. The TMC has worked closely with the Thai courts to assist in diverting cases from the courts to mediation and in developing regulations to govern the process.

With regard to international mediation cases, the Thailand Arbitration Centre (THAC) based in Bangkok has been heavily promoted by the Thai government as a regional dispute resolution centre.[64] The original purpose of the THAC was

[61] See https://pmn.or.id/pmn/.
[62] See https://pmn.or.id/pmn/the-5th-asian-mediation-conference/.
[63] Fahmi Shahab, Chairman PMN, Speech, Asian Mediation Association Conference, Jakarta, 21 October 2018.
[64] See http://thac.or.th/.

to support and promote the international system of arbitration and to become a centre of arbitration in the region. However, due to the increasing popularity of commercial mediation in Asia, the THAC decided to open the THAC Mediation Centre, which is currently building up its capacity by training mediators and promoting the use of mediation.

In May 2018, the THAC and the Regional Centre for Asia and the Pacific of the United Nations Commission on International Trade Law (UNCITRAL) hosted the first 'International ADR Conference'. Each year, the conference will address relevant issues in ADR, including the latest mediation developments.[65] The THAC noted that it is held in the backdrop of the One Belt One Road (OBOR) initiative and Thailand's development of the Eastern Economic Corridor, which forms part of OBOR.

F. Japan

Japan has a long tradition of using mediation to settle disputes. Like China, it draws on the Confucian preference for conflict to be resolved through negotiation, rather than confrontation, in a legal setting. In spite of this cultural inclination for more informal methods of resolving disputes, modern arbitration practice has grown over the last 15 years to be an acceptable forum for commercial disputes and is widely utilized in international cases.

However, in the last three years the use of modern mediation practice has been studied, promoted, and developed by leading ADR and university entities in Japan, e.g. the Japan Association of Arbitrators (JAA), which formed a committee to examine the feasibility of establishing a mediation centre, and Kobe University, which carried out mediation training in conjunction with the Centre for Effective Dispute Resolution (CEDR).[66]

Initiatives like these have led to exciting recent developments, including the opening of the new Japan International Mediation Centre–Kyoto (JIMC–Kyoto), which was inaugurated and officially opened in November 2018. The author is an adviser to the JIMC, and it was explained to him that the reason for choosing Kyoto (and not Tokyo or Osaka—Japan's two largest cities) was that it is the former capital of Japan, easy to get to, a beautiful location, and would be an attractive venue in which mediation participants can spend time.

The JIMC–Kyoto Mediation Centre is based at the main campus of Doshisha University in central Kyoto. The Centre will focus on international commercial mediations and administer the cases, including providing rooms and interpretation

[65] See http://thac.or.th/en/events/1st-international-adr-conference-2018/.
[66] Centre for Effective Dispute Resolution (CEDR) https://www.cedr.com/.

facilities. An international panel of mediators is currently being chosen, and mediation rules, codes of conduct, and others matters are being finalized.[67]

G. Korea

Koreans, like the Chinese and the Japanese, traditionally have avoided lawsuits.[68] As in other parts of Asia, Koreans' preference for mediation comes in part from their strong Confucian heritage, which holds that the very existence of unlawful behaviour indicated a failure of the moral system. Historically, the two types of ADR that are most used in Korea are arbitration and mediation in the form of court-annexed or statutory conciliation.[69] Court-annexed conciliation was underpinned by the enactment of the Judicial Conciliation of Civil Disputes Act of 1990 (JCCDA). In 2009, the Korean Supreme Court launched the Court-Annexed Mediation Center (CMC) as a pilot programme and expanded it in 2011 in order to reduce the overloaded caseworks and provide better legal services to the public.[70]

The conciliation system is classified as either judicial conciliation or non-judicial conciliation, i.e. statutory conciliation administered by governmental agencies. The difference between general mediation and statutory conciliation is in the enforcement procedure, since a settlement agreement made at statutory conciliation has the same effect as a judicial compromise, making it enforceable, unlike its general mediation counterpart, which has no such effect. Under court-annexed conciliations, the judge may undertake the conciliation procedure by himself or refer to a conciliation committee composed of three members: a judge and two other non-judges.[71]

As in other Asian jurisdictions, e.g. Japan, a modern non-court annexed mediation service has been created in Korea as an offshoot of an arbitration body, the Korean Commercial Arbitration Board (KCAB). The KCAB has long kept a close eye on the development of mediation in commercial hubs like Hong Kong and Singapore, including inviting speakers and ADR experts to hold workshops in Seoul.[72] However, recently this has now translated into a 'full steam ahead'

[67] Nicholas Brown, Pinsent Masons, 'International Dispute Resolution Centre will be Good for Japan' Mondaq, updated 5 March 2018, http://www.mondaq.com/x/679508/Arbitration+Dispute+Resolution/International+Dispute+Resolution+Centre+Will+Be+Good+For+Japan.

[68] Linda Lewis, 'The Korean Judge' Asiasociety.org, https://asiasociety.org/education/korean-judge 2018.

[69] Kyung-Han Sohn, 'Alternative Dispute Resolution System in Korea', Aram International Law Offices, 2006, 13 https://www.softic.or.jp/symposium/open_materials/11th/en/Sohn.pdf.

[70] Yonghwan Choung, *Achieving Justice Through ADR: An Analysis of the Korean Mediation System* (2017). PhD. Indiana University Maurer School of Law, https://www.repository.law.indiana.edu/etd/39.

[71] https://www.softic.or.jp/symposium/open_materials/11th/en/Sohn.pdf.

[72] See http://www.kcab.or.kr/jsp/kcab_eng/mediation/medi_01_ex.jsp.

approach with the creation of mediation panels, mediation rules, and other administrative documents needed to support commercial mediation. It is still early days for modern fee-paying commercial mediation in Korea, but as elsewhere it is acknowledged that to encourage international cases or lawyers to consider Korea as a venue for dispute resolution, mediation must be part of the service offered to lawyers and their clients. To promote Korea to the ADR world in 2017, the KCAB sponsored the 1st Asia Pacific Mediation Conference in Seoul, which was attended by practitioners and mediation experts from around the globe.[73]

III. Investment Disputes in the Asia Pacific Region

Any dispute resolution professional or litigation lawyer living in the Asia Pacific region cannot escape the barrage of information or invitations to events surrounding the Belt and Road (BR)[74] initiative. For example, in Hong Kong each week seems to bring announcements that one organization or another is holding events around investment disputes that always highlight the BR. For example, Hong Kong's pitch for BR work includes the offer of arbitration and mediation:

> For Hong Kong, Belt and Road offers a historic opportunity to leverage its status as China's most cosmopolitan city—a modern financial hub combining efficient infrastructure, well-regulated markets and Western-style legal institutions with deep understanding of Chinese culture and business practices. [75]

For some years but with increasing intensity, similar articles will have appeared in Singapore and other major Asian cities and where there is business there is inevitably conflict, which needs dispute resolution. Cities all over Asia are busily strengthening or creating new commercial mediation models and bodies to cater for this anticipated influx of cases. The foundations for this optimism would appear to be a fact, not a plan existing only on paper, and the need for investment in infrastructure throughout Asia is also genuine.

[73] See http://www.kcab.or.kr/jsp/kcab_eng/noticebrd/eng_noticebrd_2020_s.jsp?pageno=1&pagesize=10&search_word=&search_word_kind=&SEQ=1375&BRWSCNT=&file_no=&NOTI_CLSF=&file_no=&titl=&dwloadcnt=.

[74] Please note that previously the full term One Belt One Road (OBOR) was used to describe this initiative, but recently a consensus does seem to be emerging to use a shorter name Belt and Road (BR). However, in Chinese newspapers published in Chinese written script, the former version is still used.

[75] Kevin Sneader, South China Morning Post, 17 May 2016, http://www.scmp.com/comment/insight-opinion/article/1946161/chinas-one-belt-one-road-perfect-stage-hong-kong-showcase March 2106.

A. The Asia Pacific Economy

The Asia–Pacific region continues to be the world leader in growth, and recent data from the IMF points to an increase in momentum. Growth was projected to reach 5.5 percent in 2017 and 5.4 percent in 2018.[76] Despite volatile capital flows, Asian financial markets have been resilient, reflecting strong fundamentals. Recent additional policy stimulus, especially US fiscal policy, could provide further support. On the downside, a possible shift toward protectionism in major trading partners also represents a risk to the region.[77] Asia is vulnerable to a decline in global trade because the region has significant participation in global supply chains.[78] In spite of this potential for a slowing down in the growth of trade, the region is abuzz with activity and excitement regarding China's new Belt and Road initiative.

1. Background

According to the Asian Development Bank (ADB), developing Asia will need to invest 1.7 trillion US dollars per year in infrastructure until 2030 to maintain its growth momentum, tackle poverty, and respond to climate change. The ADB estimates Asia will need to invest 26 trillion US dollars from 2016 to 2030. Even without climate change mitigation and adaptation costs, 22.6 trillion US dollars will be needed or 1.5 trillion US dollars per year (baseline estimate).[79] The funding for these projects is currently not available and many countries in the region are looking to China, which has the capital, expertise, and excess capacity to bridge funding gaps by investing in Asia's infrastructure needs, primarily through the BR initiative.

2. The New Silk Road

In what has been called a New Silk Road, the BR is an exciting initiative to revive an ancient trade route and commercial network spanning half the world. The original Silk Road was a network of trade routes formally established during the Han Dynasty. The road originated from Chang'an (now Xian) in the East and ended in the Mediterranean in the West, linking China with the Roman Empire. It was not just one road, but rather a series of major trade routes that helped build trade and cultural ties between China, India, Persia, Arabia, Greece, Italy, and the Mediterranean countries. These East–West routes eventually joined up to form the

[76] International Monetary Fund (IMF), 'Asia at the Forefront: Growth Challenges for the Next Decade and Beyond', Regional Economic Outlook: Asia Pacific, October 2018, https://www.imf.org/en/Publications/REO/APAC/Issues/2018/10/05/areo1012.

[77] 'The Looming Global Trade War', The Economist, 8 March 2018, https://www.economist.com/briefing/2018/03/08/the-looming-global-trade-war.

[78] International Monetary Fund (IMF), 'Preparing for Choppy Seas', Regional Economic Outlook: Asia Pacific, May 2017, www.imf.org/en/Publications/REO/APAC/28/04/2017.

[79] Asian Development Bank, 'Meeting Asia's Infrastructure Needs' (February 2017), https://www.adb.org/publications/asia-infrastructure-needs.

4,000 mile-long Silk Road. The Silk Road became a conduit, not just for silk and jade from the East, but for wool, silver, and gold from the West, and for the transfer of ideas in both directions. It reached its height during the Tang Dynasty and declined in the Yuan dynasty.[80]

BR will cover nearly two-thirds of the world's population and one-third of global GDP. The initiative is a departure from broader trends in Chinese outbound investment, which is increasingly being led by private firms. At least in the initial stages, the state, China's state-owned enterprises (SOEs), and the largest financial institutions will be taking the lead. In its discussion of BR, a national government work report encouraged active involvement in overseas infrastructure investment and construction, e.g. through the export of equipment and machinery.[81]

To support this huge undertaking, China has set up several financial mechanisms that are funded by its foreign-exchange reserves. A 40 billion US dollars Silk Road Infrastructure Fund has been established to finance the project, in addition to the Asian International Infrastructure Bank (AIIB) as a new Multilateral Development Bank (MDB). This bank will complement and cooperate with existing MDBs to support infrastructure needs in Asia. These infrastructure projects are characterized by complex structures and arrangements, and they involve payments of considerable amounts of money over extended time periods, often in countries that are politically or economically unstable. As this investment activity will inevitably sometimes produce conflict between the investment partners, the Asian dispute resolution community has been quick to respond to this potential need. Many organizations and regional centres sense an opportunity to provide services to the investors in BR projects. Although it is not yet clear as to which institutions will be eligible to offer mediation to potential disputants, this has not prevented the creation of bodies wishing to service investment disputes and future BR cases.

B. Investor–State Mediation in Asian Belt and Road Projects

As noted, the demand for infrastructure development coupled with the new BR initiative has fast forwarded the plans by many Asian jurisdictions to either strengthen or create new ADR hubs and to include mediation as an important dispute resolution option for parties seeking resolution of commercial disputes. Apart from the exciting drive to strengthen mediation in countries like Japan and Thailand, other developments have been taking shape.

[80] Cyril Aydon, *The Story of Man* (Constable Press, 2007) 107.

[81] 'Prospects and Challenges on China's 'One Belt, One Road': A Risk Assessment Report, The Economist Intelligence Unit 2015, http://www.eiu.com/Handlers/WhitepaperHandler.ashx?fi=One-Belt-One-Road-report.

For example, the International Centre for Settlement of Investment Disputes (ICSID) has recently launched programmes to highlight the potential of mediation in investment disputes. This has included conferences tailored for mediators in investor–state disputes on investor–state mediation with the American University Washington and training with the CEDR. This training has also taken place in Paris and, in October 2018, the Hong Kong Department of Justice hosted this course in Hong Kong. It was attended by lawyers, barristers, and arbitrators from many jurisdictions.[82]

Many institutions already have bespoke rules that can be used for investor–state mediation, and these institutions are promoting their utilization for BR cases, e.g. the International Bar Association (IBA) released its Investor–State Mediation Rules in 2012.[83] Similarly, both the Stockholm Chamber of Commerce (SCC) and the International Chamber of Commerce (ICC) have released their own revamped Mediation Rules, which are in addition to their pre-existing rules for mediation.[84] In the Asia Pacific region, mediation service providers like the CEDR, the Hong Kong International Arbitration Centre (HKIAC), and the SIMC all have rules that are adaptable and suitable for investment cases.[85]

C. Mediation and Investor–State Belt and Road Projects

Since the establishment of the BR, Asian ADR bodies and mediators have been actively seeking ways to interact with BR initiatives. On an institutional level, the AIIB is establishing a complaints system for those adversely affected by infrastructure programmes it supports, which will include mediation as part of the grievance process. The AIIB is considering appointing a panel of in-house mediators and external on-call mediators from different jurisdictions. The mediation process will be similar to that currently used by the International Finance Corporation (IFC) in its infrastructure projects.[86]

Hong Kong is keen to engage in promoting itself as a hub for dispute resolution. At present, Hong Kong has an investment agreement signed under the Closer Economic Partnership Arrangement (CEPA) between the Mainland and Hong Kong SAR Government. One of the dispute settlement mechanisms available is

[82] Held in Hong Kong 16–21 October 2018, https://www.doj.gov.hk/mediatefirst/eng/pdf/flyer_e.pdf.

[83] ICSID, 'Considering the Future of Investor State Mediation,' (15 June 2015), https://icsid.worldbank.org/en/Documents/process/IBA%20Rules%20for%20Investor-state%20Mediation%2.pdf.

[84] Stockholm Chamber of Commerce, 'New Mediation Rules in Stockholm' (2014), http://www.sccinstitute.com/about-the-scc/news/2014/new-mediation-rules-in-stockholm/ and ICC, 'New Mediation Rules' (2014), https://iccwbo.org/dispute-resolution-services/mediation/mediation-rules/.

[85] ICSID (n 83).

[86] This author interviewed AIIB staff members and arrived at this conclusion based on his knowledge of working within the IFC.

mediation pursuant to the Mediation Mechanism for Investment Disputes.[87] The Secretary of Justice, Ms Teresa Cheung, is championing the use of this mechanism and hopes that this will enhance Hong Kong's position as a business centre that will provide a raft of services, including dispute resolution.[88]

There are other initiatives in Hong Kong, such as the Mainland-Hong Kong Joint Mediation Centre, which was set up by the China Council for the Promotion of International Trade (CCPIT)/China Chamber of International Commerce (CCOIC) Mediation Centre, and the Hong Kong Mediation Centre, which was established to provide a platform for resolving cross-boundary commercial disputes and will promote Hong Kong as the centre of dispute resolution. Singapore's SIMC has also signed a cooperation agreement with the CCPIT Mediation Centre to promote the use of mediation in BR projects. [89]

In mainland China it has been announced that courts will be established to handle disputes arising from projects carried out under BR, [90] and as of writing, the courts will be based in Beijing, Shenzhen, and Xian. The BR Memorandum of Understanding (which China has signed with over seventy countries) does not specifically mention mediation, but rather refers to 'friendly consultations'. Whether these consultations will include mediation is not yet clear, and there is currently a degree of confusion. [91]

D. The Singapore Mediation Convention

The latest exciting development for international mediation is the UNCITRAL Convention on International Settlement Agreements Resulting from Mediation (the Convention), also called the Singapore Convention.[92] At its 51st session, UNCITRAL approved the final draft of the Convention on 26 June 2018. The Convention is scheduled to open for signature in August 2019 and it is hoped that sufficient member states will sign it for it to come into force. This Convention is intended to make it easier for businesses to enforce mediated settlement agreements with their cross-border counterparts. Unlike arbitration, which is enforced

[87] Trade and Industry Department, Government of Hong Kong Special Administrative Region, Mainland and Hong Kong Closer Economic Partnership Arrangement (CEPA): Mediation Mechanism for Investment Disputes, https://www.tid.gov.hk/english/cepa/investment/dispute.html.

[88] Ibid.

[89] Herbert Smith Freshfields, 'The Role of Mediation in the Resolution of Belt and Road Disputes', Asia Disputes Notes [blog], (11 October 2017), https://hsfnotes.com/asiadisputes/2017/10/11/the-role-of-mediation-in-the-resolution-of-belt-and-road-disputes/.

[90] Nicholas Groffman, 'Meet the 8 Judges Who Will Sit on Belt and Road Cases', South China Morning Post (25 September 2018), https://www.scmp.com/week-asia/economics/article/2165567/meet-8-chinese-judges-wholl-sit-belt-and-road-cases.

[91] Dezan Shira and Associates, 'Confusion over Dispute Resolution at China's New Belt and Road Courts', China Briefing [online] (February 2018), http://www.china-briefing.com/news/bilateral-confusion-dispute-resolution-chinas-new-belt-road-courts/.

[92] See Chapter 19, this volume.

by what is referred to as the Convention on the Recognition and Enforcement of Foreign Arbitral Awards (New York Convention), mediation has never had an internationally recognized law on the enforcement of settlement agreements. The new Convention is especially relevant for Asia, especially for China, where parties have often been reluctant to mediate because any agreement reached cannot be enforced in a local or overseas court. Currently, parties who conclude a mediated settlement outside the context of court proceedings or arbitration can generally only enforce the settlement as a contract. Thus, usually they need to obtain a court judgment for breach of contract, and then enforce the judgment in a chosen jurisdiction.

IV. Conclusion

This is an exciting time for mediation in Asia. Although Hong Kong and Singapore were early adopters of modern commercial mediation models, it is clear that other jurisdictions, especially China, are determined to introduce and promote commercial mediation within their own legal frameworks. Although the incentive to do so has always existed, the potential for disputes arising from new upcoming investor state and BR projects perhaps has turbo-charged the efforts of countries in the Asian region to create mediation services hubs sooner, rather than later. Furthermore, once the Singapore Convention comes into force, parties in Asia will find it easier to try mediation, knowing that any settlement reached at mediation can be enforced in a court. Ben Giaretta believes that the Convention 'will most likely change the language of international dispute resolution and make mediation a default option for commercial parties in international disputes.'[93] This remains to be seen, but demonstrates the high hopes that some have for the Convention.

In non-investor state commercial cases, the rivalry to be acknowledged as the premier hub for international commercial dispute resolution and mediation in Asia will continue as before, with Singapore and Hong Kong jockeying for the number one position. However, China and other Asian countries are not allowing this contest to be limited to the early adopters of commercial mediation; their efforts are already energizing the mediation sector throughout Asia.

[93] Ben Giaretta, 'The Singapore Convention: A Game Changer?', Mishcon de Reya, Briefings [online] (18 August 2018), https://www.mishcon.com/news/briefings/the-singapore-mediation-convention-a-game-changer.

10

Mediation of Cross-Border Commercial Disputes in the European Union

*Karen Vandekerckhove**

I. Introduction

This chapter maps the landscape of mediation in commercial matters at European level, including European Union (EU) action at the international level. It presents the main instruments in this area, in particular, the general instrument Directive 2008/52 of 21 May 2008 on certain aspects of mediation in civil and commercial matters, and specific instruments focused on consumer matters, in particular, Directive 2013/11 on consumer alternative dispute resolution and Regulation 524/2013 on consumer online dispute resolution, including the evaluations or first experiences with these instruments. It also considers a sector-specific initiative at EU level—the cross-border out-of-court complaints network for financial services. It further highlights relevant initiatives by the EU at international level, especially the ongoing preparation of a worldwide convention on the recognition and enforcement of judgments in civil and commercial matters (which is envisaged to include enforcement of judicial settlements) and of an international convention and/or model law on the enforcement of settlement agreements. It studies the relation between these various initiatives and instruments and reflects on the future of cross-border commercial mediation in the EU.

II. Mediation Directive 2008/52

A. Context of the European Mediation Directive

Directive 2008/52 of the European Parliament and of the Council of 21 May 2008 on certain aspects of mediation in civil and commercial matters (hereafter the 'Mediation Directive')[1] contributes to the creation, in the EU, of an area of freedom, security, and justice, as foreseen in Title V, Chapter 3 of the Treaty on

* Any views expressed in this contribution are personal and should not be attributed to the European Commission. The text of this contribution was finalized in May 2018.

[1] OJ of 24 May 2008, L 136, 3 ff.

the Functioning of the European Union (TFEU). More specifically, the Mediation Directive forms part of judicial cooperation in civil matters that the Treaty foresees among the EU member states. This cooperation constitutes the legal framework for the proper functioning of the internal market, one of the pillars of the Union. Article 81 of the TFEU provides explicitly for the possibility of taking measures at EU level to develop alternative methods of dispute settlement (see Article 81(2)(g)).

B. Short Overview of the Mediation Directive

1. Scope of application of the Directive

The Mediation Directive applies to civil and commercial matters (Article 1 of the Directive). The term 'civil and commercial matters' is an autonomous concept that must be interpreted in light of the objectives and the scheme of the legislation concerned as well as the general principles that stem from the corpus of the national legal systems.[2] It covers not only commercial disputes but also other types of civil law disputes, e.g. those concerning family law. Within the area of commercial disputes, it includes the broad range of consumer-to-business disputes, consumer-to-consumer disputes, and business-to-business disputes. Although the material scope of the Mediation Directive could potentially have been very broad, it is substantially limited by the provision stipulating that it only applies to cross-border disputes. The latter are mainly defined as disputes in which 'at least one of the parties is domiciled or habitually resident in a member state other than that of any other party' (Article 2).

The Mediation Directive applies to 'mediation', which is defined as a structured process, however named or referred to, whereby two or more parties to a dispute attempt by themselves, on a voluntary basis, to reach an agreement on the settlement of their dispute with the assistance of a mediator (Article 3(a)). As such, the Mediation Directive does not cover all possible types of alternative dispute resolution (ADR); in particular, it does not cover informal negotiations between parties without intervention of a third person.

2. Content of the Directive

The Mediation Directive does not aim to regulate mediation comprehensively. Rather, it limits itself to certain aspects of mediation, in particular, those concerning the access to mediation, the quality of the mediation services offered, and the interface between mediation and judicial proceedings. The Mediation Directive foresees an obligation for the member states to ensure the quality of mediation and to encourage the training of mediators (Article 4). Mediation is further promoted

[2] See Case C-29/76, *LTU Lufttransportunternehmen GmbH & Co KG v Eurocontrol*, ECR 1976, 1541.

by obliging the member states to ensure that the courts, in all cases coming within the scope of the Directive, can refer the parties to mediation (Article 5). Member states must also ensure that the agreement reached between the parties can be rendered enforceable (Article 6). This concerns the enforceability of the agreement or settlement at national level; the cross-border enforceability is governed by the applicable instruments of EU law.[3]

The interface between mediation and judicial proceedings is dealt with in Articles 7 and 8 concerning the confidentiality of mediation and the effect of mediation on limitation and prescription periods. Member states must ensure that information exchanged in the context of mediation remains, in principle, confidential. In addition, mediation may not have a negative impact on the running of limitation or prescription periods. Finally, the Mediation Directive requires member states to promote mediation by making public information concerning mediators and organizations providing mediation services (Article 9), and to inform the citizens on the authorities before which they can obtain the declaration of enforceability of a settlement agreement.

C. Evaluation of the Implementation of the Mediation Directive in National Law

1. Timing of the evaluation

The Mediation Directive was implemented in national law by 1 May 2011. Article 11 of the Directive provides that by 21 May 2016 the European Commission (EC) shall submit to the European Parliament, the Council and the European Economic and Social Committee a report on its application. That report must consider in particular the development of mediation throughout the EU and the impact of the Directive in the member states.

2. Basis for the evaluation

In order to prepare the evaluation, the EC asked two external contractors to carry out two studies, one in 2013 and one in 2016.[4] The methodology involved literature research and stakeholder consultations on the basis of a questionnaire. The consultations took place at both EU and national level by 28 national rapporteurs.

[3] In commercial matters, the main instruments concerned are Regulation 1215/2012 of 12 December 2012 on Jurisdiction and the Recognition and Enforcement of Judgments in Civil and Commercial Matters (Recast) (the so-called 'Brussels I Regulation Recast'), OJ 20.12.2012, L 351, 1–32, and Regulation 805/2004 of 21 April 2004 Creating a European Enforcement Order for Uncontested Claims, OJ 30.4.2004, L 143/15, 15–39.

[4] These studies are available (2013) at http://bookshop.europa.eu/nl/study-for-an-evaluation-and-implementation-of-directive-2008-52-ec-themediation-directive--pbDS0114825/ and (2016) https://publications.europa.eu/en/publication-detail/-/publication/bba3871d-223b-11e6-86d0-01aa75ed71a1/language-en/format-PDF/source-61097803.

Stakeholders were identified among ministries of justice, mediators, mediation trainers and institutes, judges/courts, and users of mediation services. Stakeholders at EU level included, for instance, umbrella organizations of the traditional law professionals, e.g. the Council of Bars and Law Societies of Europe (CCBE) and the European Network of Councils for the Judiciary (ENCJ), as well as organizations focusing on mediation, e.g. the International Mediation Institute (IMI) and the European Association of Judges for Mediation (GEMME).

The application of the Directive was furthermore discussed in the European Judicial Network in Civil and Commercial Matters, at a dedicated meeting organized in July 2015. The framework of the Judicial Network allows information to flow directly from the member states to the EC and, vice versa, member states to be mutually inspired about possible improvements in the implementation, e.g. by way of exchange of best practices.

Finally, the EC launched a public consultation that took place towards the end of 2015 and the beginning of 2016. The Commission received 562 contributions, mainly from mediators (67.1 percent), but also from organizations specialized in mediation (8.2 percent) and lawyers (7.9 percent). From a geographical point of view, the contributions originated principally in Romania (20.7 percent), Spain (17.2 percent), and France (16.5 percent). Substantial contributions were also received from Belgium (9.5 percent) and Germany (9 percent).[5] In general, almost 70 percent of contributors found that the Mediation Directive has reached its objective and has been implemented in national law in an effective manner.

In evaluating the Directive, the Commission was confronted by the lack of statistical data. In the great majority of member states no data are recorded concerning the average duration of a mediation procedure, the success rate of mediation, or its cost. As a result, it remains difficult to demonstrate the effectiveness of mediation and the possible savings in terms of time and costs for the parties. This lack of data may be expected to be partially remedied, at least in the area of consumer disputes, on the basis of Directive 2013/11 on alternative dispute resolution for consumer disputes, amending Regulation 2006/2004, and Directive 2009/22 (the so-called Directive on consumer ADR).[6]

3. General evaluation of the Directive

The Commission's report was adopted on 26 August 2016.[7] It concludes that, in general, the Mediation Directive has had an important impact on the awareness about mediation as an alternative form of dispute resolution. In that sense, the

[5] For the results of the public consultation, see https://ec.europa.eu/eusurvey/publication/MEDIATION2015.

[6] OJ L 165 of 18 June 2013, 63–79.

[7] Report from the Commission to the European Parliament, the Council and the European Economic and Social Committee on the Application of Directive 2008/52/EC of the European Parliament and of the Council on Certain Aspects of Mediation in Civil and Commercial Matters, COM(2016) 542final (Evaluation Report) .

Directive has, without doubt, constituted a step forwards in the promotion of access to ADR.

The impact of the Directive varies geographically depending on the extent to which individual member states possessed comprehensive regulated mediation systems *before* the implementation of the Directive. In fifteen member states with an extensive system of mediation in place before 2011, the Directive has had a limited or no impact, e.g. Belgium, where no specific implementation was carried out in light of the existing legislation. In nine member states, which prior to 2011 had disparate rules concerning mediation or which only provided for self-regulation, the Directive brought about a substantial modification in the existing legislative framework. Finally, four member states had no system whatsoever for mediation prior to 2011; in these member states, the Directive triggered a completely new legislative framework for mediation.[8]

Nevertheless, it appears from the report that mediation and the advantages linked to it remain insufficiently known among the public. In many member states, a 'culture' of dispute resolution based on mediation is lacking. Judges remain reticent to refer parties to mediation. The advantages of mediation are mainly recognized in the area of family law, particularly in disputes concerning parental responsibility over children, rights of access to children, and child abduction.[9] These are typically disputes where parties need to continue to cooperate in the long term—a specific incentive to make a success of mediation.

4. Specific evaluation of the Mediation Directive

a. Scope of application

A first positive point regarding the implementation of the Directive is that most member states have not limited the scope of application of the national provisions implementing the Directive to cross-border cases as this is foreseen in the Directive, but rather have extended its provisions to purely internal or national cases. As a result, the Directive has a much broader scope of application than was foreseen by the European legislator. This broad implementation not only has a positive effect on the overall impact of the Directive, but also it ensures equal treatment of cases submitted to mediation. It would indeed be difficult to understand why certain rules on mediation would only apply when one party has its domicile or residence abroad and not when all parties live in one and the same member state. It may be recalled that the EC in its original proposal had proposed to cover all cases, irrespective of where the parties are domiciled or reside. The Council and the European Parliament, however, thought it appropriate to reduce its scope, as they had done shortly before in two other instruments in the area of civil procedural law, particularly in the European Small Claims and the European

[8] Ibid., 3.
[9] Ibid., 4.

Order for Payment Regulations.[10] The reason behind this limitation lays in the reticence on the side of member states to see an interference of EU law in their national procedural law.

b. Quality control

The evaluation of the implementation of the Directive shows that member states generally have good quality control mechanisms in place. The establishment and the enforcement of codes of conduct for mediators constitute an important contribution to the quality of mediation. Such codes of conduct are available in all member states, either drawn up by the member state itself, or issued by organizations for mediation or mediators. While compliance with codes of conduct is generally voluntary, in a number of member states compliance is compulsory. Many codes of conduct are inspired by the European Code of Conduct for Mediators.[11]

The quality of mediation is furthermore ensured through procedures for the accreditation of mediators. However, these procedures, as well as the conditions for the provision of mediation services, differ substantially from one member state to the other. In the public consultation, a large number of respondents pleaded for the establishment of quality standards at EU level in order to ensure a certain minimum level of quality in all member states. However, this suggestion was not supported by the member states. Given the diverging opinions on the matter, the report suggests that the development of EU-wide quality standards could be steered by stakeholders, possibly supported by financing made available in the context of the European Committee for Standardization (CEN).

Finally, to a great extent the quality of mediation is ensured through a solid and continued training of those offering mediation services. The report shows that all member states provide for such training. Training is usually mandatory. Organizations interested in providing training services can make use of the financing opportunities existing under the European civil justice programme.[12]

c. Recourse to mediation

The Directive foresees that the courts must have the possibility of inviting the parties to use mediation (Article 5(1)). The evaluation of the implementation of the Directive shows that this possibility now exists in all member states.[13] In some member states, participation in an information session about mediation is mandatory for the parties, in all or in specifically defined disputes. In other member states, lawyers are required to inform their clients about the possibility of using

[10] Regulation 1896/2006 of 12 December 2006 Creating a European Order for Payment Procedure, OJ L 399 of 30 December 2006, 1–32; Regulation 861/2007 of 11 July 2007 Establishing a European Small Claims Procedure, OJ L 199 of 31 July 2007, 1–22.

[11] See http://ec.europa.eu/civiljustice/adr/adr_ec_code_conduct_nl.pdf.

[12] See http://ec.europa.eu/justice/grants1/programmes-2014-2020/justice/index_en.htm.

[13] Evaluation Report (n 7) 7.

mediation; in still other member states, the document introducing court proceedings must mention whether an attempt to mediate was undertaken or, in cases where it was not, why mediation was not an option. Many member states promote the use of mediation by way of financial incentives, e.g. through a reduction or reimbursement of court fees if an agreement is reached or through legal aid. On the other hand, some member states impose sanctions when the parties refuse mediation without justified reason or when they do not comply with a mediated agreement, starting legal proceedings on the matter covered by the agreement.[14]

One of the most contested issues in this regard is the question of whether mediation should be imposed mandatorily by law.[15] Opinions on this matter vary widely. While stakeholders, in particular mediators and mediation organizations, defend an obligation to mediate, member states and academics are highly sceptical. In the latter view, mediation can only be successful if it remains voluntary; a mandatory mediation would constitute an unjustified interference with the right of access to court. The Directive itself does not answer this question (see Article 5(2)). It is therefore up to the national legislator to determine whether and in which cases the imposition of an obligation to mediate may be appropriate.

Although the member states thus provide for stimuli aimed at promoting recourse to mediation, the public consultation shows that the majority of respondents believe that the measures taken in this respect are not sufficiently effective.[16] Many think that judges have insufficient knowledge of the possibilities offered by mediation or do not sufficiently trust mediation. The report therefore encourages member states to consider best practices in other member states in order to bring about domestic improvements.[17] In particular, the positive incentives, e.g. making mediation financially attractive for the parties, seem to be successful. In a recent study carried out for the European Parliament, the practice requiring parties to participate in an initial mediation session is especially considered as best practice in this regard.[18]

d. Confidentiality of mediation; limitation and prescription

The confidentiality of mediation is guaranteed in all member states, as required by the Directive. In some member states, the mediator is prevented from divulging whether an agreement was reached during mediation, unless the parties expressly

[14] Ibid., 8–9.

[15] Italy provides the most prominent example of a member state where a mandatory mediation process exists for a broad range of disputes. In some other member states, mandatory mediation exists or is being considered for a few specific categories of disputes, principally those involving children (see 2016 study (n 4), para. 3.1.3).

[16] Evaluation Report (n 7) 8.

[17] Ibid.

[18] See http://www.europarl.europa.eu/RegData/etudes/IDAN/2016/571395/IPOL_IDA(2016)571395_EN.pdf.

agree in writing. A number of mediators nevertheless regret that no 'mediator/client privilege' exists as it exists for lawyers.

In all member states, parties attempting mediation are protected against the expiry of limitation or prescription periods during the mediation process. At EU level, such protection is not only foreseen in the Mediation Directive, but also in sector specific legislation, e.g. in Article 18 of Directive 2014/104 on damages actions for infringements of competition law.[19]

e. Enforceability of agreements resulting from mediation

All member states provide for the enforceability at national level of agreements resulting from mediation. The public consultation shows that it is rarely necessary to proceed to enforcement, since mediated agreements are usually complied with voluntarily.[20]

The cross-border enforceability is governed by the existing instruments of EU law (mainly the Brussels I Recast and European Enforcement Order Regulations, see text to (n 58) ff). In their study for the European Parliament, Carlos Esplugues and Jose Luis Iglesias plead for a more far-reaching mechanism of cross-border enforcement based on a so-called 'EU Mediation Settlement Certificate'[21] modelled on the basis of the certification system of the European Enforcement Order (Regulation 805/2004).[22] At the international level, reference may be made to the project of Working Group II of the United Nations Commission on International Trade Law (UNCITRAL), which aims to regulate the enforcement of mediated agreements in commercial matters.[23] These matters are considered more in detail in section IV.

f. Informing the public

The evaluation of the application of the Directive has shown that much information is available concerning mediation, its benefits, and its practical elements, e.g. costs and procedure. Nevertheless, it also shows that, in general, the awareness of the public in regard to mediation is low and that the information does not easily reach potential users.[24] The challenge therefore remains for member

[19] Directive 2014/104/EU of the European Parliament and of the Council of 26 November 2014 on Certain Rules Governing Actions for Damages under National Law for Infringements of the Competition Law Provisions of the Member States and of the European Union, OJ L 349, 5 December 2014, 1–19.

[20] Evaluation Report (n 7) 11.

[21] Carlos Esplugues and Jose Luis Iglesias, 'Mediation and Private International Law: Improving Free Circulation of Mediation Agreements across the EU', in European Parliament (ed.), *The Implementation of the Mediation Directive*, Compilation of in-depth analyses for the workshop held on 29 November 2016, 44 ff, see http://www.europarl.europa.eu/RegData/etudes/IDAN/2016/571395/IPOL_IDA(2016)571395_EN.pdf.

[22] Regulation 805/2004 (n 3).

[23] See http://www.uncitral.org/uncitral/en/commission/working_groups/2Arbitration.html.

[24] Evaluation Report (n 7) 12.

states to raise awareness among the general public about mediation as an alternative form of dispute resolution. The EC contributes, for instance, through the European Judicial Network in Civil and Commercial Matters, which provides information on its website about mediation at European level and in each individual member state.[25] The European e-justice portal further contains a significant amount of information about the existing mechanisms for mediation and contact details.[26]

5. Conclusion

The report of the EC concludes that the Directive has been implemented correctly in the national legislation of the member states. It has reached its objective to regulate a few crucial elements regarding mediation, in particular confidentiality, limitation and prescription, and enforceability, and to promote the quality of mediation services. As a result, the Directive has given a boost to the general acceptance of mediation as a method of dispute resolution.[27]

The effect of the Directive on the use in practice of mediation seems more difficult to evaluate due to a persisting lack of statistics. The benefits of the Directive in terms of costs are mainly defined by reference to the actual costs of mediation compared to the costs of court proceedings. Personal benefits for the parties, or more generally the benefits for society as a whole, remain vague. Nevertheless, Klaus Hopt and Felix Steffek note that the positive effects of the Mediation Directive go far beyond its mere transposition. It has prompted thought, debate, and countless initiatives in the member states in relation to the laws and practices of dispute resolution.[28]

This does not mean that access to mediation is optimal and could not be improved. The Commission is of the opinion that further improvement should not be pursued at this time by way of legislative initiatives at EU level, but rather should be triggered by initiatives at the level of the member states. Such initiatives should strive to promote a 'culture' of mediation, raising awareness of the different possibilities relating to mediation and providing for legal and financial incentives to use these possibilities. At EU level, the Commission continues to finance projects aimed to promote mediation in the context of the European civil justice financial programme.[29]

[25] See https://e-justice.europa.eu/content_mediation-62-en.do?init=true.
[26] See https://e-justice.europa.eu/home.do?action=home&plang=en&init=true.
[27] Evaluation Report (n 7) 13.
[28] Klaus Jürgen Hopt and Felix Steffek, 'Mediation: Comparison of Laws, Regulatory Models, Fundamental Issues', in Klaus Jürgen Hopt and Felix Steffek (eds), *Mediation: Principles and Regulation in Comparative Perspective* (OUP, 2013), 7.
[29] Evaluation Report (n 7) 13.

III. Mediation in Consumer Disputes

The gradual development of the internal market in the EU has shown a particular need to boost consumers' and traders' confidence in buying and selling on the European marketplace. The possibility of settling disputes in an efficient and appropriate manner through out-of-court procedures is an element that can contribute to creating such confidence. Following two non-legislative measures aimed specifically to enhance consumers' trust in the bodies under national law responsible for out-of-court settlement of consumer disputes[30] or simply to bring parties together to convince them to find a solution through common consent,[31] the Union legislator decided, in 2013, to enact binding legislation in the area of consumer dispute resolution. Two major new instruments were adopted on 21 May 2013: Directive 2013/11 on alternative dispute resolution for consumer disputes, amending Regulation 2006/2004 and Directive 2009/22 (the so-called 'Directive on consumer ADR', hereafter referred to as the 'ADR Directive');[32] and Regulation 524/2013 on online dispute resolution (ODR) for consumer disputes, equally amending Regulation 2006/2004, and Directive 2009/22 (the so-called 'Regulation on consumer ODR', hereafter referred to as the 'ODR Directive').[33] The two instruments are complementary and constitute a key action under the EC's Single Market Act[34] and Digital Single Market Strategy.[35]

A. The ADR Directive

1. The ADR Directive: an overview

The ADR Directive aims to ensure access to simple, efficient, fast, and low-cost resolution of both domestic and cross-border disputes between consumers and

[30] Commission Recommendation 98/257/EC of 30 March 1998 on the Principles Applicable to the Bodies Responsible for Out-of-Court Settlement of Consumer Disputes, OJ L 115, 17 April 1998, 31 ff. The Recommendation laid down certain minimum standards with which these bodies (independence, transparency) or the procedure itself (adversarial principle, effectiveness, legality of the outcome) should comply.

[31] Commission Recommendation 2001/310/EC of 4 April 2001 on the Principles for Out-of-Court Bodies Involved in the Consensual Resolution of Consumer Disputes, OJ L 109, 19 April 2001, 56 ff. The 2001 Recommendation extended the principles of the 1998 Recommendation to bodies bringing parties together without necessarily proposing or imposing a solution of the dispute and specified the existing principles on certain points.

[32] OJ L 165 of 18 June 2013, 63–79.

[33] Ibid., 1–12.

[34] Communication from the Commission to the European Parliament, the Council, the Economic and Social Committee, and the Committee of the Regions of 13 April 2011, Single Market Act—Twelve Levers to Boost Growth and Strengthen Confidence—Working Together to Create New Growth, COM(2011) 206 final.

[35] Communication from the Commission to the European Parliament, the Council, the Economic and Social Committee, and the Committee of the Regions of 6 May 2015, A Digital Single Market Strategy for Europe, COM(2015) 192 final.

traders arising from sales or service contracts. It obliges member states to establish national ADR infrastructures that give EU consumers access to ADR entities for their contractual disputes in virtually all economic sectors[36] independent of whether the purchase was made online or offline (Article 5). The Directive builds on the existing infrastructures of out-of-court procedures in the member states, which are quite diverse (e.g. mediation, conciliation, arbitration, ombudsmen, complaint boards).

The ADR Directive further ensures that all ADR entities notified to the Commission by national authorities offer high quality services by respecting binding quality requirements such as independence, impartiality, transparency, effectiveness, and fairness (Articles 6–9). Compliance with these quality requirements is monitored by national competent authorities. Finally, the ADR Directive ensures that consumers and traders are aware of the possibility to settle their disputes through ADR by imposing information obligations on traders.

The ADR Directive has been in force since 9 July 2015 (Article 25). By 9 January 2016, member states had to communicate to the Commission the list of competent ADR entities complying with the quality requirements of the Directive. This notification was a pre-condition for the start of the online dispute resolution system foreseen in the ODR Regulation. A first evaluation of the application of the ADR Directive is foreseen for 9 July 2019 (Article 26). It will pay particular attention to the development, functioning, and use of ADR entities, as well as the impact of the Directive on consumers and traders, particularly in terms of awareness among consumers and level of acceptance by traders.

2. The ADR Directive and the Mediation Directive

The respective scopes of application of the ADR and the Mediation Directive differ substantially. Firstly, while the Mediation Directive covers all civil and commercial matters, the ADR Directive only applies to certain types of consumer disputes arising from sales or service contracts. Second, while the Mediation Directive applies to all disputes between traders and consumers, between traders, and between consumers (B2C, C2B, C2C, and B2B), the ADR Directive only covers consumer-to-business (C2B) disputes. Third, while the Mediation Directive covers only cross-border disputes defined in a narrow way, the ADR Directive applies to all disputes, wherever the parties are resident or established in the EU. Furthermore, while the Mediation Directive covers 'mediation' as defined in its Article 3(a), the ADR Directive covers a broader range of out-of-court dispute resolution methods. Finally, the Mediation Directive, adopted on the basis of current Articles 67(4) and 81 of the TFEU (previously Articles 61(c) and 67), applies to all EU member states except Denmark. The ADR Directive, on the other hand, applies to all EU

[36] Some sectors are excluded, such as health services and public providers of further or higher education (Article 2(2) of the ADR Directive).

member states without exception and has been extended to the countries of the European Economic Area (Iceland, Liechtenstein, and Norway). Also, the purpose of the ADR and Mediation Directives differs. Even if both instruments aim to promote alternative forms of dispute resolution, the Mediation Directive mainly does this by streamlining the interface between mediation and court proceedings while the ADR Directive principally aims to ensure access by consumers to high-quality ADR entities and procedures.

B. The ODR Directive

1. The ODR Directive in a nutshell

The ODR Directive complements the ADR Directive by providing for the creation of an EU-wide platform for the online resolution of contractual disputes between EU consumers and traders arising from online purchases of goods or services.[37] While the ODR Directive's scope is aligned with that of the ADR Directive (domestic and cross-border disputes concerning sales or service contracts between a consumer resident in the EU and a trader established in the EU through the intervention of an ADR entity listed pursuant to the ADR Directive; extension to the countries of the European Economic Area), there are two important differences in scope between the two instruments. First of all, the ODR Directive only applies to disputes concerning transactions concluded online; second, the ODR Directive does not only apply to complaints brought by a consumer against a trader, but also includes complaints brought by a trader against a consumer, at least insofar as the legislation of the member state where the consumer habitually resides allows for such disputes to be resolved through the intervention of an ADR entity.

The ODR platform constitutes a single point of entry for traders and consumers; it is accessible in all EU official languages and transmits complaints submitted to it to ADR entities that have been notified under the ADR Directive. ODR advisors offer assistance to consumers and traders throughout an ADR procedure taking place via the platform and for which an electronic case management tool is available. Electronic translation tools allow for the handling of cross-border disputes. While ADR entities act in accordance with the national procedural rules applicable to them, the Directive does set certain minimum standards regarding the submission, processing, and transmission of complaints, ensuring, for instance, that no physical presence of the parties or their representatives is required. In order to increase awareness among consumers and traders, traders are obliged to provide a link to the platform on their website. As a result of the late notification of the national lists of ADR entities and the late implementation of the ADR Directive in some member states, the platform was launched as foreseen on 9 January 2016,

[37] The platform is available at https://ec.europa.eu/consumers/odr.

but in a limited fashion only. It became accessible to consumers and traders on 15 February 2016.

2. First evaluation of the functioning of the ODR platform

Article 21 of the ODR Directive provides for an annual report from the Commission to the European Parliament and the Council on the functioning of the ODR platform. On 13 December 2017, the Commission published the first such report; it describes the steps taken for the establishment of the ODR platform and its first year of operation.[38] By mid-December 2017, the ODR platform offers access to more than 300 ADR bodies from twenty-six member states. At the end of its first year of operation, the platform had received some 1.9 million visitors, with an average of 160,000 visits per month. More than 2,000 complaints were submitted on average per month, totalling 24,000 complaints during the first year. These numbers have been increasing since then, reaching over 180,000 visitors per month and a filing of over 2,300 complaints per month by the end of 2017. The platform is most popular among consumers and traders in Germany and the United Kingdom—the member states with the highest proportion of online shoppers. However, it is also increasingly used in other member states, e.g. Spain, France, Italy, and the Netherlands. Most of the complaints handled through the platform concern transactions regarding clothing and footwear (11.5 percent), airline tickets (8.5 percent), and information and communication technology goods (8 percent). This coincides with the main e-commerce sectors in the EU. The legal problems underlying the complaints concern delivery (21 percent), non-conformity (15 percent), and defective goods (12 percent). About one-third of the complaints relate to cross-border transactions, and two-thirds to domestic transactions.

Concerning the outcome of the ODR procedure, the Commission's report notes that in 85 percent of the cases, the complaint was automatically closed within 30 days after submission. In 40 percent of these cases, the consumer had been contacted by the trader directly to solve the dispute and there was therefore no need to pursue the online dispute resolution. This shows, according to the report, that the use of the platform by consumers has a behavioural effect on traders as it incites them to settle the dispute rapidly so as to avoid the ODR procedure. Despite this positive note, in 60 percent of the cases the trader did not respond to the invitation to propose an ADR body. Reasons why the procedure was not pursued, besides bilateral negotiation, may be that the trader was not registered on the platform or that the notification did not reach the trader properly.

[38] Report from the Commission to the European Parliament and the Council on the functioning of the European Online Dispute Resolution Platform Established under Regulation (EU) No 524/2013 on Online Dispute Resolution for Consumer Disputes, COM(2017) 744final. Following finalization of this chapter, the European Commission adopted its second report, see https://ec.europa.eu/info/sites/info/files/2nd_report_on_the_functioning_of_the_odr_platform_3.pdf.

Nine percent of complaints were refused by the trader from the outset. However, also in most of these cases (two-thirds) it seems that the trader made direct contact with the consumer to solve the matter. In 4 percent of the cases, the parties withdrew from the procedure voluntarily. In 2 percent of the cases, the complaint was finally submitted to an ADR body. In half of these cases, the body concerned refused to deal with the case on procedural grounds. In the end, the procedure reached a final outcome in less than 1 percent of cases, mostly within the 90-day deadline set in the ADR Directive.

With this in mind, it may be concluded that the ODR platform has reached positive results. Even if very few cases have led to a solution mediated by an ADR body, the overall success rate is estimated at 44 percent of complaints, which have been resolved in one way or another through negotiation between the parties. The platform has thus mainly had an incentive effect, contributing to solving cases outside the platform.[39]

However, there exists one serious downside. Through a scraping exercise of more than 20,000 web shops across the Union, the Commission discovered that only 30 percent of traders established in the EU comply with the obligation to provide an easily accessible link to the platform. Large traders tend to comply better than small traders; traders in some member states have a better compliance record (e.g. 66 percent in Germany) than in others (e.g. 1 percent in Latvia); traders in certain sectors (e.g. insurance) comply better than traders in other sectors (e.g. online reservation of leisure). This finding, combined with other elements showing a lack of engagement on the part of traders with regard to the platform, shows that more needs to be done to engage traders and render the platform fully operational and capable of reaching its full potential.

C. Resolution of Consumer Disputes Concerning Retail Financial Services

A specific ADR scheme at EU level exists for the handling of cross-border disputes between consumers and retail financial service providers (banks, insurance companies, investment funds, payment service providers, etc.).[40] The scheme, called FIN-NET, has existed since 2001, but on a voluntary basis. It covers (potentially) all EU member states and the EEA countries.[41] The EC provides secretarial services for the group (such as the organization of steering and plenary committee meetings

[39] Report (n 38) 8.

[40] See https://ec.europa.eu/info/business-economy-euro/banking-and-finance/consumer-finance-and-payments/consumer-financial-services/financial-dispute-resolution-network-fin-net_en.

[41] Switzerland and the Channel Islands participate as FIN-NET affiliates in the network on a best-efforts basis.

for the exchange of best practices); it does not act as a member nor does it perform any tasks in relation to the resolution of disputes itself.

FIN-NET brings together out-of-court ADR schemes that deal with complaints in the area of financial services. It focuses on assisting consumers to solve cross-border complaints by providing a mechanism that allows them to contact an out-of-court scheme in their home country in case of a dispute with a foreign financial services provider.[42] The 'competent scheme' is the appropriate body responsible for the out-of-court settlement of consumer disputes for financial services in the country where the service provider is established. The 'nearest scheme' is a body responsible for the out-of-court settlement of consumer disputes for the appropriate financial services sector in the consumer's country of residence. The mechanism allows the consumer to contact the ADR scheme in his/her home state; the latter will inform the consumer about the competent ADR scheme in the service provider's country or transfer the complaint directly to that scheme. The competent ADR scheme carries out the investigation and issues a decision or recommendation.

FIN-NET addresses a clear need to raise consumer confidence in buying cross-border financial services. Indeed, confidence levels in this area are particularly low as a result of language barriers, incomplete information, and consumers' preference for potential face-to-face interaction with the financial service provider.[43] According to the 2015 FIN-NET activity report, FIN-NET members handled almost 4,200 cross-border cases, of which 1,300 were in the banking sector, 699 in the insurance sector, and 559 in the investment sector. Compared to 2014, this represented a net increase of almost 700 cross-border cases.[44] One issue that was raised, at least in the past, was the problem of language: many consumers do not speak the language of the foreign financial service provider and therefore found themselves in a weak position in case of a complaint. In such cases, the network operation does not make the resolution of disputes easier.[45] The ODR platform might address this specific problem in the light of specific language support that it provides.

Following the entry into force of the ADR/ODR Directives, FIN-NET decided to amend its operating rules in order to ensure compliance by its members with the quality requirements of the ADR Directive.[46] As a result, many FIN-NET members have already ensured such compliance and have notified their scheme to the EC

[42] While the definition of 'cross-border dispute' seems to refer to the residence/establishment of the parties in different member states, a somewhat broader definition is included in FIN-NET's 2015 Activity Report, (https://ec.europa.eu/info/sites/info/files/2015-activity-report_en.pdf), which refers to cases 'where consumers were located in a country different from that of the financial service provider or which involved the help of an ADR scheme situated in another Member State', 6.

[43] Centre for Strategy and Evaluation Services (CSES), *Evaluation of FIN-NET*, June 2009.

[44] See FIN-NET's Activity Report 2015 (n 42) 5. From 2007 to 2015, the number of cross-border disputes handled by FIN-NET members quadrupled—from around 1,000 cases handled in 2007 to over 4,000 cases in 2015.

[45] CSES (n 43). On this point, consumers may have easier access to justice before the courts, as they are able to claim before the courts of the member state where they are habitually resident (see Articles 17 ff. of the Brussels I Regulation Recast (n 3).

[46] See https://ec.europa.eu/info/sites/info/files/memorandum-of-understanding_en.pdf.

pursuant to Directive 2013/11.[47] The entry into force of the ADR Directive has also been a stimulus to increase FIN-NET's coverage, e.g. in member states where no ADR schemes existed in the retail financial services sector or where certain parts of the financial sector (i.e. banking, insurance, investments, payments) were not yet covered.[48] Nevertheless, as with many ADR schemes, FIN-NET continues to suffer from a lack of awareness; the latest activity report also questions whether a redress system where the powers of ADR schemes are largely defined at national level is still adequate for a fully integrated retail financial services market.[49]

IV. Cross-Border Enforceability of Settlement Agreements

The legal frameworks described herein aim to establish ADR mechanisms, ensure their quality, and provide a smooth interface with legal proceedings. Importantly, however, the legal effect of the outcome of an ADR procedure still needs to be considered. Such legal effect must be considered both at the national and at the cross-border level.

A. Domestic Effect of Dispute Resolution Outcomes

A wide variety of ADR schemes exists in the EU's member states and beyond. Legal effects also vary widely, depending on the scheme and the country concerned. Effects range from a simple suggestion or recommendation to a more or less binding decision. In some schemes/countries, the outcome may have preclusive effect, meaning that parties are not allowed to invoke the agreement as a procedural defence to a claim before the courts in relation to the matter covered by the agreement; in other schemes/countries, the outcome is enforceable but does not prevent the parties from having access to the courts in case the content of the agreement itself is contested and one of the parties files a claim regarding the matter covered by the agreement.

At EU level, Article 6 of the Mediation Directive is the only provision dealing with the effect of mediated agreements. It obliges member states to ensure that a mediated agreement in a cross-border dispute as defined in the Directive is enforceable at the domestic level, unless the agreement would be contrary to the law

[47] FIN-NET (n 42). The Memorandum of Understanding entered into force as of 12 May 2016. Bodies adhering to FIN-NET that are not notified under the ADR Directive have been excluded from FIN-NET as of 16 May 2018.

[48] The network currently covers sixty members in twenty-seven countries. Not all EU member states have members yet (e.g. no members exist in Bulgaria and Romania).

[49] FIN-NET (n 42) 3.

of the member state where the request for enforceability is made or that law does not provide for enforceability of the agreement in question. The declaration of enforceability may be given by a court or other competent authority (e.g. a notary). Within this broad framework, the conditions under national law to grant enforceability, as well as the role played by the authority in charge of the approval or confirmation of the agreement, and the grounds for refusal of the approval or confirmation differ among member states.

The requirement of an intervention by an authority to grant enforceable effect to mediated agreements is in line with the legal traditions in most EU member states; when the agreement is not voluntarily performed, the settlement is usually considered to be a contract which, even if binding on the parties, can only be enforced through court action (or arbitration).[50] The Mediation Directive does not provide for a preclusive effect of mediated agreements. This is based on the assumption that an agreement between the parties reached through mediation is by its very nature voluntary and will therefore be performed by the parties voluntarily. If this is not the case, then there is an evident lack of agreement between the parties on the substance of the matter which must be considered by an authority (e.g. a court).

B. Cross-Border Effect of Dispute Resolution Outcomes

1. Cross-border effect within the European Union

The cross-border effect of settlements among EU member states is governed by Articles 57 and 58 of Regulation 1215/2012 on jurisdiction and the recognition and enforcement of judgments in civil and commercial matters (recast).[51] The Brussels I Regulation Recast provides for direct cross-border enforcement of certain types of agreements between the parties to a dispute, particularly in commercial matters. In order to benefit from cross-border enforceability, the agreement in question must either be drawn up in an authentic instrument that is enforceable in the member state in which it was formally drawn up or registered, or it must have been approved by or concluded before a court of a member state in the course of proceedings (court settlement). The latter category includes not only settlements approved or concluded before a court in the course of court proceedings, but also agreements reached between the parties outside court proceedings, whether with the assistance of an ADR body or not, which are subsequently approved or confirmed by a court. If these conditions are fulfilled, the agreement/settlement may

[50] Hopt and Steffek (n 28) 46.

[51] Brussels I Regulation Recast (n 3). For Switzerland, Norway, and Iceland, cross-border enforceability of authentic instruments and court settlements is foreseen in Articles 57 and 58 of the 2007 Lugano Convention; however, these provisions do still require a declaration of enforceability in the State where enforcement is sought.

be enforced directly, i.e. no declaration of enforceability must be obtained in the member state where enforcement is sought.

The Brussels I Regulation Recast thus provides for a certain control, or at least a confirmation, by an authority in the member state of origin as a precondition for the enforceability of the agreement or settlement in other member states. The only defence against the cross-border enforcement of the agreement is a violation of public policy in the member state where enforcement is sought. In addition, if the settlement or agreement has been certified as a European Enforcement Order pursuant to Articles 24 or 25 of Regulation 805/2004 creating a European Enforcement Order for uncontested claims, its cross-border enforcement cannot be opposed on any ground.[52] Agreements or settlements that do not comply with these conditions may not circulate among member states pursuant to the discussed instruments. This does not mean, however, that they may not circulate at all among EU member states; such circulation may be possible but only pursuant to national law.

2. Cross-border effect at the international level

No regime ensuring the cross-border effect of an outcome of an ADR procedure currently exists at international level. The 1958 New York Convention on the Recognition and Enforcement of Foreign Arbitral Awards could ensure circulation if the agreement or settlement is incorporated in an arbitral award. Beyond this limited regime, efforts are ongoing to establish an international legal framework in the context of the Hague Conference on Private International Law and UNCITRAL.

a. Draft Convention on the Recognition and Enforcement of Judgments in Civil and Commercial Matters

The Draft Convention on the Recognition and Enforcement of Foreign Judgments relating to Civil and Commercial Matters currently being prepared under the auspices of the Hague Conference on Private International Law provides in its Article 12 for the cross-border enforcement of judicial settlements (*transactions judiciaires*), which a court of a contracting state has approved, or which have been concluded in the course of proceedings before a court of a contracting state, and which are enforceable in the same manner as a judgment in the state of origin. The conditions for the cross-border effect of settlements in the draft text thus largely compare to those applicable among EU member states. A cross-border enforcement of authentic instruments is not envisaged at the international level due to the uncertain scope that such a provision would have.

[52] Regulation Creating a European Enforcement Order for Uncontested Claims (n 3).

b. Draft Instrument on the Enforcement of International Commercial Settlement Agreements Resulting from Conciliation/Mediation

Another international instrument was prepared in the context of UNCITRAL.[53] This instrument concerns the enforcement of international commercial settlement agreements resulting from conciliation or mediation.[54] The instrument would be developed in double form, first, as draft model law complementing the 2002 UNCITRAL Model Law on international commercial conciliation, and, second, as an international convention. Both instruments would have substantially equivalent provisions.

The UNCITRAL instrument would aim to cover business-to-business settlements, explicitly excluding consumer disputes.[55] It would cover international settlement agreements, defined as in Article 1(4) of the 2002 Model Law, i.e. agreements between parties having their place of business in different states; if parties have their place of business in the same state, a substantial part of the obligations under the settlement agreement would have to be performed in another state or the subject-matter of the agreement should be most closely connected to another state. The settlements covered are those resulting from conciliation (in the most recent documents referred to as 'mediation') within the meaning of Article 1(3) of the 2002 UNCITRAL Model Law, requiring in particular the participation of one or more third persons (conciliator(s)); these conciliators do not have the authority to impose a solution on the parties. States adopting the future model law or contracting parties to the future convention would be able to declare that the instrument only applies if the parties to the agreement have provided for its applicability in their settlement agreement.

The draft UNCITRAL instrument would follow a different philosophy from the currently prevailing one in the EU. It would provide for the cross-border enforcement of settlement agreements without prior control in the country where the agreement is concluded. The controls would mainly take place in the country where enforcement is sought, such as by way of a declaration of enforceability. Enforcement of the settlement could be refused on the basis of certain defences, such as those related to the capacity of the parties, the validity of the agreement, the standards applicable to the mediation, the impartiality or independence of the mediator, as well as the traditional defences of public policy of the state where enforcement is sought, or the fact that the law of that state does not allow the dispute to be settled by conciliation/mediation due to its subject matter. The draft instrument should be coordinated with the draft Convention on the Recognition

[53] Following the finalization of this chapter, the work in UNCITRAL was finalized and resulted in the Convention on the Recognition and Enforcement for Mediated Settlements (Singapore Convention), see Chapter 19, this volume.

[54] The terms conciliation and mediation are used on an interchangeable basis in the UNCITRAL notes (see in particular the note prepared for the February 2018 meeting of Working Group II, available at http://www.uncitral.org/uncitral/en/commission/working_groups/2Arbitration.html).

[55] Also, family law and employment law disputes would be excluded.

and Enforcement of Foreign Judgments mentioned earlier and with the New York Convention by excluding from its scope judicial settlements and settlements incorporated in arbitral awards.

V. Concluding Remarks: The Future of Cross-Border Commercial Dispute Resolution in the European Union

The value of mediation as a form of dispute resolution has been broadly recognized at EU level, as the legal framework discussed herein shows. The Mediation Directive applies broadly to all civil and commercial matters (including family law); the ADR Directive and ODR Regulation focus specifically on consumer contracts. However, the various instruments at EU level have been developed at different times and separately from each other, and it is not always clear how they relate to each other. Questions could be raised, for instance, regarding the scope of the various instruments. Is it necessary to limit the scope of application of the Mediation Directive to cross-border cases? It is difficult to argue that the quality of mediation, its confidentiality, its effect on limitation and prescription periods, and the enforceability of the mediated agreement should not also extend to purely domestic or cross-border cases beyond those provided for in the Directive, especially where the agreement needs to be enforced abroad. Extending the scope of application of the Mediation Directive would ensure that minimum standards are applicable to all mediations across the Union in civil and commercial matters, wherever the parties are domiciled or reside. It would also align the Mediation Directive with the ADR Directive and the ODR Regulation on this particular point. In addition, the geographical scope of the various instruments could be aligned; in particular, it would be worthwhile considering the extension of the Mediation Directive, as a parallel instrument to the ADR Directive and ODR Regulation, to the EEA states.

As regards the ADR Directive, it could be questioned why its scope should be limited to sales and service contracts only. An extension to all contractual obligations, including, e.g. licensing agreements, could ensure a broader impact of mediation across Europe. As regards the ODR Regulation, why should its scope of application should be limited to online purchases; particularly as regards domestic cases, the use of the platform may also be helpful to consumers purchasing off-line. Also, the use of the platform could be opened up to traders; if this entails cost increases, it could be provided that traders would not benefit from financial assistance which would be reserved for consumers.

At EU level, it is common practice to regularly evaluate and review existing legislation. However, such evaluation is usually carried out for each separate instrument concerned (see the evaluation of the Mediation Directive and the first report on the ODR Directive). A more horizontal critical evaluation covering all the existing instruments in the area of mediation would permit an overview of the entire mediation landscape at EU level and could form the basis for a better coordination between the various instruments.

In his study for the European Parliament, Steffek suggests that the relationship between not only the various EU instruments but more broadly different forms of dispute resolution could be improved either by a horizontal instrument concentrating on the relationship between forms of dispute resolution or by integrating provisions on the relationship among different instruments in the individual instruments regulating specific forms of dispute resolution. More importantly, Steffek pleads for a general framework instrument regulating dispute resolution, establishing principles ensuring coherence both within and across specific forms of dispute resolution and both in a domestic and in a cross-border context.[56]

Regarding the cross-border enforcement of settlement agreements, it seems that the current EU instruments, in particular, the Brussels I Recast and European Enforcement Order Regulations, operate satisfactorily. These instruments cover the bulk of commercial settlements insofar as these are confirmed by a court or drawn up in an authentic instrument. An extension of these instruments to cover the cross-border enforcement of purely private agreements, not confirmed by a court or notary, would probably require a minimum harmonization of the procedure and safeguards surrounding mediation.

A tentative proposal in this direction has been made by Esplugues and Iglesias.[57] These authors propose the creation of an EU mediation settlement certificate: this proposal is based on the finding that the current regime regarding the circulation of agreements/settlements, which requires authentication by a public authority or confirmation by a court and entails costs and time for the parties. A less time- and cost-consuming mechanism could be set up whereby an authority in the country where the settlement originated would certify compliance with certain minimum standards regarding, for instance, the subject-matter of the dispute and the participation of an accredited mediator. The creation of the certificate would be accompanied by minimum standards regarding the quality and formation of mediators. This certificate could also be granted to merely private agreements that are not enforceable in the country of origin. In this proposal, the agreement/settlement would still be subject to control in the country where enforcement is sought, in particular, public policy control.

The question does arise, however, whether the certification process proposed would remedy the problem of cost and time of the existing confirmation by a court or authentication by a notary. Its added value would depend on whether the type of certification would be cheaper and less time-consuming than the current

[56] Felix Steffek, 'The Relationship between Mediation and Other Forms of Alternative Dispute Resolution', in European Parliament (ed.), *The Implementation of the Mediation Directive* (n 21) 44 ff.

[57] Carlos Esplugues and Jose Luis Iglesias, 'Mediation and Private International Law: Improving the Free Circulation of Mediation Agreements Across the EU', in European Parliament (ed.), *The Implementation of the Mediation Directive* (n 21) 71 ff.

control carried out by the court of notary. In addition, careful thought would need to be given to the minimum standards that would need to be complied with in the country of origin. Such standards should probably include not only rules relating to the question whether the dispute may be solved by mediation or the accreditation of the mediator, but also rules relating to the capacity and the consent of the parties (including questions of choice of law), and perhaps also a certain minimum harmonization of competences and powers of ADR bodies. Such minimum harmonization could substantially enhance confidence in ADR schemes/bodies and create more legal certainty about the procedures and their outcome.[58]

Finally, the EU's conclusion of the future Convention on the Recognition and Enforcement of Foreign Judgments and its adoption of the new UNCITRAL Model Law (or, alternatively, the conclusion of the UNCITRAL Convention) would ensure the circulation of settlement agreements beyond the EU. The EU may have an interest in participating in these international instruments; businesses may benefit from alternative dispute resolution mechanisms, particularly in third states where the court system does not (yet) function adequately or does not inspire the necessary confidence. In such cases, enforcement of a settlement agreement may be the sole realistic remedy in a commercial dispute.

[58] See also ibid., 74.

PART III

SUBJECT-MATTER MEDIATION OF COMMERCIAL AND INVESTMENT DISPUTES

11
Mediation of Financial Disputes

*Ilaria Forestieri and Philipp Paech**

I. Introduction

The global financial crisis of 2008–2009 had a significant impact on financial institutions determining a broad array of claims, including debt recovery, enforcement of collateral, and claims based on negligence or breach of duty of care. The heavy litigation caseload fuelled interest in the use of alternative dispute resolution proceedings (ADR), including arbitration and mediation,[1] although, traditionally, financial institutions have preferred the recourse to national courts in key financial centres like New York, London, Frankfurt, or Hong Kong.

Still, while the use of ADR, especially arbitration, is not new in finance,[2] mediation of disputes arising in this context is just developing. Although the impact of mediation is expected to increase in the future, often, relevant contractual documentation does not generally refer disputes to mediation or other ADR methods. At the same time, only a few jurisdictions provide specific laws and dedicated alternative dispute resolution methods for financial services. There may be a general trend here: legislators are neglecting the fact that mediation may have the potential to improve the market environment, both in terms of efficiency and in terms of reputation. Hence, the driver for change is the desire to improve conditions for transacting and to increase liquidity and growth in a more stable market.

Mediation is a consensual procedure rooted in party autonomy and by default, the parties can agree to initiate a mediation process at any point in time during

* Although all the chapters have been discussed in depth and shared by both authors, Ilaria is the original drafter of sections I and II, paragraphs A, B, and E. Philipp is the original drafter of section II, paragraphs C, D, F, and section III. Section IV was jointly drafted.

[1] See International Chamber of Commerce (ICC), Commission on Arbitration and ADR, 'Financial Institutions and International Arbitration Report. Task Force on Financial Institutions and International Arbitration' (2017), iccwbo.org/publication/financial-institutions-international-arbitration-icc-arbitration-adr-commission-report/. Task force members found that the 2008 financial crisis resulted in a noticeable increase in financial disputes. In most cases, financial service providers preferred to resort to arbitration (the ICC had 1,548 arbitration cases pending in 2017). An earlier survey by Queen Mary University Law School and PwC confirmed arbitration's overall popularity. On average, 69 percent of companies in the banking/finance industry support arbitration, with 25 percent declaring arbitration as their 'most preferred option'. Mediation is the best option for almost the 20 percent of companies in the same sector. See PwC, 'Corporate Choices in International Arbitration Industry Perspectives' (2013), http://www.pwc.com/gx/en/arbitration-dispute-resolution/assets/pwc-international-arbitration-study.pdf.

[2] See ICC Commission (n 1) 8.

their relationship. There are many reasons to resort to mediation, although there are some that are more evident. First, mediation is, in its essence, a private process that responds better to the contractual nature of financial transactions.[3] Second, the procedure is flexible and it can be tailored to parties' needs, both at an early stage when drafting a dispute resolution clause and including it in the contractual framework and during the ongoing execution of the relationship.[4] Third, is an essential advantage of mediation is maintaining confidentiality of financial information, which is extremely important in the context of financial litigation.[5] Considering the potential connection with the judicial system in cases of court-annexed mediation, mediation represents a valid case-management technique, which can be used by the judges to select disputes suitable to be settled out of courts, avoiding time and costs of litigation.[6]

This chapter sheds light on the potential of mediation and related arrangements in wholesale finance, to the exclusion of arbitration. In recent years there has been growing interest in mediation in finance, although mediation is said to lag behind its potential,[7] due, above all, to unawareness among market participants or to the impression that mediation is unsuitable per se for resolving financial disputes. To prove this claim, the potential benefits (section II) and the limits (section III) of

[3] Mediation's advantages are often pointed out in the context of a more general debate about the appropriateness of resorting to ADR procedures as an alternative to litigation; see Klaus Hopt and Felix Steffek (eds), *Mediation: Principles and Regulation in Comparative Perspective* (OUP, 2013); Felix Steffek and Hannes Unberath, *Regulating Dispute Resolution: ADR and Access to Justice at the Crossroads* (OUP, 2013); Henry Brown and Arthur Marriot, *ADR: Principles and Practice* (Sweet & Maxwell, 2011); Nadia Alexander, *Global Trends in Mediation* (Kluwer Law International, 2006).

[4] There are various international institutions, such as the ICC and the United Nations Commission on International Trade (UNCITRAL) that have developed mediation and arbitration model clauses for use in financial contracts. These model clauses have been used by the International Swaps and Derivatives Association (ISDA) in its *2013 ISDA Arbitration Guide*, https://www.isda.org/a/6JDDE/isda-arbitration-guide-final-09-09-13.pdf. The American Arbitration Association (AAA) has prepared a booklet *Drafting Dispute Resolution Clauses: A Practical Guide*, which sets forth examples of specific provisions that can be included in a mediation or arbitration clause, https://www.adr.org/sites/default/files/document_repository/Drafting%20Dispute%20Resolution%20Clauses%20A%20Practical%20Guide.pdf.

[5] According to ICC Commission's survey on the use of mediation in the financial sector, confidentiality is a determining factor in a financial institution's preference for ADR (n 1) 9.

[6] Since the Pound Conference, held in the United States in 1976, a series of studies on ADR have supported the general advantages of court-annexed mediation; see Frank E. A. Sanders, 'Varieties of Dispute Processing' in Leo Levin and Russel R. Wheeler (eds), *The Pound Conference: Perspectives on Justice in the Future*, (St. Paul, 65–87, 1979). Barbara McAdoo and Nancy Welsh, 'Court-Connected General Civil ADR Programs: Aiming for Institutionalization, Efficient Resolution and the Experience of Justice', in Donna Stienstra and Susana M. Yates (eds), *ADR Handbook for Judges* American Bar Association, Section of Dispute Resolution, January 2004).

[7] According to the Dispute Resolution Statistics provided by the US Financial Industry Regulator Authority (FINRA), a number of 426 closed mediation cases compare to 2177 closed arbitration cases in 2018, https://www.finra.org/arbitration-and-mediation/dispute-resolution-statistics#mediationstats. The number of dispute resolution cases handled by the Hong Kong International Arbitration Centre (HKIAC), including both arbitration and mediation, reached 532 in 2017; parties have opted for mediation only in fifteen cases, http://hong-kong-economy-research.hktdc.com/business-news/article/Hong-Kong-Industry-Profiles/Arbitration-and-Mediation-Industry-in-HongKong/hkip/en/1/1X000000/1X006N9U.htm.

mediating wholesale financial disputes appear at the centre of this chapter. The chapter concludes that the ambit of mediation in financial markets is limited to the non-financial aspects of the relevant relations between financial institutions and that there is a need for legislators to clarify and support the use of mediation in respect of wholesale financial disputes, including the case of court-annexed mediation (section IV).

II. Rationales for Mediation in Finance

The reasons for which parties agree to refer their disputes to mediation are manifold. These rationales are similar across the various sectors of the economy. However, some of the rationales underlying the idea of mediation may be particularly important to finance, as compared to other sectors of the economy, because they respond to the specific nature of financial transactions better than to the nature of other types of transactions. For instance, whereas cost may be the prevailing criterion from the perspective of parties active in some sectors of the economy, the cost argument might be less important for actors in other sectors. Similarly, for parties in a given sector of the economy, it may be worth trying to preserve workable relationships beyond a dispute, whereas in other sectors market participants might not care because business relationships are short term and random anyway.

Although mediation is still not yet used on a large scale, in some parts of the financial market mediation is now increasingly accepted. In recent times, trade associations active in the financial market, e.g. the International Swaps and Derivatives Association (ISDA), have started promoting the use of mediation, particularly by providing relevant standard contractual terms, or by setting up dedicated mediation service providers. Also, market organizations and dispute resolution service providers have introduced industry-specific ADR initiatives, including those relating to mediation, to better serve these industry needs, including PRIME Finance in The Hague,[8] the Financial Dispute Resolution Centre (FDRC) in Hong Kong,[9] and the Financial Industry Regulatory Authority (FINRA—a self-regulatory organization) in the United States.[10] The China International Economic and Trade Arbitration Commission (CIETAC), which also provides mediation services, has recently included financial disputes in its portfolio of services.[11]

In a number of jurisdictions, legislators have enacted relevant legislation, encouraging or sometimes even mandating mediation of financial disputes in some way. An independent ombudsman-based system is in place in the United

[8] See http://www.primefinancedisputes.org/page/mediation.
[9] See http://www.fdrc.org.hk/en/html/resolvingdisputes/resolvingdisputes_mediationarbitration.php.
[10] See http://www.finra.org/arbitration-and-mediation/learn-about-mediation.
[11] See http://www.cietac.org.

Kingdom and Ireland,[12] whereas the US, Singapore, and Hong Kong have opted for a model based on arbitration and mediation.[13] Italy has adopted a hybrid system with a *quasi*-judicial body at its centre.[14] Most of these schemes aim at consumer disputes. The difference with voluntary ombudsman schemes, e.g. that of the Association of German Banks,[15] lies in the fact that the aforementioned jurisdictions legally mandate mediation for certain financial disputes. Parties choose mediation for specific reasons, and legislators have their specific motives to support it. These rationales are not necessarily congruent; however, they are difficult to separate from each other. They can be grouped into seven categories.

A. Timely Resolution of Disputes and the Matter of Cost

It seems that legislators in many jurisdictions support the use of mediation above all to make up for suboptimal access to traditional judicial dispute resolution. In other words, the rationales typically cited refer to the time and cost of proceedings and reducing the backlog of cases in the court system.[16] The argument of mediation as an appropriate method to save time and cost is, in principle, no different across all economic sectors. Mediation—to a certain extent—enhances market efficiency by reducing the amount of resources that need to be dedicated to the judicial dispute resolution, on both the side of the judicial system and of the parties (note that unsuccessful mediation followed by judiciary proceedings increases costs). With regard to this argument, there is a current trend in many jurisdictions towards mediation, including the introduction in some of a compulsory (pre-filing) mediation stage for certain types of disputes, or the option that the court suggests mediation or refers the case to mediation.[17] Legislators justify their approach referring to

[12] In 2017, the UK Financial Ombudsman Service received 1,932 complaints regarding financial services: of the total number of cases, around 0.8 percent have been resolved through alternative proceedings, http://www.financial-ombudsman.org.uk/publications/annual-review-2017/index.html. In Ireland in 2017, 4,538 new complaints were received by the Financial Services Ombudsman (FSO), https://www.fspo.ie/documents/FSO_Annual_Review2017.pdf.

[13] The Financial Industry Regulator Authority (FINRA) operates the largest securities dispute resolution forum in the United States, using both arbitration and mediation. The Monetary Authority of Singapore created the Financial Disputes Resolution Centre (FIDRec), which was launched on 31 August 2005 to resolve financial consumer disputes. The Hong Kong government introduced the Financial Dispute Resolution Scheme (FDRS) and established the Financial Dispute Resolution Centre (FDRC) in February 2010, providing arbitration and mediation services for consumers and SMEs on the claimant's side.

[14] The Italian Arbitro Bancario e Finanziario (ABF) is an out-of-court settlement scheme for disputes between customers and banks and other financial intermediaries. Decisions are entrusted to the panels and are made according to the law, see Banca d'Italia, '*The Banking and Financial Ombudsman Annual Report*', *Abridged Version*, No. 7 (July 2017), https://www.bancaditalia.it/pubblicazioni/relazione-abf/index.html?com.dotmarketing.htmlpage.language=1.

[15] See https://en.bankenverband.de/tasks/ombudsman-scheme/.

[16] See Stephen B. Goldberg, Frank E.A. Sander, and Nancy H. Rogers, *Dispute Resolution: Negotiation, Mediation, and Other Processes* (Aspen Casebook Series, 2013) 336.

[17] The term 'court-connected' mediation is used to describe the process in which the court incorporates mediation as part of its procedural system, making the arrangements for the appointment of

scarce resources of the judicial system, provoking the critique that parties' access to justice is made dependent on available resources.[18]

For instance, in recent years in the context of finance, the Italian legislator has taken this line and supported mediation as the preferred ADR mechanism.[19] However, mediation is still struggling to gather pace in the Italian financial sector.

Some argue that financial institutions do not have confidence in mediation, which induces them, *ex ante*, to be more sceptical even towards good cases for settlement. However, this scepticism may also be owed to the absence of precedent setting[20] or to the lack of interest in starting a mediation process for one of the reasons set out in section III. In particular, the benefit of speedy and cost-efficient proceedings is significantly smaller for financial institutions, as they are typically secured or collateralized and benefit from special privileges to terminate and close-out their relationships with defaulting counterparties. Sophisticated risk management mechanisms are recognized by the insolvency law of most mature financial markets. As a consequence, financial institutions frequently are not dependent on a judicial decision to enforce their right and would not benefit from a (speedier) mediation either.

The Italian example of financial mediation suggests that the efficiency and effectiveness of mediation may be compromised by practical problems and by the relevant legal culture implementing it.[21] Thus, the shortcomings of mediation could well lead to an adverse effect not only on financial institutions' confidence toward mediation, but also on market inefficiency, consuming time and money when parties have to start a second process before a court. In other words, attempts by legislators to cure an overburdened judicial system by forcing more private dispute resolution may backfire—especially when mediation and other ADR procedures are unable to overcome fundamental structural problems.[22]

the mediator; the term 'court-annexed' mediation is used to describe the process in which the court provides for the mediation, usually involving judges to settle the case, see Brown and Marriot (n 3) 84.

[18] Goldberg, Sandern, and Rogers (n 16) 336.

[19] See Article 5 of the Italian Mediation Law (Legislative Decree no. 28 of 4 March 2010 amended by the Law Decree no. 69 of 21 June 2013).

[20] See ICC Commission (n 1) 10.

[21] Given the strong litigation culture, the Italian legislator opted for a strong approach introducing mandatory mediation. A prior mediation attempt is now a precondition for admissibility before the court and the law allows the court to order the initiation of the mediation process. In addition, change agents among the Italian legal community were instrumental in the insertion of mediation into the dispute resolution system. See Paola Lucarelli (ed.), *Mediazione su ordine del giudice a Firenze* (Utet, 2015).

[22] The Italian Ministry of Justice's statistics, however, prove that mandatory mediation has a role in relieving overburdened courts, with overall savings on time and costs, thus improving the justice system. During the first semester of 2018 there were approximately 7,152 mediations for banking contract-related disputes and 1,695 mediation for financial contract-related disputes. Of these numbers, a sample analysis shows that mediation success rate was 9 percent for banking contracts and 11 percent for financial contracts, https://webstat.giustizia.it/Analisi%20e%20ricerche/Mediazione%20Civile%20-%20Anno%202018%20(primo%20trimestre).pdf.

B. The Multi-Party Scenario

The nature of finance as a highly interconnected part of the economy seemingly makes it an ideal candidate for mediation. Wholesale finance, in particular, can only be understood as a network, where actors transact with one another regularly, and often on a long-term basis. The multi-party nature is particularly visible in certain types of transactions, e.g. syndicated loans and securitizations. In these transactions, the overall arrangement comprises bilateral or multilateral contractual arrangements at various levels that are dependent on one another. For example, the complete transactional set up of a syndicated loan may comprise, in addition to the basic multilateral loan agreement, an inter-creditor agreement, a security trustee arrangement, parent-company guarantees, and risk participations by third parties.

Securitization offers an even more complex picture, which consists of the basic risk-transfer mechanism between the debt originator and the special purpose vehicle. This agreement is supplemented by a number of arrangements with third parties, e.g. credit enhancement providers, rating agencies, security trustees, mono-line insurers and liquidity providers, and the ultimate buyers of the securitized bond.

The common pattern consists of one or more basic contractual relationships supplemented by several ancillary contractual arrangements, which may or may not involve the same parties, and which are all, in some way, dependent on one another as parties would enter none of them in isolation. Also, there is a significant probability that disputes simultaneously arise under more than one of those agreements.

Using mediation to settle disagreements arising inside these complex multiparty relationships may have an immense advantage: the multi-party nature can be mirrored in the dispute settlement process. In other words, parallel or intertwined disputes can be discussed during a mediation process, which brings together all the different parties involved, upon the sole condition that they agree to start negotiations. By contrast, it is difficult and inefficient to take into account, let alone consolidate, the positions of different parties connected through different contracts in the same way in traditional bankruptcy proceedings. This would typically require additional procedural steps, interventions, submitting petitions, etc. As a result, cost increases and the resolution takes considerably more time. As mediation is voluntary and entirely based on party autonomy, there is a high degree of flexibility in terms of personal and material scope.

C. Restructuring and Bank Resolution

As opposed to liquidation proceedings, other processes addressing situations of corporate distress, e.g. restructuring or rehabilitation procedures, may leave room for party agreements. The success of certain types of procedures even depends on certain issues being solved on the basis of party agreement, e.g. a debt restructuring to avoid bankruptcy. Mediation may a useful tool to help structure those parts of the process that are not formalized by the relevant statute.[23]

However, while this may apply to the scenario of distressed real-economy actors, it may be less relevant in relation to financial institutions. Rehabilitation or restructuring proceedings in respect of financial institutions are comparatively rare exceptions. In the past, smaller banks, as a rule, underwent liquidation, whereas big, interconnected (and hence systemically relevant) ones were generally bailed out by governments (the insolvency of Lehman Brothers was an exception to this pattern, with the known consequences). The resulting catch-22 situation for governments provoked the adoption of a number of specific regulatory measures in the aftermath of the financial crisis. Among these measures is a new type of procedure, called bank resolution. The result of a bank resolution strongly resembles that of restructuration or rehabilitation procedures: debt is restructured (bail-in) and partly written down, or the financial institution is acquired, wholly or in parts, by competitors or a bridge institution. However, as opposed to traditional restructuring or rehabilitation proceedings, there is no involvement of the relevant counterparties. The competent authorities manage the restructuring and break-up of the distressed institution using sweeping administrative law powers bestowed on them by legislation, and the process of resolving a bank typically takes a few days only. Hence, as opposed to restructuring of real-economy corporations, there is no room for mediating in the new bank resolution procedures.

D. Long-Term Contracts

Financial institutions use a number of long-term contracts. There are, on the one hand, genuine long-term transactions, such as long-term loans or bonds. On the other hand, there are more short-term transactions, such as, in particular, derivative and repurchase contracts. Some of them are very short term, or just 'overnight'. However, even these short-term deals are documented as part of all-encompassing master agreements, which typically remain in place between the parties for several years. Master agreements are the backbone of a financial institutions risk management. They provide for termination and set off in the event of default and cater for the relevant documentation regarding the provision of collateral.

[23] See Paola Lucarelli and Ilaria Forestieri, 'The Three Targets of Insolvency Mediation: Dispute Resolution, Agreement Facilitation, Corporate Distress Management' (2017) in Laura Carballo Piñeiro and Katia Fach Gómez (eds), 14(4) Transnational Dispute Management: Special Issue on Comparative and International Perspectives on Mediation in Insolvency Matters, https://www.transnational-dispute-management.com/article.asp?key=2494.

Often, re-interpretation and renegotiation of contractual terms as a consequence of an open discussion between parties in the context of a mediation seem more meaningful then terminating that relationship and simply settling accounts. The flexibility to maintain the contract despite deviating from the original agreement is much higher in the context of mediation, as no specific provision is needed to allow for that flexibility. By contrast, in judicial proceedings, the court can only look into hardship, *force majeure*, or good faith mechanisms, which must either be made available from the beginning in the contract itself or must be provided by the relevant legal order.

Furthermore, there is a positive side effect: mediation is particularly effective because it requires parties to long-term contracts to aggregate all relevant information on their relationship. In this way, the mediator's intervention helps the parties to evaluate whether to continue the contract or to re-invest resources in other ventures, instead of tying them up uselessly for a long time.

E. Preservation of Business Relationships

Finance is a business strongly relying on reputation and relationships. Court proceedings are by their nature conflict induced and parties only exceptionally settle under an amicable agreement once having commenced proceedings. Mediation provides more room for maintaining or rebuilding mutual trust. In that, mediation offers the possibility of a brighter future of a commercial relationship between the parties since they avoid the confrontational aspects of litigation or arbitration proceedings.

Mediation is not an assurance that the disputing parties will be future business partners. But it is in many respects about improving communication and parties' cooperation. By airing their differences in an informal, non-binding setting, the parties often are able to see, in part, the adversary's point of view and come to a financial arrangement that nobody is happy with, but everybody can live with. If the parties have a long-term commercial relationship, this relationship is not affected by prolonged litigation or arbitration hearings, which may have winners and losers. The communication between the parties may not be established in adversarial methods. In particular, the wholesale market is strongly based on long-term relations and good reputation. Therefore, it would benefit highly from the reconciliatory nature of mediation.

F. Cross-Border Enforcement

Wholesale finance is highly internationalized. The parties may be located in different countries—as a consequence, there is little clarity regarding which laws would apply in a future insolvency. Also, contracts may be concluded under the law of third-country jurisdictions, or collateral assets may be located or held by a custodian in a third jurisdiction.

Court orders aimed at the enforcement of rights governed by the law of a foreign jurisdiction may be difficult or cumbersome to enforce. For instance, collateral located in a third-country jurisdiction will often be governed by the relevant third jurisdiction's law. Unless special arrangements are in place between the relevant jurisdictions (which is the case in the EU)[24] it can be cumbersome to enforce the collateral. Worse, in the meantime, the collateral assets may lose their value. Litigation cannot address this potential difficulty, but mediation potentially can avoid it. As the outcome is amicable, enforcement in the proper sense is unnecessary. Hence, in an industry with a considerable percentage of cross-jurisdictional transactions, amicable dispute resolution may assist in removing part of the territorial limitations that apply to court decisions.

III. The Limits of Mediation in Finance

Financial transactions are different in a number of ways when compared to transactions occurring in other markets. Section II discussed to what extent the relevant special characteristics make *a case for* mediation specifically in relation to financial transactions. This section looks at mediation in finance from the opposite viewpoint and asks to what extent the special character of financial transactions makes mediation appear a *less suitable* alternative as compared to judicial proceedings. It identifies issues in relation to third-party rights (section A), risk-management of financial institutions (section B), their interconnectedness (section C), and the fact that privileged treatment of financial institutions comes at a cost (section D).

It does not delve into criticism that is generally raised in respect of mediation, referring to, among other things, the risk that the mediator may not be sufficiently impartial, with the consequence that mediation masks inbuilt power inequalities between the parties, particularly with regards to consumer involvement. Also, it does not discuss the inability to set precedents, or any other of the more general critiques of mediation. These issues are discussed in other chapters of this volume.[25]

[24] Directive 2001/24/EC of 4 April 2001 on the reorganization and winding up of credit institutions, OJ L125/15 of 5.5.2001. See also Chapter 10, this volume.

[25] See Chapter 1 and Chapter 2, this volume.

A. Third-Party Rights

Mediation is aimed at settling disputes on the basis of a new party agreement. However, such an agreement cannot impinge on any pre-existing rights of third parties. This can be avoided solely in a scenario where all parties concerned are also party to the new agreement. This principle translates into the situation of liquidation of an insolvent corporation. Mediation cannot resolve the priority contest among its creditors, nor can it shift around these priorities. This is reflected in the character of insolvency law as mandatory. As a consequence, the capacity of an insolvent to enter mediation is restricted to agreements that do not impinge on the availability of assets for distribution (size of the estate) or on the principles that determine the performance of privileged, secured, and general creditor claims (distribution of the estate).[26] These 'core' insolvency matters are not negotiable. Thus, the commencement and administration of liquidation proceedings, the rescheduling of the debtor's liabilities, the verification of creditors' claims, and the distribution of the debtor's assets are typically reserved for the competent court, i.e. the court of the forum.[27]

This incapacity of an insolvent to enter a mediation aiming to renegotiate debt is relatively obvious. However, this fundamental principle has a much broader effect: pre-insolvency transactions that cause an outflow of value from the estate are typically liable to be retroactively voided by the court, provided that they fall within a certain 'suspect' period prior to insolvency (depending on the jurisdiction, a period of three months to two years) and provided that other criteria are met, such as preferential treatment of a creditor or insufficient consideration.

Consequentially, the court can also avoid those transactions that are intended to implement the outcome of a mediation process and that took place prior to the insolvency but within the suspect period, to the extent that the other material requirements for avoidance, e.g. creditor preference, are met. Therefore, a mediation resulting in transfer of value remains under the sword of Damocles in the guise of insolvency avoidance, until the relevant suspect period is over.

In principle, these determinants apply to the financial sector in the same way as to any other part of the economy. However, in practical terms, they are much more relevant for the financial than for any other sector, reducing or nearly eliminating the scope for mediating financial disputes among wholesale market participants. This is because the threat of subsequent voidance of a transaction clashes with two important characteristics of the modern financial market, which the following sections analyse in turn.

[26] See Michael Bridge and Joanne Braithwaite, 'Private Law and Financial Crisis' (2013) 13 Journal of Corporate Law Studies 367–70.

[27] See Philipp Paech, 'Close-out Netting, Insolvency Law and Conflict-of-Laws' (2013) 14 (2) Journal of Corporate Law Studies 419.

B. Risk Management

The core characteristic of finance is that risk taking—speculation—generates returns. Financial institutions use sophisticated processes to manage their resulting financial risks. These techniques include, in particular, contractual rights to terminate and close out all outstanding mutual exposures and enforce relevant collateral without the necessity to undertake any further formal steps. These mechanisms, however, very much work in a 'binary' way. As long as both parties are 'healthy', the transactions are alive and the party that is 'in the money' can reap the returns. As soon as one of the parties default, the solvent counterparty benefits from the aforementioned termination and close-out rights. It is hence well protected against counterparty risk, as it can walk away with the relevant collateral, which typically covers 100 percent of the remaining close-out amount. This 'clean break' removes any exposure to the defaulting party from the solvent party's books. No future risk flows from this relationship.[28]

This mechanism is deeply entrenched in modern market practice and it is an integral part of the risk management and capital requirements imposed on market participants by regulation.[29] Mediation, very much like any other process by which contractual obligations are adjusted, would complicate that binary clean-break logic. It does not make much sense for the solvent counterparty to renegotiate positions because it already benefits from a more effective protection. In other words, mediation of financial transactions would only distort financial institutions' risk management.

This result is particularly poignant in respect of mediation that intervenes during (still) solvent times. If one of the parties becomes subsequently insolvent, the mechanisms of insolvency avoidance would apply to transactions that implement the mediation outcome, i.e. the transactions may not be enforceable in insolvency and are hence liable to claw-back. By contrast, the 'clean break' achieved through close-out and collateral is protected under insolvency law and cannot be voided retroactively.[30]

These considerations apply to all bulk transactions that are entered into on the basis of master agreements, e.g. interest rate or currency derivatives, credit default swaps, other derivatives, repurchase as well as securities lending arrangements, or any other transaction involving the provision of collateral.[31] They may or may

[28] See Philipp Paech, 'The Value of Financial Market Insolvency Safe Harbours' (2016) 36 (4) Oxford Journal of Legal Studies 855.

[29] Ibid.

[30] Ibid.

[31] Derivatives are generally (but not necessarily) documented under the master agreement promoted by the International Swaps and Derivates Association (ISDA), which is not publicly available. Repos are functionally akin to a secured loan but different from the legal perspective: an asset is sold against a cash payment and bought back at a later point in time at a slightly different price. Repos are often documented under the Global Master Repurchase Agreement (GMRA), http://www.icmagroup.org/assets/documents/Legal/GMRA-2011/GMRA-2011/GMRA%202011_2011.04.20_formular.pdf.

not apply to tailor-made agreements underlying other types of transactions. As a consequence, there seems to be little room for mediating in the context of these transactions.

C. Interconnectedness

The financial market is highly interconnected through constantly changing exposures that exist between all its participants. Interconnectedness cannot be 'stopped' outside formalized liquidation or resolution proceedings, even in the event of corporate distress. A financial institution cannot be disentangled from its cobweb of transactions, nor could it attempt to 'cool down' and enter into new transactions.

This is because a financial institution, as long as it is a going concern, regularly needs to enter a minimum of new transactions to stay afloat, notably in order to satisfy its constantly changing refinancing needs through repurchase agreements, and to cover its exposure to counterparty and market risk on the basis of derivatives. The liquidity and risk management process of a financial institution looks like an organic, constantly adapting and evolving process. As a consequence, every financial institution has a permanently changing portfolio of transactions with an equally evolving group of counterparties.

This phenomenon is further complicated by the fact that exposures between two parties can alter due to changes in market prices, up to the point where they invert. A party may at some point be a net creditor, and, sometime later, a net debtor to the relevant other party. Hence, the idea of involving 'all creditors' into a mediation of contractual obligations to avoid any violation of third-party rights is not realistic. The set of creditors and relevant exposures will change as from the moment the mediation process is finished. Later, should one of the parties become insolvent, there will be new exposures that will have occurred in the meantime, and new creditors (third parties) that did not exist at the moment of the mediation. As it is impossible to guarantee that all interests concerned are taken into consideration, transactions implementing the outcome of the mediation process will remain fully subjected to insolvency avoidance.

D. Privileges Induce Risk Taking

Mediation is a private alternative to justice, or a form of 'informal justice'. As discussed in the previous sections, mediation does not seem to be suitable to address the situation of a defaulting financial institution or, more generally, restructure rights that concern third parties. However, legislators might gradually tackle these issues and allow more room for mediation, even where third-party rights and insolvency are concerned, as they may adhere to the view that the advantages of mediation are important and that its disadvantages can be contained. For example, legislators may conclude that a wider scope for mediation in finance served the goals of financial and systemic stability. Or, they could adhere to the view that moving more financial disputes from the judiciary to mediation would enhance liquidity and growth due to the reduced cost and time of the process.

However, this would entail exempting financial institutions to some extent from principles that otherwise apply to all non-financial market participants. Affording special treatment in insolvency translates into a privilege for financial institutions, particularly in scenarios where the insolvent and its counterparties are all financial institutions.

Yet, such privileges afforded to a specific type of market participant typically come at a price for other types of market participants, i.e. in the present case, by non-financial counterparties of an insolvent financial institution. As creditors that have little levy to adjust their positions, they assume a weaker position as a consequence of the privilege afforded to financial institutions, bearing a bigger share of the cost of the insolvency as a consequence.[32] All non-financial market participants would be concerned, i.e. small, medium, and large non-financial enterprises, consumers, and ultimately the state and its welfare systems as a last resort.[33]

However, although it appears surprising, this policy has a long tradition. The privilege of obtaining an insolvency-proof security interest is probably the earliest and most basic example of a legislative decision that favours 'big fish' rather than small ones. In recent years, sweeping insolvency privileges have been granted to the financial industry, on grounds of its fundamental role in terms of prosperity and growth. The most significant are the contractual termination, setoff, and enforcement rights (section B), which are nearly universally accepted by insolvency laws.[34]

However, risks shifted elsewhere in the short term may reflect back on the financial market itself, notably through a negative feedback loop comparable to a phenomenon commonly called 'moral hazard'. Since the last financial crisis, it has become clear that being better protected than real-economy actors has always exacerbated the risk appetite of financial institutions: famously, the prospects of being bailed out by the state in times of severe financial distress ('too big to fail') made banks and their counterparties behave in an even riskier way.[35]

This argument can similarly be applied to mediation: if financial institutions were afforded the privilege of allowing their mediation outcome to be enforceable

[32] See Mark J. Roe, 'The Derivatives Market's Payment Priorities as Financial Crisis Accelerator' 63 (3) Stanford Law Review 558–9. Riz Mokaland and Edward Janger (2011) 'Financial engineering meets Chapter 11 safe harbours and the Bankruptcy Code', Report presented at 85th Annual National Conference of Bankruptcy Judges, Tampa, Florida, 12. See also more generally Katharina Pistor, 'A Legal Theory of Finance' (2013) 41 (2) Journal of Comparative Economics 323.

[33] Paech (n 28) 855.

[34] Ibid.

[35] Ibid.

in insolvency, even though they fall within the suspect period and even though they concern third-party rights, this would constitute yet another privilege for financial institutions, paid for by non-adjusting, non-financial third parties. At the same time, an additional perverse incentive would kick in, as the privilege may provoke further risk-taking by financial institutions as they will typically exploit any room for manoeuvre, allowing them to take on more risk.

E. Policy after the Financial Crisis

In political terms, it seems difficult in finance to argue in favour of an effectively supportive framework for mediation. Both non-financial market participants and consumers will typically have little sympathy for further privileges afforded to financial institutions, especially if these privileges flow from informal, confidential agreements. Hence, a reinforced framework for mediation would probably be regarded with distrust. In other words, an increased use of mediation in finance may fuel reservations towards the financial sector even further.

IV. Conclusion: A Hybrid Solution

Section II discussed potential benefits flowing from the use of mediation in the context of financial transactions and juxtaposed them in section III to the relevant limits and potential disadvantages. A number of typical characteristics of finance, e.g. the multi-party and long-term character of transactions, seem to suggest that mediation could be a very effective means of dispute resolution, improving market agents' interactions, creating additional liquidity, and bringing down cost and risk. However, other traits of finance, particularly the intrinsic focus on counterparty credit risk and the consequential, *quasi*-universal connection to a potential future insolvency of one of the parties, limit the use of mediation to the boundaries set by the axioms of insolvency, especially as regards the principle of equal treatment of creditors. Still, the positive aspects—greater speed, lower cost, preservation of relationships, informality and confidentiality—should be made available to financial market participants, to the extent that it is possible.

The initial assumption was that the necessary framework for the effective use of mediation is currently underdeveloped. Hence, this section discusses the relevant choices legislators will need to take if they intend to foster the use of mediation in financial markets, despite its significant limitations.

Most fundamentally, there must be clarity about the ambit of mediation in financial markets. Mediation ideally results in a new contractual agreement which, in principle, allows the parties to settle on any kind of outcome, including to maintain, modify, or put an end to it. However, it is of crucial importance to parties and regulators that any resulting transactions are not subject to invalidity or unenforceability should one of the parties become insolvent, as that outlook would endanger the parties' risk management. The benchmark comes in the form of the relevant jurisdiction's insolvency avoidance rules. Any transaction resulting from a mediation that might be subject to subsequent insolvency avoidance as a creditor preference or similar is worthless at best, but probably constitutes a danger in terms of risk management.

For this reason, relationships including financial transactions can be mediated in principle only. The uncertainty about risk thus created probably outweighs the benefits of mediation. Therefore, there would be no role for mediation in finance without special legal protection, i.e. a 'safe harbour' for mediation results. Yet, as discussed in sections E and F, there would be knock-on effects of such safe harbour, ranging from a danger to provoke moral hazard among financial institutions, leading to more risk taking, to difficulty explaining such further privilege for financial institutions to the wider market and to voters. Providing privileges in terms of material protection of mediation results achieved between financial markets seems therefore excluded.

More promising seems the use of procedural safeguards. The suitable institution to implement such safeguards is the court. The court alone is competent to ensure that the demarcation lines between aspects suitable and those aspects unsuitable are drawn correctly, as they have to be drawn on a case-by-case basis. The presence of the judge marks the control of the judiciary over contractual freedom and hence safeguards the rights of third parties, and counters moral hazard and public distrust towards big financial institutions. It is important, though, as a prerequisite, that judges play the central role in selecting the cases suitable to be resolved through mediation,[36] and determining the parties concerned.

First, the court can ensure that mediation in finance is limited to those aspects of the parties' relationship that are not directly connected to financial flows and risk-taking, e.g. improving communication, information flows, solving of operational or standardization issues, requirements for accessing a specific market infrastructure. Some jurisdictions have already adopted such court-connected mediation programmes that are used to handle civil and commercial litigation outside situations of corporate distress.[37] In Italy, court-connected mediation has been mandated for financial consumer disputes (see introduction to section II).

The scope of the mediation would not extend to the financial aspects of the relevant transactions, and thus there would be little danger of affecting third-party creditor rights. As the judge can resort to mediation on a case-by-case (in

[36] See Tania Sourdin, 'Five Reasons Why Judges Should Conduct Settlement' (2011) 37 Monash University Law Review 145–70.

[37] Recently, certain jurisdictions have introduced rules that allow debtors to seek the appointment of a mediator both in pre-insolvency situations and after the commencement of insolvency proceedings, see Carballo Piñeiro and Fach Gómez (n 23).

accordance with the characteristics of the dispute and the needs of the parties) this approach would counter the problem that enforceable outcomes of 'solvent' mediation would still create an unjustified privilege that might imperil the risk management of financial institutions.

In respect of the risk-related content of a transaction, already in certain jurisdictions can courts refer parts of *ongoing* proceedings to mediation, particularly with a view to reaching agreements to restructure debts on the basis of a debtor-negotiated restructuring plan. In this case, the framework of the court proceedings must ensure that all relevant interests in the insolvency process are considered. Mediation can hence be a means by which to agree to a court-connected but negotiated debt restructuring within the context of judicial proceedings.

From a market-wide perspective, court-connected mediation could be an excellent solution to increase market efficiency for two reasons. First, the judicial 'filter' makes sure that mediation is used only where it can bring sustainable results. Second, mediation allows the parties to resolve separate issues on which a settlement could be reached, as opposed to questions on which the disputants are deadlocked. Both aspects save time and costs for both the parties and the judiciary.[38]

[38] On how the Lehman Brothers case can serve as an example of mediation as a dispute resolution tool in the financial context, see Andrew J. Olejnik, 'Lehman Brothers ADR Procedures for resolving its Derivative Contracts in Bankruptcy', https://insolventiemediation.nl/media/uploads/file/10-Lehman-Bros-ADR-procedures.pdf.

12
Mediating Sovereign Debt Disputes

Calliope M. Sudborough

I. Introduction

Financial crises such as the Argentine debt crisis of 2001–2002 (Argentine crisis) and the global financial crisis of 2007–2008 (GFC) cause immense instability often provoking sovereign bankruptcy and the resultant longstanding political and economic consequences on debtor state populations. At the same time, international law on sovereign bankruptcy has failed to develop and still provides no accepted definition of sovereign debt.[1] Nevertheless, it is commonly understood in the legal and financial community that sovereign default is when a government is unable to pay its debt within the time limit or grace period stipulated in the contract with its creditors.[2]

Despite mounting calls for the establishment of a unified set of international legal principles to deal with sovereign debt crises, legal scholars, financial stakeholders, and governments have so far been unable to reach agreement thereupon.[3] As a result, sovereign debt crises almost invariably result in either partial or total default, in turn producing a variety of approaches ranging from sovereign debt restructuring (whereby creditors agree to reduce their claims) to bailout (financial support given to defaulting countries).[4]

When economic crisis has left a state unable to repay its debt, sovereign bondholders and states must negotiate a new financing agreement. Yet, various factors undermine such collective negotiations, leading many creditors to seek full collection of their investments via litigation or, more recently, investment arbitration. Critics of these mechanisms have argued that they not only undermine future

[1] Michael Waibel, *Sovereign Defaults before International Courts and Tribunals* (CUP, 2013) 8–9.

[2] Juan Carlos Hatchondo, Leonardo Martinez, and Horacio Sapriza, 'Understanding Sovereign Default', in Robert W. Kolb (ed.), *Sovereign Debt: From Safety to Default* (John Wiley & Sons, 2011) 1–13. Please note that definitions of financial mechanisms in this chapter have been simplified and adapted for an audience focused on legal aspects.

[3] Kenneth Rogoff and Jeromin Zettelmeyer, 'Bankruptcy Procedures for Sovereigns: A History of Ideas, 1976–2001' (2002) 49 IMF Staff Papers 470; Steven L. Schwarcz, 'Sovereign Debt Restructuring: A Bankruptcy Reorganization Approach' (2000) 85 Cornell Law Review; Anne O. Krueger, *A New Approach to Sovereign Debt Restructuring* (International Monetary Fund, 2002) 1–2.

[4] International Monetary Fund, Reviewing the Process for Sovereign Debt Restructuring within the Existing Legal Framework (report prepared by Policy Development and Review, International Capital Markets, and Legal Departments, 2003) 3–7.

restructuring efforts, but also that they further deplete the state's much-needed funds at a time of economic crisis and postpone economic recovery. This chapter examines whether, and how, investment mediation could offer an advantageous, supplementary means for resolving sovereign debt disputes.

II. Challenges to Sovereign Debt Restructuring

Despite the global financial instability that followed the GFC, government debt levels are expected to hit a record 66 trillion US dollars in 2018, which is 80 percent of global GDP, pursuant to the credit rating firm Fitch Ratings.[5] Dominating the international financial market for sovereign lending are sovereign bonds, debt instruments by which creditors advance money in exchange for the promise of repayment of principal (i.e. the original amount of the loan) and interest.[6] The providers of financing are either so-called 'official creditors', such as other states and international development institutions like the World Bank, the International Monetary Fund (IMF), or bilateral governmental agencies, or 'private creditors' including private banks, funds, or retail commercial creditors.[7] After being issued on the primary market, sovereign bonds may subsequently be traded on the secondary market by 'underwriters' or 'intermediaries' to virtually anyone, producing a large number of highly varied creditors around the world.[8]

However, contrary to the private debt market, there is no national or international bankruptcy procedure to ensure an orderly restructuring of the debt of a sovereign that has defaulted on its bonds, despite the numerous suggestions that have been made to that effect.[9] Thus, when a state is unable to repay its debts, it is the sovereign debtor's responsibility to enter into voluntary negotiations with its numerous and diverse creditors around the world and to reach a consensus despite their different agendas in order to obtain an acceptable restructuring of its debts.[10]

Since the debt restructuring process is voluntary, a creditor may refuse to accept a 'haircut' (a reduced reimbursement of their loan) and instead 'hold out' and seek a legal strategy to enforce their contractual rights via state litigation.[11] Whenever one or more creditors agrees to relieve a country's debt by reducing its claims, the value of the remaining creditors' claims increases, creating a free rider problem in which there is an incentive for the 'holdout creditors' to benefit at the expense

[5] Kate Allen, 'Agency Fitch warns governments of credit rating risks' (23 January 2019), https://www.ft.com/content/cf9fc00e-1ef9-11e9-b126-46fc3ad87c65.
[6] Waibel (n 1) 7–11.
[7] Ibid.
[8] Philip J. Power, 'Sovereign Debt: The Rise of the Secondary Market and Its Implications for Future Restructurings' (1996) 64 Fordham Law Review 2715–19.
[9] Rogoff and Zettelmeyer (n 3) 470–500.
[10] Mark L. J. Wright, 'Sovereign Debt Restructuring: Problems and Prospects' (2012) 2 Harvard Business Law Review 172.
[11] Ibid., 172–3.

of the creditors who have reduced their claims by seeking full payment through various legal remedies.[12]

Moreover, in recent decades the secondary sovereign debt market has produced new players known as 'vulture funds'. Vulture funds are generally hedge funds that seek to recover compensation at many times their investment by buying distressed sovereign bonds at a discounted price with a high risk of default, refusing to participate in restructuring, and then engaging in protracted litigation until they win or the state settles the case.[13] Using such tactics, vulture funds achieve exorbitant profits, on average obtaining recovery rates of 3 to 20 times their investment, or 300 to 2000 per cent.[14]

As demonstrated during the aftermath of the Argentine economic crisis and default, which sparked decades of litigation, holdout behaviour makes restructuring slower, more difficult, and uncertain. States in the middle of economic crisis are further harmed by having to repay individual creditors significantly greater sums than those agreed upon with cooperating creditors in restructuring negotiations. Moreover, litigation is costly for these debtor countries, siphoning away financial and political resources from other important policy issues.[15] In parallel, Argentina's creditors were the first to open the door to a different legal tool for resolving sovereign debt disputes in their search for a more efficient means of obtaining a favourable judgment: investment arbitration.

III. Investment Arbitration of Sovereign Disputes

International investment law is based on international investment agreements (IIAs) in which countries sign treaties (often bilateral investment treaties, or BITs) committing to accord certain protections to foreign investments.[16] Almost invariably, IIAs include a dispute resolution procedure that foresees arbitration for conflicts arising from investment activity within their scope.[17] Such investment arbitration proceedings may take place under the rules of the International Centre for the Settlement of Investment Disputes (ICSID), the UN Commission of International Trade Law (UNCITRAL), the International Chamber of Commerce

[12] Wright (n 10) 172; Michael Waibel, 'Opening Pandora's Box: Sovereign Bonds in International Arbitration' (2007) 101 (4) The American Journal of International Law 722.

[13] Jonathan I. Blackman and Rahul Mukhi, 'The Evolution of Modern Sovereign Debt Litigation: Vultures, Alter Egos, and Other Legal Fauna' (2010) 73 Law and Contemporary Problems 49–50; Jean Ziegler, 'Draft Progress Report on the Activities of Vulture Funds and the Impact on Human Rights' (2015), UN Human Rights Counsel Advisory Committee.

[14] Ziegler (n 13) 5.

[15] Ibid.

[16] Campbell McLachlan, Laurence Shore, and Matthew Weiniger, *International Investment Arbitration: Substantive Principles* (OUP, 2008).

[17] Joachim Pohl, Kekeletso Mashigo, and Alexis Nohen, 'Dispute Settlement Provisions in International Investment Agreements: A Large Sample Survey' (2012) 2 OECD Working Papers on International Investment 10–12.

(ICC), and other competent legal bodies.[18] Investment arbitration presents various advantages; in particular, it provides for heightened enforceability. For example, parties that engage in investment arbitration proceedings conducted under the Convention on the Settlement of Investment Disputes between States and Nationals of Other States (ICSID Convention), to which 153 countries are parties, are guaranteed that member states shall enforce the arbitral award without appeal.[19] In other words, an award under the ICSID Convention is the same as a final judgment.

Bondholders seeking to file arbitration claims do so by categorizing their bonds as 'investments' in order to benefit from the arbitration clauses within a particular IIA.[20] Although the language of BITs varies, most set forth that investors can initiate arbitration proceedings under the ICSID Convention.[21] However, for sovereign bond creditors to establish jurisdiction or the right to file an investment arbitration claim under the ICSID Convention, they must first persuade the arbitral tribunal that their purchase of sovereign bonds constitutes an 'investment' pursuant to Article 25(1) of the ICSID Convention as well as the underlying BIT providing for ICSID arbitration.[22] In a series of three ICSID arbitration cases involving claims brought by Italian creditors against Argentina, which issued sovereign bonds pursuant to the Italy–Argentina BIT, the tribunals' decisions on jurisdiction consistently concluded that holders of sovereign bonds could qualify as 'investors' pursuant to Article 25(1) of the ICSID Convention, thus finding that the bondholders have standing to bring investment treaty-based claims.[23] However, doubt lingers on the jurisdictional issue of sovereign bonds qualifying as investments as is evidenced by the dissenting opinions in the decisions, the numerous academic articles debating the validity of the majority's decisions in these cases, and the more recent award in *Poštová banka and Istrokapital v Hellenic Republic*.[24]

[18] Ibid.

[19] See 'Database of ICSID Member States', https://icsid.worldbank.org/en/Pages/about/Database-of-Member-States.aspx.

[20] Karen Halverson Cross, 'Arbitration as a Means of Resolving Sovereign Debt Disputes' (2006) 17 American Review of International Arbitration 337.

[21] See 'Database of Bilateral Investment Treaties', https://icsid.worldbank.org/en/Pages/resources/Bilateral-Investment-Treaties-Database.aspx/.

[22] Article 25(1) of the ICSID Convention.

[23] *Abaclat and others v Argentine Republic*, ICSID Case No. ARB/07/5 Decision on Jurisdiction and Admissibility, 4 August 2011; *Ambiente Ufficio S.p.A. and others v Argentine Republic*, ICSID Case No. ARB/08/9, Decision on Jurisdiction and Admissibility, 8 February 2013; *Giovanni Alemanni and others v Argentine Republic*, ICSID Case No. ARB/07/8 Decision on Jurisdiction and Admissibility, 14 November 2014.

[24] In the *Abaclat* and *Ambiente* cases, see the dissenting opinions of ICSID tribunal members Georges Abi-Saab and Santiago Torres Bernárdez; *Poštová banka, a.s. and Istrokapital SE v Hellenic Republic*, ICSID Case No. ARB/13/8 Award of 9 April 2015, para. 350; Luke Eric Peterson, 'Majority Opinion in ICSID Bondholders Claim Has Broader Lessons for Defaulting Sovereigns, Fractured Tribunals, Shareholder Groupings, and Would-Be Claimants Needing Help Getting ICSID Claims Registered' (2011) Investment Arbitration Reporter 4; Andrew Newcombe, 'Mass Claims and the Distinction between Jurisdiction and Admissibility', Kluwer Arbitration Blog [blog] (25 October 2011), http://kluwerarbitrationblog.com/2011/10/25/mass-claims-and-the-distinction-between-jurisdiction-and-admissibility; S. I. Strong,

In the latter case, the arbitral tribunal unanimously decided that bonds are not a covered investment under the applicable Slovakia–Greece BIT.[25] Furthermore, adding to the uncertainty of investment arbitration's promise in the sovereign debt dispute context is the fact that the arbitral tribunals in all of these cases never proceeded to the phase of rendering a decision on the merits, since the cases were settled or otherwise discontinued.[26]

In addition to the aforementioned lack of consensus on the standing of sovereign bondholders to file investment arbitration claims against debtor states and the untested waters of arbitral decisions on the merits of such cases, outspoken criticism of investment arbitration has increased in recent years, which could undermine its attractiveness as a dispute resolution tool in the sovereign debt arena.[27] The growing number of investor–state dispute settlement (ISDS) cases and the broad range of policy issues they raise have put the system of investment arbitration under intense scrutiny by states, non-governmental organizations, and other stakeholders.[28] This has given rise to calls for examining alternative approaches to resolving investment and sovereign debt disputes.

IV. Mediating Sovereign Debt Disputes

As a by-product of the backlash against investment arbitration, ISDS stakeholders are advocating for the increased use of mediation to supplement investor–state arbitration.[29] This section focuses on investment mediation as a tool for resolving sovereign debt disputes.

To fully appreciate the potential of mediation to resolve investment treaty disputes, mediation must be differentiated from other forms of dispute resolution. This is complicated by a debate among practitioners and scholars as to the correct definition of mediation, some favouring either a more restrictive or a broader definition. For the purposes of clarity, this chapter refers to the definition provided

'Mass Procedures in *Abaclat v Argentine Republic*: Are They Consistent with the International Investment Regime?' (2013) 3 Yearbook on International Arbitration 21–31.

[25] *Poštová banka and Istrokapital* (n 24) para. 350

[26] *Abaclat* (n 23) Consent Award, 29 December 2016; *Ambiente* (n 23) Order of Discontinuance of the Proceeding, 28 May 2015; *Giovanni Alemanni and others v Argentine Republic*, 14 December 2015.

[27] Katia Fach Gómez, 'Foreign Direct Investment in Latin America' in Markus Krajewski and Rhea Tamara Hoffmann (eds), *Research Handbook on Foreign Direct Investment* (Edward Elgar, 2019) 502; Catharine Titi, 'Investment Arbitration in Latin America: The Uncertain Veracity of Preconceived Ideas (2014) 30 (2) Arbitration International, 383–4; Emmanuel Gaillard, 'Anti-Arbitration Trends in Latin America' (2008) 239 (108) New York Law Journal 1–3; James X. Zhan (ed.), *World Investment Report 2015: Reforming International Investment Governance* (United Nations, 2015) 127–63.

[28] UNCTAD, 'Improving Investment Dispute Settlement: UNCTAD Policy Tools' (2018) 4 IIA Issues Note 1–14, http://unctad.org/en/PublicationsLibrary/diaepcb2017d8_en.pdf.

[29] Anna Joubin-Bret and Jan Knörich (eds), 'Investor–State Disputes: Prevention and Alternatives to Arbitration' (United Nations, 2010) 1–9.

in the Guide on Investment Mediation of the Energy Charter Conference, which describes mediation as:

> a process in which a neutral third party, a mediator, meets with the disputing parties and actively assists them in reaching a settlement based on their business interests and risk assessments or policy considerations and not only their legal positions.[30]

Therefore, unlike a judge or an arbitrator, a mediator has the responsibility of assisting the parties to come to an amicable accord of their own design based on the parties' interests. Accordingly, the mediation process is quite distinct from a judicial or arbitral process because the focus is not on establishing who is 'right' in the eyes of the applicable law, but rather on negotiating a practical agreement that best fulfils the parties' various interests for a mutually beneficial outcome.

Mediation is often associated with conciliation as part of the various non-binding forms of dispute resolution and the terms are frequently interchanged. However, it is a mistake to employ conciliation and mediation as synonyms because the two mechanisms are not by any means identical. As Frauke Nitschke explains,[31] conciliators are empowered to issue reports with settlement recommendations. This means that conciliators employ a more formal and evaluative process focused on the parties' legal rights that is akin to a non-binding arbitration. By contrast, mediation is more informal and less institutionalized than conciliation, placing the emphasis on open communication between the parties.[32] The mediator usually takes a facilitative approach that operates as a form of assisted negotiation in which the mediator refrains from suggesting terms of settlement but rather focuses on identifying ways in which the parties can build an agreement that satisfies their interests.[33]

A. Advantages

This section discusses the use of mediation for resolving sovereign debt disputes, and specifically, the possible advantages of doing so. To begin, mediation could redress several of the criticisms aimed at the use of investment arbitration in this domain. For example, critics have claimed that investor–state arbitrations often lead to purportedly inconsistent awards, which, in the context of sovereign lending,

[30] 'Dispute Resolution through International Arbitration' in Anna Joubin-Bret and Jan Knörich (eds), *Guide on Investment Mediation of the Energy Charter Conference* (United Nations, 2010) 10–21, http://unctad.org/en/docs/diaeia200911_en.pdf.

[31] See Chapter 7, this volume.

[32] Joubin-Bret and Knörich (n 29) xiii, xix.

[33] Ibid.

could undermine market confidence.[34] Since mediation is more focused on the parties' interests than an analysis of their legal rights, and since it is aimed at producing a contractual agreement between them rather than a decision interpreting the law, there is no reason to be concerned about an unpredictable body of law emanating from mediation of sovereign debt disputes.[35] Furthermore, since mediation maintains the parties' power over the outcome, this element of control should further assuage creditors' concerns about arbitrary judicial decisions or arbitral awards that increase the market risk of purchasing sovereign bonds.[36]

Another popular critique of the use of investment arbitration generally takes aim at the alleged exclusive club of investment arbitrators whose continued 'club membership', or repeated selection to investment arbitration tribunals, is contended to favour the interests of investors.[37] Mediation can also redress this concern. Unlike the decision-making role of the arbitrator, the responsibility of the mediator is to facilitate the parties' negotiations using various tools for fostering open communication, trust, and problem-solving creativity to ensure that the parties' negotiations are fruitful.[38] Thus, the impartiality (both real and perceived) of the mediator is critical for the parties' confidence in the mediator and active cooperation in the process. [39] Accordingly, a mediator has little to gain from favouring the interests of creditors or states' interests, as it would undermine the success of his or her career.

A third criticism of investment arbitration proceedings that mediation might redress targets the enormous investment in time and cost which, particularly in the context of sovereign default, diverts government funds needed for public services during a time of economic crisis.[40] This reproach is especially biting from a public policy perspective in the context of sovereign debt disputes where the sovereign state must often employ austerity policies on its citizens in order to pay off its debts.[41] Although a direct comparison of costs is not yet possible, given that insufficient data is available on investor–state mediations, it is possible to compare the statistics for the relative cost of international commercial arbitration and

[34] Josef Ostransky, 'Sovereign Default Disputes in Investment Treaty Arbitration: Jurisdictional Considerations and Policy Implications' (2015) 3 Groningen Journal of International Law 55.

[35] Guide on Investment Mediation (n 30).

[36] Ibid.

[37] Pia Eberhardt, Cecilia Olivet, Tyler Amos, and Nick Buxton, 'Who Guards the Guardians? The Conflicting Interests of Investment Arbitrators' in *Profiting from Injustice: How Law Firms, Arbitrators and Financiers are Fuelling an Investment Arbitration Boom* (Corporate Europe Observatory, 2012) 34–55, https://corporateeurope.org/sites/default/files/publications/profiting-from-injustice.pdf.

[38] Christopher W. Moore, *The Mediation Process* (4th edn, John Wiley and Sons, 2014) 43–84.

[39] Ibid.

[40] Joachim Pohl, 'Societal Benefits and Costs of International Investment Agreements: A Critical Review of Aspects and Available Empirical Evidence', OECD Working Papers on International Investment (2018) 46, http://www.oecd-ilibrary.org/docserver/download/e5f85c3d-en.pdf?expires=1520242913&id=id&accname=guest&checksum=C5A583E38B16F4788F9981DD21A1D47F.

[41] Blackman and Mukhi (n 13) 53; Liz Alderman, James Kanter, Jim Yardley, Jack Ewing, Niki Kitsantonis, Suzanne Daley, Karl Russell, Andrew Higgins, and Peter Eavis, 'Explaining Greece's Debt Crisis', *The New York Times* (17 June 2016), https://www.nytimes.com/interactive/2016/business/international/greece-debt-crisis-euro.html.

mediation as an indicator.[42] Mediation proceedings differ from arbitration proceedings in that they do not focus on fact-finding and discovery, witness testimony, reading and writing lengthy legal briefs and judgments, as well a series of formal procedural steps and hearings.[43] Rather, mediation centres on facilitating the parties' negotiations and creative problem solving (i.e. mostly verbal communications either directly between the parties or via the mediator) and then securing agreement on the terms of the settlement, which is usually drafted by the parties and their counsel.[44] Moreover, contrary to the panels of three arbitrators common in high-value and complex commercial arbitrations, the norm is to engage only one mediator irrespective of the complexity of the claims or the amount in dispute, thus diminishing the portion of the costs relating to the third party's fees and expenses.[45] In light of the differences in the process, international commercial mediations tend to last a few months (depending on the mediator and the parties' availabilities to schedule meetings) rather than years, which is generally the pace of multifaceted, international arbitrations.[46] Consequently, the mediation invoice is almost certain to be lighter than in an investment arbitration, which saves precious public funding for debt-laden states often in the midst of austerity regimes.

Aside from answering to the criticisms of investment arbitration as a dispute resolution tool in the sovereign debt context, mediation also provides additional benefits that are not available in other dispute resolution mechanisms. First, unlike judicial or arbitral proceedings, mediation allows sovereign bondholders and the defaulting state to preserve or rebuild a positive relationship by engaging in a dialogue that could lead to a mutually beneficial solution.[47] This is particularly important for both creditors and indebted governments as it might lead on the one hand to a greater pay-out for creditors than a potential loss in litigation or arbitration, and on the other hand, it gives a greater chance of renewed investment and financing for states in economic crisis.[48] Mediation provides states and creditors the possibility to strike a new deal by allowing them to include issues in their bargain that go beyond the mere issue of compensation payment.[49]

Second, as mediation focuses on the parties' mutual interests, it gives the parties an opportunity to craft a solution that goes beyond the binary remedy of win

[42] Andrew Waters, 'The Costs Of Arbitration' (Watson Farley and Williams, 2015), http://www.wfw.com/wp-content/uploads/2015/08/WFW-ArbitrationNewsletter1-Costs.pdf; Hannah Tümpel and Calliope Sudborough, 'ICC's ADR Rules, 2001–2010: Current Practices, Case Examples and Lessons Learned' in Arnold Ingen-Housz (ed.), *ADR in Business* (Wolters Kluwer, 2011).

[43] ICSID, 'Overview of An Arbitration Under the ICSID Convention', https://icsid.worldbank.org/en/Pages/process/Arbitration.aspx.

[44] Moore (n 38).

[45] Tümpel and Sudborough (n 42).

[46] Ibid.

[47] Nancy A. Welsh and Andrea Kupfer Schneider, 'The Thoughtful Integration of Mediation into Bilateral Investment Treaty Arbitration' (2013) 18 Harvard Negotiation Law Review 82, 105–15

[48] Joubin-Bret and Knörich (n 32) 33.

[49] Ibid.

or lose.[50] Judicial and arbitral proceedings do not allow the bondholders and the issuing sovereigns to explore their broader interests, although there might be many cases in which they are unexpectedly similar. For example, both parties might share an interest in expediting the settlement of the dispute. For the state, an efficient settlement would limit the damage to its reputation on the financial markets, and for the creditors, it would save time and costs in the collection process.[51]

Third, as mediation does not involve jurisdictional requirements or oblige parties to indicate legal standing for participating in the proceedings, it allows a broader range of participants to be involved in the process, should the disputing parties agree.[52] In the context of sovereign debt disputes in which important policy issues related to debt restructuring, economic crisis, austerity measures, and bailout programs are at stake, it may be necessary to involve participants who represent other stakeholder groups to express their interests for consideration in the negotiations, making it more likely that the settlement agreement will be accepted more widely by the electorate.[53]

B. Disadvantages

Like litigation or arbitration, mediation is not a panacea for sovereign debt disputes. To employ mediation in the most optimal manner, it is necessary to prepare for its potential disadvantages. One of the first obstacles that mediation faces in being used more systematically in the investor–state and sovereign debt context is that it remains essentially theoretical. To date, although there have been a handful of investor–state conciliation cases, only one investor–state mediation case has been confirmed and the outcome is still unknown.[54] Without more cases to demonstrate a proven track record and make statistics available, it is difficult to market mediation as a dispute resolution tool. In turn, this lacuna makes it all the more difficult for one party to convince another to participate in mediation where no prior mediation clause exists, as wary parties may decline due to lack of familiarity with the process.

[50] Welsh and Schneider (n 47).

[51] Joubin-Bret and Knörich (n 32) 32.

[52] Articles 2–3 of the IBA Mediation Rules, providing that a party seeking to commence mediation proceedings must submit the request to the administering institution as well as an invitation to the other party or parties.

[53] UNCITRAL Rules on Transparency in Treaty-Based Investor-State Arbitration (2014).

[54] According to the Centre, the Request for Mediation was filed pursuant to Article 3 of the ICC Mediation Rules (which applies when there is no prior agreement to mediate between the parties) pursuant to the applicable BIT which provided for the opportunity to amicably resolve disputes. After the Centre submitted notice of the Request filed by the requesting party investor, the responding State party agreed to refer the dispute to ICC Mediation Rules together with the IBA Rules for Investor-State Mediation. See Chapter 7, this volume.

Furthermore, investor–state mediation is often scoffed at by members of the litigation and arbitration community, who view it as being a waste of time. Rationalizing this cynical point of view, sceptics point to the statistics on Conciliation Proceedings under the ICSID Convention and Additional Facility Rules, wherein the small number of cases, for the most part, have failed to result in a settlement agreement.[55] However, reference to these statistics is misleading since they refer to ICSID-specific conciliation proceedings and not mediation proceedings specifically which, as mentioned, present important differences. In reality, ICSID conciliation proceedings are far more akin to non-binding, rights-based arbitration proceedings than interest-based mediation proceedings because they focus on an evaluative, fact-finding process that involves the conciliator(s) requesting documents, hearing witnesses, making site visits, and issuing recommendations.[56] Instead, 'pure' mediation proceedings seek to facilitate the parties' negotiations by focusing on their interests. Moreover, commercial mediations in fact have a greater rate of success than ICSID conciliation proceedings, with the great majority of cases reaching settlement.[57]

Another challenge for mediating sovereign debt disputes is the political risk and institutional obstacles for states.[58] Negotiations during a mediation can be obfuscated for states by the constraints of existing laws and regulations as well as political issues, involvement of lobbyists, and harsh publicity. For instance, it might be more damaging for a politician's career to enter into a voluntary, early settlement with immediate compensation to foreign bondholders than to be subjected to an arbitral award imposing a similar cost on the state some years later.[59] Furthermore, voluntary settlements can generate internal, organizational conflicts wherein discords may arise as to whether the protection of foreign creditors' investment rights is of greater importance than the safeguard of the state's economic sovereignty or any number of the state's other governing powers.[60] Moreover, domestic creditors may perceive such a mediated settlement between the state and its foreign creditors as unfair, special treatment that puts the domestic creditors at a disadvantage.[61] Finally, a successful mediation requires that there be at least one representative having the mandate to negotiate on behalf of the government to reach a settlement. Should several government departments become involved in the dispute it may be difficult to identify one agent with the authority to negotiate the settlement on

[55] ICSID, 'The ICSID Caseload—Statistics' (2017/2) 8,13. For further information on ICSID Conciliation proceedings, interested readers are referred to Chapter 7, this volume.

[56] ICSID, 'Overview of Conciliation Under The Additional Facility', https://icsid.worldbank.org/en/Pages/process/ICSID-Additional-Facility-Conciliation.aspx. See also Chapter 7, this volume.

[57] CEDR News, 'Mediation Market Grows By 5%: The 2016 Mediation Audit' (2016), https://www.cedr.com/news/?item=Mediation-Market-grows-by-5-percent-The-CEDR-2016-Mediation-Audit, citing 86 per cent of mediation proceedings resulted in settlement.

[58] Joubin-Bret and Knörich (n 32) 32.

[59] Ibid.

[60] Ibid.

[61] Ibid.

behalf of all.[62] Overall, there is no simple answer to the political and institutional obstacles to mediating sovereign debt disputes. To some degree, the remedy may lie in adopting a different attitude, i.e. one that shifts the focus away from the short-term agendas of individual political actors and more on the long-term benefits for the state and its people. Moreover, some of these state-specific issues might also be resolved with the help of the mediator.

Another barrier to mediating sovereign debt disputes is that it seemingly runs counter to the current trend for increased transparency in ISDS, as evidenced by the adoption in 2014 of the UNCITRAL Rules on Transparency in Treaty-Based Investor–State Arbitration. Transparency standards now necessitate that ISDS arbitration proceedings be rendered more public in a number of ways, e.g. making available the notice of arbitration, the response, the claims and counterclaims, submitted documents, and exhibits as well as any decisions made by the arbitral tribunal.[63] To further the inclusiveness of ISDS proceedings, non-disputing parties (such as concerned interest groups) may now also apply to the arbitral tribunal to make submissions for the arbitral tribunal's consideration.[64] Consequently, should sovereign debt disputes now be redirected from ISDS arbitration proceedings with enhanced transparency standards to less transparent mediation proceedings, there is a risk that this would detract from the legitimacy of any settlement agreement stemming therefrom and thus render the process less attractive. Therefore, it is important that similar increased transparency standards also apply to sovereign debt mediation proceedings.

Perhaps the most frequently cited obstacle to the more widespread use of mediation in ISDS and, concomitantly sovereign debt disputes, is the lack of an available enforcement mechanism akin to the New York Convention.[65] Although mediated settlement agreements are legally binding contracts, parties fear that without a means of ensuring immediate enforcement of the settlement deal, they will be required to engage in further legal proceedings should one of the parties fail or refuse to carry out performance of the mediated accord.[66] In the context of sovereign debt disputes, creditors may understandably be sceptical of any voluntary dispute resolution outcome resulting in a new contract, since the purpose of their claim against the debtor state is to seek compensation from the sovereign for its incomplete performance of the original bond agreement in the first place. However,

[62] Barton Legum, 'The Difficulties of Conciliation in Investment Treaty Cases: A Comment on Professor Jack C. Coe's 'Toward A Complementary Use of Conciliation in Investor-State Disputes—A Preliminary Sketch' (2006) 21 Mealey's International Arbitration Report 4.

[63] Articles 1–8 of the UNCITRAL Rules on Transparency in Treaty-Based Investor–State Arbitration.

[64] Article 4 of the UNCITRAL Rules on Transparency in Treaty-Based Investor–State Arbitration.

[65] Natasha Mellersh, 'Can We Enforce Mediation Agreements?', JAMS ADR Blog [blog] (Jams International, 22 September 2017) http://adrpartners.rs/en/can-enforce-mediation-agreements/ ; Lorraine Brennan, 'Do We Need a New York Convention for Mediation/Conciliation?' (February 2015), https://www.mediate.com/articles/BrennanLbl20150227.cfm. See also Chapter 19, this volume.

[66] Ibid. See also Chapter 1, this volume.

the parties can circumvent this issue by requesting an arbitral tribunal to render an award that embodies the terms of their accord, known as an 'award by consent'.[67] An award by consent would thus effectively transform the parties' settlement agreement into an arbitral award enforceable under the ICSID Convention or the New York Convention.[68] In addition, in a recent and major development, the newly-adopted United Nations Convention on International Settlement Agreements Resulting from Mediation, also known as the Singapore Convention on Mediation (Singapore Convention), provides for the recognition and enforcement of mediated settlement agreements resolving international commercial disputes.[69] Accordingly, once the Singapore Convention takes effect upon ratification by at least three member states, it will provide an enforcement mechanism similar to the framework established by the 1958 New York Convention for the recognition and enforcement of arbitral awards.[70]

V. Practical Considerations of Mediating Sovereign Debt Disputes

This section turns to some practical aspects of mediating sovereign debt disputes, e.g. how mediation can be introduced into the sovereign default dispute resolution process as well as various procedural considerations, including whether to engage in ad hoc or institutional proceedings and the selection of a competent mediator.

A. Commencing Mediation Proceedings

The first procedural question is how to commence mediation proceedings between sovereign bondholders and states in default. There are several possibilities. The most effective means of ensuring that the parties commence mediation proceedings is to have a pre-existing agreement to mediate that would obligate the parties to participate at least until the first meeting with the mediator. This agreement could be included as a mediation clause directly in the sovereign bond contract

[67] See, for example, Rule 43(2) of the ICSID Arbitration Rules ('If the parties file with the Secretary-General the full and signed text of their settlement and in writing request the Tribunal to embody such settlement in an award, the Tribunal may record the settlement in the form of its award') and Article 33 of the ICC Arbitration Rules ('If the parties reach a settlement after the file has been transmitted to the arbitral tribunal in accordance with Article 16, the settlement shall be recorded in the form of an award made by consent of the parties, if so requested by the parties and if the arbitral tribunal agrees to do so').

[68] Ibid.

[69] See also Chapter 19, this volume.

[70] UNCITRAL Report of Working Group II (Dispute Settlement) on the work of its sixty-seventh session (Vienna, Austria, 2–6 October 2017). See also Chapter 19, this volume.

or in the language of the applicable investment treaty.[71] Such a clause could deny the parties the right to file for judicial or arbitral proceedings until the first mediation meeting has taken place, or at least require that mediation proceedings be initiated in parallel to arbitration proceedings.[72] For example, Clause C of the ICC Mediation Rules creates an obligation to refer a dispute to mediation under the ICC Mediation Rules while permitting parallel arbitration proceedings if required, whereas Clause D states that the parties may not commence arbitration proceedings, if necessary, until an agreed period has elapsed following the filing of the request for mediation. The advantage of such a compulsory, prior mediation agreement is that it forces the parties to at least attempt mediation, which in turn gives the parties the greatest chance of reaching settlement.[73] However, the mediation clause could also provide for non-compulsory mediation in which the parties would be invited to consider mediation prior to filing for judicial or arbitral proceedings, but would not be obligated to do so.[74] Even where no mediation clause exists, the parties could nevertheless enter into a subsequent agreement to mediate.[75] However, in such a case there is no guarantee that they will reach such an agreement. Therefore, the party seeking to propose mediation to the other party would probably benefit from filing the request for mediation through an institution that could help persuade the other party to accept the proposal by explaining the mediation process and ensuring that it is a neutral, productive, and time- and cost-efficient process.[76]

B. Choice of Procedural Rules

It is also important to establish what procedural rules would govern the mediation proceedings. In any dispute resolution proceedings, including mediation, the parties have the choice whether to conduct the proceeding ad hoc or under the administration of an institutional body. In ad hoc proceedings, the parties will have to determine all aspects themselves, such as the governing rules, the selection of the mediator, the division of costs, etc.[77] Although this approach might save on

[71] Waibel (n 1) 162–7; See also Article 9.18 of the Comprehensive and Progressive Agreement for Trans-Pacific Partnership (CPTPP) (2018).

[72] Article 9.19 of CPTPP provides that the parties cannot file for arbitration before six months have passed since filing a request for amicable dispute resolution proceedings as described in Article 9.18.

[73] Tümpel and Sudborough (n 42) 269.

[74] Clause B of the ICC Mediation Rules requires the parties to discuss and consider submitting their dispute to the ICC Mediation Rules without obliging the parties to commence mediation proceedings.

[75] Article 1(a) of the IBA Mediation Rules states that the IBA Mediation Rules can apply where the parties have so agreed even after the dispute arises.

[76] Tümpel and Sudborough (n 42) 270.

[77] Michael McIlwrath and John Savage, *International Arbitration and Mediation: A Practical Guide* (Kluwer Law International, 2010) 64–7.

the costs of fees to an administering institution, the parties are likely to spend a considerable amount of time seeking to resolve unexpected hurdles without any guarantee that they will manage to do so, particularly once the dispute has arisen.[78] Nevertheless, parties may still involve the limited assistance of an administering institution at some point during the proceedings, even where they prefer to conduct the proceedings ad hoc, e.g. as an appointing authority for the mediator.[79]

Where parties choose to conduct the mediation under the administration of an institutional body, the administering institution will be responsible for either obtaining the agreement of the parties on the various procedural issues that might arise, or in making a decision in the absence of an agreement in order to ensure that the proceedings are conducted as efficiently as possible.[80] Accordingly, although the costs of such proceedings will include fees to be paid to the administering body, that institutional body in turn will have the responsibility to ensure that the overall costs of the proceedings remain low, e.g. by scrutinizing any expenses the mediator seeks to have reimbursed and by making decisions necessary to expedite the process, as might be the case where the parties are unable to agree on the place of the mediation meetings or seek to replace the mediator.[81]

Several institutions have published rules that could apply to mediating investor–state sovereign debt disputes, including the International Bar Association (IBA) Rules for Investor State Mediation, the ICC Mediation Rules, and the Mediation Rules of the Arbitration Institute of the Stockholm Chamber of Commerce. As mentioned previously, the ICSID Conciliation Rules provide for *conciliation*, and not mediation, proceedings.[82] Although a worthwhile exercise, the purpose of this chapter is not to conduct a detailed comparison of these rules, but it would be wise to examine the various options before including any particular set of rules into a dispute resolution clause or before filing for mediation with any particular institution. In considering the choices, it would also be prudent to take the following factors into consideration: the international reputation of the institution in terms of neutrality, training, quality of services and international network; the amount of assistance provided by the administering organization to facilitate the process where procedural obstacles occur; the process for the selection of the mediator; the process for replacing the mediator if necessary; the costs and how they are allocated and controlled; the flexibility of the process where the parties envision combining mediation; and other dispute resolution mechanisms such as arbitration or expertise.[83]

[78] Ibid.
[79] ICC Rules for the Appointment of Experts and Neutrals 2015.
[80] McIlwrath and Savage (n 77).
[81] Appendix Article 3 of the ICC Mediation Rules setting out that the Centre shall decide whether the mediator's fees and costs are reasonable and thus payable by the parties.
[82] ICSID (n 56).
[83] McIlwrath and Savage (n 77) 187–204.

C. Selecting the Mediator(s)

Additionally, the parties need to select a mediator. As the focus is on sovereign debt mediation, we must ask what particular skills a mediator should possess for such disputes. Sovereign debt disputes are specific because they involve private parties (creditors) and sovereign states. Furthermore, sovereign debt disputes involve major issues of public policy, international finance, states' international obligations, transparency, and national sovereignty. As such, not all capable mediators may be suitable for mediating disputes between states and their bondholders. Fortunately, several bodies have established guidelines in selecting and evaluating the criteria of potential mediators for investment disputes, including the IBA, the Energy Charter Conference and the International Mediation Institute (IMI), providing a useful reference.[84] Although each body lists different useful criteria for consideration, the various competency standards listed by all of these bodies converge on the following important points:

i. thorough training and experience as a mediator;
ii. experience with investor-state disputes or dispute resolution proceedings involving states or state agencies;
iii. skill in handling cross-cultural negotiations;
iv. international reputation and credibility and,
v. experience dealing with government representatives, politicians and/or diplomats.[85]

Further, in light of the technicalities of sovereign debt disputes, it would be beneficial to engage a mediator capable of quickly understanding the complexities of international sovereign financing and investment law.

Although international commercial mediation continues to flourish, parties to investment disputes do not yet benefit from a recognized body of investment mediators in making their appointments. In addition, it has not yet been verified whether similar competency criteria as those listed in the preceding paragraph were the basis for selecting the proposed panel of ICSID Conciliators.[86] Hence, parties to sovereign debt disputes would be wise to not rely solely on the listing of a proposed conciliator or mediator's name in a particular institution's panel, but rather to examine his or her proven mediation skills and experience in settling disputes of a similar nature in light of the aforementioned suggested criteria. Lastly,

[84] IBA Mediation Rules; Energy Charter Conference Mediation Guide; International Mediation Institute Competency Criteria for Investor–State Mediators 2016.

[85] Ibid.

[86] ICSID, 'Selection and Appointment Of Conciliators: Additional Facility Conciliation' (2018), https://icsid.worldbank.org/en/Pages/process/Selection-and-Appointment-of-Commission-Members---AF-Conciliation.aspx.

given that investor–state sovereign debt disputes require a very specific combination of skills that might not be present in one particular mediator at any given time, parties should be open to the possibility of naming co-mediators whose combined qualifications could be particularly helpful.

VI. Conclusion

Although a trickle of investment arbitration proceedings has been filed to resolve conflicts between sovereign bondholders and debtor states, mediation proceedings in this domain remain largely theoretical. However, stakeholders and legal scholars in the sovereign finance arena have expressed doubts as to whether investment arbitration is the most appropriate dispute resolution tool for sovereign debt claims as well as their concerns about the cost of such legal proceedings for debtor state's taxpayers, who are usually subject to austerity measures as a result of the state's default.

Given the lack of any normative legal framework for sovereign bankruptcy and the need to facilitate sovereign debt restructuring as efficiently as possible to minimize financial instability, it is time to employ newer tactics. Mediation addresses some of the shortcomings of investment arbitration for sovereign debt disputes by providing the parties with the flexibility to focus on their common interests, rather than solely on their legal positions for a more efficient solution. Moreover, mediation proceedings are likely to be less costly for sovereign states in bankruptcy, freeing resources for important services that the state must provide to its citizens.

At the same time, as mediation is new to the investment dispute arena and does not yet benefit from a treaty recognizing the enforcement of mediated settlement agreements, it is viewed with a heavy dose of scepticism. To overcome this and other hurdles, creditors and states would benefit from the assistance of experienced dispute resolution institutions in investment disputes and from the use of an established set of procedural rules for the mediation.

13
Mediating International Energy Disputes

Peter D. Cameron and Abba Kolo

I. Introduction

Conventional approaches to the classification of disputes tend to reinforce the often tacit assumption that mediation is neither of much relevance to energy disputes nor is it much in use. We argue that a different approach, taking into account the changing character of the international energy industry, and noting the practice of combining different techniques in tackling particular disputes, reveals that mediation is already in use in diverse ways, with varying degrees of success and in different forms of energy. Apart from an extensive review of the available literature, we use several case studies to support this view. We also argue that mediation could be more effective if four issues were addressed.

The modern internationally operating energy industry is a very different creature from the fossil fuels-based industry associated with the Age of Oil, with its geographic focus on the Middle East and parts of the southern hemisphere, dominated by large, internationally operating, multinational companies. Several seminal awards in international arbitration, e.g. *Aminoil* and the various Libya cases,[1] emerged from this bygone energy world. Like their counterparts in the regionally focused gas industry, which has also generated many arbitrations but fewer publicly available awards, these energy companies typically concluded long-term contracts with states or state agencies and sought to keep them stable over decades despite changing circumstances. The long-term, capital-intensive and risky nature of this energy investment meant that disputes often arose (e.g. caused by change in economic circumstances, change in government policies, gaps in contract, and disagreements among partners on operational matters) as did the need to resolve such disputes amicably to preserve the parties' long-term business relationships. A pattern emerged: energy disputes can typically have a state-to-state character, or

[1] *The Government of the State of Kuwait v The American Independent Oil Company*, 21 International Legal Materials (1982) 976; *Texaco Overseas Petroleum Co/California Asiatic Oil Co. v Libyan Arab Republic*, (1978) 17 International Legal Materials 1; *BP Exploration v Libyan Arab Republic*, (1973) 53 International Law Report 297; *Libyan American Oil Co. (LIAMCO) v Libyan Arab Republic*, 20 International Legal Materials (1981) 1.

can arise between investors and states, companies against other companies, or individuals against companies.[2]

In the twenty-first century there have been two major changes to this picture: one concerns the players and the other concerns the contracts. Firstly, internationally operating energy firms may well be concerned with wind or solar power rather than fossil fuels. Their investments may be made in Europe or North America, rather than in the southern hemisphere and most importantly, their capital structure will usually be of a more modest nature than that of the successors to Standard Oil. The fossil fuel-based players are—after a period of oil price collapse between 2014 and 2017—very concerned about the costs of doing business. Secondly, the era of long-term contracts in the international energy industry is not over, but has experienced a sharp decline. In the gas industry, changes in end-user markets have undermined the pricing mechanism in long-term contracts, triggering a series of gas pricing arbitrations in recent years. Changes in long-term petroleum contracts are more common as market volatility and other changes of circumstance have become more frequent.

Of course, the impact of this on mediation[3] is indirect. In our view, there are three broad impacts. Firstly, there is a trend for players to be more aware than ever of the benefits of amicably settling the differences that inevitably arise in any relationship over time, fostering a spirit of cooperation that a mediator can use to benefit both parties. This is facilitated by the role of international organizations like the Energy Charter Conference and its Secretariat, which can promote awareness and understanding of this approach in the context of investment disputes.[4] Second, there is greater pressure than ever before to ensure that costs—including reputational as well as direct costs—of settling disputes are kept to the minimum. Finally, there is a willingness to review the traditional approach[5]—primarily, even

[2] Timothy Martin, 'Dispute Resolution in the International Energy Sector: An Overview' (2011) 4 (4) Journal of World Energy Law and Business 332. They can also involve criminal proceedings, of course, which are not considered in this chapter.

[3] Notwithstanding the conceptual difference between mediation and conciliation, for purposes of this chapter and in line with other the usage of commentators, the two terms are used interchangeably. See Energy Charter Secretariat, *Guide on Investment Mediation* (2016) 2, https://energycharter.org/fileadmin/DocumentsMedia/CCDECS/2016/CCDEC201612.pdf; Esme Shirlow, 'The Rising Interest in the Mediation of Investment Treaty Disputes, and Scope for Increasing Interaction between Mediation and Arbitration' Kluwer Arbitration Blog [blog] 29 September 2016 (noting that: 'Mediation is frequently likened to conciliation. In fact, both the ECT Guide and PCA Conciliation Rules specifically use "mediation" and "conciliation" interchangeably'), http://arbitrationblog.kluwerarbitration.com/2016/09/29/the-rising-interest-in-the-mediation-of-investment-treaty-disputes-and-scope-for-increasing-interaction-between-mediation-and-arbitration/.

[4] In this context, it may be noted that the Energy Charter Secretariat has initiated courses on mediation in connection with investor–state disputes, driven by the growing practice of including provisions on mediation to settle disputes in modern investment treaties. These are jointly organized with the International Centre for Settlement of Investment Disputes (ICSID) and the Centre for Effective Dispute Resolution and the International Mediation Institute. They are mainly designed to deliver benefits to government officials seeking to develop skills in this area.

[5] It is difficult to believe that this is unconnected with the current critique of arbitration in investor–state disputes, which among other claims, argues that this mode of dispute settlement in international treaty instruments puts states at a significant disadvantage. For a recent critique of the current or

if not exclusively, arbitration in this key economic sector—and ask if elements of cooperation cannot be incorporated into an adversarial process. Even if arbitration is pending, mediation can still be initiated, and indeed may be initiated at any time once the arbitration has started.[6] This much is assured by the current legal

traditional approach to international arbitration, see Muthucumaraswamy Sornarajah, *Resistance and Change in the International Law on Foreign Investment* (CUP, 2015).

[6] Mediation Guidance Notes to the International Chamber of Commerce (ICC), Mediation Rules 2014 (Guidance 28), which states that : 'Mediation under the Rules may take place either before arbitration (or litigation) proceedings have been commenced, or in the course of those proceedings', https://cms.iccwbo.org/content/uploads/sites/3/2014/12/icc-mediation-guidance-notes-english.pdf. A review of the principal rules governing arbitration suggests that mediation or conciliation may be initiated either before or after the arbitration has started and allow for mediated settlements to be recorded as an arbitral award ('consent award' or 'award on agreed terms'): these include Article 43 of the International Centre for Settlement of Investment Disputes Convention Arbitration Rules 2006 (ICSID Arbitration Rules), Article 36 of the United Nations Commission on International Trade Law Arbitration Rules 2010 (UNCITRAL Arbitration Rules); Article 33 Rules of Arbitration of the International Chamber of Commerce 2017 (ICC Arbitration Rules); Article 26 London Court of International Arbitration Rules 2014 (LCIA Arbitration Rules); Article 34 Permanent Court of Arbitration Optional Rules for Arbitrating Disputes between two parties of which only one is a State 1993 (PCA Optional Arbitration Rules); Article 34 Permanent Court of Arbitration Optional Rules for Arbitration of Disputes Relating to Natural Resources and/or the Environment 2001 (PCA Optional Arbitration Rules Relating to Natural Resources); Article 39 Arbitration Rules of the Arbitration Institute of the Stockholm Chamber of Commerce (SCC Arbitration Rules); Article 47.5 China International Economic and Trade Arbitration Commission Arbitration Rules 2015 (CIETAC Arbitration Rules), Article 43 China International Economic and Trade Arbitration Commission Investment Arbitration Rules 2017 (CIETAC Investment Arbitration Rules); Article 32.10 Arbitration Rules of the Singapore International Arbitration Centre, 2016 (SIAC Arbitration Rules). However, most of the above arbitration rules 'make no comment as to whether a tribunal may assist the parties in reaching a settlement.' See Clyde Croft, Christopher Kee, and Jeff Waincymer, *A Guide to the UNCITRAL Arbitration Rules* (CUP, 2013) 408. The exception is Article 47.1 of the CIETAC Arbitration Rules, which states that where both parties consent, the 'arbitral tribunal may conciliate the dispute during the arbitral proceedings' and that the 'parties may also settle their dispute by themselves.' See also Article 47(10), which states that where the parties have reached a settlement agreement by themselves before the commencement of an arbitration, 'either party may request CIETAC to constitute an arbitral tribunal to render an arbitral award in accordance with the terms of the settlement agreement.' Cf. Article 21(1) ICSID Arbitration Rules, which provides for the possibility of a pre-hearing conference between the tribunal and parties 'to consider the issues in dispute with a view to reaching an amicable settlement'. The disputing parties may also reach a settlement after the award is rendered to avoid the cost of enforcement and/or maintain their future business relationships. In *Slovak Gas Holding v Slovak Republic* (ICSID Case No. ARB/12/7), the claimants instituted arbitration proceedings at ICSID in March 2012, alleging that certain measures taken by the Slovak Republic and certain of its organs, including a change in price regulation in the gas sector implemented by means of Decree 4/2008, violated their rights under the Energy Charter Treaty. The proceedings were suspended in December 2012 at the instance of the parties to allow an amicable settlement. In January 2014, the parties filed their settlement and requested the Tribunal to embody the settlement agreement in an award, pursuant to ICSID Arbitration Rule 43(2). Reducing such settlement agreements into consent awards gives them legal force, thereby enabling their enforcement under the New York Convention or other international instrument, as applicable. It can also enhance the legitimacy of the agreement and makes it much easier for political leaders to obtain support from their constituents. See Wolf von Kumberg, Jeremy Lack, and Michael Leathes, 'Enabling Early Settlement in Investor–State Arbitration: The Time to Introduce Mediation Has Come' (2014) 29 ICSID Review–Foreign Investment Law Journal 1, 8. On consent awards generally, see Yaraslau Kryvoi and Dmitry Davydenko, 'Consent Awards in International Arbitration: From Settlement to Enforcement' (2015) 40 Brooklyn Journal of International Law 827; Alan Redfern and Martin Hunter, *Law and Practice of International Commercial Arbitration* (Sweet and Maxwell, 2010) sections 9.33–9.38; Loukas Mistelis, 'The Settlement-Enforcement Dynamic in International Arbitration' (2008) 19 American Review of International Arbitration 377.

framework for mediation (in investment treaties,[7] national investment laws, energy/oil and gas contracts,[8] and institutional procedural rules on mediation, e.g. those of the ICC, ICSID, PCA, and the LCIA).[9]

In the literature on types of international dispute settlement, there is—unsurprisingly—a tendency to separate the main types to examine them analytically.[10] Of course, there is nothing reprehensible about a practice aimed at providing clarity about the various options to assist the reader's understanding, but it can imply that the diverse approaches inhabit different worlds, which they do not (nor would the authors probably intend or sanction this interpretation). The reality is that elements of mediation are already incorporated into some formal dispute settlement clauses in energy contracts, and if interest in them is a guide, the trend is growing. One caveat here is that in largely national settings the picture may differ. In energy terms, the largest consumer and producer of energy, the United States, has long used mediation in its oil and gas disputes.[11] However, on the international

[7] Although most investment treaties contain provisions on a 'cooling-off' period (usually 60–180 days), which require the parties to attempt an amicable settlement of the dispute before resorting to arbitration, very few explicitly require the parties to attempt to settle the dispute through conciliation or mediation during the cooling-off period. The few exceptions include: Article 8.20(1) Chapter Eight of the European Union–Canada Comprehensive Economic and Trade Agreement (2016), Article 9.18(1) of the Comprehensive and Progressive Agreement for Trans-Pacific Partnership (CPTPP) (2018), Article 3.4 and Annex 6 of the EU–Singapore Investment Protection Agreement (IPA) (2018), Article 3.29 and Annex 10 of the EU–Vietnam IPA (2018), and Article 42(1)(b) of the Draft Pan-African Investment Code, December 2016. See Gabriel Bottini and Veronica Lavista, 'Conciliation and BITs', in Arthur Rovine (ed.), *Contemporary Issues in International Arbitration and Mediation: The Fordham Papers* (Koninklijke Brill, 2009) 354; Chunlei Zhao, 'Investor-State Mediation in a China-EU Bilateral Investment Treaty: Talking about Being in the Right Place at the Right Time' (2018) 17 Chinese Journal of International Law 111.

[8] For example, Article 42(1)(b) of the Iraq Kurdistan Region Model Production Sharing Contract (2007) states that where a dispute cannot be resolved through negotiations, 'within sixty (60) days after the date of the receipt by each party to the Dispute of the Notice of Dispute or such further period as the parties to the Dispute may agree in writing, any party to the Dispute may seek settlement of the dispute by mediation in accordance with the London Court of International Arbitration (LCIA) Mediation Procedure, which Procedure shall be deemed to be incorporated by reference into this article, and the parties to such Dispute shall submit to such mediation procedure', http://www.eisourcebook.org/cms/December%202015/Iraq%20Kurdistan%20Model%20Production%20Sharing%20Contract.pdf.

[9] International Chamber of Commerce Mediation Rules 2014; Rules of Procedure for Conciliation Proceedings (the Conciliation Rules) of the International Centre for the Settlement of Investment Disputes (ICSID Conciliation Rules); Mediation Rules of the Arbitration Institute of the Stockholm Chamber of Commerce 2014 (SCC Mediation Rules); Conciliation Rules of the United Nations Commission on International Trade Law 1980 (UNCITRAL Conciliation Rules); Permanent Court of Arbitration Optional Conciliation Rules 1996 (PCA Conciliation Rules), Permanent Court of Arbitration Optional Rules for Conciliation of Disputes Relating to Natural Resources and/or the Environment 2002; London Court of International Arbitration Mediation Rules 2012 (LCIA Mediation Rules); International Bar Association Rules for Investor–State Mediation 2012 (IBA Rules for Investor–State Mediation).

[10] For example, Nigel Blackaby and Constantine Partasides, *Redfern and Hunter on International Arbitration* (OUP, 2015); Anthony Connerty, *A Manual of International Dispute Resolution* (Commonwealth Secretariat, 2006).

[11] For example, see Gary McGowan, 'Mediating International Oil & Gas Disputes' in James M Gaitis (ed.), *The Leading Practitioners' Guide to International Oil & Gas Arbitration* (Juris, 2015) 967–82, 967: 'In the United States, and to an increasing extent throughout the world, many, if not most, of those (oil and gas) disputes are mediated before proceeding to a hearing before an international arbitral

scene this is not typical practice, and indeed, where foreign investors are involved, the pattern will tend to arbitration as the preferred option by the parties to energy contracts.

II. Energy Disputes and Mediation Requirements

In many parts of the world, governments and their agencies are heavily involved in the energy business, whether this concerns oil and gas, wind, solar, nuclear energy, or coal. The only exception to this is the United States and Canada. Government involvement can occur as owner of resources and grantor of rights to them, provider of regulatory oversight, and sometimes as participant in contracts with private parties through a state entity.[12] In many countries, locally owned companies are encouraged by the host state to take a role in the energy sector, to promote jobs, to grow local skills, and to diversify the wider economy from dependence on the energy sector. There are very few areas of energy sector activity where the state is absent.[13]

For the settlement of disputes, this broad role of the state means that a purely commercial approach has limited applicability, since one of the parties will have at least some non-commercial goals and interests. A mediator, skilled in commercial mediation practice, may find it challenging to deal with the very different priorities of a state party. Discussion of a settlement will almost always involve parties not present in the room and require consultation with them. The powerful driver to a settlement in the commercial world—time is money and a dispute uses up time—may not figure in the same way, or even at all, when a state party is involved.[14]

tribunal'. McGowan's emphasis on the sequential nature of mediation and arbitration gives us a clue to how mediation is typically likely to be evident in energy disputes generally.

---

[12] Ernest Smith, John Dzienkowski, Owen Anderson, John Lowe, Bruce Kramer, and Jacqueline Weaver, *International Petroleum Transactions* (Rocky Mountain Mineral Law Foundation, 2010) 30–54, 180–91, 214–15; Peter Cameron and Michael Stanley, *Oil, Gas, and Mining: A Sourcebook for Understanding the Extractive Industries* (World Bank, 2017) 58–60, 63–5, https://openknowledge.worldbank.org/bitstream/handle/10986/26130/9780821396582.pdf?sequence=2&isAllowed=y; Michael Bunter, *The Promotion and Licensing of Petroleum Prospective Acreage* (Kluwer Law International, 2002) 40–56.

[13] In most cases, host states try to achieve these objectives by including in the exploration and exploitation contracts they sign with foreign investors relevant provisions on these issues, and sometimes by enacting specific legislation such as local content laws to supplement the contract and the more general legislative framework: See Smith et al. (n 12) 442–525; Cameron and Stanley (n 12) 65–6; Thomas Hickey, 'Production Sharing Contracts, Licenses and Concessions: A Comparative Look at Where We Are and How They Are Evolving', in Rocky Mountain Mineral Law Foundation, *Proceedings of the Fifty-Eighth Annual Institute on Oil and Gas Law held by the Centre for American and International Law* (Lexis Nexis, 2007) Chapter 18; Theophilus Acheampong, Marcia Ashong, and Victoria Crystal Svanikier, 'An Assessment of Local Content Policies in Oil and Gas Producing Countries' (2016) 7 (3) Journal of World Energy Law and Business 220.

[14] Nancy A. Welsh and Andrea K. Schneider, 'The Thoughtful Integration of Mediation into Bilateral Investment Treaty Arbitration' (2013) 18 Harvard Negotiation Law Review 71, 86–7.

Indeed, the *scope* for mediation will be influenced by this factor. At its most constraining, a commercial dispute with a host government or a state-owned enterprise may not be amenable to conciliation or mediation for the simple reason that government officials who agree to settle a significant dispute open themselves to accusations of corruption, loss of their jobs, and criminal proceedings.[15] The word 'significant' is important here. Often, energy disputes involve very large amounts of money and so their sensitivity to this consideration is greater. However, the 'public' aspect of many (but not all) energy disputes does *not* mean that states or state agencies will be averse to some form of conciliation or mediation and, indeed, there is some evidence that they are becoming more common.[16]

The advantages of mediation are reasonably well known, but it is worth summarizing the main ones before examining how they are used in the energy sector.[17] Among the advantages of mediation are that parties can maintain control over the outcome of the dispute and are enabled to maintain their business relationship. It is also generally faster and cheaper relative to arbitration and litigation.[18] Mediation

[15] Concern over taking personal responsibility tends to be more pronounced in state officials because the actions of such officials are more open to public scrutiny. However, executives in public companies may also be subject to criticism or punishment by shareholders 'for decisions that compromise financial or other ownership expectations.' See Jack J. Coe, Jr, 'Toward a Complementary Use of Conciliation in Investor-State Disputes—A Preliminary Sketch' (2005) 12 University College Davis Journal of International Law and Policy 7, 29. As Reisman puts it, 'all large and complex organizations in which authority is allocated among many different departments will experience difficulty in making major decisions. This seems especially to be the situation with respect to governments in international investment law disputes. Indeed, in States in which there are active political oppositions waiting for an opportunity to pounce on the incumbents for having "betrayed" the national patrimony by settling with an investor, modalities other than transparent third-party decisions can undermine or even bring down governments and destroy personal careers. [. . .] It is often easier for governments to have the right decision imposed by an outside tribunal rather than "conceded" by the government.' See William Reisman, 'International Investment Arbitration and ADR: Married but Best Living Apart', in Susan D. Franck and Anna Joubin-Bret (eds), *Investor-State Disputes: Prevention and Alternatives to Arbitration II* (United Nations, 2011) 22, 26; Thomas Waelde, 'Efficient Management of Transnational Disputes: Mutual Gain by Mediation or Joint Loss in Litigation' (2006) 22 Arbitration International 205, 217; Louis Wells and Rafiq Ahmed, *Making Foreign Investment Safe: Property Rights and National Sovereignty* (OUP, 2007) 220; Jeswald W. Salacuse, 'Is There a Better Way? Alternative Methods of Treaty-Based, Investor-State Dispute Resolution' (2007) 31 Fordham International Law Journal 138, 150–1. Nigeria is an example of the vulnerability of both private and public officials in this area. Nine former executives of international oil companies Shell and Eni, together with the companies, are currently facing criminal prosecution in Italy over alleged bribery and corruption in connection with a settlement agreement the two companies reached with the Nigerian government in 2011. In Nigeria, three former state officials, including two ministers, are also being prosecuted for their alleged role in the transaction. See 'Malabu Scandal: Trial of nine Shell, Eni executives starts June 20', Premium Times (Nigeria), (21 May 2018), https://www.premiumtimesng.com/news/top-news/269124-malabu-scandal-trial-of-nine-shell-eni-executives-starts-june-20.html, and Sahara Reporters (New York), 'President Buhari Disagrees With Attorney General Malami, Orders EFCC To Ensure Prosecution Of Diezani, Adoke, Others Involved In Malabu Scam,' Sahara Reporters (20 February 2018), http://saharareporters.com/2018/02/20/president-buhari-disagrees-attorney-general-malami-orders-efcc-ensure-prosecution-diezani.

[16] For example, from 2002 to 2013, there has been a settlement agreement in at least eight investment cases involving claims of violation of the Energy Charter Treaty by the host state. See Energy Charter Secretariat (n 3) 4.

[17] See Chapters 1 and 2, this volume, which address the pros and cons of mediation.

[18] Energy Charter Secretariat (n 3); Joseph Shade, 'The Oil & Gas and ADR: A Marriage Made in Heaven Waiting to Happen' (1995) 30 Tulsa Law Journal 599.

can take into consideration the entirety of the parties' circumstances.[19] It 'provides parties with the opportunity to explore alternative solutions to an adjudicated outcome in a safe and confidential environment'; it enables the parties 'to invent their own solutions including those not available in adjudicated proceedings, thereby avoiding an imposed solution'.[20] It is 'a chance to gather and impart information'.[21] Edna Sussman reinforces this when she says that mediation has an ability to explore underlying interests, and to explore creative solutions.[22] As one arbitrator notes, it offers to resolve a dispute on a 'without prejudice' basis.[23]

However, on the downside, several commentators observe that it does not always provide a decision or an outcome, and invariably entails a compromise. In Salmon's view, mediation adds to the time and costs if there is no settlement.[24] If unsuccessful, it is potentially 'a waste of time'.[25] Other criticisms commonly made include that the outcome is not binding (so either party can refuse to reach agreement or reject any recommendation a mediator may make); mediators cannot compel parties to disclose documents or issue interim measures (so they lack teeth); the settlement agreement is not automatically enforceable unless it takes the form of a consent award, and the outcome has no precedent value for future similar disputes between parties or with third parties.[26]

A curiosity of mediation use is that while there is an extensive legal framework for it, there are not many reported cases of successful mediated disputes in energy. Barriers to mediation may include: a lack of familiarity with mediation among small- and medium-sized businesses; cultural and self-interest of the legal profession; confidentiality of such procedures and outcomes; the need for parties to maintain secrecy to avoid the risk of an internal and external backlash; and scepticism over the effectiveness of mediation—seen as a delaying tactic or a 'waste' of time and energy due to the non-binding nature of its outcome.[27] Finally, a factor

[19] Simeon H. Baum, 'Hawking Our Wares in the Marketplace of Values - Sell Quality Not Cost When Promoting Mediation: The Interplay of Global Norms of Justice and Harmony in the Mediation Forum', in Arthur Rovine (ed.), *Contemporary Issues in International Arbitration and Mediation: The Fordham Papers* (Martinus Nijhoff, 2011) 317.

[20] Ibid.

[21] Ken Salmon, 'Mediation: Advantages and Disadvantages' (2014) 25 (2) Construction Lawyer 23.

[22] Edna Sussman 'The Advantages of Mediation and the Special Challenges to its Utilization in Investor State Disputes' (2014) 1 TDM [online] https://www.transnational-dispute-management.com/article.asp?key=2081.

[23] Anthony Connerty, 'Alternative Dispute Resolution' (2007) 5 TDM [online] https://www.transnational-dispute-management.com.

[24] Salmon (n 21) 23.

[25] Connerty (n 23).

[26] Coe (n 15) 25–32; Thomas Gaultier, 'Cross-Border Mediation: A New Solution for International Commercial Dispute Settlement?' (2013) 26 (1) NYSBA International Law Practicum 38, 47–50; Fabio Solimene, 'Dispute Resolution in Energy-Related Agreements: How to Choose the Right Means and Draft a Proper Clause' (2015) International Energy Law Review 108, 111–12.

[27] Waelde (n 15); Mauro Rubino-Sammartano, 'Visible and Invisible Barriers to Mediation: Speaker Notes' (2012) 9 (4) TDM [online] https://www.transnational-dispute-management.com. See generally, von Kumberg et al. (n 6) 3 (noting: 'lack of familiarity with (and therefore distrust of) mediation; uncertainty about how to find the right competent and suitable mediators for the case in hand; lack of time to mediate within the arbitration process steps; not being convened by the arbitral organizations

that plays a role is probably the lack of an international enforcement mechanism, which is likely to remain a shortcoming at least until the recently proposed United Nations Commission on International Trade Law (UNCITRAL) Convention on the enforcement of international commercial settlement agreements is negotiated and enters into force.[28]

A. Mediation Promotion by Treaty and by Contract

Yet, there are pointers as to its use in the energy sector. There is evidence of the promotion of mediation by both treaty and contract instruments. For the former we need look no further than Article 26.1 of the Energy Charter Treaty (ECT), which states that investment disputes concerning Part III (Investment Promotion and Protection) 'shall, if possible, be settled amicably'. Although the ECT is silent as to the particular mechanisms that might be used to facilitate an 'amicable settlement' within the three-month cooling off period, the parties are nonetheless free to choose mediation or conciliation using existing mechanisms, as well as 'good offices', whereby a trusted third party facilitates the parties to establish contact and commence an exploration of ways in which an amicable settlement may be reached, a structured negotiation or some bespoke mechanism relevant to their dispute.[29] A *request* for amicable settlement by either party to the dispute and a failure to resolve the dispute within a period of three months following the request are procedural requirements, rather than jurisdictional conditions under the ECT, before the investor may proceed to submit it to formal settlement under Article 26.2. This is *not* tantamount to a duty to mediate, since there are other mechanisms available to parties seeking to resolve a dispute amicably, but it does imply that mediation is one of several options to meet the direction given in Article 26.1.[30]

to consider mediation; not being proactively encouraged to seriously focus on settlement using skilled neutrals; and lack of adequate enforcement procedures'); Martin (n 2) 332, 337–8.

[28] See Chapter 19, this volume.

[29] Energy Charter Secretariat (n 3) at section 2.1.

[30] For example, in *Stati v Kazakhstan*, the tribunal observed that, 'By the express reference in subparagraphs (1) and (2), it is clear that the intention of Art. 26 ECT is to provide an opportunity of three months to the Parties to settle the dispute. In view of this obvious intention, the Tribunal considers that to be a procedural requirement rather than one of jurisdiction, at least as long as the Parties have indeed had such a three months opportunity.' The tribunal then noted that the parties had failed to reach a settlement during the three-month period it granted them as such, there was 'no reason to deny jurisdiction.' *Anatolie Stati, Gabriel Stati, Ascom Group SA and Terra Raf Trans Traiding Ltd v Kazakhstan*, SCC Case No. 116/2010, Award of 19 December 2013, paras 829, 830; cf. *Mohammad Ammar Al-Bahloul v The Republic of Tajikistan*, SCC Case No. 064/2008, Partial Award on Jurisdiction and Liability, 2 September 2009, paras 154–6; Energy Charter Secretariat (n 3) paragraph 2.1 (noting that: '[w]hile available arbitral awards under the ECT have not confirmed the existence of a duty to mediate in Article 26.1 of the ECT, they confirmed that parties need to seriously attempt to reach an amicable settlement'); Thomas Roe and Matthew Happold, *Settlement of Investment Disputes under the Energy Charter Treaty* (CUP, 2011) 137.

With respect to contract, a common feature of many energy contracts is the use of escalation clauses. As one authority has pointed out, these have long been common in construction contracts.[31] They can be called variously 'multi-tiered,' or 'stepped' clauses. The Association of International Petroleum Negotiators (AIPN) has used these in several of its Model Form Agreements based on industry practice and designed largely by industry professionals.[32]

In a nutshell, the idea is that the parties are required to submit disputes to an increasingly rigorous and formal series of dispute resolution methods. This allows the parties to encourage and allow opportunities for an agreed settlement, either through mediation or (in the AIPN models) negotiation by senior executives on each side. The parties retain control over their own destinies in the initial stages and the process also ensures that if these relatively informal efforts at a settlement fail, the next step will be one that allows a third party to render a binding decision.

Multi-tiered dispute resolution provisions are very common in the petroleum industry. They are frequently included in various types of petroleum contracts across the world, including the Middle East, Africa, and Latin America. In the petroleum sector (and in the energy sector more generally), the parties' cooperation and continued performance of their obligations is essential. The multi-tiered dispute resolution provisions are frequently included to maximize the parties' chances to reach an amicable resolution of any disagreements that may arise during the performance of their long-term contracts and avoid the risk that their commercial relationship might suffer if the dispute goes to the formal processes of arbitration or court litigation. The value of a long-term relationship is especially important in the energy sector, which typically requires close cooperation between the parties and can be highly capital intensive at various stages. Normally, parties to oil and gas contracts view arbitration or court litigation as a last resort solution.

The multi-tiered dispute resolution clauses require the parties to define at an early stage what their complaints are with some specificity, and what relief they seek. This serves two important purposes: 1) achieving containment of the scope of the dispute by defining the issues in dispute; and 2) because of this procedure of defining the issues in dispute, and what issues could be amicably agreed, enabling the parties to discuss the practical steps as to how to continue operations and performance of their long-term contract. The parties have an interest in working out constructively how to contain their dispute and ensure continuous performance of their contract and avoid disruption of petroleum operations pending resolution of their differences (even if their dispute escalates).

[31] Klaus P. Berger, 'Law and Practice of Escalation Clauses' (2006) 22 Arbitration International 1–17; see also Didem Kayali, 'Enforceability of Multi-Tiered Dispute Resolution Clauses' (2010) 27 (6) Journal of International Arbitration 551–77.

[32] For example, in the Association of International Petroleum Negotiators (AIPN) International Model Form Dispute Settlement Agreement 2004; and the International Model Form Joint Operating Agreement 2002, http://www.aipn.org.

In sum, the multi-tiered dispute resolution clauses in petroleum contracts are aimed at: minimizing/containing the escalation of disputes that arise between the parties; preserving the parties' long-term relationship; maximizing cost efficiency; ensuring that the parties can agree on mechanisms for maintaining the performance of ongoing obligations under the contract, pending resolution of their dispute; and ensuring that by means of a notification procedure the other party is fully aware of the timing of a distinct stage in the process, without which the multi-tier approach would become difficult to implement.

Where a contract requires notification of the dispute, the commercial purpose of this requirement is to clearly define and contain the scope of the parties' dispute, thus allowing it to streamline the parties' attempts to amicably resolve their dispute. It is of particular significance in a multi-tier process. The principal reason for its importance was identified in the Guidelines to the AIPN Model Form Agreement on Dispute Settlement as follows:

> To avoid creating more problems than are solved by this multi-step process, it is imperative that the parties make clear in their agreement when the transition occurs from one dispute resolution method to the next. Otherwise, a party may attack the process in the courts on the grounds that a condition precedent to moving on to the next step has not been fulfilled.

The key to defining the moment of transition with precision is the Notice of Dispute. Its receipt supplies an objectively verifiable event from which an agreed time to exhaust a specified method of dispute resolution can be measured.[33] An example of text on this from a recent petroleum agreement is as follows:

> A Party who desires to submit a Dispute for resolution shall commence the dispute resolution process by providing the other parties to the Dispute written notice of the Dispute ('*Notice of Dispute*'). The Notice of Dispute shall identify the parties to the Dispute, shall contain a brief statement of the nature of the Dispute and the relief requested and shall request negotiations among Senior Representatives.
>
> If the Dispute cannot be resolved by negotiation within sixty (60) days after the date of receipt by each party to the Dispute of the Notice of Dispute any party to the Dispute may seek settlement of the dispute by mediation in accordance with the London Court of International Arbitration (LCIA) Mediation Procedure, which Procedure shall be deemed to be incorporated by reference into this Article, and the parties to such Dispute shall submit to such mediation procedure:
>
> (a) If the Dispute is not settled by mediation within sixty (60) days of the appointment of the mediator, or such further period as the parties to the

[33] Association of International Petroleum Negotiators (AIPN), International Model Form Dispute Settlement Agreement (2004) 16.

> Dispute may otherwise agree in writing, any party to the Dispute may refer the Dispute to, and seek final resolution by, arbitration under the LCIA Rules, which Rules shall be deemed to be incorporated by reference into this Article.[34]

This type of clause can be particularly relevant to the commercial setting of an agreement between various energy companies. For example, the 2002 AIPN Model Joint Operating Agreement and the 2004 Model Agreement on International Dispute Settlement[35] provide for a multi-stage approach to the resolution of disputes arising between the parties, and require a formal, written notice of dispute that sets out the scope of the dispute, followed by an initial period of negotiations among higher management of the parties (typically subject to a defined time limit). These model contracts then anticipate a transition towards a second stage, involving mediation. If all other means fail, the final step is to resort to arbitration.[36] Such structure is particularly important for joint operating agreements because it provides practical steps for the parties to resolve disputes in a way that achieves the purposes outlined previously—i.e. containment of the dispute; cost efficiency; preservation of a long-term relationship; and ensuring that the parties have agreed on mechanisms for ongoing obligations to be met.

Such stepped clauses also have a darker side, which merits a brief comment. If the pre-action procedures, e.g. mediation, are mandatory, they can be used by a dilatory and recalcitrant party to delay the arbitration or even to prevent arbitration by accusing the other party of acting in bad faith during the pre-arbitration phase. For this reason, the drafter of such clauses must make certain that the transitions from one stage to the next are clearly defined. It could also be argued that having such procedures is inconsistent with providing for emergency arbitrator procedures or expedited arbitration. Our preference would be to provide for mediation concurrently with the commencement of arbitration, rather than as a pre-condition to arbitration.

[34] Unpublished production sharing agreement (authors' copy).

[35] The AIPN International Model Form Dispute Settlement Agreement was developed in the early 2000s for two reasons: firstly, it aimed to reconcile the many different versions of dispute resolution provisions that have been included over the years in AIPN Model Form Agreements; secondly, it was intended as a 'state of the art' dispute resolution agreement that could be incorporated into future AIPN Model Form Agreements. In this case, the drafting committee was expanded to include not only AIPN members, but also experts in dispute resolution with experience as advocates and arbitrators in upstream international energy disputes. These model provisions have therefore an authority that allows them to set a standard which at this stage in industry practice—since they are frequently used—should be seen as a minimum standard.

[36] See Article 18.2 of the AIPN Model Joint Operating Agreement (2002), http://www.aipn.org.

III. Energy Mediation in Practice

The following awards provide examples of reported mediated energy disputes. The next sections discuss the issues and the lessons that may be drawn from them.

A. Electricity: Vattenvall–PSE

In the mediation of a dispute involving a Power Purchase Agreement (PPA), Vattenfall (a Swedish energy company) and Polskie Sieci Elektroenergetyczne (PSE, a Polish integrated electricity company) had a mediation in 2002/2003 concerning the SwePol submarine interconnector contractual regimes. The PPA was entered into in 1995 under which PSE agreed to purchase electricity from Vattenfall for twenty years at a fixed price aimed at enhancing Polish energy security and reducing the country's reliance on electricity supplies from Russia. However, by the year 2000/2001 changes in economic, political, and regulatory circumstances had rendered the PPA uneconomical for PSE, and as a result, it 'refused to continue to take any of the power it was obligated to take and pay'.[37] Based on the advice of external counsel to PSE, the parties agreed to submit the dispute to mediation, rather than arbitration. A sole mediator was appointed supported by 'three senior specialists in electricity regulatory economics, electricity engineering, and financial analysis' (mediation team), who 'provided expertise on technical, modelling and regulatory economics issues'.[38] The parties made clear to the mediator their aim of achieving a reasonable renegotiation of the deal within a specified time duration and agreed to pay the mediator a success fee if these objectives were achieved.

To facilitate the process, the parties provided the mediator relevant negotiating documents, rather than selected documents, which enabled the mediator to understand not only how close the parties were to an agreement but also identified the obstacles or 'blockages' to an agreement and thereby tried to solve such blockages. Aside from meeting with the parties separately, the mediator also consulted other relevant external players, including the 'Polish energy regulator, the Swedish network operator and the EU Competition Directorate' as part of the 'intelligence gathering' process. The information gathered by the mediator and the technical teams was then synthetized by the mediation team, which produced an outline proposal to be presented to the parties, the elements of which consisted of a new contractual regime and a system of risk/investment sharing. This proposal was based on what the mediation team considered a 'fair and practical deal' that the disputing parties would have reached themselves, assuming they had 'jointly developed and funded the interconnector originally'.[39] The outline proposal together

[37] Waelde (n 15) 219.
[38] Ibid., 223. The following paragraphs draw upon the account given in this article.
[39] Ibid., 226–7.

with case assessments prepared by the mediator was presented to the senior executives of both parties' companies at series of caucus meetings with the mediator. After about seventy-five days of 'shuttle-diplomacy' by the mediator and his team, the parties met face-to-face in St Andrews (Scotland) for two and a half days, far away from their respective places of business and distraction, during which a preliminary agreement was reached, and thereafter a detailed agreement was negotiated, agreed, and signed by the parties within four months without further involvement of the mediator.

Aside from the time and cost savings (the mediation cost both parties about 1 million euros), other lessons to be drawn from this case study include: the 'advantage [of] conver[ting] [...] a lose-lose situation into a win-win situation', the 'significant value that can be generated by professional, interdisciplinary and scientifically oriented transnational mediation', the advisability of not handing over control of commercially significant disputes related to long-term business relationships to external litigation lawyers whose inclination would be to litigate rather than mediate.[40] This case also illustrates the need to involve Chief Executives and/or senior officials (who have the authority to take decisions on behalf of their respective organization) in the mediation process as they were more likely to view the disputes from their companies' broader commercial and long-term interests, rather than be shaped by the narrow interest of winning the case.

B. Oil and Gas, and Maritime Boundary: East Timor–Australia Conciliation

Before East Timor regained its independence in 2002, Indonesia and Australia had tried unsuccessfully to negotiate a boundary between the two countries in the Timor Sea, known to contain very large petroleum deposits. Unable to resolve their boundary dispute after a period of several years, the two nations entered into a Joint Development Agreement (JDA) in 1989 that provided a legal framework for the sharing of revenues derived from petroleum development in the area. After gaining its independence, East Timor and Australia signed a new treaty, which was substantially the same as the 1989 JDA. However, the parties were not able to reach a unitization agreement that would allow development to proceed in respect of the Greater Sunrise gas field because of the unresolved boundary dispute between the two countries. In 2006, the two nations signed a new treaty known as Certain Maritime Arrangements in the Timor Sea (CMATS), which modified the 2002 treaty in two key respects, one of which was that it 'extended the duration of the treaty period for 50 years from the date the CMATS entered into force in 2006 [i.e. until 2057] or until five years after the exploitation of the Greater Sunrise

[40] Ibid., 231–2.

field ceased, whichever occurred first. It also declared that neither country would pursue or assert any claims to sovereign rights and maritime boundaries during this period'.[41]

Although the two nations were not able to resolve their boundary dispute, nevertheless, the two treaties created sufficient stability in the Timor Gap for 'massive LNG development to proceed',[42] at least for some time.

However, in April 2016 East Timor initiated conciliation proceedings at the Permanent Court of Arbitration (PCA) to resolve the maritime boundary dispute with Australia. The conciliation was initiated under Annex V of the United Nations Convention on the Law of the Sea (UNCLOS), which allows for a 'compulsory conciliation' to be 'initiated where a state has exercised its right to exclude disputes relating to sea boundary delimitation from compulsory arbitration and judicial settlement—as Australia did in 2002, two months before East Timor regained its independence from Indonesia.'[43]

A five-member commission was constituted to hear the case,[44] and the opening session held at the Peace Palace in The Hague on 29 August was webcast live, but subsequent sessions were held behind closed doors 'in order to provide an "environment conducive to facilitating the eventual success of the conciliation." '[45] That was after the Commission in September 2016 had rejected Australia's objection that the commission lacked competence to hear the case.[46]

Prior to initiating the conciliation, East Timor had filed two separate arbitrations against Australia at the PCA. The first claim was filed in April 2013 under the Timor Sea Treaty alleging that CMATS was void because of the allegation that

[41] Smith et al. (n 12) 179–80; Centre for International Law (CIL), National University of Singapore, Working Conference on Conciliation: What Is It and When to Use It, 17–18 January 2017, 12, https://cil.nus.edu.sg/wp-content/uploads/2017/10/Conciliation-Background-Paper.pdf.

[42] Ibid., 180.

[43] Tom Jones, 'Australia Fails to Halt Conciliation with East Timor' Global Arbitration Review [online] 26 September 2016, https://globalarbitrationreview.com/article/1068790/australia-fails-to-halt-conciliation-with-east-timor. Article 298(1)(a)(i) of UNCLOS provides:1) in instances where a State declares that it does not accept any one or more of the dispute resolution procedures provided for in Annex V, section 2 of UNCLOS with respect to disputes concerning the interpretation or application of UNCLOS Articles 15, 74 and 83 relating to sea bed boundary delimitations; 2) when such a dispute arises subsequent to the entry into force of UNCLOS; and 3) no agreement within a reasonable period of time is reached in negotiations; any party to the dispute can request a State to accept submission of the matter to conciliation under Annex V section 2. Annex V section 2 provides that a party notified in accordance with the above provisions 'shall be obliged to submit to such proceedings' and that a failure of a party or parties to reply to a notification of institution of proceedings or submit to such proceedings 'shall not constitute a bar to the proceedings'.

[44] Two members of the Commission were appointed by East Timor and Australia each, while the chairman was appointed by the four party appointed members. See CIL (n 41) 12; Lacey Yong, 'East Timor and Australia Reach Deal on Maritime Border', Global Arbitration Review [online] 4 September 2017, https://globalarbitrationreview.com/article/1147052/east-timor-and-australia-reach-deal-on-maritime-border; Lacey Yong, 'Australia and East Timor Sign Treaty on Maritime Border', Global Arbitration Review [online] 6 March 2018, https://globalarbitrationreview.com/article/1166345/australia-and-east-timor-sign-treaty-on-maritime-border.

[45] Jones (n 43).

[46] Yong, 2017 (n 44); Yong, 2018 (n 44); CIL (n 41) 13.

'during the negotiation of CMATS, Australian intelligence operatives covertly listened in on Timor-Leste's negotiating team.'[47] In the second arbitration filed in 2015, East Timor sought to 'challenge [. . .] Australia's right to tax a subsea pipeline transporting gas from the Bayu-Undan gas field in the Timor Sea to a liquefied natural gas facility in the Australian city of Darwin.'[48]

In order to facilitate the conciliation process and as part of 'a confidence building measure', East Timor 'withdrew the two arbitrations before the awards had been reached.'[49]

East Timor and Australia reached an agreement in August 2017 on the 'central elements' of a permanent maritime boundary in the Timor Sea,[50] and the two nations signed a Maritime Boundaries Treaty on 6 March 2018, which 'defines a permanent boundary between the two countries and a pathway for each to the Greater Sunrise gas field in formerly disputes waters. [. . .] It also addresses the legal status of the gas field and establishes a "special regime" for the development of the field and the sharing of revenues.'[51]

Notwithstanding the formality of the proceedings and costs in legal fees incurred by the parties, the conciliation provided East Timor and Australia an opportunity to resolve their disputes in a manner they would otherwise not have achieved through arbitration or litigation before the PCA or the International Court of Justice (ICJ) respectively. More importantly, the conciliation afforded the parties the opportunity to reach a comprehensive agreement that resolved not only the legal issues concerning sharing revenues, but also the underlying political dispute concerning their maritime boundaries. The conciliation also 'demonstrate(s) that States are becoming increasingly creative in seeking to have even the most intractable maritime boundary disputes resolved under the principles of international law and through [less adversarial] third party means.'[52]

C. Oil and Gas: Tesoro–Trinidad and Tobago

In another dispute, involving Tesoro Petroleum Corporation and the Government of Trinidad and Tobago, concerning a joint venture entered into in 1968 to develop oil and gas in the host country on a fifty-fifty share ownership basis, the agreement

[47] Ryan Cable, 'In Search of Permanent Maritime Boundaries: Timor-Leste Commences First Ever Compulsory Conciliation under UNCLOS', Kluwer Arbitration Blog [blog] 4 October 2016, http://arbitrationblog.kluwerarbitration.com/2016/10/04/in-search-of-permanent-maritime-boundaries-timor-leste-commences-first-ever-compulsory-conciliation-under-unclos-2/; Yong, 2017 (n 44).

[48] Ibid.

[49] Yong, 2018 (n 44).

[50] Yong, 2017 (n 44).

[51] Yong, 2018 (n 44).

[52] Cable (n 47); Avnita Lakhani, 'The Strategic Use of Mediation for Resolving Maritime Territorial Disputes' (2013) Journal of International Maritime Law 60–73.

provided that, in the event Tesoro wished to sell its shares, the government had a right of first refusal. The agreement also provided that no dividends would be declared in the first five years of the joint company. A dispute settlement clause in the agreement provided for conciliation under the auspices of ICSID within a period of six months, failing which it was to be submitted to arbitration. Disputes arose between the parties in 1981 over taxation and the refusal by the government to give its approval to a declaration of dividends for 1981 and 1982. Following an unsuccessful negotiation between the parties for possible sale of Tesoro's shares to the government, the former invoked the dispute settlement clause by initiating conciliation proceedings with ICSID.

The parties appointed a sole conciliator, and proceedings commenced on 9 March 1984; each party was represented by lawyers. The proceedings were conducted more or less like arbitration, with submissions of memorials and counter-memorials, including an objection to jurisdiction raised by the government, which was joined to the merits by the conciliator. However, with the consent of the parties, the conciliator decided that no oral hearings would be necessary, and that he would decide the matter based on the written submissions of the parties.

On 5 February 1985, the conciliator issued his recommendation, which provided a basis of negotiation between the parties over the next eight months and via which the parties were able to reach a settlement agreement in November 1985. The conciliation cost the parties about 11,000 US dollars in administrative charges and fees of the conciliator, excluding legal costs, at a time when ICSID arbitration cost from 120,000 to 170,000 US dollars.[53]

Just like the Vattenfall–SPE case discussed earlier, the Tesoro–Trinidad case study demonstrates the time and cost advantages of mediation relative to arbitration or court litigation. Another lesson to be drawn was the strong likelihood that the parties would resolve the dispute in a manner that maintained their commercial relationships than was likely to be achieved through arbitration. Furthermore, on the one hand, the case demonstrates the benefits of expressly providing for mediation or conciliation in an oil and gas and energy investment agreement to encourage the parties to request mediation in the event of a dispute arising without the fear of appearing weak. On the other hand, the case demonstrates the risks of how to resort to institutional conciliation that might take an otherwise informal and flexible process into legalistic proceedings when lawyers are allowed to take control of the process.

[53] Lester Nurick and Stephen Schnably, 'The First ICSID Conciliation: *Tesoro Petroleum Corporation v Trinidad and Tobago*' (1986) 1 ICSID Review–Foreign Investment Law Journal 340; CIL (n 41).

D. Oil and Gas: RSM–Cameroon

In another oil and gas conciliation conducted under the auspices of ICSID, RSM Production Corporation filed a request in 2011 based on a conciliation clause in a five-year concession agreement it entered into with the Republic of Cameroon to explore for a natural gas field in Doula. The investor alleged that Cameroon illegally transferred a portion of the concession to a UK company, Victoria Oil and Gas. The claimant also alleged that Cameroon breached a provision in the contract that provided a mechanism for fixing the price of natural gas under the concession. A Commission consisting of three conciliators was appointed by the parties. Both parties were represented by counsel. Following a proceeding that lasted from February 2012 to June 2013, including four days of a hearing in Paris, the Commission issued its report on 11 June 2013, declaring the proceedings closed because in its opinion, there was 'no likelihood of agreement between the parties'.[54] The lesson to be drawn from this case study is that, where the disputing parties were not willing to settle, neither the existence of a conciliation clause in the contract nor the appointment and efforts of a distinguished panel of conciliators or mediators can help them reach a settlement. As noted earlier, in such cases the conciliation process could be described as a futile use of time and resources.

E. Oil and Gas: CMS Energy–Equatorial Guinea

Another unsuccessful conciliation filed pursuant to an ICSID Conciliation clause in an oil, gas, and mining contract involved Equatorial Guinea and the CMS Energy Corporation where the host state filed the request for conciliation in June 2012. A sole conciliator was appointed by the parties and the first session of the proceedings was held in March 2013, following which the parties exchanged written statements of their respective positions. The sole conciliator then visited the place connected with the dispute from 18–19 October 2013. Subsequently, the parties filed a second written statement of their respective positions. In March 2014, a hearing was held for three days in New York and in May 2015, following which the conciliator issued his report declaring that in his view, 'there [was] no likelihood of settlement between the parties'.[55] Thus, after three years of effort, the conciliation came to naught.

On the one hand, the last two case studies demonstrate that, aside from the willingness of the parties to submit the dispute to conciliation, the success of the

[54] CIL (n 41); Kyriaki Karadelis, 'RSM Files against Cameroon after Conciliation Fails', Global Arbitration Review [online] 25 June 2013, https://globalarbitrationreview.com/article/1032440/rsm-files-against-cameroon-after-conciliation-fails.

[55] *Equatorial Guinea v CMS Energy Corporation and others*, ICSID Case No. CONC(AF)/12/2; CIL (n 41) 16.

process depends very much on the parties' willingness to compromise in order to reach a settlement. Otherwise, the whole process might turn out to be a futile exercise. Thus, '[i]f the political and/or economic incentives are insufficiently attractive, it is unlikely that parties will agree to settle'.[56] On the other, the Vattenfall–PSE and Tesoro case studies (and to a limited extent the East Timor–Australia) illustrate the benefits of mediation/conciliation in resolving energy disputes quickly and cheaply relative to arbitration or court litigation, as well as providing the parties with an opportunity to recalibrate their commercial relationships in a manner they may not achieve through arbitration or litigation. The case studies also indicate that when the disputing parties hand over control of the mediation/conciliation to their legal counsel, they may end up having a process akin to arbitration, with all its legal technicalities, as well as time-consuming activity and perhaps high financial costs, especially if the panel consists of more than one mediator/conciliator.

IV. Issues in Mediation and the Future of Energy Mediation

This final section reflects on how the effectiveness of mediation in energy disputes might be enhanced. As the case studies illustrate, and contrary to some popular assumptions that question its relevance to the various energy industries, mediation is already in use, albeit in diverse ways, with varying degrees of success, and with respect to various kinds of energy. Data about other investor–state mediations is not readily available in the public domain; as such, any conclusions on the basis of what we have presented here must be tentative. To the extent that mediation offers to the parties in a dispute potential savings in terms of costs in time and funds, it seems entirely appropriate to seek ways in which its use can be enhanced and, indeed, even promoted.

At the ground level, the parties should ensure that there is a legal basis for mediation by expressly providing in investment treaties, national investment legislation, and in the relevant energy agreements that there is a requirement to attempt mediation either as a pre-condition for submitting the dispute to arbitration, or, preferably, concurrently with the commencement of arbitration. The existence of such a clause in the applicable law would encourage the parties to resort to the mechanism without the requesting party appearing weak.[57] That said, we have noted firstly that in the energy sector one of the parties is often a state body, subject to

[56] CIL (n 41) 17; Stephen Schwebel 'Is Mediation of Foreign Investment Disputes Plausible?' (2007) 12 ICSID Review–Foreign Investment Law Journal 237.

[57] Salacuse (n 15) 182 (noting that 'investment contracts between multinational corporations and host governments might provide for specific alternative dispute settlement in the event that conflict arises. Such contracts might stipulate, for example, that no arbitration may be launched until corporate executives and government officials have attempted and failed to negotiate or mediate disputes'); von Kumberg et al. (n 6) 5.

quite different and often non-commercial constraints and pressures than a commercial party, complicating the tasks of a mediator, and secondly, that there are advantages in considering the option of mediation even after an arbitration process has begun.

At the next level, mediation could be enhanced by making its benefits and availability better known. As noted, one of the reasons for the lower frequency of mediation use is the lack of familiarity among small- and medium-sized businesses both with its benefits and where to access it. This problem might be overcome by more awareness campaigns by dispute service providers such as ICSID, PCA, the International Mediation Institute, and other institutions. A wider publicity for the success stories of mediation might also help.[58]

Furthermore, at present, there is no international legal framework that provides for *enforcement* of mediation agreements and mediated settlement agreements akin to the New York Convention. Obviously, this applies to all kinds of mediation and not only those with an energy or energy-related subject matter. Consequently, a party to a mediation agreement may refuse to take part in a mediation, prevaricate, or take other measures to delay proceedings (and anecdotal evidence suggests this is not an uncommon abuse of conciliation requirements). Instead, it may resort to arbitration or court litigation in another jurisdiction. Similarly, unlike an arbitration award, which may be enforced under the New York Convention in all member states, a mediated settlement agreement can only be enforced as a contract or by taking steps to have it ratified as a consent award by the arbitral tribunal hearing the case.[59] Currently, the UNCITRAL Working Group on Arbitration and Conciliation is working to develop a convention on the international enforcement of commercial settlements, which will (when it comes into force) ease the difficulties of enforcing a settlement agreement.[60] Such a convention will enhance the prospects of mediation in general.[61]

[58] Markus Petsche, 'Mediation as the Preferred Method to Solve International Business Disputes: A Look into the Future' (2013) International Business Law Journal 251, 258; Thomas Stipanowich, 'The International Evolution of Mediation: A Call for Dialogue and Deliberation', (2015) 46 Victoria University of Wellington Law Review 1191, 1241, http://ssrn.com/abstract=2712457. On recent initiatives by ICSID to promote investor–state mediation through education, outreach, and case administration, see 'ICSID Secretariat, Considering the Future of Investor-State Mediation,' https://icsid.worldbank.org/en/Pages/resources/ICSID%20NewsLetter/2017-Issue3/Considering-the-Future-of-Investor-State-Mediation.aspx; and 'ICSID hosts half-day event, "Investor-State Mediation: Perspectives from States, Mediators & Practitioners on 15 June 2017', https://icsid.worldbank.org/en/Pages/News.aspx?CID=243.

[59] Edna Sussman, 'A Path Forward: A Convention for the Enforcement of Mediated Settlement Agreements' (2015) 6 TDM [online] www.transnational-dispute-management.com; Bobette Wolski, 'Enforcing Mediated Settlement Agreements (MSAs): Critical Questions and Directions for Future Research' (2014) 7 Contemporary Asia Arbitration Journal 87; Chang-Fa Lo, 'Desirability of a New International Legal Framework for Cross-Border Enforcement of Certain Mediated Settlement Agreements' (2014) 7 Contemporary Asia Arbitration Journal 119.

[60] See Chapter 19, this volume.

[61] Sussman (n 59); Gaultier (n 26) 48 (noting that 'in the context of international disputes, being able to use mediation and have its resulting agreement be able to be applied almost worldwide definitely is an attraction, and underlines the concrete effectiveness of cross-border mediation, even though

Finally, as noted, one of the reasons that dissuades business executives and state officials from resorting to mediation is a concern about, at best, being accused of giving in to the opponent or, at worst, of being a party to corruption. This is more so in the case of investor–state disputes in highly politicized sectors, e.g. oil and gas, and indeed in most other forms of energy. In such cases, public officials would rather shift responsibility for a decision to an arbitral tribunal or a court of law, rather than take personal responsibility. Such concerns may be assuaged by creating an inter-ministerial or inter-departmental agency vested with the authority to endorse settlement agreements, thereby enhancing the legitimacy of such agreements in the eyes of the public, in a way that is analogous to an arbitral award or a court decision. Alternatively, the mediator formally can endorse the settlement agreement, thereby lending his/her authority to the final agreement.[62]

In conclusion, we believe that the practice of mediation in energy disputes is far greater than textbooks on dispute settlement and energy law would have us believe, and moreover, that its future can be—and indeed ought to be—greater, as a way of enhancing the parties' options for amicable and speedy settlement. These prospects would surely be brighter if the above issues were sufficiently well addressed.

the process is still at an early stage.'); S. I. Strong, 'Realizing Rationality: An Empirical Assessment of International Commercial Mediation', (2016) 73 Washington & Lee Law Review 1973, 2014–16.

[62] Waelde (n 15) 217 (noting that 'the mediator, if vested with sufficient authority, can endorse more formally the negotiated outcome').

14

WIPO Mediation

Resolving International Intellectual Property and Technology Disputes Outside the Courts

Heike Wollgast and Ignacio de Castro

I. Introduction

The use of alternative dispute resolution (ADR) procedures—mediation, arbitration and expert determination—to settle disputes between private parties outside the courts has a long tradition in legal systems around the world. While traditionally ADR options have not been widely used to settle intellectual property (IP) and related disputes, such procedures are becoming increasingly popular.[1]

IP and related disputes have distinctive characteristics. With the globalization of trade and the increasingly international creation and exploitation of IP, these disputes often span multiple jurisdictions and involve highly technical matters, complex laws, and sensitive information. In these circumstances, parties often look for flexible dispute resolution processes that can be customized to their needs and that enable them to control the time and cost of proceedings. The 2013 World Intellectual Property Organization (WIPO) International Survey on Dispute Resolution in Technology Transactions confirmed that the ability to limit the time and cost of proceedings were top priorities (Figure 14.1) when selecting dispute resolution options.[2]

This chapter explains the key features of procedures under the WIPO Mediation Rules, and how these procedures have been applied in case examples. This chapter also provides a WIPO model dispute resolution clause and discusses key elements of clause drafting.

[1] See Queen Mary University of London, School of International Arbitration, Pinsent Masons, 'Pre-Empting and Resolving Technology, Media and Telecoms Disputes (International Dispute Resolution Survey)' (November 2016), http://www.arbitration.qmul.ac.uk/media/arbitration/docs/Fixing_Tech_report_online_singles.pdf.

[2] See http://www.wipo.int/export/sites/www/amc/en/docs/surveyresults.pdf.

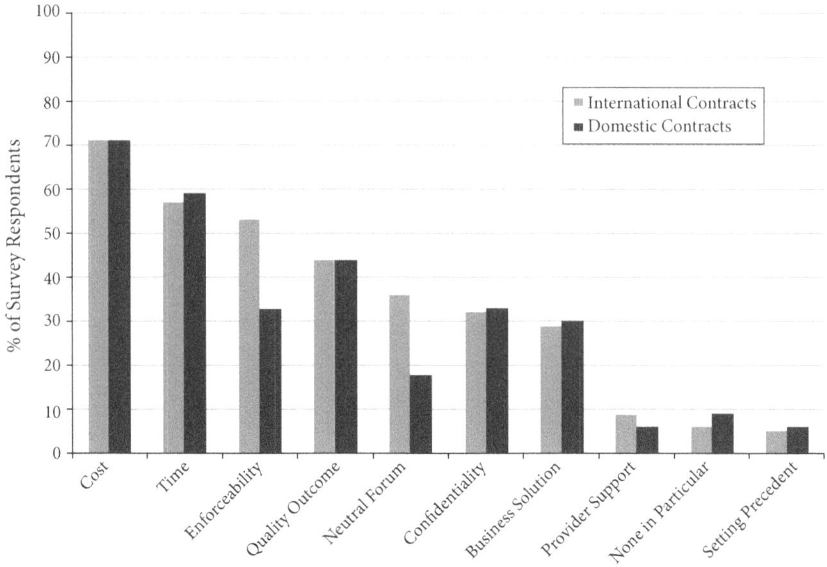

Figure 14.1 Top priorities when considering dispute resolution clauses.
Source: WIPO International Survey on Dispute Resolution in Technology Transactions.

II. Main Features of ADR

Parties' choices among different dispute resolution options will depend on the circumstances of the case, and the parties' needs and expectations. While there is no general answer whether mediation, arbitration, or another form of ADR might be preferable over conventional court-based IP litigation, each type of ADR has features that, if well managed, may translate into substantial time and cost savings for parties, and therefore can offer an affordable and accessible avenue for parties.

Such features offered by ADR include the following:

A single procedure. Parties can use ADR to settle in a single forum disputes involving several jurisdictions, avoiding the expense and complexity of multi-jurisdictional litigation, and the risk of inconsistent results.

Party autonomy. As opposed to court litigation, ADR allows parties to exercise greater control over the way their dispute is resolved because of its private nature. The parties themselves can select the most suitable neutral (specialized in the subject matter in dispute) for their dispute. Additionally, the parties may choose the place and language of the proceedings and the applicable law.

Expertise. The parties can appoint arbitrators, mediators, or experts with specific knowledge and experience in the relevant legal, technical, or business area. This will help achieve high-quality solutions while limiting time and cost of the proceedings that might otherwise be required for external expertise.

Neutrality. ADR can be neutral to the law and language of the parties, preventing any home court advantage that one of the parties may enjoy in court-based litigation.

Cost and time efficiency. Economically viable and speedy dispute resolution is essential in IP and related commercial disputes. ADR methods allow parties to save significant costs that they would otherwise undergo in multi-jurisdictional court proceedings. In this regard, ADR mechanisms provide for short timelines, which the parties can further adapt. Specific fast-track methods exist to provide for even faster solutions, such as expedited arbitration.

Confidentiality. ADR proceedings and their results are confidential, allowing the parties to focus on the merits of the dispute without concern about its public impact. This may also be of particular relevance where commercial reputations and trade secrets are involved.

Preserving long-term relationships. By using ADR mechanisms, particularly mediation, parties may preserve their business relationships as business interests can be taken into consideration and viable long-term solutions can be adopted in a less confrontational forum.

III. WIPO Arbitration and Mediation Center

With offices in Geneva, Switzerland and in Singapore, the WIPO Arbitration and Mediation Center (WIPO Center), established in 1994, is a neutral, international, and non-profit dispute resolution provider specialized in IP and related commercial disputes.[3] Developed by leading experts in cross-border dispute settlement, the arbitration, mediation, and expert determination procedures offered by the WIPO Center are recognized as particularly appropriate for technology and other disputes involving IP. The WIPO Center maintains a database of over 2,000 neutrals, independent WIPO mediators, arbitrators, and experts globally who are skilled in IP and ADR. To date, the WIPO Center has administered over 600 mediation, arbitration, and expert determination cases; most of these cases were filed in recent years.

The WIPO Center pays particular attention to helping parties contain time and cost of proceedings conducted under WIPO Rules. This includes the WIPO Center's assistance to parties in selecting and appointing the mediator, arbitrator, or expert; active case management, including WIPO Center guidance regarding the application of relevant procedural rules; the availability, at the parties' option, of an Electronic Case Facility (WIPO eADR);[4] and of meeting and hearing facilities where the proceedings take place at WIPO in Geneva. A 25 percent reduction

3 See http://www.wipo.int/amc/en/.

4 See http://www.wipo.int/amc/en/eadr/index.html.

on the WIPO Center's fees applies if a party (or both parties) to the dispute is (are) users of other WIPO IP Services.[5] A typical WIPO mediation takes four and a half months, but has been completed in much shorter timelines where requested by parties, for example, to ensure compliance with deadlines in court referrals.

WIPO ADR procedures are organized to stimulate positive opportunities for party settlement. To date, 70 percent of the mediation procedures administered by the WIPO Center have been settled. Even in arbitration, some 40 percent of WIPO cases settle before any tribunal award is issued.

The subject matter of WIPO cases includes a wide range of IP and related commercial matters, e.g. patents, know-how and software licenses, franchising and distribution agreements, trademarks (including trademark coexistence agreements), distribution contracts, joint venture agreements, research and development (R&D) contracts, technology transfer agreements, technology-sensitive employment contracts, mergers and acquisitions involving IP assets, sports marketing agreements, publishing, and music and film contracts. Over 70 percent of WIPO cases (and over 90 percent of patent-related WIPO cases) have an international dimension, involving, for example, technology protected by patents in several jurisdictions in Asia, Europe, and the US, or parties based in different jurisdictions. Amounts in dispute in WIPO cases have ranged from 15,000 US dollars to 1 billion US dollars.[6]

There are no restrictions on who may use the WIPO Center's services. They have been used by companies of all sizes across various industries and sectors, artists and inventors, R&D centres, universities, producers, and copyright collecting societies, from more than 40 jurisdictions around the world.[7] WIPO mediations have been conducted in several languages, including Chinese, English, French, German, Italian, Korean, Portuguese, and Spanish.

The parties decide where they wish the mediation to take place. It is not necessary for a mediation conducted under the WIPO Mediation Rules to take place at WIPO's premises in Geneva or Singapore. The most common venues of WIPO ADR proceedings have included France, Germany, Ireland, Italy, Netherlands, Singapore, Spain, Switzerland, United Kingdom, and United States. The WIPO Center also is a leading provider of time- and cost-efficient

[5] For example, users of the Patent Cooperation Treaty (PCT) for the international registration of patents http://www.wipo.int/pct/en/, the Hague System for the International Registration of Industrial Designs http://www.wipo.int/hague/en/, or the International Trademark System (the Madrid System) http://www.wipo.int/madrid/en/.

[6] For general up-to-date information on the WIPO Center's caseload, as well as descriptive examples of WIPO mediation and arbitration cases, see http://www.wipo.int/amc/en/center/caseload.html.

[7] Including Algeria, Australia, Austria, Belgium, Belize, Brazil, Canada, China, Colombia, Cyprus, Denmark, Finland, France, Germany, Greece, Hungary, India, Indonesia, Ireland, Israel, Italy, Japan, Lebanon, Malaysia, Malta, Mexico, Morocco, Netherlands, Nigeria, Norway, Panama, Philippines, Poland, Portugal, Republic of Korea, Romania, Russian Federation, Singapore, Spain, Switzerland, Trinidad and Tobago, Tunisia, Turkey, United Arab Emirates, United Kingdom, and United States of America. See http://www.wipo.int/amc/en/center/caseload.html.

mechanisms to resolve Internet domain name disputes without the need for court litigation. This service includes the WIPO-initiated Uniform Domain Name Dispute Resolution Policy (UDRP), under which the WIPO Center has processed over 44,000 cases.[8]

IV. WIPO ADR Options

The WIPO Center offers rules, clauses, and neutrals for mediation, arbitration, expedited arbitration, and expert determination (Figure 14.2). WIPO expedited arbitration is an arbitration procedure that is carried out in a shorter timeframe and at reduced cost. Depending on the parties' choice, expedited arbitration may be preceded by mediation or expert determination. WIPO expert determination is a procedure in which a technical, scientific, or related business issue between the parties is submitted to one or more experts who make a determination about the matter. Under the WIPO Expert Determination Rules, the determination is binding, unless the parties have agreed otherwise.

The WIPO Mediation, Arbitration, Expedited Arbitration and Expert Determination Rules are appropriate for all commercial disputes. However, they contain provisions on matters like confidentiality in relation to technical and experimental evidence that are of special interest to parties to IP and technology disputes.

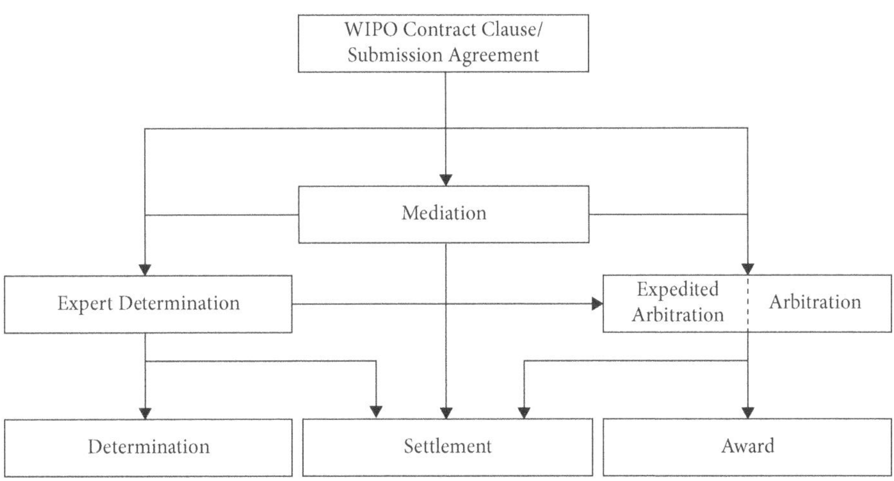

Figure 14.2 WIPO Alternative Dispute Resolution (ADR) options.

[8] See http://www.wipo.int/amc/en/domains/.

V. The Role of the WIPO Center

While parties can handle ADR proceedings themselves directly with the neutral, such ad hoc procedures require considerable ADR experience and effective cooperation between all parties to avoid delays and unnecessary costs. In an institutional ADR proceeding, the selected institution provides a tested framework for initiating and conducting the procedure, case management services, and access to qualified arbitrators and mediators. Administrative fees do vary and may be a factor in selecting an institution.

In administering disputes, the WIPO Center provides the following administrative services:

- Assistance to the parties that wish to commence a mediation, arbitration, expedited arbitration, or expert determination;
- Facilitating the parties in selecting and appointing the mediator, arbitrator(s), or expert if necessary, with reference to the Center's database of more than 1,500 neutrals globally with expertise in commercial, IP, and information and communications technology dispute resolution;
- Guidance regarding the application of the relevant procedural rules;
- Liaising between the parties and the arbitral tribunal, mediator, or expert with a view to ensuring optimal communications and procedural efficiency;
- Making available, at the parties' option, the WIPO Electronic Case Facility (WIPO ECAF);
- Assisting the parties in organizing any other support services that may be needed, such as translation, interpretation, or secretarial services;
- Fixing the fees of the neutrals, in consultation with parties and the neutrals;
- Administering the financial aspects of the proceedings by obtaining a deposit from each party of the estimated costs and paying out of the deposit the fees of the neutrals and any other support services or facilities, such as fees for interpreters, where they are required;
- Where the proceedings take place at WIPO in Geneva, providing a meeting room and party retiring rooms free of charge;
- Where the proceedings take place outside Geneva, assisting the parties in organizing appropriate meeting rooms and other required facilities;
- Providing such other services or functions as may be required to ensure that the WIPO procedures are conducted efficiently and expeditiously.

VI. WIPO Mediation Rules

By agreeing to submit a dispute to WIPO mediation, the parties adopt the WIPO Mediation Rules[9] as part of their agreement to mediate. The Rules, last updated

[9] See http://www.wipo.int/amc/en/rules/.

in 2016, are available in several languages, including Chinese, English, French, German, Japanese, Korean, Russian, and Spanish. They have the following main functions: establishing the non-binding nature of the procedure;[10] (defining the way in which the mediator will be appointed;[11] setting out the way in which the mediator's fees will be determined;[12] guiding the parties as to the way in which the mediation can be commenced and the process can be established;[13] providing the parties with assurances about the confidentiality of the proceedings and the disclosures made during the proceedings;[14] and determining how the costs of the proceedings will be borne by the parties.[15]

VII. Submission of disputes to WIPO Mediation

A. Mediation Agreement

Normally, the starting point of a WIPO mediation is the agreement by the parties to submit a dispute to mediation. Such an agreement may be contained in a contract governing a business relationship between the parties, such as a license, in which the parties provide that any disputes occurring under the contract will be submitted to WIPO mediation. Or, it may be specially drawn up in relation to a particular dispute after the dispute has occurred, e.g. in patent, trademark, or copyright infringement disputes, including in cases pending before the courts.

To date, some 60 percent of WIPO cases were based on contract dispute resolution clauses in, for example, licensing agreements (relating, e.g. to trademarks, patents, copyright, and software), R&D agreements, technology transfer agreements, distribution agreements, franchising agreements, joint venture agreements, consultancy agreements, as well as cases arising out of agreements in settlement of prior court litigation. About 40 percent of WIPO cases were based on submission agreements concluded by the parties to an existing non-contractual or sometimes even contractual dispute. These statistics reflect the difficulty in agreeing to resolve a dispute once it has arisen. It also highlights the importance of including and carefully drafting contract dispute resolution clauses at the stage when the respective contract is negotiated by the parties.

[10] Articles 14(a) and 19(iii) of the WIPO Mediation Rules.
[11] Article 7 of the WIPO Mediation Rules.
[12] Article 23 of the WIPO Mediation Rules.
[13] Articles 3–6, 13 of the WIPO Mediation Rules.
[14] Articles 15–18 of the WIPO Mediation Rules.
[15] Article 25 of the WIPO Mediation Rules.

B. Unilateral Request for Mediation

Under the WIPO Mediation Rules a party may submit a unilateral request for mediation to the WIPO Center where one party wishes to submit a dispute to mediation, but no mediation agreement can be concluded.[16] The WIPO Center may then assist the parties in considering the request or, upon request, appoint an external neutral to provide such assistance.[17] If the other party agrees to submit the dispute to WIPO mediation, the WIPO Center proceeds with the appointment of a mediator; otherwise, the mediation will be terminated. In WIPO cases, this process is frequently used and may be of interest for parties that wish to formalize their willingness to submit a dispute to mediation. The WIPO Center is available to assist parties that wish to commence a WIPO mediation or arbitration through its good offices services.

C. Combining ADR Procedures

Parties may combine mediation and arbitration to allow for an efficient resolution of a conflict at appropriate escalation levels.[18] This may increase the likelihood of settling the dispute. As noted, 70 percent of WIPO mediations settle, and even if no agreement can be reached in the mediation, the process helps to prepare any subsequent arbitration. This may explain the high settlement rates in WIPO arbitrations (40 percent); such settlement agreement in an arbitration is then usually reflected in a consent award. Some 40 percent of the ADR cases filed with the WIPO Center included an escalation clause providing for WIPO mediation, followed, in the absence of a settlement, by WIPO arbitration or expedited arbitration. A number of model agreements that propose WIPO dispute resolution also opt for the multi-tier approach.[19]

D. WIPO Model Clauses

The use of model ADR clauses and submission agreements is encouraged to ensure that the important elements of a dispute resolution clause are provided for and to avoid any ambiguity that may later lead to difficulties and delays in the dispute

[16] Article 4(a) of the WIPO Mediation Rules.

[17] Article 4(b) of the WIPO Mediation Rules.

[18] Trevor Cook and Alejandro I. Garcia, *International Intellectual Property Arbitration* (Kluwer Law International, 2010) 133.

[19] See 'WIPO mediation in the area of R&D'.

resolution process. WIPO model clauses and submission agreements[20] have been carefully drafted by experts to allow parties to define principal elements, such as the place of arbitration or mediation, applicable law, language of proceedings, and appointment of mediator or arbitrator. The model clauses are available in several languages, including Chinese, English, French, German, Japanese, Korean, Russian, and Spanish. There are model clauses for each WIPO ADR procedure as well as for combinations of these procedures. The following is an example of a frequently used combined clause, including a brief explanation of the more relevant elements of the clause:

> Mediation Followed, in the Absence of a Settlement, by [Expedited] Arbitration
>
> Any dispute, controversy or claim arising under, out of or relating to this contract and any subsequent amendments of this contract, including, without limitation, its formation, validity, binding effect, interpretation, performance, breach or termination, as well as non-contractual claims, shall be submitted to mediation in accordance with the WIPO Mediation Rules. The place of mediation shall be [specify place]. The language to be used in the mediation shall be [specify language].
>
> If, and to the extent that, any such dispute, controversy or claim has not been settled pursuant to the mediation within [60][90] days of the commencement of the mediation, it shall, upon the filing of a Request for Arbitration by either party, be referred to and finally determined by arbitration in accordance with the WIPO [Expedited] Arbitration Rules. Alternatively, if, before the expiration of the said period of [60][90] days, either party fails to participate or to continue to participate in the mediation, the dispute, controversy or claim shall, upon the filing of a Request for Arbitration by the other party, be referred to and finally determined by arbitration in accordance with the WIPO [Expedited] Arbitration Rules. [The arbitral tribunal shall consist of [a sole arbitrator] [three arbitrators].] The place of arbitration shall be [specify place]. The language to be used in the arbitral proceedings shall be [specify language]. The dispute, controversy or claim referred to arbitration shall be decided in accordance with the law of [specify jurisdiction].[21]

This WIPO model clause allows parties to move from the mediation to the arbitration phase if a party fails to participate in the mediation. Also, setting a timeline for mediation in a multi-tiered clause helps the case stay on track towards a settlement or agreed follow-up procedure. The place where the mediation will take place should be named. As noted, meetings or hearings may take place anywhere in the world at the convenience of the parties and the mediator.

[20] See http://www.wipo.int/amc/en/clauses/index.html.

[21] See http://www.wipo.int/amc/en/clauses/index.html.

Furthermore, the parties should decide the language in which the mediation will be conducted. They may choose any language, or even several languages. Parties are strongly advised to use model ADR clauses and submission agreements; however, where deemed useful, they can adapt model clauses and submission agreements to their further needs. For such specific cases, the WIPO Center offers the WIPO Clause Generator, an online tool that proposes additional elements based on WIPO case experience.[22]

VIII. Stages of a Dispute at which WIPO Mediation May Be Used

WIPO mediation can be used at any stage of a dispute. It can be chosen as the first step towards seeking a resolution of the dispute after negotiations between the parties have failed. WIPO ADR also may present a suitable opportunity for cases pending before national courts or arbitral tribunals where the parties are willing to explore settlement or need the assistance of an expert in a technical or scientific matter. The WIPO Center administers cases referred to WIPO mediation by national courts as well as by other adjudicative bodies.[23] In such a case, pending court proceedings would normally be suspended under the applicable national law.

Another common use of mediation is more akin to dispute prevention than dispute resolution. Parties may seek the assistance of a mediator in the course of negotiations for an agreement, or the renegotiation of an agreement that has become obsolete, where such negotiations have reached an impasse but where the parties consider it to be in their commercial interests to conclude the agreement, e.g. in the context of trademark and IT agreements, or concerning the determination of fair, reasonable, and non-discriminatory (FRAND) licensing terms.[24]

IX. Principal Stages in a WIPO Mediation

There are few formalities associated with mediation. The conduct of a WIPO mediation is decided by the parties with the mediator, who together work out, and agree upon, the procedure that is to be followed.

[22] See http://www.wipo.int/amc-apps/clause-generator/.
[23] See http://www.wipo.int/amc/en/clauses/national_court.html.
[24] See text to (n 43–n 45).

A. Request for Mediation

The request for mediation should set out summary details concerning the dispute, including the names and communication references of the parties and their representatives, a copy of the agreement to mediate, and a brief description of the dispute.[25] These details are not intended to perform the legal function of defining arguments and issues, but to supply the Center with sufficient information to enable it to proceed to commence the mediation process. Thus, the Center will need to know who is involved and the subject matter of the dispute in order to assist the parties in selecting a mediator appropriate for the dispute.

B. Appointment of the Mediator

Unless the parties have agreed among themselves on the person of the mediator, the WIPO Center will contact the parties (or their representatives) to commence discussions on the appointment of the mediator. The appointment will take place pursuant to the 'list procedure'.[26] Under that procedure, the WIPO Center will propose several names of prospective mediators, together with their biographical details, to the parties for their consideration, taking into account any qualifications that the parties may have identified, as well as other relevant factors, e.g. subject-matter of the dispute, applicable law, and nationality of the parties.

In selecting candidates, the WIPO Center draws on its list of neutrals that comprises seasoned dispute resolution generalists and specialized practitioners and experts who cover the entire legal and technical spectrum of IP. The WIPO list of neutrals also includes the members of International Trademark Association's (INTA) panel of trademark mediators.[27] Parties are invited to number the candidates in order of preference, and return the marked lists to the WIPO Center within seven days. Taking into account the preferences and objections expressed by the parties, the WIPO Center will then proceed to appoint a person from the list.

Prior to the appointment, the WIPO Center requests the selected mediator candidate to undertake a conflict check and to sign a statement of independence and impartiality[28] that will be communicated to the parties, together with the notification of the appointment of the mediator. At this stage, the WIPO Center will also fix, in consultation with the mediator and the parties, the fees of the mediator.[29]

[25] Article 3(b) of the WIPO Mediation Rules.
[26] See Article 7 of the WIPO Mediation Rules.
[27] See http://www.wipo.int/amc/en/neutrals/.
[28] See Article 8 of the WIPO Mediation Rules.
[29] See Article 23 of the WIPO Mediation Rules; see also text to (n 30–n 32).

C. Initial Contacts between the Mediator and the Parties

Following appointment, the mediator conducts a series of initial discussions with the parties, which normally take place by telephone. The purpose of these initial contacts is to set a schedule for the subsequent process. The mediator indicates what documentation, if any, he or she considers should be provided by the parties prior to their mediation session, and sets the timetable for the supply of any such documentation and the holding of the mediation session. The mediator also discusses with the parties if additional documentation by the parties should be provided, and the need for any assistance by experts.

D. Mediation Session

Depending on the issues involved in the dispute, including the complexity and the economic importance of the dispute, the mediation may involve meetings held on one day or across several days. Normally, WIPO mediation sessions are conducted within one day. In some WIPO cases, parties agree with the mediator to hold mediation sessions over the phone.

At the mediation session, the mediator first establishes with the parties the ground rules that are to be followed in the process. In particular, the mediator discusses with, and obtains the agreement of, the parties about whether all meetings between the mediator and the parties will take place with both parties present, or whether the mediator may, at various times, hold separate meetings (caucuses) with each party alone; and he or she ensures that the parties understand the rules on confidentiality set out in the WIPO Mediation Rules.

The mediation session normally involves the following steps: the gathering of information concerning the dispute and the identification of the issues involved; the exploration of the respective interests of the parties underlying the positions that they maintain in respect of the dispute; the development of options that might satisfy the respective interests of the parties; the evaluation of the options that exist for settling the dispute in the light of the parties' interests and each party's alternatives to settlement; and if the parties reach a settlement, the recording of the settlement in an agreement. Throughout the process of the mediation, each party can undertake, at various stages, private consultations with its advisors and experts for the purpose of evaluating options.

E. Costs of WIPO Mediation

The request for mediation is subject to the payment of an administration fee to the WIPO Center. In principle, that fee amounts to 250 US dollars if the amount in dispute is less than 250,000 US dollars, and in other cases it amounts to 0.1 percent of the value in dispute, up to a maximum of 10,000 US dollars. Where the request for mediation does not indicate any claims for a monetary amount or the dispute concerns issues that are not quantifiable in monetary amounts, an administration fee of 1,000 US dollars shall be payable, subject to adjustment. As mentioned, a 25 percent reduction on the administration fee applies if a party (or both parties) to the dispute is (are) users of certain other WIPO IP services.[30]

The fees of the mediator are fixed at 2,500 US dollars if the amount in dispute is less than 250,000 US dollars. In other cases, these fees are negotiated and fixed at the time of the appointment of the mediator. They are usually calculated on an hourly basis at a rate that takes into account the circumstances of the dispute, e.g. the complexity of the dispute and its economic importance, as well as the experience of the mediator.[31]

The WIPO Mediation Rules provide for the costs of the mediation (the registration fee of the Center, the mediator's fees, and all other expenses of the mediation) to be borne in equal shares by the parties.[32] The parties are free to agree to change this allocation of costs. In practice, given the high rate of settlement and the cost/benefit advantages that mediation generally offers in comparison to court litigation, the allocation of the costs of a mediation is rarely a significant issue between the parties.

F. Time and Cost-Efficiency through Tailored WIPO ADR Processes

In its case experience, the WIPO Center noted that specific areas of IP transactions can benefit from targeted adaptations of the standard ADR framework, e.g. in relation to rules, neutrals, fees, and clauses. To offer guidance to parties in this respect, the WIPO Center has developed tailored ADR schemes in a number of areas, including information and communication technology (ICT), R&D, procedures before Intellectual Property and Copyright Offices (IPOs), film and media, and art and cultural heritage.[33] The next three subsections discuss some examples.

1. Mediation for proceedings pending before IPOs

The WIPO Center collaborates with IPOs to raise awareness among users of the services provided by IPOs and of the advantages of ADR options to prevent and

[30] Additional fee reductions may apply in the context of the WIPO Center's collaborations with other organizations; see http://www.wipo.int/amc/en/center/specific-sectors/.

[31] See WIPO Schedule of Fees http://www.wipo.int/amc/en/mediation/fees/.

[32] Article 25 of the WIPO Mediation Rules.

[33] See http://www.wipo.int/amc/en/center/specific-sectors/.

resolve IP and technology disputes.[34] Some IPOs have developed ADR options, or encourage parties to use such options, in the context of proceedings pending before them, notably trademark or patent opposition proceedings. For example, under its collaboration with the IPO of Singapore (IPOS), the WIPO Center has participated in the development of a mediation option for trademark and patent proceedings, and an expert determination option for patent proceedings pending before IPOS, and administers such proceedings.[35] The Trademark Trial and Appeal Board (TTAB) and the Patent Trial and Appeal Board (PTAB) of the United States Patent and Trademark Office (USPTO) encourage parties to consider WIPO ADR as a means of settling the issues raised in any trademark or patent proceedings. The WIPO Center is one of the listed dispute resolution services providers for TTAB and PTAB proceedings.[36]

In the area of copyright, some IPOs administer ADR proceedings in domestic disputes and designate the WIPO Center as administrator of cases where one or both parties are domiciled outside the country. Such collaboration is, for example, in place between the WIPO Center and the Ministry of Culture, Sports and Tourism (MCST),[37] and the National Copyright Directorate of Colombia (DNDA).[38]

2. Mediation for R&D and technology transfer disputes

International and domestic R&D and transfer of technologies involve a rich variety of contracts and transactions, including research contracts, collaborative projects, licensing, joint ventures, alliances, spin-offs, and buyer-supplier relationships. Such collaborations can involve complex legal, commercial, or management issues, often including related IP rights. Also, research partners from different institutional backgrounds may have diverging expectations and understandings of creating, using, and exploiting IP rights. Efficient dispute avoidance and resolution practices are key in such complex situations. Providing time- and cost-effective options, ADR may help parties to find solutions to their disputes without the need for court litigation, contributing to the continuation of research activities and commercialization of research results.

The WIPO Center regularly administers R&D and technology transfer-related disputes under its Mediation, Arbitration and Expedited Arbitration Rules. The WIPO Center also maintains an open-ended Panel, including mediators, arbitrators, and experts from around the world with expertise in R&D and technology

[34] See overview of WIPO Center collaborations at https://www.wipo.int/amc/en/center/specific-sectors/ipoffices/. The WIPO Center makes available a Guide on ADR Options for IPOs and Courts; see https://www.wipo.int/edocs/pubdocs/en/wipo_pub_guide_adr.pdf.

[35] See http://www.wipo.int/amc/en/center/specific-sectors/ipos/mediation and http://www.wipo.int/amc/en/center/specific-sectors/ipos/expert-determination/.

[36] See https://www.uspto.gov/trademarks-application-process/trademark-trial-and-appeal-board and https://www.uspto.gov/patents-application-process/patent-trial-and-appeal-board-0.

[37] See https://www.wipo.int/amc/en/center/specific-sectors/ipoffices/.

[38] See http://www.wipo.int/amc/es/center/specific-sectors/dnda/.

transfer. They can be appointed by parties in cases under the WIPO Rules, but parties are also free to select mediators, arbitrators, or experts from outside the WIPO Panel.

A number of R&D model agreements recommend WIPO mediation and/or WIPO expedited arbitration. For example, the Spanish Patent and Trademark Office has developed contract templates for R&D collaborations that the Office makes available to interested users.[39] These contract templates include model dispute resolution clauses, including referral of disputes to WIPO mediation followed by WIPO expedited arbitration. Other model R&D agreements that recommend WIPO mediation followed by expedited arbitration clauses include the European Development of a Simplified Consortium Agreement (DESCA) 2020 Model Consortium Agreement[40] and the Intellectual Property Agreement Guide (IPAG) model agreements in Austria.[41]

3. Mediation in the context of fair, reasonable, and non-discriminatory (FRAND) disputes

Another recent example relates to standards-related disputes involving telecom patents in multiple jurisdictions. Technical standards play an increasing role in today's economy. Standard development organizations (SDOs) typically require their members to license standard-essential patents (SEPs) on FRAND terms. In recent years, courts in several jurisdictions have dealt with the determination of FRAND licensing terms under different applicable laws, and have developed different approaches and methodologies.

ADR offers flexible, accessible options for parties wishing to conclude a FRAND agreement (Figure 14.3), including small and medium-sized enterprises (SMEs). This has been recognized by some SDOs that include ADR procedures in their IP policies[42]. ADR, including WIPO ADR, also has been identified by courts and authorities in the United States and in Europe as a suitable option to facilitate the determination of FRAND licensing terms.[43]

To facilitate submission of FRAND disputes to WIPO ADR, the WIPO Center makes available tailored model submission agreements that parties may use to refer

[39] See http://www.oepm.es/es/propiedad_industrial/transferencia_de_tecnologia/Modelos_de_Contratos/index.html.

[40] See http://www.desca-2020.eu/.

[41] See http://www.wipo.int/amc/en/center/specific-sectors/rd/ipag/.

[42] See Digital Video Broadcasting (DVB), https://www.dvb.org/members/iprpolicy; Blu-Ray Disc Association (BRDA), http://blu-raydisc.com/Assets/Downloadablefile/BDA_Bylaws_%28v2.0%29-18618.pdf; Open Mobile Alliance Ltd (OMA), http://openmobilealliance.org/wp-content/uploads/2013/01/Member_IPRGuidelines_v53006.pdf.

[43] See European Commission Communication, Setting out the EU Approach to Standard Essential Patents, COM(2017) 712 final, 29 November 2017, Section 3.4, http://www.europarl.europa.eu/RegData/docs_autres_institutions/commission_europeenne/com/2017/0712/COM_COM(2017)0712_EN.pdf; see also reference to the WIPO Center in Motorola Mobility LLC and Google Inc., FTC File No. 121 0120, http://www.ftc.gov/opa/2013/07/google.shtm.

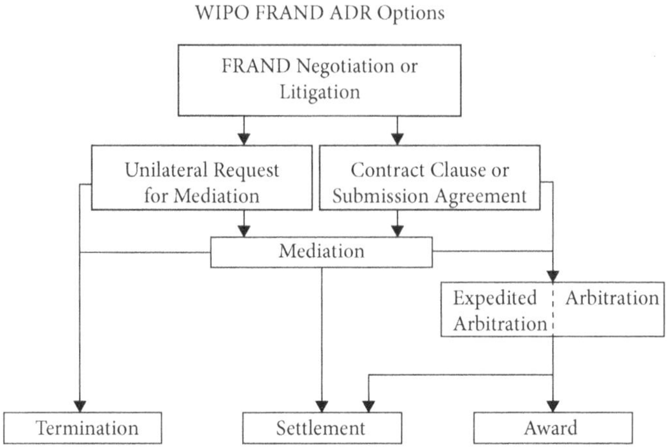

Figure 14.3 WIPO FRAND ADR options.

such disputes, including the determination of FRAND licensing terms, to WIPO mediation, arbitration, or expedited arbitration.[44] Developed in consultation with the European Telecommunication Standards Institute (ETSI) as well as experts in patent law, standardization, and arbitration from a number of jurisdictions, the WIPO model submission agreements put emphasis on a cost- and time-effective determination of FRAND terms, including through mediation.

The WIPO Center also recently published the Guidance on WIPO FRAND ADR.[45] The WIPO Guidance aims to help parties and neutrals to understand and make use of procedural options that are available at different stages of the process, including where large SEP portfolios are involved. The Guidance addresses matters such as scope, appointment procedure, procedural schedule, evidentiary issues, confidentiality, interim measures, and appeal.

G. Recent WIPO Mediation Case Examples

1. A WIPO patent mediation

A technology consulting company holding patents on three continents disclosed a patented invention to a major manufacturer in the context of a consulting contract.[46] The contract neither transferred nor licensed any rights to the manufacturer. When the manufacturer started selling products which the consulting company alleged included the patented invention, the consulting company threatened to file

[44] See http://www.wipo.int/amc/en/center/specific-sectors/ict/frand/.
[45] See http://www.wipo.int/export/sites/www/amc/en/docs/wipofrandadrguidance.pdf.
[46] See http://www.wipo.int/amc/en/mediation/case-example.html.

patent infringement court proceedings in all jurisdictions in which the consulting company was holding patents.

The parties started negotiating a patent license with the help of external experts but failed to agree on the royalty as the multimillion-dollar damages sought by the consulting company significantly exceeded the amount the manufacturer was willing to offer.

The parties submitted their dispute to mediation under the WIPO Mediation Rules. The WIPO Center suggested to the parties potential mediators with specific expertise in patents and the relevant technology. The parties chose one of those mediators, who conducted a two-day meeting in which the parties eventually reached a settlement that not only covered the royalty issue, but also included agreement on future consulting contracts.

The mediation was thus instrumental in transforming a hostile situation in which the parties were preparing to engage in prolonged and expensive litigation into one in which they were able to conclude an arrangement which suits the business interests of both parties and ensures the profitable use of the technology in the service of those interests.

2. A WIPO mediation of a trademark coexistence dispute

After a dispute arose between them, a North American company requested mediation with two Italian companies and one Spanish company on the basis of an agreement which the parties had reached for mediation under the WIPO Mediation Rules. The goal of the mediation was to help the parties avoid confusion and misappropriation of their similar trademarks and to regulate future use of their trademarks. Although Italian was agreed as the language of proceedings, any settlement agreement would be recorded in both Italian and English.

The Center suggested to the parties mediator candidates with expertise in European trademark law and fluency in Italian and English. The parties selected an Italian mediator with a trademark practice. The mediator conducted an initial telephone conference with the lawyers of the parties in which he scheduled the mediation meeting, and agreed on the procedure.

Two months later, the mediator met with the parties in a two-day session in Milan. The meeting was held in joint session with the exception of two brief caucuses. At the end of the second day the parties—with the assistance of the mediator—were able to draft and sign a settlement agreement covering all of the pending issues in dispute.

3. A WIPO mediation of a biotech dispute

A French and a German company entered into a collaboration agreement for the development of a human antibody for the treatment of a major disease. Two years later, a US corporation acquired the French company. Alleging that the US corporation shortly thereafter caused certain payments required under the collaboration agreement to be withheld, the German entity filed an action for breach of contract against the US corporation in a district court in the United States of America. The US corporation filed counterclaims of rescission and breach of contract against the German company. After more than one year of court proceedings, the parties accepted the suggestion of the judge to submit their dispute to mediation and filed a joint request for mediation with the WIPO Center.

When the parties could not agree on the name of the mediator, the Center submitted for consideration of the parties a list of five possible candidates, meeting criteria set forth by the disputants in their mediation agreement. After some discussion, the parties agreed on one of the nominees proposed by the Center, an American IP lawyer with considerable mediation experience.

The mediator conducted meetings with the parties in the United States of America. As a direct consequence of the facilitative role played by the mediator in the course of the case, the parties settled their dispute six months after the commencement of the mediation.

4. WIPO mediation in the area of research and development

A major European research institute and a French company entered into a license agreement. The agreement involved a technology in the area of building materials relating to an application for patent pending before the European Patent Office (EPO). The parties included in their contract a multi-tier dispute resolution clause providing for WIPO mediation, followed by court litigation.

Three years after the conclusion of the agreement the company alleged the invalidity of the license agreement and requested a refund of royalty payments in light of the rejection of the patent application by the EPO. The research institute commenced mediation proceedings requesting payment of the royalty rates. The parties invited the WIPO Center to provide them with a list of mediator candidates experienced in mediation, drafting licensing agreements and specialized in patent law.

One of those mediators was selected by the parties. The mediator conducted a preparatory telephone conference with the parties including an explanation of mediation principles, the submission of documents as well as details of the mediation meeting, such as the timetable, venue and party representation. […] a one-day mediation session took place in Munich, Germany. At the end of the mediation session the parties were able to conclude a settlement agreement. This settlement agreement included options for the amendment of the license agreement and payment of royalty rates, based on future decisions on the patent application, and the additional option to conclude a research and development agreement between the parties. The mediation settled within less than three months after its commencement and enabled further extended collaboration between the parties.

5. A WIPO mediation of an IT dispute

A Lebanese and a United States-based start-up company entered into a license agreement on the use of mobile phone applications; the agreement contained a dispute resolution clause referring to WIPO mediation followed, in the absence of a settlement, by WIPO arbitration. The mediation location was Paris, and the language used English. A dispute arose between the parties regarding the use of the application under the license. Following the commencement of the mediation, the WIPO Center proposed several candidates and appointed a mediator in accordance with the parties' choice. The mediator was a French lawyer experienced in technology cases and who was fluent in English and French.

Parties agreed that the mediator should lead the oral proceedings in French, while written communications were produced in English. Given the parties' confirmed willingness to cooperate in the mediation, and the costs for parties to travel to a physical meeting in Paris, the parties agreed with the mediator to hold mediation sessions entirely through telephone conversations. The mediator worked with the parties in caucus telephone sessions and joint calls towards a settlement agreement. Within two months of the appointment of the mediator, such settlement agreement was concluded and formed the basis for the parties' further collaboration.

X. Conclusion

In light of the increasing internationalization and complexity of IP transactions, the WIPO Center has experienced a considerable increase in IP ADR cases in recent years, together with a continued rise in demand for adapted ADR services in specific industry sectors. Notably, business sectors such as telecommunications, life sciences, and R&D experience specific recurring types of disputes with particular features, including FRAND, and needs that can best be addressed by specially tailored ADR services. At the same time, a growing number of national procedural laws and legal authorities encourage, or even require, the use of mediation to release pressure from national courts, which may not always be sufficiently equipped to deal with the technical and legal complexity and increasing volume of IP disputes. With twenty-five years of experience handling such disputes, the WIPO Center endeavours to promote further efficiency gains through dedicated ADR dispute resolution schemes at the cutting edge of IP dispute resolution needs and techniques.

15
Mediation and Other ADR in International Construction Disputes

*Alberto Fortún and Alfonso Iglesia**

I. Introduction

Anytime we dare to approach the use of alternative dispute resolution (ADR) mechanisms in construction disputes, we confront the same dilemma: on the one hand, experiences differ regionally and are limited in number; on the other hand, the theoretical propositions available in books and articles about the advantages of ADR are far from reality. Accordingly, our remarks and observations cannot be too ambitious, but the reader will find a combination of an academic description of some ADR mechanisms that we believe could play a relevant role in the near future, as well as other remarks based on our experience.[1]

Nevertheless, when examining the parties' perspectives and expectations, it is evident that a public entity developing a project will be reluctant to negotiate or use ADR alien to its national practice; the same goes for contractors travelling abroad with low exposure to international projects.

The parties resolve the vast majority of construction disputes through negotiation. When that is not possible, international arbitration is preferred to other ADR, and certainly preferred to litigation.[2] In international projects, litigation is uncommon, although it appears in construction projects where the owner is a public entity and the project does not have any international financing.

In general, time and costs are key concerns in any ADR. In its 2016 *Global Construction Report* the consultancy group Arcadis concluded that 'with uncertainty reigning in markets around the world and projects more complicated than ever before, disputes are taking longer to resolve, which can have far-reaching

* The authors thank Ms Elena Vela (*Cuatrecasas associate*) for her assistance in the research and preparation of this chapter.

[1] Our opinions are mainly based on disputes related to projects in Latin America, Middle East, North Africa, and Europe.

[2] Queen Mary University of London, White and Case and School of International Arbitration, '2015 International Arbitration Survey: Improvements and Innovations in International Arbitration' (2015). According to this survey, '90 % of respondents indicate that international arbitration is their preferred dispute resolution mechanism, either as a stand-alone method (56%) or together with other forms of ADR (34%)'; see http://www.arbitration.qmul.ac.uk/media/arbitration/docs/2015_International_Arbitration_Survey.pdf.

consequences'.[3] Solving a dispute takes long, and given all difficulties and economic consequences attached, construction professionals are becoming increasingly involved in mediation, adjudication, dispute boards, expert determination, and other ADR.

This chapter first identifies the most common construction disputes (section II) and provides a general overview of alternative dispute resolution methods (section III). When describing the different methods, it explores both service providers and trends. Section IV refers to dispute boards, as their use has increased in recent years, and section V specifically considers adjudication as a statutory mechanism. Section VI discusses mediation's significance, and that, in spite of its multiple advantages, contractors and counsel are not sufficiently aware of them. Lastly, it provides basic advice and references from which to choose and draft dispute resolution clauses (section VII). It concludes by suggesting that dispute avoidance is preferable to dispute resolution and that early involvement of neutrals benefits the final completion of the project (section VIII).

II. Construction Disputes

The construction industry is intrinsically contentious. The sheer complexity of construction projects requires coordination and inter-dependence of numerous factors, making construction agreements propitious for disputes. Whether related to cost, design, materials, procurement, time, payment, differing site conditions, property damage, or any other related issue, the potential of ADR mechanisms for preventing and resolving disputes is enormous.

Every dispute and every project have their own features and singularities. Both the vastness of the industry and the complexity of the supply chain do not allow for general principles or statements, but in spite of all disclaimers, cases over the last two decades present relevant similarities.

According to Joseph C. Levigne, the most common owner-and designer-initiated changes that tend to result in dispute include:

i. numerous last-minute addenda during the bidding period;
ii. delayed access to the site;
iii. delay in submitting approved-for-construction design drawings or clarifications;
iv. delay in submitting owner-furnished items;
v. defects in plans or specifications, including errors and omissions;
vi. major design changes;

[3] Arcadis is a multinational company providing design and consultancy services worldwide; see *Global Construction Disputes Report* (2016), www.arcadis.com/media/3/E/7/%7B3E7BDCDC-0434-4237-924F-739240965A90%7DGlobal%20Construction%20Disputes%20Report%202016.pdf.

vii. scope additions;
viii. scope deletions;
ix. schedule improvement directives;
x. acceleration directives;
xi. suspension of work;
xii. interference by owner or designated representative; and
xiii. non-performance by owner.[4]

On the contractor's side, the most common contractor-initiated changes that tend to result in disputes include:

i. failure to start work as planned;
ii. failure to supply sufficient work force;
iii. schedule delay and subcontractor schedule delay;
iv. financial failure;
v. contractor performance failure;
vi. subcontractor performance failure;
vii. supplier performance failure;
viii. technical inadequacy;
ix. defective works;
x. poor workmanship; and
xi. poor quality of works.[5]

In 2014, Emre Cakmak and Pinar Cakmak concluded that delays in work progress, time extensions, inadequate or incomplete specifications, design error,[6] and contract interpretation problems complete the list of the top five most-common disputes.[7] Their conclusions are consistent with our own experience.

In all types of construction projects (e.g. infrastructure, electric networks, process plants, and civil works), we usually encounter ambiguities in contract documents, different interpretations of the contract provisions, inconsistencies and contradictions among contractual documents, or—a key element—the wrong contract form. Owners underestimate the consequences of choosing a model form that is excessively burdensome on the contractors. However, a disproportionate allocation of risks can jeopardize the project and render completion of the contract impracticable.

[4] Joseph C. Lavigne, *Construction Contract Claims and Methods of Avoiding Contract Litigation through Dispute Resolution Alternatives* (National Technical Information Service, 1993), 25–6.

[5] Ibid., 26.

[6] In design errors, we could also include inadequate or incomplete specifications, poor quality of design, and lack of available information.

[7] Emre Cakmak and Pinar Irlayici Cakmak, 'An Analysis of Causes of Disputes in the Construction Industry Using Analytical Network Process' (2014) 109 Procedia: Social and Behavioral Sciences 183–7.

Human behaviour can be a source of conflicts, and it is tempting to focus on the fact that disputes result from lack of communication, lack of team spirit, or conflicting cultures. However, in our experience, well-prepared professionals work on international projects, so it is very rarely that a dispute results only from poor personal relationships. It is true that language and cultural differences may cause misunderstandings where the owner or developer may not be used to working with international contractors. But on most occasions, we find that culture-related conflicts are exaggerated with the aim of generating arguments that are not related to the substance of the dispute. It is easier to argue that 'you do not understand the local practices' than to recognize failure to fulfil a contractual obligation.

III. Alternative Dispute Resolution Methods

The range of ADR services aiming at preventing and resolving construction disputes has steadily increased over the last two decades. Some ADR providers have echoed the possibilities of applying a variety of ADR techniques in construction projects and have tailored their rules to specific construction disputes. This section describes ADR mechanisms that the parties usually discuss and agree on when executing the agreements or after the dispute has arisen.

Dispute resolution clauses increasingly combine arbitration with another ADR technique, either negotiation or mutual consultation, mediation or conciliation, expert determination or standing dispute boards, either in the form of adjudication boards or neutral evaluations issuing non-binding recommendations. Following international model contracts such as the International Federation of Consulting Engineers' (FIDIC), Engineering Advancement Association of Japan's (ENAA), or the New Engineering Contract (NEC), some construction agreements require that, before resorting to arbitration, disputes be submitted to expert determination or dispute boards, which are constituted at the start of the project or when the dispute arises. Most of them require that the parties negotiate in good faith for a limited time, and some may establish mandatory mediation[8] or conciliation before submitting the dispute to arbitration.

Statistically, we cannot demonstrate how successful each formula is. We submit, however, that any legal practitioner working in the construction industry should, at least, consider the possibility of including mutual consultation, mediation, dispute boards, expert evaluation (including any form of third-party neutral evaluation),

[8] The 2014 ICC Mediation Guidance Notes described mediation as '[…] a flexible settlement technique, conducted privately and confidentially, in which a mediator acts as a neutral facilitator to help the parties try to arrive at a negotiated settlement of their dispute. The parties have control over both the decision to settle and the terms of any settlement agreement'; see International Chamber of Commerce (ICC), '2014 ICC Mediation Guidance Notes' (2014) 4, https://cdn.iccwbo.org/content/uploads/sites/3/2014/12/icc-mediation-guidance-notes-english.pdf.

or adjudication when drafting a dispute resolution clause. Of course, the parties must contractually agree on whether the mechanism of last resort to settle a dispute should be arbitration or litigation.

When it comes to construction, the project third-party neutral is available not only to mediate disputes as they arise, but also to identify and resolve other potential problems. The intervention of the neutral may be required before or after formalizing the dispute. When a dispute arises, practitioners should also master and understand the circumstances where it could be useful to apply one of the ADR techniques, even if these were not agreed upon and established in the terms and conditions of the agreement. The main disadvantage of not including ADR in the agreement is that, if ADR is not contractually required, seeking the intervention of a neutral after the dispute arises could be perceived as a sign of weakness.

In our experience, the use of dispute boards, either in the form of dispute review boards (DRBs), issuing non-binding recommendations, or dispute adjudication boards (DABs), issuing binding decisions has significantly increased, particularly in Latin America and Eastern Europe. The use of expert advisory opinions[9] or expert evaluation has also been proposed and accepted occasionally for projects in North Africa, and calling a third-party neutral to act as facilitator or mediator has also been considered and accepted in disputes with state entities. In long-term projects, appointing a standing board of senior managers has been successfully implemented in a few projects in North Africa between Spanish investors and national entities.

Arbitration is seen as the last remedy, and the parties are tempted to think that they should go to arbitration only if there is no other possibility for solving the problem. Sometimes, arbitration is triggered with the purpose of formalizing a dispute and changing the dynamics of the project. It is interesting to note that the parties are not always aware that they are using ADR techniques. In practice, however, before a dispute is formalized, it has been escalated to higher management, presentations have been made in front a joint committee (very similar to a simplified mini-trial),[10] or a third-party expert has been jointly engaged by the parties to

[9] Expert advisory opinion may be defined as a technique consisting of 'having an independent, neutral expert meet with the parties, both together and separately, obtain information from both parties, and then render a non-binding decision, evaluation or prediction as to the ultimate outcome of the dispute'. It favours the resolution of disputes between partners of a joint venture as well as typical situations in which the foreign investor should operate the project after construction. The intervention of an expert contributes to showing a more accurate picture of each party's claims, as well as, usually, lower economic expectations. See James P. Groton 'Alternative Dispute Resolution in the Construction Industry' in Thomas E. Carbonneau and Philip J. Mcconnaughay (eds), *Handbook on Construction Arbitration and ADR* (American Arbitration Association, 2007) 13.

[10] The International Institute for Conflict Prevention & Resolution (CPS) defines mini-trials as '[a] hybrid process by which the parties present their legal and factual contentions to a panel of representatives selected by each party, or to a neutral third party, or both. The presentations are strictly limited and, at the end of the presentations, the party representatives and/or neutral meet and confer. The utility of the process is to provide senior party representatives with an opportunity to balance the strength of their client's claims against the contentions of their adversary, with an eye to resolving the matter on commercial rather than legal terms'. See International Institute for Conflict Prevention & Resolution (CPR), 'Services Offered', www.cpradr.org/dispute-resolution-services/services-offered.

re-evaluate the claim 'without prejudice'. It seems that all these methodologies and techniques should also be considered ADR techniques even if the parties, due to their cultural backgrounds, do not shape them exactly as the books described.

One of the Gordian knots in the use of ADR techniques is the appointment of neutrals.[11] Currently, several institutions offer a roster of neutrals. Services for the appointment of mediators, adjudicators, or experts are highly valuable for the parties, especially if they had not been able to include a 'project neutral contract clause'[12] in their agreements. If we review the set of rules that the main ADR providers have specifically drafted for the construction industry, we can see that US and UK providers have been particularly active in this area. We should mention the American Arbitration Association (AAA)[13] and its international division, the International Centre for Dispute Resolution (ICDR), as well as Judicial Arbitration and Mediation Services, Inc. (JAMS)[14] and the Chartered Institute of Arbitrators (CIArb).[15]

In Asia, the China International and Economic Trade Arbitration Commission (CIETAC) approved the Construction Project Disputes Review Rules,[16] and the same set of rules is offered by the Beijing Arbitration Commission/Beijing International Arbitration Center (BAC/BIAC).[17] The Hong Kong Construction Arbitration Centre (HKCAC) provides a set of construction mediation and arbitration rules,[18] and very similar projects have been established in the *Centro de Arbitraje de la Industria de la Construcción* in Mexico,[19] and in India and Singapore at the Construction Industry Arbitration Council (CIAC), set up by the

[11] See Chapter 16, this volume.

[12] For illustrative purposes, see Judicial Arbitration and Mediation Services, Inc. (JAMS), 'Sample Construction Project Neutral Contract Clause', https://www.jamsadr.com/construction-project-neutral-clause/.

[13] AAA, 'Construction Industry Arbitration Rules and Mediation Procedures including Procedures for Large Complex Construction Disputes' (2015), https://www.adr.org/sites/default/files/Construction%20Rules.pdf.

[14] JAMS, 'Engineering and Construction Arbitration Rules & Procedures' (2014), https://www.jamsadr.com/rules-construction-arbitration/. JAMS is a private ADR provider founded in 1979 in the United States by the Hon. H. Warren Knight.

[15] CIArb, 'Construction Adjudication Guidelines' (2013), https://www.ciarb.org/resources/guidelines-ethics/adjudication/; 'CIArb Dispute Board Rules' (2014), https://www.ciarb.org/resources/rules; 'Dispute Board Rules Practice & Standards Committee' (2014), www.ciarb.org/docs/default-source/ciarbdocuments/das/ciarb-dispute-board-rules-practice-amp-standards-committee-august-2014.pdf?sfvrsn=2; 'Expert Determination', https://www.ciarb.org/das/dispute-appointment-service/expert-determination/; and 'Adjudication', https://www.ciarb.org/das/dispute-appointment-service/adjudication/.

[16] CIETAC, 'Construction Project Disputes Review Rules' (2014).

[17] Beijing Arbitration Commission, 'Construction Dispute Board Rules' (2009). See also Chapter 9, this volume.

[18] HKCAC, 'HKCAC Construction Mediation Rules', and 'HKCAC Construction Arbitration Rules'.

[19] Centro de Arbitraje de la Industria de la Construcción (CAIC), 'Reglamento de Arbitraje de CAIC' 'Reglamento de Conciliación de CAIC; 'Reglamento de Paneles de Solución de Disputas de CAIC; and 'Reglamento de Peritaje de CAIC.

Construction Industry Development Council (CIDC) in India, in cooperation with the Singapore International Arbitration Centre (SIAC).[20]

The International Chamber of Commerce (ICC) published its Dispute Board Rules with the main purpose of satisfying the needs of the construction industry,[21] and other arbitration centres have very quickly understood that a set of rules for dispute boards and adjudication was necessary (e.g. Hong Kong International Arbitration Centre).[22]

More specifically, JAMS proposes 'Dispute Resolution Rules for Surety Bond Disputes' (effective since February 2015). Surety disputes are very frequent, and either contractor or owner usually requires advice to protect its position ahead of the execution or calling of a surety.[23] The 2015 JAMS Engineering and Construction Arbitration Rules and Procedures for Expedited Arbitration[24] also incorporate very interesting—but unknown—features in Rules 32 (Bracketed or High-Low arbitration option)[25] and 33 (Final Offer or Baseball Arbitration Option).[26]

[20] CIAC, 'CIAC Arbitration Manual and Rules' (2013), www.ciac.in/download/ciac_manual.pdf; and 'CIAC Mediation & Conciliation' (2014), www.ciac.in/rules.html.

[21] ICC, 'ICC Dispute Board Rules' (2015).

[22] HKIAC, 'HKIAC Adjudication Rules' (2009).

[23] JAMS, 'Dispute Resolution Rules for Surety Bond Disputes' (2015).

[24] JAMS, 'Engineering and Construction Arbitration Rules and Procedures for Expedited Arbitration' (2015), www.jamsadr.com/files/Uploads/Documents/JAMS-Rules/JAMS_construction_expedited_rules-2015.pdf. The JAMS Expedited Arbitration Procedures address such issues as control of discovery and document admissibility, use of hearing 'chess clock' procedures, expert witness examination, prompt rulings on motions, maintenance of hearing schedules with minimum delays, and issuance of detailed reasoned awards to assure settlement of all issues.

[25] According to Rule 32 (Bracketed (or High-Low) Arbitration Option):

(a) At any time before the issuance of the Arbitration Award, the Parties may agree, in writing, on minimum and maximum amounts of damages that may be awarded on each claim or on all claims in the aggregate. The Parties shall promptly notify JAMS and provide to JAMS a copy of their written agreement setting forth the agreed-upon maximum and minimum amounts.
(b) JAMS shall not inform the Arbitrator of the agreement to proceed with this option or of the agreed-upon minimum and maximum levels without the consent of the Parties.
(c) The Arbitrator shall render the Award in accordance with Rule 24.
(d) In the event that the Award of the Arbitrator is between the agreed-upon minimum and maximum amounts, the Award shall become final as is. In the event that the Award is below the agreed-upon minimum amount, the final Award issued shall be corrected to reflect the agreed-upon minimum amount. In the event that the Award is above the agreed-upon maximum amount, the final Award issued shall be corrected to reflect the agreed-upon maximum amount.

[26] According to Rule 33 (Final Offer (or Baseball) Arbitration Option):

(a) Upon agreement of the Parties to use the option set forth in this Rule, at least seven (7) calendar days before the Arbitration Hearing, the Parties shall exchange and provide to JAMS written proposals for the amount of money damages they would offer or demand, as applicable, and that they believe to be appropriate based on the standard set forth in Rule 24(c). JAMS shall promptly provide a copy of the Parties' proposals to the Arbitrator, unless the Parties agree that they should not be provided to the Arbitrator. At any time prior to the close of the Arbitration Hearing, the Parties may exchange revised written proposals or demands, which shall supersede all prior proposals. The revised written proposals shall be provided to JAMS, which shall promptly provide them to the Arbitrator, unless the Parties agree otherwise.

Certainly, it is not our purpose to establish an exhaustive list of ADR for construction disputes. We stress, however, that some ADR tools that originated in the construction industry are especially suitable for this sector, e.g. dispute boards and adjudication.

IV. Dispute Boards

Excluding mutual consultation and negotiation between the parties and arbitration, in our experience dispute boards (DBs) are the preferred ADR mechanism in engineering and construction agreements. DBs are agreed in projects financed by multi-lateral investment banks, and they are used in Europe,[27] the Middle East, and, increasingly but to a lesser extent, in some Latin American projects.

DBs may be set up when executing medium- and long-term contracts as standing bodies that exist throughout the course of the project and periodically monitor its progress, irrespective of whether disputes arise. Alternatively, DBs may be established by the parties after a dispute arises to resolve that particular issue. If they are appointed at the beginning of the project, we would use the term 'standing dispute board'. If the DB is appointed after the dispute arises, we would call it an 'ad hoc dispute board'. Considering the type of decision DBs may issue, we can distinguish between DABs, whose decisions are immediately binding on the parties, and DRBs,[28] whose decisions (sometimes called 'recommendations') are not immediately binding but may become so, depending on the provisions set out in the applicable rules.

A combined formula has been proposed in the second edition of the FIDIC Red, Yellow and Silver Books, which appeared in December 2017. In its Clause 21 of the General Conditions (*Avoidance of Disputes*), the International Federation

(b) If the Arbitrator has been informed of the written proposals, in rendering the Award the Arbitrator shall choose between the Parties' last proposals, selecting the proposal that the Arbitrator finds most reasonable and appropriate in light of the standard set forth in Rule 24(c). This provision modifies Rule 24(h) in that no written statement of reasons shall accompany the Award.
(c) If the Arbitrator has not been informed of the written proposals, the Arbitrator shall render the Award as if pursuant to Rule 24, except that the Award shall thereafter be corrected to conform to the closest of the last proposals, and the closest of the last proposals will become the Award.
(d) Other than as provided herein, the provisions of Rule 24 shall be applicable.

[27] The Arcadis 2017 'Global Construction Disputes Report' points out that expert determination ranked second after negotiation; see images.arcadis.com/media/D/B/0/%7BDB0605C1-66EE-4648-A6F1-7451A34A881E%7DGlobal%20Construction%20Disputes2017-Online.pdf?_ga=2.42187173.1897240039.1515777404-1024009092.1515777404.

[28] These are envisioned in AAA, 'Construction Industry's Guide to Dispute Avoidance and Resolution' (2009), www.adr.org/sites/default/files/document_repository/The%20Construction%20Industry%27s%20Guide%20to%20Dispute%20Avoidance%20and%20Resolution.pdf; '[T]he DRB's determination is generally presented as a recommendation or a non-binding decision. Although the recommendations are non-binding, they are generally admissible in future proceedings—such as arbitration or litigation—if the issue is not resolved at the DRB level', 12).

of Consulting Engineers (FIDIC) provides for a *Dispute Avoidance/Adjudication Board (DAAB)*. This DAAB is a standing dispute board which can either 1) provide assistance to the parties, and/or informally discuss and attempt to resolve any issue or disagreement if the parties make a joint request pursuant to Clause 21.3; or 2) render a binding decision acting as an adjudication board.[29] This is a DAAB, which FIDIC defines as 'the preferred option proposed in the FIDIC model contracts'.[30]

Most international sets of rules contain provisions for both DABs and DRBs, leaving the choice to the parties.[31] Terminology is confusing in some cases, so the practitioner should pay special attention to the parties' agreement.[32] Standing dispute boards are constituted at the beginning of the project with the purpose of either rendering mere recommendations (DRB) or binding decisions (DAB) if a dispute arises. In our experience, it is more common for the parties to agree on DABs.

The interim binding nature of the DAB's decision results from the parties contractually agreeing that they will implement and abide by the panel's decision until the dispute is finally resolved.[33] This means that even when the applicable rules explicitly provide for the DAB's decision to be binding on the contracting parties,[34] its enforceability depends on a contractual agreement. Unlike arbitral awards or court judgments, the DAB's decision is not compulsorily enforceable. To be able to enforce the DAB's decision, the party benefitting from it must pursue a contractual claim against the non-fulfilling party.

[29] Pursuant to Clause 21.4.3, 'The decision shall be binding on the parties, who shall promptly comply with it whether or not a Party gives a NOD with respect to such decision under this Sub Clause' (FIDIC, 2nd edn, 2017).

[30] In its 1999 edition, dispute adjudication boards are recommended in Sub-Clause 20.2 to 20.8 of the Red, Yellow and Silver Books and in Sub-Clauses 20.3 to 20.11 of the Gold Book. In 2005, FIDIC and the World Bank (along with other development banks) published a special Multilateral Development Bank (MDB) harmonized edition of the Construction Contract for MDBs (the Pink Book), which supports the use of standing dispute adjudication boards. In its 2017 edition, Clause 21 of the Red, Yellow and Silver Books provide for DAABs.

[31] Among others, the ICC Dispute Board Rules, the CIArb's Dispute Board Rules, the Mexican Construction Arbitration Center (CAIC)'s Reglamento de Paneles de Solución de Controversias, the CIETAC's Construction Project Disputes Review Rules, or the Beijing Arbitration Commission (BIAC)'s Construction Dispute Board Rules.

[32] For instance, the ICC Dispute Board Rules have DBs appointed at the start of the project and remaining throughout it. They make a distinction between DRBs and DABs, depending on the type of conclusion they issue: under the ICC Dispute Board Rules, DRBs issue recommendations, which are not immediately binding on the parties but become so if no party objects within 30 days (Article 4), whereas DABs issue decisions that must be complied with immediately (Article 5). Article 6 of the ICC Dispute Board Rules also provides for the establishment of combined dispute boards (CDBs) that offer an intermediate solution between the DRBs and the DABs: they normally issue recommendations but may issue decisions if a party requests it and no other party objects, or the dispute board so decides on the basis of criteria set out in the Rules.

[33] Jane Jenkins, 'Dispute Avoidance and Resolution' in Jane Jenkins (ed.), *International Construction Arbitration Law* (2nd edn, Kluwer Law International, 2014) 60.

[34] See e.g. Clause 20.4 of the FIDIC contracts (1999) or Clause 21.4.3 (2017).

In some ICC cases dealing with Clause 20 of the FIDIC contracts, it has been successfully pleaded that the party's non-compliance with a binding DAB decision constitutes a contractual breach (i.e. breach of Clause 20.4), and the arbitrators are entitled to declare such a breach of contract in a final partial award. In such final partial award, the arbitrators are not granting any provisional measures but a final decision on that particular breach that does not prejudice the arbitrators' final decision on the merits.[35]

In its 2017 edition of the Red, Yellow and Silver Books, the FIDIC recommends standing dispute boards that could assist the parties in either the avoidance of the dispute or in the 'real-time' resolution of the disputes– if they arise—by way of binding decisions, and encourages parties to reach amicable settlements including the use of mediation.[36] ICC Arbitration remains the final resort to settle a dispute.

The main advantages of standing DBs are drawn from the fact that their members are familiar with the project's development and its technical and practical conditions from the very beginning. The common approach adopted by popular model rules in this matter foresees that standing DB members regularly conduct on-site visits and meet with stakeholders so as to closely monitor the project's progress and promptly address potential problems before these become full-on disputes.[37] Therefore, in the event that a dispute arises, standing DB members are best suited to satisfy the need for timely action, insofar as they are extensively informed about and experienced in the project.

In addition, since standing DBs are closely interacting with the contracting parties throughout the project's progress, they may also play a dispute preventive role by easing tension, de-escalating the dispute, encouraging the parties to overcome potential disagreements on their own, or assisting them in coming to an agreed

[35] In 2017 ICC cases we have worked on, the arbitrators' decision follows a reasoning similar to the Singapore Court of Appeal's Decision of 2015 in the case of *PT Persusahaan Gas Negara (Persero) TBK v CRW Joint Operation SGCA 30* (*Persero II*) regarding the 'final' nature of the award as opposed to a provisional or interim measure. This approach has also been shared by the arbitrators in ICC Case No. 10619 of March 2001 published in the ICC International Court of Arbitration Bulletin Vol. 19, No. 2. C. For additional support, see also Christopher R. Seppala, 'Enforcement by an Arbitral Award of a Binding but not Final Engineer's or DAB Decision under the FIDIC Conditions' (2009) International Construction Law Review 414.

[36] See e.g. FIDIC, *Conditions of Contract for Plant & Design Build, Guidance* (2nd edn, FIDIC, 2017), 50–5.

[37] Although not exclusively intended for the construction industry, the AAA's 'Dispute Resolution Board Guide Specifications' provide for the board members to periodically visit the project site and meet with representatives of the contracting parties to discuss progress of the works and facilitate conversation among the parties in order to resolve any pending claims which may become disputes. The frequency and scheduling of these visits will be every three months or as agreed upon among the parties with the board (Section 1.3.C). The International Federation of Consulting Engineers (FIDIC, 1st edition) follows a similar line in its model contracts: the DAB envisioned in Clause 20 therein 'shall visit the site at intervals of not more than 140 days, including times of critical construction events, at the request of either the Employer or the Contractor [. . .] The purpose of site visits is to enable the DAB to become acquainted with the progress of the Works and of any actual or potential problems or claims', Annex: Procedural Rules. See also Articles 10 to 12 of the CIArb's Dispute Board Rules.

resolution,[38] without the need for the DB to issue a decision. In this regard, their role would be similar to that of a mediator or facilitator. This is especially true in view that this type of project is usually extended in time and thus requires the parties to maintain ongoing relations under the best possible atmosphere.

Conversely, since ad hoc DBs are only constituted once a dispute has arisen, their usefulness as dispute avoidance mechanisms from this perspective is more limited, although they may also achieve the purpose of avoiding recourse to arbitration or litigation, provided that the parties consider the decision acceptable. Besides, while ad hoc DB members will not be as familiar with the project as standing DB members, the positive aspect is that the parties will be able to appoint professionals especially experienced in the specific issue in dispute once it has developed, whereas standing DB members need to be able to deal with any and all aspects of the project at the expense of expertise in particular issues. And predictably, ad hoc DBs are significantly less costly than standing DBs, whose members are employed and paid, regardless of whether there are any disputes.[39]

V. Adjudication

Adjudication originated in the United Kingdom in the 1970s, primarily to resolve subcontractor payment disputes in the building sector.[40] Under the Housing Grants, Construction and Regeneration Act of 1996,[41] which applies to most commercial contracts entered into after May 1998, a party is entitled to refer a dispute arising under the contract to adjudication. The adjudicator's decision is binding until the dispute is finally determined by judicial proceedings or arbitration (if the contract provides for arbitration or the parties otherwise agree to arbitrate), similar to the DAB's decisions mentioned earlier.

[38] The Foreword to the ICC Dispute Board Rules sets out three basic functions of dispute boards: 'upon perceiving a potential disagreement, the dispute board may (1) encourage the parties to overcome it on their own. If this is impossible or the disagreement too entrenched, the dispute board can (2) intervene with informal assistance to help the parties resolve the matter by agreement or (3) determine a dispute through a recommendation or a decision issued after a procedure of formal referral. Each of these functions is of equal value in helping to reduce the risk and cost of disruption to the parties' contract'. These functions are developed in Articles 16–18.

[39] As an alternative to avoid the expense of a three-person standing DB without giving up the benefit of familiarity and first-hand knowledge of its members, the AAA's 'Construction Industry's Guide to Dispute Avoidance and Resolution' suggests appointing an individual as a 'single dispute resolver', who would perform all the functions of a traditional standing DB or an 'on-site neutral', whose role would be that of a mediator or facilitator not issuing a formal decision or recommendation.

[40] See James P. Groton, Robert A. Rubin, and Bettina Quintas, 'Comparing Dispute Review Boards and Adjudication' in Thomas E. Carbonneau and Philip J. Mcconnaughay (eds), *Handbook on Construction Arbitration and ADR* (American Arbitration Association, 2007) 287–92.

[41] Please note that the adjudication section applies only to England, Scotland, and Wales.

The World Bank includes adjudication provisions in its Standard Bidding Documents—Procurement of Works (2015),[42] which is the standard contract form used in large-scale civil works projects funded by the World Bank. Other multilateral development banks and international financing institutions (e.g. the Asian Development Bank and the European Bank for Reconstruction and Development), which have prepared a Master Bidding Document for Procurement of Works and User's Guide (2005) including adjudication, also include these provisions.

In international transactions, adjudication was recommended as a first step in the NEC model contracts.[43] Namely, the NEC3 Engineering and Construction Agreement, Option W1[44] foresees a tiered dispute resolution procedure, providing that disputes arising under or in connection with the contract must be settled by first, referral to an adjudicator, whose decision must be binding on the parties unless and until reviewed by courts or arbitral tribunals. Second, only if a party is dissatisfied with the adjudicator's decision, and after that party has notified the other party of its intent to refer to a tribunal, can it resort to arbitration or litigation.[45]

June 2017 saw a new suite of NEC contracts (NEC4) published, which revised the former Dispute Resolution section (Options W1 and W2 under NEC3), now entitled Resolving and Avoiding Disputes. According to Matthew Garrat, these changes reflect NEC's consensual dispute resolution approach towards improving the chances of reaching a negotiated solution and maintaining collaboration between the parties.[46]

In the new models, NEC4 includes an escalation and negotiation step, which must be completed before referring the dispute to adjudication in transactions to which the Housing Grants, Construction and Regeneration Act of 1996 is not applicable (Option W1). In the negotiations, senior representatives have a four-week period to agree on a negotiated solution and this period must be completed before referring the dispute to adjudication (which thus becomes the second step to be completed prior to resorting to arbitration or litigation).[47]

In addition, NEC4 introduces a new Option W3 to be chosen instead of Option W1, which keeps a two-tier clause but replaces adjudication (the former first step under Option W1) by the appointment of a dispute avoidance board. Therefore, under Option W3, the dispute avoidance and resolution scheme provides 1) for the dispute to be referred to the dispute avoidance board, which shall assist the parties

[42] World Bank, 'Standard Bidding Documents: Procurement of Works' (2015), http://www.worldbank.org/en/projects-operations/products-and-services/brief/procurement-standard-documents-archive.

[43] Institution of Civil Engineers (ICE), New Engineering and Construction Contract (NEC3) (June 2005, amended as of June 2006).

[44] To be used unless the Housing Grants, Construction and Regeneration Act applies

[45] ICE (n 43) 27–32.

[46] Matthew Garrat, 'The Next Generation: An Explanation of Changes and Benefits', NEC4 Whitepaper (2017) 6–7.

[47] Practical Law Construction, 'NEC4: Disputes under Options W1, W2 and W3', Practice Note w-009-1492 (2018).

in the settlement of the dispute and may provide a non-binding recommendation; and 2) if either party is not satisfied with such recommendation, for a formal referral to arbitration or litigation within four weeks.[48]

Overall, the degree of satisfaction in the use of statutory adjudication in the United Kingdom is high. In Ireland, however, some have criticized the introduction of statutory adjudication in 2013 (effective since July 2016) and insisted on the advantages of conciliation as a non-binding mechanism, where the conciliator actually brought about a settlement.[49] It seems that the new standard international contracts support this view.

VI. Mediation and Conciliation

The advantages and suitability of using mediation for resolving construction disputes are irrefutable. Mediation and conciliation are used as synonymous in the majority of cases, but the role of the third-party neutral (i.e. mediator or conciliator) may be different and should require specific attention not to frustrate the parties' expectations.

According to different scholarly works, mediation is used in construction disputes as much as arbitration, dispute boards or adjudication.[50] In the United States, Ireland, and the United Kingdom (at least, until implementing statutory adjudication in 1998), mediation has been fairly popular in settling commercial disputes. However, in our experience, this is not the case in other countries. Its predominance and use around the construction world are yet quite heterogeneous.

The European Union and its member states have introduced statues and legislative measures in support of mediation.[51] In Spain, for example, Act 5/2012 incorporated into Spanish Law Directive 2008/52/EC of the European Parliament and of the Council of 21 May 2008 on certain aspects of mediation in civil and commercial matters.[52] The Spanish Act is applicable to cross-border and domestic cases. One of the key obstacles to mediation may lie with local counsel. Because some local lawyers do not know about the advantages of mediation, they may avoid advising clients regarding its use. Owners and contractors' lack of familiarity with

[48] Ibid.

[49] See Brian L. Bond, 'Alternative Methods of Resolving Construction Disputes: Is Statutory Adjudication Really the Best Way?' (2016) 82 (3) International Journal of Arbitration, Mediation and Dispute Management 239–49.

[50] The Arcadis 2017 *Global Construction Disputes* points out that mediation was the second ADR mechanism used in North America after negotiation and ahead of arbitration. In the United Kingdom, mediation ranks third after adjudication and negotiation. In Asia, mediation is third on the list, after arbitration and negotiation. In the Middle East, adjudication is preferred to mediation but stands behind negotiation and arbitration; see images.arcadis.com/media/D/B/0/%7BDB0605C1-66EE-4648-A6F1-7451A34A881E%7DGlobal%20Construction%20Disputes2017-Online.pdf?_ga=2.42187173.1897240039.1515777404-1024009092.1515777404.

[51] See Chapter 10, this volume.

[52] Act 5/2012, of 6 July, of mediation in civil and commercial matters (BOE 162, 07/07/2012).

mediation may be an additional hurdle. On some occasions, selecting experts, dispute boards or arbitration is considered more effective.

We do not think that mediation should be immediately excluded; quite the contrary. Choosing an ADR requires a case-by-case analysis. In a construction project, the resolution of the dispute is key to completing the project. If the parties choose mediation early on, they may prevent the conflict from escalating beyond the original issue. Mediation allows relationships to be preserved, prevents excessive costs, and saves management time. Moreover, mediation enables the parties to shape the process and control its outcome, leading to a degree of party autonomy and self-determination that is not present in adjudication processes, e.g. arbitration and litigation.

Mediation has many advantages for the parties. Mediation provides a fast conflict resolution procedure at a low cost. Mediation is confidential and therefore, it does not prejudice the parties' position in case an agreement is not reached. The procedure is flexible and the mediator, who is and must remain impartial and neutral, hears of the parties' interests and positions, beyond legal issues. Even if mediation fails, preparing and conducting the mediation process provides clients with the perfect scenario to clarify their position and re-evaluate the consequences of the conflict. Mediation also helps to reduce the number of claims. It prevents further disputes and avoids the spiral effect of cumulative claims minimizing the impact of a dispute that could finally end up in arbitration or litigation.

In preparing the mediation, the client's team (either contractors, owners, or designers) should be reassured that this is a voluntary process. Before going to mediation, the client's decision-makers should be aware of their best alternative to a negotiated agreement (BATNA) and worst alternative to a negotiated agreement (WATNA). The client should be encouraged to have an open mind with regard to how the mediation process may develop and what the mediator or the other party may recommend. They should have a deep understanding of the distinction between the law, facts, and interest defining their position and their arguments. The client should be assured that they will have time to speak with the mediator privately in caucus, and that this is a very flexible process. It is also important that they be encouraged to take responsibility for their own actions and act in good faith. While the clients should under no circumstance be pressured or coaxed into settling, it is also important that they are made aware of the consequences of not settling, especially since, in some cases, this may lead to a long litigation process.

From the perspective of the client, especially in complex construction disputes, it is wise to request a litigation estimate from their counsel in case the dispute goes to court or arbitration. A semi-detailed estimate of the finances and time that may be dedicated to a legal battle may be valuable to the client to better understand and appreciate the advantages of the mediation process in itself.

The individual characteristics and experience of each mediator are among the most crucial factors that determine the relative success, coherence, productivity, and effectiveness of the mediation process. The mediator's appointment process depends entirely on the individual characteristics of each case, largely on the relationship and approach of the parties, the nature of the dispute (if it is factual, legal or a combination of both), and the type of contract. It is important for the parties to do their research and discuss in good faith about the appointment of the mediator. However, in many situations, the parties will not be able to reach consensus, and, in such cases, it is necessary to designate an appointing authority that could be able to break the deadlock.

Parties also need to consider the type of mediation that may be best suited to their requirements. While facilitative mediators would aid in resolving the dispute, they would not make recommendations like evaluative mediators. In general, it is important that evaluative or facilitative mediators have specialized knowledge in the area of the dispute. Importantly, mediators should also possess extensive awareness of the individual cultural elements of doing business in different regions. This is vital, as these cultural elements may have been a factor in the cause of the dispute or may be intrinsic to its resolution.

VII. Choosing and Drafting Dispute Resolution Clauses

The introduction of dispute resolution clauses in construction agreements requires specialized knowledge and expertise. Drafting dispute resolution clauses is not an easy task. Most arbitration courts and ADR providers offer standard clauses for arbitration and mediation.[53] In addition, there are some model clauses specifically drafted for construction disputes that combine dispute boards and adjudication with negotiation and arbitration.

The dispute resolution clause should be negotiated and read systematically and consistently with the rest of the terms and conditions of the agreement. By way of example, it could be inconsistent to draft a Clause X, in which some disputes are referred to expert determination, as well as a Clause Y, which refers all disputes to arbitration preceded by negotiations or mediation. In the agreements, it is also important to identify whether the engineer or the owner's representative is competent to render binding determinations in relation to specific issues. If a claim is brought before the engineer, and the engineer does not resolve the claim right away, the parties should be able to skip that requirement and have an available mechanism within the dispute resolution clause.

To avoid unnecessary risks, it is advisable to either adapt standard dispute resolution clauses or implement model contracts. In case of drafting multi-tier clauses, we suggest that the drafter should establish time limits running

[53] See Centre for Effective Dispute Resolution (CEDR), 'Model International ADR Contract Clauses,' http://www.cedr.com/about_us/modeldocs/.

from a clear and well-defined event, and should use unambiguous language as to its binding nature.[54] In *Emirates Trading Agency LLC v Prime Mineral Exports Private Ltd*,[55] the High Court of England held that multi-tier clauses are binding, and the parties must comply with all agreed ADR. Furthermore, it held that there was a public interest in favour of ADR clauses. The rest of this section considers some dispute resolution clauses that users can find in ADR rules or in model contracts: 1) mediation–arbitration clauses; 2) consultation–expert determination and arbitration; 3) dispute boards–arbitration, and 4) adjudication–arbitration.

A. Mediation–Arbitration

Mediation is becoming a requirement for dispute resolution in construction. In the United States, organizations like the American Institute of Architects and the Design Build Institute of America have now prescribed mediation as a requirement before binding arbitration in their standard documentation.[56] Similarly, in Ireland, the Irish Construction Industry Federation (CIF) has introduced mediation clauses into their construction sub-contracts, as has the Canadian Construction Documents Committee.[57] In Hong Kong, where the government has specific mediation rules aimed at the construction industry, if the parties do not come to an agreement as to who they would like to appoint, the Hong Kong International Arbitration Centre is given the responsibility under the government mediation rules to make the appointment as the mediation administering agency.

Commonly, negotiations are included as a first tier, before mediation and arbitration. Remarkably, the multi-step dispute resolution clause that the Institute for Conflict Prevention & Resolution (CPR) proposes that executives at a higher level of management than the persons with direct responsibility for administration of the contract participate in the negotiations.[58] Two examples of mediation–arbitration

[54] See Soledad Marco, 'La mediación en cláusulas escalonadas', Revista de la Corte Aragonesa de Arbitraje y Mediación, www.cortearagonesadearbitraje.com/docs/Documentacion/Documentacion100.pdf.

[55] *Emirates Trading Agency Llc v Prime Mineral Exports Private Ltd* [2014] EWHC 2104 (Comm) (1 July 2014).

[56] Sections 15.2, 15.3, and 15.4 of the model contract document 'A201—General Conditions for the Contract of Construction' (2017), published by the American Institute of Architects, set forth a 'stepped' dispute resolution procedure whereby a claim must first be decided by an 'initial decision-maker', whose determination is binding but subject to mediation and binding dispute resolution (i.e. arbitration or court litigation, depending on what the parties have agreed on).

[57] Canadian Construction Documents Committee, 'CCDC 40 - 2005 Rules for Mediation and Arbitration of Construction Disputes' (2005).

[58] International Institute for Conflict Prevention & Resolution, International Administered Arbitration [online] II. *Multi-Step Clause with Administered Arbitration*, https://www.cpradr.org/resource-center/model-clauses/international-model-clauses.

(med–arb) clauses can be found in the ICDR and SIAC–Singapore International Mediation Centre (SIMC) proposals.

According to the ICDR Standard Mediation–Arbitration Step Clause:

> In the event of any controversy or claim arising out of or relating to this contract, or the breach thereof, the parties hereto agree first to try and settle the dispute by mediation, administered by the International Centre for Dispute Resolution under its Mediation Rules. If settlement is not reached within 60 days after service of a written demand for mediation, any unresolved controversy or claim arising out of or relating to this contract shall be settled by arbitration in accordance with the International Arbitration Rules of the International Centre for Dispute Resolution.

According to the SIAC–SIMC Arb–Med–Arb Model Clause:

> Any dispute arising out of or in connection with this contract, including any question regarding its existence, validity or termination, shall be referred to and finally resolved by arbitration administered by the Singapore International Arbitration Centre ('SIAC') in accordance with the Arbitration Rules of the Singapore International Arbitration Centre ('SIAC Rules') for the time being in force, which rules are deemed to be incorporated by reference in this clause [. . .]
>
> The parties further agree that following the commencement of arbitration, they will attempt in good faith to resolve the Dispute through mediation at the Singapore International Mediation Centre ('SIMC'), in accordance with the SIAC–SIMC Arb–Med–Arb Protocol for the time being in force. Any settlement reached in the course of the mediation shall be referred to the arbitral tribunal appointed by SIAC and may be made a consent award on agreed terms.

Interestingly, in the SIAC–SIMC example the model clause proposes that mediation be attempted after commencing arbitration. SIAC–SIMC does also have a proposal for mediation prior to arbitration, which is more common in other jurisdictions, e.g. Spain, France, and Mexico. In situations where the conflict is too contentious, proposing mediation after arbitration could be useful as it requires that the parties to re-evaluate their respective claims without waiving any credibility or right to pursue their primary claim in the arbitration.[59]

[59] See Chapter 4, this volume.

B. Consultation–Expert Determination–Arbitration

Under the auspices of the Engineering Advancement Association of Japan, General Condition 6 of ENAA's Model Form International Contract for Process Plant Construction standardizes a multi-tiered approach for settlement of disputes arising in connection with or out of the contract. According to it, i) the parties must seek to resolve any such disputes by mutual consultation; ii) if this fails, after formal notice of dispute is given, a further consultation period of 30 days is established; and iii) once this 30-day period for further consultation has elapsed, the dispute must be referred to arbitration under the ICC Rules. As an alternative to the consultation prerequisite, the parties can resort to expert determination under the Rules for Expertise of the ICC, before referring the dispute to be finally settled by arbitration.[60]

C. Standard Clauses for Dispute Boards

In addition to model clauses combining mediation and arbitration, it is also common to find model clauses referring to dispute boards. Although not exclusively intended for the construction industry, the ICC publishes Standard ICC Dispute Board Clauses[61] for parties who wish to set up and operate a dispute board under the ICC Dispute Board Rules.[62] The ICC distinguishes between: (i) ICC Dispute Review Board followed by ICC arbitration, if required; (ii) ICC Dispute Adjudication Board followed by ICC arbitration, if required; and (iii) ICC Combined Dispute Board followed by ICC arbitration, if required.[63]

In August 2014, the CIARb published its Dispute Board Rules including a set of recommended Dispute Board Clauses.[64] The Rules envisage a Dispute Board Scheme with three key elements:

i. a dispute board clause inserted into the substantive commercial contract;
ii. the rules themselves; and
iii. a three-part agreement between the dispute board and the two parties to the substantive commercial contract.[65]

[60] Engineering Advancement Association of Japan (ENAA), 'Model Form International Contract for Process Plant Construction' (2010) 5–7.

[61] The Standard ICC Dispute Board Clauses (2015) are available at https://cdn.iccwbo.org/content/uploads/sites/3/2015/09/Standard-ICC-Dispute-Board-Clauses-in-English.pdf.

[62] The ICC Dispute Board Rules (2015) are available at https://cdn.iccwbo.org/content/uploads/sites/3/2015/09/icc-dispute-board-rules-english-version.pdf.

[63] See (n 61).

[64] CIArb (n 15) Article 2.

[65] See Michael O'Reilly, 'The Chartered Institute of Arbitrators' Dispute Board Rules' (2015) 81 (2) International Journal of Arbitration, Mediation and Dispute Management 197–8.

The CIArb has distinguished between DRBs[66] and DABs.[67] The main difference is that if the parties have chosen to implement a DRB, they are not bound by the DRB's Recommendations (Article 3.1), whereas the decision of a DAB is binding on the parties (Article 4.3). Since 1999, the FIDIC contract provides the most typical combination of dispute boards and arbitration in Clause 20 (dispute resolution).[68]

D. Standard Clauses for Adjudication

The CIArb proposes a Construction Adjudication Clause that essentially adopts the requirement of the Housing Grants, Construction and Regeneration Act 1996.[69] In the HKCAC, there is also a standard Dispute Resolution Clause providing for three steps: i) negotiation, ii) mediation or adjudication, and iii) arbitration.[70] The new FIDIC and NEC4 model contracts of 2017 insist on using ADR as a mechanism for avoiding disputes, keeping open the possibility of negotiations at the highest management level even after the adjudicator's decision. FIDIC refers to DAABs (FIDIC 2017) and NEC4 to 'Resolving and Avoiding Disputes'. Therefore, it seems obvious that the settlement of construction disputes will require a full command of ADR.

[66] CIArb (n 15) Article 2.3.a: 'The Parties hereby agree to establish a Dispute Review Board in accordance with the Dispute Board Rules of the Chartered Institute of Arbitrators (the "Rules"). The DRB shall have [one/three] member[s] appointed in accordance with the Rules, which are incorporated herein by reference. Any disputes between the Parties arising out of or in connection with this Contract shall be submitted to the DRB pursuant to the Rules. If the DRB issues a Recommendation and one of the Parties rejects it, either Party may submit the dispute to arbitration, if the Parties have so agreed, or to the courts. Pending a ruling by the arbitral tribunal or the court, the Parties may voluntarily comply with the Recommendation.'

[67] Ibid., Article 2.3.b: 'The Parties hereby agree to establish a Dispute Adjudication Board in accordance with the Dispute Board Rules of the Chartered Institute of Arbitrators (the "Rules"). The DAB shall have [one/three] member[s] appointed in accordance with the Rules, which are incorporated herein by reference. Any disputes between the Parties arising out of or in connection with this Contract shall be submitted to the DAB pursuant to the Rules. If the DAB issues a Decision and one of the Parties rejects or fails to comply with it, either Party may submit the dispute to arbitration for summary or other expedited relief, if the Parties have so agreed, or to the courts without prejudice to any other rights it may have. Pending a ruling by the arbitral tribunal or the court, the Parties must comply with the DAB's Decision.'

[68] Dispute Boards are recommended in Sub-Clause 20.2 to 20.8 of the Red, Yellow and Silver Books and Sub-Clauses 20.3 to 20.11 of the Gold Book. Furthermore, in 2005 FIDIC and the World Bank (along with other development banks) published a special Multilateral Development Bank (MDB) harmonized edition of the Construction Contract for MDBs (the Pink Book), which provides for the use of standing dispute adjudication boards.

[69] The CIArb's Dispute Resolution Clauses are available at https://www.ciarb.org/docs/default-source/ciarbdocuments/das/recommended-clauses/contract-clause.pdf?sfvrsn=8.

[70] The HKCAC Standard Dispute Resolution Clause (2015) is available at: 116.48.140.240/HKCACL/images/phocagallery/OfficialDoc/SDRC%202015%20Standard%20English.pdf.

VIII. Conclusion

Disputes are inherent in construction projects; it would be too optimistic to think that the use of ADR will prevent all disputes among owners, designers, contractors, subcontractors, and suppliers. However, the parties capable of resorting to suitable dispute resolution mechanisms such as mediation, expert determination, or dispute avoidance/adjudication boards will save costs, foster a timely completion of the works, reduce the number of disputes, and prevent critical situations in which the accumulation of unresolved claims may jeopardize the financial viability of the entire project.

In 2017, both the NEC and the FIDIC sent a clear message to all users and practitioners: prevention of disputes starts at the negotiation stage. It is not enough that the project teams discuss and negotiate over potential claims. As soon as there is a conflict that could easily become a formal claim, the parties' higher management should be involved and both parties should attempt to settle the dispute in good faith. Reaching an amicable settlement should be the main goal for both parties at any time, even after obtaining a binding decision from the adjudicator or in the course of arbitration. Settling the dispute will be for their common benefit as well as for the benefit of the project.

In cases where this kind of partnering or collaborative attitude appears difficult, the early involvement of a third-party neutral will be key. S/he could adopt the role of mediator, expert, or dispute board. If the third-party neutral is appointed at the commencement of the project and the contract defines the neutral's role, the possibilities of settlement are higher. The use of neutral evaluation is growing steadily and so is mediation or conciliation. In our experience, however, dispute boards are more frequently used. The ADR services offered at an international level are ample and of great quality. Practitioners and clients can opt for many different choices. It is for the parties to agree on the most suitable combination of ADR, but it is no longer acceptable to ignore their existence.

PART IV

SPECIAL TOPICS IN THE MEDIATION OF COMMERCIAL AND INVESTMENT DISPUTES

16

Selection of Mediators

Charles H. Brower II

I. Introduction

Selection of mediators represents one of the most common[1] and most important[2] questions for parties involved in, or contemplating, international commercial mediation. When addressing this topic, however, it is necessary to begin with an appreciation of context. Although recourse to international commercial mediation has increased in recent years,[3] the absolute number of controversies submitted to international commercial mediation remains fairly low.[4] Observers continue to refer to the incipient nature of the discipline,[5] the absence of an extensive body of practice,[6] and continuing resistance to mediation in geographically important

[1] Michael McIlwrath and John Savage, *International Arbitration and Mediation* (Kluwer Law International, 2010) 187; see also Herbert Smith Freehills, 'Selecting Your Mediator and Drafting the Mediation Agreement' (2014) 4 ADR Practical Guide Series 1, https://www.herbertsmithfreehills.com/latest-thinking/adr-practical-guide-series-and-guide-to-improving-conflict-management.

[2] See Lorraine M. Brennan, 'Preparing the Client in an International Mediation: What to Expect from the Process', in Arthur W. Rovine (ed.), *Contemporary Issues in International Arbitration and Mediation: The Fordham Papers 2014* (Brill Nijhoff, 2015) 141, 145–6.

[3] McIlwrath and Savage (n 1) 187; Josefa Sicard-Mirabal and Rachel Clarke, 'The Effect of Culture on International Mediation', in Rovine (n 2) 167; S. I. Strong, 'Beyond International Commercial Arbitration? The Promise of International Commercial Mediation' (2014) 45 Journal of Law and Policy 11, 15. According to one survey, recourse to international commercial mediation increased following the 2008 financial crisis due in large part to declining litigation budgets. See Queen Mary School of International Arbitration & PwC, '2013 International Arbitration Survey: Corporate Choices in International Arbitration' 10 (2013), https://www.pwc.com/gx/en/arbitration-dispute-resolution/assets/pwc-international-arbitration-study.pdf.

[4] McIlwrath and Savage (n 1) 187; Harold I. Abramson, 'Time to Try Mediation of International Commercial Disputes' (1998) 4 International Law Student Association Journal of International and Comparative Law 323; see also (n 142–n 146) and accompanying text. Not surprisingly, the popularity of international commercial mediation varies by industry. In a recent survey, only 5 percent of respondents in the energy industry listed mediation as their most-preferred mechanism for resolving disputes, whereas 68 percent of respondents listed mediation as their least-preferred mechanism for resolving disputes. Queen Mary School and PwC (n 3) 7. In the financial services industry, only 9 percent of respondents listed mediation as their most-preferred mechanism for resolving disputes, whereas only 18 percent of respondents listed mediation as their least-preferred mechanism for resolving disputes, suggesting at least a little more enthusiasm and a lot less resistance to mediation in that sector. In the construction industry, views seemed more evenly split, with 22 percent of respondents listing mediation as their most-preferred mechanism for resolving disputes, and an equal percentage of respondents listing mediation as their least-preferred mechanism for resolving disputes (n 3).

[5] McIlwrath and Savage (n 1) 187.

[6] Ibid.

regions, including Europe.[7] Given these facts, it should come as no surprise that potential users of international commercial mediation will find only a small body of literature addressing selection of mediators,[8] with writers often expressing conflicting (or at least different) perspectives on important topics.[9]

This chapter seeks to distil and to enhance the understanding of mediator selection by examining the qualities that users should consider when choosing international commercial mediators, the processes for gathering information about potential candidates, the processes for vetting shortlisted candidates, and special problems associated with the selection of mediators for international commercial disputes. Section II discusses the goals that parties should consider when selecting mediators for international commercial disputes. Its subsections identify a number of threshold requirements for mediators in such matters,[10] and describe a range of professional qualifications that parties should consider when selecting international commercial mediators.[11] Additionally, they explore certain personal characteristics that parties should also consider in the selection process,[12] and identify process orientations that parties should consider when selecting international commercial mediators.[13] Section III discusses mechanisms that parties may use to gather information about mediators and, thus, build a pool of suitable candidates.[14] Section IV examines mechanisms for vetting shortlisted candidates,

[7] See Carrie Menkel-Meadow, 'Variations in the Uptake of and Resistance to Mediation Outside of the United States', in Rovine (n 2) 189, 192; see also James M. Rhodes, 'The Current Status and Future of International Mediation', in Rovine (n 2) 177.

[8] See generally Harold I. Abramson, *Mediation Representation* (2nd edn, OUP, 2011) 151–83 (Abramson, *Mediation Representation*); Nadja Alexander, *International and Comparative Mediation* (Kluwer Law International, 2009) 115–27; McIlwrath and Savage (n 1) 187–204; Harold I. Abramson, 'Mining Mediation Rules for Representation Opportunities and Obstacles' (2004) 14 American Review of International Arbitration 103, 103–8 (Abramson, 'Mining Mediation Rules'); Harold Abramson, 'Selecting Mediators and Representing Clients in Cross-Cultural Disputes' (2006) 7 Cardozo Journal of Conflict Resolution 253 (Abramson, *Selecting Mediators*); Brennan (n 2) 145–7; Dr Luis Miguel Diaz and Nancy A. Oretskin, 'Mediation Furthers the Principles of Transparency and Cooperation to Solve Disputes in the NAFTA Free Trade Area' (2001) 30 Denver Journal of International Law and Policy 73, 80–2; Claudia T. Salomon and Peter D. Sharp, 'Selecting a Mediator in International Disputes: Dare We Speak of Mediation as Winnable?' (2006) 61 Dispute Resolution Journal 69.

There is a separate literature on the qualities of successful mediators in the context of inter-state conflicts, which lacks direct relevance but may stimulate thought if one keeps the contextual differences in mind. See e.g. Jacob Bercovitch, 'Third Parties in Conflict Management: The Structure and Conditions of Effective Mediation in International Relations' (1985) 40 International Journal 736, 749–51; Jacob Bercovitch, J. Theodore Anagnoson and Donnette L. Wille, 'Some Conceptual Issues and Empirical Trends in the Study of Successful Mediation in International Relations' (1991) 28 Journal of Peace Research 7, 14–15; Jacob Bercovitch and Allison Houston, 'The Study of International Mediation', in Jacob Bercovitch (ed.), *Theory and Practice of International Mediation: Selected Essays* (Routledge, 2011) 35, 44–6 (Bercovitch and Houston, 'The Study of International Mediation'); Jacob Bercovitch and Allison Houston, 'Why Do They Do It Like This?' (2000) 44 Journal of Conflict Resolution 170, 180–1 (Bercovitch and Houston, 'Why Do They Do It Like This?'); Marieke Kleiboer, 'Understanding Success and Failure of International Mediation' (1996) 40 Journal of Conflict Resolution 360, 368–73.

[9] See (n 30–n 32, n 41–n 44, n 67, n 71–n 74, n 86–n 95) and accompanying text.

[10] See (n 21–n 64) and accompanying text.

[11] See (n 65–n 95) and accompanying text.

[12] See (n 96–n 108) and accompanying text.

[13] See (n 109–n 126) and accompanying text.

[14] See (n 127–n 163) and accompanying text.

including interviews with candidates and references.[15] Finally, section V addresses two special problems relating to selection of mediators: the initial failure to agree on candidates, and the loss of trust and confidence in mediators following appointment.[16]

II. What to Consider When Selecting Mediators

International commercial mediation involves a voluntary process.[17] It will succeed only in an atmosphere of trust and confidence that facilitates cooperation between the disputing parties.[18] Proper selection of a mediator should aim at identifying individuals who can encourage and support the disputing parties' own efforts to reach settlement.[19] Although the importance of any particular factor will depend on the parties and the facts of the particular case,[20] the following four categories seem generally relevant to the selection of mediators for international commercial disputes:

i. threshold, gatekeeping requirements that any candidate must satisfy as a condition for appointment;
ii. desirable professional qualifications;
iii. personal qualities that support the development of trust and confidence; and
iv. process orientations that might or might not be well suited to particular kinds of disputes.

A. Threshold Requirements

When selecting mediators, the parties may have threshold requirements that any candidate must satisfy as a condition for appointment.[21] Some of these involve logistical and practical considerations, while others relate to the integrity of the process. For example, with respect to logistical and practical considerations, a candidate's availability at the time and place for mediation represents a fundamental requirement for appointment.[22] Unlike arbitration proceedings, which can take at least a year or two and involve weeks of

[15] See (n 164–n 182) and accompanying text.
[16] See (n 183–n 192) and accompanying text.
[17] See Bercovitch (n 8) 749; Bercovitch and Houston, 'The Study of International Mediation' (n 8) 44.
[18] Ibid.
[19] See McIlwrath and Savage (n 1) 188; see also Bercovitch and Houston, 'Why Do They Do It Like This?' (n 8) 181.
[20] Abramson, *Mediation Representation* (n 8) 181; Salomon and Sharp (n 8) 70; see also Brennan (n 2) 151.
[21] Cf. Alexander (n 8) 123, 125.
[22] McIlwrath and Savage (n 1) 195; see also Brennan (n 2) 146.

hearings,[23] international commercial mediation occurs in a more compressed timeframe, with the whole process taking just a few weeks or months, and the mediation itself often taking just one day.[24] Given this difference, some observers advise disputing parties first to select the time (or a range of acceptable times) and place of mediation, and only then to seek candidates whose availability conforms to the parties' expectations.[25] In their view, organizing the mediation around the availability of candidates might be possible, but generally becomes a frustrating and unworkable task.[26] Thus, the parties should make availability one of the very first questions put to candidates during the selection process.[27]

Language skills constitute a second practical threshold requirement for appointment. In order to build an atmosphere of trust and confidence, mediators must have the capacity to speak directly to counsel and party representatives on both sides.[28] As a result, viable candidates should have professional fluency in the language selected by the parties for pre-mediation communications and for plenary meetings at the mediation.[29] Some observers go further, claiming that fluency in the native languages of *both parties* functions as a hallmark of impartiality and 'has more influence than any factor in developing a party's trust and confidence in the mediator'.[30] Other commentators express the view that effective mediators need not speak the native languages of both parties, or even the native language of *any* party, so long as the mediator and all stakeholders share a common working language.[31] In fact, requirements for fluency in multiple languages could unduly restrict the pool of potential mediators,[32] especially when layered on top of the parties' preferences with respect to professional qualifications, personal qualities, and process orientations. Thus, while language skills represent an important threshold requirement, this probably constitutes an area where the parties may wish to impose fewer, more sensible conditions.

The parties may also wish to consider the extent to which they want billing rates to figure into their consideration of threshold requirements. While billing rates may not constitute a major concern in large, complex, or bet-the-company cases,

[23] See Justyn Jagger and Peter Cheong, 'SIAC Publishes Average Cost and Duration of Arbitrations' (12 October 2016), https://www.morganlewis.com/pubs/siac-publishes-average-cost-and-duration-of-arbitrations; Hong Kong International Arbitration Centre, 'Costs and Duration', http://www.hkiac.org/content/costs-duration; see also Margaret L. Moses, *International Commercial Arbitration* (CUP, 2008) 150; Chris Mackay and Richard Farndale, 'International Arbitration—Preparation. Planning. Proceedings.' [blog] (14 November 2013), https://burnesspaull.com/blog/2013/11/international-arbitration---preparation-planning-proceedings; cf. Stockholm Chamber of Commerce, 'Hearings in SCC Arbitrations', http://www.sccinstitute.com/dispute-resolution/hearings/.

[24] McIlwrath and Savage (n 1) 187–8.

[25] Ibid., 187.

[26] Ibid.

[27] Ibid., 187, 195; Salomon and Sharp (n 8) 73.

[28] Ibid.; see also McIlwrath and Savage (n 1) 198.

[29] Ibid.

[30] Salomon and Sharp (n 8) 73.

[31] McIlwrath and Savage (n 1) 198.

[32] Ibid.

they can quickly become an issue for smaller cases in which the parties principally hope to avoid the cost of litigation or arbitration.[33] In this context, parties should consider that the fees of top mediators can vary substantially within a single jurisdiction.[34] For example, two observers cite a 2008 survey of thirty leading British mediators, who quoted between 3,500 and 8,000 GB pounds to mediate disputes with 1,000,000 GB pounds in controversy.[35] When considering mediators from different national jurisdictions, the variations can become even more significant.[36] For example, the same observers describe a matter involving Asian and European parties, in which the amounts in controversy came to less than 4,000,000 US dollars.[37] During the selection process, the parties considered candidates who quoted as little as 500 US dollars for a one-day mediation, and as much as 60,000 US dollars for a three-day mediation, plus the cost of first-class travel from Europe to Asia and five days in a hotel.[38] Ultimately, the parties settled on an individual who charged 10,000 US dollars for a one-day mediation, plus travel costs.[39] Regardless, the point is that the parties should consider the extent to which they will regard fees (or an appropriate range of fees) among their threshold requirements, keeping in mind that they can vary substantially without reflecting much (if any) difference in experience or qualifications.[40]

Turning from logistical and practical considerations to the integrity of the process, the parties may further wish to consider the extent to which they desire neutrality, impartiality, independence, and the appearance of those qualities, to constitute threshold requirements for appointment. This also raises the question of whether a party should consciously promote candidates who, while formally neutral, seem more likely to sympathize with that party's perspective on the underlying business relationship, the dispute, or settlement options.[41] In this context, mediators can serve no useful function if they lose the trust of either party.[42] Thus, a mediator who lacks neutrality or impartiality in the sense of subjectively favouring and advancing the interests of one side will alienate the other side and, by doing

[33] Ibid., 203.
[34] Ibid., 201–2.
[35] Ibid.; see also Centre for Effective Dispute Resolution, 'The Sixth Mediation Audit' (22 May 2014), https://www.cedr.com/docslib/TheMediatorAudit2014.pdf (indicating that the average daily fee for experienced UK mediators amounted to 3,820 GB pounds, emphasizing that averages 'conceal a wide degree of variation' and providing a table listing the daily mediator fees charged by all survey respondents, which ranged from pro bono to between 6,001 and 6,500 GB pounds); Grant Morris, 'From Anecdote to Evidence: The New Zealand Commercial Mediation Market' (2016) 22(1) New Zealand Business Law Quarterly 10, https://papers.ssrn.com/soL3/papers.cfm?abstract_id=2923901 (indicating that daily mediation fees among New Zealand commercial mediators general range between 2,500 and 7,500 NZ dollars).
[36] McIlwrath and Savage (n 1) 201, 203.
[37] Ibid., 203.
[38] Ibid.
[39] Ibid.
[40] Ibid.
[41] See Salomon and Sharp (n 8) 70.
[42] Bercovitch and Houston, 'The Study of International Mediation' (n 8) 44.

so, destroy any prospects for cooperation and settlement.[43] For similar reasons, it seems counterproductive for parties to promote candidates who appear likely to slant their way.[44] In fact, each party has a strategic interest in promoting candidates that the *other* side will like and trust, inasmuch as cooperation and settlement remain the goals in mediation.[45]

Building on this point, while neutrality and impartiality likely constitute fundamental threshold requirements, the picture becomes more complicated when it comes to independence and the *appearance* of impartiality. While somewhat counterintuitive, a number of observers advise parties to consider appointment of mediators suggested by the adverse party,[46] possibly even mediators who have pre-existing relationships with the adverse party.[47] In their view, this may enhance the adverse party's sense of trust,[48] commitment to the process,[49] and flexibility.[50] It may also increase the mediator's influence when encouraging the adverse party to moderate its expectations.[51] According to one observer, this format works best when the mediator has a pre-existing relationship with the party who has more leverage, on the theory that the mediator will use his or her influence not to advance the interests of the more powerful party, but to encourage concessions that the more powerful party might not otherwise make.[52] In other words, leverage may sometimes count for more than independence and the appearance of impartiality in building momentum for settlement.[53]

When discussing neutrality and related concepts, observers often address the extent to which nationality should function as a threshold requirement when selecting mediators for international commercial disputes.[54] In arbitration, the nationality of sole arbitrators and tribunal chairs generally constitutes either an important consideration,[55] or a firm requirement in the sense that those individuals must not have the nationalities of any party,[56] and possibly their controlling shareholders.[57] In mediation, it may constitute a rule of thumb and an acceptable

[43] See Salomon and Sharp (n 8) 71; see also Abramson, 'Mining Mediation Rules' (n 8) 103.
[44] See McIlwrath and Savage (n 1) 190.
[45] Ibid.
[46] Abramson, *Mediation Representation* (n 8) 165; McIlwrath and Savage (n 1) 190; Salomon and Sharp (n 8) 71.
[47] Abramson, *Mediation Representation* (n 8) 154; Bercovitch and Houston, 'The Study of International Mediation' (n 8) 46; Bercovitch and Houston, 'Why Do They Do It Like This?' (n 8) 181.
[48] McIlwrath and Savage (n 1) 190, 199.
[49] Abramson, *Mediation Representation* (n 8) 165.
[50] Bercovitch and Houston, 'The Study of International Mediation' (n 8) 46.
[51] McIlwrath and Savage (n 1) 195.
[52] Kleiboer (n 8) 370.
[53] See Bercovitch and Houston, 'The Study of International Mediation' (n 8) 44–5.
[54] McIlwrath and Savage (n 1) 198–9; Salomon and Sharp (n 8) 71.
[55] Article 12(4) of the International Arbitration Rules of the American Arbitration Association (2014); Article 6(7) of the Arbitration Rules of the United Nations Commission on International Trade Law (UNCITRAL) (2010).
[56] Article 13(5) of the Arbitration Rules of the International Chamber of Commerce (ICC) (2017); Article 6.1 of the Arbitration Rules of the London Court of International Arbitration (LCIA).
[57] Article 6.2 of the LCIA Arbitration Rules.

starting point to favour candidates having nationalities other than those of the disputing parties,[58] subject to three qualifications. First, unless the parties place great importance on nationality,[59] this criterion probably functions a secondary or tertiary consideration when compared to factors like experience, credentials, training, rapport-building, patience, and persistence.[60] Second, nationality requirements may limit the pool of qualified candidates,[61] especially if applied in conjunction with language requirements. Third, as already suggested, parties may have incentives to agree to candidates having the nationality of the adverse party,[62] inasmuch as shared experience and background can promote trust[63] and thus enhance the mediator's influence over the adverse party.[64]

In short, parties should consider availability and fluency in the language of the mediation as threshold requirements for appointment. They may also want to consider the extent to which they view fees as a threshold requirement. Likewise, they may wish to consider the extent to which they regard neutrality, impartiality, independence, and the appearance of those qualities, as threshold requirements. While neutrality and impartiality probably constitute fundamental threshold requirements, people may have differing views at the margins when it comes to independence and the appearance of impartiality. In particular, parties may have good reasons to consent to mediators having the nationality of, and possibly a pre-existing relationship with, the adverse party.

B. Professional Qualifications

In selecting candidates for appointment as mediator in international commercial disputes, the parties should consider what professional qualifications would help to inspire a sense of trust and confidence in a mediator for the particular dispute.[65] As discussed in more detail later, these may include experience as mediator, subject-matter expertise, reputation and standing, as well as training and certification, including training and certification in mediating cross-cultural disputes.

One should begin by observing that the essential function of mediators involves a process of identifying differences and encouraging settlement of those differences. Because this process calls for skills that improve with practice,[66] the extent of mediation experience probably represents the most important professional

[58] Salomon and Sharp (n 8) 71.
[59] See McIlwrath and Savage (n 1) 198.
[60] See Abramson, *Mediation Representation* (n 8) 157.
[61] McIlwrath and Savage (n 1) 198.
[62] See (n 45–n 53) and accompanying text.
[63] See (n 48) and accompanying text.
[64] See (n 51) and accompanying text.
[65] See Alexander (n 8) 116.
[66] McIlwrath and Savage (n 1) 200.

qualification. Mediators who handle only a few matters per year probably lack sufficient opportunities to hone and improve their skills.[67] In addition, parties may find it difficult to solicit a robust body of feedback regarding candidates with slim track records. Therefore, parties should ask candidates the number of mediations they handle per year.[68] On the theory that relevant experience matters most,[69] they should also ask candidates about their experience in mediating commercial disputes of a 'similar type and complexity'.[70]

Closely related to the last point, parties may wish to consider the extent to which they prefer candidates with subject-matter expertise. While parties may reasonably focus on candidates having expertise in mediation as a process,[71] counsel often express a preference for mediators who also have experience in the subject matter of the dispute.[72] For example, where controversies largely involve disagreements over legal issues, the parties might prefer mediators who have some experience with the governing law.[73] However, because facts drive most disputes and because the factual context differs across industries, parties and counsel may prefer mediators who have experience in the relevant sector.[74] Particularly for complex matters in the construction,[75] energy, financial,[76] and technology fields,[77] a degree of subject-matter experience helps to ensure the parties and counsel that the mediator can get up to speed quickly and understand *their* dispute in the proper context.[78] However, while a degree of subject-matter expertise seems preferable,[79] the parties may wish to avoid too much of a good thing. As Hal Abramson has warned, a mediator who has too much subject-matter expertise may see himself or herself as the authority on the topic and, thus, tend to offer evaluations of the parties' respective cases, whether they want it or not.[80] Also, the more the parties insist on subject-matter expertise, the smaller the pool of mediators on which they have to draw.[81]

Experience and subject-matter expertise seem related to reputation and standing in the sense that the most popular mediators with the most relevant subject-matter

[67] Abramson, *Mediation Representation* (n 8) 152. But see Herbert Smith Freehills (n 1) 1.
[68] Ibid.
[69] See Salomon and Sharp (n 8) 72.
[70] McIlwrath and Savage (n 1) 200; see also Herbert Smith Freehills (n 1) 1.
[71] See Brennan (n 2) 146.
[72] Abramson, *Mediation Representation* (n 8) 153. But see Herbert Smith Freehills (n 1) 2.
[73] McIlwrath and Savage (n 1) 201. But see Salomon and Sharp (n 8) 72; Herbert Smith Freehills (n 1) 2.
[74] McIlwrath and Savage (n 1) 201. However, just because the parties are involved in specialized fields does not mean that the particular dispute necessarily requires a mediator with specialized knowledge; see Herbert Smith Freehills (n 1) 2. For example, 'insurers, construction companies, and financial institutions […] all routinely have commercial disputes with suppliers which have little to do with the industry sector in which they operate' (ibid.).
[75] McIlwrath and Savage (n 1) 201; Brennan (n 2) 146; Salomon and Sharp (n 8) 72.
[76] McIlwrath and Savage (n 1) 201.
[77] Brennan (n 2) 146; Salomon and Sharp (n 8) at 72.
[78] McIlwrath and Savage (n 1) 200–1; see also Herbert Smith Freehills (n 1) 2.
[79] Abramson, *Mediation Representation* (n 8) 153.
[80] Ibid., 153–4.
[81] Herbert Smith Freehills (n 1) 2.

expertise seem likely to enjoy a good reputation and high standing in the particular field. Regardless of whether this correlation exists, mediators who have developed substantial reputations and standing seem (at least marginally) better placed to inspire trust and confidence, all things being equal. Of course, the importance of reputation and standing may depend on the situation.[82] Certain parties may value reputation and standing more than others. Also, the importance of reputation and standing may wax or wane depending on the type of mediation that the parties want. For example, reputation and standing may play a significant role in evaluative mediations, where the mediator must give his or her opinion on one or more aspects of the case.[83] In these situations, the mediator's reputation and standing may increase the weight of his or her pronouncements. Viewed from this perspective, parties with strong cases may favour candidates with reputation and standing because they will want people with authority to communicate the strength of their cases to the other side.[84] By contrast, reputation and standing arguably have less importance in facilitative mediations where the mediators focus more on discussions about problem-solving and the interests of the parties.[85]

With respect to professional qualifications, parties should finally consider the extent to which they value mediator training and certification. According to some observers, training and certification represent important professional qualifications that rank high on the list of factors that one should take into account when selecting mediators.[86] While it seems difficult to argue against the relevance of training and certification, one might still question the value or weight to be given such factors. For example, in the absence of a clearly recognized gold standard in an emerging field, training and certification may only ensure a basic level of competence.[87] Although not useless, that level of accomplishment may, by itself, do little to inspire trust and confidence. Nor does it provide any assurance that the parties will get an exceptional, or exceptionally well-suited, mediator.[88]

In weighing the relative importance of training and certification, the author considers the following perspective to be helpful. One can imagine appointing experienced mediators who have relevant subject-matter expertise and strong reputations, but no recent training or any certifications. By contrast, one can hardly imagine appointing inexperienced mediators who have no relevant subject-matter expertise and no particular reputation, even if those individuals have received extensive mediation training and multiple certifications. Viewed from this perspective, one may suggest two propositions. First, training and certification

[82] See Salomon and Sharp (n 8) 70.
[83] Ibid.
[84] Ibid.
[85] Ibid.
[86] See Abramson, *Mediation Representation* (n 8) 151; Herbert Smith Freehills (n 1) 1.
[87] See Abramson, *Mediation Representation* (n 8) 152; McIlwrath and Savage (n 1) 193.
[88] See Diaz and Oretskin (n 8) 81.

almost certainly count for less than substantial experience. Second, by themselves, training and certification seem unlikely to make candidates suitable for appointment to mediate complex international commercial disputes.

In addition to generalized mediator training, some observers advise parties to seek candidates who have training in the cross-cultural aspects of international commercial disputes.[89] Again, one may concede the relevance of such training while still questioning the value or weight that it deserves in selecting mediators. To begin with, most disputes between sophisticated businesses from different national jurisdictions involve legitimate commercial differences.[90] Cultural differences almost never lie at the heart of such disputes.[91] Furthermore, while cultural misunderstandings can lead to gaffes and peripheral impasses in international mediations,[92] one should not exaggerate the extent to which cultural issues arise uniquely in the international context.[93] In culturally pluralistic societies, domestic mediations frequently involve participants from disparate cultural, ethnic, and regional backgrounds.[94] To the extent that experienced mediators have already encountered and navigated problems associated with cross-cultural interactions, one arguably may perceive less need for training aimed at the manifestation of similar phenomena in the context of cross-border disputes. Those issues may differ in degree, but they do not differ in kind. However, regardless of whether s/he acquires it through *training*, the mediator should possess appropriate cultural *knowledge* of both parties, not because cultural differences rank among the likely sources of conflict, but because knowledge of culture may improve the chances for settlement, both by promoting trust and by identifying values that may seem important to stakeholders in formulating creative settlement proposals.[95]

In short, when it comes to promoting trust and confidence, mediator experience probably represents the most important professional qualification. Counsel also tend to regard a degree of subject-matter expertise as an important factor to consider when selecting mediators for international commercial disputes. Depending on the situation, one or both parties might see reputation and standing as important factors. Although training and certification certainly have relevance, the importance of such qualifications seems more debatable. This observation applies both with respect to generalized training for international mediators, and with respect to training directed specifically at the cross-cultural aspects of international commercial mediation.

[89] See, e.g. Abramson, *Mediation Representation* (n 8) 156; Abramson, 'Selecting Mediators' (n 8) 254.
[90] McIlwrath and Savage (n 1) 199.
[91] Ibid., 199–200.
[92] Ibid., 200.
[93] Strong (n 3) 18.
[94] Ibid.
[95] See McIlwrath and Savage (n 1) 200.

C. Personal Qualities

Despite the emphasis on professional qualifications, mediation involves a social process and requires personal qualities likely to support the development of trust and confidence.[96] According to some observers, these personal qualities matter more than training and, possibly, even experience.[97] Perhaps the most important quality involves a concept that some describe fuzzily as 'people skills',[98] and that others describe more concretely as 'bonding',[99] or the capacity for 'rapport' building.[100] When mediators connect with them, the disputing parties tend to be 'more forthcoming with the information that the mediators need' to shape discussion.[101] Bonding also enhances trust, credibility, and the capacity of mediators to influence the disputing parties.[102]

In addition to rapport building, important personal characteristics include patience and persistence.[103] One might also describe this as a sense of optimism that allows the mediator to continue with equanimity, hope, and enthusiasm, even in the face of setbacks.[104] Other important qualities include preparation,[105] intelligence,[106] and creativity.[107] It goes without saying that all these qualities support the development of rapport, trust, and confidence.[108] In other words, these are not discrete qualities, but connected indicators of broader concepts associated with effective mediation.

D. Process Orientations

In addition to professional qualifications and personal qualities, parties should consider the kind of processes that seem most likely to assist them in reaching settlement, and they should seek mediators with compatible orientations. While not unique to the international context, consideration of process should address

[96] See Bercovitch (n 8) 751; see also Abramson, *Mediation Representation* (n 8) 154.
[97] See Diaz and Oretskin (n 8) 81.
[98] Ibid., 80.
[99] Abramson, *Mediation Representation* (n 8) 155.
[100] Ibid., 154–5.
[101] Ibid., 155.
[102] Ibid.
[103] Ibid., 155–6; see also Alexander (n 8) 116; Bercovitch (n 8) 750; Bercovitch and Houston, 'The Study of International Mediation' (n 8) 44.
[104] See Lela P. Love and Joseph B. Stulberg, 'The Uses of Mediation', in Andrea Kupfer Schneider and Christopher Honeyman (eds), *The Negotiator's Fieldbook: The Desk Reference for the Experienced Negotiator* (American Bar Association, 2006) 573, 574.
[105] Abramson, *Mediation Representation* (n 8) 155.
[106] Ibid.; Bercovitch (n 8) 750; Bercovitch and Houston, 'The Study of International Mediation' (n 8) 44.
[107] Abramson, *Mediation Representation* (n 8) 156; see also Bercovitch and Houston, 'The Study of International Mediation' (n 8) 44.
[108] Ibid., 155.

the type of mediation desired (facilitative versus evaluative), the mediator's perspective (viewing the dispute narrowly versus broadly), the level of client participation, and the frequency of caucuses.

Starting with the type of mediation, most readers probably understand the difference between facilitative mediation, in which mediators facilitate communication between the parties to help them problem-solve and bridge differences, and evaluative mediation, in which mediators express their opinions on the situation and how the dispute would turn out in the event of litigation or arbitration.[109] While facilitative mediation represents the prevailing trend,[110] parties from some cultures may be less familiar with this Western, problem-solving approach and may prefer a more directive style.[111] According to Abramson, this may hold true for parties from Islamic and Chinese cultures.[112] In addition, evaluative mediation can become useful when disagreements seem rooted in one party's misjudgement or selection bias.[113]

Although it can make sense to choose an evaluative process based either on cultural preferences or the nature of the dispute, sensitivity to the consequences of selecting an evaluative format is vital. First, in evaluative mediations, the mediator may express opinions before one or both parties are ready to accept negative assessments of their case.[114] Second, in evaluative mediations, counsel and party representatives are less likely to engage in problem solving and candid conversation.[115] To the contrary, they are more likely to withhold damaging information, hide flexibility, and present slanted arguments.[116] While these consequences might or might not seem acceptable, the point is that the parties should discuss and agree in advance on the type of mediation that will assist them, and they should seek candidates with compatible orientations.[117]

Turning to the mediator's perspective, will the mediator focus narrowly on the strengths and weaknesses of the legal case, or expand his or her perspective to include important business interests that would not be addressed in adjudication, and possibly the personal and relational interests of stakeholders?[118] Of course, a narrow focus makes more sense for evaluative mediations, whereas a broader perspective seems better suited to facilitative mediations.[119] In addition, the broader perspective may have more appeal to parties from Asian and South American

[109] Ibid., 161–2; McIlwrath and Savage (n 1) 189; Brennan (n 2) 146; Herbert Smith Freehills (n 1) 2.
[110] Cf. McIlwrath and Savage (n 1) 189.
[111] Abramson, *Mediation Representation* (n 8) 157.
[112] See Abramson, 'Selecting Mediators' (n 8) 265–8; see also Alexander (n 8) 117.
[113] Abramson, *Mediation Representation* (n 8) 162.
[114] McIlwrath and Savage (n 1) 189; see also Herbert Smith Freehills (n 1) 2.
[115] Abramson, 'Selecting Mediators' (n 8) 274.
[116] Ibid.
[117] According to Abramson, '[t]here is no more important decision in mediation representation than choosing the roles of your mediator', Abramson, 'Mining Mediation Rules' (n 8) 104.
[118] Abramson, *Mediation Representation* (n 8) 165–6.
[119] Cf. ibid., 166.

cultures, which place greater emphasis on relationships than on the details of contractual provisions.[120]

Turning to the level of client participation, one would expect lower levels of direct client involvement to be the norm in evaluative mediations and higher levels of direct client involvement to be the norm in facilitative mediations.[121] However, to the extent that one's clients present poorly, aggravate the other side, feel intimidated, or simply lack confidence, one might prefer mediators who can manage the process with little or no client participation.[122] Conversely, to the extent that one's clients come from cultures that place great value on relationships, one might prefer mediators who know how to involve clients actively in the process.

Finally, with respect to the frequency of caucuses, the question comes down to whether the parties prefer to work with the mediator separately or together in joint sessions.[123] According to some observers, parties from common law countries prefer mediators who make greater use of caucuses.[124] The same holds true for Japanese parties, who try to avoid direct conflict and who have long traditions of using intermediaries in the course of conflict resolution.[125] By contrast, some observers indicate that parties from continental European countries prefer mediators who do not caucus, or who do so only selectively.[126] Again, the point is that the parties should discuss and agree in advance on the format that seems most likely to assist them, and they should seek candidates with compatible orientations.

III. Gathering Information About Candidates

Having identified the desired constellation of threshold requirements, professional qualifications, personal qualities, and process orientations, the parties must undertake one of the most challenging parts of international commercial mediation: finding candidates who actually meet those, or at least most of those, criteria.[127] Given the emerging nature of international mediation practice,[128] the parties may have to draw on a patchwork of sources, including dispute-settlement institutions, mediator databases, word-of-mouth, and recommendations made by the adverse party.

Starting with dispute-settlement institutions, a number of institutions that focus on mediation and international commercial arbitration can assist the parties in

[120] See Abramson, 'Selecting Mediators' (n 8) 253–4.
[121] See Abramson, *Mediation Representation* (n 8) 166.
[122] Ibid.
[123] Ibid., 167.
[124] McIlwrath and Savage (n 1) 197.
[125] Abramson, *Mediation Representation* (n 8) 173.
[126] See McIlwrath and Savage (n 1) 197; see also ibid., 167, 171.
[127] See McIlwrath and Savage (n 1) 188; Herbert Smith Freehills (n 1) 1.
[128] See (n 4–n 9) and accompanying text.

identifying candidates and appointing mediators. Certain mediation institutions, e.g. JAMS in the United States and the Centre for Effective Dispute Resolution (CEDR) in London, maintain lists of mediators and are willing to propose suitable candidates at no cost.[129] Others, such as the International Institute for Conflict Prevention and Resolution (CPR) in New York, charge for access to their lists.[130] On the positive side, mediation institutions generally have access to feedback about the individuals on their lists, can exclude poorly performing mediators, and can promote better performing mediators, all of which ensures a measure of quality control.[131] However, some observers caution that these institutions generally focus on domestic mediations, meaning that candidates may have little or no experience in mediating international commercial disputes.[132]

As an alternative to mediation institutions, parties can seek assistance from institutions that focus on international commercial arbitration, but that also administer international commercial mediations. For example, the American Arbitration Association's International Center for Dispute Resolution (ICDR), the International Chamber of Commerce (ICC), and the London Court of International Arbitration (LCIA) all fall into this category.[133] These institutions do not maintain lists or pools of international commercial mediators, but take a 'go-to-market' approach in identifying candidates suitable for particular disputes.[134] On the positive side, these institutions specialize in the resolution of international commercial disputes and have strong reputations, meaning that they also have incentives to maintain and enhance their standing in the field. However, international arbitration institutions charge substantial fees for their services, including for mediation services.[135] For example, as of this writing, the ICC requires a non-refundable deposit 2,000 US dollars for mediations conducted under its rules, which the parties can apply to administrative expenses that can range between 5,000 and 30,000 US dollars depending on the amounts in controversy.[136] These do not include the fees of the mediator.[137] The LCIA requires a non-refundable filing fee of 750 GB pounds, plus hourly charges for time incurred by LCIA administrative staff, which can range from 100 to 225 GB pounds per hour, depending on the person and the activity involved.[138] The ICDR requires a non-refundable 250 US dollar deposit, which the parties can apply to administrative expenses equal to 75 US dollars for each hour charged by the mediator.[139]

129 McIlwrath and Savage (n 1) 191; Brennan (n 2) 146.
130 Ibid.
131 See McIlwrath and Savage (n 1) 191.
132 Ibid.
133 Ibid., 192.
134 Ibid.
135 Ibid.
136 Appendix on Fees and Costs to the ICC Mediation Rules (2014) , Articles 1–2.
137 Ibid., Article 3.
138 Schedule of LCIA Mediation Costs (2012), paras 1(a)–(b).
139 ICDR Mediation—Administrative Fee Schedules (2017).

In addition to cost, another potential drawback of relying on international arbitration institutions involves their comparatively low levels of experience in appointing mediators.[140] While the mediation caseload of these institutions has grown quickly,[141] the number of mediations that they handle remains low,[142] whether measured in absolute or relative terms. For example, one observer suggests that the number of new mediations administered by the ICC during 2013 probably amounted to a number somewhere in the upper 20s,[143] whereas the corresponding number for new arbitrations for the ICC in 2013 came to 767 new matters.[144] The same observer reports that the number of new mediations administered by the ICDR during 2012 and 2013 totalled 105 and 74,[145] respectively, whereas the corresponding number for new arbitrations for the ICDR in 2012 and 2013 came to 996 and 1,165 new matters, respectively.[146] These numbers do not suggest the existence of any shortfall in quality with respect to the mediation services provided by international arbitration institutions. The numbers only indicate that international arbitration institutions naturally have less experience with mediation than institutions that have made mediation their *raison d'être*.[147]

In addition to mediation institutions, a number of organizations maintain publicly searchable databases of mediators.[148] For example, the Netherlands-based International Mediation Institute (IMI) maintains a database of individuals who have satisfied the organization's criteria for certification as meditators.[149] As of this writing, that database includes 671 profiles.[150] To the extent that parties may find it valuable, the IMI database also permits users to search for individuals who have earned an additional certification in 'intercultural competence', although the search function returns no names as of this writing.[151] Some observers have also mentioned Mediate.com as a source of information about potential candidates.[152] On both sites, users may search for mediators by geographical location. On the IMI website, users may also search by languages spoken and, on the Mediate.com website, users may search by type of matter. On both sites, most entries have detailed biographical information. Some entries also include names

[140] McIlwrath and Savage (n 1) 192.
[141] Ibid.; Sicard-Mirabal and Clarke (n 3) 167–8.
[142] E.g. McIlwrath and Savage (n 1) 187, 192.
[143] See Rhodes (n 7) 178–9.
[144] Markus Altenkirch and Jan Frohloff, 'International Arbitration Statistics 2016—Busy Times for Arbitral Institutions' Global Arbitration News [online] 26 June 2017, https://globalarbitrationnews.com/international-arbitration-statistics-2016-busy-times-for-arbitral-institutions/.
[145] Rhodes (n 7) 182.
[146] Altenkirch and Frohloff (n 144).
[147] See McIlwrath and Savage (n 1) 192.
[148] Ibid., 193.
[149] Ibid.; see also Abramson, *Mediation Representation* (n 8) 152; Alexander (n 8) 122–3; Brennan (n 2) 146.
[150] See International Mediation Institute, 'Find a Mediator', https://www.imimediation.org/find-a-mediator/.
[151] Ibid.
[152] McIlwrath and Savage (n 1) 193.

and contact information for references. They do not, however, appear to include user feedback.[153]

While database entries may provide helpful information about professional qualifications, they do not capture the personal qualities that may be even more important to parties, and at the front of their minds.[154] Also, to the extent that database entries provide qualitative information relating to things like process orientation, candidates tend to describe themselves so broadly that the entries provide few candid and helpful insights into their default or preferred mediation styles. To collect information about personal qualities and mediation styles, one may at least initially have to direct 'word-of-mouth' inquiries to trusted peers, who may or may not have direct experience with the candidates.[155] While the same sort of phenomenon exists in international commercial arbitration,[156] one ventures to say that the public and private information networks probably are more robust in that field than in international commercial mediation.[157]

As a final source of information about candidates, a number of observers support consideration of individuals proposed by the adverse party.[158] As already indicated, this approach offers several advantages.[159] First, every party has an interest in selecting mediators that the other side will like and trust.[160] Second, deferring to reasonable nominations made by the other party manifests the trust and cooperation needed to settle disputes.[161] Third, if allowed to nominate the mediator, the adverse party may feel more invested in the mediation process.[162] And fourth, a mediator nominated by the adverse party may have greater influence over that party when it comes to moderating settlement expectations.[163]

In short, gathering information about potential candidates represents one of the most challenging parts of international mediation due both to the importance of generating a suitable pool and to the difficulty of piecing together helpful intelligence from a patchwork of imperfect sources. These sources include mediation institutions, international arbitration institutions, public databases, and

[153] Contra ibid.

[154] Ibid., 190.

[155] Ibid.

[156] See Susan D. Franck, 'The Role of International Arbitrators' (2006) 12 International Law Student Association Journal of International and Comparative Law 499, 516; Lucy Greenwood and Ann Ryan Robertson, 'Choosing the Right Energy Arbitrator' CIArb News [online] 3 February 2017, http://www.ciarb.org/news/ciarb-news/news-detail/features/2017/02/03/choosing-the-right-energy-arbitrator; Arbitrator Intelligence, 'About', https://www.arbitratorintelligence.org/about-us/.

[157] Ibid.; see also Eric Gottwald, 'Leveling the Playing Field: Is it Time for a Legal Assistance Program for Developing Nations in Investment Treaty Arbitration?' (2007) 22 American University International Law 237, 257.

[158] Abramson, *Mediation Representation* (n 8) 165; McIlwrath and Savage (n 1) 190; Salomon and Sharp (n 8) 71.

[159] See (n 48–n 53, n 62–n 64) and accompanying text.

[160] See (n 45) and accompanying text.

[161] See (n 48) and accompanying text.

[162] See (n 49) and accompanying text.

[163] See (n 51) and accompanying text.

word-of-mouth. In addition, parties should at least remain open to candidates proposed by the other side, just as they would want the other side to respond with sympathetic consideration to any candidates suggested.

IV. Vetting Shortlisted Candidates

Having assembled a shortlist of candidates who meet the threshold requirements and who possess the desired professional qualifications, the parties will want to vet the finalists to get a better sense of their personal qualities and mediation styles. Ideally, this process should include interviews both with the finalists[164] and with references who have had direct experience in mediations conducted by the finalists.[165]

In international commercial arbitration, the process of interviewing candidates has become mainstream,[166] but even so remains controversial.[167] When it comes to interviews in the context of arbitration, the concern is that counsel or party representatives will engage arbitrator candidates in *ex parte* discussions regarding the merits of the case or other sensitive topics, with the result that the discussions may compromise the candidates' independence or impartiality.[168] The same concern does not apply to interviews conducted with candidates in international mediation for the simple reason that most parties expect to engage mediators in at least some *ex parte* discussions regarding the merits and other sensitive topics.[169] In fact, the success of the mediation may depend on this.[170] Nevertheless, to avoid misunderstandings and even the appearance of impropriety, parties should disclose that they intend to interview shortlisted candidates and that they expect the other side to do the same.[171]

In his book, *Mediation Representation*, Abramson identifies several lines of questions that parties may wish to pursue with candidates for appointment in international commercial mediation.[172] These include some basic questions relating to threshold requirements, such as conflicts of interest.[173] Topics might include prior

[164] Abramson, *Mediation Representation* (n 8) 177; McIlwrath and Savage (n 1) 194.

[165] Abramson, *Mediation Representation* (n 8); Alexander (n 8) 116; Herbert Smith Freehills (n 1) 1.

[166] See Nigel Blackaby, Constantine Partasides, Alan Redfern, and Martin Hunter, *Redfern and Hunter on International Arbitration* (5th edn, OUP, 2009) 264; Julian D. M. Lew, Loukas A. Mistelis, and Stefan M. Kröll, *Comparative International Commercial Arbitration* (Kluwer Law International, 2003) 232.

[167] Catherine Rogers, 'A Window into the Soul of International Arbitration: Arbitrator Selection, Transparency and Stakeholder Interests' (2015) 46 Victoria University of Wellington Law Review 1179, 1186; see also Blackaby et al. (n 166) 264; Lew et al. (n 166) 233; Moses (n 23) 129.

[168] Blackaby et al. (n 166) 26; Lew et al. (n 166) 232; Moses (n 23) 128, 130.

[169] McIlwrath and Savage (n 1) 194; see also Herbert Smith Freehills (n 1) 1.

[170] Ibid.

[171] Ibid.

[172] Abramson, *Mediation Representation* (n 8) 179–81.

[173] Ibid., 179–80.

knowledge of the parties, their lawyers, and the facts of the dispute.[174] In addition, parties may wish to inquire about conceptual issues, e.g. how candidates deal with impasses that arise in the course of mediation.[175] Topics might include their approach to impasses due to incompatible predictions about the merits of the case, as well as impasses due to interpersonal frictions between stakeholders.[176] Finally, the parties may wish to ask a series of questions about process. These might include general topics, e.g. the frequency of caucuses, the extent of direct client involvement, the candidates' disposition to provide evaluations, as well as the reasons that candidates favour particular approaches.[177] While probably less important, parties might also inquire about anticipated procedural steps, such as pre-mediation contacts with the parties and the use of opening statements during the mediation, as well as the candidates' reasons for valuing those steps. To ensure candid responses, parties should take care not to ask these questions in a way that telegraphs their preferences.[178] While recognizing that the importance of any topic may depend on the facts of the particular case, Abramson sensibly advises that the candidates' approach to impasses probably represents the most important topic, inasmuch as the parties clearly have experienced impasses and must overcome them in order for the mediation to succeed.[179]

In addition to the questions for candidates, Abramson identifies a number of lines of questions that parties may wish to pursue during reference calls.[180] Not surprisingly, the topics generally call for objective assessments of personal qualities, which candidates cannot directly provide and which may be difficult to glean from relatively short interviews with the candidates themselves. Topics include the candidates' ability to cultivate rapport, as well as their patience and persistence, preparedness, intelligence, and creativity in terms of reframing the dispute.[181] While recognizing that the importance of any topic may depend on the facts of the particular case, Abramson sensibly advises that the capacity for rapport building and persistence generally represent the most important topics to address during reference calls.[182]

In short, the vetting of shortlisted candidates should include two sets of interviews and should focus on collecting information about personal qualities and mediation styles. Due to the expectation that parties will have *ex parte* discussions of the merits with mediators during the mediation process, they can interview candidates with fewer constraints than would be the case for international

[174] Ibid.
[175] Ibid., 180.
[176] Ibid.
[177] Ibid.
[178] Ibid., 179.
[179] Ibid., 181.
[180] Ibid., 181–2.
[181] Ibid.
[182] Ibid., 182.

arbitration. In those interviews, the most important questions may relate to how the candidates handle impasses. By contrast, when interviewing references, the most important questions may relate to the capacity for rapport building and persistence.

V. Special Problems Related to Mediator Selection

In an ideal world, the parties would identify candidates, formulate a shortlist, agree on their preferred candidate, and feel a growing sense of trust and confidence in that person throughout the mediation. In reality, however, things can go wrong. Two variations deserve particular attention because they relate either to the ability to get the mediation off the ground, or to the feasibility of continuing the proceedings. In the first variation, the parties may find themselves unable to agree on which mediator to appoint. In the second variation, the parties may initially agree on the choice of mediator, but subsequently one party may reach the conclusion that it placed its trust and confidence in the wrong person.

When the parties fail to agree on a mediator there is, and there is not, an easy solution to the impasse. For mediations conducted under institutional rules, the easy technical solution is for the institution to appoint the mediator based either on the candidate with the highest overall favourability rating among the disputing parties,[183] or based on the institution's exercise of discretion.[184] While technically a feasible way to get a mediator in place, institutional appointments hardly represent an appealing option. Simply put, the parties' failure even to agree even on a candidate bodes poorly for the mediation, the mediator's influence, and the cooperation required to bring the parties to settlement.[185] Thus, in the event that the parties initially cannot agree on a mediator, they might wish to reconsider either their positions on the topic of appointment, or the utility of continuing with the mediation process.

Even when parties initially agree on a mediator, it sometimes happens that one side subsequently concludes that it placed its trust and confidence in the wrong person. While the loss of trust and confidence in the neutral does not constitute a desirable state of affairs, the consequences of this development loom much smaller in mediation than in arbitration.[186] In arbitration, dissatisfied parties cannot challenge arbitrators except for cause,[187] and such efforts do not often succeed.[188] Nor

[183] Rule 4(b) of the ICDR Mediation Rules (2014).
[184] Rule 4(c) of the ICDR Mediation Rules (2014); see also Article 5(2) of the ICC Mediation Rules (2014); Brennan (n 2) 146.
[185] See McIlwrath and Savage (n 1) 191.
[186] Abramson, 'Mining Mediation Rules' (n 8) 104.
[187] Ibid.; see also Blackaby et al. (n 166) 274–7; Lew et al. (n 166) 303–7; Moses (n 23) 140–1.
[188] Ibid., 141–2; see also Lew et al. (n 166) 303.

can dissatisfied parties unilaterally terminate arbitration proceedings,[189] which may continue for months or even years.[190] By contrast, in mediation, dissatisfied parties can unilaterally withdraw at any point and, thus, terminate the proceedings.[191] Even if they choose not to take that drastic step, the entire process may last only a few weeks, and the mediation itself often lasts only a day.[192] In other words, the compressed time frame and the possibility of exit help to ensure that international commercial mediation constitutes a low-risk dispute settlement option, even when things do not go according to plan.

VI. Conclusion

International commercial mediation involves a collaborative process that assists parties in settling differences while preserving relationships and avoiding the time, cost, and uncertainties associated with adjudication. While it has grown in popularity,[193] and even become a focus in the dispute settlement policies of some leading multi-national corporations,[194] international commercial mediation remains an emerging field.[195] Whether measured in absolute or relative terms, the number of matters submitted to international commercial mediation continues to be low.[196]

Under these circumstances, it should come as no surprise that potential users will find only a small body of literature on selection of mediators, with commentators often expressing different views on important topics.[197] Hopefully, this chapter contributes to the understanding of the mediator selection process, articulates a fresh perspective on structural approaches to this critical step, and supplies potential users with helpful practical tools and insights relating to the qualities that they should seek in mediators, the process of collecting information about candidates, the vetting of individuals on the shortlist, and the navigation of problems when things do not go according to plan.

[189] See Blackaby et al. (n 166) 426. An exception involves the highly unusual case where a claimant initiates proceedings but fails to communicate its statement of claim, which can result in dismissal of the proceedings. Ibid., 163.

[190] See (n 23) and accompanying text.

[191] Abramson, 'Mining Mediation Rules' (n 8) 104.

[192] See (n 24) and accompanying text.

[193] See (n 3) 141 and accompanying text.

[194] Strong (n 3) 38; see also Tibor Varady, John J. Barceló, and Arthur Taylor Von Mehren, *International Commercial Arbitration* (5th edn, Thomson/West, 2012) 27–8.

[195] See (n 4–n 9) and accompanying text.

[196] See (n 4) 142–6 and accompanying text.

[197] See (n 8–n 9) and accompanying text.

17

The Confidentiality and Transparency Debate in Commercial and Investment Mediation

*Chester Brown and Phoebe Winch**

I. Introduction

It is often said that an important feature of mediation is that confidentiality attaches to mediation proceedings.[1] This is said regardless of whether mediation takes place in a commercial or investment setting, as confidentiality is seen as enabling the frank discussions necessary for parties to reach a negotiated settlement, facilitated by a mediator. Confidentiality can (obviously) be contrasted with the concept of transparency, which, by its nature, is likely to reduce the confidentiality of a mediation process.[2] At the outset, it should be noted that the importance of transparency in the context of investment mediation is arguably far greater than it is in the context of commercial mediation. By their very nature, investor–state proceedings demand the involvement of the host state as an actor, and put in issue the host state's ability to adopt regulatory measures as part of its sovereign functions, and therefore invariably concern subject matter that sparks a public interest frequently lacking in the commercial context. Thus, the tensions that exist between the imperatives of confidentiality and transparency give rise to different considerations in commercial mediation as compared with investment mediation.

This chapter firstly explores the genesis of the confidentiality and transparency debate—in international arbitration—and how it has unfolded in the arbitral

* Any views expressed in this chapter are personal in nature and do not necessarily reflect the views of the authors' employers or any organizations with which the authors are presently or have in the past been affiliated.

[1] See, e.g. Tania Sourdin, *Alternative Dispute Resolution* (4th edn, Thomson Reuters, 2012) 389–405; Laurence Boulle, *Mediation: Principles, Process, Practice* (3rd edn, LexisNexis Butterworths, 2011) 669–74; Hilary Astor and Christine Chinkin, *Dispute Resolution in Australia* (2nd edn, LexisNexis Butterworths, 2002) 178–86.

[2] Often used to refer to a number of concepts in the mediation context, the concept of 'transparency' discussed in this chapter is used to focus on the transparency of mediation proceedings, as opposed to the broader notion of transparency, touching on issues such as transparency in third-party funding and in the appointment and compensation of arbitrators: UNCITRAL, 'Report of Working Group III (Investor–State Dispute Settlement Reform) on the work of its thirty-fourth session – Part I', UN Doc A/CN.9/930, Vienna, 27 November–1 December 2017, paras 78–81.

setting. As with mediation, a widely understood characteristic of arbitration is the confidentiality that frequently attaches to arbitration proceedings, whether by way of the parties' agreement or the operation of the *lex arbitri* (which may differ from jurisdiction to jurisdiction). While the confidentiality of arbitral proceedings continues to exist in the commercial context in many jurisdictions, the last two decades have seen a demonstrable trend towards increased transparency in investor–state dispute settlement (ISDS). To enhance transparency in the investment sphere, various mechanisms have been adopted that have led to an improvement in transparency levels.[3] These include the revisions of institutional rules, such as the International Centre for Settlement of Investment Disputes (ICSID) Rules of Arbitration, the development of the United Nations Commission on International Trade Law (UNCITRAL) Rules on Transparency in Treaty-Based Investor–State Arbitration (Transparency Rules), and the incorporation of transparency standards into international investment agreements, or IIAs (section II).

Section III discusses the manner in which the debate over confidentiality and transparency has developed in the context of commercial and investment mediation. For the purposes of this chapter, the term 'mediation' refers to a process in which a neutral third party assists the parties by promoting through various activities an amicable accord resolving a dispute.[4] The term is employed in its broadest sense, to encompass 'conciliation', notwithstanding the distinction international law may draw between the two processes.[5] Mediation has become an attractive alternative to arbitration, often resulting in earlier settlement of disputes and an associated decrease in time and cost. In light of its confidential nature, however, mediation use by parties to resolve their differences suffers from the same criticisms that can be levelled at arbitration: that it favours secrecy at the expense of transparency. This tension is explored, as is the balance struck between the two values in the current framework governing mediation. As will become apparent, there has been greater preservation of confidentiality in mediation than in arbitral proceedings. Section IV justifies the heightened protection afforded to confidentiality in

[3] Steffen Hindelang, 'Study on Investor–State Dispute Settlement (ISDS) and Alternatives to Dispute Resolution in International Investment Law' (2016) 1 TDM, www.transnational-dispute-management.com/article.asp?key=2313.

[4] Jack Coe, Jr, 'Settlement of Investor–State Disputes through Mediation: Preliminary Remarks on Processes, Problems and Prospects', in R. Doak Bishop (ed.), *Enforcement of Arbitral Awards against Sovereigns* (JurisNet/LLC, 2009) 81–2.

[5] E.g. the Permanent Court of Arbitration (PCA) Optional Conciliation Rules expressly use the words 'conciliation' and 'mediation' interchangeably; see Guide to Enactment and Use of the UNCITRAL Model Law on International Commercial Conciliation, 2002, para. 20; see also Jack Coe, Jr, 'Toward a Complementary Use of Conciliation in Investor–State Disputes: A Preliminary Sketch' (2005) 12 (7) University of California Davis Journal of International Law and Policy 7, 14. In contrast, Article 33(1) of the United Nations Charter refers to 'mediation' and 'conciliation' as distinct methods of international dispute settlement. See also Christian Tomuschat, 'Article 33', in Bruno Simma, Daniel Erasmus-Kahn, Georg Nolte, and Andreas Paulus (eds), *The Charter of the United Nations: A Commentary*, vol. I (3rd edn, OUP, 2012) 1078.

mediation and advocates the increased use of mediation in settling international disputes, in particular, investor–state disputes.

II. The Confidentiality and Transparency Debate

A. Origins of the Debate

The origins of the confidentiality and transparency debate in international mediation may be traced back to the origins of investor–state arbitration and, even, international commercial arbitration.[6] The initial framework for ISDS, established primarily by IIAs, such as bilateral investment treaties (BITs) and the investment chapters in free trade agreements (FTAs), provided for dispute resolution governed by mechanisms and rules inspired by international commercial arbitration.[7] Since confidentiality has been, and continues to be, a prominent feature of international commercial arbitration in many jurisdictions and under many sets of institutional rules, these mechanisms arguably resulted in the assumption that the same level of confidentiality also attached to investor–state proceedings. An inevitable conflict arose when these mechanisms were transposed to the investor–state context, in which a trend towards transparency was emerging, since the 'notion that any part of the arbitral process should be exposed to public view runs directly counter to a deeply ingrained perceived advantage of international commercial arbitration, which is that it exists for the *confidential* resolution of the dispute, as between the parties to it.'[8]

1. Investor–state arbitration

In the last three decades, there has been a proliferation in investor–state disputes. The primary form of resolving these disputes is arbitration, with a total of 817 publicly known cases commenced under treaties to date.[9] Notwithstanding its apparent popularity, certain participants in the ISDS regime, as well as other stakeholders, have recently expressed a growing dissatisfaction with features of the arbitral process which is used to settle investment disputes. One such criticism—the focus of this chapter—is its perceived lack of transparency.[10]

[6] Hindelang (n 3).

[7] UNCITRAL, 'Settlement of Commercial Disputes: Preparation of Rules of Uniform Law on Transparency in Treaty-Based Investor–State Dispute Settlement', UN Doc A/CN.9/WG.II/WP.160, 5 August 2010, para. 5; Campbell McLachlan, 'Investment Treaty Arbitration: The Legal Framework', in Albert Jan van den Berg (ed.), *50 Years of the New York Convention: ICCA International Arbitration Conference*, vol. 8 (Kluwer Law International, 2009) 98–100.

[8] Ibid., 130 (emphasis in original).

[9] UNCTAD, 'Special Update on Investor–State Dispute Settlement: Facts and Figures', 3 IIA Issues Note (November 2017).

[10] Gabriele Ruscalla, 'Transparency in International Arbitration: Any (Concrete) Need to Codify the Standard?' (2015) 3 (1) Groningen Journal of International Law 1, 2.

Transparency in ISDS is considered desirable in light of the involvement of the host state in the proceedings and the public interest in the subject matter of the dispute. The nature of investor–state arbitration is such that highly sensitive political issues will often be considered by the investment tribunals.[11] Indeed, there is usually a question of public policy at the core of an investor–state dispute concerning the conduct of the host state in taking certain measures that are challenged by the investor as constituting a breach of the host state's treaty obligations. It has been said that the public has a 'vital interest' in securing the integrity of such proceedings, which review administrative, judicial, and legislative acts of the host state.[12] Equally, enhanced transparency could alleviate possible concerns on the part of the host state of criticism and 'losing face' by settling a dispute on confidential terms. According to a 2017 Survey on Obstacles to Settlement of Investor–State Disputes conducted by the National University of Singapore's Centre for International Law, allegations of future prosecution for corruption and public and/or political criticism were among the primary obstacles preventing the state from settling a dispute.[13]

In addition, the disputes could lead to large potential monetary liability for public treasuries due to legal costs incurred by the state,[14] and substantial claims made by the investor,[15] as expenditure of public funds would usually be required to satisfy such liability.[16] For these reasons, among others, calls were increasingly made for the adoption of additional transparency measures which would serve to enhance public acceptance of investment arbitration (explored in section B).[17]

2. International commercial arbitration

Participants in international commercial arbitration proceedings have not experienced a similar trend towards greater transparency. The commercial sphere

[11] E.g. investment tribunals have been called upon to rule on the phasing out of nuclear power in Germany (*Vattenfall AB and others v Federal Republic of Germany*, ICSID Case No. ARB/12/12) and the introduction of plain packaging for cigarettes to address health risks related to smoking in Australia (*Philip Morris Asia Limited v The Commonwealth of Australia*, UNCITRAL, PCA Case No. 2012-12); see also, generally, Hindelang (n 3).

[12] Ibid.

[13] Centre for International Law, National University of Singapore, 'Report: Survey on Obstacles to Settlement of Investor–State Disputes' (26 May 2017), 11–13.

[14] UNCITRAL (n 2), para. 29.

[15] In 2017, the average amount claimed in investor–state arbitrations was 1.35 billion US dollars, and the average amount awarded to successful claimants was 522 million US dollars: UNCTAD Annual Report 2017, 5.

[16] Jeswald Salacuse, 'Is There a Better Way? Alternative Methods of Treaty-Based, Investor–State Dispute Resolution' (2007) 31 Fordham International Law Journal 401, 403–5; see also, Roberto Echandi, 'Complementing Investor–State Dispute Resolution: A Conceptual Framework for Investor–State Conflict Management' in Roberto Echandi and Pierre Sauvé (eds), *Prospects in International Investment Law and Policy* (CUP, 2013) 270, 291–3.

[17] See OECD, 'Transparency and Third-Party Participation in Investor–State Dispute Settlement Procedures' (OECD Working Papers on International Investment 2005/01, OECD Publishing). UNCITRAL, 'Report of the Working Group on Arbitration and Conciliation on the work of its forty-eighth session' UN Doc A/CN.9/646, New York, 4–8 February 2008, 41st Session, para. 69.

generally lacks the same public interest element warranting increased transparency as in investor–state arbitration.[18] Accordingly, it has been said that confidentiality remains an 'essential feature' of international commercial arbitration,[19] upon which users of this form of dispute resolution place the 'highest value'.[20] While national legal systems do not have a uniform approach to finding that there is an implied duty of confidentiality in international commercial arbitration, the general acceptance of confidentiality is greater than in the investment context, subject to broadly recognized exceptions, e.g. where there is consent, express or implied, where there is an order, or leave of the court, or where the interests of justice require disclosure.[21] It has therefore been said in the context of international commercial arbitration that the adoption of measures to enhance transparency, e.g. a publication policy or indeed 'any other policy which would mitigate or diminish the strict insistence on confidentiality', may constitute a deterrent to the use of commercial arbitration.[22]

B. Transparency Mechanisms

In recent years, treaties and institutional rules have been amended and new instruments have been developed to combat the criticisms outlined and to increase transparency in ISDS. These initiatives to promote transparency generally address public access to documents and hearings, and the participation of third parties (*amicus curiae*) in proceedings.[23] In light of the focus of this chapter on mediation, three key initiatives to increase transparency are noted but not explored in great detail.

The first initiative lies in the recent revisions to the procedural rules most frequently used in investor–state disputes, being those contained in the ICSID Convention, namely the ICSID Arbitration Rules and the ICSID (Additional

[18] Cf Gary Born, *International Commercial Arbitration* (2nd edn, Kluwer Law International 2014) 2823 ff, arguing that the differences between the two contexts are less significant than might appear and the rationale for differing treatments is less compelling than sometimes suggested.

[19] UNCITRAL (n 17) para. 57.

[20] Stephen Bond, 'Expert Report of Stephen Bond Esq (in *Esso/BHP v Plowman*)' (1995) 11 (3) Arbitration International 273. According to the 2018 International Arbitration Survey published by the Queen Mary University of London and White & Case LLP, confidentiality and privacy are considered to be amongst the most valuable characteristics of international arbitration: 'International Arbitration Survey: The Evolution of International Arbitration' (2018) 7, available at https://www.whitecase.com/publications/insight/2018-international-arbitration-survey-evolution-international-arbitration.

[21] See William Kenny, 'Transparency in Investor State Arbitration' (2016) 33 (5) Kluwer Law International 471, 481–9; exceptions recognized in *Emmott v Michael Wilson & Partners Limited* (2008) EWCA Civ 184, [93]–[102], [107].

[22] Bond (n 20) 273–4, former Secretary General of the Court of International Arbitration of the International Chamber of Commerce (ICC) speaking in the context of ICC arbitration.

[23] UNCITRAL, 'Report of Working Group II (Arbitration and Conciliation) on the work of its fifty-third session' UN Doc A/CN.9/712 Vienna, 4–8 October 2010, 44th session, para. 31.

Facility) Arbitration Rules,[24] which did not originally deal extensively with the issues of confidentiality and transparency.[25] In 2006, amendments were made to the ICSID Rules addressing, inter alia, the use of *amicus curiae* briefs from non-disputing parties,[26] and the participation of non-parties to the arbitration.[27]

The second initiative is the adoption in 2013 of the Transparency Rules by UNCITRAL Working Group II, and by UNCITRAL and the United Nations General Assembly.[28] The Transparency Rules are the first to have 'mandated transparency throughout the arbitral process'.[29] Like the ICSID Arbitration Rules, the Transparency Rules provide for public hearings,[30] and the participation in the arbitral proceedings of *amici curiae* and non-disputing parties to the relevant IIA.[31] However, the Transparency Rules go further by requiring the disclosure of a wide range of information submitted to and issued by the tribunals, to be made public by a central repository.[32] The rules provide for two exceptions to transparency: confidential or protected information and integrity of the arbitral process.[33]

A notable drawback of the Transparency Rules is their limited application.[34] Progress has, however, been made through the entry into force of the United Nations Convention on Transparency in Treaty-Based Investor–State Arbitration,[35] which

[24] Because the ICSID Arbitration Rules and the ICSID (Additional Facility) Rules are in relevant respects identical, they are treated together as 'the ICSID Arbitration Rules' for the sake of convenience.

[25] See Articles 36(3), 48(5) of the ICSID Convention; Rule 32(2) of the ICSID Arbitration Rules (1984).

[26] A new paragraph was inserted into existing Rule 37 to provide authority for the tribunal, after consulting both parties, to allow a non-disputing party to file written submissions following inconsistent decisions from ICSID tribunals: see *Aguas del Tunari v Bolivia* (ICSID Case No ARB/02/3, Decision on Jurisdiction of 21 October 2005), para. 17; *Suez, Sociedad General de Aguas de Barcelona SA, and Vivendi Universal SA v Argentine Republic* (ICSID Case No ARB/03/19, Order in response to a Petition for Transparency and Participation as Amicus Curiae of 19 May 2005), para. 16.

[27] See, generally, Antonio R Parra, 'The Development of the Regulations and Rules of the International Centre for Settlement of Investment Disputes' (2007) 22 (1) ICSID Review–Foreign Investment Law Journal 55–68, 65 ff.

[28] UNGA Resolution 68/109 (16 December 2013), "United Nations Commission on International Trade Law Rules on Transparency in Treaty-Based Investor–State Arbitration and Arbitration Rules (as revised in 2010, with new article 1, para. 4), as adopted in 2013)", available at http://www.uncitral.org.

[29] Lise Johnson and Nathalie Bernasconi-Osterwalder, 'New UNCITRAL Arbitration Rules on Transparency: Application, Content and Next Steps' (2013) 4 (4) Investment Treaty News (IISD) 3.

[30] Article 6 of the UNCITRAL Transparency Rules; subject to confidentiality and logistics.

[31] Articles 4, 5 of the UNCITRAL Transparency Rules.

[32] Articles 2, 3, 8 of the UNCITRAL Transparency Rules.

[33] Article 7 of the UNCITRAL Transparency Rules; Julia Salasky and Corinne Montineri, 'UNCITRAL Rules on Transparency in Treaty-Based Investor–State Arbitration' (2013) 31 (4) ASA Bulletin 774, 793–4.

[34] The Transparency Rules apply to investor–state arbitrations initiated under the UNCITRAL Arbitration Rules pursuant to a treaty concluded after 1 April 2014, unless the states parties to the treaty have agreed otherwise. For treaties concluded before this date, the Rules shall apply to such arbitrations only when the disputing parties or the states parties to the investment treaty have agreed to their application.

[35] The Convention goes further than the Transparency Rules, which generally only apply to arbitrations under the aegis of the UNCITRAL Arbitration Rules, by providing that the Transparency Rules shall apply to 'any investor–State arbitration, whether or not initiated under the UNCITRAL Arbitration Rules' (Article 2(1), see also Article 5); this broad application may, however, be curtailed by the set of reservations available (Article 3).

operates to constitute the consent of states to the application of the Transparency Rules in proceedings brought under pre-April 2014 investment treaties to which they are parties,[36] the voluntary adoption of the Transparency Rules by parties themselves,[37] and the inclusion of the rules in investment chapters of IIAs concluded after 1 April 2014, which will now be considered.[38]

Thirdly, as foreshadowed, there has been an attempted codification of transparency standards in some IIAs in recent years, generally effected either by drafting novel transparency standards or by adopting the Transparency Rules.[39] The genesis of more detailed and complete transparency standards can be traced back to the entry into force of the North American Free Trade Agreement (NAFTA) in 1994 (which may be replaced by the 'United States–Mexico–Canada Agreement' signed on 30 November 2018, which is not yet in force and is not focused on in this chapter). While the NAFTA itself did not expressly deal with the issue of transparency and confidentiality or *amici curiae*, with the benefit of interpretive decisions issued by the NAFTA Free Trade Commission (FTC)[40] and decisions of Chapter 11 (Investment) tribunals,[41] the Agreement's position in respect of these issues has been clarified.[42]

[36] For a detailed discussion on the application of the Rules under the Convention, see N. Jansen Calamita and Ewa Zelazna, 'Chapter V: Investment Arbitration, The Changing Landscape of Transparency in Investor–State Arbitration: The UNCITRAL Transparency Rules and Mauritius Convention', in Christian Klausegger, Peter Klein, Florian Kremslehner, Alexander Petsche, Nikolaus Pitkowitz, Jenny Power, Irene Welser, and Gerold Zeiler (eds), *Austrian Yearbook on International Arbitration* (Manz'sche Verlags- und Universitätsbuchhandlung, 2016) 286–8.

[37] The first known instances of the application of the Transparency Rules in investor–state arbitration are *Iberdrola, S.A. and Iberdrola Energía. S.A.U. v Bolivia* (PCA Case No. 2015-05) and *BSG Resources Limited v Republic of Guinea* (ICSID Case No. ARB/14/22). In both cases, the parties had agreed to the application of the Rules to their proceedings; see Christian Leathley and Daniela Paez, 'UNCITRAL Transparency Rules Applied for the First Time in investor–State Arbitration' HSF Notes (26 October 2015), https://hsfnotes.com/publicinternationallaw/2015/10/26/uncitral-transparency-rules-applied-for-the-first-time-in-investor-state-arbitration/.

[38] Article 8.36 of the CETA; Article 3.46 of the EU–Vietnam investment protection agreement (IPA); Article 10(3) of the Georgia–Switzerland BIT (2014); Article 14(3) of the Austria–Kyrgyzstan BIT (2016) (signed, not yet in force).

[39] Ruscalla (n 10) 23.

[40] The FTC is formally empowered to express the views of Mexico, Canada and the US, and its interpretation is binding on tribunals constituted under Chapter 11; see Jack Coe, Jr, 'Transparency in the Resolution of Investor–State Disputes – Adoption, Adaptation and NAFTA Leadership' (2006) 54 University of Kansas Law Review 1339, 1366.

[41] See NAFTA FTC, 'Notes of Interpretation of Certain Chapter 11 Provisions', 31 July 2001, which confirmed the view of the Tribunal's in *Metalclad Corp v United Mexican States* (ICSID Case No. ARB(AF)/97/1, Decision on a Request by the Respondent for an Order Prohibiting the Claimant from Revealing Information, 27 October 1997), para. 9 (reproduced in the Award, para. 13); *SD Myers, Inc v Canada* (UNCITRAL, Procedural Order No. 16 of 13 May 2000), paras 8–9; NAFTA FTC, 'Statement of the Free Trade Commission on non-disputing party participation', 7 October 2003, confirming the position adopted by the tribunals in two contemporaneous proceedings, in which it was held that neither NAFTA nor the UNCITRAL Arbitration Rules precluded a limited role for amici curiae: *Methanex Corporation v United States of America* and *United Parcel Service v Canada*. In both proceedings, the petition for amicus standing was opposed to by Mexico, but supported by the US and Canada. See also Coe (n 40) 1370 ff.

[42] The NAFTA does not impose a general duty of confidentiality on disputing parties; provides for the publication of documents (subject to redaction for confidentiality and privilege); and permits the tribunal to accept written submissions from a person or entity that is not a disputing party.

In keeping with the NAFTA policy towards greater transparency, the Canadian and US Model BITs[43] were the first to introduce provisions addressing public access to investment dispute hearings, submissions by non-disputing parties and extensive disclosure of a range of documents not traditionally in the public domain.[44] Recent treaty practice demonstrates that an increasing number of IIAs have followed the American and Canadian lead by providing for transparency standards based on their model provisions.[45] In addition to this drafting of novel transparency standards, a number of IIAs concluded after 1 April 2014 have incorporated the Transparency Rules,[46] the first being the Comprehensive Economic and Trade Agreement (CETA) between Canada and the EU,[47] making the Rules mandatory for all disputes commenced under the treaty, considered to be a 'revolutionary' step.[48]

As a result of these initiatives, increased transparency is fast becoming an 'international best practice' in investor–state arbitration.[49] Such initiatives do not, however, apply to international mediations, which continue to enjoy an increased protection of confidentiality.

III. Confidentiality and Transparency in Commercial and Investment Mediation

Mediation is recognized as a mechanism available for the settlement of international disputes.[50] It may be used as a means to assist in the resolution of both international commercial and investment disputes, either as a stand-alone process or integrated into international arbitration.[51] By its very nature, mediation is generally understood to require confidentiality. For in order for a mediation to

[43] The Canadian term used to refer to BITs is 'Foreign Investment Protection Agreements', or 'FIPAs'. For ease of reference, the term 'BIT' will be employed in a broad sense to include FIPAs.

[44] Articles 35, 38, 39 of the Canadian Model BIT (2004); Articles 28, 29 of the US Model BIT (2004); UNCTAD, 'Transparency: UNCTAD Series on Issues in International Investment Agreements II' (2012), 37.

[45] See, e.g. Articles 9.23.2–3, 9.24.1–2 of the Comprehensive and Progressive Agreement for Trans-Pacific Partnership; Articles 26.2, 27, 28.1–2 of the Chile–Hong Kong, China SAR BIT (2016) (signed, not yet in force); Articles 10.25.3, 10.26.1, 10.27.1–2 of the Republic of Korea–New Zealand FTA (2015); Articles 11.20.4–5, 11.21.1–2 of the Australia–Republic of Korea FTA (2014); Articles 31, 32 of the Canada–Senegal BIT (2014); Canada recently concluded several BITs with African nations containing similar provisions: Rainbow Willard and Sarah Morreau, 'The Canadian Model BIT: A Step in the Right Direction for Canadian Investment in Africa?', Kluwer Arbitration Blog [blog] (18 July 2015), http://arbitrationblog.kluwerarbitration.com/2015/07/18/the-canadian-model-bit-a-step-in-the-right-direction-for-canadian-investment-in-africa/; UNCTAD, 'Transparency: UNCTAD Series on Issues in International Investment Agreements II' (2012), 37.

[46] UNCITRAL (n 2), para. 75.

[47] Article 8.36 of CETA.

[48] August Reinisch and Lukas Stifter, 'European Investment Policy and ISDS' (13 November 2014) 13 https://ssrn.com/abstract=2564018.

[49] See Calamita and Zelazna (n 36) 272.

[50] Article 33(1) of the United Nations Charter.

[51] Edna Sussman, 'The Arbitrator Survey: Practices, Preferences and Changes on the Horizon' (2015) 26 American Review of International Arbitration 517, 536. See also Dilyara Nigmatullina, 'The

succeed, the parties and mediator must be able to frankly discuss and explore the issues at the core of the dispute, the true position of the respective parties, and the possibilities available for settlement. That is, the participants must traverse topics that would not normally be disclosed with any candour in arbitral or judicial proceedings. Such full and frank disclosure is made possible by affording confidentiality to the mediation proceedings, removing the risk of disclosure.[52] Requiring increased transparency would undermine the environment in which mediation operates, which may, in turn, reduce the likelihood that the mediation process will succeed.[53]

The question of the appropriate level of confidentiality that should apply in mediation receives a different answer depending on the context in which it is posed. As with the relationship between commercial arbitration and investment arbitration, commercial mediation and investment mediation share common roots, but possess important differences that must be recognized.[54] The use of international commercial mediation is growing, with the possibility of becoming as popular as international commercial arbitration.[55] It is often a precondition to litigation or arbitration due to the benefits it can offer private parties and its ability to diffuse disputes at an early stage. Commercial mediation, like commercial arbitration, lacks the public interest element inherent in investment mediation and, as such, the confidentiality of mediation proceedings has been retained by relevant governing national laws and rules, generally subject to well-established exceptions.

Mediation has not enjoyed the same success in the settlement of investment disputes.[56] This is not because it lacks utility in investor–state disputes,[57] but, rather, because it has been 'undervalued and overlooked' as a form of dispute resolution.[58] As in the commercial context, mediation has the potential to reduce the cost and length of disputes, increase the rate of early settlement, and help to maintain a

Combined Use of Mediation and Arbitration in Commercial Dispute Resolution: Results from an International Study' (2016) 33 (1) Journal of International Arbitration 37, 28–9.

[52] Guide to Enactment and Use of the UNCITRAL Model Law on International Commercial Conciliation, 2002, para. 58.

[53] James H. Carter, 'Part II: Issues Involving Confidentiality', in Albert Jan van den Berg (ed.), *New Horizons in International Commercial Arbitration and Beyond*, vol. 12 (Kluwer Law International, 2005) 485.

[54] Coe (n 40) 1340.

[55] S. I. Strong, 'Use and Perception of International Commercial Mediation and Conciliation: A Preliminary Report on Issues Relating to the Proposed UNCITRAL Convention on International Commercial Mediation and Conciliation' (17 November 2014) University of Missouri School of Law Legal Studies Research Paper 2014-28 17 https://ssrn.com/abstract=2526302.

[56] Silvia Constain, 'Mediation in Investor–State Dispute Settlement: Government Policy and the Changing Landscape' (2014) 29 (1) ICSID Review–Foreign Investment Law Journal 25, 25–6.

[57] Susan D. Franck, 'Using Investor–State Mediation Rules to Promote Conflict Management: An Introductory Guide' (2014) 29 (1) ICSID Review–Foreign Investment Law Journal 66, 77; Nancy Welsh and Andrea Kupfer Schneider, 'The Thoughtful Integration of Mediation into Bilateral Investment Treaty Arbitration' (2013) 18 Harvard Negotiation Law Review 71, 77, 82–3.

[58] Anna Spain, 'Integration Matters: Rethinking the Architecture of International Dispute Resolution' (2010) 32 University of Pennsylvania Journal of International Law 1, 19.

business relationship between the investor and the host state. Notwithstanding its advantages, critics of mediation rely on the fact that mediation falls victim to the same conflict as does arbitration, in that its inherent secrecy renders it an inappropriate form of investor–state dispute resolution. As a response to this conflict, there has been a shift towards increased transparency led by the International Bar Association (IBA) Council in its adoption of the IBA Rules on Investor–State Mediation (IBA Rules), and the European Union (EU) in its recent treaty negotiations. However, the level of transparency will not, and should not, reach the same level as that attained in investment arbitration.[59]

A. The Protection of Confidentiality in Mediation

Confidentiality in mediation is often afforded cumulative protection. The first layer of protection is likely to be found in the parties' agreement itself. This will be reinforced if the parties have adopted a set of institutional rules that contain a provision on confidentiality. Should the institution administer the mediation, the mediator may be bound by a duty to maintain confidentiality contained in any ethical rules or codes adopted by the institution.[60] Finally, national legislation will be essential in times of requiring the assistance of courts to uphold the contractual nature of the confidentiality obligation.[61]

The concept of confidentiality in mediation is multi-faceted.[62] The first, and the most common, feature of confidentiality, is the general duty of confidentiality vis-à-vis external parties. Participants in the mediation (such as the parties, experts, and mediator) are subjected to a general obligation not to make prohibited disclosures to external parties. Secondly, confidentiality extends to the flow of information within the mediation itself, in particular, in relation to private (or 'caucus') sessions. In practice, the flow of communication is managed in one of two ways: there is the 'open communication' approach, whereby information passed to mediators in private is not considered confidential unless specifically requested by the parties;[63] and there is also the more widely accepted 'in-confidence' approach, whereby all information disclosed privately is treated as confidential unless the

[59] Coe (n 4) 27.

[60] See, e.g. Article 4 of the Singapore Mediation Centre, Mediation Procedure; Article 5 of the International Mediation Institute Code of Professional Conduct.

[61] Lawrence Boo, 'Commentary on Issues Involving Confidentiality' in van den Berg (n 53) 523–4.

[62] See the tripartite classification of confidentiality posited in Nadja Alexander, 'Confidentiality', in Nadja Alexander (ed.), *International and Comparative Mediation, Global Trends in Dispute Resolution* (Kluwer Law International, 2009) 245, 248–51; the classification was adopted in the twelve criteria of the Regulatory Robustness Rating System in Nadja Alexander, Sabine Walsh, and Martin Svatoš (eds), *EU Mediation Law Handbook* (Kluwer Law International, 2017).

[63] See, e.g. the approach adopted by the Australian Centre for International Commercial Arbitration (ACICA) Mediation Rules 2007, UNCITRAL Conciliation Rules, PCA Optional Conciliation Rules, and Model Law on International Commercial Conciliation.

disclosing party indicates otherwise.[64] Thirdly, and finally, confidentiality extends to the rights and obligations associated with protecting mediation communications from being legally discovered or admitted in evidence in subsequent court and arbitral proceedings, which includes calling the mediator to give evidence.

B. Confidentiality Framework

1. National regimes

The regulation of confidentiality in mediation is a matter for each state.[65] In general, the protection afforded to confidentiality in mediation by national laws is not uniform.[66] Indeed, the legislation regulating mediation has been adopted in a 'hodge-podge manner', creating what has been described as a 'confusing quilt of laws that create different rules for all the different areas in which mediation and conciliation is (sic) supposed to take place'.[67] This lack of uniformity in the form of legal safeguards provided to protect against unwanted disclosure of certain information has prompted efforts to create a harmonised approach generally to mediation, including the treatment of confidentiality.[68]

In 2008, the European Parliament and the Council of the European Union issued a Directive on Mediation promoting the use of mediation in civil and commercial matters.[69] The Directive recognized the importance of confidentiality in the mediation process and included an article on confidentiality, albeit dealing only with the protection at the level of the disclosure of information in subsequent judicial or arbitral proceedings,[70] leaving member states to enact stricter measures in respect of other aspects of the mediation. Consequently, there continues to be great diversity in the regulation of mediation confidentiality within the EU.[71]

[64] See, e.g. the approach adopted by the London Court of International Arbitration (LCIA), World Intellectual Property Organisation (WIPO) and International Centre for Dispute Resolution (ICDR); Nadja Alexander, 'Chapter 8: UNCITRAL and International Mediation' in Alexander (n 62) 348.

[65] Hindelang (n 3).

[66] Guide to Enactment and Use of the UNCITRAL Model Law on International Commercial Conciliation, 2002, para. 17; see, generally, Carter (n 53); Michael Pryles, 'Commentary on Issues Involving Confidentiality', in van den Berg (n 53).

[67] Eric van Ginkel, 'The UNCITRAL Model Law on International Commercial Conciliation: A Critical Appraisal' (2004) 21 (1) Journal of International Arbitration 1, 2–3.

[68] Guide to Enactment and Use of the UNCITRAL Model Law on International Commercial Conciliation, 2002, para. 58.

[69] See Chapter 10, this volume.

[70] Article 7.

[71] Nadja Alexander, 'Harmonisation and Diversity in the Private International Law of Mediation' in Klaus J. Hopt and Felix Steffek (eds), *Mediation: Principles and Regulation in Comparative Perspective* (OUP, 2013) 131, 182. See also European Parliament 2014–2019, 'Report on the Implementation of Directive 2008/52/EC of the European Parliament and of the Council of 21 May 2008 on certain aspects of mediation in civil and commercial matters' (A8-0238/2017), 27 June 2017; on 12 September 2017, a resolution was passed addressing the recommendations in the report.

In 2002, UNCITRAL adopted its Model Law on International Commercial Conciliation (Model Law), which was intended to be a tool for harmonizing legislation.[72] The default provision on confidentiality, considered by the former Secretary of UNCITRAL to be one of the three pillars of the Model Law,[73] is drafted in broad terms, referring to 'all information relating to the conciliation proceedings', subject only to two exceptions.[74] The Model Law also contains provisions addressing the admissibility of evidence in other proceedings,[75] and the disclosure of information.[76] However, UNCITRAL's approach in drafting the Model Law was to take the 'path of minimum regulation of the foundations of mediation (primarily confidentiality)', to permit diversity in regulation beyond the minimum standards.[77] To date, legislation based on or influenced by the Model Law and the principles on which it is based has been adopted in thirty-three states in a total of forty-five jurisdictions.[78]

Notwithstanding these developments, national approaches to confidentiality still differ. Instead of embarking on a comparative study of the legal treatment of confidentiality in mediation in differing jurisdictions, this chapter instead focuses on the treatment of confidentiality and transparency under institutional rules that are often agreed to by the parties.

2. Institutional rules: commercial mediation

A number of institutions have adopted rules designed for international commercial mediation, each with slightly different approaches in their treatment of confidentiality.[79] Insofar as the general duty of confidentiality is concerned, the approach adopted under most rules is to impose on the parties and the mediator an obligation not to disclose any information regarding the mediation proceedings in the absence of any agreement of the parties to the contrary and/or subject to applicable law.[80] This duty tends to extend to any settlement agreement reached between

[72] Guide to Enactment and Use of the UNCITRAL Model Law on International Commercial Conciliation (2002), para. 13.

[73] 'When your Multi-Cultural Dinner Party Conversation becomes an International Mediation: An interview with Mr. Jernej Sekolec, Secretary of UNCITRAL, on the 29th September 2003' (2004) 15 World Arbitration and Mediation Report 105.

[74] Namely, where disclosure is required by law or for the purposes of implementation or enforcement of a settlement agreement: see discussion in Nadja Alexander, 'Chapter 9: The UNCITRAL Model Law on International Commercial Conciliation (2002)' in Alexander (n 62) 419–21.

[75] Article 10.

[76] Article 8.

[77] See (n 72).

[78] Current as of 19 April 2018, http://www.uncitral.org/uncitral/en/uncitral_texts/arbitration/2002Model_conciliation_status.html.

[79] For the purposes of this discussion, the following rules have been considered: the ICC Mediation Rules (2014), ICDR International Mediation Rules (2014), LCIA Mediation Rules (2012), UNCITRAL Conciliation Rules (1980), Stockholm Chamber of Commerce (SCC) Mediation Rules (2014), ACICA Mediation Rules (2007), and the Singapore International Mediation Centre (SIMC) Rules.

[80] Rule 10.3 of the LCIA Mediation Rules; Articles 10(1), (3) of the ICDR Rules; Article 9.1(a) of the SIMC Rules; Article 3(1) of the SCC Mediation Rules (exception only where parties have agreed otherwise); Rule 15.2 of the ACICA Mediation Rules (exception only where parties' prior written consent).

the parties, subject to disclosure where necessary for its implementation or enforcement.[81] Derogations from this general approach are seen in the International Chamber of Commerce (ICC) Mediation Rules, which permit disclosure of the fact of the existence of mediation proceedings,[82] and the UNCITRAL Conciliation Rules, which do not provide for any exceptions to the general duty of confidentiality (except in respect of the settlement agreement).[83]

The common approach to dealing with the admissibility of mediation communications as evidence in subsequent judicial, arbitral, or similar proceedings is to provide a list of prohibited disclosures that shall only be produced as evidence when agreed to by the parties or required by applicable law.[84] Such disclosures invariably include any admissions, views, or suggestions made by either party in respect of a possible settlement, proposals for settlement put forward by the mediator, and any indications of willingness on the part of either party to accept such proposals.[85] As to the role of the mediator in future proceedings as a witness or otherwise, it is less common to see regulation in this respect.[86]

Few institutional rules regulate the flow of information within the mediation itself, leaving this to be determined by the mediator and the parties.[87] In general, where the rules regulate this aspect of confidentiality, the open communication approach is more commonly adopted. It has been suggested that amendments should be made to 'bring [the rules] into line with current thinking', which favours the default position of confidentiality, subject to the party's request that information be passed onto those outside the private session.[88]

3. Institutional rules: investment mediation

To date, only two sets of investment-specific mediation rules have been developed: the IBA Rules and the ICSID Conciliation Rules.[89] In light of the unique conciliation procedure required by the ICSID Conciliation Rules,[90] the absence of

[81] Article 9(1)(b) of the ICC Mediation Rules; Article 14 of the UNCITRAL Conciliation Rules; Rule 15.2 of the ACICA Mediation Rules; Article 9.1(b) of the SIMC Rules.

[82] Article 9(1)(a) of the ICC Mediation Rules.

[83] Article 14 of the UNCITRAL Conciliation Rules.

[84] Article 9(2) of the ICC Mediation Rules; Article 10(3) of the ICDR Rules; Articles 10.4, 10.6 of the LCIA Mediation Rules; Article 20 of the UNCITRAL Conciliation Rules; Rule 21 of the ACICA Mediation Rules; Article 9.2 of the SIMC Mediation Rules.

[85] Article 20 of the UNICTRAL Conciliation Rules; see similar wording in Article 9(2) of the ICC Mediation Rules; Article 10(3) of the ICDR Mediation Rules; Rule 21 of the ACICA Mediation Rules.

[86] Article 10(2) of the ICDR Rules; Article 11.2 of the LCIA Mediation Rules; Rule 20 of the ACICA Mediation Rules; Article 9.3 of the SIMC Mediation Rules.

[87] Article 5.3 of the LCIA Mediation Rules; Article 10 of the UNCITRAL Conciliation Rules; Rule 11 of the ACICA Mediation Rules.

[88] Nadja Alexander, 'Chapter 8: UNCITRAL and International Mediation' in Alexander (n 62) 348, comments made in respect of the UNCITRAL Conciliation Rules.

[89] While not specifically drafted to apply to mediations concerning an investment, the PCA Optional Conciliation Rules may be used in 'conciliating disputes [...] between two States and also in disputes between two parties only one of which is a State.' (PCA Optional Conciliation Rules, 'Introduction').

[90] Ch 3 of the ICSID Convention; Frauke Nitschke, 'The IBA's Investor–State Mediation Rules and the ICSID Dispute Settlement Framework' (2014) 29 (1) ICSID Review–Foreign Investment law Journal 112, 113 ff.

express provision for confidentiality in the Rules,[91] and the very few conciliations that have taken place under their auspices,[92] they will not be discussed in depth. Rather, it is of greater relevance to consider the impact of the IBA Rules.

The IBA Rules were adopted by the IBA Council on 4 October 2012. The Rules are specifically designed to 'assist investors and States in settling disputes under investment treaties, investment contracts or investment laws.'[93] The twelve articles serve as default rules that create a baseline of procedures to be used in connection with investor–state mediation.[94] In this manner, the Rules preserve one of the touchstones of mediation—flexibility—permitting modifications or derogations by party agreement, while providing a 'check list' for parties tailoring a mediation procedure to their needs.[95] Such flexibility is desirable for governments approaching decisions that entail budgetary or policy implications.[96]

In respect of confidentiality and transparency, '[a] most important feature' of the Rules,[97] a different balance is struck between these two values than compared with the balance reached by the institutional rules governing commercial mediation. Like their commercial counterparts, the IBA Rules provide for the privacy of the mediation,[98] the confidential communication of information to the mediator during the proceedings,[99] and a general prohibition on the disclosure of mediation communications and documents.[100] Where the Rules differ, however, is in their express carve-out from the confidentiality obligation of the fact of the existence of the mediation, any resulting settlement and its terms (unless the parties agree in writing), and the disclosure of specified documents or information. Save in two respects, any disclosure made shall be in a manner that protects the confidentiality of information to the greatest extent feasible and permissible.[101]

In addition, the IBA Rules regulate the confidentiality of the flow of communications between the parties and the mediator during the mediation. The Rules distinguish between oral communications between a party and the mediator during separate private meetings, or caucuses, and written communications provided by one party to the mediator. The former communications are treated as confidential unless the party explicitly authorizes their disclosure (in-confidence approach),

[91] Provision is made to prohibit reliance on conciliation communications in subsequent arbitral, judicial or other proceedings (Article 35 of the ICSID Convention) and to ensure that hearings 'shall take place in private and [. . .] remain secret' (Rule 27(1) of the ICSID Conciliation Rules).

[92] According to ICSID's latest caseload statistics, of the 650 cases ever registered under the ICSID Convention and Additional Facility Rules, only ten have been Conciliation cases: ICSID, 'The ICSID Caseload: Statistics' (Issue 2018–1), 7–8.

[93] Anna Joubin-Bret and Bart Legum, 'A Set of Rules Dedicated to Investor–State Mediation: The IBA Investor–State Mediation Rules' (2014) 29 (1) ICSID Review– Foreign Investment Law Journal 17.

[94] Franck (n 57) 80.

[95] Joubin-Bret and Legum (n 93) 21; ibid.

[96] Constain (n 56) 38–9.

[97] Joubin-Bret and Legum (n 93) 23.

[98] Article 10(1) of the IBA Rules.

[99] Article 8 of the IBA Rules.

[100] Article 10(2) of the IBA Rules.

[101] Article 10(3) of the IBA Rules.

while the latter must be labelled as 'Confidential—For Mediator's Use Only' in order to be treated as such (open communication approach).[102]

To date, there has been only one reported mediation conducted under the IBA Rules, albeit it is difficult to know precisely how many mediations are in existence in light of their confidential nature.[103] Aside from parties agreeing to their application, the IBA Rules may apply by virtue of their incorporation in IIAs, which is an effective method to expand their use in ISDS. It remains to be seen how widely the Rules will be used. Despite their relatively slow uptake, the provisions are an early example of an attempt to reconcile the need for confidentiality of the mediation process with the demonstrable trend towards increased transparency in ISDS. While it remains up to the parties to agree otherwise in writing, the default position under the IBA Rules is one of greater transparency.

4. Position under IIAs

Traditionally, IIAs have not expressly mentioned mediation as a means of investment dispute settlement. Rather, they have provided for the use of preliminary non-confrontational dispute settlement procedures, often during 'cooling-off' periods. According to a statistical survey published by the Organisation for Economic Co-operation and Development (OECD) in 2012, over thirty different designations of these preliminary procedures were found in the 1,600 BITs, the subject of the survey, with a 'slightly declining majority' providing for a period of amicable settlement, and an 'increasing share' of the treaties specifying settlement through negotiations or consultations. Settlement methods such as conciliation and mediation were, however, mentioned very rarely.[104]

In the wake of complaints concerning ISDS, some states have chosen to not renew or terminate investment instruments altogether.[105] Other states have, however, decided to conclude new or modernize old investment agreements in an effort to reform the ISDS regime by providing for a greater use of mediation.[106] Increasingly in recent treaty practice, specific reference is either being made to mediation (as well as to conciliation or recourse to other third-party neutrals) as an

[102] Article 8(4) of the IBA Rules; see also Franck (n 57) 84.

[103] Administered by the ICC International Centre for Alternate Dispute Resolution, the mediation was commenced following submission of a claim to arbitration under the France-Philippines BIT by a French engineering and consulting services company. In an 'effort to avert arbitration', the Republic of Philippines subsequently agreed to mediation pursuant to the IBA Rules (Luke Peterson, 'In an Apparent First, Investor and Host-State Agree to Try Mediation under IBA Rules to Resolve an Investment Treaty Dispute' 9 (9) *Investment Arbitration Reporter* (20 April 2016)). The mediator was reportedly J Christopher Thomas QC.

[104] Joachim Pohl, Kekeletso Mashigo, and Alexis Nohen, 'Dispute Settlement Provisions in International Investment Agreements: A Large Sample Survey' *OECD Working Papers on International Investment*, 2012/02, OECD Publishing, 17–18.

[105] E.g. South Africa and Indonesia resolved to terminate, or not renew, a majority of their BITs. Several Latin American countries have rejected the use of investor–state arbitration in investment instruments, favouring the use of domestic courts. See Hindelang (n 3).

[106] See Phase 1 and 2 reform actions in UNCTAD, 'World Investment Report 2017: Investment and the Digital Economy' (2017).

available form of pre-arbitration dispute settlement,[107] or to the use of mediation as an alternative or supplement to arbitration.[108] At the forefront of this reform is the EU, with its recently concluded investment protection agreements (IPAs) and CETA with Canada.

a. EU–Canada Comprehensive Economic and Trade Agreement (CETA)

On 30 October 2016, after eight years of negotiation, Canada and the EU completed and signed the CETA. While the agreement is novel in more than one respect,[109] this section focuses on the incorporation of mediation into the ISDS regime established by CETA. Pursuant to the stand-alone provision on mediation in Article 8.20 of the investment chapter, either party may elect to have recourse to mediation at any time of the proceedings. If mediation is commenced simultaneously with arbitration, the agreement to mediate shall be disclosed to the public as it is included in the list of documents to be made publicly available pursuant to the UNCITRAL Transparency Rules, which are incorporated into the CETA.[110] The parties are at liberty to agree on a set of rules to govern the procedure, for example, the IBA Rules. Theoretically, it may be possible for the parties to agree to the application of the rules of procedure for mediation set out in Annex 29-C of CETA (with any necessary modifications), which govern the mediation procedure in any dispute between two state parties to the treaty.[111] However, as they are not tailored for investment disputes, it may still be preferable to adopt other investment-specific rules, such as the IBA Rules.

If the Annex applies to an investment mediation under the CETA, the position on confidentiality starts with the general proposition that 'all stages of the proceeding, including any advice or proposed solution, are confidential.'[112] This obligation does not, however, extend to the existence of the mediation nor to any factual information already existing in the public domain. It is also subject to any agreement of the parties and is without prejudice to Article 4.6, which provides that:

[107] See, e.g. Pt III, Article 26 of the Investment Agreement for the COMESA (Common Market for Eastern and Southern Africa) Common Investment Area; Article 9.18 of the Comprehensive and Progressive Agreement for the Trans-Pacific Partnership; Article 8.19 of the Peru–Australia FTA.

[108] Joubin-Bret and Legum (n 93) 18; see, e.g. Article 30 of the ASEAN Comprehensive Investment Agreement; according to the Guide on Investment Mediation adopted by the Energy Charter Conference, under Article 26.1 of the Energy Charter Treaty, investors and Contracting Parties are free to agree on mediation using existing or tailor-made mechanisms to settle investment disputes 'amicably' (see sections 2, 7 of the Guide).

[109] E.g. the CETA introduces a new two-tier investment tribunal system; see, generally, Elsa Sardinha, 'The New EU-Led Approach to Investor–State Arbitration: The Investment Tribunal System in the Comprehensive Economic Trade Agreement (CETA) and the EU–Vietnam Free Trade Agreement' (2017) 32 (3) ICSID Review–Foreign Investment Law Journal 625.

[110] Article 8.36(2) of the CETA; Article 3(1) of the Transparency Rules.

[111] Article 29.5 of the CETA.

[112] Annex 29-C, Article 6 of the CETA.

> Mutually agreed solutions shall be made publicly available. However, the version disclosed to the public may not contain any information that a Party has designated as confidential.

Finally, the parties are prohibited from relying on or introducing as evidence in other dispute settlement proceedings the positions adopted by either party in the mediation, any advice given or proposals made by the mediator, and the indication of willingness on the part of one party to accept such a proposal.[113] Together, these provisions strike a balance between the confidentiality of the mediation proceedings and the competing interest of transparency similar to that found in the IBA Rules. While it is open to the parties to agree otherwise in writing, the default position under Annex 29-C permits disclosure of the fact that the mediation is taking place, any mutually agreed solution, and any information already existing in the public domain.

b. The EU–Singapore IPA and the EU–Vietnam IPA

The EU's treaties with Vietnam and Singapore adopt a similar approach to mediation. The dispute settlement regime contained in the EU–Singapore IPA and the EU–Vietnam IPA specifically provide for mediation (and alternate dispute resolution generally) at any time of the proceedings.[114] Again, recourse to mediation may be governed by the rules agreed to by the parties, including the investment-specific mediation rules set out in an Annex.[115] Unlike the mediation mechanism set out in Annex 29-C of the CETA (which applies to inter-state mediations, but which could be modified for investor–state mediations), the procedures provided for under these treaties are specifically tailored to investment disputes. Parties may be more inclined to select these rules to govern their mediation.

The position adopted insofar as confidentiality is concerned under the mediation rules is similar to the position under Annex 29-C of the CETA. The starting point is the general proposition that 'all steps of the procedure, including any advice or proposed solution, shall be confidential. However, any disputing party may disclose to the public that mediation is taking place.'[116] This proposition is subject to any agreement of the disputing parties and is without prejudice to Article 4.6 which provides for the disclosure of any mutually agreed solutions, subject to redaction of confidential information. Such solutions 'shall' be made publicly available pursuant to the EU–Singapore IPA,[117] while under the EU–Vietnam IPA, they

[113] Annex 29-C, Article 6(4) of the CETA.

[114] Ch 3, Article 3.4 of the EU–Singapore IPA; ch 3, Article 3.31, of the EU–Vietnam IPA; both articles are drafted in similar terms to Article 8.20 of the CETA.

[115] Annex 6 of the EU–Singapore IPA; Annex 10 of the EU–Vietnam IPA.

[116] Annex 6, Article 6(3) of the EU–Singapore IPA; Annex 10, Article 6(3) of the EU–Vietnam IPA is in substantively similar terms.

[117] Annex 6, Article 4(6) of the EU–Singapore IPA.

'may' be made available only by the EU, one of its Member States or Vietnam.[118] In a similar fashion to the CETA, a prohibition is also placed on the reliance or introduction as evidence in future dispute settlement procedures of the position taken by the disputing parties in the course of the mediation, any advice or proposals made by the mediator, and the indication of willingness on the part of one party to accept such proposals.[119]

Finally, confidentiality is dealt with in the Code of Conduct applicable to any mediator who conducts a mediation initiated under the investment chapter, regardless of the governing rules agreed to by the parties.[120] The provision governing confidentiality contained in the Code prohibits a mediator or former mediator from disclosing a settlement, his or her deliberations, any information concerning a proceeding or acquired during a proceeding, except for the purposes of that proceeding, and using any such information for reasons of personal gain.[121] While the CETA contains a similar Code of Conduct for mediators with a similar provision for confidentiality, that Code only applies to mediators who conduct a mediation in accordance with the provisions governing disputes between two state parties to the treaty, not the investment chapter provisions.[122]

The EU–Singapore IPA and the EU–Vietnam IPA appear to go further than the CETA. They incorporate an investment-specific mediation mechanism in their respective chapters on investment protection, providing a more viable stand-alone procedure to govern investor–state mediations than the general mediation rules provided for in Annex 29-C of the CETA. In addition, by including a Code of Conduct applicable to a mediator conducting any mediation under the ISDS regime, regardless of the type of rules adopted by the parties, they ensure a base level of confidentiality on the part of the mediator in any investment mediation. Current negotiations between the EU and other countries concerning the drafting of investment agreements indicate that further treaties are poised to follow these 'state-of-the-art procedural and substantive innovations'.[123]

[118] Annex 10, Article 4(6) of the EU–Vietnam IPA.

[119] Annex 6, Article 6(1) of the EU–Singapore IPA; Annex 10, Article 6(1) of the EU–Vietnam IPA.

[120] Annex 7, Article 1 of the EU–Singapore IPA; Annex 11, Article 1 of the EU–Vietnam IPA.

[121] Annex 7, Articles 19–21, 23 of the EU–Singapore IPA; Annex 11, Articles 7, 9 of the EU–Vietnam IPA.

[122] See Annex 29-B, Article 1 of the CETA: 'mediator means a person who conducts a mediation in accordance with article 29.5'.

[123] See, e.g. EU–Mexico FTA negotiations, EU Textual Proposal, April 2017, 'Investment and Trade in Services Title', ch II, s C, Article 2.21 and Annex I; the EU included a similar mediation mechanism in its textual proposal for the 'Trade in services, investment and e-commerce' chapter in Transatlantic Trade and Investment Partnership (TTIP) with the US (ch II, s 3, Article 3, and Annex I); see generally Elsa Sardinha, 'Towards a New Horizon in Investor–State Dispute Settlement? Reflections on the Investment Tribunal System in the Comprehensive Economic Trade Agreement (CETA)' (2017) 54 CYIL 311.

IV. Future Role for Mediation in International Commercial and Investment Dispute Settlement

It is likely, and preferable, that mediation should continue to play an important role in the settlement of international commercial and investment disputes, in light of its significant advantages concerning flexibility and party control, the enhanced likelihood of business relationships being maintained, the reduced length and cost of mediation proceedings as compared to international arbitration proceedings, and the possibility of early settlement of the dispute. These advantages can, in part, be attributed to the assurance provided to parties that any admissions and disclosures made during the facilitated negotiation will be kept confidential, regardless of its outcome. A want of privacy and confidentiality in mediation risks undermining its benefits, which, in any event, arguably outweigh its reduced transparency.

Investment mediation and commercial mediation will likely continue to develop as two distinct branches of the same tree. The use of international commercial mediation will continue to steadily increase as its participants become more familiar with the effectiveness and conduct of the procedure, made possible, for example, through various educational initiatives.[124] The future of mediation in ISDS similarly appears to be bright. Support for mediation continues to grow as participants in ISDS become aware of its benefits and as mechanisms are adopted to encourage and facilitate its use, such as the IBA Rules. Indeed, the inclusion of mediation as a means to reduce duration and cost of investment proceedings was recently encouraged by the latest UNCITRAL Working Group on ISDS reforms.[125]

The same mechanisms as have been adopted in the context of ISDS, relating to public hearings, disclosure of documents, and the involvement of *amici curiae*, would not all appear to be suitable for mediation; in this regard, the two mechanisms should not function with the same levels of transparency.[126] Introducing similar transparency mechanisms would reduce the perceived benefits of mediation, namely, the possibility of frank and candid settlement discussions. The current approach to confidentiality under the IBA Rules, as well as under the EU–Singapore IPA and the EU–Vietnam IPA, is a step in the right direction in respect of accommodating the public interest in investor–state disputes. Privacy and confidentiality in mediation should be 'preserved to an appreciable degree'.[127] However, deference should be given to policies of transparency by rendering investment mediations more open than purely private commercial mediations.

124 Strong (n 55) 29–31.
125 UNCITRAL (n 2) paras 45, 67.
126 Coe (n 5) 27.
127 Ibid.

The IBA Rules and the EU's recent treaty practice in this area facilitate this outcome by providing for disclosure of the fact of the occurrence of any mediation and the terms of any settlement agreement reached, subject to redaction of confidential information, while preserving the privacy of negotiations that take place during the mediation itself and private sessions or caucuses. These requirements should not be seen as eroding the confidentiality of proceedings, as this base level of disclosure may be justified by government accountability. Many governments may already be required, by virtue of national reporting obligations, to report on and account for in budgetary decisions any mediations and settlement agreements reached in disputes with foreign investors.

In addition, the stance adopted under these instruments leaves the parties with a large degree of discretion, retaining the flexibility of the process. Flexibility is particularly desirable in the investment context to permit adaptation of the mediation procedure depending on the nature of the dispute. On the one hand, such flexibility would allow the tribunal, in consultation with the parties, to invite the participation of third parties in the proceedings, should this be of assistance.[128] On the other hand, some investment disputes may be purely contractual in nature and not attract the same public interest as other disputes, warranting less transparency.

V. Conclusion

Confidentiality is rightly regarded as an important feature of mediation, whether it be in the context of settling commercial or investment disputes. Indeed, a large part of the success of mediation proceedings is attributed to their private and confidential nature. It is somewhat inevitable that a debate has arisen, given the tension between the desire of some participants in international dispute settlement proceedings for confidentiality and the increasingly vocal calls for enhanced transparency. As discussed, this debate has unfolded in a different manner in the realm of commercial mediation, in which the confidentiality of mediation proceedings has been largely preserved, as opposed to the sphere of ISDS, in which one observes an increasing encroachment of the desire for transparency. In the latter context, one must acknowledge the arguments in favour of heightened transparency. Accountability of the state and the public interest in disclosure is of great importance, and the mediation procedure should adapt to respect these concerns. However, any such adaptations should respect the nature of mediation. Progress in line with the approach taken in the IBA Rules, the EU–Singapore IPA, and the EU–Vietnam IPA is a good example of striking an adequate balance between these competing considerations.

[128] Ibid., 40.

While it is anticipated that mediation will continue to be regularly used in the settlement of international commercial disputes, there are uncertainties as to how it will be embraced in ISDS. But the benefits offered by mediation suggest that it should be actively considered by parties to investor–state disputes. If the resort to mediation can assist in the amicable resolution of investor–state disputes, that would arguably serve not only the interests of the parties, but also the health of the ISDS regime.

18

Codes of Conduct for Commercial and Investment Mediators

Striving for Consistency and a Common Global Approach

Joe Tirado and Elisa Vicente Maravall

I. Introduction

As the use of mediation has grown and developed around the world, the question of how best to ensure mediators adhere to a common set of standards becomes ever more important. This is seen by many stakeholders as essential for building confidence in mediation and establishing mediator credibility, which are in turn fundamental requirements for the continued adoption and growth of mediation. This chapter aims to provide a selective European (section II) and global (section III) overview of some of the key codes of conduct for mediators that exist at the time of writing. In particular, it looks at how the adoption of such codes may promote greater consistency.

II. Europe: A Regional Overview

A. Preliminary Remarks: The EU Framework

In 2008 the European Parliament and the Council of the European Union issued Directive 2008/52/EC with the aim of both encouraging the use of mediation and of ensuring a balanced relationship between mediation and judicial proceedings (EU Mediation Directive).[1] Nine years later, the European Comission (EC) concluded in its report on the EU Mediation Directive's implementation, dated 27 June 2017 (EC 2017 Report) that the EU Mediation Directive had had a substantial impact

[1] Directive 2008/52/EC of the European Parliament and of the Council of 21 May 2008 on certain aspects of mediation in civil and commercial matters (EU Mediation Directive). See also Chapter 10, this volume.

on the laws of several Member States of the European Union (Member States). In some countries it had even triggered the adoption of significant changes to the existing mediation regulation.[2] Of particular note, the EC 2017 Report found that, 'with regard to codes of conduct, the implementation of the Directive is overall satisfactory'.[3]

The EU Mediation Directive seeks to encourage the development and adherence to codes of conduct, rather than impose on EU Member States certain specific mandatory measures. This approach acknowledges the fact that, while ensuring the quality of mediation via a code of conduct is indeed a policy to be followed by all Member States, there are different opinions among them on whether the market or the member state itself is best equipped to develop such a code. Article 4(1) of the EU Mediation Directive requires that Member States

> shall encourage, by any means which they consider appropriate, the development of, and adherence to, voluntary codes of conduct by mediators and organisations providing mediation services, as well as other effective quality control mechanisms concerning the provision of mediation services.

In practice, as shown by the EC 2017 Report, the implementation of Article 4(1) of the EU Mediation Directive has had the following effects: nineteen Member States have required the development of and adherence to codes of conduct for mediators, whereas in other Member States providers of mediation have set their own codes of ethics;[4] while there are Member States that already have a national code of conduct for mediators, in others several codes of conduct are applied in practice without being prescribed by law; [5] and, overall, most stakeholders are of the opinion that the encouragement, development, and adherence to voluntary codes of conduct by mediators and organizations providing mediation services required by the Directive has been effective.[6]

In particular, as highlighted by the EC 2017 Report, the European Code of Conduct for Mediators developed by a group of stakeholders with the European Commission and launched on 2 July 2004 (European Code of Conduct) played a key role in implementing Article 4(1) of the EU Mediation Directive, either

[2] European Commission, Report on the Implementation of Directive 2008/52/EC of the European Parliament and of the Council of 21 May 2008 on certain aspects of mediation in civil and commercial matters (2016/2066(INI)), 27 June 2017.

[3] Ibid., Section III of the first part of the Report entitled 'Summary of Facts and Findings'.

[4] Specifically, said nineteen member states are Austria, Belgium, Bulgaria, Cyprus, Estonia, Spain, Finland, France, Ireland, Italy, Lithuania, Latvia, Malta, Poland, Portugal, Romania, Sweden, Slovenia, and Slovakia.

[5] Specifically, an example of a member state that has a national code of conduct for mediators is Finland, while an example of a member state where several codes of conduct are applied in practice without being prescribed by law is Spain.

[6] EC 2017 Report, section III of the first part of the Report entitled 'Summary of Facts and Findings'.

because it is directly used by stakeholders or because it has inspired national codes of conduct.[7]

As indicated in its Preamble, the European Code of Conduct aims to apply to all kinds of mediation, either in civil or commercial matters. It sets out several principles to which individual mediators 'may voluntarily decide to commit, under their own responsibility'. Moreover, organizations providing mediation services may also commit to such principles; namely, by asking mediators acting under the auspices of their organization to abide by the European Code of Conduct. Nonetheless, the Preamble also acknowledges that organizations providing mediation services may wish to develop more detailed codes adapted to their specific context or the types of mediation services they offer, as well as to specific areas such as family mediation or consumer mediation.

The European Code of Conduct addresses the following topics: competence, the appointment and the fees of mediators and the promotion of their services; independence and impartiality; the mediation agreement, the mediation process and settlement; and confidentiality.[8] It is noteworthy that the adherence to the European Code of Conduct is without prejudice to any national legislation or rules regulating individual professions. [9]

Overall, within Europe, the general trend as regards codes of conduct for mediators may be characterized as either a jurisdiction where a national code of conduct for mediators has been developed by the State itself (Category A jurisdiction) or a jurisdiction where a code or codes of conduct have been developed at an institutional or an organizational level (Category B jurisdiction). In either case of a Category A or B jurisdiction the code(s) of conduct generally follow the European Code of Conduct. This chapter considers five representative jurisdictions falling within each of the two categories of jurisdiction described. They are France and Finland (Category A), and France, Finland, Spain, England and Wales, and Germany (Category B).

As a preliminary comment, the codes of conduct that have been developed within Europe generally contain provisions covering the following areas:1) mediator training, including initial and continuous training both in theory and practice as well as accreditation mechanisms; 2) independence, neutrality, impartiality, loyalty, and honesty of mediators; 3) confidentiality (as such, mediators cannot disclose any information obtained during the course of mediation save for public policy provisions or otherwise expressly agreed); 4) a mediator´s right to refuse to mediate, for example, if the mediation goes against his/her beliefs; 5) mediator fees; 6) parties' agreements to mediate, since the parties need to make informed decisions; 7) enforcement of the parties' mediated settlement agreements; 8) mediator

[7] The full text and status of the European Code of Conduct for Mediators is available at http://ec.europa.eu/civiljustice/adr/adr_ec_code_conduct_en.htm.

[8] European Code of Conduct for Mediators, sections 1–4.

[9] Ibid., Preamble.

duties and obligations (while there is naturally no obligation for the mediation to be successful, the mediator nonetheless needs to inform parties on his/her duties and obligations, since he or she may be sanctioned in case of violation of his/her duties under the code); 9) terms of reference for mediation (fixing the procedural timetable, timing, place, fees, party representatives, and the general conduct of the mediation); and 10) parties' assistance.[10] At long last, these codes of conduct also generally provide that the parties may modify their provisions (most often, by way of written agreement) in order to adapt the same to their particular case.

B. France

French regulation on mediation is one of the most thorough and robust within the European Union.[11] Civil mediation was first regulated in France by Law No. 95-125, dated 8 February 1995, regarding the organization of jurisdictions and civil, criminal, and administrative procedure. Subsequently, the EU Mediation Directive was transposed into French law through Order No. 2011-1540, of 16 November 2011, and Decree No. 2012-66, dated 20 January 2012, regarding amicable dispute resolution.

Within the current framework, both mediation and conciliation are currently defined under French law as a structured process whereby two or more parties to a dispute attempt to reach a settlement with the assistance of a neutral party. Further, the current system distinguishes between i) where the neutral party is jointly chosen by the parties outside of court proceedings (conventional mediation/conciliation) (Articles 1532 and 1535 of the French Code of Civil Procedure), or ii) selected by the judge seized during court proceedings if the parties agree (court-ordered mediation/conciliation) (Articles 131-1 ff of the Code of Civil Procedure and Article 2238 of the French Civil Code). Case law, specially that of the Cour de Cassation (Supreme Court), has further reinforced and provided guidelines as to the interpretation and application of this regulation.[12]

France stands as one of the few EU Member States where a national code of ethics for the mediator has been issued. The *Code national de déontologie du médiateur* (National Code of Mediator Ethics) dated 5 February 2009 has been adopted by various domestic mediation centres, including the *Association nationale des médiateurs européens* (AME), the *Association nationale des médiateurs* (ANM), the *Centre de médiation et d'arbitrage de la Chambre de commerce et d'industrie de*

[10] Nadja Alexander, 'Introducing Regulatory Robustness Ratings for Mediation Regimes in the EU', in Nadja Alexander, Sabine Walsh, and Martin Svatos (eds), *EU Mediation Law Handbook, Global Trends in Dispute Resolution* (Kluwer Law International, 2017) 5. Albeit not so recently, see also Nadja Alexander, 'International and Comparative Mediation', *Global Trends in Dispute Resolution* (Kluwer Law International, 2009) 215.

[11] Delphine Wietek, 'France', in Alexander, Walsh, and Svatos (n 10) 299.

[12] Ibid.

Paris (CMAP), the *Chambre nationale des practiciens de la médiation* (CNPM), the *Fédération nationale pour la médiation familiale* (FENAMEF), the *Fédération nationale des centres de médiation* (FNCM), the *Consulte des médiateurs d'entreprises and the réseau des médiateurs en entreprise* (RME). Overall, the National Code aims to be the baseline code of ethics for the practice of mediation in France.[13] Moreover, some of these mediation centres (e.g. the CNPM and the CMAP), have elaborated their own mediation rules or code of ethics in addition to the National Code.[14] Likewise, other mediation centres, such as *the Institut français de la médiation and the Chambre professionnelle de la médiation et de la négociation* also have their own codes of ethics.[15]

In addition to the French domestic mediation centres, there is also the International Chamber of Commerce (ICC), which is based in Paris, France. While the ICC has not adopted, together with its Mediation Rules in force as of 1 January 2014, any code of conduct, it has issued a Mediation Guidance Note that aims to provide guidelines to practitioners in the field of mediation.[16] Bearing in mind that mediation may be conducted in various ways depending on the background of the parties, their advisors, the mediator, and the nature of the dispute, the Mediation Guidance Note does not prescribe a mediation process, but rather encourages parties to work out the best arrangements for their particular case in light of common mediation practices and the flexibility of the process.[17]

C. Finland

In Finland mediation is regulated by a combination of legislation and other alternative soft law regulation. As such, while the main aspects of mediation are regulated by legislation, out-of-court mediation is left to a significant extent to institutional self-regulation, as well as to regulation by the market itself.[18] The first law on mediation in Finland entered into force at the start of 2006 with the Act on Court Mediation (663/2005) and the Act on Mediation in Criminal and Certain Civil Cases (1015/2005). In particular, court mediation has been influenced by developments in both Denmark and Norway, where mediation within

[13] See http://www.anm-mediation.com/images/anm/documents/code-de-deontologie.pdf.
[14] See http://www.cnpm-mediation.org/la-mediation/charte-de-la-mediation (CNMP) and http://www.cmap.fr/le-cmap/reglements/ (CMAP).
[15] See http://www.institut-francais-mediation.fr/index.php/la-mediation/code-de-deontologie, and http://cpmn.info/wp/ethique-et-de-deontologie/.
[16] 2014 Mediation Guidance Notes of the International Chamber of Commerce, https://iccwbo.org/publication/icc-2014-mediation-guidance-notes/.
[17] Preamble to the Mediation Guidance Note. See Chapter 5, this volume.
[18] Please note that this is the first reference. Petra Hietanen-Kunwald, 'Finland', in Nadja Alexander, Walsh, and Svatos (n 10) 274.

the courts has been used since 1998 (Norway) and 2003 (Denmark).[19] The Act on Court Mediation (663/2005) was later replaced by the Mediation Act (394/2011), entered into force in May 2011. The current Mediation Act is complemented by Government Bill 2010, which provides further additional guidance as to its interpretation. Moreover, in respect of court mediation, guidance can also be found in Government Bill 2004, which formed the basis of the (repealed) Act on Court Mediation (663/2005).

As is the case in France, there is also a national code of conduct for mediators in Finland. The national Code of Conduct for Lawyers applies in respect of mediation conducted by any member pertaining to the Finnish Bar Association.[20] As such, mediators registered with the Finnish Bar Association are subject, together with the Advocates Act, to a set of rules adopted by the Finnish Bar Association, which includes the Mediation Rules and the Code of Conduct. Section 2 of the Mediation Rules expressly states that mediators are in a client relationship with both (all) parties to the dispute and that the Code of Conduct applies *mutatis mutandis*. The fact that lawyer/mediators are deemed to be in a client relationship with both parties implies a general loyalty obligation towards both parties. Yet, this obligation raises questions about how the Code of Conduct will be interpreted in respect of this specific relationship as regards mediators, which evidently differs from usual client relationships, where lawyers represent only one party.[21]

Also, while the Code of Conduct allows lawyers/mediators to contractually limit their liability, they do not have legal immunity. Nevertheless, any limitation of liability must, at any rate, not be unreasonable, considering both the nature of the assignment and other circumstances.[22] In this regard, it is noteworthy that mediators are obliged to have mandatory professional indemnity insurance and that, specifically, in relation to consumers, the lawyers/mediators liability may only be restricted in exceptional cases.[23] In addition to the national code of conduct for mediators, there are other sectoral codes of conduct for mediators in Finland (namely, classified by area of specialization such as family law mediators, medical, or construction).[24]

[19] Ibid.

[20] Available only in Finish at https://www.asianajajaliitto.fi/files/1980/Hyva_asianajajatapa_fi_www.pdf.

[21] Hietanen-Kunwald (n 18) 286.

[22] See Section 5.2 of the Code of Conduct for mediators registered in Finland.

[23] See Commentary on the Code of Conduct for mediators registered in Finland, published on 31 January 2011. The Commentary is available at https://www.asianajajaliitto.fi/viestinta/muut_julkaisut/tapaohjekommentaari. Available at https://www.asianajajaliitto.fi/viestinta/muut_julkaisut/tapaohjekommentaari.

[24] See https://e-justice.europa.eu/content_mediation_in_member_states-64-fi-en.do?member=1.

D. Spain

Where mediation regulation existed in Spain before the EU Mediation Directive, both at a national and regional level, its focus was mainly on family mediation. The first initiative to regulate mediation in Spain can be traced back to the early twentieth century when several regional acts on family mediation were passed. Subsequently, the first progress in mediation regulation at a national level was accomplished through the enactment of the State Act 15/2005 of 8 July 2005 which amended some rules of the Spanish Civil Code and the Spanish Code of Civil Procedure on separation and divorce, and imposed an obligation to draft a law on family mediation on the Spanish government.[25]

This obligation would not be fulfilled for nearly another seven years, when the law implementing the EU Mediation Directive was finally enacted, albeit somewhat late and under a threat of penalties from the EU Commission. Specifically, Royal Decree-Law 5/2012 was enacted on 6 July 2012 as Act 5/2012, some aspects of which were later supplemented by Royal Decree 980/2013 of 13 December 2013 and by Order JUS/746/2014 of 6 May 2014 (jointly, 'the Spanish Mediation Act').

The Spanish Mediation Act's scope is broader than that of the EU Mediation Directive, since it encompasses both domestic and cross-border mediation on civil and commercial matters. In particular, according to Article 2(1) of the Act, it applies when the parties have explicitly or implicitly agreed on its application or, if no agreement exists, where at least one of the parties is domiciled in Spain and the mediation is going to be conducted in Spain.

While there is no national Spanish mediation code, there are several codes of conduct that influence the practice of mediation in Spain. For instance, the Mediation Committee of the Spanish Arbitration Club, whose main aim is to promote the development of mediation and its practice in Spain, adopted the Code of Good Practice for Mediation (CEA Code) in August 2013.[26] The CEA Code has been mostly influenced by the European Code of Conduct; by the revised Model Standards of Conduct for Mediators adopted by the American Arbitration Association, the American Bar Association and the Association for Conflict Resolution in 2005; and by the Code of Professional and Ethical Conduct for Members adopted by the Chartered Institute of Arbitrators in 2009. Overall, the CEA Code strives to provide a framework of security and trust for mediators, mediation institutions, and lawyers representing parties in mediation.[27]

Additionally, other codes of conduct have been adopted by some local chambers of commerce and mediation institutions in Spain: for instance, the codes of conduct adopted by the Mediation Institution of the Balearic Islands (*Institución*

[25] Mercedes Tarrazón and Marian Gili Saldaña, 'Spain', in Alexander, Walsh, and Svatos (n 10) 743.
[26] The CEA Code is available at http://www.clubarbitraje.com/en/mediation-commission.
[27] Ibid.

de Mediación de les Illes Balears),[28] the Mediation Centre of the Valencia Bar Association (*Centro de Mediación del Ilustre Colegio de Abogados de Valencia*),[29] and the Mediation Centre of Murcia (*Centro de Mediación de Murcia*).[30]

E. England and Wales

Mediation in England and Wales[31] has a long-standing tradition. What is more, England stands today as a major European hub for cross-border mediation, for the a number of reasons. First, historically, English law has been often the contract law selected between the parties thanks to its widespread respect internationally. Given that the courts in England are therefore a frequent forum, mediation practice has also followed accordingly. Second, the country's geographical position makes it a frequent choice of mediation venue for international disputes between parties from America and Europe. Third, the fact that English is, broadly speaking, the international language of business further enhances England and Wales as a major hub. Fourth, the development of the mediation practice in England and Wales has generally been significantly ahead in comparison with that of the rest of Europe, with the result that English-based mediators have had the opportunity to develop substantial experience and expertise.[32]

A notable feature of mediation practice in England and Wales, including for cross-border disputes, is the lack of a detailed and specific governing regulation. Such feature compares in contrast with the vast majority of professions—law, accountancy, and medicine, by way of example—that do have specific regulation. Yet, this reflects the pattern of development of mediation in England and Wales. Whereas many countries began issuing laws and other regulation for mediation to encourage the use of mediation, mediation in England and Wales began with the practice of it, and voices advocating for specific regulation in this field have only come later.[33]

Actually, mediation in England and Wales has grown mainly out of the business environment, and not through the introduction of regulatory reforms. As such, overall, it has been essentially 'demand-led' and not 'supply-led': for instance, the Centre for Effective Dispute Resolution (CEDR) was founded in 1990 with the

[28] See https://www.imibalears.es/files/Codigo-Deontologico-mediadores-IMIB.pdf.

[29] See http://www.mediacion.icav.es/codigo-deontologico-cmicav-2012/.

[30] See http://www.centrodemediacionmurcia.com/component/azurapagebuilder/?view=page&id=32.

[31] We note that Scotland and Northern Ireland, while part of the United Kingdom, are separate legal jurisdictions and have their own provisions governing mediation.

[32] Bill Marsh and others, 'England and Wales', in Alexander, Walsh, and Svatos (n 10) 207–8. Ewald Filler, 'Commercial Mediation in Europe', in *Commercial Mediation in Europe: An Empirical Study of the User Experience, Global Trends in Dispute Resolution* (Kluwer Law International, 2012) 229.

[33] Ibid., 208.

support of The Confederation of British Industry (CBI) and leading law firms, business, and the public sector.[34]

On the whole, what some civil lawyers may view as a potential lack of certainty, common lawyers tend to embrace as enabling both the preservation of party autonomy and the flexibility and choice that comes with it.[35] In fact, although precise statistics are practically impossible to obtain, it is estimated that there are approximately 10,000 commercial mediations being conducted each year in England and Wales.[36]

A number of important developments have impacted on mediation practice in England and Wales. These include the EU Mediation Directive, the Rome I Regulation on the law applicable to contractual obligations (to the extent it may be relevant to determining the applicable law of most mediation contracts),[37] Directive 2013/11/EU on alternative dispute resolution (ADR) for consumer disputes (to the extent it may be relevant as regards cross-border consumer disputes submitted to mediation),[38] and the Civil Procedure Rules (1998) in England and Wales (CPR).

Furthermore, while there is no national code of conduct for mediators, there is a range of available codes of conduct under which mediators can operate. By way of example, the CEDR Code of Conduct for Third Party Neutrals, which applies to any person who acts as a mediator or other neutral third party in any dispute resolution process conducted under the auspices of the CEDR and which is consistent with the European Code of Conduct for mediators.[39] Moreoever, other relevant examples are the Code of Practice of UK Mediation,[40] the Code of of Professional and Ethical Conduct of the Chartered Institute of Arbitrators (Part 2 relates to the conduct of its members as mediators),[41] and the Code of Practice and Guidance from the UK Family Mediation Council.[42]

While no particular code is legally mandatory, most mediators act in accordance with a particular one, and many do incorporate it into the mediation agreement, even if often only by reference. In principle, incorporation into the mediation agreement will eventually provide parties with a cause of action against the mediator for breach of the contract.[43] Even if most mediation organizations have

[34] See https://www.cedr.com/about_us/.
[35] Filler (n 32) 203.
[36] See the Centre for Effective Dispute Resolution Biannual Mediation Audit (11 May 2016) 3, https://www.cedr.com/docslib/The_Seventh_Mediation_Audit_(2016).pdf.
[37] Regulation (EC) No 593/2008 of the European Parliament and of the Council of 17 June 2008 on the law applicable to contractual obligations (Rome I).
[38] Directive 2013/11/EU of the European Parliament and of the Council of 21 May 2013 on alternative dispute resolution for consumer disputes, amending Regulation (EC) No 2006/2004 and Directive 2009/22/EC (Directive on Consumer ADR).
[39] Available at https://www.cedr.com/about_us/modeldocs/.
[40] See https://www.ukmediation.net/about-us/code-of-practice/.
[41] Available at https://www.ciarb.org/resources/guidelines-ethics/.
[42] See https://www.familymediationcouncil.org.uk/us/code-practice/.
[43] Filler (n 32), 222.

their own code of conduct, many mediators also often use the European Code of Conduct for Mediators as a guide.

F. Germany

The first codification of mediation and related provisions in Germany was accomplished by transposing the EU Mediation Directive into national law in July 2012 with the passing of the German Mediation Act (*Mediationsgesetz*, MediationsG).[44] Despite the EU Mediation Directive's focus on cross-border mediation, in transposing it into German national law, the German legislature focused almost exclusively on domestic mediation. As a result, cross-border disputes are frequently determined in Germany with the aid of institutional mediation rules.[45] For instance, the German Institution of Arbitration (*Deutsche Institution für Schiedsgerichtsbarkeit*) provides comprehensive mediation rules, among other alternative dispute resolution services, that may be used as regards cross-border disputes.[46] The development of the framework for cross-border mediation and mediation practice in general in Germany is still ongoing and may be revisited in future legislative initiatives. For now, Germany has resisted undertaking more ambitious reform to pass a comprehensive law on mediation.[47]

While MediationsG did not enact any code of conduct for mediators, many private mediation organizations have issued their own codes of conduct or directly refer to the European Code of Conduct for Mediators and incorporate them into their set of mediation rules. Germany has a large number of mediation organizations, both at a national and regional level, some of which are also part of umbrella organizations, such as the *Deutsches Forum für Mediation*.[48] Some prominent mediation organizations have issued their own codes of conduct, e.g. the Federal Association for Economic and Professional Mediatio (*Bundesverband Mediation in Wirtschaft und Arbeitswelt*).[49] Other mediation organizations, such as the Federal Association for Mediation (*Bundesverband Mediation*),[50] the Federal Association for Family Mediation (*Bundes-Arbeitsgemeinschaft für Familien-Mediation*),[51] or the German Centre for Mediation (*Centrale für Mediation*)[52] refer to the European Code of Conduct.

[44] 2012 German Mediation Act (*Mediationsgesetz*, MediationsG).
[45] Kristina Osswald and Gustav Flecke-Giammarco, 'Germany', in Alexander, Walsh, and Svatos (n 10) 223.
[46] Available at http://www.disarb.org/de/16/regeln/dis-mediation-rules-id31.
[47] Oswald (n 45), 223.
[48] See http://www.deutscher-mediationsrat.de/.
[49] Available at http://www.bmwa-deutschland.de/index.php/de/downloads/17.html.
[50] See https://www.bmev.de/ueber-den-verband/ethik/eu-verhaltenskodex.html.
[51] See https://www.bafm-mediation.de/internationales/english-information/european-code-of-conduct-for-mediators/.
[52] See https://www.centrale-fuer-mediation.de/verhaltenskodex.htm.

Given that MediationsG does not encompass a code of conduct for mediators, and there are currently no effective means of enforcing other codes of conduct, any possible breach of the mediator's duties or the mediation agreement may only be addressed via a law suit for breach of the mediator's contractual obligations. Some German practitioners have advocated for mediation institutions to introduce procedures to allow breaches to be assessed by an independent body.[53] The Statutory Order on Training and Further Education of Certified Mediators (*ZMediatAusbVO*) was passed on 21 August 2016 and came into force on 1 September 2017.[54] Time will tell whether the Statutory Order will further encourage both the use of mediation and its regulation in Germany.

III. Global Overview: Main Trends

A. Preliminary Remarks: The International Mediation Institute Framework

In the previous section two categories of jurisdiction were distinguished as regards the current regulation of codes of conduct for mediators within the Europe; namely, either a national code of conduct for mediators existing within a jurisdiction (Category A) or codes of conduct issued by various organizations (Category B). Globally, as is the case in the Europe, jurisdictions falling within Category B (e.g. Brazil and the US) also outnumber those falling within Category A (e.g. Hong Kong).

As it is beyond the scope of this chapter to analyse each jurisdiction at a global level as regards their respective regulation as to codes of conduct for mediators, it focuses instead on the three jurisdictions mentioned by way of example. However, before doing so, on a global perspective, it first briefly refers to the International Mediation Institute (IMI), which launched its revised Code of Professional Conduct in March 2017.[55]

Founded in 2007, the IMI is a non-profit charity registered in The Hague, The Netherlands. It is supported financially and practically by a group of corporate users and by a group comprising of the main international alternative dispute resolution service providers. 'Professional mediation worldwide' sums up the vision of the IMI, which aims to i) set and achieve high mediation standards; ii) convene stakeholders and parties; iii) promote understanding and adoption of mediation

[53] Peter Tochtermann, 'Mediation in Germany: The German Mediation Act', in Klaus J. Hopt and Felix Steffeck (eds), *Mediation: Principles and Regulation in Comparative Perspective* (OUP, 2012) 565.

[54] 2016 Statutory Order on Training and Further Education of Certified Mediators (*ZMediatAusbVO*).

[55] Available at http://www.imimediation.org/2017/03/10/launch-revised-imi-code-professional-code-conduct-mediators/.

among users and their advisers, and iv) disseminate skills for parties, counsel, and mediators.[56]

The IMI Code of Professional Conduct provides users of mediation services with a brief statement of the ethical standards expected from IMI Certified Mediators. Furthermore, users who believe the standards established in this Code have not been met may activate the IMI Professional Conduct Assessment Process.[57]

The IMI Code of Professional Conduct covers the following topics: mediator appointment; mediators' diligence and impartiality; mediators' conduct of the mediation process; confidentiality; and professional conduct issues and complaints.[58] Overall, the codes of conduct mentioned here generally cover the aforementioned topics, too.

B. Hong Kong

Hong Kong has enacted Mediation Ordinance (Cap 620), which is applicable to the mediation of both domestic and international cases and which came into effect on 1 January 2013.[59] Although there is no specific civil procedure legislation as regards mediation, Hong Kong's judiciary has issued several practice directions (PDs) for the conduct of various court proceedings related to both domestic and international mediation. The following PDs should be noted for their key influence in shaping mediation practice in Hong Kong: mediation (PD 31); voluntary mediation in petitions presented under Sections 168A and 177(1)(f) of the Companies Ordinance (PD 3.3); construction and arbitration list (PD 6.1); family mediation (PD 15.10); the personal injuries list (PD 18.1); the Employees' compensation list (PD 18.2); probate and administration of estate proceedings (other than applications under the non-contentious probate rules (PD 20.2); mediation for compulsory sale cases under the land (compulsory sale for redevelopment) (LTPD CS No.1/2011); and case management and mediation for nuilding (LTPD BM No.1/2009). [60]

In early 2010 the Hong Kong Mediation Code of Conduct was promulgated by the Hong Kong Department of Justice with the double goal of setting a common standard among mediators and serving as a key quality assurance function.[61] Among the forty-eight recommendations included in a report released later that year by the Working Group on Mediation of the Hong Kong Department of Justice was the recommendation to promote its endorsement among mediation

[56] See http://www.imimediation.org/about-imi/vision-and-mission/.
[57] Available at http://www.imimediation.org/practitioners/code-professional-conduct/.
[58] Ibid.
[59] 2013 Hong Kong Mediation Ordinance.
[60] Available at http://mediation.judiciary.hk/en/practice_directions.html.
[61] Available at http://www.doj.gov.hk/eng/public/pdf/2010/med20100208e_annex7.pdf.

organizations: 'there should be wide promulgation of the Hong Kong Mediation Code which is a code of conduct for mediators in Hong Kong and mediation service providers are encouraged to adopt the Code and set up robust complaints and disciplinary processes to enforce the Code'.[62]

Indeed, two years later, a single accreditation body, the Hong Kong Mediation Accreditation Association Limited (HKMAAL), was established in the form of a limited company to be a non-statutory, industry-led body responsible for accreditation and dealing with disciplinary matters as regards mediators practicing in Hong Kong.[63]

Among the most prominent organizations that have endorsed the Hong Kong Mediation Code of Conduct is the Hong Kong International Arbitration Centre (HKIAC).[64] Nonetheless, HKIAC also has its own General Code of Ethics for Mediators that, albeit largely similar, is not identical to the Hong Kong Mediation Code of Conduct.[65] In fact, the HKIAC's Code of Ethics has inspired other codes in turn, e.g. the Hong Kong Institute of Architects and the Hong Kong Institute of Surveyors, which with the permission of the HKIAC, have used its General Ethical Code for Mediators as a starting point.[66]

C. United States

In the United States, not only has each state and their administrative bodies adopted their own rules regarding mediation, but also local courts often have their own individual rules pertaining to mandatory and voluntary mediation. Given the disparity of approach, there have been several attempts to develop uniform mediation laws in the United States. These include the Alternative Dispute Resolution Act, which was adopted in 1998 by the United States Congress, and the Uniform Mediation Act.

As such, on the one hand, it must be noted that the Alternative Dispute Resolution Act requires all federal trial courts to implement ADR and authorizes them to send a case to mandatory ADR procedures, including mediation.[67] On the other hand, as regards the Uniform Mediation Act, it must be noted that several states have attempted to coordinate their legislation by adopting the Uniform Mediation Act or by adopting the state's own mediation statute with similar provisions. Drafted by the American Bar Association Section on Dispute Resolution and the National Commissioners on Uniform State Laws on 2001, the Uniform

[62] Available at http://www.doj.gov.hk/eng/public/pdf/2010/med20100208e.pdf. See Recommendation 27.
[63] Available at http://www.hkiac.org/mediation/rules/hong-kong-mediation-code.
[64] See also Chapter 9, this volume
[65] Available at http://www.hkiac.org/mediation/rules/general-ethical-code.
[66] See http://www.jdrc.com.hk/CodeConductMediator.htm.
[67] 1998 Alternative Dispute Resolution Act.

Mediation Act was first adopted by Nebraska in 2003, followed a few months later by Illinois. At the time of writing, eleven states and the District of Columbia have adopted the Uniform Mediation Act, and bills to enact it have been introduced in New York and Massachusetts. Other states, e.g. California, have not adopted the Uniform Mediation Act, but instead have adopted similar legislation.[68]

Furthermore, a number of different efforts have been made to establish codes of mediator ethics in the United States. Some of these attempts have been localized to particular mediation programmes, while others attempt a very broad approach designed to encompass all mediators. Specifically, at least two primary codes of conduct of widespread use exist at the time of writing in the United States: the Model Standards of Conduct for Mediators (Joint Standards), and the Model Standards of Practice for Family and Divorce Mediation.

As regards the former, it must be noted that they were initially developed and adopted by the American Arbitration Association, the American Bar Association Section of Dispute Resolution, and the Society of Professionals in Dispute Resolution (now called Association for Conflict Resolution) in 1994. These standards were revised on August 2005 and approved by all three participating organizations.[69]

Furthermore, as regards the latter, it must be noted that their current version was approved in August 2000 by the Association of Family and Conciliation Courts, Association for Conflict Resolution and Mediation following an update of the 1984 ABA Model Standards of Practice for Family and Divorce Mediation. The current Model Standards of Practice for Family and Divorce are generally applicable to the mediation of family and divorce disputes.[70]

Additonally, other ethical guidelines have been issued by the dispute resolution committees or sections of state and local bar associations, and most community mediation programs or mediation oganizations have their ethical guidelines, too. For example, JAMS, one of the largest private alternative dispute resolution providers in the world, has issued its own Mediators Ethics Guidelines, which provide basic guidance—without prejudice to the applicable law—to JAMS mediators as regards ethical issues that may arise during or related to the mediation process.[71]

Despite the need for and attention placed upon mediator ethics, practitioners have identified several difficulties as regards the establishment, implementation, and enforcement of a national code of ethics for mediators in the United States. As such, while the current dispersion of rules calls for the enactment of a national code of ethics (considering, for instance, that the aforementioned JAMS Mediators

[68] 2003 California Rules of Conduct for Mediators in Court-Connected Mediation Programs for Civil Cases. See the legislative tracking of the Uniform Mediation Act, http://www.uniformlaws.org/Act.aspx?title=Mediation%20Act.

[69] Available at www.mediate.com/articles/model_standards_of_conflict.cfm.

[70] Available at https://www.mediate.com/articles/afccstds.cfm.

[71] Available at https://www.jamsadr.com/mediators-ethics/.

Ethics Guidelines are necessarily subject to the applicable law), practitioners have pointed out that the interdisciplinarity of the field and the inherent flexibility of the process make it quite difficult to establish strictly common standards, since (in most settings) mediators are a diverse group.[72] Moreover, practitioners have also argued that no real enforcement authority exists, and that, as such, until the profession is subject to some form of licensing or regulation, the ability to include all mediators within a single code at a national level appears a daunting task.[73]

There is currently no register of certified mediators in the United States, nor is there a state-imposed national common mediator accreditation. In any state, a mediator can practise in private settings without being licensed, certified, or listed. Yet, while there are generally no limitations regarding their professional background—for example, a mediator is required to be a lawyer in the District of Columbia to mediate civil court cases other than family disputes—many mediators are former judges.[74] Most state courts maintain a 'roster of neutrals' or list of mediators for court referrals and at least twenty-eight states have statewide standards for those mediators who seek recognition by courts and who wish to maintain their status on such rosters.[75]

D. Brazil

Mediation is currently regulated in Brazil through two specific Acts: the Mediation Act, published on 26 June 2015, which came into force on 23 December 2015, and the new Civil Procedure Code, published on 16 March 2015, which came into force on 17 March 2016.[76] Prior to the introduction of this recent regulation, the most relevant instrument regulating mediation in Brazil was an administrative regulation from the National Council of Justice (Resolution No. 125/2010), as amended on 17 March 2016,[77] so as to establish that mediators and any other specialists involved in consensual methods of settling disputes must be subject to a permanent recurring training programme and public evaluation and to determine that certain schools and training institutions would undertake such training programmes for judicial mediators. Accordingly, Brazilian courts have regulated the recognition of these schools and institutions in each state.[78]

[72] Kimberlee K. Kovach, 'The Evolution of Mediation in the United States: Issues Ripe for Regulation May Shape the Future of Practice', in Nadja Alexander (ed.), *Global Trends in Mediation, Global Trends in Dispute Resolution* (2nd edn, Kluwer Law International 2006) 389–450.

[73] Ibid.

[74] See https://gettingthedealthrough.com/area/54/jurisdiction/23/mediation-2017-united-states/.

[75] See http://nvms.us/wp-content/uploads/2014/11/us-mediation-certification-standards.pdf.

[76] 2015 Mediation Act and 2016 Civil Procedure Code.

[77] 2010 National Council of Justice Resolution no. 125.

[78] See http://www.cnj.jus.br/atos-normativos?documento=156.

While mediation regulation has been advanced significantly with these 'ten years in one' developments,[79] codes of conducts for mediators still remain varied. At the time of writing, at least three primary codes of conduct of widespread use exist in Brazil.

First, the Code of Conduct of the National Council of the Arbitration and Mediation Institutions (*Conselho Nacional das Instituições de Mediação e Arbitragem*, CONIMA) was issued in 1997 by an organization of entities dedicated both to the teaching of and to the practice of mediation.[80] This Code of Ethics has been adopted by prominent mediation organizations at a national level, such as the Brazilian Centre of Mediation and Arbitration (*Centro Brasileiro de Mediaçao e Arbeitragem*, CBA).[81] Second, the Code of Conduct of the National Council of Justice (*Conselho Nacional de Justiça*, CNJ) was issued in 2010 as Annex III to the afore-mentioned Resolution No. 125/2010. This Code's application is limited to judicial mediation.[82] Third, the Code of Conduct of the National Forum of Mediation (*Fórum nacional de Mediação*, FONAME) was issued in 2011 by an organization encompassing institutions devoted to the teaching of and to promoting the practice of mediation in Brazil[83]

All the Codes of Ethics referred to above share the following key characteristics: autonomy of the will of the parties as a fundamental principle; impartiality, independence, credibility, competence, and diligence of the mediator; and preservation of secrecy as an ethical guide concerning the issues brought to mediation. In accordance with the applicable law, mediators should be qualified theoretically and practically and should work permanently to improve in both fields.[84]

IV. Conclusion

Lord Woolf of Barnes' astute commentary on the evolution of the mediation practice is particularly relevant in drawing conclusions from the above overview at both a European regional and a global level on the current trends on the codes of conduct available for commercial and investment mediators:

> Mediation has come a long way, but still has much further to go. The field now needs to evolve quickly into a true profession. High minimum practice and

[79] See http://mediationblog.kluwerarbitration.com/2017/03/03/brazilian-mediation-ten-year-in-one/.

[80] It is currently only available in Portuguese. See http://www.conima.org.br/codigo_etica_med.

[81] See http://www.cbma.com.br/us/codigo_de_etica.

[82] It is currently only available in Portuguese. See http://www.tjrj.jus.br/documents/10136/1077812/cod-etica-mediador-conciliador.pdf.

[83] It is currently only available in Portuguese. See https://fonamecombr.files.wordpress.com/2015/10/cc3b3digo-de-c3a9tica.pdf.

[84] See http://mediationblog.kluwerarbitration.com/2017/03/03/brazilian-mediation-ten-year-in-one/.

> ethical standards need to be set, made transparent and achieved internationally; users—customers—of mediation need to see these standards operating effectively. More and better information must be made available by individual mediators about their skills, capabilities and personalities. Quality and Transparency together will enable mediation to grow. [85]

Mediation practice has certainly come a long way in the last few years. It is today not only generally practised worldwide, but also supported by its own specific frameworks at a national or regional level. The importance of mediation was specifically recognized in the EC 2017 Report:[86]

> In line with the Justice for Growth agenda and the Europe 2020 Strategy, mediation could be seen as a means to improve the efficiency of the justice system and to reduce the hurdles that lengthy and costly judicial procedures create for citizens and businesses; it can therefore contribute to economic growth. Mediation may also contribute to maintaining good relationship between the parties as, contrary to judicial proceedings there is no 'winning' or 'losing' party, which is particularly important, e.g. in family law cases.

Yet, while many states both in Europe and globally have enacted a national act to regulate the mediation practice (although in most occasions they do so in quite broad, rather than specific, terms), a remarkable variation still remains, particularly as regards the issuance of codes of conduct for mediators. As such, at a global level, as is the case within Europe, jurisdictions that fall within Category B (i.e. systems with several codes of conduct issued by various organizations) currently outnumber those jurisdictions falling within Category A (i.e. systems with a national code of conduct for mediators). In this regard, while the current codes of conduct for mediators strive to favour mediation practice and increase transparency, remarkable variations in these codes may ultimately have the opposite effect.

With this in mind, it is submitted that among the next key steps in order to further promote the use of mediation is to push—in those jurisdictions where there are multiple codes of conduct for mediators issued by different mediation organizations—for the development of one national code of conduct for mediators. Indeed, as UC Berkeley Professor Harold J. Wilensky notes, 'any occupation wishing to exercise authority must find a technical basis for it, assert an exclusive jurisdiction, link both skill and jurisdiction to standards of training, and convince

[85] Woolf of Barnes, Lord Chief Justice of England & Wales in 2000–2005, as cited in Patrick Deane, Wolf von Kumberg, Michael Leathes, Deborah Masucci, Michael McIlwrath, Leslie Mooyaart, and Bruce Whitney, 'Making Mediation Mainstream: A User/Customer Perspective', in Arnaud Ingen-Housz (ed.) *ADR in Business: Practice and Issues Across Countries and Cultures* (Kluwer Law International, 2010) 49–59.

[86] See EC 2017 Report, Section IV, 'A Balanced Relationship between Mediation and Judicial Proceedings'.

the public that its services are uniquely trustworthy and tied to a set of professional norms'.[87] In effect, the current disparity existing between codes of conduct for mediators within most jurisdictions does not assist mediation in accomplishing these goals.

Further, enacting one national code of conduct for mediators within the respective jurisdictions would have a number of benefits, including: encouraging more consistent and transparent mediation practice, upon setting common standards of conduct; avoiding increasing bureaucracy both for mediators and for the parties; boosting the quality of the mediator services, in accordance with clear and homogenous standards of practice as set by the code; and, avoiding any potential conflicts that may inevitably arise within a system where several codes of conduct for mediators coexist. In fact, in those jurisdictions where a national code of conduct exists, e.g. France, Finland, or Hong Kong, mediation practice and its regulation appear particularly well developed and robust.

While it is possible to have an interim period where both a national code of conduct for mediators and other codes could potentially coexist, the ultimate optimal goal would be that only a single national code would exist in each jurisdiction. And then, ultimately, a common international code of conduct for mediators could be established. For now, it will be interesting to see whether the current Category B mediation jurisdictions will further develop and become Category A mediation jurisdictions. If so, this is likely to bring more consistency and transparency to the regulation of the mediation practice. Both the European Code of Conduct and the EU Mediation Directive have managed to foster such a trend at least within the area of the European Union. Time will tell if such a trend can ultimately also be accomplished on a global level.

[87] Harold J. Wilensky, 'The Professionalization of Everyone' (1964) 70 The American Journal of Sociology 2.

19

New Singapore Convention on Cross-Border Mediated Settlements

Key Choices

*Hal Abramson**

I. Introduction

On 9 February 2018, Working Group II of the United Nations Commission on International Trade Law (UNCITRAL) finished three years drafting a convention on cross-border mediated settlement agreements.[1] The Convention, which is designed to facilitate compliance with agreements, offers a more expeditious alternative to relying on expensive and uncertain breach of contract lawsuits. The backstory of this milestone is really two stories: one on the multi-party negotiation process that produced the result and one on the substantive choices in the result. The two stories also illustrate the relationship between a well-designed process and result.

This brief description is intended to help those less familiar with UNCITRAL before reading anything else. UNCITRAL was established by the UN General Assembly (UNGA) to help harmonize and modernize the law of international trade and commercial law. UNCITRAL's sixty state members are elected by the UNGA and selected to ensure representation by geographic regions and principal economic and legal systems. As an organ of the UNGA, UNCITRAL follows the UNGA's rules of procedures for its sessions and those of its working groups. UNCITRAL determines its work programme based on proposals received from

* The author recognizes the valuable comments on earlier drafts by Corinne Montineri and Tim Schnabel. The author also thanks Cardozo Law School research assistants Nicholas Gliagias and Farzana Khaleda for their diligent work checking and formatting footnotes.

[1] NB: the word 'enforcement' is not used in the title of this chapter, within this chapter (with a couple of exceptions), or in the title of the Convention. The Convention is formally entitled 'United Nations Convention on International Settlement Agreements Resulting from Mediation' and will likely be known as the 'Singapore Convention on Mediation.' Common law attorneys will likely be surprised by this language choice, even though the Convention fashions a process for 'enforcing' cross-border mediated settlement agreements. Civil law lawyers also are likely to be surprised that the familiar phrase 'recognition' is omitted in the Convention and replaced by a functional definition in the Convention. The background on this language choice is explained under section IV, which describes the five-point compromise called 'The Compromise.'

States or organizations. It sets its own agenda, reviews the work of its various working groups to which the Commission assigns projects, and prepares reports, model laws, and conventions for the UN.

This mediated settlement initiative was assigned by the Commission to Working Group II, which formerly focused on 'Arbitration,' then was expanded to cover 'Arbitration and Conciliation,' and currently is named 'Dispute Settlement.' Any recommendations from Working Group II are sent to UNCITRAL for its adoption, and any proposed conventions, as occurred in this case, are first sent to UNCITRAL and then to the UNGA for consideration and adoption.[2] This chapter focuses primarily on the deliberations of Working Group II when drafting the mediation settlement convention.

At the outset, I should explain my vantage point. I present these two stories from the perspective of an active 'observer' not as a member of a country delegation. I represented two non-governmental organizations (NGOs) with observer status, the International Mediation Institute (IMI) and the International Academy of Mediators (IAM),[3] attended most of the drafting meetings over the three-year process, and participated in multiple discussions. I also served as an 'expert consultant'. In that capacity, I organized and moderated three mediation education programmes for delegates and the public under the auspice of UNCITRAL.[4] Finally, I also bring the perspective of an arbitrator, mediator, and full-time academic in the field of dispute resolution for over twenty-five years who has written regularly on negotiations, mediation, and international conflict resolution.

I feel a need to explain the writing style that includes a disproportionate use of pronouns and passive voice over my preference for active voice and acknowledging the contributions of others. The writing style respects the norms of the UNCITRAL deliberative process where reports are written with pronouns, in passive tense, and with few references to individuals or organizations.[5] Even though the public documents omit names, I mention some key players and unreported exchanges thanks to the permission that I was given. Nevertheless, many of the heroes in these stories are sadly omitted, although these heroes are known to people who participated in the drafting process.

With these writing guidelines in mind, I expound in the chapter on the process and substantive stories that resulted in the new Convention.

[2] UNCITRAL, *A Guide to UNCITRAL: Basic Facts About the United Nations Commission on International Trade Law* (United Nations, 2013) 6, para. 48.

[3] IMI is an international organization that develops global standards for mediators, advocates and others in dispute resolution. See https://www.imimediation.org/. IAM is an organization of peer-selected top commercial mediators from around the world. See https://iamed.org/.

[4] See section C (the three programmes are briefly described in (n 10)).

[5] When preparing this article, I was advised that I could safely discuss any information that is publicly available, but asked not to refer to any discussions that were not expected to be public. Consultations and informal discussions during breaks are productive in part because participants can speak freely without public attribution and need to anticipate reactions of constituencies as they are working through problems.

II. Initiating the Mediated Settlement Project

This Project officially started on Friday, 21 March 2014 at 3:54 pm, at least for me, when I received an email from a Tim Schnabel with the US Department of State. He introduced himself as the US representative to UNCITRAL's Arbitration and Conciliation Working Group. His office, he indicated, was considering a project on the enforcement of mediated settlement agreements. He was interested in my thoughts on whether such a project would be desirable to pursue. In our telephone call, he mentioned that the project idea was initially raised at a State Department's advisory committee meeting by Professor S. I. Strong.[6] I learned that Mr. Schnabel was systematically reaching out to various people to figure out whether the enforcement project was worth proposing to UNCITRAL. After several months of consulting with various interest groups and experts, he prepared a proposal for future work to UNCITRAL for its July 2014 Session. The proposal, formally submitted on behalf of the US, was referred by UNCITRAL to Working Group II for evaluation.[7]

At the Working Group II Session in New York in February 2015, the delegates along with non-governmental organizations (NGOs) and other observer groups engaged in a thorough review of the US proposal. The week-long session was conducted by Michael Schneider from Switzerland who served as a diligent and disciplined Chair. I sat in the room in awe as a first-time observer. The Chair tightly managed the substantive discussions among more than hundred people representing ninety-one states and organizations. I was especially impressed by his skill in summarizing what he heard to clarify he understood each point and in his incisive follow-up questions. He usually posed one or two probing questions to test the understanding of the speaker and to delve deeper, although I was less enamoured with his technique when I was in the hot seat.

Mr. Schneider seemed sceptical about the wisdom of this project as he engaged with speakers from topic to topic. For those of us favouring the project, the meeting was a cliff hanger. I recall us trying to guess whether the Chair was inclined toward or against the project by the questions he would ask, his tone, and his body language—variables that those of us in the dispute resolution field think we are pretty good at reading. During the breaks, we shared our guesses and tried to read the tea leaves, rarely confident about each of our predictions. We were acutely

[6] The idea for the convention was generated at a public meeting of the Department of State's Advisory Committee on Private International Law in February 2014. At that meeting, Professor S. I. Strong of the University of Missouri Law School presented her article comparing the legal environment surrounding international commercial arbitration with the surrounding international commercial mediation and suggested creating a new convention in the area of international mediated settlements. See S. I. Strong, 'Beyond International Commercial Arbitration? The Promise of International Commercial Mediation' (2014) 45 Washington University Journal of Law & Policy 11.

[7] United Nations General Assembly, '47th Session, July 2014, Planned and Possible Future Work – Part III, Proposal by the Government of the United States of America: Future Work for Working Group II' (2 June 2014) UN Doc A/CN.9/822.

aware of how the meeting would end: depending on how the Chair reads the group, he would declare a consensus to proceed or not. We were pleased that the week ended with a recommendation that the project be adopted by the Commission.

You can gain an understanding of the thoroughness and range of discussion by reviewing the detailed Work Group II report after the session. It neatly divided the discussion into General Remarks, Legal and Practical Questions, Feasibility and Possible Form of Future Work, and Recommendation to the Commission.[8] Working Group II concluded that:

> After discussion, the Working Group agreed to suggest to the Commission that it be given a mandate to work on the topic of enforcement of settlement agreements, to identify the relevant issues and develop possible solutions, including the preparation of a convention, model provisions or guidance texts. Considering that differing views were expressed as to the form and content, as well as the feasibility, of any particular instrument, it was also agreed to suggest that a mandate on the topic be broad enough to take into account the various approaches and concerns.[9]

III. Process Story: Multi-Party Negotiations at Working Group II

Before exploring the next section on the substantive choices in the Convention, you might find helpful this brief description of the underlying multi-party process that produced the result. In my view it was well-designed to fully engage participants in a robust deliberative process.

Working Group II selected as Chair of this project Natalie Morris-Sharma, a member of the Singapore delegation. Under her watchful and skilful supervision, she chaired this almost three-year deliberative process in collaboration with the expert assistance of UNCITRAL's Secretary to Working Group II, Corinne Montineri. Ms. Morris-Sharma proved to be an impressive Chair due to her thoughtful use of 'consultations' discussed further on and active listening skills. I was astonished to learn afterwards that she had no formal mediation or facilitation training. She was a natural. She summarized comments succinctly, checked-in with speakers to verify that she accurately understood what she heard, and proficiently used open and close questions to promote sharing and clarifying information among participants. She also effectively used instinctive humour that helped lubricate the serious deliberations. For example, when the discussions were moving too quickly at

[8] UN General Assembly (UNGA), 'Report of Working Group II (Arbitration and Conciliation) on the Work of its Sixty-Second Session' (11 February 2015) UN Doc A/CN.9/832, IV. D.

[9] See Recommendation to the Commission after February Working Group II Session. See A/CN.9/832, IV. D. Paragraph 59 (11 February 2015).

one point, she triggered collective laughter when apologizing for her hyperactivity while proclaiming that she had not yet drunk her first cup of coffee that day.

The Working Group met twice a year for one to two weeks sessions to deliberate issue by issue, and draft section by section, with input from the EU Commission and various NGOs in the room. The consensus-building process featured six methods that were employed to produce a productive process. I thought it illustrated best practices for managing a large multi-party negotiation.

A. Whole Group Meetings

Working Group II members primarily met together to deliberate in a UNGA-style room. The Chair guided the discussions for each session by following an agenda and the numbered paragraphs in a report that was published in advance of each session. She piloted the Working Group with an attentive ear for any emerging consensus, opportune moments to break for a 'consultation', and differences that may warrant deferring a topic.

The room set-up placed the state delegations in the front half at their delegation tables, while the NGOs, regional representatives, and international organizations sat at their tables in the second half of the room. Each seat included an electronic or plastic placard that displayed the name of the country or organization and headsets to connect with one of five simultaneous translators. Behind each seat were other chairs with headsets to accommodate other members of a delegation or organization. Some of the state delegations included two to six members; the number of people in the front of the room could sometimes reach a hundred, and the number of NGOs and regional representatives could add another fifty to seventy-five participants.

The procedure for contributing was simple. Anyone wishing to speak could press a speaker button in New York or turn the plastic placard upright in Vienna and wait to be called by the Chair. In New York, where there was no screen that listed speakers waiting for their turn, a speaker did not know how many speakers were in the queue. In Vienna, speakers could gauge when they would be called by seeing the number of placards upright. Speakers were by and large savvy in diplomatic language, respectful, substantive, and worked at maintaining the deliberative thread by referring to prior presenters' remarks. This approach left me feeling that speakers were mostly listening to each other and not just giving speeches.

B. Consultations

The Chair strategically adjourned meetings for a 'consultation' when she thought that no consensus was emerging on a significant issue and informal discussions might help. She would frame the issue and invite delegates to meet for 30 minutes (or more) in small groups to develop proposals for the full group. These consultations, which were used several times for each session, would lead to small group meetings, mini-negotiations, and draft proposals. The Chair would move around the floor listening unobtrusively to small group discussions and gently offer prompts to help keep the consultations on track. The method was exceptionally effective in resolving some of the most contentious issues. I think the consultations succeeded in part because key participants approached these opportunities for engagement with a mindset to learn from each other and reconcile differences.

C. Educational Programmes for the Delegates and Public

Mediation programmes were conducted to educate delegates and the public about issues relevant to key stages of the drafting process. UNCITRAL hosted or co-sponsored three mediation education programmes that were organized at the initiative of mediation organizations. I was asked to organize each of the programmes that were each scheduled to coincide with a concurrent Working Group II session.[10] Like other UNCITRAL educational programmes, the goal was to help inform the ongoing deliberative process. These programmes appeared valuable for state delegations that were more expert on arbitration than mediation. I leave to others who attended the programmes to judge their benefits.

[10] After the first Working Group Session in Vienna in September 2015, the Executive Director of IMI, Irena Vanenkova, offered to put together a mediation education programme for delegates who might be interested in gaining more background on mediation to help inform their contributions. UNCITRAL responded positively to the offer. IMI asked me to put together a programme and recruited Professor Janet Martinez at Stanford Law School to participate. We designed this first programme for the second working group session on 2 February 2016 at the UN in New York. It compared mediation with the more familiar arbitration process. After the New York meeting, there was a sense that another programme might be helpful. The second educational programme was held during the next session at the UN in Vienna on 21 September 2016. That programme was well-timed personally because I went to Vienna on the way to my son's wedding in Cyprus the following week! The programme was hosted by the Vienna International Arbitral Center and co-sponsored with IMI and IAM. It included the following panelists: Eileen Carroll QC (Mediator, Co-founder, CEDR, London), Birgit Sambeth Glasner (Mediator, Geneva), Michel Kallipetis (Mediator, London), Allan Stitt (Mediator, Member of Canadian Delegation, Toronto), Josephine Wan-Wen Hadikusumo (Senior Counsel, Asia, Texas Instruments, Singapore), Norris Yang (Mediator, Former Chair of Hong Kong Mediation Council, Hong Kong). I moderated the programme that was entitled an opportunity to ask questions to mediators and users. After the Vienna meeting, some felt that one more programme might be useful. The third programme was held at the next session at the UN in New York on 8 February 2017. It was hosted by JAMS, and co-sponsored by IMI and IAM. The panel included Michel Kallipetis (Mediator, London), Louise Otis (Mediator, retired justice of the Quebec Court of Appeals, President of the Administrative Tribunal of OECD, Montreal), Dr. Karl Mackie (Mediator, President, Co-founder, CEDR, London), Pedro Ribeiro (MCIArb, Arbitrator and Mediator, Vice President of CAMARB—Câmara de Arbitragem, Empresarial, Brazil), Roland Schroeder (General Electric Global Litigation Counsel, United States), and Allan Stitt (Mediator, Member of Canadian Delegation, Toronto). Similar to the previous programme, I moderated it, and we invited participants to ask questions to mediators and users.

D. Contributions by NGOs and the EU

UNCITRAL encourages NGOs to attend and contribute to working group meetings. UNCITRAL values their experience and expertise because NGOs reflect the audience that will ultimately use the texts. When this new mediation project was announced, a number of mediation-related groups registered with UNCITRAL for observer status and sent representatives to the meetings. The format at the sessions made it easy for NGOs to contribute because they had access to documents, were assigned seats with microphones and headsets, and could talk with state delegates on the floor during breaks and consultations. NGO representatives participated in multiple formal and informal ways as issues emerged. I will cite several examples as illustrations although there were many more.

An early issue was whether a mediation settlement instrument was even needed when Working Group II was assessing whether to recommend proceeding with the mediation project. At that February 2015 session, Professor S. I. Strong of the University of Missouri Law School,[11] representing the American Society of International Law, helped bolster the case for the initiative when she presented an empirical study she conducted as supporting evidence.[12] A second original study that offered further supporting evidence was conducted by the Institute for Dispute Resolution at New Jersey City University. It was undertaken for IMI and presented at the September 2016 Vienna Session. The study found that the majority of users and stakeholders in the survey and at the Global Pound Conference believe that a global mechanism to enforce mediation settlements would improve commercial dispute resolution in international business transactions.[13]

[11] See Chapter 3, this volume.

[12] The delegates were provided with a preliminary report that was subsequently published as a law review article. S. I. Strong, 'Realizing Rationality: An Empirical Assessment of International Commercial Mediation' (2016) 73 Washington and Lee Law Review 1973. See also S. I. Strong, 'Use and Perception of International Commercial Mediation and Conciliation: A Preliminary Report on Issues Relating to the Proposed UNCITRAL Convention on International Commercial Mediation and Conciliation' (2014) University of Missouri School of Law Legal Studies Research Paper 2014-28, https://papers.ssrn.com/sol3/papers.cfm?abstract_id=2526302. Preliminary findings from the study had previously been reviewed by the UNCITRAL Secretariat and the United States and were referenced in documents circulated prior to the February 2015 meeting. See Note by Secretariat, 'Settlement of Commercial Disputes: Enforceability of Settlement Agreements Resulting From International Commercial Conciliation/Mediation' (27 November 2014) U.N. Doc. A/CN.9/WG.II/WP.187 at 6 (n 16). See also Comments Received From States, 'Settlement of Commercial Disputes: Enforceability of Settlement Agreements Resulting From International Commercial Conciliation/Mediation—Revision of the UNCITRAL Notes on Organizing Arbitral Proceedings' (23 December 2014) U.N. Doc. A/CN.9/WG.II/WP.188 at 6 (n 7).

[13] Michael R. Griffith and David S. Weiss, 'Report On International Mediation And Enforcement Mechanisms: Issued by the Institute for Dispute Resolution (IDR) NJCU School of Business to the International Mediation Institute for the Benefit of Delegates Attending the UNCITRAL Working Group II (Dispute Settlement) 67th Session' (UNCITRAL Working Group II (Dispute Settlement) 67th Session, Vienna, September 2017), https://www.imimediation.org/wpfd_file/imi-njcuidr-wgii-report2017v4-0-pdf.

Another issue that got my personal attention was whether the compliance instrument should apply to only monetary terms. At the first Working Group II meeting in February 2015, several delegations and at least one NGO representative asserted that any instrument should be limited because of the practical difficulties of enforcing non-monetary terms. This suggestion was alarming, in my view. If an international treaty restricted enforcement to only monetary terms, parties may view mediation primarily for resolving this narrow class of disputes. This narrow view would foreclose the full benefits of the mediation process for uncovering other terms that may better meet parties' interests. After much research on the parallel issue under the Convention on the Recognition and Enforcement of Foreign Arbitral Awards (New York Convention), I presented precedent for a broader instrument and the substantive and policy reasons favouring that approach. Other speakers also spoke in support of a broader instrument. Fortunately, this view was ultimately adopted by Working Group II and the final convention covers compliance with all the settlement terms.[14]

Mediation-related NGOs especially rallied at the Vienna meetings in September 2016 when several difficult questions converged for discussion: Would the convention apply to private parties on an opt-in or opt-out basis? Should an enforceable agreement be certified as one that was the product of a private mediation, and if so, how would it be certified? And, whether a defence to enforcement would include certain types of misbehaviour by the mediator, and if so, how narrow would the defence be framed? These questions fell clearly within the bailiwick of the mediation-related NGOs and their representatives, and they offered much formal and informal input into various proposals. These three questions were ultimately resolved as part of the break-through 'compromise' discussed in the next section.[15]

As these several examples illustrate, NGOs contributed in various ways during the drafting process. They were welcomed by many state delegations, in my experience. However, like any multi-party process, it can be difficult to assess the impact of most contributors. Nevertheless, I think NGOs can safely claim that their participation enriched the discussion.

In addition to various NGOs participating, the EU, as a regional economic integration organization represented by the European Commission, participated actively throughout the three years. EU member states made up more than 25 percent of the delegates on the floor at any meeting.[16] They were ably represented by

[14] One delegation, in an effort to find a solution that may appeal to all sides, proposed that the convention cover non-monetary features with the option for a state to file a reservation to exclude enforcement of long-term or complex obligations.

[15] See section IV.

[16] UNCITRAL membership of sixty states included thirteen members from the EU (21.6 percent). For the Working Group II meetings, attendance varied. For the February 2017 Session in New York, for example, twelve out of the forty-one members in attendance were members of the EU (29 percent) plus nine more EU countries as observers. UNGA, 'Report of Working Group II (Dispute Settlement) on the Work of its Sixty-Sixth Session' (16 February 2017) UN Doc A/CN.9/901 II. In the last meeting in February 2018, when the final draft was adopted, twelve out of the thirty-three members in attendance were members of the EU (36 percent) plus four more countries as observers. See UNGA, 'Report of

Norel Rosner, Legislative Officer, who contributed much in the whole group meetings, during consultations, and in informal discussions.

E. The *Travaux Préparatoires* (Official Record of a Negotiation)

The *travaux préparatoires*, known as travaux, reports, and secretariat notes, were prepared before each session and at the end of each meeting day. These documents aided the deliberations as they unfolded by creating a record so that participants could track where they have been and where they were going. These documents standout for two reasons. First, they offer a detailed contemporaneous record of what transpired (issues that were considered and what was discussed). Second, there are no personal names, countries, or NGOs associated with the remarks and exchanges. The entire written record is anonymous in order to promote candid exchanges and reduce the need to grandstand for constituencies back home.

As the secretary of UNCITRAL Working Group II, Corrinne Montineri performed the herculean task of preparing the numerous lengthy documents that aided the working group's deliberations. Ms. Montineri, with help from her colleague Jae Sung Lee, prepared before each session a provisional agenda, a Report of Working Group II that covered what happened at the prior session, and a Note by the Secretariat as background and guide for the upcoming session. Then when the session convened, Ms. Montineri with her colleague prepared daily 'draft' reports of what transpired and distributed them before the next day of meetings. At the end of each day, she returned to her office to meticulously prepare the draft report for the next day while the delegates and other representatives took a break for the evening to socialize and meet informally before returning for another work day. These *travaux préparatoires* are posted on the UNCITRAL website, making them a widely available source for clarifying and interpreting the final model law and convention. You will see many references to these sources in this chapter.

F. Voting

Decisions were made by consensus. I was surprised to learn at my first meeting that, as a general rule, no formal voting took place. The Chair, Ms. Morris-Sharma, had the responsibility of recognizing when the working group reached a consensus. She used various techniques to test for one. For example, she would declare 'that not hearing any more comments or disagreements' she was ready to move on. That comment would ferret out further concerns if there were any. Or, she would

Working Group II (Dispute Settlement) on the Work of its Sixty-Eighth Session' (19 February 2018) UN Doc A/CN.9/934 II.

invite other comments with the remark that if there are no more, she would declare a consensus. These types of prompts helped surface an emerging consensus or an occasion for consultation or deferring an issue. This form of decision-making imposed a heavy responsibility on the Chair to listen attentively, astutely read the group, and proactively build consensus.[17]

These six methods to engage participants were used throughout the week-long sessions over the almost three years of deliberations.

IV. Substantive Story: Key Issues and How They Were Resolved

This section explains key provisions of the Convention, including the five-point compromise that likely will be of interest to mediation-savvy readers and states that are contemplating adopting the Convention.[18] The full Convention can be found in Appendix A. For states that might not be ready to ratify the Convention, the working group prepared, as an alternative, an amendment to the Model Law on International Commercial Conciliation. The Model Law is not discussed in this chapter.

A. Article 1. Scope of Application

Article 1 frames the narrow scope of the Convention. Presumably to little surprise, Article 1(1) limits its application to disputes that are international, and it includes a definition of international that focuses on the place of a party's business, where a substantial part of the obligations is performed, or where the subject matter is most closely connected.[19] Articles 1(2) and 1(3) further limit the scope by specifying what disputes and settlement agreements are *not* covered, with limits that will surprise and disappoint some. Article 1(2) states that the Convention does not apply to settlement agreements that arise out of consumer transactions or relate to family, inheritance, and employment law. Article 1(3) tries to avoid overlap with other regimes that apply to mediated settlement agreements. Some delegations wanted to avoid duplicating other regimes, e.g. the Hague Conference instruments, while others were fine with states providing multiple avenues for relief under different instruments. They were less concerned with overlap and more concerned about

[17] UNCITRAL, *A Guide to UNCITRAL: Basic Facts About the United Nations Commission on International Trade Law* (United Nations, 2013) 6, para. 14.

[18] Timothy Schnabel, who represented the US at UNCITRAL and initially proposed the mediation project, recently posted on SSRN a draft article on the new treaty. See 'The Singapore Convention on Mediation: A Framework for the Cross-Border Recognition and Enforcement of Mediated Settlements', https://papers.ssrn.com/sol3/papers.cfm?abstract_id=3239527 (September 2018).

[19] See full text in Appendix A.

avoiding gaps by other instruments imposing ceilings, not floors. The working group decided to restrict the scope so that it would not apply to settlement agreements approved by a court or concluded in the course of a court proceeding and enforceable as a state court judgment. Also, it would not apply to settlement agreements enforceable as an arbitral award.

B. Article 2. Definitions

Article 2(3) offers a definitions section with a surprise that I suspect will be embraced by much of the contemporary mediation world. It replaced the word 'conciliation' with the word 'mediation'. Even though UNCITRAL used the word 'conciliation' in the Conciliation Rules (1980) and in the Model Law on International Conciliation (2002), Working Group II made this long overdue change. It then labelled the convention as 'United Nations Convention on International Settlement Agreements Resulting from *Mediation*' (emphasis added). The Working Group offered the following explanation:

> [T]he Commission decided to use the term 'mediation' instead in an effort to adapt to the actual and practical use of the terms and with the expectation that this change will facilitate the promotion and heighten the visibility of the instruments. This change in terminology does not have any substantive or conceptual implications.[20]

Although some might object because they think there is a worthwhile distinction to maintain between mediation as a more facilitative process and conciliation as a more evaluative process, I would expect most of the mediation audience to welcome this change.

C. Article 4. Requirements for Reliance on Settlement Agreements

Parties must supply evidence of a 'settlement agreement that resulted from mediation'. This unexpected proof requirement was subject to considerable discussion and reflects what the drafting group characterized as a 'balance between, on the one hand, the formalities that are required to ascertain that a settlement agreement result from mediation and, on the other hand, the need for the draft convention to

[20] UNGA, 'Settlement of Commercial Disputes—International Commercial Mediation: Draft Convention on International Settlement Agreements Resulting from Mediation' (2 March 2018) UN Doc A/CN.9/942, II.B(1) .

preserve the flexible nature of the mediation process'.[21] It is in this spirit that this proof requirement should be interpreted.

This requirement was born out of the concern that the Convention apply only to settlements from a legitimate mediation process. Some delegates wanted to be sure that the treaty would not be used for illegal purposes like money laundering or for mediations that are not genuine, e.g. when a couple of friends in a dispute meet in a pub. It is for these reasons that the Convention not only requires that the agreement be signed by the parties, but also that there is 'evidence that the settlement agreement resulted from mediation' by one of four ways: the mediator's signature on the settlement agreement, the mediator's signature on a separate document indicating a mediation was carried out, an attestation by an administering institution, or 'any other evidence acceptable to the competent authority'.[22]

D. Article 5. Grounds for Refusing to Grant Relief

Article 5 on defences posed the risk of crippling the Convention by establishing facially sound grounds for refusing relief that could be abused. Delegates argued that preserving defences was vital for protecting parties with a valid reason for not complying with a settlement agreement. At the policy level, they offered a persuasive argument. But if all or most possible defences were preserved, the Convention would fail to serve its primary purpose of expediting compliance. Article 5 was subject to multiple rounds of discussion at different meetings, including a gallant effort in the final session to regroup and refine the grounds to avoid overlap. I had hoped that this last discussion would have further refined the grounds and reduced the risk of misuse. The failure to gain consensus was due to the 'need to accommodate the concerns of different domestic legal systems'[23] and left disconcerting space for abuse, in my view.

Preserving several limited defences made sense, like the opportunity to present proof that the party 'was under some incapacity' or that the settlement agreement was not binding, was subsequently modified, or has been performed. Other defences, however, left space to ferment trouble by defendants who want to avoid compliance. Two troublesome defences stand out. One is the defence that an agreement is 'null and void, inoperative or incapable of being performed under the law to which the parties have validly subjected it'.[24] Another is the defence that the obligations in the agreement are 'not clear or comprehensible'.[25] By asserting these

[21] Ibid.
[22] Articles 4(a) and 4(b) of the Convention.
[23] UNGA (n 20) UN Doc A/CN.9/942 II.B., para. 8.
[24] Article 5(1)(b)(i) of the Convention.
[25] Article 5(1)(c)(ii) of the Convention.

defences, defendants may be able to transform this new expedited process into a more protracted and expensive one similar to the one before the Convention. Courts should construe narrowly these defences[26] and others in view of the purpose of the Convention.

E. 'The Compromise'

As the deliberations progressed from semi-annual meeting to semi-annual meeting, Working Group II resolved the easier issues while deferring the difficult ones. Among those favouring a Convention, we feared that when deliberations reached the remaining more controversial and complex issues, the resolutions risked gutting the instrument. The fears were palpable in the hallways. Several worrisome questions occupied me. Would the Convention include a large hole for a stream of legal claims based on mediator misconduct that would be difficult to prove and would prolong the compliance process? Would the benefits be limited to only parties that elect to opt-in to the Convention? If so, only diligent parties who overcome the status quo bias will likely elect what is supposed to be a better enforcement process. Would the entire enterprise for a convention be derailed by the argument that formulating global standards is premature for what opponents view as an incipient field?

These sort of questions, among others, moved different sides toward a 'compromise proposal'. The compromise was the result of numerous informal and formal discussions among delegates, NGO representatives, and the EU in full working group meetings, consultations, hallways, and over meals. The five elements of the compromise were initially 'cobbled' together by about a dozen delegates during lunch on Tuesday 7 February 2017 and presented after lunch to the full Working Group. The timing left the remaining three days to flesh out the details. And then a blizzard on Thursday 9 February prompted closing the UN for the day. This lost day turned into an opportunity. Instead of enjoying the snow in Central Park, some delegates and others met at a private law office near the UN. They worked together to overcome some final hurdles and solidify details that could be presented to the full Working Group. [27] The five-point 'compromise', as it became known, created a pathway for resolving the remaining most contentious issues.

[26] For the 'null and void', etc. defence, Working Group II specifically states that it intends a narrow interpretation based on adopting language from the New York Convention. See UNGA, 'Settlement of Commercial Disputes—International Commercial Conciliation: Preparation of an Instrument on Enforcement of International Commercial Settlement Agreements Resulting from Conciliation' (14 July 2017) UN Doc A/CN.9/WG.II/WP.202, para. 43.

[27] UNGA (n 16) UN Doc A/CN.9/901, Section E. Proposal, paras 51–93.

1. Opt-out provision (Articles 8(1)(a) and (b) of the Draft Convention)

Should the Convention apply automatically with an opt-out provision? Those favouring opt-out argued that the instrument should apply automatically, as the New York Convention applies to enforcement of arbitral awards. This approach also would be consistent with the objective of the instrument to make it easier to secure compliance with settlement agreements. Others argued for party autonomy. Parties should opt-in only after they understood how the Convention operates and made an informed choice to do so.

This party autonomy argument appealed to several mediation experts, as I learned when preparing for the Vienna expert panel programme in September 2016. During the evening before the programme, some panelists expressed concern that an opt-out provision ran counter to the basic principle of party self-determination. Parties should make an informed choice to use the Convention, so they argued as some state delegates did during the meetings. I was stunned by the resistance because the benefits of an opt-out provision seemed so obvious. Instead of the after-dinner meeting offering a congenial opportunity to get acquainted over drinks and prepare for the next day, it turned into an intense, lively, and educational discussion. We met late into the night as we explored the pros and cons of opt-in and opt-out and the foundational principle of party self-determination.

By the end of the evening, I struggled to succinctly frame the issue: would the new instrument offer a better default process than the one now in place without the instrument? If not, I suggested, we should not be supporting the new instrument. When we reconvened our planning meeting over lunch the next day, the panel unanimously favoured the opt-out approach. It became apparent to all of us that opt-out favoured the default process, and this enterprise was aiming to fashion a better default process.

Ultimately, the Working Group adopted the policy of automatically applying the Convention with an opt-out option for a party to the settlement agreement.[28] Even though the Convention omits explicitly authorizing private opt-outs, the understanding is that parties to a settlement agreement can agree to exclude the application of the convention, and the clause would be upheld under Article 5(1)(d) as a defence based on the settlement terms.[29]

However, Article 8 authorizes a state party to the Convention to opt-out of the Convention's automatic application in a declaration. If a state opts-out, private parties can still opt-in to the Convention by private agreement (such as in the settlement agreement or the agreement to mediate).

[28] Article 8 distinguishes between 'parties to the convention,' which are Contracting States, and 'parties to the settlement agreement,' which are private parties. See further explanation in UNGA (n 20) A/CN.9/942 II.B (3).

[29] UNGA (n 16) UN Doc A/CN.9/934, para.78; UNCITRAL Report, 51st session (25 June–13 July 2018) III.B.1., A/73/17, paras 37–40.

2. Grounds for refusing to grant relief based on mediator behaviour (Articles 5(e) and (f) of the Draft Convention)

Some delegates wanted to include a defence to enforcement based on bad mediator behaviour. They saw a need to protect parties against unfair treatment by a mediator or failure of a mediator to disclose information that calls into question his or her impartiality. Initial concerns related to the impact of a mediator's non-compliance with professional conduct standards or domestic law. For people in the mediation field, this defence roused fears of abuse by parties looking for an excuse to get out of an agreement. Although it is rare that these mediator misbehaviours occur and have an impact, the claims are theoretically possible, and some delegates thought they should be guarded against. For many in the mediation field as advocates or mediators, these claims are familiar ones that can be asserted by a party trying to avoid a commitment. These claims also can make the compliance process costlier as leverage for negotiating a revised settlement.

When discussing these concerns at the February 2016 New York session, it was considered how mediation is different than arbitration. It was recognized that parties voluntarily use mediation; a mediator lacked authority to impose a settlement; any resulting agreement is voluntarily entered; and parties are free to withdraw from the process at any time. At the end of the discussions, delegates were encouraged to consider whether these mediator misconduct risks might be covered by other defences, such as the public policy defence in the instrument, and to review practical and judicial experiences in their jurisdictions before the next meetings in Vienna.[30]

At the following Vienna session in September 2016, a drafting process began with the goal of providing protection from these mediator risks while limiting the opportunity for abuse and leverage to get out of commitments by threatening lengthy and costly litigation. One of the early drafts that stimulated an energetic drafting process stated:

> Draft provision 8 (Grounds for refusing [recognition] and enforcement) (key language in italics)[31]
>
> (1) [Recognition and] enforcement may be refused [...] if that party furnishes [...] proof that:
>
> (e) *The conciliator failed to maintain fair treatment of the parties, or did not disclose circumstances likely to give rise to justifiable doubts as to its impartiality or independence.*

[30] UNGA, 'Report of Working Group II (Arbitration and Conciliation) on the Work of its Sixty-Fourth Session' (10 February 2016) UN Doc A/CN.9/867, paras 170–5 (Report prepared after the February 2016 meetings).

[31] Note by the Secretariat, 'Settlement of Commercial Disputes – International Commercial Conciliation: Preparation of an Instrument on Enforcement of International Commercial Settlement Agreements Resulting from Conciliation' (30 June 2016) UN Doc A/CN.9WG.II/WP.198 II.D(35). The final draft became Article 5 in the Convention.

After much discussion of divergent views, exchange of multiple drafts, and parsing of language that included active participation by NGOs, the emerging view was that serious mediator misconduct could probably be covered by other defences in the instrument. The delegates that wanted an additional protective provision emphasized the significant role of the mediator and the need to retain a defence even if it is difficult to prove that a party has been treated unfairly. Unlike arbitration, it was asserted by those favouring a protective provision, there was no means to challenge the mediation process or the conduct of the conciliator.

As delegates searched for a proposal that met everyone's concerns, it was suggested that the scope of challengeable behaviour be limited to when it has a 'direct impact on the settlement agreement', to 'exceptional circumstances', and to when the conduct has a 'material impact' or 'undue influence'. It also was suggested that subparagraph (e) be divided into two separate subparagraphs: one on fair treatment and another on disclosure.[32]

The final version approved by the Working Group adopted the two subparagraphs approach. It also retained narrow defences that addressed the underlying goal of protecting parties from a badly behaving mediator while fashioning language that reduced the risk of parties exploiting defences to evade commitments. The final language of Article 5, with italics to highlight safeguards against abuse, are:

> Section 1(e) There was a *serious* breach by the mediator of standards applicable to the mediator or the mediation *without which breach that party would not have entered into the settlement agreement*; or
>
> (f) There was a failure by the mediator to disclose to the parties circumstances that raise *justifiable* doubts as to the mediator's impartiality or independence and such *failure to disclose has a material impact or undue influence on a party without which failure that party would not have entered into the settlement agreement.*

3. Avoid Overlap with Other Enforcement Regimes (Article 1(3) of the Draft Convention)

Another issue was whether the compliance mechanism in the Convention should avoid overlap with other compliance regimes. As discussed, under Article 1(3) on Scope of Application, the Working Group decided to try to minimize overlap by not applying the Convention to settlement agreements enforceable as a court judgment or an arbitration award.[33]

[32] See UNGA, 'Daily Minutes' (16 September 2016) UN Doc A/CN.9/WG.II/LXV/CRP.1/Add.4, paras 5–11 (Draft report, addendum, distributed day after discussions); UNGA, 'Daily Minutes' (21 September 2016) UN Doc A/CN.9/WG.II/LXV/CRP.1/Add.7, paras 15–18 (para. 18 refers to compromise solution) (distributed day after discussions).

[33] See section A.

4. Defining 'Recognition and Enforcement' (Article 3 of the Draft Convention)

Another issue was whether to use the language 'recognition and enforcement' of settlement agreements in the Convention, a phrase that figures prominently and frequently in the New York Convention on arbitral awards including in its title.[34] Because part of the phrase, 'recognition,' has a different meaning in civil law jurisdictions than in common law jurisdictions, delegates needed to draft a convention that would reduce the risk of confusion. It was not easy at the meetings to understand each other's explanations and reconcile them. The solution was to omit the term 'recognition' and fashion a new article, which became Article 3.

Article 3 separates the two concepts. The concept 'enforcement' is used under Article 3(1) that provides for enforcing a settlement agreement under the terms of the Convention.[35] The word 'recognition' is not used. Instead, the 'recognition' concept is replaced in Article 3(2) with a functional definition that uses other words to address key aspects of recognition, e.g. the ability to assert a mediated settlement as a complete defence if another party tries to raise the underlying settled claims.

Other articles in the Convention do not repeat Article 3's meticulously negotiated and intricate language. Instead, the articles use the blanket term 'relief' when referring collectively to the concept of enforcement in Article 3(1) and the functional recognition description in Article 3(2).[36]

5. Two options for states: convention or model law

Central to the five-point compromise was the dual instruments proposal. It resolved a distributive choice that was blocking progress: Would there be a convention or model law? The compromise proposal avoided a choice that would have produced a clear winner and loser. It offered something to both sides. For those states that opposed a convention because they wanted more time to gain experience with mediation and compliance issues, they could adopt the model text in their domestic law and join the convention later. For those states that favoured a convention because they are ready for its benefits, they could ratify it under the dual instruments resolution. The UNGA, it also was suggested, should not express any preference between the two options.[37]

In an effort to encapsulate its goals, the Working Group formulated this formal resolution for adoption by UNCITRAL and the UNGA:

[34] 'Convention on the Recognition and Enforcement of Foreign Arbitral Awards', Articles I –VII (New York City, 1958).

[35] The term 'enforcement' shows up in a few other places but for other purposes. See Appendix A, Articles 1(3)(a)(ii) and (b), and Article 12(4).

[36] See use of 'relief' in Appendix A, Articles 4, 5, 6, and 12.

[37] UNGA (n 16) UN Doc A/CN.9/901, paras 89–93; Note by the Secretariat, 'Settlement of Commercial Disputes—International Commercial Mediation: Draft Convention on International Settlement Agreements Resulting from Mediation' (2 March 2018) UN Doc A/CN.9/942, II.B Annotations, para. 12.

> Recalling that the decision of the Commission to concurrently prepare a convention on international settlement agreements resulting from mediation and an amendment to the UNCITRAL Model Law on International Commercial Conciliation was intended to accommodate the different levels of experience with mediation in different jurisdictions, and to provide States with consistent standards on cross-border enforcement of international settlement agreements resulting from mediation, without creating any expectation that interested States may adopt either instrument.[38]

After the 'compromise' was reached, the delegates wrapped up the drafting process by addressing some standard and not particularly controversial provisions, although one routine provision provoked an entertaining exchange with substantive implications. It was proposed in the draft provision that the Convention become effective six months after the third state ratifies it. Then a delegate suggested that the number should be ten states, followed by other delegates suggesting other numbers ranging from three and ten. The Chair, using her instinctive humour to make a point, remarked that things were beginning to sound like a bingo game or haggling at a bazaar. She then asked delegates to support any proposed number with a rationale. In a very short time, the discussion returned to the original number of three and the delegates reached a consensus.[39]

During this last discussion, one of the delegates raised a point worth noting. The Convention is not a bilateral treaty. It is not limited to compliance with settlements 'from' a state that is also a party. This means that settlements are subject to the Convention in any country that is a party, even if the person or entity suing is not from a country that ratified the Convention.

V. Conclusion—What's Next?

The recommendations of Working Group II were adopted by UNCITRAL on 25 June 2018. On that warm day at the UN in New York, delegates and representatives sang a celebratory song composed for the occasion.[40] It was entitled 'Good Memories' and sung to the melody of *Home on the Range*. It also paid tribute to Mr. Schnabel's leadership for moving this initiative forward and to Singapore for offering to host opening the Convention for signature.

Oh give me a forum
Where mediation is at home

[38] See A/CN.9/942, II.B Annotations, Paragraph 12 (2 March 2018).
[39] Article 14 of the Convention.
[40] The song was composed by three UNCITRAL members who are too modest to be publicly recognized for their authorship of this original composition for the 51st Commission of UNCITRAL, New York, 25 June 2018.

Where debate and amendments flow free
Where seldom is heard, a discouraging word
And results are here for us to see
Ohhhhh forum to engage,
Where each of us wrote a page,
Where Tim took the lead
And we followed with speed
Mediation convention hurray

When the work first begun
And the quorum was found
With the New York Convention as guide
We all shared our views
And now we share the news
The Singapore convention is live
Ohhhh forum to engage …

Next, the Convention was presented to the UNGA for approval in the fall of 2018. At the 25 June Commission meeting, the Commission adopted by consensus the following decision and recommendation to the UNGA:[41]

> *The United Nations Commission on International Trade Law,*
>
> *Recalling* its mandate under General Assembly resolution 2205 (XXI) of 17 December 1966 to further the progressive harmonization and unification of the law of international trade and in that respect to bear in mind the interests of all peoples, in particular those of developing countries, in the extensive development of international trade,
>
> *Recognizing* the value of mediation as a method of amicably settling disputes arising in the context of international commercial relations,
>
> *Recalling* General Assembly resolution 57/18 of 19 November 2002 noting the adoption of the UNCITRAL Model Law on International Commercial Conciliation and expressing the conviction that the Model Law, together with the UNCITRAL Conciliation Rules recommended by the General Assembly in its resolution 35/52 of 4 December 1980, contributes significantly to the establishment of a harmonized legal framework for the fair and efficient settlement of disputes arising in international commercial relations,
>
> *Convinced* that the adoption of a convention on international settlement agreements resulting from mediation that is acceptable to States with different legal,

[41] UNCITRAL (n 29), para. 68.

social and economic systems would complement the existing legal framework on international mediation and contribute to the development of harmonious international economic relations,

Recalling that the decision of the Commission to concurrently prepare a convention on international settlement agreements resulting from mediation and an amendment to the UNCITRAL Model Law on International Commercial Conciliation was intended to accommodate the different levels of experience with mediation in different jurisdictions, and to provide States with consistent standards on cross-border enforcement of international settlement agreements resulting from mediation, without creating any expectation that interested States may adopt either instrument,[42]

Noting that the preparation of the draft convention on international settlement agreements resulting from mediation was the subject of due deliberation in the Commission and that the draft convention benefited from consultations with Governments and interested intergovernmental and international non-governmental organizations,

Having considered the draft convention at its fifty-first session, in 2018,

Drawing attention to the fact that the text of the draft convention was circulated for comment before the fifty-first session of the Commission to all Governments invited to attend the meetings of the Commission and the Working Group as members and observers,

Considering that the draft convention has received sufficient consideration and has reached the level of maturity for it to be generally acceptable to States:

1. *Submits* to the General Assembly the draft convention on international settlement agreements resulting from mediation, as it appears in annex I to the report of the United Nations Commission on International Trade Law on the work of its fifty-first session;
2. *Recommends* that the General Assembly, taking into account the extensive consideration given to the draft convention by the Commission and its Working Group II (Dispute Settlement), consider the draft convention with a view to (a) adopting, at its seventy-third session, on the basis of the draft convention approved by the Commission, a United Nations Convention on International Settlement Agreements Resulting from Mediation; (b) authorizing a signing ceremony to be held as soon as practicable in 2019 in Singapore, upon which the Convention would be open for signature; and (c) recommending that the Convention be known as the 'Singapore Convention on Mediation';

[42] *Official Records of the General Assembly, Seventy-Second Session, Supplement No. 17* (A/72/17) paras. 238 and 239. See also UNGA (n 16) UN Doc A/CN.9/901, para. 93.

3. *Requests* the Secretary-General to publish the Convention, upon adoption, including electronically and in the six official languages of the United Nations, and to disseminate it broadly to Governments and other interested bodies.

After approval by the UNGA, the Convention is scheduled to be open for signature in Singapore in early August 2019.[43] The Commission unanimously expressed its support for the convention to be referred to as the 'Singapore Convention on Mediation.'[44]

The opening for signature launches the final stage of 'ratification, acceptance, approval, or accession' by the states.[45] Then, each state will have an opportunity to decide whether to adopt the Convention in accordance with the state's local legal requirements and procedure.

I hope that this chapter will help inform that discussion and choice.

Appendix A
United Nations Convention on International Settlement Agreements Resulting from Mediation

Preamble

The Parties to this Convention,

Recognizing the value for international trade of mediation as a method for settling commercial disputes in which the parties in dispute request a third person or persons to assist them in their attempt to settle the dispute amicably,

Noting that mediation is increasingly used in international and domestic commercial practice as an alternative to litigation,

Considering that the use of mediation results in significant benefits, such as reducing the instances where a dispute leads to the termination of a commercial relationship, facilitating the administration of international transactions by commercial parties and producing savings in the administration of justice by States,

Convinced that the establishment of a framework for international settlement agreements resulting from mediation that is acceptable to States with different legal, social and economic systems would contribute to the development of harmonious international economic relations,

Have agreed as follows:

[43] See Appendix A, Article 11.
[44] UNCITRAL (n 29) paras 43–5.
[45] See Appendix A, Article 14.

Article 1. Scope of Application

1. This Convention applies to an agreement resulting from mediation and concluded in writing by parties to resolve a commercial dispute ('settlement agreement') which, at the time of its conclusion, is international in that:
   (a) At least two parties to the settlement agreement have their places of business in different States; or
   (b) The State in which the parties to the settlement agreement have their places of business is different from either:
      (i) The State in which a substantial part of the obligations under the settlement agreement is performed; or
      (ii) The State with which the subject matter of the settlement agreement is most closely connected.
2. This Convention does not apply to settlement agreements:
   (a) Concluded to resolve a dispute arising from transactions engaged in by one of the parties (a consumer) for personal, family or household purposes;
   (b) Relating to family, inheritance or employment law.
3. This Convention does not apply to:
   (a) Settlement agreements:
      (i) That have been approved by a court or concluded in the course of proceedings before a court; and
      (ii) That are enforceable as a judgment in the State of that court;
   (b) Settlement agreements that have been recorded and are enforceable as an arbitral award.

Article 2. Definitions

1. For the purposes of article 1, paragraph 1:
   (a) If a party has more than one place of business, the relevant place of business is that which has the closest relationship to the dispute resolved by the settlement agreement, having regard to the circumstances known to, or contemplated by, the parties at the time of the conclusion of the settlement agreement;
   (b) If a party does not have a place of business, reference is to be made to the party's habitual residence.
2. A settlement agreement is 'in writing' if its content is recorded in any form. The requirement that a settlement agreement be in writing is met by an electronic communication if the information contained therein is accessible so as to be useable for subsequent reference.
3. 'Mediation' means a process, irrespective of the expression used or the basis upon which the process is carried out, whereby parties attempt to reach an

amicable settlement of their dispute with the assistance of a third person or persons ('the mediator') lacking the authority to impose a solution upon the parties to the dispute.

Article 3. General Principles

1. Each Party to the Convention shall enforce a settlement agreement in accordance with its rules of procedure and under the conditions laid down in this Convention.
2. If a dispute arises concerning a matter that a party claims was already resolved by a settlement agreement, a Party to the Convention shall allow the party to invoke the settlement agreement in accordance with its rules of procedure and under the conditions laid down in this Convention, in order to prove that the matter has already been resolved.

Article 4. Requirements for Reliance on Settlement Agreements

1. A party relying on a settlement agreement under this Convention shall supply to the competent authority of the Party to the Convention where relief is sought:
   (a) The settlement agreement signed by the parties;
   (b) Evidence that the settlement agreement resulted from mediation, such as:
      (i) The mediator's signature on the settlement agreement;
      (ii) A document signed by the mediator indicating that the mediation was carried out;
      (iii) An attestation by the institution that administered the mediation; or
      (iv) In the absence of (i), (ii) or (iii), any other evidence acceptable to the competent authority.
2. The requirement that a settlement agreement shall be signed by the parties or, where applicable, the mediator is met in relation to an electronic communication if:
   (a) A method is used to identify the parties or the mediator and to indicate the parties' or mediator's intention in respect of the information contained in the electronic communication; and
   (b) The method used is either:
      (i) As reliable as appropriate for the purpose for which the electronic communication was generated or communicated, in the light of all the circumstances, including any relevant agreement; or
      (ii) Proven in fact to have fulfilled the functions described in subparagraph

(a) above, by itself or together with further evidence.

3. If the settlement agreement is not in an official language of the Party to the Convention where relief is sought, the competent authority may request a translation thereof into such language.
4. The competent authority may require any necessary document in order to verify that the requirements of the Convention have been complied with.
5. When considering the request for relief, the competent authority shall act expeditiously.

Article 5. Grounds for Refusing to Grant Relief

1. The competent authority of the Party to the Convention where relief is sought under article 4 may refuse to grant relief at the request of the party against whom the relief is sought only if that party furnishes to the competent authority proof that:
   (a) A party to the settlement agreement was under some incapacity;
   (b) The settlement agreement sought to be relied upon:
      (i) Is null and void, inoperative or incapable of being performed under the law to which the parties have validly subjected it or, failing any indication thereon, under the law deemed applicable by the competent authority of the Party to the Convention where relief is sought under article 4;
      (ii) Is not binding, or is not final, according to its terms; or
      (iii) Has been subsequently modified;
   (c) The obligations in the settlement agreement:
      (i) Have been performed; or
      (ii) Are not clear or comprehensible;
   (d) Granting relief would be contrary to the terms of the settlement agreement;
   (e) There was a serious breach by the mediator of standards applicable to the mediator or the mediation without which breach that party would not have entered into the settlement agreement; or
   (f) There was a failure by the mediator to disclose to the parties circumstances that raise justifiable doubts as to the mediator's impartiality or independence and such failure to disclose had a material impact or undue influence on a party without which failure that party would not have entered into the settlement agreement.
2. The competent authority of the Party to the Convention where relief is sought under article 4 may also refuse to grant relief if it finds that:
   (a) Granting relief would be contrary to the public policy of that Party; or
   (b) The subject matter of the dispute is not capable of settlement by mediation under the law of that Party.

Article 6. Parallel Applications or Claims

If an application or a claim relating to a settlement agreement has been made to a court, an arbitral tribunal or any other competent authority which may affect the relief being sought under article 4, the competent authority of the Party to the Convention where such relief is sought may, if it considers it proper, adjourn the decision and may also, on the request of a party, order the other party to give suitable security.

Article 7. Other Laws or Treaties

This Convention shall not deprive any interested party of any right it may have to avail itself of a settlement agreement in the manner and to the extent allowed by the law or the treaties of the Party to the Convention where such settlement agreement is sought to be relied upon.

Article 8. Reservations

1. A Party to the Convention may declare that:
   (a) It shall not apply this Convention to settlement agreements to which it is a party, or to which any governmental agencies or any person acting on behalf of a governmental agency is a party, to the extent specified in the declaration;
   (b) It shall apply this Convention only to the extent that the parties to the settlement agreement have agreed to the application of the Convention.
2. No reservations are permitted except those expressly authorized in this article.
3. Reservations may be made by a Party to the Convention at any time. Reservations made at the time of signature shall be subject to confirmation upon ratification, acceptance or approval. Such reservations shall take effect simultaneously with the entry into force of this Convention in respect of the Party to the Convention concerned. Reservations made at the time of ratification, acceptance or approval of this Convention or accession thereto, or at the time of making a declaration under article 13 shall take effect simultaneously with the entry into force of this Convention in respect of the Party to the Convention concerned. Reservations deposited after the entry into force of the Convention for that Party to the Convention shall take effect six months after the date of the deposit.
4. Reservations and their confirmations shall be deposited with the depositary.

5. Any Party to the Convention that makes a reservation under this Convention may withdraw it at any time. Such withdrawals are to be deposited with the depositary, and shall take effect six months after deposit.

Article 9. Effect on Settlement Agreements

The Convention and any reservation or withdrawal thereof shall apply only to settlement agreements concluded after the date when the Convention, reservation or withdrawal thereof enters into force for the Party to the Convention concerned.

Article 10. Depositary

The Secretary-General of the United Nations is hereby designated as the depositary of this Convention.

Article 11. Signature, Ratification, Acceptance, Approval, Accession

1. This Convention is open for signature by all States in Singapore, on 1 August 2019, and thereafter at United Nations Headquarters in New York.
2. This Convention is subject to ratification, acceptance or approval by the signatories.
3. This Convention is open for accession by all States that are not signatories as from the date it is open for signature.
4. Instruments of ratification, acceptance, approval or accession are to be deposited with the depositary.

Article 12. Participation by Regional Economic Integration Organizations

1. A regional economic integration organization that is constituted by sovereign States and has competence over certain matters governed by this Convention may similarly sign, ratify, accept, approve or accede to this Convention. The regional economic integration organization shall in that case have the rights and obligations of a Party to the Convention, to the extent that that organization has competence over matters governed by this Convention. Where the number of Parties to the Convention is relevant in this Convention, the regional economic integration organization shall not

count as a Party to the Convention in addition to its member States that are Parties to the Convention.

2. The regional economic integration organization shall, at the time of signature, ratification, acceptance, approval or accession, make a declaration to the depositary specifying the matters governed by this Convention in respect of which competence has been transferred to that organization by its member States. The regional economic integration organization shall promptly notify the depositary of any changes to the distribution of competence, including new transfers of competence, specified in the declaration under this paragraph.
3. Any reference to a 'Party to the Convention', 'Parties to the Convention', a 'State' or 'States' in this Convention applies equally to a regional economic integration organization where the context so requires.
4. This Convention shall not prevail over conflicting rules of a regional economic integration organization, whether such rules were adopted or entered into force before or after this Convention:
   (a) if, under article 4, relief is sought in a State that is member of such an organization and all the States relevant under article 1(1) are members of such an organization; or
   (b) as concerns the recognition or enforcement of judgments between member States of such an organization.

Article 13. Non-Unified Legal Systems

1. If a Party to the Convention has two or more territorial units in which different systems of law are applicable in relation to the matters dealt with in this Convention, it may, at the time of signature, ratification, acceptance, approval or accession, declare that this Convention is to extend to all its territorial units or only to one or more of them, and may amend its declaration by submitting another declaration at any time.
2. These declarations are to be notified to the depositary and are to state expressly the territorial units to which the Convention extends.
3. If a Party to the Convention has two or more territorial units in which different systems of law are applicable in relation to the matters dealt with in this Convention,
   (a) Any reference to the law or rule of procedure of a State shall be construed as referring, where appropriate, to the law or rule of procedure in force in the relevant territorial unit;
   (b) Any reference to the place of business in a State shall be construed as referring, where appropriate, to the place of business in the relevant territorial unit;

(c) Any reference to the competent authority of the State shall be construed as referring, where appropriate, to the competent authority in the relevant territorial unit.

4. If a Party to the Convention makes no declaration under paragraph 1 of this article, the Convention is to extend to all territorial units of that State.

Article 14. Entry into Force

1. This Convention shall enter into force six months after deposit of the third instrument of ratification, acceptance, approval, or accession.
2. When a State ratifies, accepts, approves or accedes to this Convention after the deposit of the third instrument of ratification, acceptance, approval or accession, this Convention shall enter into force in respect of that State six months after the date of the deposit of its instrument of ratification, acceptance, approval or accession. The Convention shall enter into force for a territorial unit to which this Convention has been extended in accordance with article 13 six months after the notification of the declaration referred to in that article.

Article 15. Amendment

1. Any Party to the Convention may propose an amendment to the present Convention by submitting it to the Secretary-General of the United Nations. The Secretary-General shall thereupon communicate the proposed amendment to the Parties to the Convention with a request that they indicate whether they favour a conference of Parties to the Convention for the purpose of considering and voting upon the proposal. In the event that within four months from the date of such communication at least one third of the Parties to the Convention favour such a conference, the Secretary-General shall convene the conference under the auspices of the United Nations.
2. The conference of Parties to the Convention shall make every effort to achieve consensus on each amendment. If all efforts at consensus are exhausted and no consensus is reached, the amendment shall, as a last resort, require for its adoption a two-thirds majority vote of the Parties to the Convention present and voting at the conference.
3. An adopted amendment shall be submitted by the depositary to all the Parties to the Convention for ratification, acceptance or approval.
4. An adopted amendment shall enter into force six months after the date of deposit of the third instrument of ratification, acceptance or approval. When an amendment enters into force, it shall be binding on those Parties to the Convention that have expressed consent to be bound by it.

5. When a Party to the Convention ratifies, accepts or approves an amendment following the deposit of the third instrument of ratification, acceptance or approval, the amendment shall enter into force in respect of that Party to the Convention six months after the date of the deposit of its instrument of ratification, acceptance or approval.

Article 16. Denunciations

1. A Party to the Convention may denounce this Convention by a formal notification in writing addressed to the depositary. The denunciation may be limited to certain territorial units of a non-unified legal system to which this Convention applies.
2. The denunciation shall take effect twelve months after the notification is received by the depositary. Where a longer period for the denunciation to take effect is specified in the notification, the denunciation shall take effect upon the expiration of such longer period after the notification is received by the depositary. The Convention shall continue to apply to settlement agreements concluded before the denunciation takes effect.

DONE at ---- this [X] day of [X] ------, in a single original, of which the Arabic, Chinese, English, French, Russian and Spanish texts are equally authentic.

Index

For the benefit of digital users, indexed terms that span two pages (e.g., 52–53) may, on occasion, appear on only one of those pages.

The manufacturer's authorised representative in the EU for product safety is Oxford University Press España S.A. of El Parque Empresarial San Fernando de Henares, Avenida de Castilla, 2 - 28830 Madrid (www.oup.es/en or product.safety@oup.com). OUP España S.A. also acts as importer into Spain of products made by the manufacturer.
Printed and bound by CPI Group (UK) Ltd, Croydon, CR0 4YY
14/09/2026
02216306-0013